M000283080

THE GOOD HOTEL GUIDE 2022

GREAT BRITAIN & IRELAND

THE GOOD HOTEL GUIDE 2022

GREAT BRITAIN & IRELAND

Editors
Jane Knight
Nicola Davies
Kate Quill
M Astella Saw

THE GOOD HOTEL GUIDE LTD

The Good Hotel Guide Ltd

This edition first published in 2021 by
The Good Hotel Guide Ltd

Copyright © 2021 Adam and Caroline Raphael
Maps © 2021 David Perrott

Chief executive: Richard Fraiman

Contributing editors:
Rose Shepherd
Helen Pickles
Bonnie Friend

Production: Hugh Allan
Managing editor: Alison Wormleighton
Designer: Stuart Sutch
Text editor: Daphne Trotter
Computer consultant: Vince Nacey
Digital agency: Umi Digital
Researcher: Cristina Recio-Corral

A CIP catalogue record for this book may be found in the British Library.

ISBN 978-0-9932484-6-7

Cover photograph: The Blakeney Hotel, Blakeney

Printed and bound in Malta by Gutenberg Press Ltd

MIX
Paper from
responsible sources
FSC
www.fsc.org
FSC® C022612

*'A good hotel is where
the guest comes first'*

Hilary Rubinstein, founding editor
(1926–2012)

goodhotelguide.com

The Pig at Combe, Gittisham

CONTENTS

goodhotelguide.com

Our website has many handy features to help you get
the most out of your Guide.

- Explore offers and discounts
- View special collections
- Read the latest news
- Search for a hotel near you
- Search for a hotel near a particular destination
- Submit a review
- Join the Good Hotel Guide Readers' Club
- Order a copy of the printed Guide

DESKTOP

TABLET   SMARTPHONE

Make it even easier to get on the Good Hotel Guide website while
you're on the go: add an icon to the home screen of your iPhone or iPad
for one-touch smartphone access. Go to **goodhotelguide.com** on your
mobile browser. Tap on the rectangle with an arrow pointing upwards,
at the bottom of the screen. Then tap on the + sign
('Add to Home Screen') that pops up.

INTRODUCTION

Publishing an independent hotel guide in the middle of a pandemic is not for the faint-hearted. This year's Guide has been researched and edited in challenging circumstances. Despite forecasts of mass closures, most of our selected hotels, inns and B&Bs not only have survived but have enjoyed record numbers of guests over the summer. As for the Guide, the enthusiasm of readers as they once again experience the joys of staying away has encouraged us in our role of sorting out the exceptional from the ordinary.

This year's edition, our 45th, with more than 650 selections, has once again been edited by two experienced travel journalists, Jane Knight, former travel editor of The Times, and Kate Quill, who was her deputy. They head a talented group of writers led by Rose Shepherd. Together with Niki Davies and Astella Saw who edited the Shortlist, they have brought their detailed knowledge of hospitality to discovering new properties such as a stylish West Country restaurant-with-rooms and a brilliant new Scottish guest house.

I am sometimes asked what sort of people read the Guide. I replied to one such enquiry: 'At the last count we have one duke, one duchess, one viscount, one countess (Italian), five dames, nine lords, 31 ladies, 46 knights and roughly 20,000 odds and sods.' These numbers may no longer be accurate – aristocrats kick the bucket from time to time – but the fact is that the Guide appeals to all sorts, from people who want to stay in a humble B&B to those whose tastes and the depth of their pockets tend to grand country houses.

The Guide is proud of not only its wide appeal but also its fierce independence. It has campaigned (some have unkindly called them rants) on a wide variety of topics, from 'save the kipper' and 'the curse of muzak' to more serious issues, such as the high cost of commissions paid to online travel agencies and the advantages to guests and the hotels of direct booking.

As Caroline and I are well into our ninth decade, it is time for us to go. Richard Fraiman, who has worked closely with us over the past seven years, will take on the responsibility for publishing the best and most trusted independent guide on the market. We are confident it has a great future because he will professionalise the business and strengthen the Guide's reputation as a trusted source of information about the best places to stay, without fear or favour.

We have much enjoyed our 21 years at the helm. Thanks to all our thousands of readers who have encouraged and supported us with reviews and criticism. We could not do without you because the GHG is, and always will be, a guide for readers. There are more than 50,000 hotels and B&Bs in the UK and Ireland. We have space for only a fraction, which is why we refine our selections every year. The ultimate judges of which places get an entry – the pick of the bunch – are you, our readers. So please keep writing.

Adam and Caroline Raphael
July 2021

HOW TO USE THE GOOD HOTEL GUIDE

MAIN ENTRY

The 406 main entries, which are given a full page each, are those we believe to be the best of their type in Great Britain and Ireland.

Colour bands identify each country; London has its own section.

An index at the back lists hotels by county; another lists them by hotel name.

Hotels appear alphabetically under the name of the town or village.

The maps at the back of the book are divided into grids, with a small house indicating a main entry, and a triangle a Shortlist entry.

If a hotel has received one of our César awards either this year or in the last ten years, that is indicated here. If a hotel is making its first appearance, is returning after an absence or has been upgraded from the Shortlist, this is indicated by a 'new' emblem.

The panel provides useful information, such as contact details, number of bedrooms and facilities.

We try to indicate whether a hotel is wheelchair-accessible or is unsuitable for the disabled. It's always worth calling the hotel to check the details of this.

We name readers who have endorsed a hotel; we do not name inspectors, readers who ask to remain anonymous, or those who have written a critical report.

If the Shortlist (see opposite) also has one or more entries for this village or town, a cross-reference to the Shortlist appears here.

We give the starting price for room, bed-and-breakfast and/or dinner-bed-and-breakfast prices. The price for dinner is for a set meal, or the average cost of three courses from an à la carte menu.

Sample entry shown:

228   ENGLAND   goodhotelguide.com

LUDLOW Shropshire   MAP 3:C4

OLD DOWNTON LODGE

César Previous César winner

'Pheasants scatter as you edge your way down the lanes' to Pippa and Willem Vlok's restaurant-with-rooms, occupying medieval and Georgian farm buildings around a flower-filled courtyard. It is a 'super-peaceful place, renovated and furnished to a high standard', readers write. 'The attention to detail is faultless.' Bedrooms, two with oak floor-poster, are a study in rustic chic. A 'high-raftered' stables room had 'lighting so elaborately digitised, it took most of the evening to work out which switches to activate'. A log-burner warms a sitting room in an old milking barn, where local cheeses, including Remembered Hills ('blue, of course') went down well with a good bottle of wine. In the 'pseudo-baronial' dining room, chef Nick Bennett's short market menu might bring a choice of venison, squash and chestnut, savoy; hake, saag aloo, lemongrass and fennel; duck, chicory and orange. Most nights there is also a tasting menu. Give them notice of any dietary needs. 'We couldn't get enough of the food,' another reader writes. As for the service, 'the entire team are the most genuine, lovely, kind people'. (LH and JF, and others)

Downton on the Rock
Ludlow SY8 2HU

T: 01568 771826
E: bookings@olddowntonlodge.com
W: olddowntonlodge.com

BEDROOMS: 9. In buildings round courtyard.
OPEN: all year, except Christmas, dinner nightly, lunch Thurs–Sun.
FACILITIES: sitting room, dining room, 'museum' (function room), in-room TV (Freeview), civil wedding licence, 1-acre courtyard, EV charging, unsuitable for disabled.
BACKGROUND MUSIC: soft classical in sitting and dining rooms.
LOCATION: 6 miles W of Ludlow.
CHILDREN: over-12s only.
DOGS: allowed in some bedrooms by prior arrangement (£15 per dog), not in public rooms.
CREDIT CARDS: Amex, MC, Visa.
PRICES: B&B doubles from £165. Market menu (2–3 courses) £40–£50, tasting menu (6 courses) Tues–Sat £65.

SEE ALSO SHORTLIST

HOW TO USE THE GOOD HOTEL GUIDE

SHORTLIST ENTRY

The Shortlist complements our main section by including interesting
new entrants and a selection of places in areas in which we have limited choices.
It also includes some hotels that have previously been in the Guide but have
not had sufficient feedback this year.

This hotel is
making its first
appearance in
the Shortlist or is
returning after
an absence.

Shortlist hotels
are included in
both indexes at
the back of the
book, where (S)
indicates that it is
a Shortlist entry.

Many readers
tell us they find
background music
irritating. We say
whether music
is played and
where you might
encounter it.

We list the principal
credit cards accepted
by the hotel (with
MC standing for
Mastercard).

We give the range
of room, bed-and-
breakfast and/or
dinner-bed-and-
breakfast prices. The
price for dinner is
for a set meal, or the
average cost of three
courses from an à la
carte menu.

goodhotelguide.com ENGLAND SHORTLIST 523

[NEW]

LUDLOW Shropshire
THE FEATHERS
A local landmark, this Grade I listed Jacobean
building with an ornate, timber-framed façade
stands in a 'wonderful position' in the heart
of town, a few minutes' walk from the main
square and castle. 'The hotel has been completely
revamped internally without losing its renowned
historical features,' a regular Guide reader, and
return visitor, reports. Inside are 'huge fireplaces',
'fine timberwork' and restored oak panelling; it is
'immaculately clean' throughout. The bedrooms
are pleasingly modern: while some may be snug,
all have a 'very comfortable' bed and a choice of
pillows, plus a mini-fridge, coffee and loose-leaf
teas. Service at mealtimes is 'fast and cheerful';
there is 'decent variety' at breakfast.

MAP 6C4
24–25 Bull Ring
Ludlow SY81AA
T: 01584 875261
W: feathersatludlow.co.uk

BEDROOMS 42. Some suitable for disabled.
OPEN all year.
FACILITIES lift, lounge, bar, tea room, restaurant, function rooms, in-room smart TV, civil wedding licence, courtyard, limited parking (charge).
BACKGROUND MUSIC jazz in public areas.
LOCATION in town centre.
CHILDREN all ages welcomed.
DOGS allowed, not in restaurant.
CREDIT CARDS MC, Visa.
PRICES per room £95–£219. Breakfast £10, à la carte £30.

LYME REGIS Dorset
GREENHILL HOUSE
'If Lyme Regis is the pearl of the Dorset coast,
then this beautiful B&B is surely one of its
diamonds.' Sara and Ed Hollway's 'restful,
relaxing' 1930s home overlooking Lyme Bay
offers guests 'a blissful experience'. 'Everything
has been carefully thought out to provide the
utmost comfort and convenience': there are maps,
books, jigsaw puzzles and board games in the
sitting room; in the well-equipped bedrooms,
'top-quality design, with a hint of the '30s, is
executed with panache and a touch of humour'.
A generous breakfast is served in the dining room
or the 'delightful' garden, where the views to
Golden Cap and the Jurassic Coast are 'sublime'.
The walk back from town is steep – let the bus or
a taxi take the strain.

MAP 1C6
Somers Road
Lyme Regis DT7 3EX
T: 01297 445492
W: greenhillhousebandb.co.uk

BEDROOMS 3.
OPEN all year except 20–29 Dec.
FACILITIES sitting room, dining room, in-room TV (Freeview), ½-acre garden.
BACKGROUND MUSIC none.
LOCATION on a hillside, above the town.
CHILDREN all ages welcomed (but no special facilities).
DOGS not allowed.
CREDIT CARDS not accepted.
PRICES per room: B&B £155–£180.

CÉSARS 2022

We give our César awards to the ten best hotels of the year. Named after César Ritz, the most celebrated of hoteliers, these are the Oscars of hotel-keeping.

🏵 NEWCOMER OF THE YEAR
Locanda on the Weir, Porlock Weir
Italian foodie flair meets West Country charm at this uber-stylish restaurant with rooms on Exmoor's coast, where chef Pio Catemario di Quadri cooks up a storm while Cindy Siu creates eclectic, appealing interiors worthy of the food. (Page 267)

🏵 ISLAND HOTEL OF THE YEAR
Hillside, Ventnor
There's plenty of Scandi chic at Gert Bach's thatched cottage with its stripped-back pale interiors highlighted by colourful abstract art canvases and Solent views. The terraced gardens supply the kitchen, which produces simple but superb dishes. (Page 323)

🏵 WELSH INN OF THE YEAR
The Bell at Skenfrith, Skenfrith
A firm favourite with readers, The Bell faced a challenging time when the River Monnow flooded and flowed through its ground floor. Now the dog-friendly pub is better than ever, with a fresh look, great food and riverside walks. (Page 425)

🏵 COUNTRY HOUSE HOTEL OF THE YEAR
Askham Hall, Penrith
It's relaxed rather than grand at Charles Lowther's comfortably cluttered ancestral pile, with its classic English country garden, a 17th-century pele tower, family heirlooms and a Michelin-starred restaurant. Dogs and children are welcome. (Page 258)

🏵 SMALL HOTEL OF THE YEAR
Plantation House, Ermington
Chef/patron Richard Hendey cooks as much as possible on the premises at his small hotel, from bread to truffles. Readers rave over his nightly-changing menus, which feature local Devonshire produce and fresh food from the kitchen garden. (Page 176)

🏆 SCOTTISH GUEST HOUSE OF THE YEAR
Woodcroft House, Perth
The scenic setting, spacious rooms, warm welcome
and fine cooking stood out for our inspectors at this Arts
and Crafts-style Victorian guest house with three rooms.
Take your own wine to dinners ordered in advance from
extensive menus. (Page 376)

🏆 INN OF THE YEAR
Helen Browning's Royal Oak, Bishopstone
There's character aplenty at this pub on an organic
farm, with bedrooms named after different fields,
a communal area called The Wallow with table football,
and everything from milk to meat supplied from the
surrounding fields. (Page 101)

🏆 ECCENTRIC HOTEL OF THE YEAR
Rayanne House, Holywood
On certain nights, chef/patron Conor McClelland replicates
the entire nine-course meal served on the Titanic the night
she sank. Lavish rooms include the golf-themed Rory
McIlroy bedroom, and a breakfast of titanic proportions
is served. (Page 452)

🏆 B&B OF THE YEAR
Newbegin House, Beverley
Guests receive a warm welcome plus a garden tour at
Walter and Nuala Sweeney's refined Georgian town house.
Bedrooms are supplied with sherry, fresh milk and flowers,
there's a superb choice at breakfast, and everything is
great value. (Page 95)

🏆 FAMILY FRIENDLY HOTEL OF THE YEAR
Porth Tocyn Hotel, Abersoch
It's the relaxed atmosphere together with everything
from a games room and outdoor pool to cots and baby-
listening devices that make this hotel a firm family
favourite. There is no charge for children sharing
their parents' room either. (Page 403)

REPORT OF THE YEAR COMPETITION

Readers' contributions are the lifeblood of the Good Hotel Guide. Everyone who writes to us is a potential winner of the Report of the Year Competition. Each year we single out the writers of the most helpful reports. These correspondents win a copy of the Guide.

This year's winners are:
Peter Anderson, of Newbury
Elspeth and John Gibbon, of St Ives, Cambridgeshire
David Hampshire, of Stoke Poges
Mary Hewson, of Oldham
Andrew and Moira Kleissner, of Cardiff
Max and Susan Lickfold, of Olney
Kevin and Victoria Seymour, of Seaford
Frances Thomas, of Aylesbury
Andrew Warren, of Cambridge
Ian White, of Haywards Heath

JOIN THE GOOD HOTEL GUIDE READERS' CLUB

Send us a review of your favourite hotel.
As a member of the club, you will be entitled to:
- A pre-publication discount offer
- Personal advice on hotels
- Advice if you are in dispute with a hotel
- Monthly emailed Guide newsletter

The writers of the ten best reviews will each win a free copy of the Guide. The winner of our monthly web competition will win a free night, dinner and breakfast for two at one of the Guide's top hotels.

Send your review via
our website: goodhotelguide.com
or email: editor@goodhotelguide.com
or write to:
Good Hotel Guide
94 Church Lane
London N2 0TB
England

EDITOR'S CHOICE

From glamorous spa hotels to great-value B&Bs and dog-friendly pubs with treats behind the bar, here are some of the places that have caught our eye this year. Turn to the full entry for the bigger picture.

The Pig at Harlyn Bay, Padstow

BARASET BARN
ALVESTON
There is something to tempt all palates on the Asian–Mediterranean menu of this atmospheric restaurant with rural views. Share small plates (harissa cauliflower, tempura squid) or try Goan vegetable curry or a Baraset chop steak burger. (Page 67)

THE OLLEROD
BEAMINSTER
Chris Staines, who has a Michelin background, puts his judicious skills to good use in this pale-stone Dorset house. Dishes range from the pleasingly simple – fish of the day with lemon – to the more exotic, such as spiced minced lamb. (Page 89)

BROCCO ON THE PARK
SHEFFIELD
A 'modern smorgasbord', with a Nordic twist, is served at this switched-on establishment. Lamb neck fillet with cherries, and seared scallops with pea velouté, feature on the menu, which is laid out to appeal to lovers of meat, fish or veg. (Page 289)

THE PIG AT HARLYN BAY
PADSTOW
The 'uncomplicated British garden food' served here includes Cornish mackerel tartare and Kernow lamb loin. Or drink in the sea air at the Lobster Shed, where seafood is cooked in the wood oven or on the charcoal-fired grill. (Page 255)

MORSTON HALL
HOLT
Galton Blackiston's Michelin-starred tasting menus run to seven courses – butternut squash velouté, Middle White suckling pig – served in the conservatory restaurant with doors opening out onto a lavender-scented garden. (Page 204)

THE GEORGE OF STAMFORD
STAMFORD
Tradition rules in the clubby Oak Room restaurant, from the roast beef carved at the table to the trolleys heaving with puddings and cheeses. Feast on whole Atlantic lobster or mint-crusted rack of Herdwick lamb. (Page 299)

YALBURY COTTAGE
LOWER BOCKHAMPTON
This oak-beamed restaurant is strong on Dorset produce. Jamie Jones's menus include brill 'Cordon Bleu', and beef brisket with Jerusalem artichoke purée. Readers praise the wine list. Across the road is Thomas Hardy's former schoolhouse. (Page 227)

THE RED LION FREEHOUSE
EAST CHISENBURY
This welcoming thatched Wiltshire inn is no ordinary country pub. Guy and Brittany Manning's inspiring menus rely heavily on home-grown and foraged produce; expect herb-roasted guineafowl breast, or roast black cod with aubergine caviar. (Page 166)

THE CROSS AT KINGUSSIE
KINGUSSIE
Readers pour lavish praise on this 'sensational' – and peaceful – oasis in the Cairngorms. Dishes include venison with creamed cabbage, and wild sea bass with roast root vegetables, and there's a six-course tasting menu with paired wines. (Page 371)

FOREST SIDE
GRASMERE
Paul Leonard's Michelin-starred menus combine the flavours and ingredients of Cumbria to exacting perfection: try his beef tartare with caviar or slow-cooked beetroot with yogurt and locally picked green juniper. (Page 188)

THORNBURY CASTLE
THORNBURY
Even if you don't bag the top suite with its ten-foot blue and gold bed at the top of the turret you can't help feeling the romance of this Tudor castle, complete with arrow slits, crenellated walls, and four-posters. (Page 313)

PENALLY ABBEY
PENALLY
Floor-to-ceiling cusped windows frame views over Carmarthen Bay at this 'Strawberry Hill Gothic' house with rooms in soft pastels and an incredibly stylish restaurant. Expect toile de Jouy wallpaper, parquet floors and a ruined chapel in the gardens. (Page 423)

THE OLD RAILWAY STATION
PETWORTH
What could be more romantic than returning to the golden age of steam travel and staying in a Pullman carriage with mahogany fittings and colonial-style furniture? Sip champagne under a parasol on the platform for a first-class break. (Page 265)

THE DIAL HOUSE
REEPHAM
Choose between rooms resembling a Venetian palazzo, the mysterious east or a Parisian garret with slipper bath at the foot of the bed (oh là là). They all have record players, and a revolving bookcase reveals a secret dining room. (Page 271)

FISCHER'S AT BASLOW HALL
BASLOW
There are just 11 bedrooms at this Edwardian manor with period furnishings, fine food and beautiful grounds. It's a short stroll to Chatsworth House, aka Pemberley in Pride and Prejudice, should you wish to channel your inner Jane Austen. (Page 82)

STAR CASTLE
ST MARY'S
With an idyllic location on the Isles of Scilly, this Elizabethan castle within star-shaped fortress walls is pretty special. Castle rooms have beams and half-testers, and you can take tea on the ramparts or sip gin in the Dungeon bar. (Page 282)

MONACHYLE MHOR
BALQUHIDDER
If your idea of romance is less four-posters and velvet, more modern design in a remote setting, this is the place for you. Stylish rooms include a pod in the trees, a cool cabin and a wagon, and there are wild walks from the door. (Page 348)

HAZLITT'S
LONDON
It's lavishly luxurious in this Soho retreat, with four-posters and silk curtains, baroque mirrors and antiques. There's even a suite where the bed is adorned with gilded cherubs and another with a private garden beneath a sliding roof. (Page 56)

THE COACH HOUSE AT MIDDLETON LODGE
RICHMOND
Some of the rooms in cottages, former stables and outbuildings here come with outdoor hot tubs but all are rustic chic boltholes, perfect for snuggling up in after exploring the 200-acre estate with its appealing double-height restaurant. (Page 272)

CARY ARMS & SPA
BABBACOMBE
New England chic meets seaside inn at the Cary Arms, where you can stay in a stylish beach hut with sea views from the glass doors and the porthole on the mezzanine. Feast on seafood in the restaurant, then sip sloe gin in the rooms. (Page 74)

The Coach House at Middleton Lodge, Richmond

DRIFTWOOD HOTEL
PORTSCATHO

Seaside views don't get much better than from this dreamily located hotel overlooking Gerrans Bay – and you can get to the beach easily along its own pathway. All but one of the comfortable, boho-chic rooms look out on to the coast. (Page 268)

TREFEDDIAN HOTEL
ABERDOVEY

With a welcome as large as the stupendous views from its perch above Cardigan Bay, this family-run hotel is perfectly situated for hearty outdoor activities, from golf (with a view of the sea) to sailing, paddle-boarding and pony-trekking. (Page 401)

TRESANTON
ST MAWES

All the bedrooms in this shipshape former yacht club have glittering sea views, and you can dine outside on its waterside terraces. The nautical feel – even the staff wear blue and white uniforms – adds a touch of Riviera glamour. (Page 284)

ROSLEAGUE MANOR
LETTERFRACK

Go wild on the Atlantic Way at this pink Regency house, with sloping lawns and views across Ballinakill Bay in Connemara. Interiors are filled with antiques, plump sofas, brass beds and log fires. Seven rooms have sea views. (Page 453)

THE HENLEY
BIGBURY-ON-SEA

There's a touch of nostalgia at this Edwardian bolthole with a panorama of the Avon estuary from its sun terrace. Tumbling plants and towering potted palms, Lloyd Loom chairs, vintage wallpapers and velvet quilts recall a gentler era. (Page 97)

THE GALLIVANT
CAMBER

This adults-only hotel over the road from the sand dunes is a seriously funky little place, with a cool Californian vibe. It offers half-board-only overnight stays, which include elevenses, English vino and a yoga session on the beach. (Page 134)

THE COLONSAY
COLONSAY

Escape to this harbourside hotel, which enjoys views across to Jura and welcomes the locals in the bar and well-regarded restaurant. A restful sleep is assured in the modern rooms; awake refreshed to explore the island's white-sand beaches. (Page 353)

VIEWFIELD HOUSE
PORTREE

Sweeping views of the Sound of Raasay from the 20-acre grounds are complemented by fine Victorian interiors – stuffed eagles, Turkey carpets, antique furniture, a grand piano. After a full Scottish, go sailing aboard the family yacht. (Page 382)

ROMNEY BAY HOUSE
NEW ROMNEY

Marsh wetlands, a long shingle beach for head-clearing walks, and vast skies form the landscape in which this white mansion sits. Noel Coward and the Astors used to party here, and the house retains its 1930s charisma. (Page 243)

THE PIG ON THE BEACH
STUDLAND

You will love being beside the seaside at this eccentric, gabled and turreted villa, with shabby-chic bedrooms, vintage bric-a-brac, excellent food served in the conservatory and sun-squinting views of the chalk cliffs of Studland Bay. (Page 302)

Driftwood Hotel, Portscatho

Calcot & Spa, Tetbury

GILPIN HOTEL AND LAKE HOUSE
WINDERMERE

Not only do the garden suites have their own cedarwood hot tubs, but there are lodges with steam rooms and saunas, and even more pampering spa suites, with bedrooms 'floating' over a pond. The private Lake House has its own swimming pool. (Page 334)

SEAHAM HALL
SEAHAM

Seaham's superlative Asian-themed spa has swish, spacious facilities, including a 20-metre pool, hammam, salt sauna, eucalyptus steam room, herbal sanarium and Zen lounge. Celebrate peace of mind with a manicure and bubbly in the nail bar. (Page 286)

THE NEWT IN SOMERSET
BRUTON

Spas sometimes look like clumsy add-ons, but the half-indoor, half-outdoor pool here, with its timber roof and stone walls, complements the aesthetics of this Palladian manor. After a treatment, meditate in the medieval herb garden. (Page 126)

THE SCARLET
MAWGAN PORTH

This chic, eco-friendly hotel spa on the Cornish coast keeps 'getting things right', say readers. Enjoy the clifftop wooden sauna, lounge in a hot tub to the sound of crashing waves and really relax in a cosy, suspended cocoon pod. (Page 235)

CALCOT & SPA
TETBURY

Combine a Cotswold break at this 16th-century house with some me-time in the heated indoor pool and courtyard hot tub. In addition to the sauna, steam rooms and treatments, there are tennis courts and bike rides through the 220-acre estate. (Page 310)

LIME WOOD
LYNDHURST

Swanky, in a hippy-chic sort of way, and inspired by its forested, flowered and scented setting, the Herb House Spa has a glamorous pool overlooking the garden, an outdoor hot pool, a mud house, and a high-tech rooftop gym and yoga deck. (Page 231)

BODYSGALLEN HALL AND SPA
LLANDUDNO

Restore mind and body at this 17th-century country house with over 200 acres of gardens and parkland. The spa has a 15-metre pool, gym, sun garden and treatments ranging from an Aching Foot Relaxer to a 'non-surgical facelift'. (Page 416)

HOMEWOOD
BATH

A pretty outdoor pool and cosy, sheltered divans to lounge on are a highlight of the spa at this stylish hotel. Refresh tired limbs in the hydrotherapy pool or steam room, and have a Tibetan 'five elements' massage. (Page 83)

CONGHAM HALL
KING'S LYNN

Renowned for its extensive herb garden, Congham makes use of home-grown herbs and flowers in its signature treatments, such as a Herbal Facial or Rosemary Muscle Melt Massage. There is also a 12-metre indoor pool and a bio sauna. (Page 212)

MULLION COVE HOTEL
MULLION COVE

There is plenty to rejuvenate you here, from the outdoor pool and appealing range of treatments – Organic Seaweed Leaf Wrap or Jade Wave Stone massage – to the spectacular clifftop views. There is a dedicated vegan menu in the restaurant. (Page 239)

OLD DOWNTON LODGE
LUDLOW

Readers love this rural haven for its 'faultless attention to detail'. Sip English fizz in the parterre garden before dining on Nick Bennett's 'exquisite' menus: halibut with nasturtium root, or lamb with pea, mint and wild garlic. (Page 228)

THE COTTAGE IN THE WOOD
BRAITHWAITE

Enjoy Michelin-starred dining at this 17th-century cottage with views of England's highest mountain forest. Ben Wilkinson's menus are brief, and his cooking blessedly unpretentious – hogget with lentils, or cured trout with oyster cream. (Page 113)

READ'S
FAVERSHAM

This is an established favourite with Guide regulars, who say it's like paying a visit to a more civilised era. Roast loin of Kentish lamb, potato gnocchi fricassée, and the freshest vegetables feature on Frederick Forster's classic menus. (Page 181)

THE ANGEL INN
HETTON

Michael Wignall prides himself on a 'contemporary, less formal approach to fine cuisine' in his Michelin-starred gastro pub, with dishes such as turbot with courgette tempura, and potatoes cooked in seaweed. (Page 202)

THE CRAB & LOBSTER
SIDLESHAM

Go birdwatching in Pagham Harbour Local Nature Reserve before dining at this picturesque 17th-century pub. The menus specialise in locally caught fish, but you'll also find roast lamb alongside the beer-battered loin of hake and crab cakes. (Page 290)

LLYS MEDDYG
NEWPORT

This Georgian inn has a convivial restaurant with art and rustic furniture. Ed Sykes, a keen forager, cooks traditional dishes with an imaginative twist (local lobster with seaweed butter) and there is home-smoked salmon at breakfast. (Page 422)

TYDDYN LLAN
LLANDRILLO

Bryan and Susan Webb's dining room in the Vale of Edeyrnion has built a loyal following over the years, and no wonder. Local meat, such as aged Welsh black beef, comes from their 'vigilant butcher'; the fish 'straight from the coast'. (Page 415)

THE PEAT INN
PEAT INN

The modern Scottish cuisine served in this attractive restaurant, decorated in soft teals and greys, is so good it has held a Michelin star since 2010. Expect home-cured sea trout pastrami, or roe deer with butternut squash. (Page 375)

THE NEPTUNE
OLD HUNSTANTON

Kevin and Jacki Mangeolles' welcoming coaching inn, a stone's throw from the sea, has held a Michelin star since 2009. Kevin's contemporary British menus use the best Norfolk produce, served in a crisp, elegant dining room. (Page 249)

MOOR HALL RESTAURANT WITH ROOMS
AUGHTON

Mark Birchall's Scandi-style dining room in five acres of gardens has two Michelin stars and features delicately balanced dishes such as baked carrots with Doddington cheese and chrysanthemum. There is a tasting menu at breakfast. (Page 70)

Llys Meddyg, Newport

Paschoe House, Crediton

THE HARPER
LANGHAM

With a roll-top bath and shower to wash dirty paws after a romp on Norfolk's beaches, towels in the lobby to dry them, and a plush dog bed in the bar, The Harper clearly cares for its four-legged guests as much as its two-legged ones. (Page 217)

MOOR OF RANNOCH –
RESTAURANT & ROOMS
RANNOCH STATION

There's no charge for dogs staying at this remote outpost amid miles of moorland. When you return from exploring, there are towels for mucky puppies, comfy cushions in front of the fire, and a free sausage the next day for breakfast. (Page 383)

PASCHOE HOUSE
CREDITON

Doggie day or dinner care is on offer here, and there's plenty of together time, too, with pets allowed in the library bar, morning room and some bedrooms. There's a dog bin by the front porch, towels to wipe dirty paws, and treats and toys. (Page 154)

THE OLD COASTGUARD
MOUSEHOLE

Furry friends can sit with you while you eat in the bar and join you on the Sun Deck in this Cornish pub. Blankets and biscuits, treats and towels are supplied, and there's no charge for well-behaved dogs to stay in your room. (Page 238)

THE HARE AND HOUNDS
TETBURY

Dine with your dog at your side in sight of an enormous canine mural in Jack Hare's bar, or in the garden, with its doggie bins and dog wash. You can go for walks at Westonbirt Arboretum, too, which is just ten minutes away. (Page 311)

THE SUN INN
KIRKBY LONSDALE

Four-legged guests receive a 'pooch pack' with towel, bowl, treat and dog-trail map. They can clean up in the dog and boot shower before curling up by the fire in the bar or joining their owners in the dog-friendly dining area. (Page 213)

WIDBROOK GRANGE
BRADFORD-ON-AVON

They even host doggie birthday parties here, but if your pup isn't celebrating, just book it into a special afternoon tea, with wet food, organic dog biscuits, a puppichino and a tennis ball to take home. There's optional Pawsecco, too. (Page 111)

TY MAWR
BRECHFA

Biscuits, bowls and a warm welcome await four-legged friends at this hotel with gardens bordering the River Marlais with plenty of good local walks. Owners Paul Bennett and Melissa Hurley don't charge for Fido to stay either. (Page 404)

NO.15 GREAT PULTENEY
BATH

Just over the road from dog-friendly Henrietta Park, this city hotel can organise walkies and doggie day care should you want a break. Back at base, there are unlimited dog treats in the pantry and blankets in the bedrooms. (Page 84)

THE THREE BLACKBIRDS
WOODDITTON

While their owners enjoy excellent pub meals, pampered pooches can tuck into items from their own menu, including venison jerky and Tailwagger Creek wine (0% alcohol). Six bedrooms are dog friendly and there are walkies from the door. (Page 337)

Hambleton Hall, Hambleton

LANGAR HALL
LANGAR
At the end of a long avenue of lime trees, this golden-hued Georgian house offers 'quietly eccentric' rooms decorated in pretty prints and filled with antiques, paintings and books. Couples can book a chalet by the croquet lawn. (Page 216)

SUMMER LODGE
EVERSHOT
This sprawling dower house – enlarged with the help of local architect Thomas Hardy in 1893 – has traditional bedrooms in florals and stripes, and grand public rooms heaving with antiques. (Page 178)

PEN-Y-DYFFRYN
OSWESTRY
Set among flower-filled gardens in a secluded, green valley, this old rectory is a highly pleasing prospect. There's tea and cake on arrival, individually styled bedrooms, 'superb food' in the restaurant, and smoked haddock at breakfast. (Page 251)

GRASMERE HOTEL
GRASMERE
The Winsland family run this handsome Victorian house in a riverside setting with unfailing dedication. Guests love the views of Helm Crag, the well-appointed bedrooms, the lounges to relax in, and excellent Cumbrian breakfasts. (Page 189)

HAMBLETON HALL
HAMBLETON
The sumptuous bedrooms here have fabulous views of Rutland Water and are filled with luxury fabrics, plump cushions and sofas – all kept to perfection by tip-top housekeeping. The restaurant has the UK's longest-held single Michelin star. (Page 195)

TUDOR FARMHOUSE
CLEARWELL
This beautifully converted stone farmhouse in the Forest of Dean has sleek, contemporary rooms with just a touch of rusticity in the beams and exposed stone walls. Book a foraging or wildlife safari, returning to buttered crumpets for tea. (Page 145)

HOTEL ENDSLEIGH
MILTON ABBOT
The Grade I listed parkland, with its dells, follies and grottoes, was designed by Humphry Repton, and would be a draw on its own, but Olga Polizzi has completed the pastoral idyll with her exquisite interiors in this cottage orné. (Page 237)

THE MILLSTREAM
BOSHAM
In a pretty harbourside village, these former 17th-century workers' cottages are set in gardens with a stream running through. Bedrooms are light and restful, the restaurant highly praised. (Page 109)

KINLOCH HOUSE
BLAIRGOWRIE
An imposing Victorian mansion in large grounds, Kinloch has an oak-panelled hall, library and portrait gallery, but it also manages to be a snug, homely sort of place, with roaring fires and plush bedrooms with views of Marlee Loch. (Page 349)

LLANGOED HALL
LLYSWEN
Art lovers will love this romantic place, which has works by Sickert, Whistler and Augustus John. Staying here feels like an Edwardian country house weekend, with aristocratic, antique-filled interiors and 17 acres of landscaped gardens. (Page 419)

THE FALCON
CASTLE ASHBY
With parkland designed by Capability Brown, an Italian garden, orangery, arboretum and meerkats menagerie, Castle Ashby's gardens are pretty impressive. Guests of the Falcon get free access and can swim in the lake in front of the castle. (Page 141)

BARNSLEY HOUSE
BARNSLEY
The renowned garden designer Rosemary Verey created the perfect example of an English country garden at her old home, with a laburnum walk, statues and a potager, which supplies the restaurant. There's even a spa in this magical place. (Page 79)

THE PIPE AND GLASS INN
SOUTH DALTON
The Michelin-starred cuisine tells you they're serious about food in James and Kate Mackenzie's pub. Now they have added a garden, with sculptures, hidden arbours, a kitchen garden and a herbarium, where every plant is edible, even the roses. (Page 295)

GLENAPP CASTLE
BALLANTRAE
The Gulf Stream warming this part of the Scottish coast means exotic plants flourish at Glenapp, with its Italian garden designed by Gertrude Jekyll, a walled garden with 150-foot glasshouse, and plenty of picturesque pathways in between. (Page 347)

BALLYMALOE HOUSE
SHANAGARRY
The Loire's Château de Villandry was the inspiration behind Ballymaloe's herb garden, with 70 plant varieties in its formal parterre. It's one of a number of gardens here, including a Celtic Maze. Tours or gardening courses can be booked. (Page 463)

GLIFFAES
CRICKHOWELL
There's everything from oaks to ornamental species, including Japanese maples and handkerchief trees, in the arboretum at this Italianate Victorian manor on the banks of the River Usk. Take a copy of the tree walk map and explore. (Page 407)

GRAVETYE MANOR
EAST GRINSTEAD
The 19th-century visionary gardener William Robinson developed his ideas on wild gardens at his Sussex home. Now eight full-time gardeners are kept busy maintaining Gravetye's flower garden, meadows, orchards and kitchen garden. (Page 167)

LONGUEVILLE MANOR
ST SAVIOUR
A Victorian kitchen garden with glasshouses and potting sheds supplies Jersey Royals and other produce for the restaurant at this manor house hotel. The 18-acre estate also includes a lake, formal gardens, beehives and unspoilt woodland. (Page 435)

GOLDSTONE HALL
MARKET DRAYTON
At the heart of the flower-filled gardens with small woodland area on this Shropshire estate is the one-acre kitchen garden with herbal walkways. One of the largest in Britain, it supplies an abundance of fresh produce for the restaurant. (Page 232)

LE MANOIR AUX QUAT'SAISONS
GREAT MILTON
Raymond Blanc's Oxfordshire hotel is famed for its food, but also has sculpture-studded gardens, from a mushroom valley and wildflower meadow to a potager, pond and Japanese tea garden. There's both a gardening school and a cookery school. (Page 192)

Le Manoir aux Quat'Saisons, Great Milton

THE HACK & SPADE
RICHMOND
Hearty breakfasts at Jane Ratcliffe's former Georgian ale house with hotel-standard bedrooms set you up for the day, but be sure to return in time for tea and home-made cakes. Horse riding, fishing and shooting can be arranged. (Page 274)

DORSET HOUSE
LYME REGIS
Lyn and Jason Martin describe their eco-friendly B&B as 'breakfast with rooms' and take great care with the daily-changing menu of local, organic produce. Add boutique-style bedrooms and a willingness to go out of their way to help guests. (Page 229)

NO. 33
HUNSTANTON
Jeanne Whittome's smart B&B ticks all the boxes for a special stay. Breakfasts and picnic hampers come from sister venture the Thornham Deli, rooms are beautifully decorated, and there is even a concierge service to book bikes or boats. (Page 208)

THE OLD RECTORY
HASTINGS
It's seriously stylish in Lionel Copley's Georgian rectory B&B, with wood floors and hand-painted wallpapers. As well as a treatment room and honesty bar, there's a weekend supper club. Breakfast features house-smoked kippers and bacon. (Page 199)

23 MAYFIELD
EDINBURGH
Guests are entrusted with their own key during their stay at Ross and Kathleen Birnie's Victorian house with antique furniture and period features. Bedrooms might have a four-poster or half-tester and breakfast is a slap-up spread. (Page 359)

AEL Y BRYN
EGLWYSWRW
Readers report that this much-loved B&B is 'first class in every respect', with spacious rooms, glorious views to the Preseli hills and superb attention to detail. Breakfasts and dinners are equally good, and you can take your own wine. (Page 410)

TREWORNAN MANOR
WADEBRIDGE
In gardens and pastureland near the Camel estuary, Paul and Lesley Stapleton's Grade II listed manor house B&B wins high praise from readers for its smart bedrooms, complimentary cream tea, superb breakfasts and relaxed air. (Page 326)

UNDERLEIGH HOUSE
HOPE
Vivienne Taylor's Derbyshire longhouse offers a restful stay with its large, pretty bedrooms, peaceful garden and views across the Peak District's Hope valley. Breakfasts get a big thumbs up, with home-made bread and a full grill. (Page 205)

THE QUAY HOUSE
CLIFDEN
Run as a B&B for almost 30 years, Paddy and Julia Foyle's former harbourmaster's house has become a Connemara institution. Antiques, curios, mirrors and paintings abound downstairs, and some of the spacious bedrooms have harbour views. (Page 445)

LINDETH FELL
BOWNESS-ON-WINDERMERE
Far from your average B&B, the Kennedy family's luxury guesthouse offers picnics, cream teas and cold plates as well as an outstanding breakfast. The seven-acre gardens and some of the elegant rooms overlook Windermere. (Page 110)

No. 33, Hunstanton

The Lord Poulett Arms, Hinton St George

BROCKENCOTE HALL
CHADDESLEY CORBETT
Looking for all the world like a Loire château overlooking a lake, Brockencote has smart contemporary rooms, a well-regarded restaurant and grounds you can roam with four-legged friends. B&B doubles from £120. (Page 142)

SEA MIST HOUSE
CLIFDEN
Sheila Griffin is your genial hostess at her pretty Georgian home with a flower-filled garden, wood-burner-warmed sitting rooms, artworks and antiques. At breakfast, she serves a full Irish, with eggs from her own hens. B&B doubles are €90. (Page 446)

BROOKS GUESTHOUSE
BRISTOL
In the heart of the city, this uber-cool guesthouse not only has a rooftop garden, but also has Airstream-style caravans parked in it. Otherwise, rooms are smart but simple, with B&B doubles from £69, and caravans from £94. (Page 118)

AYNSOME MANOR
CARTMEL
With B&B doubles from £99, this 400-year-old manor house offers superb value close to the attractions of the Lake District. A tranquil base with traditional comforts, it has simple country-style bedrooms and excellent cuisine. (Page 140)

LLANTHONY PRIORY HOTEL
LLANTHONY
There's a monastic simplicity to the rooms in this former prior's lodging, with the ruins of a medieval Augustinian abbey outside. You won't get TV, Wi-Fi or en-suites, but you can enjoy this romantic setting from £100, B&B, for two. (Page 418)

BIGGIN HALL
BIGGIN-BY-HARTINGTON
You get the Peak District without peak prices at this 17th-century country house, with beams, wood panelling and a vast fireplace in the comfy lounge. Some bedrooms have a four-poster or half-tester. B&B doubles from £110. (Page 98)

THE GUNTON ARMS
THORPE MARKET
It's got all the trappings of a posh country hotel, with a 1,000-acre estate and oodles of original artwork, but this is very much a proper pub, with blazing fires, flagstone floors, and rooms from a very reasonable £95, with breakfast. (Page 314)

THE CASTLEMAN
CHETTLE
There's plenty of charm in Niki and Jez Barfoot's 18th-century former dower house, with a Jacobean fireplace and ornate carved woodwork in one of the drawing rooms. Bedrooms are country style, with B&B doubles from £120. (Page 143)

THE LORD POULETT ARMS
HINTON ST GEORGE
It's both chic and cheap at this thatched 17th-century inn, with plenty of exposed brick, beams and mix-and-match furniture in the bar and dining area and the uncluttered bedrooms upstairs. B&B doubles from £95. (Page 203)

THE PIERHOUSE
PORT APPIN
Gordon Campbell Gray's tranquil lochside hotel comes with spectacular sea views and delicious seafood. If you don't mind only seeing the views from the public rooms, comfortable cliff-facing doubles cost from £125, B&B. (Page 380)

The Felin Fach Griffin, Felin Fach

THE PEACOCK AT BARLOW
BARLOW
They don't just serve local ale at The Peacock – they brew it, at the onsite Collyfobble Brewery. This tasteful reinvention of the village local, in a village once named Barley, has eight high-spec bedrooms named after different hops. (Page 78)

THE DOG AT WINGHAM
WINGHAM
Foodies delight in Marc Bridgen's village gastropub, with its passion for Kent produce and a dining club. Golfers, too, are catered for, with transport to nearby clubs, while the stylish rooms include a seriously romantic bridal suite. (Page 335)

THE ACORN INN
EVERSHOT
There's literary history in this atmospheric village inn with its oak-panelled bar, which featured in Thomas Hardy's Tess of the d'Urbervilles. Bedrooms are Hardy themed, acorn motifs abound and there's even a skittle alley. (Page 177)

THE DABBLING DUCK
GREAT MASSINGHAM
Saved from redevelopment by two farmers, this gastropub with rustic-chic bedrooms overlooking the village green uses as much produce as possible from its owners' land. There's plenty of game on the menu – and the pub's own Mucky Duck gin. (Page 191)

THE HARCOURT ARMS
STANTON HARCOURT
It's not just pints and pillows at this 17th-century pub – it also runs its own deli with fresh produce, coffee and cakes. The beamed bar comes with flagstone floors and wood burners, and modern bedrooms have statement fabric headboards. (Page 300)

THE FELIN FACH GRIFFIN
FELIN FACH
Between the Black mountains and the Brecon Beacons, this dog-friendly pub with smart but casual bedrooms is perfect for walkers. Enjoy a Welsh real ale before the fire in the cosy bar before dining on a nightly-changing menu of superb food. (Page 411)

SIGN OF THE ANGEL
LACOCK
The olde-worlde charm of this 15th-century half-timbered coaching inn with its flagstones and fireplaces earned it a place in the Harry Potter films and in the BBC's Cranford series. Upstairs are five rustic-chic bedrooms. (Page 215)

THE SHIP INN
ELIE
Rachel and Graham Bucknall's white and blue dog-friendly gastropub comes with its own beach cricket team. Bedrooms, though, have a coastal rather than a cricket theme, in breezy blues and whites, with sea views. (Page 360)

PENTONBRIDGE INN
PENTON
Just half a mile from the Scottish border, this former coaching inn combines chic contemporary bedrooms and bathrooms with creative cooking. Full of style, with tweedy fabrics, slate floors and modern art, it still retains its character. (Page 262)

THE ROSE & CROWN
ROMALDKIRK
Whether you eat in the flagged-floor bar with roaring fire or in the candlelit panelled dining room, you can be sure of good food using local produce at this inn. Rooms combine character with contemporary luxury. (Page 277)

FOWEY HALL
FOWEY
It's family holiday heaven in this elegant but relaxed hotel, with everything from a crèche and cinema to a pool and playground. Add to that Cornish cuisine, a spa and a sandy cove nearby and you'll see why guests are as happy as clams. (Page 184)

SOAR MILL COVE HOTEL
SALCOMBE
Get bacon bait from the kitchen and go crabbing at the gorgeous beach which shares this hotel's name. When you're done with sand and sea, there's a pool back at the Makepeace family's hotel, as well as tennis, snooker and board games. (Page 285)

WOOLLEY GRANGE
BRADFORD-ON-AVON
Quirky decor and a laid-back atmosphere reign in this refined Jacobean mansion. There's a spa for adults and free childcare for kids, both family and formal dining, and ducks, pigs, chickens and a rabbit to pet in the extensive grounds. (Page 112)

COWLEY MANOR
COWLEY
This grand Italianate mansion decorated with 1960s pizzazz comes with wellies for woodland walks, family swimming time in the spa's two pools, and rooms for all sizes of families. Some rooms have interconnecting doors for up to seven. (Page 152)

TREFEDDIAN HOTEL
ABERDOVEY
You only need glance at the all-day menu, with its fish platters for adults, fish fingers for kids, to see that Trefeddian caters for all generations. Play tennis or golf, go swimming, sailing or pony trekking, or hit the nearby beach. (Page 401)

CHEWTON GLEN
NEW MILTON
Slick treehouse suites and fab facilities including a spa, pools, tennis courts, golf course, kids' club and cookery school are the recipe for the perfect family break in this New Forest country house. It's not cheap, but it's worth it. (Page 242)

AUGILL CASTLE
KIRKBY STEPHEN
Towers and battlements are part of the fun at this Victorian folly of a castle, where no one bats an eyelid if the tinies scatter their toys round the elegant drawing room. Everything from baby monitors to dressing-up clothes is on hand. (Page 214)

THE ROSE & CROWN
SNETTISHAM
Forget the fancy kids' club and full-on facilities – this Norfolk pub is more about its family-friendly attitude. There's a play area in the garden, a kids' menu, a miniature steam railway at Norton Hill next door, and beaches nearby. (Page 292)

TEMPLE HOUSE
BALLYMOTE
When you've been rowing on the lake near the ruins of a Knights Templar castle and explored the acres of woodland around the Perceval family mansion, kids' supper is served in the kitchen while adults eat communally in the dining room. (Page 441)

HEADLAM HALL
DARLINGTON
While there isn't a kids' club, there's plenty at Headlam to keep the youngsters busy, with gardens to explore, family-friendly slots in the pool, and both tennis and golf. Early tea and an informal atmosphere complete the picture. (Page 158)

Chewton Glen, New Milton

Glenfinnan House Hotel, Glenfinnan

THE GROVE OF NARBERTH
NARBERTH

Walking trails weave through The Grove's 28-acre grounds, while footpaths criss-cross the surrounding countryside. Hike to a deserted Welsh chapel or an ancient settlement on a nearby hill, or take longer treks in the Narberth valley. (Page 420)

THE GURNARD'S HEAD
ZENNOR

Follow the coastal path in either direction from this dog-friendly pub. Head west to Land's End, past Botallack tin mine, of Poldark fame, or hike for four hours in the other direction to St Ives before returning to the comfort of the inn. (Page 341)

DUNKERY BEACON
COUNTRY HOUSE
WOOTTON COURTENAY

A three-hour round trip from the door of this Exmoor hotel takes you to the beacon of the same name, which at 519 metres marks the national park's highest point. The hotel has a drying room, a supply of maps and plenty of walk recommendations. (Page 338)

THE CASTLE HOTEL
BISHOP'S CASTLE

On the Shropshire Way, and close to the Offa's Dyke Path, The Castle makes a superb base for walkers. It has drying and boot-cleaning facilities and can supply packed lunches as well as details of scenic walks right from the hotel door. (Page 100)

THE STAR
ALFRISTON

Borrow wellies or sun hats from the Polizzis' latest pad and hike along the pretty Cuckmere valley and to the undulating chalk cliffs of the Seven Sisters. In the South Downs national park, the dog-friendly hotel is surrounded by scenic walks. (Page 65)

GLENFINNAN HOUSE HOTEL
GLENFINNAN

It's a ten-minute walk through the deer-studded estate to the Glenfinnan viaduct railway bridge of Harry Potter fame. Don't stop there, though – there's everything from easy hikes to munro bagging on offer in the surrounding countryside. (Page 363)

SHEEDY'S
LISDOONVARNA

Midway along the Wild Atlantic Way, and not far from the Cliffs of Moher, this old farmhouse is also on the edge of the Burren's dramatic karst landscape. You can explore it on your own or book a walking package with a local guide. (Page 455)

HAZEL BANK
BORROWDALE

In pretty Borrowdale, this country house has a number of interesting walks from the door, taking in the massive Bowder Stone monolith, the Borrowdale yews celebrated in Wordsworth's poem and the tarn where Wainwright's ashes are scattered. (Page 106)

LASTINGHAM GRANGE
LASTINGHAM

After a day on the North York Moors, return to this former farmhouse to have wet clothes whisked away and to tuck into a well-earned five-course dinner. There's a scenic five-mile walk from the door to the village of Hutton le Hole. (Page 218)

ST AIDAN HOTEL AND BISTRO
SEAHOUSES

Among the coastal walks near this hotel is the three-mile yomp up the beach from Seahouses all the way to Bamburgh, with its castle. Staff can advise you on routes, and the bistro is a good place to refuel after a day's exploring. (Page 287)

THE TORRIDON
TORRIDON
This turreted, baronial-style Highland hunting lodge can arrange fishing on local lochs and rivers with a ghillie, with equipment and tuition for beginners, if required. Or hire a boat and guide to go sea fishing from nearby Gairloch. (Page 395)

DEVONSHIRE ARMS
BOLTON ABBEY
Part of the Bolton Abbey Estate in the Yorkshire Dales national park, this luxury hotel offers 4½ miles of double-bank fishing along the River Wharf, where anglers can fish for brown trout and grayling. Tuition can be arranged. (Page 105)

GLENAPP CASTLE
BALLANTRAE
You can learn how to fly-fish in the River Stinchar, which is on the doorstep of this luxurious Ayrshire country house, or venture north to the Doon or Girvan rivers. The more adventurous can book the skippered boat for sea fishing. (Page 347)

THE INN AT WHITEWELL
WHITEWELL
There are seven miles of river to explore at this traditional inn on the banks of the Hodder, with 14 pools and plenty of runs. Four rods are available for trout, sea trout and salmon in season; ghillies are available for hire. (Page 330)

NEWPORT HOUSE
NEWPORT
Fly-fishers head to this Georgian mansion on Ireland's Newport river, which runs to seven miles and has many pools and streams, with an excellent run of spring salmon, among other fish. Or hire a boat and fish from Lough Beltra. (Page 459)

ENNISCOE HOUSE
CASTLEHILL
This 18th-century mansion overlooks beautiful Lough Conn, which is renowned for brown trout and spring salmon. The owners can arrange a day's angling for you courtesy of a local fishing outfit, with boat hire and ghillies. (Page 443)

FORSS HOUSE
THURSO
The Forss river curls around this house, and the owners post a weekly fishing report on their Facebook page. They can advise on rods that may occasionally be available for weekly rent, and arrange trout fishing on nearby lochs. (Page 394)

TEMPLE HOUSE
BALLYMOTE
Hook a 'monster' pike, perch or bream on Templehouse lake, which is a mile long. The hotel offers all the fishing equipment you need, a guide or ghillie, and the use of its four boats if you fancy hosting a jolly fishing party. (Page 441)

KINLOCH LODGE
SLEAT
You will be well placed at this hotel on the lovely shores of Loch Na Dal to take advantage of Skye's excellent salmon and trout fishing; the hotel is plugged into the best local guides and ghillies to help organise your day. (Page 388)

THE TROUT AT TADPOLE BRIDGE
BUCKLAND MARSH
You can arrive by boat if you wish at this pescatarian-themed riverside pub with rooms – it has its own mooring on the Thames. It is also ideally positioned for fly fishers looking to land a trout from the area's many chalk streams. (Page 129)

The Torridon, Torridon

Each of these hotels has a tennis court (T) and/or a swimming pool (S)

Cliveden House, Taplow

ENGLAND

Hartwell House & Spa,
Aylesbury (T,S)

Homewood,
Bath (S)

The Royal Crescent Hotel & Spa,
Bath (S)

Beechfield House,
Beanacre (S)

Park House,
Bepton (T,S)

Burgh Island Hotel,
Bigbury-on-Sea (T,S)

The Blakeney Hotel,
Blakeney (S)

The Devonshire Arms,
Bolton Abbey (S)

Widbrook Grange,
Bradford-on-Avon (S)

Woolley Grange,
Bradford-on-Avon (S)

The Lygon Arms,
Broadway (S)

The Newt,
Bruton (S)

Hell Bay Hotel,
Bryher (S)

Brockencote Hall,
Chaddesley Corbett (T)

Corse Lawn House,
Corse Lawn (T,S)

North House,
Cowes (S)

Cowley Manor,
Cowley (S)

Paschoe House,
Crediton (T)

The Rectory Hotel,
Crudwell (S)

Headlam Hall,
Darlington (T,S)

Dart Marina,
Dartmouth (S)

Maison Talbooth,
Dedham (T,S)

Old Whyly,
East Hoathly (T,S)

Gara Rock,
East Portlemouth (S)

Whatley Manor,
Easton Grey (S)

Summer Lodge,
Evershot (T,S)

Moonfleet Manor,
Fleet (S)

Fowey Hall,
Fowey (S)
Hambleton Hall,
Hambleton (T,S)
The Pheasant,
Harome (S)
Walwick Hall Hotel,
Humshaugh (S)
Congham Hall,
King's Lynn (S)
Augill Castle,
Kirkby Stephen (T)
The Harper,
Langham (S)
Mallory Court,
Leamington Spa (S)
Lime Wood,
Lyndhurst (S)
Bedruthan Hotel and Spa,
Mawgan Porth (T,S)
The Scarlet,
Mawgan Porth (S)
Mullion Cove Hotel,
Mullion Cove (S)
Chewton Glen,
New Milton (T,S)
Askham Hall,
Penrith (S)
Star Castle,
St Mary's (T,S)
Soar Mill Cove Hotel,
Salcombe (S)
Seaham Hall,
Seaham (S)
Thyme,
Southrop (S)
Plumber Manor,
Sturminster Newton (T)
Cliveden House,
Taplow (T,S)
Calcot & Spa,
Tetbury (T,S)
The Royal Hotel,
Ventnor (S)
The Nare,
Veryan-in-Roseland (T,S)
Gilpin Hotel and Lake House,
Windermere (S)
Middlethorpe Hall & Spa,
York (S)

SCOTLAND
Glenapp Castle,
Ballantrae (T)
Glengarry Castle,
Invergarry (T)
Douneside House,
Tarland (T,S)

WALES
Trefeddian Hotel,
Aberdovey (T,S)
Porth Tocyn,
Abersoch (T,S)
Gliffaes,
Crickhowell (T)
Bodysgallen Hall & Spa,
Llandudno (S)
Lake Country House Hotel & Spa,
Llangammarch Wells (T,S)

CHANNEL ISLANDS
The White House,
Herm (T,S)
The Atlantic Hotel,
St Brelade (T,S)
Greenhills Country House Hotel,
St Peter (S)
Longueville Manor,
St Saviour (T,S)

IRELAND
Ballyvolane House,
Castlelyons (T)
**Killiane Castle Country House
and Farm,**
Drinagh (T)
Rosleague Manor,
Letterfrack (T)
Currarevagh House,
Oughterard (T)
Rathmullan House,
Rathmullan (S)
Coopershill,
Riverstown (T)
Ballymaloe House,
Shanagarry (T,S)

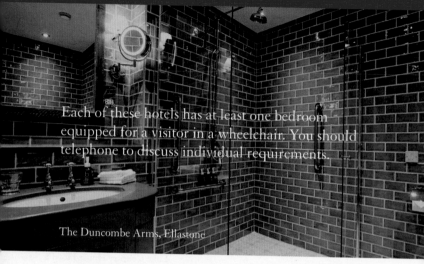

Each of these hotels has at least one bedroom equipped for a visitor in a wheelchair. You should telephone to discuss individual requirements.

The Duncombe Arms, Ellastone

LONDON
The Beaumont
The Goring
The Zetter
The Zetter Townhouse Clerkenwell
The Zetter Townhouse Marylebone

ENGLAND
The Wentworth,
  Aldeburgh
The Cookie Jar,
  Alnwick
Baraset Barn,
  Alveston
Hartwell House & Spa,
  Aylesbury
The Red Lion,
  Babcary
The George Inn,
  Barford St Michael
Barnsley House,
  Barnsley
Three Hills,
  Bartlow
The Cavendish,
  Baslow
No.15 Great Pulteney,
  Bath
Beadnell Towers,
  Beadnell
Beechfield House,
  Beanacre
Park House,
  Bepton

Helen Browning's Royal Oak,
  Bishopstone
The Blakeney Hotel,
  Blakeney
The Lord Crewe Arms,
  Blanchland
The Devonshire Arms,
  Bolton Abbey
Leathes Head Hotel,
  Borrowdale
The Millstream,
  Bosham
Lindeth Fell,
  Bowness-on-Windermere
Widbrook Grange,
  Bradford-on-Avon
Woolley Grange,
  Bradford-on-Avon
The White Horse,
  Brancaster Staithe
The Lygon Arms,
  Broadway
The Pig in the Forest,
  Brockenhurst
The Newt in Somerset,
  Bruton
The University Arms,
  Cambridge
Pendragon Country House,
  Camelford
Blackmore Farm,
  Cannington
The Pig at Bridge Place,
  Canterbury
The Falcon,
  Castle Ashby

Brockencote Hall,
  Chaddesley Corbett
Captain's Club Hotel,
  Christchurch
Beech House & Olive Branch,
  Clipsham
The Bay Hotel,
  Coverack
Hipping Hall,
  Cowan Bridge
Clow Beck House,
  Croft-on-Tees
Headlam Hall,
  Darlington
Dart Marina,
  Dartmouth
The Red Lion Freehouse,
  East Chisenbury
Whatley Manor,
  Easton Grey
The Duncombe Arms,
  Ellastone
The Ellerby Country Inn,
  Ellerby
Summer Lodge,
  Evershot
Lympstone Manor,
  Exmouth
The Carpenters Arms,
  Felixkirk
Fowey Hall,
  Fowey
The Pig at Combe,
  Gittisham
Forest Side,
  Grasmere
Le Manoir aux Quat'Saisons,
  Great Milton
The Pheasant,
  Harome
Simonstone Hall,
  Hawes
Castle House,
  Hereford
The Bath Arms,
  Horningsham
Kentisbury Grange,
  Kentisbury
Congham Hall,
  King's Lynn
Augill Castle,
  Kirkby Stephen
The Harper,
  Langham
Mallory Court,
  Leamington Spa

Lewtrenchard Manor,
  Lewdown
Lime Wood,
  Lyndhurst
Bedruthan Hotel and Spa,
  Mawgan Porth
The Scarlet,
  Mawgan Porth
Hotel Endsleigh,
  Milton Abbot
Chewton Glen,
  New Milton
Jesmond Dene House,
  Newcastle upon Tyne
The Assembly House,
  Norwich
Hart's Hotel,
  Nottingham
Old Bank Hotel,
  Oxford
Old Parsonage Hotel,
  Oxford
Tebay Services Hotel,
  Penrith
The Black Swan,
  Ravenstonedale
The Coach House at Middleton Lodge,
  Richmond
Boskerris Hotel,
  St Ives
The Idle Rocks,
  St Mawes
Seaham Hall,
  Seaham
La Fleur de Lys,
  Shaftesbury
Brocco on the Park,
  Sheffield
The Rose & Crown,
  Snettisham
Glazebrook House,
  South Brent
Thyme,
  Southrop
The Pipe and Glass Inn,
  South Dalton
The Harcourt Arms,
  Stanton Harcourt
Plumber Manor,
  Sturminster Newton
The Royal Oak,
  Swallowcliffe
Cliveden House,
  Taplow

The Horn of Plenty,
Tavistock
The Hare and Hounds,
Tetbury
The Royal Oak,
Tetbury
Thornbury Castle,
Thornbury
The Gunton Arms,
Thorpe Market
Titchwell Manor,
Titchwell
Tuddenham Mill,
Tuddenham
The Royal Hotel,
Ventnor
The Nare,
Veryan-in-Roseland
The Crown,
Wells-next-the-Sea
The Pear Tree Inn,
Whitley
Gilpin Hotel and Lake House,
Windermere
The Three Blackbirds,
Woodditton
Middlethorpe Hall & Spa,
York

SCOTLAND
Loch Melfort Hotel,
Arduaine
Boath House,
Auldearn
Glenapp Castle,
Ballantrae
Monachyle Mhor,
Balquhidder
Coul House,
Contin
The Three Chimneys and The House Over-By,
Dunvegan
Prestonfield,
Edinburgh
Kylesku Hotel,
Kylesku
The Peat Inn,
Peat Inn
The Green Park,
Pitlochry
Viewfield House,
Portree
Blackaddie House,
Sanquhar

Kinloch Lodge,
Sleat
The Inn at Loch Tummel,
Strathtummel
Douneside House,
Tarland
Forss House,
Thurso
The Torridon,
Torridon

WALES
Harbourmaster Hotel,
Aberaeron
Trefeddian Hotel,
Aberdovey
Gliffaes,
Crickhowell
Penbontbren,
Glynarthen
Tyddyn Llan,
Llandrillo
Bodysgallen Hall & Spa,
Llandudno
Lake Country House Hotel & Spa,
Llangammarch Wells
The Grove of Narberth,
Narberth
Twr y Felin Hotel,
St David

CHANNEL ISLANDS
Greenhills,
St Peter

IRELAND
The Mustard Seed at Echo Lodge,
Ballingarry
Stella Maris,
Ballycastle
Gregans Castle Hotel,
Ballyvaughan
The Quay House,
Clifden
The Wilder Townhouse,
Dublin
Castle Leslie,
Glaslough
Rayanne House,
Holywood
No.1 Pery Square,
Limerick
Viewmount House,
Longford

LONDON

St Paul's Cathedral and One New Change

LONDON

ARTIST RESIDENCE LONDON

♛ Previous César winner

You can drop in for a Pinot, Peroni or passion
fruit cooler in the café or club room or under
a striped awning on the front terrace at this
local hang-out and hip hotel in leafy residential
Pimlico. It is part of Justin and Charlotte
Salisbury's small collection of Artist Residences
(see index), which began with Justin's parents'
Brighton B&B. The public rooms serve as gallery
space, with a rotating art exhibition, pop-art
neon, a buzzy vibe and a general air of boho chic.
Bedrooms, with maybe a bare brick wall and
floorboards, are furnished with quirky vintage
and reclaimed pieces, limited-edition prints,
a Bakelite dial phone, Roberts radio, espresso
machine, organic toiletries. An Art Deco-style
suite has club chairs, a sofa, a statement bed, a
freestanding bath and walk-in shower. The Loft
has a 1930s French-style bath and walk-in shower
in an open-plan bathroom. In the Clubhouse,
brunch is served all day (perhaps potato, feta and
mint fritters or a bacon sandwich), while cocktail
hour ushers in dishes such as vegetable tagine,
harissa roast chicken, monkfish with coconut,
ginger, kefir lime and sticky rice.

52 Cambridge Street
Pimlico
London SW1V 4QQ

T: 020 3019 8610
E: london@artistresidence.co.uk
W: artistresidence.co.uk/london

BEDROOMS: 10. 2 suites.
OPEN: all year.
FACILITIES: cocktail bar, restaurant,
club room lounge, games/private
dining/meetings room, in-room TV
(Freeview), car parks (fee) nearby,
unsuitable for disabled.
BACKGROUND MUSIC: in public areas.
LOCATION: Pimlico, underground
Pimlico.
CHILDREN: all ages welcomed, cot
available for larger rooms, no extra
beds.
DOGS: in some bedrooms (£15 a night,
bed, bowl, treats), and all public
spaces.
CREDIT CARDS: Amex, MC, Visa.
PRICES: room only from £255. Cooked
breakfast dishes £6.50–£12, à la carte
£40. 1-night bookings sometimes
refused weekends.

SEE ALSO SHORTLIST

LONDON

MAP 2:D4

THE BEAUMONT

With a mix of Jazz Age glamour and New York chutzpah, The Beaumont is one of London's modern-day 'grande dame' hotels. On a quiet side street in the heart of Mayfair, it's well placed for the capital's shops and big-ticket attractions. Art Deco interiors of glossy panelling, opaque-glass lampshades and mirrored pillars give it an 'inescapable air of luxury and style', yet its warmth makes it 'intimate and inviting'. Black-and-white photographs of legendary stars add to the feeling of a private members' club. Bedrooms are sleek affairs with 1930s-style furniture, floor-to-ceiling windows and mosaic-and-marble bathrooms. Even entry-level rooms are spacious; 'definitely spaces you want to spend time in'. Cocktails in the walnut-panelled American Bar are essential before dining in the glamorous Colony Grill restaurant. With its speakeasy vibe, and weekly jazz sessions, it features a New York-influenced menu of classic dishes such as grilled Dover sole, and whiskey-braised beef short-rib. Breakfasts are full-on American with buttermilk pancakes, bagels and eggs how-you-want, as well as a full grill. A 'fun and flirtatious' hotel.

Brown Hart Gardens
Mayfair
London W1K 6TF

T: 020 7499 1001
E: reservations@thebeaumont.com
W: thebeaumont.com

BEDROOMS: 72. Some rooms suitable for disabled.
OPEN: all year.
FACILITIES: bar, restaurant, private dining room, spa, outdoor dining, electric shuttle limousine; in-room smart TV (free movies), nearby car parks (fee), public rooms wheelchair accessible, adapted toilet.
BACKGROUND MUSIC: yes.
LOCATION: Mayfair, mews parking, underground Bond Street, valet parking.
CHILDREN: all ages welcomed, free cots, extra bed £80.
DOGS: by arrangement.
CREDIT CARDS: Amex, MC, Visa.
PRICES: B&B doubles from £470 (with continental breakfast). Cooked breakfast dishes £8–£23.75, à la carte £50.

SEE ALSO SHORTLIST

LONDON

DURRANTS

'A cherishable place of curious individuality', this somewhat old-fashioned Edwardian hotel, spread across four Georgian town houses, continues to delight trusted readers with its slightly idiosyncratic charms. Owned by the Miller family since 1921, it extended a 'warm, personal welcome' with 'handshakes all round' to one faithful returnee. All rooms, from modest singles (some with shower only) to opulent suites, have a handmade Savoir bed and traditional furnishings. Service is 'ample and, if not always expert, always willing'. You can take tea in the cosy Wallace Room, have a drink by a coal fire in the panelled George bar. In the Grill Room, British classics sit alongside more modern fare on the menu – chargrilled steaks, roast partridge and shepherd's pie, pumpkin and baby spinach risotto, sea bass with wild mushrooms, roast duck with orange and golden raisin sauce. 'Breakfast can be taken until 11 am, hooray. Quality and choice excellent.' The Wallace Collection is just next door, Hyde Park and Regent's Park within strolling distance, and 'the tempting emporia of Marylebone but a step away'. (KS, RW)

26–32 George Street
Marylebone
London W1H 5BJ

T: 020 7935 8131
E: enquiries@durrantshotel.co.uk
W: www.durrantshotel.co.uk

BEDROOMS: 92. 7 on ground floor.
OPEN: all year, restaurant closed 25 Dec evening.
FACILITIES: lifts, bar, restaurant, lounge, meeting/events rooms, in-room TV (Freeview), use of nearby fitness club, public areas wheelchair accessible, no adapted toilet.
BACKGROUND MUSIC: none.
LOCATION: off Oxford Street, underground Bond Street, Baker Street.
CHILDREN: all ages welcomed, extra bed (in larger rooms only) £50.
DOGS: allowed in George bar only.
CREDIT CARDS: Amex, MC, Visa.
PRICES: B&B doubles from £230, singles from £213. À la carte £42.

SEE ALSO SHORTLIST

LONDON

MAP 2:D4

11 CADOGAN GARDENS

Through the conventional entrance – with its Union Jack proudly flying – of this smart Victorian town house in the heart of Chelsea lies a luxurious hotel brimming with character. A warren of corridors and staircases – plus tiny lift – leads to a sprawl of bedrooms and suites, sitting rooms and private retreats. 'A hidden gem,' says a Guide insider, that makes guests feel 'they're staying in a home away from home', albeit a classy one. There are gilt-framed portraits around the black-painted staircase, a clubby bar, more art in the drawing room with its coffee walls and purple sofas, leather armchairs in the library, and a plant-filled conservatory. Bedrooms are elegant, with splashes of colour in button-back armchairs and bed throws. Top-end suites are dramatic with sumptuous fabrics and marble bathrooms. All have coffee machines, and views over Cadogan Gardens or rooftops. The buzzy Hans' Bar and Grill has dishes such as pan-fried hake with chorizo and samphire, and herb-marinated grilled chicken plus brunch and vegetarian choices. Staff are 'super-friendly' and 'can't do enough'. The hotel is a member of Relais & Châteaux.

11 Cadogan Gardens
Chelsea
London SW3 2RJ

T: 020 7730 7000
E: reservations@11cadogangardens.
  com
W: 11cadogangardens.com

BEDROOMS: 56 (incl. 25 suites). Plus 6 apartments.
OPEN: all year.
FACILITIES: small lift, drawing room, library, cocktail bar, Hans' Bar and Grill (wine room, conservatory), private dining/meetings/events rooms, in-room TV (Sky), gym, decked terrace, 24-hr secure parking (£70), grill and public rooms wheelchair accessible, adapted toilet by grill.
BACKGROUND MUSIC: everywhere except the library.
LOCATION: Chelsea, underground Sloane Square.
CHILDREN: all ages welcomed, cots free, extra bed in suites £72.
DOGS: only assistance dogs.
CREDIT CARDS: Amex, MC, Visa.
PRICES: B&B doubles from £339. À la carte £40.

SEE ALSO SHORTLIST

LONDON

THE GORING

London's last grand hotel of the Edwardian era, The Goring is the epitome of old-fashioned luxury, from its silk-lined walls and liveried footmen to Michelin-starred dining and a secret garden. Owned by the fourth generation of the founding family, and in a peerless position in Belgravia – close to Buckingham Palace – it's reassuringly 'expensive', with service to match. Cases are whisked to rooms, polished shoes are returned wrapped in tissue, suites have dedicated butlers. Rooms have a low-key glamour with bespoke furniture and marble bathrooms; the best overlook the large rear garden. Public rooms are more ostentatious: carved wall-panels in the gold and red bar and lounge, Swarovski chandeliers in the dining room. Expect traditional, impeccably served food such as Dover sole, the famed Goring lobster omelette, and roast rib of beef carved from a silver trolley. There's a delightful vegetarian menu, too. Breakfast has 'plenty of choices' – eggs Benedict, pancakes, avocado on sourdough – and 'just as we wanted'. 'Plentiful' and 'courteous' staff deliver the hotel's famed 'attention to detail'.

15 Beeston Place
Grosvenor Gardens
London SW1W 0JW

T: 020 7396 9000
E: reception@thegoring.com
W: thegoring.com

BEDROOMS: 69. 2 suitable for disabled.
OPEN: all year.
FACILITIES: lifts, lounge, bar, restaurant (vegetarian menu), private dining rooms, gym, in-room TV (Sky), civil wedding licence, business centre, fitness room, veranda, 1-acre garden (croquet), public rooms wheelchair accessible, adapted toilet.
BACKGROUND MUSIC: none.
LOCATION: Belgravia, mews parking, underground Victoria.
CHILDREN: all ages welcomed, extra bed £80, interconnecting rooms.
DOGS: only assistance dogs allowed, others at hotel's discretion (ring to check).
CREDIT CARDS: Amex, MC, Visa.
PRICES: B&B doubles from £485, singles from £455. À la carte (3 courses) £65.

SEE ALSO SHORTLIST

LONDON

MAP 2:D4

THE GRAZING GOAT

The chain stores of Oxford Street are so near and yet (praise be!) so far from this gastropub with a pavement terrace for outdoor drinking and dining. An ideal place to take the weight off your feet after browsing Marylebone's independent emporia, it is trendy but not achingly so, with a relaxed, friendly vibe. The bedrooms, over three floors, have been newly refurbished, with blond wood, restful paint colours, a king-size bed, a tea-/coffee-maker and botanical toiletries. The more stairs you climb, the quieter your night, but this is not the most traffic-choked neighbourhood. In the bar, first-floor dining room or alfresco, menus of sustainably sourced ingredients include dishes such as grass-fed beef burger, a daily pie, asparagus, sweet potato and pine-nut Wellington, haddock and chips, and always a plant-based option. Breakfast, charged à la carte, includes freshly pressed juices, a breadboard with croissant, sourdough and fig-and-almond bread, coconut and oat porridge with Medjool dates and brown sugar, smashed avocado on chilli cornbread, a full English. (See its sister pub in Pimlico, The Orange.)

6 New Quebec Street
Marble Arch
London W1H 7RQ

T: 020 7724 7243
E: reservations@thegrazinggoat.co.uk
W: thegrazinggoat.co.uk

BEDROOMS: 8.
OPEN: all year.
FACILITIES: bar, dining room, patio, in-room TV, car park nearby (fees), ground-floor bar and toilet fully wheelchair accessible.
BACKGROUND MUSIC: all day in bar and restaurant.
LOCATION: central, underground Marble Arch.
CHILDREN: all ages welcomed, free cot, extra bed £30.
DOGS: allowed in public rooms, not in bedrooms.
CREDIT CARDS: Amex, MC, Visa.
PRICES: room only from £219. Breakfast mains from £7.50, full English £12.50, à la carte £35.

SEE ALSO SHORTLIST

LONDON

MAP 2:D4

HAZLITT'S

Step out of the hurly-burly of London into a
cocoon of quiet but gracious living in this historic
town house hotel. The former home of the
18th-century essayist, William Hazlitt, it's been
skilfully extended into neighbouring houses
and turned into a rich and colourful boutique
hotel, complete with wonky walls and creaky
floorboards. Lavish and luxurious, yet never stiff
and formal, it is a place of 'civilised' and 'old-
fashioned hospitality'. Bedrooms, for example,
are named after Hazlitt's friends, including
various favourite ladies. Each is richly furnished
with 17th- or 18th-century carved oak beds or
Georgian four-posters, antiques, velvet bedspreads
and thick silk curtains. Paintings and baroque
mirrors hang on panelled walls, with perhaps
a marble bust in a fireplace. Bathrooms have
restored vintage plumbing, often with roll-top
baths. In-room breakfasts are elegantly served on
bone china with posies of flowers, plus there's a
short lounge menu, which you can also take in the
panelled library. With a working fire and plenty
of books, plus a well-stocked honesty bar, this is a
quiet retreat from bustling Soho outside.

6 Frith Street
Soho
London W1D 3JA

T: 020 7434 1771
E: reservations@hazlitts.co.uk
W: hazlittshotel.com

BEDROOMS: 30. 2 on ground floor.
OPEN: all year.
FACILITIES: lift, library, private lounge/
meeting room, in-room TV (Sky,
Freeview), public rooms wheelchair
accessible, adapted toilet.
BACKGROUND MUSIC: none.
LOCATION: centre of Soho,
underground Tottenham Court Road,
Leicester Square.
CHILDREN: all ages welcomed, under-
13s free, extra bed £45.
DOGS: not allowed.
CREDIT CARDS: Amex, MC, Visa.
PRICES: room-only doubles from £239.
Breakfast £12, limited room-service
menu, dishes from £7.

SEE ALSO SHORTLIST

LONDON

THE ORANGE

Conveniently close to both Victoria station
and Sloane Square, this former brewery on the
corner of a leafy Pimlico square is a popular
neighbourhood pub and restaurant topped by
four lovely rooms. Downstairs, the relaxed pub
is the perfect hang-out for a craft beer or cocktail
accompanied by a little music, with seating (and
standing room) spilling out on to the pavement.
Like sister gastropub The Grazing Goat (see
entry), it has an appealing, shabby-chic style, with
bare floorboards, orange-themed advertising
posters, wooden chairs and tables. An enigmatic
sign reading 'Henry Guest' recalls a former
landlord. Upstairs, the rustic-chic bedrooms are
more Cotswolds in style than central London,
some with beams, a sawn-off modern four-poster.
You can eat in the bar, or in the more formal
but still friendly first-floor dining room, from
sustainably sourced menus, perhaps a wood-
fired pizza, vegetable Wellington, grilled plaice
with samphire, caper and brown-shrimp butter.
At breakfast there is home-made granola with
wild honey, brioche French toast with blueberry
compote, maple syrup, smashed avocado on chilli
corn bread, the full English.

37 Pimlico Road
Pimlico
London SW1W 8NE

T: 020 7881 9844
E: reservations@theorange.co.uk
W: theorange.co.uk

BEDROOMS: 4.
OPEN: all year.
FACILITIES: restaurant, 2 bars, private
dining room, in-room TV, rooftop
terrace, pavement seating, civil
wedding licence, ground-floor pub/
dining area wheelchair accessible,
adapted toilet.
BACKGROUND MUSIC: in public areas.
LOCATION: Pimlico, underground
Sloane Square.
CHILDREN: all ages welcomed, extra
bed £30.
DOGS: allowed in bedrooms by prior
agreement (no charge), public rooms,
except first-floor dining room.
CREDIT CARDS: Amex, MC, Visa.
PRICES: B&B doubles from £214.
À la carte £38.

SEE ALSO SHORTLIST

LONDON

MAP 2:D4

PORTOBELLO HOTEL

All is bello indeed behind a Doric portico at this one-time haunt of rock-and-rollers – it remains a veritable carnival of stylish eccentricity, occupying twin stucco mansions in raffish Notting Hill. Part of Peter and Jessica Frankopan's Curious group, it is furnished with antiques, and miscellanea from Portobello market. The stuffy old reception has been scrapped, so you now step straight into a lounge, while bedrooms have been refreshed or completely refurbished. They range from bijou third-floor singles to splendiferous signature rooms, with great variety in between. Several have a four-poster (one is a 'royal', from Hampton Court Palace) and an in-room bath. Some have an exotic mural, maybe shelves of vintage Penguin paperbacks. Lower-ground-floor rooms have a private patio. All have fresh milk, Green & Spring toiletries. You can help yourself to a drink from the honesty bar and order from the sitting-room menu, maybe Caesar salad or chicken casserole, a sandwich or sharing platter. In the morning help yourself from a buffet on the Welsh dresser, while the kitchen can rustle up a full English or boiled eggs and soldiers.

22 Stanley Gardens
Notting Hill
London W11 2NG

T: 020 7727 2777
E: stay@portobellohotel.com
W: portobellohotel.com

BEDROOMS: 21.
OPEN: all year.
FACILITIES: lift, sitting room/breakfast room with honesty bar, in-room TV (Freeview), street parking (fees), unsuitable for disabled.
BACKGROUND MUSIC: 'chill-out' in sitting room.
LOCATION: Notting Hill, underground Notting Hill Gate.
CHILDREN: all ages welcomed.
DOGS: allowed in 1 room, not in breakfast room.
CREDIT CARDS: Amex, MC, Visa.
PRICES: B&B (continental) doubles from £220, singles from £190. Cooked breakfast £6–£10, light snacks £8–£12. 1-night bookings sometimes refused Sat, public holidays.

SEE ALSO SHORTLIST

LONDON

THE ROOKERY

Everything feels so true to the past at this Georgian property that you half expect Dr Johnson to arrive in a chaise from his house, through the alleys of the City. Within is a world of rich silks and velvets, antique furniture, oil portraits, crackling fires and throne loos. Lovingly created by Peter McKay and Douglas Blain, it is situated in a now trendy neighbourhood which was dubbed 'The Rookery' in Dickensian times when it was a den of thieves. Today, a club-like calm reigns throughout. Bedrooms have either a 17th-century carved oak bed or a four-poster. The penthouse suite – the Rook's Nest – comes with a huge Victorian bathing machine on a plinth in the corner and stairs to a sitting room with antique lawyer's desk, views of St Paul's and minibar fridge (Samuel Johnson never had that, sir!). There is an honesty bar in the conservatory and seating for six in a tiny, leafy garden. Breakfast on black tea and cross buns to prevent faintness – or, better yet, freshly squeezed orange juice, granola, delicious pastries, a bacon sandwich or smoked salmon bagel. See also Hazlitt's (main entry) and Batty Langley's (Shortlist).

12 Peter's Lane
Cowcross Street
London EC1M 6DS

T: 020 7336 0931
E: reservations@rookery.co.uk
W: rookeryhotel.com

BEDROOMS: 33. 1 on ground floor.
OPEN: all year.
FACILITIES: conservatory lounge, meeting rooms, in-room TV (Sky), small patio garden, unsuitable for disabled.
BACKGROUND MUSIC: none.
LOCATION: Clerkenwell, underground Farringdon, Barbican.
CHILDREN: all ages welcomed, under-13s sharing with parents stay free in some rooms.
DOGS: not allowed.
CREDIT CARDS: Amex, MC, Visa.
PRICES: room doubles from £189, singles from £169. Breakfast from about £12, à la carte (from limited room-service menu) £28.

SEE ALSO SHORTLIST

LONDON

MAP 2:D4

THE ZETTER

In a once run-down neighbourhood of
clockmakers and communists, now a hive of
creativity, the former home of the Zetters football
pools company was reborn in 2004 as a cool,
child-friendly, eco-friendly hotel. It has its own
1,500-foot borehole to flush the loos, bikes to
borrow, and nearby Farringdon Station is now a
major transport hub. The bedrooms are 'vintage
modern' both in style and in the kind of extras
supplied – everything from hot-water bottles in
hand-knitted cosies, Penguin paperbacks and
an umbrella, to air conditioning, mood lighting,
a Hypnos bed, Bose or Marshall speakers, and
a drench shower. There are stylish nods to the
building's Victorian warehouse heritage, too.
Rooftop suites have their own furnished terrace,
some with an outdoor bathtub so you can steep
under the stars. In the bar/restaurant or at
pavement tables, casual drop-in dining options
include sharing plates, a butternut squash,
beetroot and chestnut salad, a chargrilled Dexter
beef or veggie burger and Hereford rib-eye steak
with triple-cooked chips. Breakfast on pastries,
a full English or veggie. (See also the next two
Zetter Townhouse entries.)

86–88 Clerkenwell Road
London EC1M 5RJ

T: 020 7324 4444
E: info@thezetter.com
W: thezetter.com

BEDROOMS: 59. 2 suitable for disabled.
OPEN: all year.
FACILITIES: 2 lifts, atrium, bar/
restaurant, terrace (alfresco dining),
in-room TV (Freeview, some with
smart TV), in-room spa treatments,
reduced rates at local gym, bicycles
to borrow, NCP 5 mins' walk, public
areas wheelchair accessible, adapted
toilet.
BACKGROUND MUSIC: in bar/restaurant.
LOCATION: Clerkenwell, NCP garage
5 mins' walk, underground
Farringdon.
CHILDREN: all ages welcomed, extra
bed for under-15s free of charge.
DOGS: only guide dogs allowed.
CREDIT CARDS: Amex, MC, Visa.
PRICES: room-only doubles from £153.
Breakfast, cooked dishes from £8.50,
full English £13.50, à la carte £35.

SEE ALSO SHORTLIST

LONDON

MAP 2:D4

THE ZETTER TOWNHOUSE CLERKENWELL

♕ Previous César winner

Just across the cobbled square from the mothership (see previous entry), in an area described by George Gissing in the 1880s as one of 'abortive streets, of shadowed alleys', today as hip as you please, a pair of Georgian town houses have been reinvented as a one-off small hotel. The interior, created for an imagined Great Aunt Wilhelmina, is a jewel box of eccentricity, with ticking clocks, stuffed fish and furry things, vintage books, velvet sofas and any number of curiosities. Bedrooms have a mix of antique and reclaimed furniture, perhaps a half-tester or four-poster bed. All are air conditioned, with a Hypnos bed and drench shower. Extras include bottled cocktails, fresh coffee, water from the Zetter's borehole, a retro dial phone, a hot-water bottle with knitted cosy, selected novels, a Sonos sound system. You'd be looking at the cocktail bar for a long time before the word 'minimalist' came to mind. Here is the place to enjoy afternoon tea or small plates of Modern European fare. At breakfast there is a full English, full veggie, smashed avocado, Cumberland sausage, St Ewe eggs. (See also next entry.)

49–50 St John's Square
Clerkenwell
London EC1V 4JJ

T: 020 7324 4567
E: reservations@thezetter.com
W: thezettertownhouse.com

BEDROOMS: 13. 1 suitable for disabled.
OPEN: all year.
FACILITIES: cocktail lounge, private dining room, games room, in-room TV (Freeview), civil wedding licence, cocktail lounges wheelchair accessible.
BACKGROUND MUSIC: in cocktail lounge.
LOCATION: Clerkenwell, underground Farringdon.
CHILDREN: all ages welcomed, extra bed for under-15s free of charge.
DOGS: assistance dogs only.
CREDIT CARDS: Amex, MC, Visa.
PRICES: B&B doubles from £151, room only from £119. Full English breakfast £13.50, full veggie £16, à la carte £30.

SEE ALSO SHORTLIST

LONDON

THE ZETTER TOWNHOUSE MARYLEBONE

The absurdist wit and whimsy of the Victorian poet and painter Edward Lear coupled with an imaginary wicked Uncle Seymour inspired the whacky design of these two brick-and-stucco Georgian terrace houses. Interiors are filled with objects orbicular and quadrangular, oak furniture, a grandfather clock, lamps, candlesticks, runcible spoons, diaphanous doorstops and oriental ginger jars. One bedroom has an ornate carved four-poster, another an in-room bath. Lear's Loft has a roof terrace with alfresco bath beside a bong tree. Each has modern creature comforts, with air conditioning, a Hypnos bed, a bath with drench shower, fresh coffee, organic teas, cocktails, and Bose speakers as well as a Roberts radio and hot-water bottles with hand-knitted cosy. You can drink and eat in Seymour's Parlour, with a fireplace at one end, a bar at the other, and the feel of a sophisticated gentlemen's club throughout. It's the place for afternoon tea or small plates of locally sourced food – cheeses, charcuterie, wild mushroom arancini, smoked ham croquettes with a beautiful pea-green emulsion. (See also two preceding entries.)

28–30 Seymour Street
Marylebone
London W1H 7JB

T: 020 7324 4544
E: reservations@thezetter.com
W: thezettertownhouse.com/
marylebone

BEDROOMS: 24. 2 suitable for disabled.
OPEN: all year.
FACILITIES: lift, cocktail lounge/restaurant, in-room TV (Freeview).
BACKGROUND MUSIC: all day in cocktail lounge.
LOCATION: central, underground Marble Arch.
CHILDREN: all ages welcomed, extra bed for under-15s free of charge.
DOGS: only guide dogs allowed.
CREDIT CARDS: Amex, MC, Visa.
PRICES: B&B doubles from £172 (includes £16 continental buffet). À la carte £35.

SEE ALSO SHORTLIST

ENGLAND

Kynance Cove, Cornwall

ALDEBURGH Suffolk   MAP 2:C6

THE WENTWORTH

When the Aldeburgh Festival launched in 1948, Michael Pritt's family had already run The Wentworth for 28 years, and it is this continuity and timelessness of their 'very well-managed' seafront institution that so appeals to many of our readers. 'Apart from being a lovely hotel in a beautiful location,' writes one, 'what makes it special are the staff – welcoming, helpful, cheerful, efficient, interesting and interested.' 'One of the great things is the way the staff remain,' writes another. 'Dogs made so welcome, too.' The look is hotel traditional, with light-wood furniture, softly patterned wallpaper, and maybe a bath with hand-held shower. 'We had a lovely big room overlooking the sea.' Snug inland-facing rooms are less sought after. You can take tea in one of the lounges, have a simple bar lunch, or eat more formally in the dining room, where seasonally changing menus include dishes such as chicken breast with fondant potato; sweet potato, cauliflower and chickpea curry, or salmon fillet. At breakfast there is smoked haddock or kipper, the full Suffolk. 'Good room, good food, good staff.' (SR, EG)

Wentworth Road
Aldeburgh IP15 5BD

T: 01728 452312
E: stay@wentworth-aldeburgh.co.uk
W: wentworth-aldeburgh.com

BEDROOMS: 35. 7 in Darfield House opposite, 5 on ground floor, 1 suitable for disabled.
OPEN: all year except possibly 2 weeks in Jan.
FACILITIES: 2 lounges, bar, restaurant, private dining room, conference room, in-room TV (Freeview), 2 terrace gardens, courtyard garden, parking, public rooms wheelchair accessible, adapted toilet.
BACKGROUND MUSIC: none.
LOCATION: seafront, 5 mins' walk from centre.
CHILDREN: all ages welcomed, extra bed £15.
DOGS: allowed in bedrooms (£5 per night) and public rooms, not in restaurant.
CREDIT CARDS: Amex, MC, Visa.
PRICES: B&B doubles from £200, singles from £125. Set-price dinner £25–£31 (2/3 courses). 1-night bookings refused Sat.

ALFRISTON Sussex

MAP 2:E4

THE STAR

NEW

'Olga and Alex Polizzi are the real stars here, after pulling off an amazing renovation of a 16th-century pub in a charming village in the South Downs national park,' a Guide insider writes. A first joint venture for mother and daughter, it is 'a friendly place for locals to drop in for a pint or all-day dining', in the 16th-century bar 'full of character and beams', while bedrooms, in the main building and new block, are 'classic Polizzi, mixing contemporary furniture with antique finds and a dollop of panache'. Dog-friendly rooms have a patio; those above, a Juliet balcony. A reader was happy to have a 'comfortable chair, small sofa' and 'kettle with teas' but noted there was 'no coffee option'. In the dining room, with its Elizabethan-design floor, Tim Kensett devises menus of seasonal British dishes with a Mediterranean twist. 'All the food was delicious,' from a 'simple pasta dish' to 'pink South Downs lamb'. On fine days you can dine in the welcoming courtyard. Relax in the library with its wood-burner, borrow boots to go walking; don glad rags for Glyndebourne. See also Hotel Endsleigh, Milton Abbot, and Tresanton, St Mawes. (Kevin Seymour, JK)

Alfriston
Polegate BN26 5TA

T: 01323 870495
E: thestar@thepolizzicollection.com
W: thepolizzicollection.com/the-star

BEDROOMS: 30. 1 bedroom suitable for wheelchair-users (no wet room).
OPEN: all year.
FACILITIES: bar/lounge, library, restaurant, courtyard (alfresco dining), in-room TV, parking, EV charging, restaurant wheelchair accessible, adapted toilet.
BACKGROUND MUSIC: none.
LOCATION: centre of village.
CHILDREN: all ages welcomed, extra bed £30.
DOGS: allowed in ground-floor bedrooms (£25 a night) and inn, not in restaurant.
CREDIT CARDS: MC, Visa.
PRICES: B&B doubles from £190. À la carte £54. 1-night stays refused at weekends.

SEE ALSO SHORTLIST

ALNWICK Northumberland   MAP 4:A4

THE COOKIE JAR

The name gives a hint that this intimate boutique hotel, in a former convent near Alnwick Castle, has a dash of style and fun. Public rooms have a modern country house feel with stripped-wood floors, leather armchairs and a chic shades-of-blue colour scheme on the walls and in the geometric-patterned fabrics. There are shelves of Penguin classics in the lounge, framed collections of cutlery in the dining room, and pieces of blue-and-white glassware and pottery dotted around. Bedrooms continue the blue theme, and mix vintage furnishings with modern pieces; they are inviting but uncluttered, with big beds and – of course – home-made cookies. Some overlook the castle, others have cosy sloping ceilings, while the extraordinary Chapel Suite offers a copper bath beneath stained-glass windows. All have sharply modern bathrooms. Dine on Modern British food such as lamb with sweetbread croquette and pea purée, and halibut with pearl barley risotto. Breakfast, overlooking the garden, includes home-made granola, poached egg and avocado, and a full grill. The name? It's after the owner, Debbie Cook. 'What a discovery!' concluded a guest.

12 Bailiffgate
Alnwick NE66 1LU

T: 01665 510465
E: hello@cookiejaralnwick.com
W: cookiejaralnwick.com

BEDROOMS: 11. 1 suitable for disabled.
OPEN: all year, bistro open daily Mar–end Oct, restricted opening Nov–end Feb (ring to check).
FACILITIES: lounge, bistro, drying room, secure gunroom, in-room TV (Freeview), lift, terrace with fire pit (alfresco dining), garden, parking, disabled access throughout and adapted toilet.
BACKGROUND MUSIC: in public spaces.
LOCATION: near town centre.
CHILDREN: all ages welcomed, extra bed £30.
DOGS: in some bedrooms (£30 per stay), not in public areas, 5 kennels for gun dogs.
CREDIT CARDS: MC, Visa.
PRICES: B&B doubles from £175. Set dinner 2 courses £36.50, 3 courses £44.50.

ALVESTON Warwickshire

MAP 3:D6

BARASET BARN

🏆 Previous César winner

The 'phenomenal food' served at this former 19th-century barn is matched by 'the amazing backdrop' and light-filled bedrooms overlooking sheep-filled meadows. Baraset has a reputation for its punchy dishes, often with an Asian-Mediterranean twist, such as Moroccan spiced lamb with couscous, and tempura squid with yuzu and wasabi dressing, plus 'generous' desserts such as daiquiri sundae. 'We savoured every mouthful.' The lofty barn with flagged floors, beamed roof, exposed-brick walls and vast metal-and-glass lampshades provides an 'atmospheric setting' with 'friendly service'. There's a decking area for summer dining and a courtyard with fire pit, 'the perfect spot for a drink'. 'Enormous bedrooms', across the courtyard in a modern timber and brick barn, are smart with floor-to-ceiling windows, contemporary furniture and bright-patterned headboards and fabrics. Bathrooms, with walk-in showers, are modern with black fittings and white tiling. Breakfast in the bright conservatory includes home-made muesli, scrambled eggs or avocado on sourdough, and the full works, with vegetarian option. Borrow a bike to cycle to nearby Stratford-upon-Avon.

Pimlico Lane
Alveston
Stratford-upon-Avon CV37 7RJ

T: 01789 295510
E: barasetbarn@lovelypubs.co.uk
W: www.barasetbarn.co.uk

BEDROOMS: 16. In separate annexe, 1 suitable for disabled.
OPEN: all year, hotel closed Sun nights.
FACILITIES: restaurant, conservatory, bar lobby, in-room TV (Freeview), courtyard garden, patio, meetings/private dining, EV charging, hotel bicycles, public area and restaurant wheelchair accessible, adapted toilet.
BACKGROUND MUSIC: in public rooms at mealtimes.
LOCATION: rural, 2 miles NE of Stratford-upon-Avon.
CHILDREN: all ages welcomed, free cots, extra bed £20.
DOGS: allowed in garden and conservatory, not bedrooms.
CREDIT CARDS: Amex, MC, Visa.
PRICES: B&B doubles from £120. À la carte £35.

AMPLEFORTH Yorkshire   MAP 4:D4

SHALLOWDALE HOUSE

Returning guests are received 'just like old friends' at this wisteria-clad, light-filled 1960s house with its peerless views over gardens to the Hambleton hills. Run for many years by Phillip Gill and Anton van der Horst – whose afternoon tea and home-made cakes are legendary – its ace card is its picture windows that ensure striking views from every room. 'Spacious' bedrooms are full of warm colours, brightly patterned fabrics and a late 20th-century decorative style. Comfortable, with armchairs and books, it has lots of nice touches: pot plants, binoculars, Penhaligon bathroom products, 'even a bowl of chocolates to dip into while watching the rabbits on the lawn'. The gardens of terraced lawns, borders and shrubberies are a 'lovely wonder' and excellent for birdwatching. Dinner (booked ahead), confidently cooked by Phillip, is an event with white napery, fresh flowers and four courses that might include endive gratin, hake with garlic crust and 'delicious desserts'. Breakfast is similarly satisfying. A 'deeply relaxing' stay with 'care for our welfare and comfort'. (Andrew Warren, Frances Thomas, and others)

West End
Ampleforth YO62 4DY

T: 01439 788325
E: stay@shallowdalehouse.co.uk
W: shallowdalehouse.co.uk

BEDROOMS: 3.
OPEN: all year except Christmas/New Year, 'occasional' other times.
FACILITIES: drawing room, dining room, sitting room/library, in-room TV (Freeview), 2½-acre gardens, unsuitable for disabled.
BACKGROUND MUSIC: none.
LOCATION: edge of village.
CHILDREN: not under 12.
DOGS: not allowed.
CREDIT CARDS: Amex, MC, Visa.
PRICES: B&B doubles from £155, singles from £135. Set dinner £50 (min. 48 hours' notice). 1-night bookings occasionally refused weekends.

ARKENDALE Yorkshire

THE BLUE BELL   **NEW**

Real ales in the bar, a handful of smart rooms and a deserved reputation for its food make this 'excellent value' village inn 'a great stop-over near Harrogate'. 'We were very impressed,' say readers who chanced upon it. 'The service was friendly and we really enjoyed our stay.' It's also handy if you're off to the races at Ripon, Thirsk or Wetherby. Neat and fuss-free bedrooms have 'top-quality' furnishings with super-king beds, light-oak furniture, and plaid wool headboards and throws. Two have a bath as well as shower, one a romantic double-ended affair. Although it's a roadside inn 'we did sleep well'. You can tell this place is serious about food; there's home-made focaccia to nibble on while reading the menu, a generous mix of pub classics and more elaborate dishes. As well as pub standards such as home-made beef and onion pie, you might find harissa-spiced lamb shank, or pancetta-wrapped monkfish. 'Our meal was delicious,' say readers who decreed that the home-smoked salmon with langoustine bisque risotto was 'amazing'. Breakfasts don't disappoint, either, with 'excellent' coffee and 'top-class' cooked dishes. (Jill Cox)

Arkendale
Harrogate HG5 0QT

T: 01423 369242
E: info@thebluebellatarkendale.co.uk
W: thebluebellatarkendale.co.uk

BEDROOMS: 4.
OPEN: all year.
FACILITIES: bar, restaurant, patio, in-room TV (Freeview), parking, public areas wheelchair accessible, adapted toilet.
BACKGROUND MUSIC: in public rooms.
LOCATION: 4 miles NE of Knaresborough, 10 mins from A1(M).
CHILDREN: all ages welcomed, no charge for extra bed.
DOGS: in bar area only.
CREDIT CARDS: Amex, MC, Visa.
PRICES: B&B doubles from £110. À la carte £32.

AUGHTON Lancashire   MAP 4:E2

MOOR HALL RESTAURANT WITH ROOMS

With a moat-turned-lake, walled kitchen garden and rustic barn, this Jacobean manor house is now a smart restaurant-with-rooms turning out Michelin-starred food. The sprawling house and its five acres of grounds sit amid Lancashire farmland, ideal 'terroir' for chef and co-owner Mark Birchall, who creates dishes rooted in the landscape, with a few maverick touches. Allow three hours for a menu that might include baked carrots with cheese, chrysanthemum and sea buckthorn, raw mackerel with redcurrant, and garden fruit with birch sap and woodruff. Eat more casually in The Barn on cod with crispy chicken wing, and sirloin with truffle mash. The hall combines original wood panelling and grand fireplaces with contemporary touches such as the glass-sided restaurant. Similarly, luxuriously large bedrooms mix designer pieces – a mirrored wardrobe, lacquered Louis-style desk – with beams and fireplaces. Marbled bathrooms have freestanding baths while the two gatehouse rooms are more contemporary. All have views over the lake or garden. Breakfast is a tasting-menu feast of surprises.

Prescot Road
Aughton L39 6RT

T: 01695 572511
E: enquiry@moorhall.com
W: moorhall.com

BEDROOMS: 7. 2 on ground floor in Gatehouse.
OPEN: hotel open all year except 2–26 Jan, closed Mon/Tues (The Barn only closed Mon), Moor Hall restaurant closed 25/26 Dec.
FACILITIES: bar, lounge, 2 restaurants, in-room TV (Freeview), 5-acre grounds, EV charging, ground floor public areas wheelchair accessible, lift to one restaurant, adapted toilet.
BACKGROUND MUSIC: in public areas.
LOCATION: on B5197, 2½ miles SW of Ormskirk.
CHILDREN: all ages welcomed, extra bed £50, no under-10s in Moor Hall restaurant in eve.
DOGS: not allowed.
CREDIT CARDS: Amex, MC, Visa.
PRICES: B&B doubles from £220. Moor Hall 4-course lunch £85, 8-course dinner £185, à la carte (Barn) £56.

AUSTWICK Yorkshire

MAP 4:D3

AUSTWICK HALL

From the grand hall with its flamboyant staircase to antique-furnished bedrooms and Italianate garden, this 'very beautiful' country house B&B adds an exotic touch to a Yorkshire Dales village. Everything about the 16th-century manor house, run with 'dedication' and 'kindness' by owners Eric Culley and Michael Pearson, is exuberant. Public rooms are filled with curios and art; logs burn in fireplaces (lovely for the welcoming tea and scones); walls are richly coloured; and an 'imperial' staircase leads to handsomely furnished bedrooms with 'pleasantly creaky' floorboards. Overlooking the 'really special' gardens, these are lavish with 'extravagantly thick curtains', plump sofas, fine furniture and elaborate beds including a four-poster and a rococo affair. Palatial bathrooms have roll-top bath, bathrobes and posh toiletries; most have a separate shower. One reader notes, though, that the 'house and beautiful gardens are in need of a little TLC.' Breakfasts are 'unhurried affairs' and include home-made granola, eggs from their own hens, and local bacon. Michael advises on places for supper; The Traddock (see next entry) impressed readers. Well placed for walks, or relax in the 'large and interesting' garden. (Sophie Bennett, and others)

Townhead Lane
Austwick LA2 8BS

T: 01524 251794
E: info@austwickhall.co.uk
W: www.austwickhall.co.uk

BEDROOMS: 4.
OPEN: all year except 24–26 Dec.
FACILITIES: hall, drawing room, sitting room, dining room, in-room TV (Freeview), 14-acre gardens, hot tub, unsuitable for disabled.
BACKGROUND MUSIC: none.
LOCATION: edge of village.
CHILDREN: aged 16 and upwards welcomed.
DOGS: not allowed.
CREDIT CARDS: MC, Visa.
PRICES: B&B doubles from £125, singles from £110. 1-night bookings refused weekends.

AUSTWICK Yorkshire

MAP 4:D3

THE TRADDOCK

🏵 Previous César winner

The refined yet homely atmosphere of this elegant country house hotel, amid the Yorkshire Dales national park, ensures guests keep returning for its generous comforts. 'One of my favourites,' says one reader. The creeper-covered Georgian and Victorian house, run for almost 20 years by the Reynolds family, retains a period feel with rooms of antiques, plump sofas and rich wallpapers. Comfortable lounges have fires in the grates, newspapers and magazines to browse, and 'brilliant' staff always on hand. Bedrooms are country-house style with pretty fabrics, armchairs and perhaps a window seat. Most have a bath as well as a shower; all spoil with fruit and home-made biscuits. Food is a highlight – 'unquestionably good' – with fine-dining and brasserie menus; one reader much preferred the former. Accomplished dishes include guinea hen with confit leg, asparagus and girolles, and tempting desserts such as prune and Armagnac soufflé. A big breakfast, with home-made bread, sets you up for one of many walks from the door of this dog-friendly hotel. 'We enjoyed our break enormously.' (Peter Anderson, John and Kay Patterson, FK, and others)

Graystomber Lane
Austwick LA2 8BY

T: 01524 251224
E: info@thetraddock.co.uk
W: thetraddock.co.uk

BEDROOMS: 14. 1 on ground floor, unsuitable for disabled.
OPEN: all year.
FACILITIES: 3 lounges, bar, 2 dining rooms, function facilities, in-room TV (Freeview), 1½-acre grounds (sun deck), ground-floor restaurant wheelchair accessible.
BACKGROUND MUSIC: in public areas except 1 lounge.
LOCATION: 4 miles NW of Settle.
CHILDREN: all ages welcomed, extra bed/cot £25.
DOGS: allowed in bedrooms (£10 a night) and on lead in public rooms, not in dining rooms, but owners may eat in bar area with their dogs.
CREDIT CARDS: MC, Visa.
PRICES: B&B doubles from £95, singles from £85. À la carte 3-courses £44. 1-night bookings refused Sat.

AYLESBURY Buckinghamshire   MAP 2:C3

HARTWELL HOUSE

The French king Louis XVIII set up his court in exile here in the 19th century, signing his accession to the throne in the library, and today, staff do indeed 'make you feel like royalty'. Approached by a drive through a folly-strewn landscape, the original Jacobean manor house, which has been beautifully restored for the National Trust's Historic House Hotels (see also Bodysgallen Hall and Spa, Llandudno, and Middlethorpe Hall & Spa, York), overflows with everything that is lavish and ornate. Public rooms have stucco ceilings that drip chandeliers, damask-covered walls, antiques and architectural glories. Bedrooms might feature a four-poster or half-tester. 'They upgraded us to the tapestry room, with wood-panelled walls.' There are slightly chintzier rooms in restored stables, some dog-friendly, with outdoor access. No shorts or trainers in the dining rooms, please. 'We really enjoyed the food, especially the venison, and drinks in the library with a truly special atmosphere.' In the Great Hall, a ceiling centrepiece depicts Genius Rewriting History – plasterwork allegory by the Artari brothers or a new emblem for a 'woke' National Trust? (Charlotte Clark, GB)

Oxford Road
Stone
Aylesbury HP17 8NR

T: 01296 747444
E: info@hartwell-house.com
W: hartwell-house.com

BEDROOMS: 48. 16 in stable block, some on ground floor, 1 (main house) suitable for disabled.
OPEN: all year, closed for lunch weekdays.
FACILITIES: Great Hall, morning room, drawing room, library, 2 dining rooms, function facilities, in-room TV (Sky, Freeview), civil wedding licence, spa (indoor pool), 94-acre gardens and parkland, tennis, EV charging, public rooms wheelchair accessible, adapted toilet.
BACKGROUND MUSIC: none.
LOCATION: 2 miles W of Aylesbury.
CHILDREN: not under 6, no extra beds.
DOGS: allowed in some annexe bedrooms (max. 2 small/1 large, damages charged for).
CREDIT CARDS: Amex, MC, Visa.
PRICES: B&B doubles from £220. Set-price dinner £58–£71.

BABBACOMBE Devon

MAP 1:D5

CARY ARMS & SPA

Above pebbly Babbacombe beach and bay, in the lee of tree-covered cliffs, this family-friendly hotel mixes traditional seaside inn with New England chic. Spread over several levels, to make the most of the mesmerising sea views, the core is a stone-built inn with a comfortably traditional lounge of seafaring memorabilia, and bar restaurant with exposed-stone walls, chunky wooden furniture and log-burner. Edward, Prince of Wales, once took tea on the lawn. Food is above-average pub fare with lots of local references: Brixham scallops with cauliflower and thyme purée, perhaps, local fish with pesto-nut crust as well as home-made pies, fish and chips, and good vegetarian choices. Bedrooms are light and spare with milk-white walls, breezy colours in cushions and curtains, contemporary local art, vintage posters, and all but one with a sea view. Split between main inn and chic beach chalets – the latter with mezzanine bedrooms – all have hi-tech music systems, fresh water and sloe gin. The beach-front suites sit above the water's edge. Add garden terraces, glass-fronted spa, walks and watery activities and all should be happy.

Beach Road
Babbacombe TQ1 3LX

T: 01803 327110
E: enquiries@caryarms.co.uk
W: caryarms.co.uk

BEDROOMS: 18. 6 beach huts, 2 beach suites, unsuitable for disabled. Plus 7 self-catering cottages.
OPEN: all year.
FACILITIES: saloon, bar/restaurant (vegetarian menu), in-room TV (Freeview), civil wedding licence, spa (hydrotherapy pool, gym, steam room), garden, parking, EV charging, unsuitable for disabled.
BACKGROUND MUSIC: all day in inn, saloon and spa.
LOCATION: by beach, 2¼ miles N of Torquay harbour.
CHILDREN: all ages welcomed, extra bed £25.
DOGS: allowed in some bedrooms (£20 per night).
CREDIT CARDS: Amex, MC, Visa.
PRICES: B&B doubles from £125, beach huts from £255, singles from £100. À la carte £40, vegetarian/vegan £28. 1-night bookings refused weekends.

BABCARY Somerset

THE RED LION

Locals and tourists alike enjoy the friendly atmosphere at Clare and Charlie Garrard's thatched village gastropub, ideally situated to break the journey between London and the West Country. As well as a warm greeting, you can expect oak beams, flagstone floors, with regional ales and ciders on tap. Bedrooms, in a purpose-built 'barn', are contemporary in style with a restful palette, modern artwork, a 'comfortable bed' and en suite bath and/or shower (one reader would have liked the 'and' option considering the bathroom was so spacious). A family room has a sofa bed to sleep two children. You can dine in the bar, more formally in the restaurant with its wood panelling and roaring fire, or in the garden, under cover, where the pizza oven is lit on summer weekends. The menu runs from pub classics to dishes such as slow-cooked lamb shank with garlic mash, or goat's cheese, spinach and leek filo parcels, with wines from Berry Bros. & Rudd. A locally sourced breakfast brings free-range eggs and award-winning sausages. 'Hot dishes, cooked to order, were very much enjoyed.'

Babcary TA11 7ED

T: 01458 223230
E: info@redlionbabcary.co.uk
W: redlionbabcary.co.uk

BEDROOMS: 6. All in converted barn, 1, on ground floor, suitable for disabled.
OPEN: all year.
FACILITIES: bar, snug, restaurant, private dining room, seasonal outdoor pizza bar, meeting/function facilities, in-room TV (BT), garden (with play area), bar wheelchair accessible, adapted toilet, parking.
BACKGROUND MUSIC: in bar area.
LOCATION: 5 miles E of Somerton.
CHILDREN: all ages welcomed, family room.
DOGS: allowed in bar and some bedrooms (£15 a night).
CREDIT CARDS: Amex, MC, Visa.
PRICES: B&B doubles from £115, singles from £95, family room from £150. À la carte £29.

BAINBRIDGE Yorkshire

MAP 4:C3

LOW MILL GUEST HOUSE

Spending a night on a river bank, in an 18th-century watermill, with Wensleydale's gentle hills all around … what could be more restorative for the soul? A 'total gem' is one of the many praises for Neil and Jane McNair's guest house, which they renovated with flair and imagination. The mix of original features and eclectic furnishings produces 'warm and welcoming' spaces such as the vast beamed living room with colourful rugs, oddball memorabilia, toasty range and massive grinding stone. 'Large' bedrooms are equally bright and quirky with beams, time-worn floorboards, fun wallpapers and vintage furnishings such as a sleigh bed or copper bath. All have views of garden (spot the red squirrels) or river, 'absolute peace and quiet' and delicious details of home-made fudge and cake, and fresh milk. Temple Spa products and 'massive fluffy bathtowels' await in bathrooms. 'Delicious' breakfasts include home-made bread, croissants and preserves, and cooked items from omelettes to a full grill (with veggie option). The McNairs advise on everything from walks to pubs for supper and 'they made us feel incredibly welcome'. (TS)

Bainbridge
Leyburn DL8 3EF

T: 01969 650553
E: lowmillguesthouse@gmail.com
W: lowmillguesthouse.co.uk

BEDROOMS: 3.
OPEN: all year except 24–26 Dec.
FACILITIES: lounge, dining room, small library, in-room TV (Freeview), ¼-acre riverside garden with seating, secure bicycle storage, unsuitable for disabled.
BACKGROUND MUSIC: none.
LOCATION: 5 miles E of Hawes.
CHILDREN: not under 15.
DOGS: allowed in bedrooms (£10 per stay), not in dining room, on lead in other public areas.
CREDIT CARDS: MC, Visa.
PRICES: B&B doubles from £120, singles from £100. 1-night bookings refused Sat, bank holidays.

SEE ALSO SHORTLIST

BARFORD ST MICHAEL Oxfordshire   MAP 2:C2

THE GEORGE INN   NEW

'A thoughtful restoration of a thatched 17th-century inn that combines the feel of a village pub with excellent food and well-furnished bedrooms' won our inspectors' approval this year, despite unpropitious weather. 'We'd have loved to have seen the garden on a sunny day, with its seating and raised beds for vegetables and herbs.' There are three bedrooms above the pub, six dog-friendly rooms in converted stables with 'windows at shoulder height'. All have a coffee machine, home-made treats and luxury toiletries. 'Our garden room had antique furniture, effective under-floor heating, a large bathroom with a rain shower over the bath.' Run for owners Laura and Louis Holtzhausen by manager Claire Lenkowiec and chef Valerio Grimaldi, The George has a friendly locals bar and 'buzzy dining room facing the garden'. From 'a mix of pub favourites and blackboard specials', our informants chose 'tapas-style small plates, then halibut with clam velouté, and the star of the show, steak and Guinness pie'. At breakfast, croissants, smoothies and a full English with 'a meaty sausage' got a thumbs up. 'We had a good time.'

Lower Street
Barford St Michael OX15 0RH

T: 01869 338160
E: info@thegeorgebarford.co.uk
W: thegeorgebarford.co.uk

BEDROOMS: 9. 6 in converted stable, some suitable for disabled.
OPEN: all year.
FACILITIES: bar, restaurant, wine room/chef's table, in-room TV, civil wedding licence, covered heated terrace, parking, EV charging, public areas wheelchair accessible, adapted toilet.
BACKGROUND MUSIC: 'a mix' of music in public areas, depending on time of day.
LOCATION: in village, 8 miles SW of Banbury.
CHILDREN: all ages welcomed, no charge for extra beds.
DOGS: allowed in 6 garden bedrooms (no charge at present).
CREDIT CARDS: MC, Visa.
PRICES: B&B doubles from £110, singles from £100. À la carte £45.

BARLOW Derbyshire

THE PEACOCK AT BARLOW

With its own onsite Collyfobble Brewery, this modernised old coaching inn is set in a Peak District village with the appropriate former name of Barley. A reader felt proud as a peacock of his choice to stay there. 'It is very good,' he wrote. As you enter from the car park, admiring the sculptures, nothing about the place says 'pub', but descend the stairs and you find a popular local with a 'glass-fronted extension and distant views to the east'. The air is relaxed, with dogs and children welcome. The bedrooms – four on the first floor, four in a barn conversion – are each named after a hop, and are high-spec, with a coffee machine, a minibar fridge, air conditioning and a swish bathroom with a bath or walk-in shower, or both, and touches of wit or kitsch. In the dining room, the food is good pub grub, with Derbyshire bangers and mash, fish pie, curries, a choice of vegan dishes. After a night of the Collyfobbles you will be wanting the full English with 'golden bread', or smoked salmon with scrambled eggs and tarragon, served until 11 am. 'Service was friendly, business booming, with a full house of diners (and dogs).' (RG)

Barlow
Chesterfield S18 7TD

T: 01142 890340
E: cheers@thepeacockatbarlow.co.uk
W: thepeacockatbarlow.co.uk

BEDROOMS: 8. 4 in barn conversion. 2 on lower floor with step-free access, 2-bedroom self-catering cottage.
OPEN: all year.
FACILITIES: orangery dining area, tap room (open fire and lounge area), brewery with tasting/function room, in-room TV (Sky), terraces (outdoor seating), large car park, EV charging, wheelchair accessible, adapted toilet.
BACKGROUND MUSIC: in all public areas including upper terrace, not brewery.
LOCATION: on outskirts of village, 10 miles S of Sheffield.
CHILDREN: all ages welcomed, no extra beds, children's menu.
DOGS: in cottage bedrooms only (no charge) and all pub areas.
CREDIT CARDS: MC, Visa.
PRICES: B&B doubles from £110. À la carte £30.

BARNSLEY Gloucestershire

MAP 3:E6

BARNSLEY HOUSE

Even hardened townies are seduced by the surrounds of 17th-century Barnsley House, created by visionary gardener Rosemary Verey who moved here in the 1950s. The colourful borders, clipped yews, knot gardens, a showstopping laburnum walk and a classical temple bewitch guests. Hidden in one corner is a spa with heated outdoor pool. Bedrooms, in the wisteria-draped manor house, are 'effortlessly chic' in shades of taupe, with rugs on polished-wood floors, smooth contemporary furniture, linen-covered armchairs and blanket throws. Expect coffee machines, home-baked goodies, modern bathrooms with a roll-top bath, and garden views; top-level suites spoil with a private garden or hot tub. Relax in one of the stylishly casual sitting rooms with a log fire and newspapers, or on the long terrace; a perfect spot for afternoon tea. Meals in the white-on-white dining room make the most of the kitchen garden produce with unfussy dishes such as young courgette risotto or lamb with sweet potato purée. The sister Village Pub offers pub classics. Breakfast includes home-baked bread, eggs from their own hens and gorgeous views.

Barnsley
Cirencester GL7 5EE

T: 01285 740000
E: info@barnsleyhouse.com
W: barnsleyhouse.com

BEDROOMS: 18. 7 in stableyard, 4 in courtyard, 1 in cottage, 1 suitable for disabled.
OPEN: all year.
FACILITIES: 2 lounges, bar, restaurant, cinema, meeting room, in-room TV (Sky, Freeview), civil wedding licence, 11-acre garden (spa, hydrotherapy pool), some public areas wheelchair accessible.
BACKGROUND MUSIC: in lounge and restaurant.
LOCATION: 5 miles NE of Cirencester.
CHILDREN: not under 14, extra bed £90, or family room.
DOGS: allowed in stableyard bedrooms (£30 per night), and grounds on lead, not in public rooms.
CREDIT CARDS: Amex, MC, Visa.
PRICES: B&B doubles from £369, singles from £351. À la carte £48, in pub £35. 1-night bookings sometimes refused.

SEE ALSO SHORTLIST

BARTLOW Cambridgeshire

MAP 2:C4

THE THREE HILLS   `NEW`

In a village on the River Granta renowned for
its Roman tumuli (hence 'hills'), Chris and Sarah
Field's dog-friendly pub in a sensitively updated
17th-century building is promoted from the
Shortlist this year following a thumbs up from
our inspector. 'We had a small, clean, tastefully
appointed room in an outbuilding conversion,
fine for an overnight stay.' A reader, too, felt
their room was 'well laid out' even if it was on
the 'compact side'. All have soft-hued walls, good
fabrics, a coffee machine, a modern bathroom
and luxury toiletries. You can eat good pub grub
with a twist in the 'warm and welcoming' bar
with flagstone floor, log-burner and fashionable
blue walls, in the dining room, or outside. There
are full marks for 'friendly, prompt service
of beautifully cooked food from a smallish
menu. Beef terrine was boosted by nicely sharp
horseradish, moist halibut came with colourful
supporting vegetables.' An outdoor kitchen
dispenses chargrills and pizzas. Overall, it is 'a
good venue for family dining or a short stay at
prices to please', although 'breakfast is quite basic'.
(Sara Hollowell, and others)

Dean Road
Bartlow CB21 4PW

т: 01223 890500
е: info@thethreehills.co.uk
w: thethreehills.co.uk

BEDROOMS: 8. 4 in rear annexe, 2 on
ground floor suitable for disabled.
2-bedroom self-contained flat, 1 room
suitable for disabled.
OPEN: all year, restaurant closed Sun
pm, Mon, Tues.
FACILITIES: bar, snug/library,
restaurant, in-room smart TV
(Freeview), function facilities, large
covered patio, pergola, garden and
meadow, public areas wheelchair
accessible, adapted toilet.
BACKGROUND MUSIC: soft music (light
jazz) in bar, restaurant.
LOCATION: in a small village, 12 miles
SE of Cambridge.
CHILDREN: all ages welcomed, extra
bed £10.
DOGS: allowed in all bedrooms (£10 per
stay), bar, snug.
CREDIT CARDS: Amex, MC, Visa.
PRICES: B&B doubles from £90.
À la carte £32.

BASLOW Derbyshire

MAP 3:A6

THE CAVENDISH

A stay among the spoiling country house comforts of The Cavendish is about as close as you can get to staying on the Chatsworth Estate. All but one room overlook the grounds of the Duke and Duchess of Devonshire's grand Derbyshire home, which is a stroll away by footpath. From the moment you arrive, with bags whisked away by 'very friendly and helpful' staff to your room, you feel cosseted. Bedrooms are comfortable with antique furniture mixed with smart contemporary fabrics and wallpapers, perhaps a brass bed or four-poster, art on the walls, and fresh milk and 'scrumptious' Chatsworth biscuits awaiting. One reader found the road noise disturbing on a muggy night, with the window open. Public rooms include furnishings and art from the family's collection. For dinner, there's a choice of more casual surroundings and dishes – steak, fish and chips, sharing platters – in the Garden Room or fine dining in The Gallery. The latter's menu might include estate venison with blackberries, and monkfish with crab mousse. Good cooked breakfasts are served until late in the morning. 'A relaxing stay in splendid surroundings.' (A K-H, J and MB)

Church Lane
Baslow DE45 1SP

T: 01246 582311
E: reception@cavendishbaslow.co.uk
W: devonshirehotels.co.uk/cavendish-hotel-baslow

BEDROOMS: 28. 2 on ground floor, 4 in converted coach house, 2 suitable for disabled.
OPEN: all year.
FACILITIES: lounge/bar, 2 restaurants, 2 private dining rooms, function facilities, in-room TV (Freeview), civil wedding licence, ½-acre grounds, EV charging, public rooms wheelchair accessible.
BACKGROUND MUSIC: none.
LOCATION: on edge of village.
CHILDREN: all ages welcomed, extra bed £10 (excl. breakfast).
DOGS: allowed in 1 bedroom (£20 per night), not in main house.
CREDIT CARDS: Amex, MC, Visa.
PRICES: B&B doubles from £200, singles from £180. Set 2-course menu £48, 3-course £58 (Gallery), à la carte £40 (Garden Room). 1-night bookings sometimes refused at weekends.

BASLOW Derbyshire

MAP 3:A6

FISCHER'S AT BASLOW HALL

Built in 17th-century vernacular style, with leaded, stone-mullioned windows and rich Jacobean interiors, Max and Susan Fischer's manor house hotel is a brilliant Edwardian pastiche. It stands in beautiful grounds with brimming borders, clipped yews and an arboretum. Luxurious bedrooms have period furnishings, heavy fabrics, perhaps a half-tester bed, home-made biscuits, a coffee machine and smart toiletries. 'Our suite was splendidly shaped, with an initial sitting room. The bedrooms contained – hurrah! – both a proper full-length wardrobe and a decent chest of drawers,' one reader relates. In an annexe, spacious, contemporary-style rooms have a private walled garden. Head chef Nathan Wall creates innovative dishes, using locally produced, home-grown and foraged ingredients. Maybe dry-aged duck breast, blueberry, broccoli; monkfish, leek, spelt, chanterelle; turnip, duck egg, spinach, Gruyère. 'The famous tasting menu was every bit as delicious as we had anticipated, and the wine list contained real gems.' 'The staff couldn't have been more diligent. The gardens are a delight.' (John and Kay Patterson, AW)

Calver Road
Baslow DE45 1RR

T: 01246 583259
E: reservations@fischers-baslowhall.co.uk
W: fischers-baslowhall.co.uk

BEDROOMS: 11. 5 in Garden House, 4 on ground floor.
OPEN: all year except 25/26 Dec, restaurant closed Mon, Tues.
FACILITIES: lounge/bar, main dining room (vegetarian menu), drawing room, wine room, function facilities, in-room TV (Freeview), civil wedding licence, 5-acre grounds, restaurant and lounge wheelchair accessible.
BACKGROUND MUSIC: in bar/lounge and dining rooms.
LOCATION: edge of village, 5 miles NE of Bakewell.
CHILDREN: all ages welcomed, cots £10 per stay, no under-8s in restaurant.
DOGS: not allowed.
CREDIT CARDS: Amex, MC, Visa.
PRICES: B&B doubles from £207, singles from £180. Set-price menu £78.50, tasting menu £90.

BATH Somerset

HOMEWOOD

`NEW`

'Set in rolling hills, 15 minutes from Bath, Homewood is a lovely hotel,' our inspector writes of this country house extravaganza. Part of Ian and Christa Taylor's Kaleidoscope Collection (see The Bird, Bath, in our Shortlist), it is 'eclectic, but tastefully designed'. In comfy lounges, a reader noted 'copper kettles, warming pans, Staffordshire dogs, a wall of plates . . .' Our inspector received 'a classy welcome' in a reception area lined with clocks, and was shown to an Art Deco-style room with 'a small sitting area, a king-size bed, ample closets, a striking espresso machine'. Mews rooms are 'bolder and more modern'. The best rooms have a hot tub on a terrace or balcony. 'Young, friendly staff' serve drinks in the fuchsia-pink bar or alfresco. After a few laps of the pool or a treatment in the 'Zen-like atmosphere' of the spa, you can dine on a terrace with pizza oven, or in Olio, from a 'healthy menu (lots of fish and salad)'. Maybe St Austell Bay mussels, a burger, with 'a delicious mix of breads and oils (try the paprika!), perfectly cooked asparagus, truffle and Parmesan fries to die for'. (Carol Jackson, and others)

Abbey Lane
Freshford
Bath BA2 7TB

T: 01225 723731
E: reservations@homewoodbath.
  co.uk
W: homewoodbath.co.uk

BEDROOMS: 31. 10 in annexe.
OPEN: all year.
FACILITIES: bar, lounge, restaurant (vegetarian/vegan menus), dining domes (4–6 guests), meeting rooms, in-room TV (Freeview), spa, indoor hydrotherapy pool, outdoor heated pool, 20-acre gardens, civil wedding licence.
BACKGROUND MUSIC: in restaurant.
LOCATION: 5 miles S of Bath, on A36.
CHILDREN: all ages welcomed, children's menu, no charge for extra beds.
DOGS: welcomed in bedrooms (£25 per night, dog menu), not in restaurant.
CREDIT CARDS: Amex, MC, Visa.
PRICES: B&B rooms from £208. À la carte £45.

SEE ALSO SHORTLIST

BATH Somerset

NO.15 GREAT PULTENEY

Behind a Grade I listed Georgian facade, new
owners Guest House have had designer Martin
Hulbert refresh the interiors of this characterful,
family-friendly, dog-friendly hotel, playing with
ideas of Jane Austen's Bath. There are bedrooms
to suit everyone from Fanny Price to Mr Darcy,
from bijou attic rooms to the Hideout, with its
own steam room and hot tub. Some rooms have
wallpaper screen printed with a hand-written
inventory of a Georgian house's contents, others
have a four-poster, a view over Henrietta Park. A
converted coach house with crenellated parapet
and quatrefoil windows is home to further rooms,
two with working fireplace and large bathroom
with freestanding bath and rain shower. Light
bites are served all day, while at dinner chef
Matt Gillard's self-described 'wild British food'
includes dishes such as line-caught sea bass with
lentils, spring greens and hedgerow oil; Old Spot
shoulder steak with crispy pork belly. 'The change
in ownership has not resulted in any reduction in
quality,' wrote trusted readers on a return visit.
'We would continue to thoroughly recommend
this hotel.' (Chris and Erika Savory)

15 Great Pulteney Street
Bath BA2 4BS

T: 01225 807015
E: no15@guesthousehotels.co.uk
W: guesthousehotels.co.uk

BEDROOMS: 37. 8 in coach house,
1 suitable for disabled.
OPEN: all year, restaurant Mon–Sat,
Sun lunch.
FACILITIES: lift, bar, restaurant, private
dining room, in-room TV (Sky),
spa (treatments, hot tub, sauna),
small garden terrace, complimentary
street parking permits, public rooms
wheelchair accessible, adapted toilet.
BACKGROUND MUSIC: all day in bar and
restaurant.
LOCATION: central.
CHILDREN: all ages welcomed, extra
bed free but breakfast charged for.
DOGS: allowed in some bedrooms
(£25 per night), bar, not in restaurant.
CREDIT CARDS: Amex, MC, Visa.
PRICES: B&B doubles from £195.
À la carte dinner £35. 1-night
bookings sometimes refused at
weekends.

SEE ALSO SHORTLIST

BATH Somerset

THE QUEENSBERRY

Spread across four honey-stone town houses, this characterful hotel with fine-dining restaurant, themed around the pugilist 9th Marquess of Queensberry, really punches above its weight. Owners Laurence and Helen Beere have completed an extensive refurbishment programme, while a new kitchen has risen from the ashes of the old, following a fire that put the tin lid on an annus horribilis. Smart contemporary bedrooms range from small 'club' doubles with designer wallpaper and a shower room to a suite with a modern, seven-foot-square four-poster. The original Georgian drawing rooms are now junior suites. In the Olive Tree restaurant, Michelin-starred chef Chris Cleghorn devises innovative six- and nine-course menus (omnivore, veggie and dairy-free), with items individually priced so you can pick and mix. Maybe fallow deer, mushroom ketchup, black winter truffle; potato cooked over coal, 'cream cheese'; Cornish turbot with Exmoor caviar. Or just have a drink in the Old Q bar (the nickname recalls another Q, the disreputable 4th Duke), where a spoof version of the Queensberry Rules forbids shouting into your cell phone: 'I'M IN THE BAR!'

4–7 Russel Street
Bath BA1 2QF

T: 01225 447928
E: reservations@thequeensberry.co.uk
W: thequeensberry.co.uk

BEDROOMS: 29. Some on ground floor.
OPEN: all year, restaurant closed Mon, midday Tues–Thurs.
FACILITIES: lift, residents' drawing room, bar, 2 sitting rooms, restaurant (vegetarian/vegan menus), meeting room, in-room TV (Freeview), 4 linked courtyard gardens, valet parking, unsuitable for disabled.
BACKGROUND MUSIC: in restaurant and bar.
LOCATION: near Assembly Rooms.
CHILDREN: all ages welcomed, extra bed £25 plus breakfast £25, children's menu.
DOGS: assistance dogs only.
CREDIT CARDS: Amex, MC, Visa.
PRICES: B&B doubles from £170. Tasting menus £85–£110, à la carte £75. 1-night bookings sometimes refused weekends.

SEE ALSO SHORTLIST

BATH Somerset

MAP 2:D1

THE ROYAL CRESCENT
HOTEL & SPA

The sweep of honey-stone buildings that form Bath's Georgian crescent is home to two majestic mansions which combine as one hotel, beyond which lie a leafy garden and atmospheric spa. With chandeliers, antiques and oil paintings, it's very smart, but is far from snooty. A trusted reader praises the personable staff. Families are welcome, while pet-friendly rooms have garden or courtyard access. Palatial suites might come with a four-poster or ornate ceilings, but even the least-expensive rooms are justly termed 'deluxe', with contemporary styling, queen-size bed and Noble Isle toiletries. In the restaurant, David Campbell's short menus include dishes such as saddle of venison, haggis croquette, poached pear and mulled wine, or wild-mushroom arancini. The beautifully tended garden, hidden behind the hotel, is the perfect place to relax, as is the Georgian spa, with its 12-metre pool, church-style windows and a Mediterranean-style walled garden. Breakfast – in bed, if you like – brings real OJ, pastries, tea-soaked Agen prunes, local pork sausages, free-range eggs, waffles or what you will, while the afternoon teas are legendary.

16 Royal Crescent
Bath BA1 2LS

T: 01225 823333
E: info@royalcrescent.co.uk
W: royalcrescent.co.uk

BEDROOMS: 45. 10 in Dower House, 14 in annexes, 8 on ground floor.
OPEN: all year.
FACILITIES: lift, bar, lounge, library, restaurant (vegetarian menu), in-room TV (Sky, Freeview), civil wedding licence, 1-acre garden, spa (12-metre pool), public rooms wheelchair accessible, adapted toilet, EV charging, parking.
BACKGROUND MUSIC: in library and restaurant.
LOCATION: ½ mile from High Street.
CHILDREN: all ages welcomed, under-3s free, extra bed 7–12s £50.
DOGS: allowed in some bedrooms, public rooms, garden, not in restaurant or bar (£35 per stay).
CREDIT CARDS: Amex, MC, Visa.
PRICES: B&B doubles from £330. À la carte £72, tasting menu £82. Min. 2-night stay Sat.

SEE ALSO SHORTLIST

BAUGHURST Hampshire

MAP 2:D2

THE WELLINGTON ARMS

Outstanding food and beautiful bedrooms can be found alongside some charming touches at Simon Page and Jason King's pretty pub, with its hanging baskets at the door and teapots with fluffy cosies displayed at the bar. The cosies, knitted by Simon's mum, are for sale, along with jams, organic sourdough bread and sloe gin. Produce for Jason's menus does not come more local than lamb from the Jacob sheep in the field at the back, honey from the hives, or the salad leaves, herbs and veg from the garden and allotments. His dishes might feature gnocchi with garlic, roast butternut squash, walnut and sage or herb-stuffed partridge with sticky red cabbage, served in the beamed bar. There are more beams at bedtime, in the suite above the pub and in the three pristine bedrooms housed in outbuildings. All are light and airy, with oak furniture, heated slate floor or sisal carpet, a rain shower, and extras including luxury toiletries, minibar and home-baked biscuits. Breakfast brings a feast of new-laid eggs, oak-smoked salmon, French toast with crispy bacon and maple syrup. Four-legged friends are welcomed with water and treats.

Baughurst Road
Baughurst RG26 5LP

T: 0118 982 0110
E: hello@thewellingtonarms.com
W: thewellingtonarms.com

BEDROOMS: 4. 3 in converted outbuildings.
OPEN: all year, Tues–Sat, Sun lunch.
FACILITIES: 2 dining rooms, in-room TV (Freeview), 2-acre garden, parking, dining room wheelchair accessible.
BACKGROUND MUSIC: in bar and restaurant.
LOCATION: equidistant between Reading, Basingstoke and Newbury.
CHILDREN: all ages welcomed, no extra beds.
DOGS: allowed in 2 bedrooms (£10 per night), public areas.
CREDIT CARDS: MC, Visa.
PRICES: B&B doubles from £125. À la carte £40.

BEADNELL Northumberland   MAP 4:A4

BEADNELL TOWERS   `NEW`

A 10-minute walk from the sandy curve of
Beadnell Bay, this dog and family-friendly hotel
is a cut above the average seaside place to stay,
with its boutique-smart rooms, funky touches
and buzzy atmosphere. Step inside the 'rather
unprepossessing' Georgian building and 'it's
clear a designer hand has been at work', says a
Guide insider. Denim-blue panelling, William
Morris-style wallpapers and parquet flooring
provide a chic backdrop to quirky collections of
Bakelite telephones and maritime paraphernalia.
The dining area with exposed stone and painted
brick is bright with mustard-yellow leather seats,
oversized lampshades and copper pans. 'It's
fun rather than pretentious' with 'smiley staff
and dogs enjoying treats'. Food is 'robust and
no-nonsense', such as mussels, local oysters and a
'piping-hot, cheesy-mash-topped' fish pie, though
the cooking 'lacks finesse'. Bedrooms, some with
beams, mix a town-house smartness of elegant
headboards and designer lighting with a seaside
practicality: polished floorboards and solid wood
furniture. Most have a bath and shower. Breakfast
includes kippers, and 'perfect, creamy' scrambled
eggs. (HP)

The Wynding
Beadnell NE67 5AY

T: 01665 721211
E: info@beadnelltowers.co.uk
W: beadnelltowers.co.uk

BEDROOMS: 22. 4 in coach house,
some on ground floor, 1 suitable for
disabled.
OPEN: all year.
FACILITIES: lounge, bar/restaurant,
in-room TV (Freeview), private
dining room, terrace, public rooms
wheelchair accessible, adapted toilet.
BACKGROUND MUSIC: in public rooms.
LOCATION: in Beadnell, 800 yds from
the beach.
CHILDREN: all ages welcomed, extra
bed from £35.
DOGS: allowed in some bedrooms
(£25 per stay), bar.
CREDIT CARDS: MC, Visa.
PRICES: B&B doubles from £129, singles
from £119. À la carte £35.

BEAMINSTER Dorset

MAP 1:C6

THE OLLEROD

In Hardy's 'Emminster', ten minutes from Dorset's Jurassic Coast, a historic priest's house is now a restaurant-led hotel. In 2018, industry professionals Silvana Bandini and Chris Staines took on what was then the Bridge House Hotel, relaunched it, and have been upgrading it ever since. Bedrooms blend original features with traditional touches and contemporary comforts: Frette linen, organic toiletries, a coffee machine. A dog-friendly ground-floor room has a large walk-in shower; a two-bedroom family suite has both bath and shower. Coach-house rooms have been reconfigured as two self-catering apartments. Locals drop in for a pint by the log-burner in the cosy bar, with small plates served throughout the afternoon. Lunch and dinner are taken in the dining room or on a new Moroccan-style dining terrace. Chris held a Michelin star in London and cooks a changing menu of dishes such as cod, seaweed gnocchi, mussel chowder; free-range pork, gooseberry compote, home-grown vegetables. 'The cooking is of a very high standard,' a reader writes. 'Breakfast was the best we've had in a hotel for some time.' (John Hunt)

3 Prout Bridge
Beaminster DT8 3AY

T: 01308 862200
E: enquiries@theollerod.co.uk
W: theollerod.co.uk

BEDROOMS: 9. 2 self-catering apartments in coach house.
OPEN: all year.
FACILITIES: lounge, bar, sun room, conservatory, restaurant (vegan menu), in-room TV (Freeview), treatment room, civil wedding licence, walled garden, covered terrace, parking.
BACKGROUND MUSIC: in public rooms.
LOCATION: 100 yds from centre.
CHILDREN: all ages welcomed, cots £10 per night, extra bed for ages 2–16 £20, children's menu.
DOGS: allowed in 1 bedroom in house, 1 coach-house apartment (£15 per night), bar and terrace, not in restaurant.
CREDIT CARDS: Amex, MC, Visa.
PRICES: B&B doubles from £165. À la carte £45, vegan £33.

BEANACRE Wiltshire   MAP 2:D1

BEECHFIELD HOUSE   `NEW`

A private drive leads to this Victorian gentleman farmer's Italianate country house, in wooded grounds and gardens, with 'a lovely heated outdoor pool'. Owned and run by former banker Chris Whyte since 2006, it is child-friendly, dog-friendly, relaxed, and ticked the boxes for our inspectors. Bedrooms, some in the coach house, range from cosy to a master room with four-poster. Dual-aspect Beech had views of the drive, 'a magnificent cedar and two neat parterres set into a large lawn'. Painted 'a soft grey-blue', it had 'a super-king bed, a little sofa and coffee table', plenty of storage, a Roberts radio, 'a bath with powerful shower over it'. Some of the furniture was dated; new curtains had been ordered to replace tatty ones. In a rather dark, atmospheric dining room, a short menu, partly sourced from the kitchen garden, brought 'huge portions of very good salt-baked beetroot salad, ginger crumb, pear sorbet and goat's cheese; perfectly cooked stone bass, artichoke purée, potato fondant, samphire, shellfish chowder'. Breakfast was 'substantial rather than elegant', but 'the scrambled eggs were superb'.

Beanacre
Melksham SN12 7PU

T: 01225 703700
E: reception@beechfieldhouse.co.uk
W: beechfieldhouse.co.uk

BEDROOMS: 24. 8 in coach house, 4 on ground floor suitable for disabled.
OPEN: all year (exclusive use only, New Year).
FACILITIES: morning room, bar, 4 dining rooms, in-room TV (Freeview), 8-acre grounds (12 by 6 metre heated pool, mid-Mar to early Nov), EV charging, bar, reception rooms, dining rooms all wheelchair accessible.
BACKGROUND MUSIC: light music in public areas.
LOCATION: just outside a small village, 1½ miles N of Melksham.
CHILDREN: all ages welcomed, extra bed £20.
DOGS: allowed in bedrooms (£20 per night), public rooms.
CREDIT CARDS: MC, Visa.
PRICES: B&B doubles from £129. À la carte £35.

BEAULIEU Hampshire

MAP 2:E2

THE MASTER BUILDER'S

A former shipbuilder's house in a Georgian hamlet on the Beaulieu river, where the New Forest meets the Solent, is today a shipshape and stylish dog-friendly hotel with 'very pleasant staff'. Main-house bedrooms have original features, perhaps a fireplace or four-poster, antique furniture, a garden or a river view. Two rooms under the eaves have plenty of space for a family. In the Henry Adams wing, contemporary rooms have a 'nautical but not over-insistent theme', with blue-and-white decor. There is a free-and-easy, seagoing vibe here. Footloose ponies and donkeys roam outside. Yachts ply the waters that launched warships for Trafalgar. You can dine in the new River View restaurant, with your dog in the Garden View restaurant, or alfresco. Perhaps beef stew or sausages for your best friend, and for you, pan-fried Romsey chalk-stream trout, or panzanella with Isle of Wight tomatoes, Old Winchester cheese, sourdough croutons and foraged wild garlic. 'Breakfast overlooking the ancient shipyard where Nelson's fleet was built is a fine start to any day', after which a riverside footpath will take you to the village of Beaulieu.

Buckler's Hard
Beaulieu SO42 7XB

T: 01590 616253
E: enquiries@themasterbuilders.co.uk
W: themasterbuilders.co.uk

BEDROOMS: 26. 18 in newer Henry Adams wing.
OPEN: all year.
FACILITIES: lounge, bar, restaurant, terrace with river views, in-room TV (Freeview), civil wedding licence, ½-acre garden, parking, bar and restaurant wheelchair accessible, no adapted toilet.
BACKGROUND MUSIC: in bar and restaurant.
LOCATION: 6 miles NE of Lymington.
CHILDREN: all ages welcomed, extra bed £20.
DOGS: allowed in some bedrooms (£20 a night with bed and blanket), lounge, the Yachtsman's bar, not in restaurant.
CREDIT CARDS: Amex, MC, Visa.
PRICES: B&B doubles from £155. À la carte £40.

BEAULIEU Hampshire

MONTAGU ARMS

In a lovely village roamed by New Forest ponies, this Victorian Arts and Crafts inn on the Beaulieu river is run as a luxurious, characterful hotel, with fine-dining restaurant and a pub in a 1920s wing. Leaded casements, panelling and brick fireplaces lend a historic feel. 'I love the log fires,' wrote a reader, after 'a lovely weekend'. The 'friendly, cheerful staff could not be more helpful'. 'Delightful' inn rooms and suites have restful decor, antiques, perhaps a four-poster, a modern bathroom. Two duplex suites in a converted 1820s barn overlooking the Gertrude Jekyll-inspired garden have a freestanding bath, a drench shower, and a decanter of gin to sip upstairs in the sitting room. All rooms have cut flowers and White Company toiletries (surely a nod to past guest Arthur Conan Doyle, who used Beaulieu Abbey as a setting for The White Company). In the Terrace restaurant, Matthew Whitfield works creative wonders with produce from coast, countryside and kitchen garden. Maybe Beaulieu Estate roe deer, fish from Lymington. Or pop into Monty's bar for a home-made Scotch egg if you fancy a substantial meal. (Geoffrey Bignell)

Palace Lane
Beaulieu SO42 7ZL

T: 01590 612324
E: reservations@montaguarmshotel.
  co.uk
W: montaguarmshotel.co.uk

BEDROOMS: 24. 2 in Hayloft suites.
OPEN: all year, Terrace restaurant closed Mon all day, Tues lunch.
FACILITIES: lounge, conservatory, library/bar/brasserie, restaurant, in-room TV (Freeview), civil wedding licence, 3-acre garden, public rooms wheelchair accessible, adapted toilet.
BACKGROUND MUSIC: Classic FM all day in reception.
LOCATION: village centre.
CHILDREN: all ages welcomed, under-16s extra bed £35, no under-12s for restaurant dinner, but welcome at inn.
DOGS: assistance dogs allowed.
CREDIT CARDS: Amex, MC, Visa.
PRICES: B&B doubles from £201. Tasting menu £75–£90, à la carte £60 (restaurant), £28 (Monty's). 1-night bookings sometimes refused Fri/Sat, peak season.

BEESANDS Devon

MAP 1:E4

THE CRICKET INN

The bedrooms are all named after a cricketer or cricket ground and menus are divided into first and second innings, but you're more likely to hear the sound of waves on shingle than the thwack of willow on leather at Scott Heath's pub-with-rooms. It looks onto Beesands beach rather than a village green, with the South West Coast Path running past the door and some lovely sea views. Despite the name, there's a nautical feel inside, with blue and white decor in the New England-style bedrooms – two with four-posters, some for families – and seaside trimmings everywhere. In the restaurant or on a table outside, the food is decidedly fishy, in the best possible way, with excellent locally landed fish and shellfish. When you've said W G Grace you can tuck into crab soup, flame-grilled catch of the day or steak, fish pie or a burger. 'The cooking was much improved,' say Guide insiders, returning after three years. 'A nice table by the window gave us plenty of fresh air. In the evening, people queue for fish and chips.' (C and AR)

Beesands
Kingsbridge TQ7 2EN

T: 01548 580215
E: enquiries@thecricketinn.com
W: thecricketinn.com

BEDROOMS: 7. 4 in extension.
OPEN: closed Christmas Day (no rooms Christmas Eve).
FACILITIES: bar, restaurant (alfresco dining), private dining facilities, free (intermittent) Wi-Fi, in-room TV (Freeview), parking, restaurant and bar wheelchair accessible, adapted toilet.
BACKGROUND MUSIC: all day.
LOCATION: in village, on South West Coast Path.
CHILDREN: all ages welcomed, extra bed £25, children's menu.
DOGS: allowed in bar only.
CREDIT CARDS: MC, Visa.
PRICES: B&B doubles from £120. À la carte £30. Min. 2-night stay preferred at weekends in high season.

BEPTON Sussex

PARK HOUSE, HOTEL & SPA

Recreation and relaxation are at the heart of Seamus O'Brien's spa hotel in the South Downs national park, with tennis, croquet, bowls, golf, swimming pools and all-day dining. It was first opened to guests in 1949 by Mr O'Brien's grandmother, to cater to the Cowdray Park polo set whose photographs adorn the bar walls, over time evolving into a leisure resort. Bedrooms are in country house style, with florals, checks, stripes, perhaps vintage toile wallpaper. Some have a patio or balcony, a separate seating area; all have handmade biscuits, Voya toiletries, 24-hour room service. There are further bedrooms in cottages in the grounds, most with a kitchen. At night, the seasonally changing menu runs to five main courses. 'The excellent receptionist warned us it was not long enough to offer something different every day for a week.' However, you can discuss special preferences with the kitchen, while omnivores might work their way from Sussex rib-eye steak to carrot and cumin risotto, before going round again. The breakfast menu is short, too, with local free-range eggs and oak-smoked salmon. (AW)

Bepton Road
Bepton
Midhurst GU29 0JB

T: 01730 819000
E: reservations@parkhousehotel.com
W: parkhousehotel.com

BEDROOMS: 21. 5 on ground floor, 1 suitable for disabled, 9 in cottages in grounds.
OPEN: all year, except 24–26 Dec.
FACILITIES: drawing room, bar, dining room, conservatory, function rooms, in-room TV (Sky, Freeview), civil wedding licence, 10-acre grounds, spa, heated indoor and outdoor swimming pools, tennis, EV charging, public rooms and spa wheelchair accessible, adapted toilet.
BACKGROUND MUSIC: in restaurants.
LOCATION: village centre.
CHILDREN: all ages welcomed, extra bed £25–£50.
DOGS: allowed in some bedrooms (£20 a night), not public rooms.
CREDIT CARDS: Amex, MC, Visa.
PRICES: B&B doubles from £199, singles from £184. Set-price dinner £45. Min. 2-night stay Fri/Sat.

BEVERLEY Yorkshire

MAP 4:D5

⚘ NEWBEGIN HOUSE

César award: B&B of the year

Minutes from Beverley centre, this Georgian town house whisks you off to a world of refinement with its handsome interiors, artwork and treasures, and walled garden. Walter and Nuala Sweeney welcome 'guests as friends' to share their much-loved, comfortably furnished home. Antiques, books, curios and family photographs are set against shuttered windows, polished-wood floors, chandeliers and marble fireplaces. A 'warm welcome' of a large pot of tea in the sitting room sets the tone; a guided tour of the 'lovely garden' is also offered. Big bedrooms are comfortable and eclectic rather than swish and stylish, with antiques and family heirlooms – a rocking horse in one – books, patterned carpets and floral curtains. One overlooks the garden, another has two double beds and a sweep of sash windows. Bathrooms are spacious and traditional. Thoughtful extras, including sherry, fresh milk and flowers, are praised. A generous choice at breakfast ranges from omelettes and poached eggs with prosciutto to pancakes and a full Yorkshire, plus a flush of different teas. 'Excellent value,' concludes a reader. (MM, and others)

10 Newbegin
Beverley HU17 8EG

T: 01482 888880
E: wsweeney@wsweeney.karoo.co.uk
W: newbeginhousebbbeverley.co.uk

BEDROOMS: 3.
OPEN: all year except when owners take a holiday.
FACILITIES: sitting room, dining room, small conference facilities, in-room TV (Freeview), ¾-acre walled garden, parking, EV charging, unsuitable for disabled.
BACKGROUND MUSIC: none.
LOCATION: central.
CHILDREN: all ages welcomed, no charge if own cot provided, variable charge for older children sharing with parents (contact for prices).
DOGS: not allowed.
CREDIT CARDS: none accepted.
PRICES: B&B doubles from £90, singles from £60. 1-night bookings sometimes refused during the Early Music Festival.

BIGBURY-ON-SEA Devon

MAP 1:D4

BURGH ISLAND HOTEL

♕ Previous César winner

A sea tractor ferries guests across the sands to this white concrete Art Deco edifice on a tidal island, built as a party venue in the 1930s, and what a swell party it is! Room names nod to illustrious past guests. Suites such as Noël Coward have a lounge with Deco furniture, Devon fudge, bespoke toiletries. Agatha Christie's writing retreat will sleep six. A trusted reader and a Guide insider tell separately of a compact room with poor lighting and with a metal-framed window that wouldn't shut: he hated it, and she forgave everything for the fun of it all. We hope the recent refurbishment has sorted out the glitches. The furniture in the Jane Marple room was old-fashioned, 'which is precisely the point'. There was no hospitality tray, but 'tea or coffee is delivered every morning. Room service is ordered via a Bakelite telephone.' After a dip in the sea-bathing Mermaid Pool, you can enjoy afternoon tea or cocktails under the 'peacock' ceiling of the Palm Court, eat seafood in The Nettlefold, or put on the Ritz for a black-tie dinner in the Grand Ballroom. The 13th-century Pilchard Inn is the place for fish and chips and a pint.

Burgh Island
Bigbury-on-Sea TQ7 4BG

T: 01548 810514
E: reception@burghisland.com
W: burghisland.com

BEDROOMS: 25. 1 suite in Beach House in grounds, apartment above Pilchard Inn.
OPEN: all year.
FACILITIES: lift, bar, 2 restaurants, ballroom, sun lounge, billiard room, private dining room, spa, civil wedding licence, 17-acre grounds, sea bathing pool, tennis, mainland garage, EV charging.
BACKGROUND MUSIC: period in public rooms.
LOCATION: off Bigbury beach, private garages on mainland.
CHILDREN: no under-5s, no under-13s in ballroom, extra bed £150.
DOGS: allowed in Beach House, Artist's Studio and Pilchard Inn (£25 a night).
CREDIT CARDS: Amex, MC, Visa.
PRICES: B&B doubles from £295, singles from £270. À la carte £75. 1-night bookings refused weekends, some bank holidays.

BIGBURY-ON-SEA Devon

MAP 1:D4

THE HENLEY

It's partly the lovely situation, with a 'stunning panorama' across the Avon estuary to Burgh Island, partly the warmth of the welcome that bring some of our readers back to this beachside bolt-hole time and again. Petra Lampe and Martyn Scarterfield's former Edwardian holiday cottage has seaside views from the dining room, the decked sun terrace and from each of its four bedrooms. Readers praise the wonderful beach, the 'relaxing, comfortable ambience', and not least the 'outstanding' food. From Monday to Saturday, Martyn cooks a restaurant-quality three-course dinner – maybe crab salad, asparagus ravioli, steak or sea bass with fennel sauce, served in a conservatory with Lloyd Loom chairs and potted palms. If you want to eat in, you must give three days' notice. Breakfast is of a similarly high standard – try the full Devon with Aune Valley bacon – setting you up for a round at Bigbury Golf Club, or to walk the South West Coast Path. On Sunday night you might push the boat out or, rather, take the world's only hydraulic sea tractor across to Burgh Island (see previous entry) for a black-tie affair in the Grand Ballroom.

Folly Hill
Bigbury-on-Sea TQ7 4AR

T: 01548 810240
E: info@thehenleyhotel.co.uk
W: thehenleyhotel.co.uk

BEDROOMS: 4.
OPEN: Mar–end Oct, restaurant closed Sun eve.
FACILITIES: 2 lounges, dining room, reception, in-room TV (Freeview), small terraced garden (steps to beach, golf, sailing, fishing), Coast Path nearby, unsuitable for disabled.
BACKGROUND MUSIC: jazz/classical in the evenings in lounge, dining room.
LOCATION: 5 miles S of Modbury.
CHILDREN: not under 12.
DOGS: allowed in bedrooms (not on bed, £7 per night), lounges, not in dining room.
CREDIT CARDS: MC, Visa.
PRICES: B&B doubles from £150, singles from £110. Set dinner £36. 1-night bookings sometimes refused weekends.

BIGGIN-BY-HARTINGTON Derbyshire   MAP 3:B6

BIGGIN HALL

In a beautiful setting in the Peak District, this historic country house offers a homely atmosphere and excellent value for money, which draw guests back year after year. The 17th-century building with stone mullions and leaded windows, and surrounded by gardens, is a higgledy-piggledy mix of rooms and corridors. Original features – beams, wood-panelling, vast stone fireplace in the lounge – are the backdrop to traditional furnishings, gilt-framed pictures and the odd bit of armour. Comfortably unstuffy, 'it's like staying with an old friend', comments one guest. Bedrooms are spread between characterful rooms in the main house – some with four-poster or half-tester – and a more cottagey style in converted outbuildings. All are light and include a welcome beer or Prosecco, plus fresh milk. Guests gather in the lounge or library for drinks before a 'straightforward' dinner that could include beef feather blade with bubble-and-squeak mash, and sea bream with a warm salad. At the 'plentiful' breakfast, which includes the local Derbyshire oatcakes, you might spot hens clucking around the lawn. 'Amazing value.' (JR, and others)

Biggin-by-Hartington
Buxton SK17 0DH

T: 01298 84451
E: enquiries@bigginhall.co.uk
W: bigginhall.co.uk

BEDROOMS: 21. 13 in annexes, some on ground floor.
OPEN: all year, restaurant closed Mon, Tues, Thurs, Sat lunch.
FACILITIES: sitting room, library, dining room, meeting room, in-room TV (Freeview), civil wedding licence, 8-acre grounds, restaurant and toilet wheelchair accessible.
BACKGROUND MUSIC: in restaurant.
LOCATION: 8 miles N of Ashbourne.
CHILDREN: not under 12, extra bed £25.
DOGS: allowed in annexe bedrooms (no charge unless for damage), not in main house.
CREDIT CARDS: MC, Visa.
PRICES: B&B doubles from £110, singles from £90. À la carte £32.50, Indulgence menu Fri and Sat (for whole table) £75 per person, incl. wine. 1-night bookings sometimes refused weekends.

BILDESTON Suffolk

MAP 2:C5

THE BILDESTON CROWN

Olde-worlde charm is leavened by touches of playful humour at this former 15th-century coaching inn, in a quintessential Suffolk village of half-timbered and pink-washed houses. Low beams and crackling log fires mix happily with modern paint finishes, witty wallpaper, and a check-carpeted corridor. One bedroom has a silvered French-inspired bed, a huge walk-in shower, and a double-ended bateau bath under a painting of Venice. There's more romance in a triple-aspect room with its damask-draped four-poster. Owners Hayley and Chris Lee are manager and chef respectively. Our inspectors were 'very impressed' by the dinner, served in the bar, dining room or outside (if your dog is in tow, choose the bar). 'There was plenty of choice on the menu. Food came promptly and was excellent.' 'The chef is very flexible. Let them know ahead if you want veggie options.' Typical dishes include Red Poll beef, navarin of lamb, tempura monkfish, 'all very well presented on characterful plates'. A family breakfast brought a jug of freshly squeezed orange juice, an 'ample cooked meal with delicious potatoes'.

104 High Street
Bildeston IP7 7EB

T: 01449 740510
E: reception@thebildestoncrown.co.uk
W: thebildestoncrown.com

BEDROOMS: 12. 1 suitable for wheelchair.
OPEN: all year, no accommodation 24–26 Dec, New Year's Day.
FACILITIES: 2 bars, restaurant, champagne lounge, 2 private dining areas, lift, in-room TV (Freeview), courtyard, walled garden and terrace, parking, mobile phone reception variable, restaurant and bar wheelchair accessible, adapted toilet.
BACKGROUND MUSIC: in bar, restaurant and courtyard.
LOCATION: village centre, 10 mins' drive from Lavenham.
CHILDREN: all ages welcomed, extra bed £10.
DOGS: allowed in some rooms (no charge) and in bar, not in restaurant.
CREDIT CARDS: Amex, MC, Visa.
PRICES: B&B doubles from £95, singles from £70. À la carte £40.

BISHOP'S CASTLE Shropshire   MAP 3:C4

THE CASTLE HOTEL

'We will definitely stay again' is the enthusiastic cry of many readers about this dog-friendly and walker-friendly hotel with views of the Shropshire hills. On the hilltop site of the town's former Norman castle, the 18th-century hotel charms as much with its large gardens and doggie treats as its 'uneven floors' and 'friendly staff'. 'Very comfy' bedrooms have quirky shapes, breezy colours and modern furniture; even the smallest have a couple of upholstered chairs. All have views over town and countryside; the cosier top-floor rooms, with sloping ceilings and exposed beams, have the best. Fresh bottled water delighted one guest as did 'the flask to take out with you'. A generous menu ranges from classic fish and chips, and beef and Stilton pie to vegetable tagine and slow-cooked belly pork. Eat in one of the small bars with stripped-wood floors and wood-burning stove, or in the smarter dining room. An 'excellent' breakfast includes omelettes, pancakes and a full grill served with an information sheet of suggestions of walks and drives. One couple were so taken with the hotel, they stayed an extra night. (BR, and others)

Market Square
Bishop's Castle SY9 5BN

T: 01588 638403
E: stay@thecastlehotelbishopscastle.co.uk
W: thecastlehotelbishopscastle.co.uk

BEDROOMS: 14. 2 suites in cottage and town house opposite.
OPEN: all year except 25 Dec and first week Jan.
FACILITIES: 3 bar areas, dining room, in-room TV (Freeview), in-room spa treatments, patio, terrace, garden, bars and restaurant wheelchair accessible, adapted toilet.
BACKGROUND MUSIC: in bar areas.
LOCATION: in small market town centre.
CHILDREN: all ages welcomed, extra bed £25.
DOGS: allowed in bedrooms (no charge, welcome pack), bar, at owner's side at mealtimes in dog-friendly areas, not in restaurant.
CREDIT CARDS: MC, Visa.
PRICES: B&B doubles from £125, singles from £115. À la carte £31. 1-night bookings sometimes refused Sat.

BISHOPSTONE Wiltshire

MAP 3:E6

❦HELEN BROWNING'S ROYAL OAK

NEW

César award: inn of the year

You can ride your horse to this quirky pub-with-rooms on Helen Browning's organic farm – just tell them to expect you. It is promoted from the Shortlist this year at the urging of inspectors, who received 'a warm welcome from Helen's partner, Tim Finney, and the dedicated staff, who have created a real sense of community'. Bedrooms, each named after a farm field, have a photo mural and playful rustic details. Football Field (yes, they have one, if not quite up to Wembley standard) has a smart shower room. Cuckoo Pen has 'an Art Deco feel, silver mirrors, shiny bedroom tables'. Details include 'trendy antler lamp fittings; an espresso machine'. Guests relax in The Wallow, with tea, coffee, table football. The bar and dining areas mix elements of tradition and wit. Food is big on 'hearty classics' (flame-grilled burgers, fish and chips). 'Particularly good were beef pasta gratin and plum caramel cake.' Breakfast brings eggs from the hens, 'specials such as kedgeree'. Outside you'll find 'mismatched garden furniture, gazebos strung with fairy lights', a farm shop, garden kitchen and picnic spots. (SO, and others)

Cues Lane
Bishopstone SN6 8PP

T: 01793 790481
E: royaloak@helenbrowningorganics.co.uk
W: helenbrowningsorganic.co.uk

BEDROOMS: 12. All in annexe, 100 yds from pub, 1 suitable for disabled.
OPEN: all year, lunch, dinner not served 25 Dec.
FACILITIES: lounge, pub (2 dining areas), restaurant meeting/function room, in-room TV (Freeview), ½-acre garden (rope swing, Wendy house, 'flighty hens'), EV charging, restaurant wheelchair accessible, partially adapted toilet.
BACKGROUND MUSIC: occasionally in public spaces.
LOCATION: on an organic farm, in village, 7 miles E of Swindon, 10 miles from Marlborough.
CHILDREN: all ages welcomed, extra bed £20.
DOGS: allowed in 3 bedrooms (no charge), in public rooms 'at our discretion'.
CREDIT CARDS: MC, Visa.
PRICES: B&B doubles from £93. À la carte £32.

BLAKENEY Norfolk

MAP 2:A5

THE BLAKENEY HOTEL

♔ Previous César winner

With its quayside position overlooking the boats of north Norfolk's salt marsh estuary towards Blakeney Point, this large, family-friendly hotel, established in 1922, has a loyal following. 'It is a lovely spot,' says a regular. Bedrooms, some on the cosy side, have milky and seaside colours with pretty-patterned fabrics and wallpapers, although one guest felt theirs was rather tired. The best have watery views; others overlook gardens. Guests gravitate to the two soft-hued estuary-view lounges with their big sofas and armchairs, and where tea with 'good scones, jam and butter in dishes' can be taken. On rainy days, the 'excellent pool' and games room are especially useful for families. Dinner showcases local produce such as Dover sole with brown shrimps, locally caught crab and Norfolk lamb. Desserts, such as chocolate roulade and passion fruit and lime posset, are a highlight. Breakfast includes 'delicious scrambled eggs' with smoked salmon, local kippers from Cley and a full grill. Walk it off with a breezy hike across the marshes where birds and grey seals are a treat to spot. 'My favourite hotel.' (Carol Jackson, David Sefton, DS)

The Quay
Blakeney
Holt NR25 7NE

T: 01263 740797
E: enquiries@blakeneyhotel.co.uk
W: blakeney-hotel.co.uk

BEDROOMS: 64. 16 in Granary annexe, some on ground floor, 1 suitable for disabled.
OPEN: all year.
FACILITIES: lift, 2 lounges, bar, restaurant, in-room TV (Freeview), function facilities, heated indoor pool, steam room, mini-gym, games room, terrace, ¼-acre walled garden, public rooms wheelchair accessible, adapted toilet.
BACKGROUND MUSIC: none.
LOCATION: on the quay.
CHILDREN: all ages welcomed, family rooms with bunk beds, cot £6, extra bed from £20.
DOGS: allowed in some bedrooms (£20 per night), not in public rooms.
CREDIT CARDS: Amex, MC, Visa.
PRICES: B&B doubles from £276, singles from £150. Set 3-course menu £36. 1-night bookings sometimes refused.

BLANCHLAND Northumberland

MAP 4:B3

THE LORD CREWE ARMS

♔ Previous César winner

In a postcard-perfect village of honey-stone cottages with a sparkling river, this historic building blends atmosphere with 21st-century comforts and robust food. Formerly the abbot's lodgings of a 12th-century priory, the inn crackles with character with its flagged floors, mullioned windows, a barrel-vaulted bar and dining areas that vary from cosy and fire-warmed to airy and elegant. Food is Modern British with 'handsome and punchy' flavours; perhaps own-cured salmon with horseradish crème fraîche on brioche toast, followed by pan-roasted duck breast with roast beetroot and red wine sauce. Most bedrooms are across the square or around the corner in miners' cottages, but all share a sophisticated country look with pale-washed walls, wool curtains, tartan throws and modern and antique furniture. Some have beams or a window seat, others a wood-burning stove. 'Splendid bathrooms' feature tongue-and-groove panelling, a few with a roll-top bath. Books, fudge and coffee machines are 'thoughtful touches' – as are the wellies and walking routes. (Part of the Calcot Collection; see also Barnsley House, Barnsley; The Painswick, Painswick; and Calcot & Spa, Tetbury.)

The Square
Blanchland DH8 9SP

T: 01434 675469
E: enquiries@
   lordcrewearmsblanchland.co.uk
W: lordcrewearmsblanchland.co.uk

BEDROOMS: 21. 7 in adjacent miners' cottages, 10 in The Angel across road, some on ground floor, 1 suitable for disabled.
OPEN: all year.
FACILITIES: reception hall, lounge, 3 dining rooms, bar, Gatehouse events space, in-room TV, civil wedding licence, beer garden, 1 dining area wheelchair accessible with ramp, adapted toilet.
BACKGROUND MUSIC: in dining room, bar.
LOCATION: in Blanchland village on B6306, 9 miles S of Hexham.
CHILDREN: all ages welcomed, extra bed for under-13s £25.
DOGS: well-behaved dogs allowed in bedrooms (£20 per night), public rooms, not in dining room.
CREDIT CARDS: Amex, MC, Visa.
PRICES: B&B doubles from £169, singles ring to check. À la carte £35.

BLEDINGTON Gloucestershire

MAP 3:D6

THE KING'S HEAD INN

Ducks bob on the brook that runs through the green in front of this 16th-century cider house with all the trappings of the perfect English country pub – beams, flagstones, settles, blazing fires, Hook Norton ale on draught. It has been owned for more than 20 years by Archie Orr-Ewing (ex Blues and Royals) and his wife, the milliner Nicola de Selincourt. There is certainly nothing old hat about her bedroom designs, with Cole & Son wallpaper, jazzy lampshades and headboards, arty junk-shop finds and Nicola's own Bantam Bodycare toiletries. Inn rooms are quite snug; some in the courtyard annexe are more spacious and have been redecorated since last year. 'The courtyard garden was a lovely place for pre-dinner drinks, with the chickens wandering around.' You can eat 'very good dinners' inside or out, from a menu of local, free-range and organic produce, maybe lamb rump with roast hispi cabbage, wild garlic pesto; vegetable paella, even toad-in-the-hole. There are 'large portions and plenty of choice'. The pub, which also has walks from the door, won a prestigious National Inn of the Year award for 2021, to which we say chapeau! (SP)

The Green
Bledington OX7 6XQ

T: 01608 658365
E: info@kingsheadinn.net
W: thekingsheadinn.net

BEDROOMS: 12. 6 in courtyard annexe, some on ground floor.
OPEN: all year except 25/26 Dec.
FACILITIES: bar, restaurant, snug, courtyard, in-room TV (Freeview), children's play area.
BACKGROUND MUSIC: most of the day, in bar.
LOCATION: on village green.
CHILDREN: all ages welcomed, cot £5, extra bed £25.
DOGS: allowed in 3 ground-floor bedrooms (no charge), bar, not in restaurant.
CREDIT CARDS: Amex, MC, Visa.
PRICES: B&B doubles from £110, singles from £85 (Sun–Thurs). À la carte £35. 1-night bookings refused Sat.

BOLTON ABBEY Yorkshire

MAP 4:D3

THE DEVONSHIRE ARMS

Part of the Duke of Devonshire's Yorkshire estate at Bolton Abbey, the Devonshire Arms has grown from a 17th-century inn to a country house hotel with spa, fine dining and helipads. 'Wonderfully located' and much extended, the hotel mixes contemporary furnishings with period pieces, and has artwork from the Chatsworth collection. While 'the hotel has a formal feel, the staff couldn't have been more friendly and helpful'. Bedrooms range from 'quite small' rooms near the 'not so quiet' road or overlooking the garden to four-poster rooms, with some larger rooms in the 18th-century, more traditionally furnished wing. All come with fresh milk and coffee machines, and modern bathrooms with bath and shower. Dining is a choice between the casual Brasserie – 'delicious, with good-quality traditional meals such as steak and chips' – or the fancier Burlington restaurant. The latter's short-choice menu offers 'high-order' cooking such as poached cod with razor clams and fennel, and aged Yorkshire lamb with pumpkin and oyster. After one of the 'beautiful walks from the door', return to afternoon tea. (See also The Cavendish, Baslow.)

Bolton Abbey Estate
Bolton Abbey
Skipton BD23 6AJ

T: 01756 718100
E: reception@thedevonshirearms.
    co.uk
W: devonshirehotels.co.uk

BEDROOMS: 40. Some on ground floor suitable for disabled.
OPEN: all year, restaurant closed Mon–Wed eves, brasserie open all week.
FACILITIES: 4 lounges, 2 restaurants, private dining rooms, in-room TV (Freeview), civil wedding licence, spa (indoor pool), gardens, helipads, EV charging, public areas wheelchair accessible, adapted toilet.
BACKGROUND MUSIC: in public areas.
LOCATION: 6 miles E of Skipton.
CHILDREN: all ages welcomed, extra bed £40.
DOGS: allowed in some bedrooms (£10 per night), public areas, brasserie, not spa or restaurant.
CREDIT CARDS: Amex, MC, Visa.
PRICES: B&B doubles from £169, singles from £149. Set menu £75 (restaurant), à la carte £30 (brasserie).

BORROWDALE Cumbria

MAP 4: inset C2

HAZEL BANK

♕ Previous César winner

'Relaxing' and 'luxurious' are the oft-repeated descriptions of this small country house with captivating fell views, walks from the doorstep and an intimate atmosphere. Sitting above Rosthwaite village in picturesque Borrowdale, the Victorian house has a warmth that is all thanks to owners Gary and Donna MacRae, who readers say 'made us feel instantly at home'. The interiors are comfortable, with soft carpets, polished wood and vases of flowers, but not too fussy; after all, why compete with those views! Each of the 'immaculate' bedrooms, elegant with pretty wallpaper and top-notch bathroom, looks across the valley and fells. Spoiling touches include sherry, home-made biscuits and L'Occitane products. Donna produces an 'astonishing' evening menu that starts with canapés in the lounge and continues with dishes such as home-cured salmon and lemongrass panna cotta, and roast Herdwick lamb (from neighbouring Chapel farm) with slow-roasted lamb-fat carrots. A 'sophisticated' wine list, too. Breakfast includes kippers, omelettes and a full Cumbrian (vegetarian option), and maybe a red squirrel sighting in the garden. (CS, and others)

Borrowdale
Keswick CA12 5XB

T: 01768 777248
E: info@hazelbankhotel.co.uk
W: hazelbankhotel.co.uk

BEDROOMS: 7. 1 on ground floor with walk-in shower.
OPEN: all year except mid-Dec to late Jan.
FACILITIES: lounge, dining room, drying room, in-room TV (Freeview), 4-acre grounds (croquet, woodland walks).
BACKGROUND MUSIC: Classic FM at breakfast.
LOCATION: 6 miles S of Keswick on B5289 to Borrowdale.
CHILDREN: not under 16.
DOGS: not allowed.
CREDIT CARDS: MC, Visa.
PRICES: B&B doubles from £140. Set dinner £42. Min. 2-night bookings except by special arrangement.

BORROWDALE Cumbria

MAP 4: inset C2

LEATHES HEAD HOTEL

In arguably the Lake District's most picturesque valley, Borrowdale, this Edwardian country house has spectacular views and is a favourite of outdoors lovers who like their creature comforts. Many walks can be taken from the doorstep; on return, there's tea by the log-burner in the lounge or on the terrace overlooking the garden with its birds and wildlife. Guests often report spotting red squirrels. 'Well-presented' bedrooms all have views, and are gently traditional with pale colours, soft carpets and a contemporary bathroom. One reader praised Cat Bells with its views of the eponymous fell 'one way and over fields the other'. Chef Noel Breaks's 'excellent cooking' is a big draw with a daily-changing set menu that might include treacle-cured trout with cauliflower panna cotta or duck breast with blackberries, potato and sage terrine. Lamb from nearby Yew Tree Farm is always popular. Almost all is made from scratch, including the bread, which also features at breakfast alongside dishes such as eggs Benedict and the full Cumbrian with vegetarian option. The views from the conservatory dining room guarantee a memorable meal. (SP, JB)

Borrowdale
Keswick CA12 5UY

T: 01768 777247
E: reservations@leatheshead.co.uk
W: leatheshead.co.uk

BEDROOMS: 11. Some on ground floor, 1 suitable for disabled.
OPEN: all year except 24–26 Dec.
FACILITIES: lounge, bar, conservatory restaurant, in-room TV (Freeview), drying room, terrace, 3-acre grounds, EV charging, public rooms wheelchair accessible.
BACKGROUND MUSIC: in public rooms.
LOCATION: 4½ miles S of Keswick.
CHILDREN: not under 15.
DOGS: not allowed.
CREDIT CARDS: Amex, MC, Visa.
PRICES: B&B doubles from £150. Set 4-course dinner £48.95. 1-night bookings refused Sat May–Sept.

BOSCASTLE Cornwall

MAP 1:C3

THE OLD RECTORY

Fruit and cut flowers from the organic garden, eggs from the hens, honey from the hives, and romantic associations with Thomas Hardy are among the many charms of Sally and Chris Searle's Victorian rectory B&B. It was here that Hardy met his first wife, Emma Gifford. The room he slept in has an antique carved bed, while Emma's room has an original fireplace, a king-size bed, and an original 1870s thunderbox toilet. In the author's A Pair of Blue Eyes, the rectory features as Endelstow vicarage, where Stephen Smith's first repast was taken at a table 'decked with winter flowers' and presented 'a cheerful aspect of abundance' – much like breakfast here today. The full Cornish brings sausages from the Searles' own porkers, dry-cured bacon, hog's pudding, home-grown tomatoes, peppers and courgettes in season. Or there is locally smoked fish, French toast, home-grown fruit. An evening meal is sometimes offered; on other nights, guests who book directly get a lift into Boscastle for dinner, free laundry for a stay of three nights or more, a complimentary newspaper and a tour of the three-acre garden. It's just ten minutes to the coast.

St Juliot
Boscastle PL35 0BT

T: 01840 250225
E: sally@stjuliot.com
W: stjuliot.com

BEDROOMS: 4. 1 in Stables (connected to house via conservatory and with separate entrance).
OPEN: Mar–end Oct, limited evening meals by arrangement.
FACILITIES: sitting room, breakfast room, conservatory, in-room TV (Freeview), 3-acre garden (croquet lawn, 'lookout', walled kitchen garden), EV charging, unsuitable for disabled.
BACKGROUND MUSIC: none.
LOCATION: 2 miles NE of Boscastle.
CHILDREN: not under 12.
DOGS: up to 2 allowed, only in stable room (£10 per dog per stay).
CREDIT CARDS: Amex, MC, Visa.
PRICES: B&B doubles from £95, singles from £71. 1-night bookings only accepted if there is a late vacancy or quiet period.

BOSHAM Sussex

THE MILLSTREAM

Five minutes from its own quayside, in pretty gardens with the Bosham Stream running through, this quintessentially English house is a 'real gem' of a family-run hotel. It has been owned by the Wild family since 1976, and chef Neil Hiskey is now in his 21st year here. Occupying three 17th-century workmen's cottages, with a bar in a 1970s extension, it has a lovely comfy-luxe feel to it. Bedrooms are country house in style, with contemporary touches, and range from singles to a superior double with a freestanding bath, walk-in shower and French doors to a private garden. Across the stream, two suites occupy a thatched cottage, each with its own front door and garden, ideal for a family. All rooms have a coffee machine, fresh milk in a mini-fridge, and 24-hour room service. There is a sitting room with a grand piano, with informal dining in the brasserie (maybe tempura fish and chips) and outside. In the restaurant menus include dishes such as roast monkfish, bacon, parsley and cockle sauce; feather blade steak with thyme jus; spelt and pearl barley risotto. 'Excellent service and food – will certainly go back.'

Bosham Lane
Bosham
Chichester PO18 8HL

T: 01243 573234
E: info@millstream-hotel.co.uk
W: millstreamhotel.com

BEDROOMS: 35. 2 in cottage, 7 on ground floor, 2 suitable for disabled.
OPEN: all year.
FACILITIES: lounge, bar, restaurant, brasserie, conference room, in-room TV (Freeview), civil wedding licence, front lawn (alfresco dining), residents' garden (stream, gazebo), parking, public areas wheelchair accessible.
BACKGROUND MUSIC: all day in bar, lounge and restaurants.
LOCATION: 4 miles W of Chichester.
CHILDREN: all ages welcomed, cots free, extra bed for under-13s £20, children's menu (brasserie).
DOGS: not allowed.
CREDIT CARDS: MC, Visa.
PRICES: B&B doubles from £175, singles from £130. À la carte (restaurant) £45, (brasserie) £27. 1-night bookings sometimes refused Sat.

BOWNESS-ON-WINDERMERE Cumbria   MAP 4: inset C2

LINDETH FELL

'B&B' doesn't do justice to this wisteria-clad
Edwardian country house with glorious views of
Windermere, seven acres of gardens and elegant
interiors. Run by the Kennedy family for 37 years,
the house, with its wood panelling and ornate
ceilings, is gracious yet never stuffy. Books and
family photographs can be found among the
large sofas and plump window seats, a perfect
setting for the welcoming cream tea: 'Diana
Kennedy's scones are legendary.' If it's sunny,
enjoy this on the terrace. Inviting bedrooms are
more contemporary with bold wallpapers, smart
armchairs and pale carpets, and the 'spotless
bathrooms' are well designed. 'Thoughtful extras'
include sherry, iced water, digital radio, robes
and coffee machines. Light snacks, picnics and
afternoon tea are available during the day. In the
evening, handsome supper platters can be pre-
ordered. Breakfast in the picture-window dining
room overlooking the gardens is a feast of freshly
squeezed juice, omelettes, poached haddock, pan-
fried halloumi and tomatoes, as well as a full grill.
The Kennedy family and their staff, say readers,
know how to make you feel welcome. (HP)

Lyth Valley Road
Bowness-on-Windermere LA23 3JP

T: 015394 43286
E: kennedy@lindethfell.co.uk
W: lindethfell.co.uk

BEDROOMS: 14. 1, on ground floor,
suitable for disabled.
OPEN: all year except 23–26 Dec,
2 Jan–11 Feb.
FACILITIES: 2 lounges, bar, entrance hall
with seating, dining room, in-room
TV, 7-acre grounds (terrace, gardens,
lawn games), complimentary access to
local gym, spa, pool.
BACKGROUND MUSIC: classical in dining
room, bar.
LOCATION: 1 mile S of Bowness.
CHILDREN: 12 and over, extra bed from
£28.50.
DOGS: only assistance dogs allowed.
CREDIT CARDS: MC, Visa.
PRICES: B&B doubles from £151, singles
from £75. Evening platters £15.50
(with additional 2 courses, £28). Min.
2-night stay Mar–end Oct, 3-night
min. bank holidays (ring to check
1-night availability).

BRADFORD-ON-AVON Wiltshire

MAP 2:D1

WIDBROOK GRANGE

Nick and Charlotte Dent have had a field day converting a Georgian stone farmhouse and outbuildings in 11 acres into a dog-friendly, fun hotel brimming with character and 'so many appealing, endlessly inventive features'. Upcycled agricultural paraphernalia is everywhere: here a vintage tractor, there a hay cart or old milk churns, 'mirrors created out of old door panels', a sheep fashioned from spark plugs. A stables bedroom had 'plain brown carpet, grey/brown painted walls, some of stone', no boutique pretensions, but was warm and comfortable, with the drinks tray on an old suitcase. 'The spacious bathroom was rustic, too, with panelled walls.' There is a gin bar, a cosy lounge with leather armchairs, and a conservatory perfect for afternoon tea – which is also served for dogs, with a tennis ball to take home, a choice of food and a puppichino. In the dining room, where garden tools and old fruit boxes adorn the wall, a menu of local produce includes dishes such as monkfish with saffron risotto. Readers who booked a short stay found it 'so enjoyable' that three months later they were back. (Catherine Held, and others)

Trowbridge Road
Bradford-on-Avon BA15 1UH

T: 01225 864750
E: stay@widbrookgrange.com
W: widbrookgrange.co.uk

BEDROOMS: 19. 15 in outbuildings, 1 suitable for disabled.
OPEN: all year.
FACILITIES: gin bar, snug, restaurant, conservatory, in-room TV (Freeview), civil wedding licence, function facilities, 11-acre grounds, 11-metre indoor heated swimming pool, gym, giant chess, parking, public rooms wheelchair accessible, no adapted toilet.
BACKGROUND MUSIC: soft, all day in public rooms.
LOCATION: 2 miles S of Bradford-on-Avon.
CHILDREN: all ages welcomed, family rooms, children's menu.
DOGS: allowed in certain bedrooms (£15 per night), public rooms, not restaurant.
CREDIT CARDS: Amex, MC, Visa.
PRICES: B&B doubles from £155, family from £190. À la carte £40, tasting menu £59.

SEE ALSO SHORTLIST

BRADFORD-ON-AVON Wiltshire

WOOLLEY GRANGE

Keeping both the kids amused and parents relaxed in a grand Jacobean manor is a feat, but Woolley Grange manages it – from crèche and cinema to spa and pools. Part of the Luxury Family Hotels group (see Fowey Hall, Fowey, and Moonfleet Manor, Fleet), it has thought of most things to give everyone a great break. Grown-ups like the spoiling surrounds of mullioned windows, stone terraces, oak-panelled drawing rooms and spa; kids dive into the games boxes, explore the fairy garden, play on the tree swing, or roast marshmallows and collect hens' eggs. The crèche and baby-listening service are free, too. Interiors are 'beautiful' but not precious; fairground carousel animals in corridors, saggy sofas in the lounges. Bedrooms, spread between the main building and cottages, are comfortably country house with floral curtains, and the occasional antique. Most have baths and showers. Meals are either family affairs – steaks, burgers and pasta – in the orangery, or candlelit dining on more stylish dishes such as duck with pecan granola, and monkfish tail with braised baby gem. 'The food was incredible. Everyone enjoyed it.' (FM)

Woolley Green
Bradford-on-Avon BA15 1TX

T: 01225 864705
E: info@woolleygrangehotel.co.uk
W: woolleygrangehotel.co.uk

BEDROOMS: 25. 11 in annexes, 2 on ground floor, 1 suitable for disabled.
OPEN: all year.
FACILITIES: 2 lounges, 2 restaurants, cinema, 2 private dining rooms, in-room TV (Freeview), crèche, spa, heated indoor and outdoor swimming pools, civil wedding licence, 14-acre grounds, EV charging, wheelchair accessible.
BACKGROUND MUSIC: in restaurants.
LOCATION: 1 mile NE of Bradford-on-Avon, 8½ miles SE of Bath.
CHILDREN: all ages welcomed, no additional charge for extra beds.
DOGS: allowed in bedrooms (£15 per night), public rooms, not restaurants.
CREDIT CARDS: Amex, MC, Visa.
PRICES: B&B doubles from £119, family rooms from £129. À la carte £35–£45. 1-night bookings sometimes refused weekends.

SEE ALSO SHORTLIST

BRAITHWAITE Cumbria

MAP 4: inset C2

THE COTTAGE IN THE WOOD

The woodland setting of this restaurant-with-rooms offers tranquillity and Michelin-starred dining that suits walkers as well as those looking to sit back and relax. Liam and Kath Berney's 17th-century cottage in Whinlatter Forest enjoys views to Skiddaw and surroundings teeming with wildlife. A very 'personal hotel', with 'hands-on' owners, its boutique bedrooms have shimmery wallpapers and pale-wood furnishings as well as fresh milk and home-made shortbread. Some are small but offer 'a comfy bed and a great view of the mountains'. Modern bathrooms can be a squeeze but have a decent shower and good-sized bath – ideal for sprucing up after a day's walking. Then it's canapés in the lounge before moving into the candlelit dining room to enjoy Ben Wilkinson's 'faultless cooking'. It's a very short-choice menu, as a reader points out, but there's a tasting menu option, too. 'Beautifully balanced' dishes might include hogget with lentils, spiced carrot and roast sweetbread, and cured trout with oyster cream, dill and cucumber. Breakfast includes home-made yogurt granola, omelettes and creamy scrambled eggs. (Peter Anderson, SP)

Magic Hill
Whinlatter Forest
Braithwaite CA12 5TW

T: 01768 778409
E: relax@thecottageinthewood.co.uk
W: thecottageinthewood.co.uk

BEDROOMS: 9. 1 in the garden with separate entrance.
OPEN: all year except 25/26 Dec, 2nd and 3rd week Jan, closed Sun, Mon.
FACILITIES: lounge, restaurant, in-room TV (Freeview), drying room, secure bicycle storage, terraced garden, 2 acres of woodland, restaurant and public areas wheelchair accessible, adapted toilet.
BACKGROUND MUSIC: none.
LOCATION: 5 miles NW of Keswick.
CHILDREN: not under 10.
DOGS: not allowed.
CREDIT CARDS: MC, Visa.
PRICES: D,B&B doubles from £270, singles ring to check. Set dinner £65, tasting menu £75. 1-night bookings refused weekends.

BRAMPTON Cumbria

MAP 4:B3

FARLAM HALL

This long-established country house hotel with
a walled garden, set in a peaceful Cumbrian
village, has had an elegant refurbishment without
compromising 'its sense of history and tradition'.
The creeper-covered Victorian house, in six
acres of gardens, has been lightened with soft
colours, pale-patterned wallpapers and smartly
upholstered armchairs. A Relais & Châteaux
member, it still feels comfortably traditional with
fires in sitting rooms, 'extremely pleasant' staff
and garden views from the dining room. Evening
meals are reassuringly 'proper' with canapés and
white napery while the food is 'modern country
house' and might include crab with spring pea
custard followed by roe deer with black pudding.
An excellent British cheese selection and 'a good
wine list' pleased one couple. Large bedrooms,
furnished in a 'light-touch' country house style
of gentle colours with a mix of reproduction
and antique furniture, have garden views and
armchairs; a sofa in larger rooms. Most of the
modern bathrooms include a bath and shower.
For longer stays, there are now four cottages. 'We
would definitely stay again.' (JB)

Hallbankgate
Brampton CA8 2NG

T: 01697 746234
E: farlam@farlamhall.co.uk
W: farlamhall.co.uk

BEDROOMS: 12. 2 on ground floor,
1 in stables. 4 self-catering cottages in
grounds sleep 2–6.
OPEN: all year.
FACILITIES: 2 lounges, restaurant,
cocktail bar, in-room TV (Freeview),
civil wedding licence, 6-acre grounds
(stream, walled garden), EV charging,
public rooms wheelchair accessible.
BACKGROUND MUSIC: in public areas,
restaurant.
LOCATION: on A689, 2½ miles SE of
Brampton.
CHILDREN: all ages welcomed, extra
bed £50.
DOGS: allowed in bedrooms (not
unattended, £30 per night), public
rooms, not in restaurant.
CREDIT CARDS: Amex, MC, Visa.
PRICES: B&B doubles from £209, singles
from £219. À la carte £54, tasting
menu £65. 1-night bookings may be
refused Christmas/New Year.

BRANCASTER STAITHE Norfolk

MAP 2:A5

THE WHITE HORSE

♥ Previous César winner

Amid a luminous, big-sky landscape of tidal salt marshes, with views to the sea and Scolt Head Island, the Nye family's hotel enjoys a 'brilliant location on the coast'. Floor-to-ceiling windows let you better appreciate the views from the public rooms and from some of the bedrooms, decorated in seascape shades of teal and turquoise, lavender and sand. Eight garden rooms, in an annexe with a grass and sedum roof, are very dog-friendly, with a private terrace and a wooden entrance floor area for muddy boots and mucky pups coming in from the coast path. 'The staff are helpful and kind,' wrote a reader on a return visit this year, and 'the food was still excellent'. A new marsh-side eating area with seafood bar has a clear marquee, sympathetic landscaping and furnishings. You can chow down with your pooch in the bar or eat in the restaurant, where Fran Hartshorne's 'heavily fishy' menus also include dishes such as marsh-grazed, dry-aged beef sirloin, rose harissa and feta arancini. 'The scallops were particularly memorable.' At breakfast there is fish from the smokehouse at the bottom of the garden. (Sara Price, and others)

Main Road
Brancaster Staithe PE31 8BY

T: 01485 210262
E: reception@whitehorsebrancaster.
co.uk
W: whitehorsebrancaster.co.uk

BEDROOMS: 15. 8 on ground floor in annexe, 1 suitable for disabled.
OPEN: all year.
FACILITIES: open-plan bar, lounge areas, conservatory restaurant, dining room, in-room TV (Freeview), ½-acre garden (terrace, covered sunken garden), in-room therapies, EV charging, public rooms wheelchair accessible, adapted toilet.
BACKGROUND MUSIC: 'subtle' in restaurant.
LOCATION: centre of village.
CHILDREN: all ages welcomed, extra bed £30, children's menu, high chair.
DOGS: allowed in garden rooms (£10 a night), bar.
CREDIT CARDS: Amex, MC, Visa.
PRICES: B&B doubles from £140, singles from £105. À la carte £38.

BRIGHTON Sussex

MAP 2:E4

ARTIST RESIDENCE BRIGHTON

With its outré tastes in art, Charlotte and Justin Salisbury's seafront hotel and social hub perfectly encapsulates Brighton's bohemian spirit. The template for a small collection of hotels was set here in 2008 when Justin invited street artists to stay at his parents' B&B in exchange for bedaubing and bedecking it. The cheapest bedrooms are snug, with maybe one of those runny-mascara murals by Charles Uzzell-Edwards (aka 'Pure Evil'), or a sea-facing balcony and works by local artist Joe Webb, plus a Roberts radio and rainfall shower. Some rooms have a bare brick wall, an in-room copper bath, a modern four-poster, bunks, a view of the skeletal remains of the West Pier – rather like an art installation in itself. New this year is a fourth-floor apartment in the house next door, a great base for a family stay. The restaurant has closed, but coffee and cocktails are served all day in the ground-floor bar and café spaces, along with neon admonishments ('Stop pretending'), as well as breakfast and weekend brunch. Besides, this is Brighton, with any number of places to eat.

33 Regency Square
Brighton BN1 2GG

T: 01273 324302
E: brighton@artistresidence.co.uk
W: artistresidence.co.uk

BEDROOMS: 25.
OPEN: all year, restaurant closed 25/26 Dec.
FACILITIES: small lift, bar and café, private cocktail bar (events), ping-pong/meeting room, in-room TV (Freeview), small terrace, car park opposite (fee), unsuitable for disabled.
BACKGROUND MUSIC: all day in public areas.
LOCATION: town centre.
CHILDREN: all ages welcomed, free cots, extra bed £30, under-16s not unsupervised in bedrooms.
DOGS: allowed in some bedrooms (£15 per dog per night, incl. bed, bowls and treats).
CREDIT CARDS: Amex, MC, Visa.
PRICES: room-only doubles from £129. Cooked breakfast from £7.50, full English £11, brunch (Sat, Sun) £20. 1-night bookings refused weekends.

SEE ALSO SHORTLIST

BRIGHTON Sussex

MAP 2:E4

DRAKES

Two bow-fronted Regency town houses with views of the iconic Palace Pier are home to a boutique hotel that counts Cate Blanchett and Kylie Minogue among past guests. 'Inside it is quite special,' write readers, who were 'given a warm welcome' and shown to one of the sea-facing feature rooms, with a bath beside floor-to-ceiling windows. 'We were amazed at the decor, the light pouring in. Behind frosted glass doors there was a walk-in shower/wet room. Housekeeping was immaculate.' If you're on a budget opt for a snug city-facing room with queen-size bed, a monsoon wet-room shower. A loft room has a sofa bed for a child. The staff are a delight: 'We felt they really enjoyed their work and wanted us to share that enjoyment.' In Amarillo, star-spangled, rosette-garlanded chef Ian Swainson creates a six-course fine-dining menu of beautifully presented dishes such as crab custard, white crab meat and bisque; roasted beetroots with lavender and milk curd; juniper-crusted venison, chestnut truffle purée, caramelised onion/yeast foam. The bar is the place for a cappuccino or a cocktail. (A and SA)

43–44 Marine Parade
Brighton BN2 1PE

T: 01273 696934
E: info@drakesofbrighton.com
W: drakesofbrighton.com

BEDROOMS: 20.
OPEN: all year, restaurant Tues–Sat.
FACILITIES: lounge/bar, restaurant, meeting/private dining room, in-room TV (Sky), civil wedding licence, some off-road parking £15 a night, unsuitable for disabled.
BACKGROUND MUSIC: in bar and restaurant.
LOCATION: ½ mile from centre, on seafront.
CHILDREN: all ages welcomed, no extra beds, babies 'by prior arrangement'.
DOGS: only assistance dogs allowed.
CREDIT CARDS: Amex, MC, Visa.
PRICES: room-only doubles from £125. Breakfast £7.50–£15, 6-course dinner £65. Min. 2-night stay Sat, but check availability.

SEE ALSO SHORTLIST

BRISTOL

BROOKS GUESTHOUSE

In the centre of Bristol, a stroll from the harbour, Brooks Guesthouse is a pleasant surprise, with its quirky courtyard garden, shiny rooftop caravans and excellent value. There's a 'sense of privacy' and fun, say inspectors of this three-storey 1950s office block converted by Carla and Andrew Brooks to provide cool, frills-free accommodation – though it's probably not aimed at 'older folk'. Bedrooms are 'neat and well lit' and smartly furnished with classy wallpapers, tongue-and-groove panelling, pale-wood bedsteads and hooks for clothes; space is at a premium. Housekeeping, say inspectors, is patchy. Tiled bathrooms are compact. Alternatively, the 'Airstream-style' trailers in the rooftop garden, squeezing in double bed and shower, are a funkier way for a cosy night's sleep; great 'for a young family'. 'Well-executed' breakfasts include home-made fruit compote, eggs Benedict, smoked salmon and cream cheese, as well as daily specials. They're served in the open-plan living area with its bright, eclectic mix of vintage and rustic furniture and overlooking the garden. 'It is surprisingly quiet', given the central location.

Exchange Avenue
St Nicholas Market
Bristol BS1 1UB

T: 0117 930 0066
E: info@brooksguesthousebristol.com
W: brooksguesthousebristol.com

BEDROOMS: 27. 4 in Airstream-style caravans on roof.
OPEN: all year except 24–26 Dec.
FACILITIES: lift, lounge/breakfast room, honesty bar, in-room TV (Freeview), discounted parking, courtyard and rooftop garden, unsuitable for disabled.
BACKGROUND MUSIC: in lounge and breakfast area.
LOCATION: central, next to St Nicholas Market.
CHILDREN: all ages welcomed, free cot, extra bed £20.
DOGS: only assistance dogs.
CREDIT CARDS: Amex, MC, Visa.
PRICES: B&B doubles from £69, caravans from £80. Min. 2-night stay Sat.

BRISTOL

MAP 1:B6

NUMBER THIRTY EIGHT CLIFTON

♥ Previous César winner

From its high vantage, Adam Dorrien Smith's bay-fronted Georgian town house and boutique B&B has fabulous contrasting views, with Durdham Down parkland to the fore and the roofscape of Bristol behind. 'Panelled bedrooms are painted in muted greys, greens and blues' (Farrow & Ball's Lamp Room, for example), 'with such unfussy good taste that I wanted to package them up and reinstate them at home.' All have a mini-fridge, snacks, a Roberts radio. Bathrooms are 'super stylish with powerful shower', perhaps a tin or copper bath. 'Nice touches included antique travelling chests for side tables.' For a 'spectacular outlook' choose a dual-aspect loft suite. 'There's a comfortable small sitting area off reception with an interesting mix of modern and period art, a log-burner for chilly days'; more city vistas from the terrace. The 'friendly and helpful' staff clock off at 8 pm. At that point, head for the restaurants on nearby Whiteladies Road, such as Mitch Tonks's The Spiny Lobster. Breakfast brings an excellent buffet and cooked items at a small extra cost. 'A very special place to stay.' (John and Kay Patterson, JS)

38 Upper Belgrave Road
Clifton
Bristol BS8 2XN

T: 0117 946 6905
E: info@number38clifton.com
W: number38clifton.com

BEDROOMS: 12.
OPEN: all year.
FACILITIES: lounge, breakfast room, meeting space, in-room TV (Freeview), terrace, limited number of parking permits on request, unsuitable for disabled.
BACKGROUND MUSIC: in public areas 8 am–8 pm.
LOCATION: 2½ miles from city centre.
CHILDREN: not under 12, no extra beds or cots.
DOGS: not allowed.
CREDIT CARDS: Amex, MC, Visa.
PRICES: B&B doubles from £140, single occupancy from £125. Cooked or continental breakfast (£5 surcharge to have both).

BRISTOL

MAP 1:B6

OLD CHURCH FARM

A late 16th-century manor house and former
Rolls-Royce hospitality venue is now a private
hotel owned by Christopher Trim and Kathryn
Warner, who, in the spirit of Henry Royce, strive
for excellence. 'They obviously love the place
and seem determined to give it their best shot,'
our inspectors say. A double room overlooking
the remains of medieval St Helen's church in the
grounds had antiques, a 'feature fireplace set with
logs', a smallish bathroom. A master bedroom had
'dual-aspect windows, steps down to an opulent
bathroom'. All rooms are supplied with home-
made biscuits, and there is an espresso machine
on the landing. 'Several reception rooms have a
remarkable plasterwork ceiling. Furnishings are
country house, with Dutch cowscapes, hunting
scenes, botanical drawings and John Piper prints.'
Meals are taken communally ('prepare to be
sociable'). Give 24 hours' notice if you want to
dine (72 hours if you have special requirements),
Cordon Bleu-trained Kathryn devises a three-
course, three-choice nightly menu, with home-
grown and local ingredients. A 'well-prepared
breakfast' is cooked to order.

Church Road
Rudgeway
Bristol BS35 3SQ

T: 01454 418212
E: stay@old-church-farm.co.uk
W: old-church-farm.co.uk

BEDROOMS: 7.
OPEN: all year (whole house booking
only at Christmas), kitchen closed
Sun.
FACILITIES: snug, drawing room,
breakfast room, dining room, in-room
TV, conference facilities, civil wedding
licence, 8-acre gardens, public rooms
wheelchair accessible, adapted toilet in
conference centre, parking.
BACKGROUND MUSIC: in drawing room,
dining room.
LOCATION: 12 miles N of Bristol, on
the edge of a south Gloucestershire
village.
CHILDREN: not under 12.
DOGS: not allowed.
CREDIT CARDS: Amex, MC, Visa.
PRICES: B&B doubles from £160, singles
from £145. Set-price dinner £27.50–
£32.50 (2/3 courses). 1-night bookings
refused weekends May–Sept.

BROADWAY Worcestershire

MAP 3:D6

THE BROADWAY HOTEL

With its medieval frontage, creaky-floor interiors and smart conservatory brasserie, The Broadway, named after its picturesque Cotswold location, is popular with both visitors and locals. Overlooking the village green, the half-timbering, honey stonework and latticed windows exude olde-worlde charm. Interiors don't disappoint either: oak panelling, beamed ceilings and a minstrels' gallery around the bar. It's been sympathetically jazzed up with 'bold and imaginative' decor – leather stools, bright-patterned armchairs, striking wallpapers – and throughout there's a horse-racing theme (jockeys' colours, historic photographs) in homage to nearby Cheltenham. The modern glazed-roof restaurant offers an all-day menu of brasserie classics such as bouillabaisse, chargrilled pork with potato and onion gratin, and roast onion and Brie quiche. Bedrooms mix low-beamed ceilings and quirky shapes with bright colours and dashing feature fabrics and wallpapers, often equestrian themed. Breakfasts include fresh juices, home-made preserves, smoked haddock and a full grill that will set you up for a day's exploring.

The Green
Broadway WR12 7AA

T: 01386 852401
E: reception@broadway-hotel.co.uk
W: broadway-hotel.co.uk

BEDROOMS: 19. 1 on ground floor.
3 self-catering cottages nearby.
OPEN: all year.
FACILITIES: sitting room, bar, brasserie, in-room TV (Freeview), courtyard, garden and terrace (residents only), parking, EV charging, unsuitable for disabled.
BACKGROUND MUSIC: ambient in public areas.
LOCATION: village centre, 'best to request a parking space before you arrive, especially in summer'.
CHILDREN: all ages welcomed, children's menu, up to 12 in extra bed £20.
DOGS: well-behaved dogs allowed in some bedrooms (ring for charges) and in public areas, not in restaurant.
CREDIT CARDS: Amex, MC, Visa.
PRICES: B&B doubles from £140, singles from £130. À la carte £39.

SEE ALSO SHORTLIST

BROADWAY Worcestershire

MAP 3:D6

THE LYGON ARMS

A 17th-century former coaching inn that counts Charles I and Oliver Cromwell, sundry Windsors and Hollywood royalty among past guests can fairly claim to be historic. Now with a spa and 13-metre indoor pool, and in the care of Iconic Luxury Hotels, it blends original features – inglenooks, panelled walls and beams – and period and contemporary furniture to impressive effect. There is a wide choice of bedrooms, from the Charles I suite in the main house, with a carved four-poster, to contemporary annexe rooms, open-plan courtyard suites with a landscaped terraced garden, and cottage rooms with furniture by Gordon Russell. All have a modern bathroom and a coffee machine. A reader vouches for an accessible courtyard room with 'a roll-in shower, luxurious decor'. In the showstopper Lygon Bar & Grill with barrel-vaulted ceiling and minstrels' gallery, menus of Cotswolds produce include dishes such as glazed Old Spot pork belly, black pudding, carrots and apples – among vegetarian options a beet burger or spiced lentil and spinach casserole. 'Not a cheap hotel, but it has a lovely "feel" and the staff are very pleasant and helpful.'

High Street
Broadway WR12 7DU

T: 01386 852255
E: reservations@lygonarmshotel.co.uk
W: lygonarmshotel.co.uk

BEDROOMS: 86. 26 on ground floor, some in cottages, some courtyard suites, 2 suitable for disabled.
OPEN: all year.
FACILITIES: 7 lounge areas, bar/grill (vegetarian menu), cocktail bar, in-room TV (Freeview), civil wedding licence, 3-acre garden, indoor pool, spa, EV charging, public areas (not spa) wheelchair accessible, adapted toilet.
BACKGROUND MUSIC: in lounges.
LOCATION: village centre.
CHILDREN: all ages welcomed, extra bed for 5–16s £25, over-16s £65.
DOGS: in some bedrooms (£25 a night), all lounges.
CREDIT CARDS: Amex, MC, Visa.
PRICES: B&B doubles from £255, singles from £220. À la carte £40. 1-night bookings sometimes refused Sat, bank holidays.

SEE ALSO SHORTLIST

BROADWAY Worcestershire

MAP 3:D6

RUSSELL'S

In plum position on this quintessential Cotswold town's high street, Russell's restaurant-with-rooms offers imaginative food and modern bedrooms among comforting original features. Rubbing shoulders with antique shops and art galleries, the mellow-stone building, with its people-watching terrace, has been skilfully updated from when it was the showroom of wartime utility-furniture pioneer Sir Gordon Russell. Both bar and restaurant are cool and airy with sea-blue banquettes and mid-century tables set against beams and exposed-stone walls. Bedrooms are similarly light and spacious – even the smallest have window seats and armchairs – with pale walls and carpets, contemporary furnishings and splashes of colour in suede headboards and velvet armchairs. All have natural-stone bathrooms, bathrobes and courtyard or high street views. Two huge under-eaves rooms have views of the Cotswold hills. Food is the big story here with a menu serving up imaginative dishes such as saddle of rabbit with poached quince, and stone bass with potato and spinach curry. Breakfast includes locally smoked salmon, plus a full grill.

20 High Street
Broadway WR12 7DT

T: 01386 853555
E: info@russellsofbroadway.co.uk
W: russellsofbroadway.co.uk

BEDROOMS: 7. 3 in adjoining building, 2 on ground floor.
OPEN: all year, restaurant closed Mon/ Tues evenings.
FACILITIES: bar, restaurant, private dining room, in-room TV (Freeview), patio (heating, meal service), parking, restaurant and bar wheelchair accessible, adapted toilet.
BACKGROUND MUSIC: in restaurant.
LOCATION: village centre.
CHILDREN: all ages welcomed, under-2s free, extra bed £15.
DOGS: allowed in 1 ground-floor bedroom (no charge), some areas of restaurant.
CREDIT CARDS: MC, Visa.
PRICES: B&B doubles from £140, singles from £130. À la carte £50. 1-night bookings refused weekends.

SEE ALSO SHORTLIST

BROCKENHURST Hampshire

MAP 2:E2

DAISYBANK COTTAGE

Beyond the garden gates and gravel drive, this single-storey Charles Rennie Mackintosh-inspired cottage in the heart of the New Forest is such a period gem, who would guess that it housed a spacious boutique B&B? This was Ciaran and Cheryl Maher's family home for 15 years before they opened it to guests nine years ago, and they are generous hosts, welcoming new arrivals with cupcakes. 'We don't think you could be disappointed with a stay here,' readers advise. 'From numerous DVDs, wellies and brollies, to the dressing gowns and slippers, your creature comforts are well catered for.' The bedrooms, in shades of chocolate and cream or grey, are supplied with an espresso machine, mini-fridge, handmade chocolates and 'lovely local toiletries'. Every room has its own appeal – a private terrace, a sleigh bed and French doors to a patio. Two are in the redesigned gardener's cottage. A suite overlooking the front garden has Arts and Crafts features, a volcanic-limestone bath and walk-in shower. At night pop your breakfast order in a flowerpot, and wake up to home-made granola, local free-range eggs or smoked salmon, American pancakes.

Sway Road
Brockenhurst
New Forest SO42 7SG

T: 01590 622086
E: info@bedandbreakfast-newforest.
   co.uk
W: bedandbreakfast-newforest.co.uk

BEDROOMS: 8. 2 in Gardener's Cottage, all on ground floor, plus 1-bed shepherd's hut available Apr–Sept, some suitable for disabled but not fully adapted.
OPEN: all year, except 1 week over Christmas.
FACILITIES: 2 sitting rooms, breakfast room, in-room TV (Freeview), 5-acre grounds, front and back garden, parking, EV charging.
BACKGROUND MUSIC: none.
LOCATION: ¾ mile S of Brockenhurst village.
CHILDREN: over-7s welcomed, extra bed £35.
DOGS: not allowed.
CREDIT CARDS: MC, Visa.
PRICES: B&B doubles from £110, singles from £95. 2-night min. stay preferred weekends.

BROCKENHURST Hampshire

MAP 2:E2

THE PIG IN THE FOREST

Known simply as 'The Pig' until it farrowed, the first of Robin Hutson's growing family of Pig hotels (see index) occupies a hunting lodge in the New Forest. Here the breed's signature shabby-chic style was established by Judy Hutson, who designed the interiors for an imaginary Great-Aunt Maud – a spacious sort, one feels, fond of her comfort and cocktails. It is 'one of the best and most reliable hotels that we've stayed at', say readers. 'Ask the staff for something and it will always arrive.' Everywhere there are lovely details, from vintage decanters to herbs growing in pots. The cheapest 'snug' bedrooms have a monsoon shower. There are hideaway suites in the stable yard, a forest cabin with four-poster and freestanding roll-top bath and monsoon shower room. You can have a drink in a cosy panelled bar, dine alfresco on wood-fired flatbreads from a double-decker bus. The restaurant menus feature produce from the kitchen garden, foraged in the forest or sourced within 25 miles. Maybe ramsons, garlic and potato soup and Beaulieu estate venison faggots. 'All the meals were absolutely delicious and almost impossible to fault.' (Anna Brewer)

Beaulieu Road
Brockenhurst SO42 7QL

T: 01590 622354
E: info@thepighotel.com
W: thepighotel.com

BEDROOMS: 32. 10 in stable block (100 yds), some on ground floor, 2 lodges and a cabin in the garden, 1 courtyard room suitable for disabled.
OPEN: all year.
FACILITIES: lounge, library, bar, restaurant, in-room TV (Freeview), civil wedding licence, treatment rooms, kitchen garden, 6-acre grounds, public rooms wheelchair accessible, adapted toilet.
BACKGROUND MUSIC: in public areas.
LOCATION: 1 mile E of Brockenhurst village.
CHILDREN: all ages welcomed, no charge for extra beds.
DOGS: guide dogs only.
CREDIT CARDS: Amex, MC, Visa.
PRICES: room-only doubles from £185. Breakfast £12–£16, à la carte £35. 1-night bookings refused at weekends, Christmas, New Year.

BRUTON Somerset

THE NEWT IN SOMERSET

This 800-acre country estate, centred on a Palladian manor house, is a sophisticated yet fun adventure land offering chic rooms, breathtaking gardens, spa, apple orchard and plenty more. Golden Hadspen House is the core, and former home of the Hobhouse family (revered gardener Penelope Hobhouse helped create today's gardens). Interiors mix grand architecture and antiques with designer furniture and witty touches; Karen Roos, who co-owns with billionaire husband Koos Bekker, is former editor of Elle Decoration South Africa. Expect eau-de-nil panelled walls and faux-classical portraits, open fires and polished side tables. Main-house bedrooms have a spare elegance with soft colours and marbled bathrooms while Stable Yard rooms are playful rustic-chic with exposed stone, wood-burning stoves and perhaps a mezzanine bedroom. New this year is the Farmyard, the Newt's more rustic little sister, in a former dairy farm, with its own pool. There's an all-day kitchen, or you can bike over to the Newt to eat plant-based fare in the Garden Café or menus composed according to whatever is fresh that day in the wood-panelled restaurant.

Bruton
Castle Cary BA7 7NG

T: 01963 577777
E: reservations@thenewtinsomerset.com
W: thenewtinsomerset.com

BEDROOMS: 40. 10 in converted outbuildings, 17 in Farmyard, 3 suitable for disabled.
OPEN: all year.
FACILITIES: restaurant, bar, lounge, drawing room, library, lift (main house), bar, snug, kitchen, vitality pool (Farmyard buildings), in-room TV (Sky), spa (hydrotherapy pools, swimming pool), 800-acre estate (parkland, woods, orchards, café, cyder bar, farm shop, museum), EV charging, restaurant and bar wheelchair accessible, adapted toilet.
BACKGROUND MUSIC: in public rooms.
LOCATION: on the A359 between Castle Cary and Bruton.
CHILDREN: all ages welcomed, family rooms.
DOGS: not allowed.
CREDIT CARDS: Amex, MC, Visa.
PRICES: B&B doubles from £375. À la carte £55.

BRUTON Somerset

NUMBER ONE BRUTON   NEW

'It's like staying with friends who have seriously good taste,' writes a Guide insider after a visit to Aled and Claudia Rees's welcoming hotel, occupying a Georgian town house and former ironmonger's, a forge and cottages. The 'stylishly chic' interiors are the 'perfect blend of past and present, mixing original fireplaces and wooden floors with modern artwork and artefacts'. A Venetian mosaic mirror by Claudia's godmother, the artist Candace Bahouth, graces reception, an 'enormous pink and green bedroom' is home to a pearl-inlaid chest from Syria, a claw-footed bath and candy-striped shower. Dog-friendly cottages, by the Penelope Hobhouse-designed courtyard, are more rustic, 'with exposed beams and quarry-tiled floors'. All have a welcome plate of cheese, cider and apple juice. Culinary wizard Merlin Labron-Johnson's farm-to-table menus have won a Michelin star for Osip restaurant. A meal here is 'full of surprises, from a light bite of nasturtium leaves with crispy pig's head to a duck main dish with beetroot taco'. One niggle though: the only cooked option at breakfast is boiled eggs. 'After that dinner, I expected more.' (JK)

1 High Street
Bruton BA10 0AB

T: 01749 813030
E: stay@numberonebruton.com
W: numberonebruton.com

BEDROOMS: 12. 4 in forge, 3 in cottages.
OPEN: all year, restaurant closed Mon–Wed.
FACILITIES: sitting room (honesty bar), restaurant, in-room TV, ¼-acre courtyard garden, free parking in nearby car park, EV charging.
BACKGROUND MUSIC: none.
LOCATION: at one end of the High Street.
CHILDREN: all ages welcomed, extra bed/cot £25.
DOGS: allowed in cottage and forge (£20 a night), not in restaurant.
CREDIT CARDS: MC, Visa.
PRICES: B&B doubles from £130. Set dinner menu £75. 2-night min. stay preferred at weekends.

BRYHER Isles of Scilly

MAP 1: inset C1

HELL BAY HOTEL

♿ Previous César winner

You have to island-hop to reach this New England-style hotel on the rugged Atlantic west side of the smallest of the inhabited Isles of Scilly, but once there, the sense of escape is blissful. 'A lovely hotel,' writes a reader, commending 'excellent food, great rooms, friendly, efficient staff'. It began life as a farmhouse and occupies clapboard buildings, painted white and powder blue. Interiors have a palette of blues and shell pinks, with Lloyd Loom furniture, seascapes by Cornish artists. Some have a private patio, others a balcony from which to watch the sunset. You can eat casually in the bar (maybe bouillabaisse, fish and chips or chargrilled steak), with messy glee on freshly landed shellfish in the rustic Crab Shack, or in style in the restaurant, where Richard Kearsley's short menus might bring a choice of smoked tomato risotto; treacle-cured salmon, lemongrass and ginger purée; sugar-and-citrus-smoked duck. 'We appreciated the little touches like a kitchenette in our room, the opportunity to have a "pub dinner", and a lift to the boat in the rain.' (Yvette Peart)

Bryher TR23 0PR

T: 01720 422947
E: contactus@hellbay.co.uk
W: hellbay.co.uk

BEDROOMS: 25 suites. In 5 buildings, some on ground floor.
OPEN: 11 Mar–22 Oct 2022.
FACILITIES: lounge, games room, bar, 2 dining rooms, in-room TV, gym, treatment shed, yoga studio, grounds (heated pool, playground), public rooms wheelchair accessible, adapted toilet.
BACKGROUND MUSIC: in the bar.
LOCATION: W side of island, boat from St Mary's (reached by boat/plane from mainland).
CHILDREN: all ages welcomed, under-2s free cots, under-17s £40 a night B&B, £60 incl. children's supper.
DOGS: allowed in some suites (max. 2, £15 a night), in bar, not in restaurant.
CREDIT CARDS: Amex, MC, Visa.
PRICES: B&B doubles from £190, singles from £125. Set dinner £52. Min. 2-night stay weekends.

BUCKLAND MARSH Oxfordshire

MAP 2:C2

THE TROUT AT TADPOLE BRIDGE

You can arrive by narrow boat and tie up by this Georgian pub on a peaceful stretch of the Thames with views of the stone bridge, or simply watch others messing about in boats as you sip a beer in the riverside garden. Inside, a flagstoned, beamed bar is bookended by wood-burning stoves, with a leather sofa by the fire at one end, mismatched tables and chairs in a small dining/drinking area at the other. A main dining area is hung with witty artwork. Three of the bedrooms are upstairs, three in a covered garden courtyard, all with vintage and contemporary furniture, a rain shower or claw-footed tub. Guide inspectors had a courtyard room 'decorated in muted greys, with an enormous bed, plenty of storage, an espresso machine, shortbread', fresh milk on request. At dinner, they were 'warmly greeted' by the barman and server, and enjoyed a 'perfectly cooked fillet of hake with pickled fennel and the lightest of mashed potatoes'. Pub classics come in large portions. There are kippers and smoked salmon for your breakfast, a sausage for your dog, before you set off to walk along the river bank. (D and JB)

Buckland Road
Buckland Marsh SN7 8RF

T: 01367 870382
E: info@troutinn.co.uk
W: troutinn.co.uk

BEDROOMS: 6. 3 in courtyard garden.
OPEN: all year.
FACILITIES: bar, dining area, breakfast area, private dining room, in-room TV (Freeview), civil wedding licence, 2-acre garden (pagoda, river, moorings), public areas wheelchair accessible, adapted toilet.
BACKGROUND MUSIC: in all public areas.
LOCATION: off the A420, 15 miles SW of Oxford.
CHILDREN: all ages welcomed, extra bed £15, children's menu.
DOGS: allowed in 4 bedrooms (£15 a night) and public areas.
CREDIT CARDS: MC, Visa.
PRICES: B&B doubles £120–£300. À la carte £33. 1-night bookings refused Sat.

BUDE Cornwall   MAP 1:C3

THE BEACH

Above sandy Summerleaze beach, Susie and Will Daniel's young-at-heart hotel is a great hang-out for surfers, sybarites and sun-seekers (Bude is officially one of the sunniest places in Britain). You can order cocktails to drink on the terrace and drink in the coastal view, too, while grazing on a charcuterie platter or cheeseboard. Within a 19th-century building, the bedrooms are in cool New England style, with limed oak furniture, Lloyd Loom chairs, pale paint finishes, a smart modern bathroom. Some of the rooms share the outlook over sand and sea, with glass doors to a Juliet balcony or a private terrace. Two self-catering suites are designed for a family; dogs are welcome, as well as six humans. The bar is often buzzing, and readers praise the friendly, helpful staff. The Beach no longer has a restaurant, but Bude offers a wide range of dining options, from tapas to tandoori, pub grub to pizzas. The former small port and village became a favoured resort for Victorians, when Summerleaze was a men-only beach. Today anyone is free to disport themselves in the waves or splash in the sea-bathing pool.

Summerleaze Crescent
Bude EX23 8HJ

T: 01288 389800
E: enquiries@thebeachatbude.co.uk
W: thebeachatbude.co.uk

BEDROOMS: 18. 1 on ground floor, 2 family suites.
OPEN: all year except a few days over Christmas.
FACILITIES: lift, bar, lounge area, in-room TV (Freeview), terraces, ground floor wheelchair accessible, adapted toilet.
BACKGROUND MUSIC: all day in public areas.
LOCATION: above Summerleaze beach.
CHILDREN: all ages welcomed, extra bed £30–£50.
DOGS: allowed in 2 dog-friendly suites only (£30 a night), not in public areas except the terrace.
CREDIT CARDS: Amex, MC, Visa.
PRICES: B&B doubles from £125, singles from £105, suites for 4 from £175.

BURFORD Oxfordshire

MAP 3:D6

THE LAMB INN

Occupying 15th-century weavers' cottages subsumed by an 18th-century inn on the aptly named Sheep Street, this is the kind of traditional, inclusive, tea-by-the-fire sort of place that sits so well in a historic market town. It is now owned by Fuller's, who have done nothing to compromise the character of a bar 'clearly popular with locals' with its stone floor and settles, or a beamed lounge with soot-blackened inglenook (both dog-friendly). The bedrooms, by contrast, have contemporary styling, an espresso machine, home-made flapjacks, posh toiletries and, on the pillow, a little jar of Cotswold lavender. They differ mainly in size (let them know if you prefer a bath or shower, double or twin beds), but Shepherd room has an antique four-poster and feature fireplace. In Allium suite you can watch the plasma-screen TV while steeping in a roll-top bath. For a family, it can form a duplex with Rosie, with private garden. In the restaurant or the garden, the menu includes dishes such as lobster risotto, charred sweetcorn, sorrel oil. The 'pigeon starter and the lamb were good', although the wine list is 'not very special'.

Sheep Street
Burford OX18 4LR

T: 01993 823155
E: info@lambinn-burford.co.uk
W: cotswold-inns-hotels.co.uk

BEDROOMS: 17. 1 with private garden, 1 on ground floor.
OPEN: all year.
FACILITIES: 3 lounges, bar, restaurant, in-room TV (Freeview), courtyard, ½-acre walled garden.
BACKGROUND MUSIC: subtle in all public areas.
LOCATION: 500 yds from High Street.
CHILDREN: all ages welcomed, extra bed £20.
DOGS: allowed by prior arrangement in some bedrooms (£20 per night for one, £10 for each additional dog), bar, lounges, garden, not in restaurant.
CREDIT CARDS: Amex, MC, Visa.
PRICES: B&B doubles from £150, singles from £140. À la carte £40.

SEE ALSO SHORTLIST

BURTON BRADSTOCK Dorset   MAP 1:D6

THE SEASIDE BOARDING HOUSE

There's more than an air of Cape Cod about this white clapboard hotel above Chesil Beach, which could have come straight out of an Edward Hopper painting. Mary-Lou Sturridge and Tony Mackintosh left London's Groucho Club to create this cool Jurassic Coast bolt-hole, with sea-facing bar and restaurant opening on to a terrace. Regulars tell us it's 'as good as ever, always a joy to visit'. The stripped-back interiors are enlivened with marine salvage, nautical paintings and antique-shop finds. The dashing young officer whose portrait hangs above the fire in the library is Mary-Lou's grandfather; the furniture is from her mum's house. Bedrooms, all in sight and sound of the sea, have a Roberts radio, books, a great bathroom with claw-footed bath and walk-in shower, but no TVs to detract from the views. If you fancy champagne or a cappuccino just pick up the retro dial phone. At lunch and dinner, short menus are devised by Alastair Little with new head chef Seldon Curry to appeal to all tastes. Maybe venison with beetroot ketchup; lemon sole, clams and chard; beetroot and onion tart. And how about cocktails or a cream tea outside?

Cliff Road
Burton Bradstock DT6 4RB

T: 01308 897205
E: info@theseasideboardinghouse.com
W: theseasideboardinghouse.com

BEDROOMS: 9.
OPEN: all year.
FACILITIES: cocktail bar, restaurant, library, function facilities, in-room TV on request, civil wedding licence, terrace, lawn, parking, restaurant and bar wheelchair accessible, adapted toilet.
BACKGROUND MUSIC: classical music in bar.
LOCATION: ½ mile from village centre, 3½ miles SE of Bridport.
CHILDREN: all ages welcomed, extra bed £30.
DOGS: allowed in some bedrooms (no charge unless an extra cleaning fee is warranted), bar, library, on terrace, not in restaurant.
CREDIT CARDS: Amex, MC, Visa.
PRICES: B&B doubles from £220, singles from £200. À la carte £40. 1-night bookings refused Sat.

BUXTON Derbyshire   MAP 4:E3

THE ROSELEIGH

Overlooking the Joseph Paxton-designed Pavilion Gardens in the heart of Buxton, this family-run guest house with its comfortably traditional rooms is much loved by Guide regulars, who 'strongly endorse the excellent B&B'. Maggi and Gerard Heelan's Victorian home is both richly and colourfully furnished. Public rooms have polished-wood tables, chesterfield sofas, pelmeted curtains, and Victorian prints and curios. Bedrooms are similarly traditional, with patterned carpets and curtains, wing armchairs and fuss-free bathrooms. The best ones are at the front, with views over the tree-fringed lake; there is one single room with a separate private bathroom. Breakfast is a pleasant affair – go down early to bag a window table – with home-made banana loaf and 'summer pudding' (layers of fruit and yogurt) plus cooked-to-order choices including scrambled egg and smoked salmon, a full grill, and a vegetarian option. The owners, who were both tour guides, have excellent local knowledge on everything from Buxton's Opera House, a short stroll away, to longer Peak District walks. (S and PG)

19 Broad Walk
Buxton SK17 6JR

T: 01298 24904
E: enquiries@roseleighhotel.co.uk
W: roseleighhotel.co.uk

BEDROOMS: 13. 1 on ground floor, 1 single with private bathroom (not en suite).
OPEN: 15 Jan–12 Dec.
FACILITIES: lounge (computer for guests' use), breakfast room, in-room TV (Freeview), unsuitable for disabled, parking.
BACKGROUND MUSIC: classical/baroque in breakfast room.
LOCATION: central.
CHILDREN: not under 6, no additional beds.
DOGS: not allowed.
CREDIT CARDS: MC, Visa.
PRICES: B&B doubles from £94, singles from £59. 1-night bookings usually refused weekends, bank holidays (call to check).

CAMBER Sussex   MAP 2:E5

THE GALLIVANT

Amid coastal gardens, across the road from the
important wildlife habitat of Camber dunes,
Harry Cragoe's adults-only hotel has the feel of a
Californian motel, albeit an incredibly chic one.
Now, the night rate is on a half-board basis only,
and includes elevenses, English wine at 5 pm,
and an 'experience', from yoga to kitchen skills.
Bedrooms are all on the ground floor and most
have a breezy seaside palette, with French doors
to private decking. The largest are more dramatic,
with a freestanding bathtub behind sliding doors,
a monsoon shower, and French doors to the
garden, with teak garden furniture. 'You could
watch the telly from the bath, two comfortable
chairs or the bed,' happy readers were moved
to write mid-stay. Chef Jamie Guy's seasonal
menus are sourced as locally as possible and might
include wood-roasted monkfish tail with seashore
vegetables, or wood-grilled lamb loin chops. 'We
think the food is superb – a great dinner last
night, now off to breakfast,' which might mean
smoky beans, crumpets with smoked-trout butter,
a sausage bun with tomato marmalade. Beyond
the dunes an unspoilt beach awaits. (RB)

New Lydd Road
Camber TN31 7RB

T: 01797 225057
E: enquiries@thegallivant.co.uk
W: thegallivant.co.uk

BEDROOMS: 20. All on ground floor,
12 with direct access to garden.
OPEN: all year.
FACILITIES: bar, sitting room, reading
room, restaurant, private dining room,
in-room TV (Freeview), civil wedding
licence, function facilities, spa
treatment room, terrace, car park, EV
charging, 1-acre garden, restaurant
and bar wheelchair accessible.
BACKGROUND MUSIC: in bar and
restaurant.
LOCATION: 3¾ miles SE of Rye.
CHILDREN: not under 16.
DOGS: allowed in some bedrooms
(£25–£35 per stay), sitting room, bar,
terrace.
CREDIT CARDS: MC, Visa.
PRICES: D,B&B doubles from £313. Set-
price dinner £45. 1-night stays refused
weekends.

CAMBRIDGE Cambridgeshire

MAP 2:B4

DUKE HOUSE

You can stroll from this elegant B&B on the edge of Christ's Pieces park to Cambridge's historic colleges, just as the current Duke of Gloucester did when this Victorian house was his home. Liz and Rob Cameron have notched up ten years as owners, and Liz is an accommodating hostess, assisted by manager Tina Shannon. The guest bedrooms, each named after a dukedom, are chic and individually styled. York is small but has a lovely big bathroom. Second-floor Cambridge has a sitting room, a private balcony, space for a third guest, and a large bathroom with original wooden shutters, brass fittings and a proper stand-up shower over the bath. All rooms are supplied with fine-quality natural toiletries. Complimentary tea, coffee and sweet treats are provided in the beautiful sitting room, with its embroidered linens and subtle, powdery paint finishes. Breakfast, served on fine china, includes locally pressed apple juice, fruit compote, organic yogurt, butter, bread and granola, free-range eggs, smoked salmon, award-winning sausages. For dinner, our readers highly recommend the nearby Clarendon Arms.

1 Victoria Street
Cambridge CB1 1JP

T: 01223 314773
E: info@dukehousecambridge.co.uk
W: dukehousecambridge.co.uk

BEDROOMS: 5. 1 in adjacent cottage, plus self-catering apartment.
OPEN: all year except over Christmas period.
FACILITIES: sitting room, breakfast room with courtyard, balcony, in-room TV (Freeview), limited parking (by arrangement), unsuitable for disabled.
BACKGROUND MUSIC: during breakfast.
LOCATION: city centre.
CHILDREN: babies and over-10s welcomed.
DOGS: not allowed.
CREDIT CARDS: MC, Visa.
PRICES: B&B doubles from £140, singles from £125. 1-night bookings refused weekends.

SEE ALSO SHORTLIST

CAMBRIDGE Cambridgeshire

MAP 2:B4

UNIVERSITY ARMS

Designer Martin Brudnizki had such palpable
fun in creating interiors for this large 'but still
intimate' hotel, transformed by architect John
Simpson with a portico modelled on that of the
Ritz in Paris. 'It references the university at every
turn', from the liberal use of pale blue to a library
of books by Cambridge notables, and suites named
after famous alumni such as Stephen Hawking.
'Marlowe room had an impressive turret
bathroom, with a bath overlooking Parker's Piece
green, a separate shower, Victorian-style tiles over
under-floor heating.' Cosy rooms are just that ('get
one on the top floor for the best light'), but all are
decorated in playful colours and patterns, with a
copy of Wind in the Willows by the bedside (you'll
hear a recording of it in the main loos). The look
is Edwardian, but 'everywhere the old mixes with
the new'. The fun continues in Parker's Tavern,
reminiscent of a college dining hall, where
Tristan Welch's menus give a witty spin to British
classics – maybe fishcakes, then roast turkey,
butternut squash and black garlic Wellington.
You can borrow a bike, take a panier picnic or a
punting hamper.

Regent Street
Cambridge CB2 1AD

T: 01223 606066
E: enquiries@universityarms.com
W: universityarms.com

BEDROOMS: 192. 10 suitable for
disabled.
OPEN: all year.
FACILITIES: library, bar/bistro,
ballroom, meeting rooms, fitness
centre, in-room TV, civil wedding
licence, bicycles, limited guest
parking, EV charging, public areas
wheelchair accessible, adapted toilet.
BACKGROUND MUSIC: in bar and
restaurant.
LOCATION: city centre.
CHILDREN: all ages welcomed, cots
free, extra bed £50, children's menu,
interconnecting rooms.
DOGS: only assistance dogs allowed.
CREDIT CARDS: Amex, MC, Visa.
PRICES: B&B doubles from £244
(member's rate £208). À la carte £43.

SEE ALSO SHORTLIST

CAMELFORD Cornwall   MAP 1:C3

PENDRAGON COUNTRY HOUSE

The legend of Arthur Pendragon is kept alive at Sharon and Nigel Reed's B&B, which has once again worked its magic on readers delighted by this 'wonderful find' with a 'great location, beautiful decor, wonderful hosts'. Beyond a hallway with a suit of armour, the interiors are filled with paintings and antiques, while bedrooms are named after Arthur's knights. 'Bedivere had a very comfortable four-poster' and dual-aspect Lamorak has views of both Bodmin Moor and Dartmoor. 'Extra touches made it stand out, such as an evening tipple and a home-made treat each day.' Guests gather for drinks before an 'absolutely exquisite' three-course dinner made from locally sourced products, which might include dishes such as rolled blade of beef slow-roasted in red wine. 'Nigel is in charge of starters and main course, Sharon of desserts. It was so good we promptly booked to stay another night.' 'I especially enjoyed the blackcurrant soufflé.' Breakfast brings Cornish kipper, free-range eggs, home-made preserves. 'Outstanding attention to detail, outstanding value for money.' (Sue Burman, Jane Alexander, and many others)

Old Vicarage Hill
Davidstow
Camelford PL32 9XR

T: 01840 261131
E: enquiries@
   pendragoncountryhouse.com
W: pendragoncountryhouse.com

BEDROOMS: 7. 1, on ground floor, suitable for disabled.
OPEN: all year except Christmas, restaurant closed Sun eve.
FACILITIES: sitting room, lounge with honesty bar, dining room, games room (pool table), in-room TV (Freeview), 1¾-acre grounds, EV charging.
BACKGROUND MUSIC: none.
LOCATION: 3½ miles NE of Camelford.
CHILDREN: all ages welcomed, under-2s £15 one-off charge, extra bed 3–15s £25.
DOGS: allowed in ground-floor bedroom (£5 charge), lounge but not restaurant, except guide dogs.
CREDIT CARDS: Amex, MC, Visa.
PRICES: B&B doubles from £80, singles from £68. Set menu £35 (£30 for half board). 2-night min. stay (but check for odd 1-night availability)

CANNINGTON Somerset

BLACKMORE FARM

Medieval weaponry and armour adorn the walls at this 15th-century red sandstone manor house B&B on the Dyers' dairy farm on the edge of the Quantock hills Area of Outstanding Natural Beauty. 'Wonderful hosts Ian and Ann made us very welcome,' writes a reader this year, who was given a bedroom worthy of Henry VIII, with 'a beautiful oak four-poster and stunning exposed beams'. The oak-panelled Gallery bedroom has stairs to a sitting/TV room and bathroom. The Solar has a double and a single bed. Suites in converted outbuildings are ideal for longer stays. The Cider Press, with a twin room and a double, has an open-plan lounge and kitchen/dining room, a Welsh dresser and working Aga. Suites in the Wagon House have a kettle, microwave and toaster, but you won't want to miss breakfast at the oak refectory table by a blazing fire, with free-range eggs from Blackmore hens, and award-winning local sausages. A farm shop has all the ingredients for a packed lunch, or you can put on the nosebag at the café, which now has stable huts for diners, with fairy lights, and heaters for the colder months. (CR, and others)

Blackmore Lane
Cannington TA5 2NE

T: 01278 653442
E: dyerfarm@aol.com
W: blackmorefarm.co.uk

BEDROOMS: 14. 10 in annexes, with 6 on ground floor, 1 in shepherd's hut in grounds, 1 suitable for disabled.
OPEN: all year.
FACILITIES: lounge/TV room, Great Hall/breakfast room, in-room TV (Freeview), 4-acre garden (stream, coarse fishing), children's play area, farm shop/café, lounge and dining room wheelchair accessible.
BACKGROUND MUSIC: none.
LOCATION: 3 miles W of Bridgwater.
CHILDREN: all ages welcomed, ages 2–12 £10 to share parents' room.
DOGS: allowed in some bedrooms, not in public rooms.
CREDIT CARDS: Amex, MC, Visa.
PRICES: B&B doubles from £120, singles from £75, shepherd's hut £75 per person. 1-night bookings refused bank holiday weekends.

CANTERBURY Kent

MAP 2:D5

THE PIG AT BRIDGE PLACE

Once a music venue that hosted Led Zeppelin, this Grade I listed Jacobean mansion in 'beautiful rolling countryside' has been made over with a whole lotta love as the sixth of Robin Hutson's rare-breed country house hotels (see index). Château-chic interiors are designed by Judy Hutson, with 'lashings of wood panelling' and a bar in deep burgundy, with ornate ceiling. Bedrooms, in the main house and annexes, range from very snug to a duplex suite in the old stable block, with views in four directions, a sitting room with log-burner, a bathroom with roll-top bath and monsoon shower. 'Our spacious room had moss-green panelling, a comfortable sofa, a wood floor and a bath in an alcove,' relates a Guide insider. Hop pickers' huts have 'a Little House on the Prairie feel'. In the greenhouse restaurant with its open kitchen, menus are big on produce from kitchen garden and glasshouse. Typical dishes might include foraged wild garlic risotto, Rye Bay brown crab, 'delicious aged sirloin from Ireland', one of the few products sourced from more than 25 miles away. The ethos is friendly: 'Everyone, even a gardener, greets you as you pass.'

Bourne Park Road
Bridge
Canterbury CT4 5BH

T: 0345 225 9494
E: info@thepighotel.com
W: thepighotel.com/at-bridge-place

BEDROOMS: 29. 7 in main house, 12 in coach house, 4 on ground floor, 2 suitable for disabled, 2 family-friendly lodges, converted barn, and 7 hop pickers' huts.
OPEN: all year.
FACILITIES: restaurant, bar/lounge, snugs, study, 2 treatment rooms, gardens, terrace, wheelchair access to the garden, gravel tracks round the property.
BACKGROUND MUSIC: in public areas.
LOCATION: on edge of village, 3 miles S of Canterbury.
CHILDREN: all ages welcomed, no charge for extra beds.
DOGS: not allowed.
CREDIT CARDS: Amex, MC, Visa.
PRICES: room-only doubles from £195, singles/small doubles from £109. Breakfast buffet £12, cooked £16, à la carte £42. 2-night bookings only at weekends.

CARTMEL Cumbria

AYNSOME MANOR

With views over farmland to pretty Cartmel village, and sheltered by wooded grounds, this 400-year-old manor house, run by the Varley family for 40 years, offers 'an oasis of peace and tranquillity'. These qualities, plus its reassuringly traditional comforts, keep readers returning. Lounges are comfortable with deep sofas, china ornaments and brass fenders around open fires. 'An ideal venue to relax over coffee and talk with other guests – no background music here!' 'Good-sized bedrooms' are simple country house in style with patterned wallpapers and modern oak furniture; second-floor rooms have beams and a sloping ceiling. 'Excellent' food is served in the panelled Georgian dining room. Expect classic dishes with a sophisticated touch such as Scottish mussels in garlic, cream and wine, or pan-fried duck with caramelised apple, and Calvados and thyme sauce. Diners appreciate the choice of two-to-five courses. Breakfast, too, can be simple or hearty: fruit compote and yogurt, locally smoked salmon or the full Cumbrian. Staff 'combine efficiency with first-class service in a friendly and unobtrusive manner'.

Aynsome Lane
Cartmel
Grange-over-Sands LA11 6HH

T: 01539 536653
E: aynsomemanor@btconnect.com
W: aynsomemanorhotel.co.uk

BEDROOMS: 12. 2 in cottage across courtyard.
OPEN: all year except 25–26 Dec, 2–28 Jan, lunch served Sun only.
FACILITIES: 2 lounges, bar, dining room, in-room TV (Freeview), ½-acre garden, unsuitable for disabled.
BACKGROUND MUSIC: none.
LOCATION: ¾ mile N of village.
CHILDREN: all ages welcomed, under-15s £25 additional bed, no under-5s in dining room in evening.
DOGS: in bedrooms only and must not be unattended (£7 per night).
CREDIT CARDS: Amex, MC, Visa.
PRICES: B&B doubles from £99 (bank holidays and race weekends £169). Set dinner £24–£39. 1-night bookings occasionally refused weekends.

CASTLE ASHBY Northamptonshire

MAP 2:B3

THE FALCON

NEW

'When you hear that this revamped 16th-century pub on the Castle Ashby Estate is owned by Lord and Lady Northampton, you expect it to be posh with a capital P,' writes a Guide insider – but happily no! 'Spenny and Tracy', as they style themselves, have created 'a rather lovely boutique hotel', devoted to relaxation and renewal, with a yoga studio ('You may find yourself in a downward dog next to Lady N'), juice bar and vegan-friendly menus, while retaining a separate Cellar bar. 'Designer Jackie Blakey has brought the outside indoors, with reminders of nature everywhere – wood, leather, stone, greens and russets.' A main-house bedroom had beams, a statement light, shades of moss and brown, a balcony, 'a slipper bath for a perfect wallow', toiletries developed by a clinical psychologist. Duplex cottage suites are steps away. Russell Bateman's menus are 'big on estate produce – the venison was delicious, as was the foraged mushroom mousse'. You can eat more simply alfresco, with your dog. And what to do with the day? Why, take a walking meditation in parkland, swim in the lake or visit the meerkats. Simples! (JK)

Castle Ashby
Northampton NN7 1LF

T: 01604 698005
E: reception@thefalcon-castleashby.com
W: thefalcon-castleashby.com

BEDROOMS: 22. 14 in adjacent cottages, 1 suitable for disabled.
OPEN: all year, restaurant closed Mon, Tues.
FACILITIES: reception, lounge, restaurant, cellar bar, yoga studio, juice bar, in-room TV, civil wedding licence, EV charging, private gardens within 10,500-acre Castle Ashby Estate.
BACKGROUND MUSIC: ambient, in all public spaces.
LOCATION: 9 miles E of Northampton.
CHILDREN: all ages welcomed, family suite, baby baths and cots.
DOGS: allowed in some bedrooms (£25 per night), on terraces, not in public rooms.
CREDIT CARDS: Amex, MC, Visa.
PRICES: B&B doubles from £190. Terrace menu (à la carte) £38, fixed-price dinner £60.

CHADDESLEY CORBETT Worcestershire   MAP 3:C5

BROCKENCOTE HALL

A woodland drive brings you to a lake, a 17th-century dovecote and the very image of a Loire château amid sheep-grazed pastures. A Victorian mansion, built for a carpet tycoon and remodelled in the 1940s for a member of the Butler brewing dynasty, it is part of the Eden Hotel Collection (see also Mallory Court, Leamington Spa). Bedroom style is country house contemporary. The cheapest rooms have a walk-in or over-bath shower; if you want both a bath and shower, trade up to a superior room. A welcome letter, bowl, bed, toy and chew await your dog in designated rooms; for you, there are luxury toiletries, home-made biscuits, fresh fruit and savouries. You can order light bites in the bar, ask for a picnic, or dine in the restaurant, where Tim Jenkins's short menus hit the spot with a trusted reader. 'Dinner was fantastic, from the lovely canapés amuse-bouche and pre-dessert to the actual meal.' Typical dishes: variations of pork with Madeira jus, brown-butter celeriac, garden apples, hispi cabbage; roast monkfish, mussels, curried cauliflower, samphire. 'The value was excellent and we look forward to returning.' (JC, SH)

Chaddesley Corbett DY10 4PY

T: 01562 777876
E: info@brockencotehall.com
W: brockencotehall.com

BEDROOMS: 21. Some on ground floor, 1 suitable for disabled.
OPEN: all year.
FACILITIES: lift, hall, lounge, conservatory, bar, library, restaurant, function facilities, in-room TV (Freeview), civil wedding licence, 72-acre grounds (fishing, croquet, tennis), public rooms wheelchair accessible, adapted toilet.
BACKGROUND MUSIC: all day in public areas.
LOCATION: 3 miles SE of Kidderminster.
CHILDREN: all ages welcomed, extra bed (for under-13s) £25.
DOGS: allowed in some bedrooms (£25 per night), garden and bar.
CREDIT CARDS: Amex, MC, Visa.
PRICES: B&B doubles from £120. Market menu £39–£50, seasonal menu £45–£60, tasting menu (whole table) £75.

CHETTLE Dorset

MAP 2:E1

CASTLEMAN

In an idyllic village owned by the Bourke family and run in a spirit of benevolent feudalism, this 18th-century former dower house is a one-off hotel and restaurant. Since they took over in 2020, Niki and Jez Barfoot have refreshed tired interiors. Among bedrooms, a lovely dual-aspect large double, painted a subtle, restful blue, has an antique cast iron bed, a sofa in a bay window. Guests can relax with a book and a drink by the fire in 19th-century drawing rooms, one with a Jacobean fireplace imported from a house in London. In a dining room with windows on three sides and glass doors to the garden, Richard Morris and Jez serve a seasonal menu with produce from local suppliers, kitchen garden and orchard, or foraged in the grounds and lovely countryside. For instance, salt-baked Chettle vegetables, crispy greens, confit garlic, miso cream; fish of the day, nori seaweed butter, garden potatoes, greens; roast Dorset pork chop, black pudding, quince, garden greens. A new sign outside hints at rebranding, but the Barfoots really 'get' the place, and none of its eccentric charm has been lost.

Chettle
Blandford Forum DT11 8DB

T: 01258 830096
E: enquiry@castlemanhotel.co.uk
W: castlemanhotel.co.uk

BEDROOMS: 8. 1 family room.
OPEN: all year, except 25/26 Dec, 31 Dec/1 Jan, lunch on Sun only.
FACILITIES: lounge, snug, bar, restaurant, in-room TV (Freeview), 2-acre grounds (stables for visiting horses), riding, fishing, shooting, cycling nearby, public rooms wheelchair accessible.
BACKGROUND MUSIC: low-level, often 'laid-back jazz'.
LOCATION: village, 1 mile off A354 Salisbury–Blandford.
CHILDREN: all ages welcomed, cots, extra bed £20.
DOGS: allowed in 3 bedrooms (£20 a night), not in public areas.
CREDIT CARDS: MC, Visa.
PRICES: B&B doubles from £120, singles from £100. À la carte £35, supper Mon–Wed from £20.

CHRISTCHURCH Dorset   MAP 2:E2

CAPTAIN'S CLUB HOTEL

Short of piping you aboard, they could scarcely be more welcoming at this luxurious, fun, dog-friendly hotel, with the sleek lines of a cruise ship, on the banks of the Stour. 'We had a super time. They couldn't have looked after us better,' wrote a trusted reader on a fourth visit. Accommodation ranges from cosy doubles to self-catering family suites. The style is smart contemporary, with river views through floor-to-ceiling windows. All have 24-hour room service and aromatherapy toiletries. 'The hospitality tray had assorted tea bags, coffee pods for the espresso machine, home-made ginger biscuits in a Kilner jar.' There is casual all-day dining in the Club Lounge and on the terrace; a more formal ambience in the restaurant. Typical dishes: moules frites, steak from the plancha, risotto of New Forest mushrooms. 'The quality and presentation was excellent.' On a chilly day you might have drinks and nibbles by the fire in the Quay bar, with live jazz on Sundays. Breakfast, served until 11 am, brings Loch Fyne smoked salmon, the full English, full vegetarian, eggs Benedict with Dorset ham. (JC, IM)

Wick Ferry
Christchurch BH23 1HU

T: 01202 475111
E: reservations@captainsclubhotel.com
W: captainsclubhotel.com

BEDROOMS: 29. 2 suitable for disabled.
OPEN: all year.
FACILITIES: lifts, open-plan bar/lounge/restaurant, function facilities, in-room TV (Sky, Freeview), civil wedding licence, riverside terrace, spa (hydrotherapy pool, treatments, sauna), public rooms wheelchair accessible, adapted toilet, parking, EV charging, moorings for guests.
BACKGROUND MUSIC: in public areas, live jazz every other Sun lunchtime.
LOCATION: on the river.
CHILDREN: all ages welcomed, family suites, children's menu.
DOGS: allowed in suites (£20 per dog), on terrace, areas of bar/lounge.
CREDIT CARDS: Amex, MC, Visa.
PRICES: B&B doubles from £270, suites from £360. À la carte £40. 1-night bookings normally refused Sat.

CLEARWELL Gloucestershire

MAP 3:D4

TUDOR FARMHOUSE

♻ Previous César winner

The chocolate-box charm of a centuries-old farmhouse, barn and cider house in flower-filled gardens does not immediately suggest a boutique hotel. But within, you find beautiful bedrooms, blending contemporary styling with rustic features such as beams and exposed walls. Owners Hari and Colin Fell arrived here from London in 2003, beguiled by the surrounding Forest of Dean, and our readers love what they have created. 'Idyllic visit, as always,' reads a typical report. 'Hari and her team are second to none.' Rooms range from cosy Hatchlings to spacious Cockerels and suites, with a roll-top bath, monsoon shower, maybe a four-poster. A grazing menu will see you through from lunch to a cream tea. At dinner, locally sourced dishes might include cod with mussel broth, sea vegetables, saffron potatoes or wild mushroom and summer truffle Wellington. 'The whole meal was outstanding.' Breakfast brings 'superb Wye Valley smoked salmon, an impressive array of juices including several apple varieties'. 'Lovely garden, lovely walks suggested by the hotel in ravishing countryside.' (Ann and Philip McCormack, Andrew Kleissner, and others)

High Street
Clearwell GL16 8JS

T: 01594 833046
E: info@tudorfarmhousehotel.co.uk
W: tudorfarmhousehotel.co.uk

BEDROOMS: 20. 4 on ground floor, 4 in farmhouse, 9 in barn, 7 in cider house.
OPEN: all year.
FACILITIES: lounge, bar, 2 dining rooms, treatment room, in-room TV (Freeview), 14-acre grounds (garden, ancient grassland), restaurant and lounge wheelchair accessible, adapted toilet.
BACKGROUND MUSIC: in restaurant and lounge at lunch and dinner.
LOCATION: 7 miles SE of Monmouth.
CHILDREN: all ages welcomed, extra bed £25, under-6s stay free, children's menu.
DOGS: 1 small dog allowed in 3 rooms (£10 a night).
CREDIT CARDS: Amex, MC, Visa.
PRICES: B&B doubles from £129. Tasting menu £60, à la carte £49. Min. 2-night stay at weekends, some bank holidays.

CLEY-NEXT-THE-SEA Norfolk

MAP 2:A5

CLEY WINDMILL

A Norfolk icon, this 19th-century windmill, rising from reed beds by the River Glaven, is now under new owners Natalie and Varian Bush, who say they will maintain the wonderful character of the place. The Stone Room, with high, oak-beamed ceiling, has a door to a platform that encircles the mill. The Wheat Chamber, with twin beds/king-size double is 'furnished with lovely antiques and individual touches'. The Boat House, with four-poster, has a glazed stable door to the courtyard. An amuse-bouche and three-course dinner can be delivered to your bedroom on earthenware plates, or taken by candlelight in the circular dining room at the tower base. It is supplied by respected local caterers, one a former chef here, and might include mushroom velouté, feather blade of beef, spiced fig and berry Eton mess. Let them know if you're vegetarian. Breakfast brings locally smoked fish, a full English, 'eggs in a variety of ways, a bacon or sausage sandwich'. Afterwards you might explore the 'pretty village with dinky craft and art shops', or follow the footpath through salt marshes to the beach – it's 'well worth doing'. Reports, please.

The Quay
Cley-next-the-Sea NR25 7RP

T: 01263 740209
E: info@cleywindmill.co.uk
W: cleywindmill.co.uk

BEDROOMS: 10. 1 in Boat House, 1 in Long House, 1 in Cart Shed.
OPEN: all year, usually self-catering only over Christmas.
FACILITIES: bar/lounge, dining room, in-room TV (Freeview), civil wedding licence, ¼-acre garden, ground-floor rooms suitable for more able wheelchair-users.
BACKGROUND MUSIC: in dining room, soft classical and jazz.
LOCATION: in northerly village next to River Glaven, less than a mile from the sea.
CHILDREN: all ages welcomed, extra bed £30.
DOGS: allowed in 1 room (Boat House) and Dovecote (B&B or self-catering cottage).
CREDIT CARDS: MC, Visa.
PRICES: B&B doubles from £159. Set menu £37.50, hampers £65–£95. Min. 2-night stay weekends.

CLIPSHAM Rutland

MAP 2:A3

BEECH HOUSE & OLIVE BRANCH

♔ Previous César winner

A defunct local pub, rescued by a trio of friends in 1999, is 'a wonderful place to eat', with rooms in 'gorgeous Georgian' Beech House opposite. Ben Jones, one of the original Olive Branch Three, works closely with head chef Luke Holland to maintain the ethos. The restaurant has 'a cosy cottage feel', where you can 'sit around a log fire', while alfresco dining includes gazebos on the terrace and a marquee in the paddock where produce for the kitchen is grown. Menus of locally produced and foraged ingredients include dishes such as roast 28-day mature beef, with Yorkshire pudding and roast potatoes; kelp-cured Cornish cod with wild-garlic salad cream and sea vegetables. Finish up with a rhubarb and custard mess. Bedrooms have antiques and good fabrics. Chocolate suite has a king-size and twin beds, a lounge and wet room. Ground-floor Berry has a carved French bed, patio seating, a power shower over a double-ended bath. 'Superb breakfasts' are sourced from surrounding farms – except for the oranges, which you squeeze yourself, or ask one of the 'attentive, knowledgeable' staff to do it for you. (Deborah Wooldridge, MM-D)

Main Street
Clipsham LE15 7SH

T: 01780 410355
E: info@theolivebranchpub.com
W: theolivebranchpub.com

BEDROOMS: 6. 2 on ground floor, family room (suitable for disabled) in annexe.
OPEN: all year except 25 and 31 Dec, 1 Jan, pub closed Sun night, Mon, Tues.
FACILITIES: bar, dining room, breakfast room, in-room TV (Freeview, Netflix), garden, paddock, public rooms wheelchair accessible, adapted toilet.
BACKGROUND MUSIC: classical/jazz in pub.
LOCATION: in village 7 miles NW of Stamford.
CHILDREN: all ages welcomed, cot £10 or extra bed £30 per night, children's menu.
DOGS: allowed by prior consent in ground-floor bedrooms (£10 per night) and bar.
CREDIT CARDS: MC, Visa.
PRICES: B&B doubles from £130, singles from £105. Set-price dinner (3 courses) £39.50, tasting menu (7 courses) £80.

CORSE LAWN Gloucestershire

MAP 3:D5

CORSE LAWN HOUSE

Guests can eat and drink alfresco at the Hine family's hotel, a Queen Anne-style mansion overlooking a willow-draped duck pond in a rural hamlet. In the same ownership for more than 40 years, it is run today by Baba Hine and inspires fierce loyalty among our readers. 'Love this place for its comfort, food, ambience and terrific staff,' reads a typical report this year. The look is slightly dated – one trusted reader called it 'dowdy'; fans prefer 'traditional'. But there are 'really spacious bedrooms with fresh milk for tea- and coffee-making, fresh fruit and delicious home-made shortbread'. They have period furniture and walls painted in shades of peach, pink, lavender, sienna … One suite has a carved four-poster and separate sitting room. Even standard rooms are a good size. A pool and tennis court are big pluses. In the restaurant and bistro, chef Chris Exley's varied menus include dishes such as Cornish lobster and loin of local muntjac with cherry jus. 'This hotel in the spring-green countryside is special: Baba Hine and her team have a winning formula that never ceases to delight.' (JG and PL, and others)

Corse Lawn GL19 4LZ

T: 01452 780771
E: enquiries@corselawn.com
W: corselawn.com

BEDROOMS: 18. 5 on ground floor.
OPEN: all year, Mon and Tues B&B only, by arrangement.
FACILITIES: 2 drawing rooms, snug bar, restaurant, bistro, private dining/meeting rooms, in-room TV, civil wedding licence, 12-acre grounds (croquet, tennis, indoor heated swimming pool), EV charging, unsuitable for disabled.
BACKGROUND MUSIC: none.
LOCATION: 5 miles SW of Tewkesbury on B4211.
CHILDREN: all ages welcomed, extra bed £10, 3 suites have sofa beds.
DOGS: allowed in bedrooms (£10 per stay), public rooms, not in eating areas.
CREDIT CARDS: Amex, MC, Visa.
PRICES: B&B doubles from £140, singles from £95. Fixed-price dinner £25.50–£30.50 (2/3 courses), à la carte £37.50.

COVERACK Cornwall   MAP 1:E2

THE BAY HOTEL

Set above a terraced garden, with superb views of both beach and harbour in an 'unspoilt gem' of a fishing village, this whitewashed Edwardian hotel is run with 'real care and pride'. 'I found the staff and service excellent,' wrote a trusted reader. 'The manager in particular was friendly and helpful.' You can choose a Beachcomber or Bay View room with double bed and shower, a Superior Bay View room with comfy seating and king-size or super-king bed, or a suite with French doors opening on to a private terrace. They are all contemporary in style, with a restful, muted seaside palette. Our reader's room had a 'generous, quite luxurious bathroom'. In the small restaurant that overlooks the bay, Sam Jones's menus are big on ethically sourced Cornish produce. Typically, they might feature Coverack spider crab ravioli, bisque, chive; Moorland dry-aged sirloin steak, salt-baked beetroot, za'atar, kohlrabi and pomegranate; or roasted carrot, dukkah, smoked aubergine purée, sweet potato, lime and mint yoghurt dressing. You can breakfast on omelette Arnold Bennett before broaching the South West Coast Path. 'I loved it.' (MC)

North Corner
Coverack
Helston TR12 6TF

T: 01326 280464
E: enquiries@thebayhotel.co.uk
W: thebayhotel.co.uk

BEDROOMS: 14. 1, on ground floor, suitable for disabled.
OPEN: 1 Mar–27 Dec.
FACILITIES: lounge, bar/restaurant, conservatory, in-room TV (Freeview), 2 tiered gardens, large sun terrace, parking.
BACKGROUND MUSIC: quiet classical music or blues in bar and restaurant.
LOCATION: village centre, 9 miles SE of Helston.
CHILDREN: all ages welcomed ('we are not suitable for babies or very young children'), under-3s free, extra bed for 3s and over £45.
DOGS: allowed in bedrooms (£10 a night), on lead in grounds, not in public rooms.
CREDIT CARDS: MC, Visa.
PRICES: B&B doubles from £120, singles from £96. À la carte £35. 1-night bookings sometimes refused.

COWAN BRIDGE Lancashire

MAP 4: inset D2

HIPPING HALL

Between the Yorkshire Dales and the Lake District – and just ten minutes from the M6 – Hipping Hall is a surprising foodie find with understated but luxurious bedrooms, and a relaxed atmosphere. A mix of buildings, from a medieval dining room and creeper-covered 17th-century hall to converted cottages and stables, it's surrounded by lawns, shrubbery and ponds. Some guests go walking, but most are here for MasterChef finalist Oli Martin's food. Served in the atmospheric medieval hall with beams and grand fireplace, his food is about 'purity, simplicity and freshness'. Dishes on the 12-course fortnightly-changing tasting menu sound simple but are carefully balanced to bring out flavours: scallops with smoked unripe redcurrant, lamb with wild garlic and sheep's yogurt curd, and rhubarb with lemon verbena. Comfortable accommodation ranges from a cosy cottage room with bold wallpapers, or a country house-style main-house room to the Scandi-style rooms with terraces in the converted stables. Modern bathrooms offer local Bath House products. Expect 'first-class' service. (See also sister property Forest Side, Grasmere.)

Cowan Bridge
Kirkby Lonsdale LA6 2JJ

T: 01524 271187
E: info@hippinghall.com
W: hippinghall.com

BEDROOMS: 15. 3 in cottage, 5 in stables, 1 suitable for disabled.
OPEN: all year except Christmas, restaurant closed Mon, Tues.
FACILITIES: lounge, orangery, bar, restaurant (vegetarian menu), civil wedding licence, in-room TV (Freeview), 12-acre grounds, orangery, restaurant and lounge wheelchair accessible.
BACKGROUND MUSIC: in lounge, restaurant.
LOCATION: 2 miles SE of Kirkby Lonsdale, on A65.
CHILDREN: all ages welcomed, cot £20, extra bed £70.
DOGS: allowed in stable bedrooms (max. 2, £20 per night), and orangery.
CREDIT CARDS: Amex, MC, Visa.
PRICES: B&B doubles from £199, singles from £169. Dinner tasting menu £80.

COWES Isle of Wight

MAP 2:E2

NORTH HOUSE

⚜ Previous César winner

Grotty yachts flock to Cowes during its week-long summer regatta, but this super-stylish 'very dog-friendly' hotel with a laid-back vibe provides a year-round reason to visit the nautical town. Occupying two town houses and the former Foresters Hall, once host to recitals and ventriloquist acts, it is well liked by locals, who pop in for lunch alfresco or a gottle of geer in a 'cool sitting room cum bar' with velvet tub chairs and Farrow & Ball wallpaper. The 'very hands-on' owners Lewis Green and Luke Staples also run an interiors shop – 'and it shows'. Bedrooms have a muted palette, seagrass flooring on bare boards, artfully distressed vintage pieces, a dial telephone and retro radio. Most large rooms have a freestanding bath and separate shower, perhaps a modern four-poster. From the tongue-and-groovy, flagstone-floored restaurant, hung with modern art, doors open to the garden and pool. A short seasonal menu produces 'simple and skilfully prepared' dishes such as roasted cod, mussel and razor clam chowder and duo of beef. 'Breakfast is outstanding' and during the day, guests can borrow bikes and boots. (C and ES, and others)

Sun Hill
Cowes PO31 7HY

T: 01983 209453
E: reception@northhousecowes.co.uk
W: northhousecowes.co.uk

BEDROOMS: 14.
OPEN: all year except 24–25 Dec, restaurant closed Mon, Tues (except bank holidays).
FACILITIES: bar, library, restaurant, private dining room, in-room TV (Freeview), civil wedding licence, garden, outdoor heated swimming pool, no onsite parking.
BACKGROUND MUSIC: in bar and restaurant.
LOCATION: in centre of Old Town.
CHILDREN: all ages welcomed, cot £15, extra bed £20.
DOGS: allowed in some bedrooms (£15 per night, with dog bed and treats), bar, library, in restaurant by special request.
CREDIT CARDS: Amex, MC, Visa.
PRICES: B&B doubles from £195. À la carte £36.

COWLEY Gloucestershire

MAP 3:D5

COWLEY MANOR   **NEW**

Enter 'a world of green woodland' once frequented by Lewis Carroll as you drive through the 'majestic grounds' of this Italianate mansion, which surprises with striking interiors designed with '60s pizzazz. The 'minimalist combination with classic surroundings' created for Peter and Jessica Frankopan's Curious group (see Portobello Hotel, London), together with the hotel's 'very relaxed atmosphere', pleased our inspectors. A 'lovely second-floor bedroom' was 'a quirky combination of oak panels and '60s design', with 'a huge bath and walk-in drench shower in a delightful bathroom'. Several rooms have a terrace or balcony. Those in the stables are more modern, some with an adjoining kids' room. In the 'atmospheric candlelit restaurant' or on the terrace, David Kelman's short, appealing menus include dishes such as 'delicious tuna steak and piping-hot fat chips', with good veggie options. A continental breakfast is included – 'the vegetarian full English was worth the extra expense'. Order a picnic and explore the parkland, with its lakes, sculptures, a cascade and exotic trees. 'The C-Side Spa is a highlight.'

Cowley
Cheltenham GL53 9NL

T: 01242 870900
E: stay@cowleymanor.com
W: cowleymanor.com

BEDROOMS: 31. 15 in converted stables.
OPEN: all year.
FACILITIES: bar, sitting room, billiard room, restaurant, private sitting room, garden room and dining room, in-room TV (Sky), 55-acre grounds, civil wedding licence, spa (indoor and outdoor swimming pool).
BACKGROUND MUSIC: in public areas.
LOCATION: 6 miles S of Cheltenham.
CHILDREN: all ages welcomed, extra bed £40 (includes meals).
DOGS: allowed in 7 bedrooms (£25 per night), sitting room, billiard room, terrace.
CREDIT CARDS: Amex, MC, Visa.
PRICES: B&B doubles from £185.
À la carte £45. 1-night bookings refused Sat and some holidays.

COXWOLD Yorkshire

MAP 4:D4

THE FAUCONBERG ARMS NEW

On the edge of the North York Moors, this quintessential village inn in tranquil Coxwold has locals and dogs in the bar, country fare in the dining room and fuss-free bedrooms above. The charming traditional exterior, with honey-coloured stone and tables on the cobbled terrace, is matched within, where you will find flagged floors, log fires, beams, and lots of shiny copper and brass. Eat in the bar or dining room, the latter with plaid carpet and fresh flowers, from the same menu of classic country dishes, perhaps home-made steak and ale pie, Whitby scampi or chicken supreme with wild garlic pesto. 'The food is good with a good blackboard menu to supplement,' reports a guest who praised the 'wide choice' of local beers and well-priced wines. 'Slightly quirky' bedrooms have a cottagey charm with light-oak furniture and perhaps a wrought iron or sleigh bed – a four-poster in one – floral and striped fabrics and views over the village or Howardian hills. Some are on the cosy side; all have a modern en suite bathroom, apart from the summer-only Garden Room, with a shower and eco-loo in an adjoining shed. (Alasdair Adam)

Thirsk Bank
Coxwold
Thirsk YO61 4AD

T: 01347 868214
E: reservations@fauconbergarms.com
W: fauconbergarms.com

BEDROOMS: 9. 1 log cabin in garden.
OPEN: all year.
FACILITIES: 2 bars, snug, restaurant, private dining room, 1-acre garden, in-room TV, back bar and restaurant wheelchair accessible.
BACKGROUND MUSIC: none.
LOCATION: centre of village, 6 miles N of Easingwold, 7 miles S of Thirsk.
CHILDREN: all ages welcomed, extra bed £15.
DOGS: allowed in bedrooms (£10 a night) and bars.
CREDIT CARDS: Amex, MC, Visa.
PRICES: B&B doubles from £90, singles from £70, garden room from £75, single occupancy £65. À la carte £28.

CREDITON Devon

MAP 1:C4

PASCHOE HOUSE

NEW

Hidden down a drive in remote mid-Devon,
this Victorian country house and fine-dining
restaurant blends modern design with original
features to startling effect. Tabitha Amador-
Christie has given her Tudor-Gothic family
home a bold make-over with sugar-pink walls
up the staircase, bright butterfly wallpaper in the
drawing room and a stuffed ostrich overlooking
proceedings in the powder-blue bar. Taxidermy
is a recurring theme. Despite quirky touches,
the atmosphere is quietly refined with antiques
and pretty coloured armchairs, wood-burning
stoves in grand fireplaces, and shuttered windows
overlooking the grounds. There are walks
from the doorstep, tennis and a games lawn.
Dinner is an ambitious affair with canapés and
amuse-bouche followed by dishes such as trout
with beetroot, yogurt and lime, and lamb with
Provençal vegetables, potato purée and wild
garlic. Bedrooms have a modern elegance, with
soft colours, contemporary and antique furniture,
while bathrooms have striking wallpapers. Home-
baked treats, chocolates and flowers add a homely
touch. Lazy breakfasts include fruit compote,
pancakes and eggs Florentine.

Bow
Crediton EX17 6JT

T: 01363 84244
E: theteam@paschoehouse.co.uk
W: paschoehouse.co.uk

BEDROOMS: 9.
OPEN: all year, except 3 Jan–1 Feb,
closed Mon, Tues.
FACILITIES: lift, lounge, bar, restaurant,
in-room TV (Freeview), 25-acre
grounds (tennis court, games lawn),
EV charging, civil wedding licence,
public rooms wheelchair accessible.
BACKGROUND MUSIC: light jazz in
public rooms.
LOCATION: E of Bow, off A3072.
CHILDREN: all ages welcomed, extra
bed £50, children's meals offered in
lounge/bar.
DOGS: allowed in 3 bedrooms (£15 per
night, bed, treats), in grounds, and in
public rooms apart from restaurant.
CREDIT CARDS: Amex, MC, Visa.
PRICES: B&B doubles from £179.
À la carte meal £75, tasting menu £90.

CROFT-ON-TEES Yorkshire

MAP 4:C4

CLOW BECK HOUSE

The personal welcome, horizon-stretching views, homely touches and feeling of space make this handsome former farmhouse a relaxing stay. Surrounded by gardens and farmland, it's gloriously peaceful and David and Heather Armstrong run things with a Yorkshire friendliness. The farmhouse, in David's family for more than 100 years, is smart but unpretentious with a neat, conservatively furnished lounge, and large, rustic dining room with slate floor, open beams, polished-wood tables and cheery fire. It provides an inviting setting for David's homely farmhouse-style meals chosen from a surprisingly extensive menu with good vegetarian choices. 'Spotless' bedrooms, in converted outbuildings, are comfortable and uncluttered, ranging from traditional in style, with the odd antique or elegant sofa, to more modern, with clean-lined furniture and contemporary art prints. Ground-floor rooms have small patios while all have thoughtful extras such as hot-water bottles, hairspray and home-made biscuits. At breakfast, gaze over the beautiful gardens with box hedge knot garden, pond, terrace, ornamental pigs and hidden corners with seats.

Monk End Farm
Croft-on-Tees DL2 2SP

T: 01325 721075
E: reservations@clowbeckhouse.co.uk
W: clowbeckhouse.co.uk

BEDROOMS: 6. In garden buildings, some on ground floor, 1 suitable for disabled.
OPEN: all year except Christmas and New Year.
FACILITIES: lounge, restaurant, in-room TV (Freeview), small conference facilities, 2-acre grounds on 100-acre farm.
BACKGROUND MUSIC: classical, 'easy listening' in restaurant.
LOCATION: 3 miles SE of Darlington.
CHILDREN: all ages welcomed, cot £20, extra bed £25.
DOGS: not allowed.
CREDIT CARDS: Amex, MC, Visa.
PRICES: B&B doubles from £140, singles from £90. À la carte £38.

CROSTHWAITE Cumbria

MAP 4: inset C2

THE PUNCH BOWL INN

In a quietly beautiful area of the Lake District –
the lovely Lyth valley – this smart village inn has
a deserved reputation for good food and cosseting
bedrooms. Popular with locals and visitors alike,
it's more foodie than drinkers' pub (with much
produce from their village farm), though the
bar stocks local ales as well as champagne by the
glass. New chef Aaron Lawrence (formerly of the
Lake District's Michelin-starred Gilpin Hotel)
offers dishes such as local lamb with fondant
potato and onion purée, and herb-crusted halibut
with sauté leeks. Lemon tart with local damson
sorbet is a favourite. Eat in the atmospheric slate-
floored and beamed bar with toasty log-burner,
the more formal dining room or outside on the
terrace overlooking the neighbouring church.
Contemporary country bedrooms are pleasingly
different – some with beams, others with valley
views – though all offer rich carpets and curtains,
pale-wash colours and vintage or solid-oak
furniture. Inviting bathrooms have tongue-and-
groove panelling, roll-top baths and under-floor
heating. 'Cheerful and friendly' staff welcome
guests with home-made scones and tea.

Crosthwaite
Kendal LA8 8HR

T: 01539 568237
E: info@the-punchbowl.co.uk
W: the-punchbowl.co.uk

BEDROOMS: 9.
OPEN: all year.
FACILITIES: bar, bar dining area,
restaurant, in-room TV (Freeview),
EV charging, civil wedding licence,
2 terraces, bar and restaurant
wheelchair accessible, adapted toilet.
BACKGROUND MUSIC: in public areas.
LOCATION: 5 miles W of Kendal, via
A5074.
CHILDREN: all ages welcomed, under-
12s extra bed £25, children's menu.
DOGS: allowed in bar only.
CREDIT CARDS: Amex, MC, Visa.
PRICES: B&B doubles from £160, singles
from £140. À la carte £40. 1-night
bookings usually refused 25 Dec,
31 Dec.

CRUDWELL Wiltshire

MAP 3:E5

THE RECTORY HOTEL

A Georgian rectory-turned-boutique hotel, in manicured gardens with swimming pool, is a first hospitality venture for music industry executive Alex Payne, who called in the team behind The Beckford Arms, Tisbury (see entry), with designer Natasha Hidvegi, a former plastic surgeon, to give the place a facelift. The result is a 'perfect blend of design and comfort, stylish enough to inspire interior lovers but cosy enough for guests to snuggle up with a book'. Bedrooms have subtle paint finishes, seagrass flooring; the largest has a modern four-poster, a lovely bathroom with roll-top bath. All have good toiletries, home-baked shortbread, fresh coffee, milk from a fridge on the landing. The house is set back from the road, but 'rooms that face the garden are preferable'. There are cocktails and canapés in the bar, while, in a panelled dining room, the menu brings perhaps roast lamb, potato terrine, golden turnip, kohlrabi and rainbow chard. Or pop across the road to sister outfit The Potting Shed for gastropub fare. Breakfast is taken in the glasshouse, 'which is lovely and looks out over the gardens'. (LG, and others)

Crudwell
Malmesbury SN16 9EP

T: 01666 577194
E: info@therectoryhotel.com
W: therectoryhotel.com

BEDROOMS: 18. 3 in self-catering cottage in garden.
OPEN: all year.
FACILITIES: living room, drawing room, dining room, card room, bar, in-room TV (Freeview, film library), meeting facilities, civil wedding licence, 3-acre garden, heated outdoor swimming pool (10 by 15 metres, May–Oct), restaurant and bar wheelchair accessible, no adapted toilet.
BACKGROUND MUSIC: in public areas.
LOCATION: 4 miles N of Malmesbury.
CHILDREN: all ages welcomed, extra bed £25.
DOGS: allowed in 4 bedrooms (£15 a night) and public rooms, not in dining room.
CREDIT CARDS: Amex, MC, Visa.
PRICES: B&B doubles from £150. À la carte £40. Min. 2-night bookings at weekends, usually.

DARLINGTON Co. Durham

MAP 4:C4

HEADLAM HALL

Guests continue to be delighted by this grand country house – sweeping gardens, historic features, smart bedrooms, swish spa – with a warm, down-to-earth atmosphere. 'Relaxed and unstuffy,' comments one about this family-run hotel; 'extremely helpful staff,' notes another. The creeper-covered hall, dating from Jacobean times, has flagged and polished-wood floors, panelled walls, an orangery dining room, and terraces overlooking walled gardens and beyond to the Robinson family's farmland. Yet it's 'comfortably' furnished with tartan carpets, tweed-covered armchairs, and walls with hunting prints and Victorian watercolours. There is plenty of space to relax, from the elegant drawing room and cosy library bar to the spa and gardens. Spacious bedrooms have a modern country house feel with calming colours, and range from the main hall, with original features and antiques, to contemporary spa bedrooms and more rustic mews and coach-house rooms. Austen Shaw's modern British menus offer an 'excellent' choice of dishes from roast duck or salmon with spiced risotto to tagines and pastas. 'I'd not hesitate to stay again.' (RW, HP)

Gainford
Darlington DL2 3HA

T: 01325 730238
E: reception@headlamhall.co.uk
W: headlamhall.co.uk

BEDROOMS: 38. 9 in coach house, 6 in mews, 7 in spa, 2 suitable for disabled.
OPEN: all year except 24–27 Dec.
FACILITIES: lift, bar, restaurant, brasserie, lounge, drawing room, private dining rooms, in-room TV, civil wedding licence, function facilities, 4-acre garden, spa, indoor pool, tennis, 9-hole golf course, EV charging, public rooms wheelchair accessible, adapted toilet.
BACKGROUND MUSIC: all day in bar, restaurant.
LOCATION: 8 miles W of Darlington.
CHILDREN: all ages welcomed, under-4s free, extra bed £30.
DOGS: allowed in some bedrooms (no charge), not in restaurant.
CREDIT CARDS: Amex, MC, Visa.
PRICES: B&B doubles from £135, singles from £105. À la carte 3 courses £35.

DARTMOUTH Devon

MAP 1:D4

BAYARDS COVE INN

A rare survivor, this quaint, jettied timber-frame medieval merchant's house is home to a child-friendly, dog-friendly café, bar and restaurant with rooms above. Standing close to the cobbled quayside, the historic building has put behind it the various indignities of modernisation and mixed commercial use in the care of owners Charlie and Zuzana Deuchar. It's a creaky, wonky, characterful place, with diamond-pane leaded windows. Up a 'winding staircase', the beamed Mountbatten bedroom has bare floorboards, a super-king/twin bed, a lounge with a sofa bed, and a shower room. The cheapest room is cosy double Jervis on the second floor. The street door leads straight into the café, where you check in at the bar. You can sit by the fire, or at a table outside over coffee and a cake chosen from those arrayed 'tantalisingly on the counter'. Breakfast is served until 11.30 am, with choices for vegans, vegetarians and children, and food is available all day from a seasonal menu, with a fish catch of the day, Devon steaks, maybe a tofu burger or butternut squash and spinach risotto.

27 Lower Street
Dartmouth TQ6 9AN

T: 01803 839278
E: info@bayardscoveinn.co.uk
W: bayardscoveinn.co.uk

BEDROOMS: 7. 2 family suites.
OPEN: all year.
FACILITIES: bar, restaurant, in-room TV (Freeview), bicycle storage, private parking nearby (reservation required, £15 per day), public areas wheelchair accessible, adapted toilet.
BACKGROUND MUSIC: in public areas.
LOCATION: in centre, close to waterfront.
CHILDREN: all ages welcomed, children's menu.
DOGS: allowed throughout (£12 per dog per night with prior notice, incl. bed, bowl, treats).
CREDIT CARDS: Amex, MC, Visa.
PRICES: B&B doubles from £115, family room from £165. À la carte £35. Min. 2-night stay at weekends.

SEE ALSO SHORTLIST

DARTMOUTH Devon

MAP 1:D4

DART MARINA

If there is nothing so nice as messing about on the river, there are few nicer places to do so than at Richard Seton's dog-friendly spa hotel on the Dart estuary, ever popular with our readers. 'From the moment we spotted the hotel from the far bank, waiting for the ferry, to the moment we left, the experience was first class,' writes one. There is a wide choice of chic bedrooms and suites, in pearlescent greys, with accents of blue and sand, each with a balcony, patio or sliding glass doors to a glass balustrade, from which to watch the shifting waterscape. Junior suites have a dual-aspect lounge, a freestanding bath, a wet-room drench shower, binoculars, a coffee machine. You can eat indoors or on the terrace, informally from a lounge menu. In summer Exmouth mussels and pulled-pork sliders are dispensed from a vintage bus. Best of all, push the boat out in the River restaurant with dishes such as tandoori monkfish, sole, juniper-marinated venison. 'The food was nicely presented and very tasty; I can vouch for the rib-eye steak.' 'Faultless. Sorry, nothing more to say!' (Helen Kent, IM, and others)

Sandquay Road
Dartmouth TQ6 9PH

T: 01803 832580
E: reception@dartmarina.com
W: dartmarina.com

BEDROOMS: 49. 4 on ground floor, 1 suitable for disabled, plus 4 apartments.
OPEN: all year.
FACILITIES: lounge/bar, restaurant, in-room TV (Freeview), lawn, terrace, pop-up bar, spa (heated indoor swimming pool, 8 by 4 metres, gym), parking, lounge and restaurant wheelchair accessible.
BACKGROUND MUSIC: in restaurant and lounge/bar during the day.
LOCATION: on waterfront.
CHILDREN: all ages welcomed, extra bed £30.
DOGS: allowed in some bedrooms (£10 per stay) and lounge, not in restaurant.
CREDIT CARDS: MC, Visa.
PRICES: B&B doubles from £190, singles from £150. À la carte £40. 1-night bookings usually refused weekends at peak times.

SEE ALSO SHORTLIST

DEDHAM Essex

MAP 2:C5

DEDHAM HALL

Where better for a hotel with its own art studio than a village at the heart of Constable country? But you don't have to sign up to a residential painting course to enjoy Wendy and Jim Sarton's inviting half-timbered manor house. 'We had an excellent stay,' write readers this year, impressed by the way they balance 'welcoming informality and homely atmosphere' with 'great service and professionalism'. Traditional bedrooms look out on flourishing gardens and a pond, brimming with flowers and wildlife. A fire was lit in a beamed lounge for the new arrivals, in case they should wish to sit there, 'which we did, with much pleasure, before and after the evening meal'. Wendy's menus offer a choice of dishes such as lemon sole with tartare sauce, and duck breast with green peppercorn gravy, while vegans can be catered for with notice. 'The food was absolutely freshly cooked, piping hot and ample portions.' You can breakfast on 'a remarkable selection of fresh fruit, including Wendy's notable compote', and creamy scrambled eggs, before a walk to Willy Lott's Cottage, scene of The Hay Wain. (Jonathan and Angela Dare)

Brook Street
Dedham
Colchester CO7 6AD

T: 01206 323027
E: sarton@dedhamhall.co.uk
W: dedhamhall.co.uk

BEDROOMS: 20. 16 in annexe around art studio, some on ground floor suitable for disabled.
OPEN: all year except Christmas–New Year.
FACILITIES: 2 lounges, bar, dining room, studio, in-room TV (terrestrial), 6-acre grounds (pond, gardens, fields), lounge and dining room wheelchair accessible.
BACKGROUND MUSIC: none.
LOCATION: end of village High Street (set back from road).
CHILDREN: all ages welcomed, extra bed £25.
DOGS: allowed in some bedrooms (no charge), not in public rooms.
CREDIT CARDS: MC, Visa.
PRICES: B&B doubles from £120, singles from £75. À la carte/fixed-price dinner, for residents only (or by prior arrangement), £35.

DEDHAM Essex   MAP 2:C5

MAISON TALBOOTH

'It felt like staying with friends, albeit very hip ones,' says a Guide insider, of the Milsom family's hotel outside Colchester, in a 'wonderful setting' where windows frame views of Constable's Dedham Vale. Bedrooms, each named after a poet, have 'eye-catching extras such as oversized armchairs, feature wallpaper or a huge headboard'. Shakespeare has a large sunken bath, a king-size/twin bed on which to sleep, perchance to dream. Keats has a second bedroom with bunk beds, a sunken bath and walk-through shower, and private terrace. Tennyson is, bizarrely, Beatles themed. All have complimentary soft drinks and snacks. Guests can play tennis or wander down to 'the star attraction', the lovely pool house with a lounge, open fire and honesty bar opening on to the pool, 'perfect for an atmospheric dip in the early evening'. There is an all-day bar, and brasserie dining at sister hotel Milsoms a stroll away, or they'll drive you the 650 yards to fine-dining Le Talbooth for dishes such as Dedham Vale beef and glazed short rib; for vegans maybe new-season vegetable millefeuille (see also The Pier at Harwich, Harwich). (David Verney, and others)

Stratford Road
Dedham CO7 6HN

T: 01206 322367
E: maison@milsomhotels.com
W: milsomhotels.com

BEDROOMS: 12. 5 on ground floor with walk-in shower.
OPEN: all year.
FACILITIES: lounge, Garden Room, courtesy car to restaurant 1 minute away, 5-acre grounds (tennis), outdoor heated pool, in-room TV (Sky, Freeview), spa, civil wedding licence, parking ramp, some public areas wheelchair accessible, adapted toilet.
BACKGROUND MUSIC: none.
LOCATION: ½ mile W of Dedham village.
CHILDREN: all ages welcomed, extra bed £20.
DOGS: allowed in bedrooms (£15 a night), lounge, on terrace and in area of brasserie, not restaurant.
CREDIT CARDS: Amex, MC, Visa.
PRICES: B&B doubles from £270. À la carte £70 (Talbooth), £37 (Milsoms). 1-night bookings may be refused weekends.

DEDHAM Essex

MAP 2:C5

THE SUN INN

An ancient, rambling coaching inn in a village of wonky painted houses, The Sun glows with praise for its 'genuine welcome', 'quick and affable service' and 'convivial' atmosphere. Within Piers Baker's mellow-yellow local lies an oak-panelled lounge, beamed ceilings and blazing fires, real ales on tap at the 'gorgeous, curving' burred elm counter, walls hung with works by local artists, old posters and photos. Bedrooms are smart and characterful. Spacious Elsa with a king-size oak bed, and Constable, with a half-tester, look over the street to St Mary's church, home to John Constable's 'The Ascension'. Piers's stated aim is to 'make people happy', and that includes his friendly, casually attired, youthful staff. You can eat in the split-level dining room or outside. Jack Levine's menus of fish from Mersea day boats, rare breed steaks and game might include Merrifield Farm chicken breast, girolle, gnocchi 'Cacio e Pepe'; roast cod with lentils and slow-roast San Marzano tomato. You can expect 'copious portions'. After a breakfast with freshly squeezed orange juice, set out to explore Constable country.

High Street
Dedham
Colchester CO7 6DF

T: 01206 323351
E: office@thesuninndedham.com
W: thesuninndedham.com

BEDROOMS: 7. 2 across the terrace, approached by external staircase.
OPEN: all year except 25/26 Dec.
FACILITIES: lounge, bar, dining room, in-room TV (Freeview), 1-acre walled garden (covered terrace, children's play area, garden bar), parking, unsuitable for disabled.
BACKGROUND MUSIC: all day in public areas.
LOCATION: village centre.
CHILDREN: all ages welcomed, roll-out mattress £15.
DOGS: in bar and Oak Room, in guest bedrooms by arrangement (no charge but subject to stringent terms and conditions), not in dining room.
CREDIT CARDS: Amex, MC, Visa.
PRICES: B&B doubles from £150, singles from £90. À la carte £36, weekly set menu £20.50– £25.50 (2/3 courses).

DORCHESTER Dorset

MAP 2:E1

THE KING'S ARMS

NEW

In Thomas Hardy's Casterbridge, this bow-windowed Georgian coaching inn enters the Guide after a £5 million make-over for the Stay Original group. In the 'large bar' with comfy seating and modern restaurant you can expect to hear the 'babble of voices, the jingle of glasses' that Elizabeth-Jane and her mother heard in The Mayor of Casterbridge. 'Even on a Tuesday night it was bustling.' The food is 'perhaps the real draw', with menus overseen by Tom Blake, formerly of the River Cottage, alongside head chef Steve Yates. 'Chicken confit with olives and preserved lemons was a light, tasty starter; slow-cooked, spiced shoulder of lamb perfect comfort food.' Bedrooms, styled in soft greens, greys and blues, have a king or super-king bed, a coffee machine, luxury toiletries. Our inspectors' room was 'well furnished and smartly decorated', if a 'little on the plain side', with a 'spacious drench shower'. The best two rooms have a claw-footed bath in the window. Breakfast brought 'outstanding grilled halloumi and avocado on toast', smoked salmon, scrambled eggs with crème fraîche. Hardy's house, Max Gate, is within walking distance.

30 High East Street
Dorchester DT1 1HF

T: 01305 238238
E: info@thekingsarmsdorchester.com
W: thekingsarmsdorchester.com

BEDROOMS: 20. 14 further bedrooms scheduled to open.
OPEN: all year.
FACILITIES: lift, bar, restaurant, lounge, private dining room, 1st-floor function room, terrace, secure car park, public rooms partially accessible for wheelchairs, adapted toilet.
BACKGROUND MUSIC: in public areas.
LOCATION: central.
CHILDREN: all ages welcomed, free cots for under-3s, extra bed for under-13s £20, children's menu.
DOGS: allowed in 1st-floor bedrooms (£10 per stay), bar, lounge and on terrace, subject to some restrictions, not in restaurant.
CREDIT CARDS: MC, Visa.
PRICES: B&B doubles from £105. À la carte £37.

DUNSTER Somerset

MAP 1:B5

THE LUTTRELL ARMS HOTEL

On the fringe of Exmoor national park, a short drive from the coast, in a medieval village dominated by its hilltop castle, this largely Tudor inn is today a traditional, dog-friendly hotel. 'The decor is very country eclectic, with mismatched furniture, hunting-themed pictures, lots of cushions, giving a casual, cosy feel,' an inspector writes. In the recently refreshed accommodation, a 'very spacious' bedroom had a dog bed and cot set up in readiness ('a nice touch'), a 'very attractive' but 'far-too-short' four-poster with baseboard ('my husband had to stick his feet over the side'). Some rooms have extraordinary original features, fine antiques, a private terrace. You can eat with your dog at your side in the beautiful beamed bar, in comfy fireside corners, or in an 'amazing, large secret garden with lots of seating areas (including two igloo pods) and views of the castle'. In Psalter's restaurant (named after the Luttrell Psalter), Barrie Tucker cooks 'very good, mostly classic pub food such as fish and chips (huge!), fishcakes, soup of the day and very nice salads', veggie options. 'The ambience is friendly and relaxed.'

32–36 High Street
Dunster TA24 6SG

T: 01643 821555
E: enquiry@luttrellarms.co.uk
W: luttrellarms.co.uk

BEDROOMS: 28. Some on ground floor, 1 with 'easy access'.
OPEN: all year.
FACILITIES: lounge, 2 bars, snug, restaurant, function rooms, in-room TV (Freeview), civil wedding licence, courtyard, garden (alfresco dining), lounge and restaurant wheelchair accessible, no adapted toilet.
BACKGROUND MUSIC: in restaurant.
LOCATION: village centre, 3½ miles SE of Minehead.
CHILDREN: all ages welcomed, some rooms not suitable for under-14s, extra bed £20–£30.
DOGS: allowed in most bedrooms (£10 per night), bar, not in restaurant.
CREDIT CARDS: Amex, MC, Visa.
PRICES: B&B doubles from £120, single occupancy from £107.50. À la carte £35. Min. 2-nights weekends.

EAST CHISENBURY Wiltshire   MAP 2:D2

THE RED LION FREEHOUSE

♔ Previous César winner

A thatched pub in a quiet village tucked into
the folds of Salisbury Plain is home to a highly
praised restaurant, with a swish guest house across
the road. It has been quite a journey for chef/
proprietors Guy and Brittany Manning, from
New York's vaunted Per Se restaurant, where
they met, to this leafy backwater, but our readers
are delighted that they made it. 'This place is
going from strength to strength,' runs a typical
comment. 'Highly recommended.' Within, you
will find flagstones and beams, beers on tap pulled
by friendly bar staff, all the trappings of a popular
local, and the garden is set up for outdoor dining.
Guy uses local, home-grown and foraged produce
in dishes such as herb-roasted guineafowl breast,
wild garlic gnocchi, sauce soubise, trompettes, jus
gras, while Brittany turns her hand to desserts.
Maybe chocolate financier, goat's curd, crapaudine
purée and rosemary ice cream. Spacious and
stylish bedrooms have decking beside the River
Avon, a minibar, perhaps an in-room roll-top
bath from which to contemplate the view, and
a separate rainwater shower. 'We ran out of
superlatives.' (TB, and others)

East Chisenbury
Pewsey SN9 6AQ

T: 01980 671124
E: troutbeck@redlionfreehouse.com
W: redlionfreehouse.com

BEDROOMS: 5. On ground floor, 1
suitable for disabled.
OPEN: all year except 25 Dec, kitchen
closed Sun evening, all day Mon.
FACILITIES: bar/restaurant, private
dining room, in-room TV (Freeview),
½-acre garden, restaurant wheelchair
accessible.
BACKGROUND MUSIC: in pub/restaurant.
LOCATION: in village, 6 miles S of
Pewsey.
CHILDREN: all ages welcomed, travel
cot £15, extra bed (aged 3–10) £50.
DOGS: allowed in 1 bedroom by
arrangement (£10 a night).
CREDIT CARDS: Amex, MC, Visa.
PRICES: B&B doubles from £155 (£255
Fri, Sat and peak times). À la carte
£60, pre-booked 7-course tasting
menu £85.

EAST GRINSTEAD Sussex

MAP 2:D4

GRAVETYE MANOR

♔ Previous César winner

At the end of its mile-long drive, this Elizabethan manor house with glorious gardens and superb dining is, for many guests, the ultimate country house hotel. 'Comfortable, beautiful, friendly and great food,' said one reader. Everything about it is grand and traditional, from its gables and mullioned windows to the wood-panelling, carved ceilings, plush sofas and roaring fires inside. And masses of flowers – William Robinson's Victorian gardens are famed for their visionary, natural approach. Enjoy breathtaking views of them in the restyled dining room with its walls of glass. The 'exceptional' Michelin-starred food – with produce from the garden – includes dishes such as quail with quince and pear, and Newhaven brill with butternut squash and wild mushrooms. There are more garden views from the 'beautiful bedrooms', 'old, but with everything we needed'. Expect pretty fabrics and upholstered armchairs; some have wood-panelling or a four-poster. Staff are praised for their 'outstanding and memorable' service. A Relais & Châteaux hotel. (Frances Thomas, Yvette Peart, Roderic Rennison)

Vowels Lane
West Hoathly
East Grinstead RH19 4LJ

T: 01342 810567
E: info@gravetyemanor.co.uk
W: gravetyemanor.co.uk

BEDROOMS: 17.
OPEN: all year.
FACILITIES: 2 lounges, bar, restaurant, 2 private dining rooms, in-room TV (Sky), civil wedding licence, 1,000-acre grounds (woodland, ornamental and kitchen gardens, meadow, orchard, lake, croquet lawn, glasshouses), EV charging, restaurant wheelchair accessible, adapted toilet.
BACKGROUND MUSIC: in bar.
LOCATION: 4 miles SW of East Grinstead.
CHILDREN: not under 7, extra bed £40.
DOGS: not allowed.
CREDIT CARDS: Amex, MC, Visa.
PRICES: B&B doubles from £298, single from £179. Set 4-course dinner £95. 1-night bookings sometimes refused at weekends.

EAST HOATHLY Sussex   MAP 2:E4

OLD WHYLY

Set in 'wonderful grounds which are impeccably
kept', with an orchard, hard tennis court and
swimming pool, Sarah Burgoyne's 'beautiful
house' continues to impress. The former Georgian
farmhouse is filled with antiques and artwork,
its bedrooms traditionally furnished. Two have a
separate private bathroom, two have an en suite.
At night, Paris-trained Sarah cooks a three-
course dinner of locally sourced ingredients. 'She
is a highly accomplished host and clearly a very
talented chef,' a reader relates. 'We had lamb and
sea bass, both faultless.' Another reader found
the cold beetroot soup 'a delight'. Breakfast, too,
is 'simply lovely. All kinds of goodies, with an
excellent cooked breakfast if you needed it. Juice
from real oranges. Ample toast with very nice
home-made jams and exquisite marmalade.' Both
children and dogs are welcome. There are 'lovely
walks nearby' on an adjoining estate, and on fine
days you can return to take tea alfresco. Wily old
hands book well ahead for Glyndebourne and
order a tiffin box. (Ian White, Peter and Cynthia
Boden, and others)

London Road
East Hoathly BN8 6EL

T: 01825 840216
E: stay@oldwhyly.co.uk
W: oldwhyly.co.uk

BEDROOMS: 4.
OPEN: all year.
FACILITIES: drawing room, dining
room, in-room TV (Freeview), 4-acre
garden, heated outdoor swimming
pool (14 by 7 metres), tennis,
unsuitable for disabled.
BACKGROUND MUSIC: none.
LOCATION: 1 mile N of village.
CHILDREN: all ages welcomed, extra
bed £35.
DOGS: allowed in drawing room, not
in dining room or unattended in
bedrooms (£10 charge).
CREDIT CARDS: none.
PRICES: B&B doubles from £120. Set
dinner £42, hamper £45 per person.
1-night bookings may be refused at
weekends in summer season.

EAST PORTLEMOUTH Devon

MAP 1:E4

GARA ROCK

Drive down 'tiny country lanes', putter across from Salcombe aboard a little motorboat ferry, or walk the South West Coast Path to reach this remote hotel and spa with 'a commanding cliffside position and sublime views'. However you get here, you won't regret it, says a Guide insider, though it is expensive. Built on the site of a Victorian coastguard station-turned-Edwardian hotel, it has an exciting choice of rooms and suites, some sea facing with a balcony, some with a garden patio, 'perfect for dog owners'. New junior suites have an open living space and roll-top bath. 'Apartments in the grounds are more simply furnished and more suited to families.' A lounge with 'wood-burner and sheepskin throws over squishy armchairs' shares space with a bistro with curved full-height windows, 'lights cleverly incorporated into fishing nets'. New executive head Paul Hegley creates dishes such as pan-fried halibut, Salcombe shellfish sauce, piperade and preserved fennel, but you can still have good old fish and chips. When the sun shines, dine alfresco on barbecued fare; when it rains, watch a movie in the cinema. (JK)

East Portlemouth
Salcombe TQ8 8FA

T: 01548 845946
E: info@gararock.com
W: gararock.com

BEDROOMS: 33. Accessed externally, 1 suite separate from hotel.
OPEN: all year.
FACILITIES: restaurant, private dining area, lounge bar, spa, cinema room, terrace, indoor and outdoor pool, in-room TV, civil wedding licence, EV charging, public rooms wheelchair accessible, adapted toilet on floor below, reached via lift.
BACKGROUND MUSIC: in public areas.
LOCATION: on cliff-top, 1 mile SE of East Portlemouth.
CHILDREN: all ages welcomed, no charge for extra bed.
DOGS: allowed in some rooms (£40–£60 per stay), grounds, lounge bar and restaurant.
CREDIT CARDS: Amex, MC, Visa.
PRICES: B&B doubles from £328. À la carte £45. Min. 2-night bookings.

EASTBOURNE Sussex

MAP 2:E4

BELLE TOUT LIGHTHOUSE

A beacon of hospitality in a remote situation between Beachy Head and the Seven Sisters chalk cliffs, this iconic 19th-century lighthouse, decommissioned in 1902, found new purpose in 2010 when it first opened to guests. Trusted readers, arriving in a gale, were blown away by the warmth of the welcome from general manager Ian Noall, and found 'the whole place immaculate'. The Keeper's Loft, in the tower, is strictly for the limber, with exposed brick walls, a view of the usurper Beachy Head Lighthouse through an arched window, and a ladder to a double bed. For the more faint-hearted, rooms in the adjoining house are fresh and bright, light filled, with lots of white paint and all expected facilities. At 5 pm guests are invited to mingle over drinks in the cosy lounge, where some might then settle in for a supper from the Beehive deli in the nearest village, East Dean, a drive away, before climbing stairs to the lantern to marvel at the 365-degree views of a star-filled sky. 'Breakfast was superb. I had a full English that included two sausages, which we put in a doggy bag for lunch as the plate was so full.' (RB)

Beachy Head Road
Eastbourne BN20 0AE

T: 01323 423185
E: info@belletout.co.uk
W: belletout.co.uk

BEDROOMS: 6. 5 in house, 1 in lighthouse tower (bunk bed).
OPEN: all year except Christmas/New Year.
FACILITIES: 2 lounges, breakfast room, free Wi-Fi (in some rooms and some public areas), in-room TV (Freeview), terrace, garden, unsuitable for disabled.
BACKGROUND MUSIC: none.
LOCATION: 3 miles W of Eastbourne, 2 miles S of East Dean village (pub, deli).
CHILDREN: not under 16.
DOGS: not allowed.
CREDIT CARDS: MC, Visa.
PRICES: B&B doubles from £175, singles from £122.50. Min. 2 nights, though 1-night bookings may be accepted (check for availability in the week before proposed stay).

SEE ALSO SHORTLIST

EASTON GREY Wiltshire

MAP 3:E5

WHATLEY MANOR

Once you have navigated the joys of this 'rambling building' in honey Cotswold stone, with its 'superb spa', cinema and choice of dining, there are the 26 different 'rooms' in the 'beautiful, well-tended gardens' to explore. Among them are a topiary courtyard, 'charming little retreats', a water feature, and woodland walk. Within, the decor is 'muted, leaning towards the masculine'. Wood panelling, rugs on polished floors, artwork and interesting objets create a 'welcoming' atmosphere in the lounges. For dinner, you can indulge in Niall Keating's two-Michelin-starred 'daring and innovative' taster menu, perhaps halibut with yuzukosho and black truffle, and a chocolate dessert with buttermilk and chamomile, although one reader found the ceremony of 11 courses too lengthy. Alternatively, Grey's Brasserie has a 'sophisticated city' vibe and dishes such as stone bass with mussels. Airy bedrooms have a modern elegance, and welcome with fruit, chocolates and elderflower cordial while under-floor-heated bathrooms have a bath as well as shower. Breakfast is 'beautifully presented' and 'the standard set here is extremely high'.

Easton Grey SN16 0RB

T: 01666 822888
E: reservations@whatleymanor.com
W: whatleymanor.com

BEDROOMS: 23. Some on ground floor, 1 suitable for disabled.
OPEN: all year, dining room Thurs–Sun eve, Grey's Brasserie all week.
FACILITIES: 3 lounges, 2 bars, brasserie, restaurant (vegetarian/vegan menus), cinema, gym, spa, in-room TV (Freeview), EV charging, 12-acres, civil wedding licence, public areas and restaurants wheelchair accessible, adapted toilet.
BACKGROUND MUSIC: in public areas.
LOCATION: 6½ miles from Tetbury.
CHILDREN: not under 12, extra bed £75.
DOGS: in some bedrooms (£30 per night), garden, not restaurant or bar.
CREDIT CARDS: Amex, MC, Visa.
PRICES: B&B doubles from £275. Tasting menu £145, à la carte £50. 1-night bookings usually refused at weekends.

ECKINGTON Worcestershire

MAP 3:D5

ECKINGTON MANOR

On a working farm on the edge of a village surrounded by the River Avon, Judy Gardner's stylish restaurant-with-rooms is also home to a light-filled, state-of-the-art cookery school. Bedrooms, in a timber-frame farmhouse and converted outbuildings, are a mix of stylish contemporary and rural-chic. Some have hand-painted silk wallpaper, others exposed stone, beams and rafters, and antique furniture. All have a Fired Earth shower; a junior suite has a lounge with a log-effect stove, an in-room roll-top bath and separate shower. 'We had an excellent stay in the Grain Barn,' writes a reader this year. 'With views of Bredon Hill and the Malverns, Highland cows and calves, and swallows swooping, it was a tranquil environment.' From Wednesday to Saturday, and at Sunday lunch, Greg Newman's farm-to-fork menus feature local and home-produced ingredients in dishes such as loin of Cotswold lamb, sticky lamb faggot, Evesham broccoli, anchovy and goat's curd. 'Highlights: delicate amuse-bouche, confit cod with pea purée, fine sorbets.' Stratford-upon-Avon is a 45-minute drive, and picnics are available. (Tessa Stuart)

Hammock Road
Eckington WR10 3BJ

T: 01386 751600
E: info@eckingtonmanor.co.uk
W: eckingtonmanor.co.uk

BEDROOMS: 17. All in courtyard annexes, some on ground floor.
OPEN: all year except 25/26 Dec, restaurant closed Sun evening, Mon, Tues.
FACILITIES: lift, 2 sitting rooms (1 with bar area), restaurant, function rooms, in-room TV (Freeview), civil wedding licence, cookery school, 260-acre grounds (lawns, herb garden, orchard, farm), public areas wheelchair accessible, adapted toilet.
BACKGROUND MUSIC: in garden bar and restaurant.
LOCATION: 4 miles SW of Pershore.
CHILDREN: not under 8, extra bed £35.
DOGS: allowed in 1 bedroom, not in public rooms.
CREDIT CARDS: MC, Visa.
PRICES: B&B doubles/single occupancy from £149. Set dinner £48, tasting menus (vegetarian option) £75.

EGTON BRIDGE Yorkshire

MAP 4:C5

BROOM HOUSE
AT EGTON BRIDGE

With views of moors and farmland, this smart farmhouse B&B in an acre of garden feels remote yet is only a ten-minute walk from riverside Egton Bridge. The Victorian building has been stylishly updated with slate floors, light oak doors and soothing Farrow & Ball colours: 'modern, clean and well thought through'. Bedrooms have a contemporary 'cottagey yet uncluttered feel' with pale-painted or pine furniture, creamy walls – an occasional feature wallpaper – and modern bathroom. All have garden and moorland views; the second-floor, beamed rooms have the best while the garden suite has a patio. Walk from the doorstep – the coast-to-coast path is half a mile away – and return to tea and cake in the fire-warmed sitting room or on the south-facing terrace, or something stronger from the honesty bar. Village pubs are within walking distance. Breakfast, in the French-windowed dining room, offers cooked-to-order dishes such as avocado and poached egg and a full grill. One reader particularly recommended the local sausages. Throughout guests' stay, the feeling is 'relaxed and peaceful'. (HP, Mary Hewson)

Broom House Lane
Egton Bridge YO21 1XD

T: 07423 636783
E: info@broom-house.co.uk
W: broom-house.co.uk

BEDROOMS: 7. 1 in cottage annexe.
OPEN: Mar–Oct, limited availability Nov–Feb.
FACILITIES: lounge, breakfast room, in-room TV (Freeview), 1-acre garden, unsuitable for disabled.
BACKGROUND MUSIC: in breakfast room.
LOCATION: ½ mile W of village.
CHILDREN: over-12s welcomed.
DOGS: not allowed.
CREDIT CARDS: MC, Visa.
PRICES: B&B doubles from £90, cottage suite from £145. Min. 2-night bookings for summer weekends.

ELLASTONE Staffordshire

MAP 3:B6

THE DUNCOMBE ARMS

With views over Dove valley, this village inn
combines a local feel with smart dining and
country-chic bedrooms. The bar and cosy dining
areas have the usual rural-pub credentials of
low ceilings, open fires, exposed-brick walls and
solid wood tables. Candles, and cushions and
sheepskins on chairs, lend 'intimacy'. The 'high
order' cooking mixes pub classics with more
adventurous Modern British dishes: lamb rump
with miso-baked carrot and ewe's curd, and cod
ceviche with yuzu and white grapes, as well as
home-made burger with bacon jam and cheese
sauce. However, one reader reported that the
choice was 'limited and expensive', the cod ceviche
'barely a mouthful' and 'the muzak was loud'.
Bedrooms, in a barn-style annexe, are stylishly
cosy with chic country furniture, Farrow & Ball
greiges and olive greens, and bright feature
wallpapers. 'One of the nicest hotel rooms we
have ever stayed in.' French windows and a small
patio have 'open views over undulating fields and
woods'. Most of the smart metro-tiled bathrooms
have a bath and shower. Breakfast includes
freshly squeezed juice and scrambled eggs on
home-made sourdough.

Ellastone
Ashbourne DE6 2GZ

T: 01335 324275
E: hello@duncombearms.co.uk
W: duncombearms.co.uk

BEDROOMS: 10. All in Walnut House
annexe, with 2 family rooms, 1
suitable for disabled.
OPEN: all year.
FACILITIES: bar, 2 dining rooms plus
private dining room, in-room TV
(Freeview), no mobile signal, garden
(alfresco dining, fire pit), EV charging,
bar and dining room wheelchair
accessible, adapted toilet.
BACKGROUND MUSIC: quiet in bar and
restaurant.
LOCATION: on B5032, 5 miles SW of
Ashbourne.
CHILDREN: all ages welcomed, under-
12s extra bed £30.
DOGS: allowed in some bedrooms (£20
per night), bar.
CREDIT CARDS: MC, Visa.
PRICES: B&B doubles/singles from
£195. À la carte £32–£40.

ELLERBY Yorkshire

MAP 4:C5

THE ELLERBY COUNTRY INN

In a quiet Yorkshire village, a mile from lovely Runswick Bay and on the edge of the North York Moors, this country inn is a beacon of good service, and is great value, too. Mark and Georgie Alderson seem to have thought of everything that outdoor-loving guests might want for a comfortable stay. Family and dog-friendly, the sandstone inn, with its climbing roses and window boxes, offers neat and fuss-free bedrooms with breezy colours and light oak furniture. All have fresh milk, robes and king- or super-king-size beds while modern bathrooms, most with bath as well as shower (be aware, the shower-only ones are small), have Elemis products. The best share a balcony overlooking an inviting garden with colourful planters, and sturdy wooden tables and chairs for alfresco dining. Or you can relax in a 'pretty and very comfortable residents' lounge in a conservatory'. Food, served in both bar and restaurant, includes 'superior' pub classics from home-made beef lasagne and pies to steaks and Whitby scampi, and there are good vegetarian options. Staff are 'keen to ensure you have everything you need'. (LW)

12–14 Ryeland Lane
Ellerby
Whitby TS13 5LP

T: 01947 840342
E: relax@ellerbyhotel.co.uk
W: ellerbyhotel.co.uk

BEDROOMS: 10. 4 on ground floor, 1 suitable for disabled.
OPEN: all year except Christmas Day.
FACILITIES: bar, snug, restaurant, conservatory/lounge, garden, in-room TV (Sky), public rooms wheelchair accessible, adapted toilet.
BACKGROUND MUSIC: in public areas.
LOCATION: in village, 8 miles W of Whitby.
CHILDREN: all ages welcomed, under-5s free, extra bed from £20.
DOGS: allowed in 3 bedrooms (£7.50 per night), garden and lounge/conservatory, not in bar or restaurant.
CREDIT CARDS: MC, Visa.
PRICES: B&B doubles from £105, singles from £75. À la carte 3-course £29.

ERMINGTON Devon

MAP 1:D4

♛PLANTATION HOUSE

César award: small hotel of the year

It's the commitment to cooking as much as possible on site that distinguishes this small hotel, occupying a former Georgian rectory in the rolling South Hams countryside, between rugged Dartmoor and the beautiful Erme estuary. Chef/patron Richard Hendey and John Raines create 'very tasty, well-cooked and well-presented' meals, with breads, pastries, ice cream and truffles produced on the premises. Some ingredients come from the kitchen garden, others are foraged or fished from nearby waters. A nightly-changing menu of Devon produce might include crisp-skinned, slow-cooked duckling, caramelised St Clement's jus and wild garlic dauphinoise. There's more food in the modern, 'very comfortable and well-appointed' bedrooms, with home-made cakes, biscuits and fruit as well as garden flowers. The 'excellent breakfast' runs the gamut from fruit and granola, with 'special yogurt and very tasty home-made bread', through smoked haddock and bubble and squeak, to the full Monty ('also delicious'). Guests pay half-price green fees at Bigbury Golf Club, while fishing, sailing, falconry and horse riding are all possible nearby. (Max Lickfold, SH)

Totnes Road
Ermington
Plymouth PL21 9NS

T: 01548 831100
E: info@plantationhousehotel.co.uk
W: plantationhousehotel.co.uk

BEDROOMS: 8.
OPEN: all year, restaurant (dinner only) closed some Sun evenings.
FACILITIES: lounge/bar, 2 dining rooms, in-room TV (Freeview), in-room massage, terrace, 1-acre garden, restaurant, bar and lounge wheelchair accessible, no adapted toilet.
BACKGROUND MUSIC: background jazz (sometimes live) in public rooms, classical 'when suitable'.
LOCATION: 10 miles E of Plymouth.
CHILDREN: all ages welcomed, extra bed £15.
DOGS: allowed in 1 bedroom (no charge), not in public rooms.
CREDIT CARDS: Amex, MC, Visa.
PRICES: B&B doubles from £145, single occupancy discounts. Set dinner £44.50. 1-night bookings sometimes refused on bank holiday weekends.

EVERSHOT Dorset

MAP 1:C6

THE ACORN INN

You can sink a pint of Durdle Door in the oak-panelled bar in the village inn that furnished Thomas Hardy with his 'Sow and Acorn' in Tess of the d'Urbervilles, then stay the night in one of the bedrooms named on a Hardy theme. As well as a 'great atmosphere', acorn motifs are everywhere, from a carved four-poster to the fireplace in the bar. A reader found staff 'extremely helpful' in planning a family celebration. Tess room, with an antique four-poster, proved 'smallish, but had a bay window and was entirely adequate', although 'the shower cabinet was slightly antiquated'. The loft suite was 'ideal for two adults, two teenagers and dog'. In the restaurant, with its floral furnishings, 'food was superb', with 'very tasty soups, memorable twice-baked Cornish crab and Yarg cheese soufflé'. Another reader, though, judged dinner only as 'ok', although agreed that 'breakfast was good'. 'Excellent fruit salad, delicious choice on the cooked menu.' There's a skittle alley in the pub, which is part of the Red Carnation group, and for £15 guests have use of the spa at sister hotel Summer Lodge (next entry). (Jane Thornton, and others)

28 Fore Street
Evershot DT2 0JW

т: 01935 83228
E: stay@acorn-inn.co.uk
w: acorn-inn.co.uk

BEDROOMS: 10.
OPEN: all year.
FACILITIES: 2 bars, restaurant, lounge, in-room TV (Sky, Freeview), skittle alley, beer garden, access to spa, gym at sister hotel opposite (£15 per day), parking, bar and restaurant wheelchair accessible, toilet not adapted.
BACKGROUND MUSIC: in bar and restaurant.
LOCATION: in village, 10 miles S of Yeovil.
CHILDREN: all ages welcomed, extra bed £20, childen's menu.
DOGS: allowed by prior arrangement in bedrooms (£12 a night with towels and treats), public areas, not restaurant.
CREDIT CARDS: Amex, MC, Visa.
PRICES: B&B doubles from £115. À la carte £40. Min. 2-night stay at weekends during peak season.

EVERSHOT Dorset

MAP 1:C6

SUMMER LODGE

When the Earl of Ilchester hired a certain Thomas
Hardy to extend his Georgian dower house, he
could not have foreseen the praise it would receive
as an 'extremely well-run, very comfortable,
welcoming hotel with first-class food' (Relais
& Châteaux) and spa. 'Staff are a true delight,'
write readers. 'Our room was superbly furnished
in true country house style' with 'good tea and
coffee, yummy shortbread'. Other readers were
disappointed by the view of parked cars from a
ground-floor coach house room, but beds were
'supremely comfortable', the bathroom 'splendid,
bright and spacious'. A newly 'reimagined' garden
suite has a conservatory, seating for private dining
and original artwork, including a Matisse. Steven
Titman's dishes win rave reviews. 'My starter of
wild mushroom wontons and spring rolls in miso
broth was one of the tastiest ever, and mum was
ecstatic about her main course lamb noisettes.'
'The breads were amazing.' If you want to eat
more casually, stroll to sister property The Acorn
Inn (previous entry). For lunch, maybe picnic in
the lovely gardens with tennis court. (Barbara and
Ian Dewey, Jill Cox, and others)

9 Fore Street
Evershot DT2 0JR

T: 01935 482000
E: summerlodge@rchmail.com
W: summerlodgehotel.com

BEDROOMS: 25. 6 in coach house, 4 in
courtyard, 5 in cottages, 1 on ground
floor suitable for disabled.
OPEN: all year.
FACILITIES: lounge, drawing room,
restaurant, conservatory, meeting
room, in-room TV (Sky), indoor
pool, spa, civil wedding licence, 4-acre
grounds (tennis), EV charging, public
rooms wheelchair accessible, adapted
toilet.
BACKGROUND MUSIC: in bar/whisky
lounge.
LOCATION: 10 miles S of Yeovil.
CHILDREN: all ages welcomed, cots
£25, extra bed £50, children's menu.
DOGS: allowed in some bedrooms
(£20 per dog per night, max. 2 dogs
per room), whisky lounge.
CREDIT CARDS: Amex, MC, Visa.
PRICES: B&B doubles from £235.
À la carte £65. 1-night bookings
sometimes refused.

EXETER Devon

MAP 1:C5

SOUTHERNHAY HOUSE

⚜ Previous César winner

The supremely elegant porticoed entrance of this
Grade II listed Georgian town house is a hint that
Southernhay offers a sophisticated and individual
take on a city centre hotel. Owners Deborah Clark
and Tony Orchard have created an elegant but
unstuffy atmosphere, combining original features
with sleek, modern decor. Soft Farrow & Ball
colours, quirky antiques and designer furniture
give a low-key luxurious feel. 'For such a stylish
hotel,' comments our inspector, 'the warmth was
unusually welcoming.' Bedrooms are uncluttered
spaces with large sash windows overlooking
gardens, hand-made beds and a mix of antique
and modern furnishings. A swish new apartment
is more minimalist. Bathrooms are contemporary;
smaller rooms are shower only, larger ones have
roll-top baths. Evenings kick off with a drink in
the classy cocktail bar, recently extended with a
glass pavilion. Dinner includes reliable classics
such as Devon rib-eye steak as well as lighter
dishes such as fresh tagliatelle with prawns.
'Beautifully presented' breakfasts range from
eggs and field mushrooms to buttermilk pancakes
and the full grill.

36 Southernhay East
Exeter EX1 1NX

T: 01392 439000
E: home@southernhayhouse.com
W: southernhayhouse.com

BEDROOMS: 12. 1 apartment in separate
building.
OPEN: all year.
FACILITIES: bar, restaurant, private
dining, in-room TV (Freeview),
small lawn, veranda, terrace, civil
wedding licence, street parking (free
overnight), car parks (fee), public
rooms wheelchair accessible.
BACKGROUND MUSIC: in public areas.
LOCATION: central Exeter.
CHILDREN: over-14s welcomed on an
adult basis.
DOGS: only in garden and on terrace.
CREDIT CARDS: MC, Visa.
PRICES: B&B doubles from £161.
À la carte £38.

EXMOUTH Devon

MAP 1:D5

LYMPSTONE MANOR

You cannot yet pop a cork from the sparkling wine made with grapes from the vineyard planted by Michelin-starred chef Michael Caines at his Georgian manor house in parkland on the Exe estuary, but you can drink deep of the good life. This is an utterly indulgent hotel. Even the cheapest garden-view rooms have a modern four-poster, a gin tray, coffee machine and hair straighteners. More expensive estuary-facing suites have a private terrace with a fire pit and soaking tub. Heron has side-by-side copper slipper baths and walk-in shower, Greenfinch a private garden. All are elegant, adorned with watercolours by local artist Rachel Toll, drawing inspiration from the landscape and wildlife. In a kind of Hameau de la Reine, shepherd huts sleeping up to five guests have a lounge and kitchenette – but you don't come here to cook. Michael Caines's set-price à la carte and tasting menus showcase his talent with the best of Devon produce in dishes such as Darts Farm loin of lamb, courgette and basil purée, ratatouille, roasted garlic, split lamb jus. 'An outstanding hotel – the setting, the rooms, the service and especially the food.' (A and PM)

Courtlands Lane
Exmouth EX8 3NZ

T: 01395 202040
E: welcome@lympstonemanor.co.uk
W: lympstonemanor.co.uk

BEDROOMS: 27. 5 on ground floor, 1 suitable for disabled. 6 shepherd huts.
OPEN: all year.
FACILITIES: 3 dining rooms (vegetarian/vegan menus) reception lounge, lounge, bar, 28-acre grounds, in-room TV (Freeview), civil wedding licence, EV charging, public areas wheelchair accessible, adapted toilet.
BACKGROUND MUSIC: all day in public rooms.
LOCATION: in centre, close to waterfront.
CHILDREN: all ages welcomed, extra bed £60 (no under-6s in restaurant).
DOGS: in 2 bedrooms and shepherd huts (£30 a night), not in main house.
CREDIT CARDS: Amex, MC, Visa.
PRICES: B&B doubles from £288, singles from £268. Tasting menus £150–£160, à la carte £140 (discretionary service charge of 12½%).

FAVERSHAM Kent

MAP 2:D5

READ'S

♀ Previous César winner

A Georgian manor house on the edge of a small market town close to the north Kent coast is home to Rona and David Pitchford's long-established restaurant-with-rooms. In 2020, after 45 years at the stove, David took a step back, and Frederick Forster was lured from the City to head the kitchen, but the style and ethos are timeless. To stay at this 'very special place' is 'like paying a visit to another era'. The bedrooms are in 'traditional country house style, with no modern boutique touches'. One has a four-poster, one a half-tester bed. On the landing there is 'a small pantry to make tea or coffee or buy drinks'. The staff are 'professional and delightful', the owners very present, with a sense of 'everything perfectly orchestrated'. In the dining rooms there is 'a feeling of space and of not being hurried'. Linger over roast loin of Kentish lamb with broad beans and fennel and red pepper purée; or potato gnocchi fricassée with vegetables from the kitchen garden and pumpkin velouté. 'In these penny-pinching times, one is being given, most generously and unusually, the room to breathe.' (ID, and others)

Macknade Manor
Canterbury Road
Faversham ME13 8XE

T: 01795 535344
E: enquiries@reads.com
W: reads.com

BEDROOMS: 6.
OPEN: all year Tues–Sat, except 4 days at Christmas, first 2 weeks Jan, 2 weeks Sept.
FACILITIES: sitting room/bar, 4 dining rooms, in-room TV (Freeview), civil wedding licence, 4-acre garden (terrace, outdoor dining), restaurant wheelchair accessible, toilet adapted.
BACKGROUND MUSIC: none.
LOCATION: ½ mile SE of Faversham.
CHILDREN: all ages welcomed, on sofa bed in one room, £40.
DOGS: allowed in bedrooms only (no charge).
CREDIT CARDS: MC, Visa.
PRICES: B&B doubles from £210, singles from £195. Set-price lunch £35, tasting menu £45, dinner £65, tasting menu £75.

FELIXKIRK Yorkshire

MAP 4:C4

THE CARPENTERS ARMS

A successful blend of the traditional and the modern can be found at this smart village inn, with views over the Vale of York, chalet-style bedrooms, and classy food. The beamed and flagged bar, with its copper pans and wood-burning stove, mixes scrubbed-wood tables with elegant dining chairs and pea-green walls. You can dine here, in the restaurant or on the heated terrace on food that is strong on local products, including those from its own kitchen garden. Menus mix pub classics such as steaks and posh home-made pie with more considered dishes such as sesame-crusted hake with Thai coconut sauce, or chicken with garlic and saffron aïoli. You can choose either a 'cosy' and 'rustic' bedroom in the pub or a larger and lighter, chalet-style room with glass doors to a patio and landscaped garden. There's a fire for chillier days, space for a sofa, and under-floor heating in the modern bathroom. Dogs are welcome, and some of the rooms are interconnecting for families. Breakfast includes home-grown fresh fruit salad, eggs Benedict and a full grill with vegetarian option – plus those wonderful views.

Felixkirk
Thirsk YO7 2DP

T: 01845 537369
E: enquiries@
    thecarpentersarmsfelixkirk.com
W: thecarpentersarmsfelixkirk.com

BEDROOMS: 10. 8 in single-storey garden annexe, 1 suitable for disabled.
OPEN: all year.
FACILITIES: bar/sitting area, restaurant, private dining room, in-room TV (Freeview), partially covered and heated terrace, garden, public rooms on ground floor wheelchair accessible, adapted toilet.
BACKGROUND MUSIC: at mealtimes in bar and restaurant.
LOCATION: in village, 3 miles NE of Thirsk.
CHILDREN: all ages welcomed, extra bed £30.
DOGS: welcomed in garden bedrooms (£10 a night), in bar.
CREDIT CARDS: Amex, MC, Visa.
PRICES: B&B doubles from £165, singles from £153. À la carte £32.

FLEET Dorset

MAP 1:D6

MOONFLEET MANOR

'An excellent place for a family reunion with young children', this Georgian manor house above Chesil beach, on Dorset's Jurassic coast, has a seriously impressive list of facilities. A huge indoor play area houses a skittle alley, climbing wall, indoor football, trampolines, mini-golf, and much more. There are three pools, and a spa, squash and snooker for the adults. Add in an Ofsted crèche, high tea for tiny tots and even baby-listening, and everyone is happy. The hotel is part of the Luxury Family Hotels group (see also Woolley Grange, Bradford-on-Avon, and Fowey Hall, Fowey). This year it's benefited from a spruce-up of its three spacious lounges, adding a contemporary touch to the 'very homely, welcoming atmosphere'. Bedrooms, in a variety of sizes, are next in line for a make-over, though no date has been set. In the restaurant, the menus have something for even the pickiest eater. Imaginative dishes might include Brixham crab, prawn and chilli linguine, slow-braised beef cannelloni with beef broth and truffle oil. 'Easy to have an evening meal with our grandchild, who was treated with great consideration and respect.' (DG)

Fleet Road
Fleet DT3 4ED

T: 01305 786948
E: info@moonfleetmanorhotel.co.uk
W: moonfleetmanorhotel.co.uk

BEDROOMS: 36. 3 in coach house, 3 in villa, 3 ground floor.
OPEN: all year.
FACILITIES: 3 lounges, restaurant, playroom, crèche, cinema, in-room TV (Freeview), civil wedding licence, indoor swimming pools, 5-acre garden, EV charging, public areas wheelchair accessible, no adapted toilet.
BACKGROUND MUSIC: in restaurant.
LOCATION: 7 miles W of Weymouth.
CHILDREN: all ages welcomed, no charge for extra beds, last entrance for children in dining room 7.30 pm.
DOGS: allowed in bedrooms (£15 a night), on lead in public rooms, not in restaurant
CREDIT CARDS: Amex, MC, Visa.
PRICES: B&B doubles from £109. À la carte £38. 1- and 2-night bookings sometimes refused weekends.

FOWEY Cornwall

MAP 1:D3

FOWEY HALL

♕ Previous César winner

A new 'cool contemporary look' combines with 'a huge sense of fun' at this Victorian mansion on a hilltop with 'beautiful views' over the Fowey estuary, fondly believed to have been Kenneth Grahame's model for Toad Hall. 'Period features such as baroque plasterwork and wood panelling are offset with light, modern decor and lovely details everywhere.' Rabbit figurines peer from lamps, the games room has a dramatic blue vaulted ceiling, and cloth dog heads hang on bedroom walls. Run by Luxury Family Hotels (see also Moonfleet Manor, Fleet, and Woolley Grange, Bradford-on-Avon), it is 'perfect for multi-generational visits'. Everyone is happy as clams with flexible dining, family rooms, a crèche, cinema, Wind in the Willows-themed playground, a spa and pool. Start the day with 'a delicious full English on the terrace', then explore nearby Readymoney Cove. In the dining room, menus feature a wide choice of dishes, with good vegan options. 'The crab linguine oozed flavour and freshness.' Smart bedrooms have restored antique and bespoke furniture. 'I was delighted to find a teapot as well as fresh milk in the fridge, delicious shortbread shaped like a crab.' (JK)

Hanson Drive
Fowey PL23 1ET

T: 01726 833866
E: info@foweyhallhotel.co.uk
W: foweyhallhotel.co.uk

BEDROOMS: 36. 8 in courtyard, some on ground floor, 1 suitable for disabled.
OPEN: all year.
FACILITIES: 2 lounges, library, restaurant, in-room TV (Freeview), crèche, billiard room, games rooms, civil wedding licence, spa, indoor pool, 5-acre grounds, EV charging, public rooms wheelchair accessible, adapted toilet.
BACKGROUND MUSIC: in bar, lounge, restaurant.
LOCATION: ½ mile from town centre.
CHILDREN: all ages welcomed, no charge for extra beds.
DOGS: allowed in house bedrooms (£15 a night), in lounge, not restaurant.
CREDIT CARDS: Amex, MC, Visa.
PRICES: B&B doubles from £179, family from £319. Dinner à la carte £42. 1-night bookings refused some weekends.

FOWEY Cornwall

MAP 1:D3

THE OLD QUAY HOUSE   [NEW]

Even Daphne du Maurier in her quaint house, Ferryside, did not enjoy better views of the Fowey estuary than guests have from this whitewashed former Victorian seaman's refuge. Today a 'beautiful little hotel', offering a 'friendly welcome', it is promoted from the Shortlist at the urging of readers, with particular praise for general manager Amarni Willetts: 'She handled a visit there with efficiency, incredible friendliness and ease.' Bedrooms have restful paintwork, with lots of soft greys, blues and white. Each has a shower room, a power shower, luxury toiletries, bathrobes – and macs and umbrellas. Several have a balcony. The loft is a suite with a futon, a slipper bath and walk-in shower, a lounge from which to watch the boats. The restaurant opens on to the terrace projecting over the water. Eat inside or out, maybe a lunch of mussels or a cream tea. At night chef Richard Massey's modern British menus include dishes such as Kilhallon beef fillet, herb-crusted hake, thyme gnocchi. Fowey is 'a beautiful town', with narrow streets of medieval and Georgian houses – 'like the gateway to another world', in du Maurier's words.

28 Fore Street
Fowey PL23 1AQ

T: 01726 833302
E: info@theoldquayhouse.com
W: theoldquayhouse.com

BEDROOMS: 13.
OPEN: all year.
FACILITIES: open-plan lounge, bar, restaurant, in-room TV (Freeview), civil wedding licence, terrace, parking permits supplied, bar, lounge and restaurant wheelchair accessible.
BACKGROUND MUSIC: in public areas.
LOCATION: town centre.
CHILDREN: not under 12.
DOGS: not allowed.
CREDIT CARDS: Amex, MC, Visa.
PRICES: B&B doubles from £250, singles from £210. Set-price dinner £37.50/£45 (2/3 courses).

GITTISHAM Devon

MAP 1:C5

THE PIG AT COMBE

'Down country lanes and a mile-long private drive', this Elizabethan manor house is the Miss Piggy among Robin Hutson's quirky country house hotels (see index). Like that porcine diva, it embodies fabulosity with a dash of irresistibility and a great big dollop of attitude. Choose a room to suit you, from a main-house double with a monsoon shower, to a rustic family suite in the stable yard, with king-size four-poster, freestanding bath and monsoon shower, bunks for the kids. Artfully scruffy interiors by Judy Hutson mix Zoffany fabrics with brocante finds from Paris, antiques and oil paintings. 'Our comfy luxe room was one of the few twins with a bath not in the bedroom.' There is a panelled bar with roaring fire, a 'lovely dining room' with a rococo plasterwork ceiling and mullioned windows. The menus of home-grown and local produce (from within a 25-mile radius) might feature Lyme Bay hake or 28-day-aged Dartmoor rump steak, or flatbreads alfresco in the 'stunning and vast grounds'. One reader felt the food was 'good but not special' but noted that breakfast was 'all home made with no prepacked items'. (MG, DB, and others)

Gittisham
Honiton EX14 3AD

T: 01404 540400
E: info@thepigatcombe.com
W: thepighotel.com

BEDROOMS: 30. 10 in stable yard, 5 in cottages (2 for family), 3 rooms suitable for disabled.
OPEN: all year.
FACILITIES: bar, 2 lounges, restaurant, Folly (communal dining), private dining rooms, in-room TV (Freeview), civil wedding licence, spa treatment rooms, 3,500-acre grounds, public rooms wheelchair accessible, adapted toilet.
BACKGROUND MUSIC: in public areas.
LOCATION: on outskirts of village.
CHILDREN: all ages welcomed, no charge for extra beds.
DOGS: not allowed.
CREDIT CARDS: Amex, MC, Visa.
PRICES: room-only doubles from £175, family from £305. Breakfast £10–£15, à la carte £35. 1-night bookings sometimes refused.

GRANTHAM Lincolnshire

THE BROWNLOW ARMS

Behind the door of this ironstone 19th-century village pub are chic country house interiors, buzzing dining rooms, homely bedrooms and an exuberant host. Lorraine Willoughby, who runs the pub with husband Paul, charms guests with her warmth, enthusiasm and efficiency, flitting between tables in one of the beamed dining areas. Understated and elegant, with grey-panelled walls, linen-covered chairs and white napery, these rooms feel intimate, as does the bar with its armchairs, fireplace and glowing table lamps. 'Excellent quality' food, cooked with confidence but without fuss, might include pan-roasted duck breast with cherry ketchup and salt-baked celeriac, and salmon with lemon and dill risotto, accompanied by a 'small but interesting' wine list. Bedrooms are homely affairs with pretty wallpapers, solid country furniture, good-quality fabrics and village or countryside views. One is cosily tucked under the eaves; another is in a separate barn conversion. 'Breakfast is promptly served and piping hot.' 'Within easy reach of the A1, it's well worth the detour.' (R and J Grimley, RG)

Grantham Road
Hough-on-the-Hill
Grantham NG32 2AZ

T: 01400 250234
E: armsinn@yahoo.co.uk
W: thebrownlowarms.com

BEDROOMS: 5. 1 on ground floor in barn conversion.
OPEN: all year except for all public holidays, incl. 25/26 Dec, Mon all day, Sun eve, Tues–Sat lunch.
FACILITIES: bar, 3 dining rooms (vegetarian menu), patio, in-room TV (Freeview), unsuitable for disabled.
BACKGROUND MUSIC: in public areas.
LOCATION: rural, in village 7 miles N of Grantham.
CHILDREN: all ages welcomed, extra bed £15, no under-8s in restaurant in the evening.
DOGS: only guide dogs allowed.
CREDIT CARDS: MC, Visa.
PRICES: B&B doubles from £140, singles from £85. À la carte £45.

GRASMERE Cumbria

MAP 4: inset C2

FOREST SIDE

⚜ Previous César winner

This Victorian Gothic mansion continues to delight guests with its stylish, laid-back atmosphere, enormous wooded gardens and inspired culinary creations. 'The food fully deserves its Michelin star,' declares one reader. Paul Leonard turns out dishes of startling combinations such as beef tartare with caviar and smoked bone marrow, and beetroot with yogurt, juniper and smoked roe. Vegetarian menus get equal billing; much produce comes from the walled potager. High-ceilinged public rooms are cool and airy in shades of grey jazzed up with bold wallpapers, velvet-covered sofas and modern art. The dining room makes the most of the garden views – spot the red squirrels during a cooked-to-order breakfast. 'First-rate' bedrooms are 'light, spacious and elegant' with Zoffany fabrics, Herdwick wool carpets, beds by local company Harrison Spinks, and Bramley plant-based toiletries in the limestone-tiled bathrooms. There are hikes from the doorstep, while Grasmere is just ten minutes away across the fields. A 'wonderful place to stay; we'll be back'. (Tony Hall, John and Kay Patterson)

Keswick Road
Grasmere LA22 9RN

T: 01539 435250
E: info@theforestside.com
W: theforestside.com

BEDROOMS: 20. 1 suitable for disabled.
OPEN: all year, restaurant closed Mon/Tues dinner, Mon–Thurs lunch, hotel closed Mon/Tues Nov–end Mar.
FACILITIES: lounge, bar, restaurant (vegetarian menu), function/private dining rooms, civil wedding licence, in-room TV (Freeview), terrace, 43-acre grounds, public rooms wheelchair accessible, adapted toilet.
BACKGROUND MUSIC: in public areas.
LOCATION: outskirts of village.
CHILDREN: all ages welcomed, extra bed £50, under-8s not allowed in dining room in evening.
DOGS: allowed in some bedrooms (max. 2 per room, £25 per dog, welcome pack).
CREDIT CARDS: Amex, MC, Visa.
PRICES: B&B doubles from £259. Tasting menu (for overnight guests) 4-course £50, 8-course £95.

SEE ALSO SHORTLIST

GRASMERE Cumbria

MAP 4: inset C2

THE GRASMERE HOTEL

⍟ Previous César winner

The praise keeps on coming for this family-run hotel, a 'little gem' loved for its comfort, food and welcome in postcard-pretty Grasmere. The Winslands – Kevin, Nicki and two daughters – are 'so professional and hands-on', says one reader. Their 'splendid and stylish' Victorian country house, with views to iconic Helm Crag, has a quiet garden bordering the River Rothay. Two 'beautifully decorated' lounges, both with fires, are ideal for relaxing after a day's walking or for studying the menu over drinks and canapés. 'Delicious and varied' dishes might include Herdwick lamb with rainbow courgettes and garden pea purée, and supreme of salmon with watercress velouté and poached heritage beets. The 'beautifully set' dining room with 'starched cloths and napkins', overlooking the garden, charmed readers as did the home-made bread. Breakfast 'matched the quality' of dinner with smoked salmon and haddock as well as full Cumbrian and vegetarian options, plus home-made preserves. 'Spotless' bedrooms have breezy colours, feature walls and simple furnishings with 'bright, modern' bathrooms. 'We will definitely return.' (Frances Coupe, ID)

Broadgate
Grasmere LA22 9TA

T: 01539 435277
E: info@grasmerehotel.co.uk
W: grasmerehotel.co.uk

BEDROOMS: 11. Some on ground floor.
OPEN: all year except 31 Dec–31 Jan.
FACILITIES: two lounges, restaurant, in-room TV (Freeview), ½-acre garden, unsuitable for disabled.
BACKGROUND MUSIC: in lounge and restaurant during mealtimes.
LOCATION: in village.
CHILDREN: aged 10 and over welcomed.
DOGS: not allowed.
CREDIT CARDS: MC, Visa.
PRICES: D,B&B doubles from £196, singles from £103. Set 3-course dinner £37.50. 2-night min. stay normally required (check for 1-night availability).

SEE ALSO SHORTLIST

GRASSINGTON Yorkshire   MAP 4:D3

GRASSINGTON HOUSE

Overlooking the cobbled square in one of
the Dales' most attractive villages, this smart
restaurant-with-rooms combines chic bedrooms
and creative food with a warm Yorkshire
welcome. Sue and John Rudden's handsome
Georgian house looks traditional, but the interiors
are sleek and stylish: stripped-wood floor, sea-blue
velvet seats and lemon-panelled walls in the bar;
and a bistro-style conservatory dining room with
contemporary lighting, burnished mirrors and
shimmery silver wallpaper. Luxurious bedrooms
are striking with oversized headboards, designer
wallpapers and chandeliers. Decadent touches
might include a gold-painted French-style bed
or in-room roll-top bath. Even smaller rooms
have a village view; all have home-made biscuits,
water and modern bathrooms. After a day's
walking, have a drink on the buzzy terrace
before enjoying John's creative food: inventive
dishes might include seared sea bass with charred
leeks and parsley nage, or pheasant Wellington
with beetroots, thyme lentils and blueberry jus.
Generous breakfasts include freshly squeezed
juices, home-smoked salmon, and bacon and
sausages from their own pigs.

5 The Square
Grassington
Skipton BD23 5AQ

T: 01756 752406
E: bookings@grassingtonhouse.co.uk
W: grassingtonhouse.co.uk

BEDROOMS: 9.
OPEN: all year except 25 Dec (24 Dec,
meals only), closed Mon/Tues, ring to
check Jan dates.
FACILITIES: bar, restaurant, outside
dining pod, in-room TV, civil
wedding licence, function facilities,
terrace, public rooms wheelchair
accessible.
BACKGROUND MUSIC: in public areas.
LOCATION: in village square, 16 mins'
drive from Skipton.
CHILDREN: all ages welcomed, free cot,
extra bed £35.
DOGS: allowed in bar and terrace only.
CREDIT CARDS: MC, Visa.
PRICES: B&B doubles from £135, singles
from £117.50. À la carte £40.

GREAT MASSINGHAM Norfolk

MAP 2:A5

THE DABBLING DUCK

NEW

Overlooking the green in a village known for its numerous duck ponds, the old Rose and Crown was facing conversion into housing in 2006 when two local farmers stepped up. In 2013 they brought in Mark Dobby, an industry pro, no dabbler, who now presides with his wife, Sally. 'It is a good gastropub with very satisfactory rooms,' write Guide inspectors, 'very dog- and baby-welcoming.' There are six rooms over the pub, two larger ones in an annexe. 'A friendly lad took us to our garden room. It had interesting decor, a super-king bed, a large bathroom with a rain shower over the bath, a tea/cafetière tray and biscuits.' You can eat in 'nooks in the old pub, in a library with comfy sofas and a wood-burning stove, a conservatory, or the barn with pizza ovens'. Dale Smith cooks modern pub fare, with meat and game from local smallholdings and Shorthorn beef from the owners' land. 'We enjoyed the cured trout with pickled vegetables, Cromer crab with potato salad, and the inevitable duck accompanied by deep-fried polenta and rich reduced blackberry sauce', served by 'well-trained, efficient, friendly, engaging young staff'.

11 Abbey Road
Great Massingham
King's Lynn PE32 2HN

T: 01485 520827
E: info@thedabblingduck.co.uk
W: thedabblingduck.co.uk

BEDROOMS: 8. 2 on ground floor in garden annexe.
OPEN: all year.
FACILITIES: bar, 3 private dining rooms, hallway/library, in-room TV, barn and garden (pizza oven, alfresco dining).
BACKGROUND MUSIC: jazz and soul throughout the building.
LOCATION: in village 13 miles E of King's Lynn.
CHILDREN: all ages welcomed, extra bed £20, children's menu, play castle.
DOGS: allowed in 2 bedrooms by arrangement (£10 per night, doggy menu), in bar and 1 dining room.
CREDIT CARDS: MC, Visa.
PRICES: B&B doubles from £140, single occupancy from £130. À la carte £30.

GREAT MILTON Oxfordshire   MAP 2:C3

LE MANOIR AUX QUAT'SAISONS

A man for all seasons, Raymond Blanc has created something beautiful at this 15th-century manor house where he has held two Michelin stars since 1984. 'From the minute you draw up at the honey-stone building with its prolific lavender, everything is perfect,' says a Guide insider. Bedrooms, some with private garden, draw inspiration from Blanc's travels (around the world and through life). Vettriano has deep red walls, Venetian masks; Snow Queen a four-poster and purple silk wallpaper printed with snowflakes. 'This is a wonderful hotel,' writes a reader whose 'enormous room with a giant bath and bathroom' had a real log fire. The gardens, with wild-flower meadow, mushroom valley, orchard and organic potager, supply a wealth of fresh heritage produce for the set menus. 'There were some outstanding items: artichoke hearts in tiny dice with truffles; a soupe au pistou that shows how simple ingredients can be elevated to an extraordinary level; delicious apple and Calvados sorbet.' 'If you're lucky enough to be there when Blanc is around, you're in for a treat – he stops and speaks at length to his guests.' Expensive but worth it.

Church Road
Great Milton OX44 7PD

T: 01844 278881
E: lemanoir@belmond.com
W: belmond.com

BEDROOMS: 32. 22 in garden buildings, some on ground floor, 1 suitable for disabled.
OPEN: all year, restaurant closed for lunch Mon–Wed.
FACILITIES: 2 lounges, champagne bar, restaurant (vegetarian/vegan menus), private dining room, in-room TV (Sky, BT, Freeview), cookery school, civil wedding licence, 27-acre grounds, EV charging, public rooms wheelchair accessible, adapted toilet.
BACKGROUND MUSIC: in some public areas.
LOCATION: 8 miles SE of Oxford.
CHILDREN: all ages welcomed, extra bed £65.
DOGS: allowed in some bedrooms (£20 a night) and public rooms.
CREDIT CARDS: Amex, MC, Visa.
PRICES: B&B doubles from £590. Set menus lunch £155, dinner £194, child £25.

HALNAKER Sussex

THE OLD STORE

A popular B&B in a former Georgian village bakery close to Goodwood in the South Downs has enthusiastic new owners who have been busy updating the place, inside and out. Amy and Matt Marshall are welcoming hosts, inviting guests to have a drink with them on arrival, by the fire in the cosy sitting room, or in the sunshine on a new decked terrace in the pretty garden. Bedrooms are a mix of contemporary and cottage style, with perhaps an iron bedstead, floral curtains, pastel walls. Some are under the eaves; others will sleep up to four guests. At breakfast they are happy to rustle up a full vegan, given notice, while porridge with honey, and smashed avocado on toast are already staples on a menu that includes smoked salmon, boiled eggs with soldiers, and a full English with black pudding, mushrooms and tomatoes. It is served in the light-and-airy beamed breakfast room, where cereals, yogurt, granola and fruit are set out on the dresser. Afterwards, you might make a day of it in Chichester, or take a short drive to the sands of West Wittering. Reports, please.

Stane Street
Halnaker
Chichester PO18 0QL

T: 01243 531977
E: info@theoldstoreguesthouse.co.uk
W: theoldstoreguesthouse.co.uk

BEDROOMS: 7. 1 on ground floor with step between bedroom and shower room.
OPEN: all year.
FACILITIES: sitting room, breakfast room, in-room TV (Freeview), parking, ¼-acre garden with seating.
BACKGROUND MUSIC: none.
LOCATION: 4 miles NE of Chichester.
CHILDREN: all ages welcomed, babies and toddlers stay free, extra bed £15 for 3–12s, £25 for over-12s.
DOGS: not allowed.
CREDIT CARDS: Amex, MC, Visa.
PRICES: B&B doubles from £110, singles from £70, family from £135 (higher for Goodwood 'Festival of Speed' and 'Revival' meetings). 1-night bookings refused on some weekends, and some other nights in high season.

HAM Wiltshire

MAP 2:D2

CROWN & ANCHOR

NEW

After being restored with 'a lot of care' by two local families, this village pub, in a 'dear little hamlet' close to Avebury stone circle, is 'a lovely weekend country-break sort of place', say Guide inspectors, who received a warm welcome.

You can swing by for a Detour pale ale in the traditional bar. Meals are served in a tiered dining room or on the covered terrace. From a shortish menu, a tasty meal of 'superb home-made bread, beautifully presented lamb rump, braised neck, pea-and-mint tortellini, then cherry, almond and pistachio sponge with cherry ice cream' was served by jean-clad staff. Bedrooms are approached by a separate entrance. A super-king room had walls painted 'a light olive green, orange lampshades picking up the tones of lovely prints of dissected melons', a small tub chair, 'no wardrobe, just padded hangers on the door, a useful temperature control dial'. A brand-new bathroom had 'a super walk-in shower'. Breakfast, served on 'simple country pottery', brought smoked salmon with (and in) scrambled eggs, 'lovely toast of real bread, good coffee'. Overall, 'very good value. We enjoyed our stay.'

Ham
Hungerford SN8 3RB

T: 01488 503040
E: info@crownandanchorham.co.uk
W: crownandanchorham.co.uk

BEDROOMS: 5.
OPEN: all year, closed Sun dinner, Mon, Tues.
FACILITIES: bar, restaurant, private dining room/breakfast room, beer garden, dining terrace, in-room TV, parking.
BACKGROUND MUSIC: 'nothing too loud'.
LOCATION: in centre of village.
CHILDREN: all ages welcomed, extra bed £10 per stay.
DOGS: allowed (£10 per stay), beds, towels, treats provided.
CREDIT CARDS: MC, Visa.
PRICES: B&B doubles from £110, singles from £90. À la carte £35.

HAMBLETON Rutland

MAP 2:B3

HAMBLETON HALL

🏆 Previous César winner

'We have been staying at Hambleton Hall for over 20 years and have never been disappointed; the service is impeccable, the room immaculate, and the food outstanding.' The praises keep on coming for Tim and Stefa Hart's 'star' Relais & Châteaux hotel, a Victorian mansion which embodies the classic English country house style from its 'stunning manicured gardens' overlooking Rutland Water to its sweep of public rooms with panelled walls, deep sofas and open fires. On arrival, suitcases are whisked away while you settle down to tea and biscuits. Bedrooms are classic country house: rich fabrics and wallpapers, antiques, a roll-top bath, fresh flowers and home-made treats. All have 'uplifting views' of garden or lake and 'exceptionally good' housekeeping. With the UK's longest-held Michelin star, the rich red dining room offers 'magnificent food', such as duck with peanut purée, roast venison with butternut squash and dark chocolate, and quince soufflé with almond ice cream. Service throughout the hotel is 'consistently of a very high standard – it's challenging to find anywhere else that comes near'. (Roderic Rennison, Frances Thomas, AB)

Hambleton
Oakham LE15 8TH

T: 01572 756991
E: hotel@hambletonhall.com
W: hambletonhall.com

BEDROOMS: 17. 2-bedroom suite in cottage.
OPEN: all year.
FACILITIES: lift, hall, drawing room/bar, restaurant (vegetarian menu), 2 private dining rooms, in-room TV, civil wedding licence, 17-acre grounds (tennis, swimming pool, croquet, vegetable garden), EV charging, public rooms wheelchair accessible, no adapted toilet.
BACKGROUND MUSIC: none.
LOCATION: 3 miles SE of Oakham.
CHILDREN: all ages welcomed, cot £25, extra bed £35, no under-5s in restaurant.
DOGS: allowed in bedrooms (£10 per night, not unattended), hall.
CREDIT CARDS: Amex, MC, Visa.
PRICES: B&B doubles from £295, singles from £210. Set dinner £83, tasting menu £98. 1-night bookings normally refused weekends.

HAROME Yorkshire

THE PHEASANT

Overlooking the village pond, this golden-stone group of buildings set around a pretty courtyard ticks all the boxes for country house comforts, memorable food and good service. 'It is as good as ever,' reports a reader this year. Converted from a former blacksmith's and barns, it has a deliciously informal yet stylish air, with bright, colourful lounges and an indoor pool to relax in after a day exploring the North York Moors. Jacquie Silk, the owner, is very much 'involved in the day-to-day running'. Dinners are 'consistently good' and include sophisticated dishes such as smoked haddock ravioli with duck egg yolk, or venison with salt-baked celeriac and fig purée. 'The fish was excellent, and the substantial prawn cocktail starter deserves special mention.' There is a 'good selection of wine by the glass'. Bedrooms, with a modern country house look of bold wallpapers, jazzy headboards and plaid carpets, show good attention to detail: 'complimentary fresh fruit, biscuits and bottled water were appreciated'. Breakfast doesn't disappoint, either – for one guest it proved the 'best ever' eaten in a hotel. (Peter Anderson, and others)

Mill Street
Harome YO62 5JG

T: 01439 771241
E: reservations@thepheasanthotel.
  com
W: thepheasanthotel.com

BEDROOMS: 16. 3 on ground floor, 4 in courtyard, 1 in hotel suitable for disabled.
OPEN: all year.
FACILITIES: bar, lounge, conservatory, restaurant (vegetarian menu), in-room TV (Freeview), civil wedding licence, heated indoor swimming pool, terrace, ½-acre garden, public areas wheelchair accessible, no adapted toilet.
BACKGROUND MUSIC: in public areas.
LOCATION: village centre.
CHILDREN: all ages welcomed, extra bed £40.
DOGS: allowed in 2 bedrooms (£30 per night), on terrace and in garden, not in public rooms.
CREDIT CARDS: MC, Visa.
PRICES: B&B doubles from £190, singles from £105. Tasting menu £55–£75, à la carte £50.

HAROME Yorkshire

MAP 4:D4

THE STAR INN AT HAROME

⚘ Previous César winner

Additional bedrooms in a new barn annexe will delight food lovers keen to bag a bed at this charming thatched village pub near the North York Moors, with its Michelin-starred cooking and quirky style. 'Wonderful', 'quiet and comfortable' bedrooms are tucked away across the road in converted farm buildings – characterful spaces of beams and low windows with country-scene wallpapers, tartan carpets and chunky wooden furniture. Fun objects include old riding boots, and even a piano in one, a pool table in another. Four lighter, more contemporary rooms are in the new barn addition. The lounge, with a hunting-lodge feel and log stove, is a place 'to sink back' with a drink from the honesty bar before enjoying Andrew Pern's 'Modern Yorkshire' cooking. Championing local produce, he produces 'exceptional' flavour-dense dishes of unusual combinations: Douglas fir-cured halibut with brown shrimp crumpets, roasted fallow deer with quince and elderberry preserve, and local partridge with juniper-creamed sprouts, smoked beets and clementine. 'Amazing' feast-like breakfasts are served at a giant round table. 'A fabulous experience.'

High Street
Harome
Helmsley YO62 5JE

T: 01439 770397
E: reservations@thestarinnatharome.co.uk
W: thestaratharome.co.uk

BEDROOMS: 13. All opposite pub in Cross House Lodge with Barn annexe, 6 on ground floor, unsuitable for disabled.
OPEN: all year, restaurant closed Mon lunch, last orders Sun 6 pm.
FACILITIES: bar, restaurant (veg/vegan menus), cocktail bar, 2-acre garden (all at main pub), lounge, breakfast room, terrace (at building with bedrooms), in-room TV, civil wedding licence, restaurant wheelchair accessible.
BACKGROUND MUSIC: in lounge, dining room.
LOCATION: village centre.
CHILDREN: all ages welcomed, extra bed £35.
DOGS: allowed in 3 bedrooms (£30 a night), not in restaurant or pub.
CREDIT CARDS: MC, Visa.
PRICES: B&B doubles from £150. À la carte (3 courses) £70, tasting menu £85.

HARWICH Essex

THE PIER AT HARWICH

With its belvedere and striking iron-lace balcony, this hotel is a distinctive presence on the quay of a port town on the Stour and Orwell estuaries. Owned by the Milsom family (see also Maison Talbooth, Dedham), it has a buzzy, youthful vibe. You can watch the maritime traffic come and go from the Navyärd bar and terrace over a beer and a Danish-style open sandwich, or from the upstairs restaurant, with exposed brick wall, leather banquettes and a general air of industrial chic. John Goff and co-chef Stephen Robson, who is also now general manager, cook an all-day menu of dishes which feature plenty of seafood. There's fish and chips, fish pie luxe and grilled brill with Harwich crab and herb butter as well as steaks and burgers. Bedrooms, in neutral shades with splashes of colour in the fabrics, are supplied with soft drinks and milk in a mini-fridge and posh toiletries. The Mayflower Suite, in the former Angel pub next door, has comfy seating, a telescope and panoramic views through the five-sash bay window. 'It's a particular pleasure at dusk, when the lights come on, watching the container ships and their cargo cranes.'

The Pier
Harwich CO12 3HH

T: 01255 241212
E: pier@milsomhotels.com
W: milsomhotels.com

BEDROOMS: 14. 7 in annexe, 1 on ground floor suitable for disabled.
OPEN: all year.
FACILITIES: bar, lounge (in annexe), restaurant, private dining room, small lift, in-room TV (Sky, BT, Freeview), civil wedding licence, balcony, small front terrace, parking, EV charging, restaurant, bar wheelchair accessible, adapted toilet.
BACKGROUND MUSIC: in the bar.
LOCATION: on quay, in old town.
CHILDREN: all ages welcomed, extra bed £20.
DOGS: allowed in bedrooms (no charge), bar, lounge.
CREDIT CARDS: Amex, MC, Visa.
PRICES: B&B doubles from £135. À la carte £40.

HASTINGS Sussex

MAP 2:E5

THE OLD RECTORY

You can expect a stylish stay at this Georgian rectory B&B, transformed by its designer/owner Lionel Copley, where bare wooden floors and artfully distressed furniture mix with modern pieces and hand-painted wallpapers. Arrivals are welcomed in the lounge with lavish home-made cake, and guests relax in the walled garden with a sunbathing rug and a G & T from the honesty bar or head to the treatment rooms for a massage. Each bedroom is unique, from cosy second-floor Rock-a-Nore, painted in soft greys, to Tackleway with original 1970s Sanderson wallpaper, both with a Carrara marble shower room and rainfall shower. Crown has a freestanding bath for two in the room, a secret toilet behind a bookcase. In the pretty blue-and-white hand-painted breakfast room, the mouth-watering choice includes house-smoked kippers, salmon and bacon. There is award-winning home-made marmalade to spread on home-baked bread, free-range eggs, organic apple juice, a full English with bubble-and-squeak, and toasted banana bread with vanilla mascarpone and berries. At the regular, sell-out weekend supper club, chef Rob Hills wows with his Asian-inspired dishes.

Harold Road
Hastings TN35 5ND

T: 01424 422410
E: info@theoldrectoryhastings.co.uk
W: theoldrectoryhastings.co.uk

BEDROOMS: 8. One 2-bed suite.
OPEN: all year except 2 weeks Jan, exclusive use only at Christmas and New Year.
FACILITIES: 2 lounges (honesty bar), breakfast room, treatment rooms, sauna, in-room TV (Freeview), civil wedding licence, 1-acre walled garden, limited on-site parking, unsuitable for disabled.
BACKGROUND MUSIC: 'easy listening' in breakfast room, main lounge and treatment rooms.
LOCATION: edge of Old Town (limited parking spaces, complimentary permits).
CHILDREN: not under 10.
DOGS: not allowed.
CREDIT CARDS: Amex, MC, Visa.
PRICES: B&B doubles from £115, singles from £90. Supper club £40–£45. Min. 2-night bookings weekends, 3-night on bank holidays.

SEE ALSO SHORTLIST

HAWES Yorkshire   MAP 4:C3

SIMONSTONE HALL   NEW

'The place breathes class,' says a Guide inspector
of Jake Dinsdale's Jacobean-style country house,
set high in the Yorkshire Dales on the Pennine
Way. Built in the 17th century and remodelled in
the early 19th, it is family-friendly, dog-friendly
and relaxed. 'I thought it would be rather stuffy,'
wrote a reader, 'but now we've stayed there I
highly recommend it.' Traditional-style, newly
refurbished bedrooms range from cosy to grand,
with good antiques. A four-poster room had 'a
spotless, spacious, modern bathroom' with good
toiletries, 'peafowl-pattern roman blinds'. By day
there is a grazing menu, while in the restaurant,
at lunch and dinner, a 'tempting menu' brings
dishes such as 'a delicate crab and peach salad;
rich, savoury rigatoni'. At breakfast there are
new-laid eggs from the hens, smoked haddock
Florentine. Our inspector waxed lyrical: 'To sit on
a sunlit evening, sipping excellent Forest gin (one
for connoisseurs) in beautiful gardens, with an
uninterrupted view of the Dales, while admiring
iridescent peacock plumage, is to get as near to
heaven as is possible on this earth.' (Jill Fossdyke)

Hawes DL8 3LY

T: 01969 667255
E: reception@simonstonehall.com
W: simonstonehall.com

BEDROOMS: 20. 2 on ground floor
suitable for disabled.
OPEN: all year.
FACILITIES: bar, restaurant, 3 lounges,
in-room TV, civil wedding licence,
2½-acre grounds (hot tub), EV
charging, public rooms wheelchair
accessible, adapted toilet.
BACKGROUND MUSIC: 'low key' in public
areas.
LOCATION: 1 mile N of Hawes.
CHILDREN: all ages welcomed, extra
bed for under-13s £40, for 13–16s £80.
DOGS: welcomed in some bedrooms
(1 dog £25 per stay, 2 dogs £35),
2 lounges, bar.
CREDIT CARDS: MC, Visa.
PRICES: B&B doubles from £149. Set-
price dinner £50 (£44 for pre-booked
residents). 1-night bookings usually
refused on public holidays.

HEREFORD Herefordshire

MAP 3:D4

CASTLE HOUSE

This family-owned hotel is formed of two elegant Regency mansions, with secluded gardens overlooking a moat that once belonged to Hereford Castle. Guests have a wide choice of characterful, individually styled rooms and suites, here and in a nearby town house. Some have both a bath and walk-in shower, French doors and a terrace. All are supplied with fresh milk, bottled water, a decanter of sherry and L'Occitane toiletries. 'Our room had a very comfortable bed, sofa and seating area, useful for a quiet room-service lunch,' a trusted reader relates. You can eat in the bistro, hung with works by local artists, in the restaurant, or alfresco, where you may see otters playing on the lawn. Chef Gabor Katona works with produce from local suppliers, the owners' farm and the kitchen garden to create farm-to-fork menus of dishes such as beef goulash, herb-crusted rump of lamb, roast cauliflower with Perl Las cake and soured cherries. We hear high praise of his food, and the well-trained, responsive staff. After a full Hereford breakfast with free-range pork sausages, you can stroll to the cathedral to admire the Mappa Mundi. (S and JJ)

Castle Street
Hereford HR1 2NW

T: 01432 356321
E: reception@castlehse.co.uk
W: castlehse.co.uk

BEDROOMS: 24. 8 in town house (1-min. walk), some on ground floor, 1 suitable for disabled.
OPEN: all year, restaurant closed Mon/ Tues.
FACILITIES: lift (in main house), lounge, bar/bistro, restaurant, in-room TV (Freeview), civil wedding licence, terraced garden, ground floor wheelchair accessible.
BACKGROUND MUSIC: sometimes in restaurant, bistro, reception.
LOCATION: central.
CHILDREN: all ages welcomed, family suites, cots, extra bed £25.
DOGS: only assistance dogs, others allowed in garden, on a lead.
CREDIT CARDS: Amex, MC, Visa.
PRICES: B&B doubles from £155 (No. 25), £190 (main house), singles from £140. Tasting menu £100 for two, à la carte (restaurant) £40, (bistro) £30.

HETTON Yorkshire   MAP 4:D3

THE ANGEL INN

🏵Previous César winner

In a quiet corner of the Yorkshire Dales, this creeper-covered 15th-century inn spoils guests with Michelin-starred food, luxurious but understated bedrooms and a relaxed vibe. 'I loved the warm atmosphere,' says a reader of the smart interiors where beams and log fires mix with Scandi-style furnishings. Chef Michael Wignall (ex Gidleigh Park) and his wife Johanna have created a series of light but intimate dining spaces that never feel stiff and formal. Michael describes his food as 'modern, technical and meaningful' with dishes that reflect the area but are globally inspired. Lemon sole with charred asparagus, wakami and wild garlic might be followed by quail with polenta, spring cabbage and tarragon tapioca. There are good vegetarian dishes, too. Breakfasts are 'just as sumptuous'. The bedroom choice ranges from new Scandi-style rooms in the inn and cottagey rooms in an adjoining building to rustic-chic affairs in a converted barn across the road. Suites may include a roll-top bath or private patio. All come with Dyson hairdryers and handmade chocolates; most have glorious fell views. (TL)

Hetton
Skipton BD23 6LT

T: 01756 730263
E: info@angelhetton.co.uk
W: angelhetton.co.uk

BEDROOMS: 15. 5 in barn conversion, 4 in cottage, 2 on ground floor suitable for disabled.
OPEN: all year except 24 Dec restaurant only, 25/26 Dec, 2–14 Jan, rooms/restaurant closed Tues, Wed.
FACILITIES: bar, restaurant (vegetarian menu), private dining room, civil wedding licence, terrace, in-room TV, some public areas wheelchair accessible, adapted toilet.
BACKGROUND MUSIC: in public areas.
LOCATION: village centre.
CHILDREN: all ages welcomed, extra bed for under-12s £30.
DOGS: allowed in 2 bedrooms (£15 per stay), and bar.
CREDIT CARDS: Amex, MC, Visa.
PRICES: D,B&B doubles from £295, singles from £220 (no B&B rates). À la carte 2 courses £50, 3 courses £70, tasting menu £90.

HINTON ST GEORGE Somerset

MAP 1:C6

THE LORD POULETT ARMS

In a lovely conservation village, long under the feudal sway of the Poulett family, this thatched 17th-century inn is now a stylish dining pub-with-rooms, part of the fiefdom of the trio behind The Talbot Inn, Mells, and The Beckford Arms, Tisbury (see entries). The formula is a winner: find a beautiful old boozer and strip it back to essentials; expose brick, beams, boards, mix and match bar furniture. Bedrooms are chic and uncluttered, with Welsh blankets and comfy seating. A family room has bunk beds for children. A large double with its own entrance has an in-room slipper bath and separate shower room. Since last year, Abbie Windust has taken over as landlady, while chef Philip Verden continues to devise menus of meat and game from local farms, fish landed daily on the south coast, leaves from the kitchen garden. There is a new marquee for alfresco dining, and a new garden menu of pub classics, with all-day Sunday roasts. Trusted readers had a great breakfast, which included 'the fattest, sweetest, freshest strawberries, fromage blanc and home-made granola'. Eggs are from coddled, well-fed, free-range hens.

High Street
Hinton St George TA17 8SE

T: 01460 73149
E: reservations@lordpoulettarms.com
W: lordpoulettarms.com

BEDROOMS: 6. 4 with en suite, 2 with private bathroom, 1 for family.
OPEN: all year except 25 Dec.
FACILITIES: bar, restaurant, private dining room, in-room TV (Freeview), 1-acre grounds, unsuitable for disabled.
BACKGROUND MUSIC: throughout pub.
LOCATION: in village, 4 miles NW of Crewkerne.
CHILDREN: all ages welcomed, travel cot £10, bunk beds £25 per child, Room 6.
DOGS: in some bedrooms (small charge for extra housekeeping), all public areas.
CREDIT CARDS: MC, Visa.
PRICES: B&B doubles from £95, family £160. À la carte £35.

HOLT Norfolk

MORSTON HALL

Thirty years after they first welcomed guests to
their knapped-flint former farmhouse on the
edge of the marshes, Tracy and Galton Blackiston
preside over a thriving hotel with Michelin-
starred kitchen. From his first catering venture,
a stall in Rye market, Galton moved on to work
at Miller Howe in Windermere for the late John
Tovey, whose 'Tonight at 8.30' extravaganzas set a
new style for fine dining. At Morston guests enjoy
canapés in a lounge or alfresco, before a seven-
course dinner of local and home-grown produce.
A menu might run from butternut squash velouté
to Bungay raw-milk cream and blackcurrant,
via Stiffkey sea bass with whey butter sauce, and
slow-braised belly pork. 'The food was out of this
world,' a happy reader writes. House bedrooms
– a contemporary take on the country house
look – are named after local stately homes, such
as dog-friendly, dual-aspect Sandringham. In a
garden pavilion, suites have a separate seating area
and a terrace. Breakfast on freshly squeezed pink
grapefruit juice, local apple juice, smoked kipper
or a full English with kidneys and boudin noir.
'A fantastic place.'

Morston
Holt NR25 7AA

T: 01263 741041
E: reception@morstonhall.com
W: morstonhall.com

BEDROOMS: 13. 6 on ground floor,
100 yds from house, in garden
pavilion, 1 (in main house) suitable
for disabled.
OPEN: all year except Jan.
FACILITIES: reading lounge, sun lounge,
conservatory, restaurant, in-room TV
(Freeview), civil wedding licence,
3-acre garden (pond, croquet),
restaurant wheelchair accessible,
adapted toilet.
BACKGROUND MUSIC: none.
LOCATION: 2 miles W of Blakeney.
CHILDREN: all ages welcomed, over-3s
£50 a night.
DOGS: allowed in bedrooms (£10 a
night), some public rooms, not in
restaurant.
CREDIT CARDS: Amex, MC, Visa.
PRICES: per person D,B&B doubles
from £190, singles from £260. Tasting
menu £100.

SEE ALSO SHORTLIST

HOPE Derbyshire

MAP 3:A6

UNDERLEIGH HOUSE

❡ Previous César winner

With views to the sheep-dotted fields and hills across the Peak District's Hope valley, a peaceful garden, breakfast feasts and large, pretty bedrooms, it's no surprise Underleigh wins so much praise. 'Without doubt one of the best B&Bs we have stayed at,' states one reader. Vivienne Taylor's handsome longhouse, colourful with hanging baskets, offers 'a very restful stay' with cottagey bedrooms – pretty wallpaper, pale-painted furniture, elegant armchairs, the occasional antique. Three are 'lovely comfortable suites' with large sofas; one opens to the garden. Thoughtful touches include bathrobes and fresh milk. 'First-class', 'wonderful' breakfasts, taken around a large table in the beamed and flagged dining room, include everything from home-made bread, compotes and preserves to Aga-cooked porridge, eggs Benedict and a full grill, with careful local sourcing. There is plenty to see nearby including Haddon Hall and Chatsworth: 'Vivienne went out of her way to help us enjoy the Derbyshire Dales, and recommended some great walks.' Return to tea and scones in the fire-warmed lounge or colourful garden. (Mike Clark, Ceinwen Tilley)

Lose Hill Lane
off Edale Road
Hope S33 6AF

T: 01433 621372
E: underleigh.house@btconnect.com
W: underleighhouse.co.uk

BEDROOMS: 4. 3 suites with a private lounge.
OPEN: all year except mid-Dec to mid-Feb.
FACILITIES: lounge, breakfast room, in-room TV (Freeview), ¼-acre garden, EV charging, unsuitable for disabled.
BACKGROUND MUSIC: none.
LOCATION: 1 mile N of Hope.
CHILDREN: not under 12, extra bed £20.
DOGS: allowed in 1 suite by prior arrangement (no charge), not in public rooms.
CREDIT CARDS: Amex, MC, Visa.
PRICES: B&B doubles from £100, singles from £80. 1-night bookings normally refused Fri/Sat, bank holidays.

HORNINGSHAM Wiltshire   MAP 2:D1

THE BATH ARMS   `NEW`

'A beautiful forest drive' leads to this stone inn
on the Longleat estate, where tables are set out
invitingly among pollarded limes known as 'The
Twelve Apostles'. The social hub of a pretty
village, it received a chic, less-is-more make-over
in 2020 for the Beckford group (see also The
Beckford Arms, Tisbury, et al.). 'We were greeted
by the friendly barman, who carried our bags and
brought us milk,' our inspectors report. Bedrooms,
rated by size, have simple decor, seagrass flooring,
good fabrics, no wardrobe. As they warn, if you're
tall, avoid the attic rooms. 'Room 7 had a hobbit-
like doorway, dinky casement windows, in the
bathroom a double-ended bath. Next morning we
saw other rooms, which were without hazards,
really nicely decorated, with excellent bathroom.'
Food is served in cosy dining areas and alfresco,
under canvas, including meat and game from the
estate. Ham hock and Waldorf salad with lovage
avocado purée, lamb shoulder with rosemary jus,
and dark chocolate mousse, orange, honeycomb
and sour-cherry sorbet yielded 'intense flavours'.
Breakfast brings 'delicious home-made granola',
eggs from pampered hens.

Longleat Estate
Horningsham BA12 7LY

T: 01985 844308
E: info@batharmsinn.co.uk
W: batharmsinn.com

BEDROOMS: 17. 6 in stables, 1 suitable
for disabled.
OPEN: all year, except 25 Dec.
FACILITIES: bar, restaurant, snug,
covered terrace, second terrace,
landscaped gardens (sandpit), in-room
TV (Freeview).
BACKGROUND MUSIC: 'very quiet' in bar
and restaurant.
LOCATION: between Frome and
Warminster.
CHILDREN: all ages welcomed, cot £10,
foam bed £25.
DOGS: allowed in some bedrooms
(small charge for cleaning), all public
areas.
CREDIT CARDS: MC, Visa.
PRICES: B&B doubles from £110.
À la carte £32. 1-night bookings
refused Fri.

HUMSHAUGH Northumberland

MAP 4:B3

WALWICK HALL HOTEL NEW

'If you are looking for a base to explore Hadrian's Wall this would be hard to beat,' comments a recent guest of this country house hotel with a modern elegance, smart dining and a small but swish spa. The modest entrance belies a 'surprisingly big' interior with a 'modern and elegant country house style' and public rooms lit by large sash and bay windows overlooking the terrace, 'beautiful gardens' and the Tyne valley. Bedrooms 'feel very cosseting' with Aubusson carpets, country-print wallpapers, plaid wool rugs, and thick curtains; many have a freestanding bath. It feels 'refined with Wedgwood china cups and saucers, and home-made biscuits'. 'Afternoon tea can be taken on the terrace with those gorgeous views.' The 'excellent food' at dinner can be found in the classy bar or in the main dining room, with its 'dramatic wallpaper and mirrors', and might include roast halibut with caramelised cauliflower or our reader-recommended 'trio of lamb'. 'The real triumph was the cheese selection, with five local cheeses.' Waiter-served breakfasts include 'very fine scrambled eggs', pancakes and a full Northumberland grill. (David Ganz, HP)

Humshaugh
Hexham NE46 4BJ

T: 01434 620156
E: hello@walwickhall.com
W: walwickhall.com

BEDROOMS: 10.
OPEN: all year.
FACILITIES: lift, lounge, bar, snug, restaurant, private dining room, terrace, in-room TV (Freeview), 1-acre garden, indoor pool (10 metre), spa, public areas wheelchair accessible, adapted toilet.
BACKGROUND MUSIC: in public areas and dining room.
LOCATION: 6 miles N of Hexham.
CHILDREN: all ages welcomed, 1 family room, extra beds for under-13s £35, small outdoor playground.
DOGS: allowed on terrace only, unless guide dogs.
CREDIT CARDS: Amex, MC, Visa.
PRICES: B&B doubles from £270, singles from £255. À la carte £42.

HUNSTANTON Norfolk

NO. 33

On a quiet street in the Victorian bathing resort of 'sunny Hunny', with west-facing views across the Wash, Jeanne Whittome's smart but relaxed B&B is an ideal base from which to explore north Norfolk. Everything is in place for a pleasurable stay, with breakfasts and picnic hampers from sister venture the Thornham Deli (which also offers four suites). Rooms are decorated in soft whites and greys, with a mix of antique, modern and bespoke furniture. There are tea, coffee and brownies on arrival. One rear-facing room has a white four-poster, large monsoon shower, freestanding bath, and distant sea views from a balcony. An accessible ground-floor room opens on to a courtyard. A bay-fronted ground-floor room has a bath by the old fireplace and Zoffany 'Gondolier' wallpaper. There is a sitting room, dining room with log-burner, and small garden. A concierge service can book restaurants, bicycle hire or a day's sailing. Rise to a full English with free-range eggs, home-made granola, pastries and smoked salmon bagels, which can be served in your room. There are six self-catering cottages in Hunstanton, Thornham and Brancaster Staithe.

33 Northgate
Hunstanton PE36 6AP

T: 01485 524352
E: reception@33hunstanton.co.uk
W: 33hunstanton.co.uk

BEDROOMS: 5. 1 on ground floor.
OPEN: all year.
FACILITIES: small sitting room, breakfast room, in-room TV (Freeview), small garden, lawn with tables and chairs.
BACKGROUND MUSIC: radio during breakfast.
LOCATION: town centre.
CHILDREN: well-behaved children welcomed, cot £10, extra bed for children under 14 (max. 1 per room) £30.
DOGS: allowed in bedrooms (max. 1 per room, £10 per night), not in dining room.
CREDIT CARDS: MC, Visa.
PRICES: B&B doubles from £95 (suites at Thornham Deli from £140), single occupancy discount £10 a night.

HUNTINGDON Cambridgeshire

MAP 2:B4

THE OLD BRIDGE

Wine and design are the defining features at this Georgian inn on the edge of the town centre with views across a park to the Great Ouse. Interiors have been styled by hostess Julia Hoskins, while Master of Wine John Hoskins holds daily tastings in the on-site shop. 'Comfortable, busy hotel with very good restaurant food and exceptional wine list,' a reader reports. 'Good communal areas with a buzz.' Chic bedrooms vary in size. Guide stalwarts had a 'large, light' ground-floor room with 'a sofa and chair, a small but well-appointed bathroom'. Some rooms have a four-poster. No animals were harmed in the creation of the 'tiger room', with striped and leopard-spot fabrics, a roll-top bath and walk-in shower. Snacks are served all day in the lounge, bar and on the patio. In the restaurant, Pramod Jadhav's menus might include sea bream with celeriac purée, chard, potato rösti; rack of lamb, rosemary potato cake; vegan options. At breakfast, with its smoked haddock, chive butter and sourdough toast, 'the marmalade is tremendous. I buy a pot every time I visit.' (John and Elspeth Gibbon, David Sefton, and others)

1 High Street
Huntingdon PE29 3TQ

T: 01480 424300
E: jh@huntsbridge.co.uk
W: huntsbridge.com

BEDROOMS: 24. 2 on ground floor.
OPEN: all year.
FACILITIES: lounge, bar, restaurant, private dining room, wine shop, business centre, in-room TV (Freeview), civil wedding licence, 1-acre grounds (riverside patio for private events), parking, unsuitable for disabled.
BACKGROUND MUSIC: none.
LOCATION: 500 yds from town centre, station 10 mins' walk.
CHILDREN: all ages welcomed, no extra beds.
DOGS: allowed in 2 bedrooms (no charge), lounge and bar, by arrangement, not in restaurant.
CREDIT CARDS: MC, Visa.
PRICES: B&B doubles from £130, singles from £99. À la carte £40.

ILMINGTON Warwickshire

MAP 3:D6

THE HOWARD ARMS

This ticks all the boxes for a village inn: overlooking the green, large beer garden, beams and flagstones, armchairs by the fire, country-chic bedrooms, and modern classics on the menu. Rescued by two local families, it's been updated while retaining its old-world charm, with 'log fires, nooks and crannies', report readers, 'providing a great atmosphere'. Drinkers and diners mingle in the low-beamed bar with its exposed-stone walls and window seats or in the snug with its collection of prints. Alternatively, eat in the lighter dining area off the same menu of pub classics and more creative dishes, from local sausage and mash to prawn-and-chorizo skewers or squash tagine. 'Extremely quiet' bedrooms mix modern and antique furniture with rich fabrics and bold headboards. All have space for comfy chairs, or sofas in the larger rooms; eaves rooms are tricky for taller guests. Modern bathrooms have Temple Spa products. Breakfast wins praise for its fresh juice and cooked selection: 'excellent scrambled eggs!' There are walks to Ilmington Downs, plus Stratford is eight miles away. 'Relaxing but efficient; we'd certainly return.'

Lower Green
Ilmington
Stratford-upon-Avon CV36 4LT

T: 01608 682226
E: info@howardarms.com
W: howardarms.com

BEDROOMS: 8. 4 in extension, 1 on ground floor.
OPEN: all year.
FACILITIES: snug, bar, restaurant, in-room TV (Freeview), terrace, garden (alfresco dining), parking, bar wheelchair accessible, toilet not adapted.
BACKGROUND MUSIC: all day in public areas.
LOCATION: 8 miles S of Stratford-upon-Avon, 6 miles NE of Chipping Campden.
CHILDREN: all ages welcomed, under-3s/cots free, extra bed £25.
DOGS: allowed in bar and on patio only.
CREDIT CARDS: Amex, MC, Visa.
PRICES: B&B doubles from £130, singles from £112. À la carte £36. 1-night bookings sometimes refused.

KENTISBURY Devon

MAP 1:B4

KENTISBURY GRANGE HOTEL

NEW

On the edge of Exmoor national park, a fine Victorian merchant's house – 'an odd combination of Tudor and classical details' – sits in lovely landscaped grounds that used to be a holiday park. The caravans are gone, and house bedrooms are presented in smart contemporary style. Readers' classic room was 'very small', though with 'a big, good bed, shower room, coffee machine, fridge, etc'. Upgraded to 'a much larger classic', they found 'armchairs, a chaise longue, an old marble fireplace, a huge bathroom, a big freestanding bath plus shower'. Five stand-alone, dog-friendly cottage suites have a lounge area, terrace, fridge, coffee machine, minibar, roll-top bath and deluge shower. Self-catering lodges overlook three lakes. The coach house is home to a bar and restaurant, where Ryan Hughes's modern British menus include dishes such as tandoori monkfish with baby corn and samphire; leek cannelloni with spinach, ricotta and caramelised shallot; or classic fish and chips. There are 'plenty of outdoor tables and umbrellas' for alfresco dining. The glorious north Devon coast is a short drive away. (Carol Jackson)

Kentisbury
Barnstaple EX31 4NL

T: 01271 545008
E: reception@kentisburygrange.com
W: kentisburygrange.com

BEDROOMS: 15. 5 stand-alone cottage suites, some suitable for disabled.
OPEN: all year.
FACILITIES: restaurant and bar in coach house, drawing room in main house, in-room TV (Freeview), civil wedding licence, 7-acre grounds, 3 lakes, ground-floor public areas wheelchair accessible, adapted toilet in restaurant.
BACKGROUND MUSIC: Spotify in restaurant, Classic FM in drawing room.
LOCATION: 10 miles NE of Barnstaple on A39.
CHILDREN: all ages welcomed, extra bed £30.
DOGS: allowed in cottage suites (£25 per stay), not in main house.
CREDIT CARDS: Amex, MC, Visa.
PRICES: B&B doubles from £160. À la carte £48.

KING'S LYNN Norfolk

MAP 2:A4

CONGHAM HALL

A garden of more than 400 herb varieties gives plant fanciers and pollinators a buzz at Nicholas Dickinson's Georgian country house hotel. Interiors are a well-judged blend of traditional and modish style. 'It felt nicely but not intrusively contemporary,' write trusted readers. 'It's hard to resist the stunning entrance lobby, where you can see straight out to the grounds.' Most house bedrooms have been recently refurbished. Dog-friendly rooms around the spa garden have a private terrace, a freestanding bath and waterfall shower. All rooms have an espresso machine, home-made cookies and fresh milk, complimentary use of the spa. 'Eating in the dining room with doors and windows thrown open on to tranquil grounds was close to perfection.' Menus, inspired by fruit from the orchard, home-grown vegetables and herbs, might include a salad with sweet cicely, lovage, mizuna and salad burnet; monkfish with coriander and lime; queen of puddings with lemon verbena ice cream. Breakfast brings a full English or full herbivore, treacle-smoked bacon, smoked salmon, pumpernickel. 'Highly recommended.' (Anna and Bill Brewer, A and SA, and others)

Lynn Road
Grimston
King's Lynn PE32 1AH

T: 01485 600250
E: info@conghamhallhotel.co.uk
W: conghamhallhotel.co.uk

BEDROOMS: 26. 6 garden rooms, 1 suitable for disabled.
OPEN: all year.
FACILITIES: bar, sitting room, library, restaurant, in-room TV, civil wedding licence, conference facilities, terrace, spa, 12-metre indoor pool, 30-acre grounds, EV charging, public areas wheelchair accessible, adapted toilet.
BACKGROUND MUSIC: in bar, restaurant.
LOCATION: 6 miles E of King's Lynn.
CHILDREN: all ages welcomed, free cots and extra beds for under-12s.
DOGS: allowed in some bedrooms (£10 per night, bowl, treats), some public rooms.
CREDIT CARDS: MC, Visa.
PRICES: D,B&B doubles from £249, room only from £159 (Mon–Thurs, breakfast £8–£15). À la carte £40. 1-night bookings sometimes refused Sat.

SEE ALSO SHORTLIST

KIRKBY LONSDALE Cumbria

MAP 4: inset C2

THE SUN INN

This 400-year-old inn in a market town between
the Lake District and the Yorkshire Dales comes
with beams, exposed stonework and a five-
foot bedroom doorway but has been carefully
updated with a modern touch. Step through
the whitewashed portico into the large bar with
its wood-burning stove, and there's a 'warm
welcome' and 'lovely wine'. Everything feels
'cosy but uncluttered', with light, country colours
and Windsor chairs, while the dining area has
exposed-stone and claret-red walls. Bedrooms,
gradually being refurbished, are mostly on
the small side but are stylish with handmade
furniture, local artwork and jolly checks and
tartans. Some have window seats. Bright-white
bathrooms, some with a freestanding bath, are
stocked with sweet-smelling soaps from local
producer Bath House. The 'amazing' food
is modern British, with dishes such as herb
fishcakes, lamb with smoked mash, and a rhubarb
dessert with 'just the right texture and a pleasing
amount of tartness'. Breakfast's 'generous' buffet
is followed by well-prepared hot dishes. 'Despite
the church clock chiming through the night, we
would happily stay again.'

6 Market Street
Kirkby Lonsdale LA6 2AU

T: 01524 271965
E: admin@sun-inn.info
W: sun-inn.info

BEDROOMS: 11.
OPEN: all year, restaurant closed Mon
lunch.
FACILITIES: bar, restaurant, in-room
TV (Freeview), parking, bar and
restaurant wheelchair accessible,
adapted toilet.
BACKGROUND MUSIC: in bar.
LOCATION: town centre.
CHILDREN: all ages welcomed, cots
free, extra bed £20.
DOGS: allowed in bedrooms (£20
per night, welcome pack), public
rooms (separate dog-friendly area in
restaurant).
CREDIT CARDS: MC, Visa.
PRICES: B&B doubles from £99, singles
from £95. À la carte £33. 1-night
bookings usually refused Sat (but ring
to check).

KIRKBY STEPHEN Cumbria

MAP 4:C3

AUGILL CASTLE

♔ Previous César winner

With its towers and battlements, this Victorian-folly castle in 20 acres of grounds looks the real deal yet is 'extremely laid-back – you can't fail to feel at home'. Owners Simon and Wendy Bennett have furnished the huge rooms – wood-panelling, ornate ceilings – in a grandly shabby, homely style. Family photographs and cushion-heaped window-seats complement the antiques. 'The place is not overly done up but supremely enjoyable,' our inspector reported. Bedrooms, in the castle, stables, orangery and separate buildings, range from big to vast. Eccentrically furnished with sale-room finds and bold wallpapers, they might include a four-poster or Victorian chaise longue. Bathrooms are huge, some with a roll-top bath. Plenty of activities, too, such as tennis and a games room. Evening meals in the former Music Room might include Cumbrian crab with avocado, and local lamb with gratin potatoes. There's a more casual menu, too. A 'tasty, filling' breakfast includes freshly squeezed juice, smoked salmon and scrambled egg, and field mushroom and poached egg Florentine. 'We felt like part of the family.' (Jeremy Taylor, and others)

South Stainmore
Brough
Kirkby Stephen CA17 4DE

T: 01768 341937
E: office@stayinacastle.com
W: stayinacastle.com

BEDROOMS: 13. 2 on ground floor, 9 in stables, orangery, coach house, 1 suitable for disabled.
OPEN: all year, Music Room dinner not served Sun/Mon Nov–Easter.
FACILITIES: hall, drawing room, library, sitting room, bar, dining room, conservatory, in-room TV, civil wedding licence, 20-acre grounds (tennis), EV charging, public rooms wheelchair accessible, adapted toilet.
BACKGROUND MUSIC: none.
LOCATION: 3 miles NE of Kirkby Stephen.
CHILDREN: all ages welcomed, family rooms, extra bed £25, games room.
DOGS: allowed in 2 bedrooms (£10 per night, by arrangement), not public rooms.
CREDIT CARDS: Amex, MC, Visa.
PRICES: B&B doubles from £200. À la carte 2-course £27.50, 3-course £35. 1-night bookings often refused weekends.

LACOCK Wiltshire

SIGN OF THE ANGEL

It would be 'hard to find somewhere more olde-worlde than this 15th-century coaching inn', with its fireplaces and flagstones, and wonky beams aplenty. In a National Trust village which has stood in for Cranford in the BBC drama, it is now more a restaurant-with-rooms than a pub, say Guide insiders. 'There is a small bar, but not intended for much lingering.' They were checked in by 'a pleasant young man', who showed them through a 'charming' panelled first-floor sitting room to a smallish bedroom with low doorway, beams, leaded windows and dark-wood furniture. There are just five rustic-chic bedrooms, ranging from snug to superior, with a Roberts radio, a tea/coffee-maker and a bath with a shower over it. Down the narrow stairs, head chef Ashley Jackson's menus champion local farmers, growers and artisan suppliers, with home-grown produce from the paddock and good vegan options. A typical dish might feature lamb rump with sweet potato and mint cake, or pumpkin, thyme pastry, with pecan-crusted potato. You can eat outside, too, or take afternoon tea in a 'delightful orchard garden bordered by a stream'.

6 Church Street
Lacock SN15 2LB

T: 01249 730230
E: info@signoftheangel.co.uk
W: signoftheangel.co.uk

BEDROOMS: 5.
OPEN: all year except New Year's Eve (phone to check festive dates).
FACILITIES: bar, 3 dining rooms (vegan, gluten-free menus) sitting room, private dining room, no mobile phone signal, free street parking, cottage garden, restaurant and garden wheelchair accessible.
BACKGROUND MUSIC: in restaurant, radio option in sitting room.
LOCATION: in village, 4 miles S of Chippenham.
CHILDREN: all ages welcomed, cot £20, blow-up beds, single £40, double £70.
DOGS: allowed in bedrooms (£15 charge for cleaning), public rooms.
CREDIT CARDS: MC, Visa.
PRICES: B&B doubles from £110, singles from £85. À la carte £38, tasting menu £48 (for whole tables ordering in twos or fours).

LANGAR Nottinghamshire

LANGAR HALL

The apricot-coloured Georgian house, at the end of a lime-tree avenue, adds just a touch of eccentricity to a traditional country house stay. The family home-turned-hotel of the late Imogen Skirving is run by her granddaughter, Lila Arora, with the same 'very warm' welcome. The pillared hall, sitting rooms and dining room are graciously furnished in English country house style – bookcases, wood floors, gilt-framed paintings – spiced up with a hint of India (Imogen loved the country). Bedrooms – one named after a former regular guest, Barbara Cartland – feature boldly patterned wallpapers, antiques, desks, books, upholstered armchairs and views over 'attractive parkland'. One has wood panelling, another a rocking chair and there are four-poster and half-tester beds. Most have a bath as well as a shower. For romance, try the cosy wooden 'pod' or chalet by the croquet lawn. Dinner in the 'classical' dining room is 'outstanding', raves a guest, with a 'menu full of temptation' such as wild sea bass with scallop ravioli, and crispy pork belly with barbecued aubergine and grapefruit. Throughout, the ambience is 'delightful'. (Robert Gower)

Church Lane
Langar NG13 9HG

T: 01949 860559
E: info@langarhall.co.uk
W: langarhall.com

BEDROOMS: 13. 1 on ground floor, 3 in annexe, 1 in garden chalet, 1 in pod.
OPEN: all year, closed Mon/Tues.
FACILITIES: study/sitting room, bar, garden room, main dining room, Indian room, in-room TV (Freeview), civil wedding licence, 30-acre grounds, restaurant wheelchair accessible.
BACKGROUND MUSIC: at lunch and dinner.
LOCATION: 12 miles SE of Nottingham.
CHILDREN: all ages welcomed, extra bed £30.
DOGS: in some bedrooms (£20 per stay), sitting room and bar, not in restaurant.
CREDIT CARDS: Amex, MC, Visa.
PRICES: B&B doubles from £125, singles from £110. Fixed-price dinner £54.50 (£42.50 Sun).

LANGHAM Norfolk

MAP 2:A5

THE HARPER

NEW

Just inland from Blakeney, 'the brick and flint barns where once the Langham Glass furnace raged have been transformed into a smoking-hot hotel', writes a Guide insider. The creation of Sam Cutmore-Scott and his parents, it 'pays homage to its heritage', with 'a glass menagerie in a glass-fronted reception desk', stained-glass windows and hints of industrial chic throughout. The ethos is 'laid-back yet luxurious', with wine-vending machines, 'mismatched and upcycled furniture, colourful velvet chairs and sofas'. Bedrooms, some with a modern four-poster, are supplied with coffee, and complimentary cocktails, beer, milk and snacks. Modern bathrooms feature toiletries by Irene Forte, whose unguents are used in the boutique spa. You can eat casually in Ivy's lounge, by a fire pit on a lavender-scented terrace ('lobster and samphire mac 'n' cheese was a stand-out dish'), or formally in Stanley's (perhaps haunch of Holkham venison). A continental breakfast was indifferent; cooked dishes were good. 'Special mention for manager Jules, who is a mine of local information.' Overall: 'A fantastic new addition to the Norfolk hotel scene. (JK)'

North Street
Langham
Holt NR25 7DH

T: 01328 805000
E: stay@theharper.co.uk
W: theharper.co.uk

BEDROOMS: 32. Some on ground floor, 2 suitable for disabled.
OPEN: all year.
FACILITIES: lift, bar, lounge, dining room, games room, in-room smart TV, spa (12 by 5 metre indoor swimming pool, spa bath, sauna, steam room), courtyard, bicycles, EV charging, public rooms wheelchair accessible.
BACKGROUND MUSIC: in public spaces.
LOCATION: 2 miles S of Blakeney, within the Norfolk Coast Area of Outstanding Natural Beauty.
CHILDREN: all ages welcomed, extra bed £40, no under-16s in spa.
DOGS: allowed in ground-floor bedrooms (£25 a night), in bar, games room, not in dining areas.
CREDIT CARDS: MC, Visa.
PRICES: B&B doubles from £175. À la carte £50. 2-night min. stay Fri and Sat.

LASTINGHAM Yorkshire   MAP 4:C4

LASTINGHAM GRANGE

Where the road turns into a moorland track, this country hotel offers peace, seclusion and comfort far removed from the modern world. 'One of our favourite places,' reports a regular after a visit, 'as lovely and peaceful as ever.' On the edge of the North York Moors, the former 17th-century farmhouse – all sash windows and wisteria – has been run by the Wood family for more than 60 years. Not much has changed, some might say, and that is the charm. Public rooms are traditional with floral fabrics, patterned carpets and linen cloths on tables. Guests are welcomed with home-made scones and tea, while the fires, newspapers and views over the terrace and rose garden provide relaxation – especially after a day's walking. (Wet clothes will be whisked away to the drying room.) Bedrooms are 'comfortable' rather than stylish but pin-neat and with up-to-date touches including fresh milk and coffee machines. Fine dinners are a five-course affair with starters such as pan-fried scallops with basil followed by pork in cider and cream, perhaps, or local partridge with game chips. Guests find they leave 'deeply refreshed'. (Alison Judson, and others)

High Street
Lastingham YO62 6TH

T: 01751 417345
E: reservations@lastinghamgrange.com
W: lastinghamgrange.com

BEDROOMS: 11. Plus self-catering cottage in village.
OPEN: all year except 21 Nov–7 Mar.
FACILITIES: hall, lounge, dining room, in-room TV (Freeview), 10-acre grounds (terrace, garden, orchard, croquet, boules), restaurant and garden wheelchair accessible.
BACKGROUND MUSIC: none.
LOCATION: 5 miles NE of Kirkbymoorside.
CHILDREN: all ages welcomed, under-12s free, 12s and over ring to check, high teas, adventure playground.
DOGS: allowed in bedrooms with prior consent (nominal charge), lounge, garden, but not in dining room.
CREDIT CARDS: Amex, MC, Visa.
PRICES: B&B doubles from £198, singles from £144. À la carte £42.

LAVENHAM Suffolk

MAP 2:C5

THE GREAT HOUSE

In a medieval wool town of wonky timber-frame houses, this French-style 'restaurant and bedrooms' hides its 14th-century origins behind a Georgian facade. It is owned by Dominique Tropeano, proprietor of Colchester Zoo, and is run with elan, not to say panache. Bedrooms range from seriously snug Bohème, under the eaves, to Élysée, with two king-size beds and two velvet chaises longues, perhaps a nod to the estimable military Gayer-Anderson twins, who lived here in the 1920s. Readers found attic Montmartre 'a bit of a hike', with sloping ceilings but 'lots of space, a sizeable bathroom, a walk-in wardrobe, coffee, fruit and sherry'. The bed was a little short for a man of 6ft 2in. Mind your head: in Bastille, 'the most lethal beam was padded'. In the dining room, Swann Auffray's inventive menus might include cod fillet, almond and broccoli concasse, fishy broccoli cream, almond espuma; a coco-bean stew cooked in butternut juices, scented with star anise. 'Dinner was excellent, the staff all very charming.' You can order a picnic at 24 hours' notice. (John and Elspeth Gibbon)

Market Place
Lavenham CO10 9QZ

T: 01787 247431
E: info@greathouse.co.uk
W: greathouse.co.uk

BEDROOMS: 5.
OPEN: all year except Jan, restaurant closed Sun eve–Tues lunch.
FACILITIES: restaurant/bar, in-room TV (BT, Freeview), patio dining area, street parking, unsuitable for disabled.
BACKGROUND MUSIC: in restaurant.
LOCATION: town centre (free public car park).
CHILDREN: all ages welcomed, extra bed £15, cot, high chair, children's portions.
DOGS: only assistance dogs allowed.
CREDIT CARDS: Amex, MC, Visa.
PRICES: B&B doubles from £189, small double/single from £117/£105. Set-price dinner £35.50–£39.50, tasting menus £58–£68. 1-night bookings sometimes refused Sat.

SEE ALSO SHORTLIST

LEAMINGTON SPA Warwickshire   MAP 2:B2

MALLORY COURT

A country house built in 1914 in Lutyensesque romantic vernacular style, in 'breathtakingly lovely' pleasure grounds and parkland, is today part of the Eden Hotel Collection (see also Brockencote Hall in Chaddesley Corbett) with Relais & Châteaux kudos. Bedrooms suit different purposes and pockets. Knight's Suite doubles, adjacent to the main house, are simple and straightforward – ideal for the business traveller. More romantic are the 'spacious, atmospheric period bedrooms' in the main house, with leaded, mullioned windows and, perhaps best of all, the more contemporary 'new rooms above the spa in the Orchard House'. All have a coffee machine and luxury toiletries. There are comfy lounges, a terrace on which to take tea in the sunshine. You can eat simply from the terrace and supper menu: fishcakes, pasta, charcuterie (sandwiches only from 2.30 to 5 pm). In the dining room, an 'adventurous but not too ambitious' set price Taste of the Season menu might bring Cotswold lamb with home-grown vegetables. 'The gardens are a delight, the breakfast a splendid feast, all you could wish for.' (Anna Brewer, Ian Walsh, CB)

Harbury Lane
Bishop's Tachbrook
Leamington Spa CV33 9QB

T: 01926 330214
E: info@mallory.co.uk
W: mallory.co.uk

BEDROOMS: 43. 11 in Knight's Suite, 12 in Orchard House, 2 suitable for disabled.
OPEN: all year, restaurant for dinner only.
FACILITIES: 2 lounges, restaurant, lift, in-room TV, civil wedding licence, spa (hydrotherapy pool, outdoor vitality pool), 10-acre gardens, EV charging, public rooms wheelchair accessible, adapted toilet.
BACKGROUND MUSIC: in public rooms.
LOCATION: 3 miles S of Leamington Spa.
CHILDREN: all ages welcomed, cot £15, extra bed £35.
DOGS: in some bedrooms (£25 per dog per night, cushion, bowl, treats), gardens, not public rooms.
CREDIT CARDS: Amex, MC, Visa.
PRICES: B&B doubles from £169, singles from £159. À la carte £20, 5-course tasting menu £70.

LETCOMBE REGIS Oxfordshire

MAP 2:C2

THE GREYHOUND INN

This 18th-century red brick free house was at risk of going to the dogs when Martyn Reed and Catriona Galbraith stepped in, refurbished throughout and re-established it in 2015 as a dining pub-with-rooms at the heart of a village at the foot of the downs. The beamed bar with bare floorboards and a log-burner in an inglenook is now a community hub, with a quiz night on Saturday, and regular events. You can eat here or in the garden, maybe venison tartare with smoked egg yolk, fish and chips, pork belly with cannellini beans, wild mushroom pappardelle. There is live music on Sundays, a 'mini-festival' with a cookout on bank holidays. Bedrooms have their own character, with smart fabrics, a Roberts radio, milk and home-made biscuits on the hospitality tray. Charismatic Uffington has exposed timbers and a sloping floor, while a family can have the run of the attic floor, with a super-king-size bed, painted furniture, a lounge with sofa bed, a bathroom with a turquoise roll-top bath. You can breakfast on a full English or full veggie or smoked haddock before exploring the Vale of the White Horse.

Main Street
Letcombe Regis
Wantage OX12 9JL

T: 01235 771969
E: info@thegreyhoundletcombe.co.uk
W: thegreyhoundletcombe.co.uk

BEDROOMS: 8.
OPEN: all year except 24/25 Dec, 1 week in Jan.
FACILITIES: bar with snug, 3 dining rooms (1 available for private dining/meetings), function room, in-room TV (Freeview), garden, bar/restaurant, parking, EV charging, garden wheelchair accessible, adapted toilet.
BACKGROUND MUSIC: occasionally in public rooms.
LOCATION: in village, 2 miles SW of Wantage.
CHILDREN: all ages welcomed, under-3s free, extra bed for ages 3–12 £20.
DOGS: allowed in 2 bedrooms (£15 per night), bar, garden, not dining rooms.
CREDIT CARDS: MC, Visa.
PRICES: B&B doubles from £95, family from £145. À la carte £35, 2-course Midweek Fix dinner (Wed) £16.

LEWDOWN Devon

LEWTRENCHARD MANOR

🏅 Previous César winner

In a peaceful Devon valley, this family-run historic manor house is loved for its architecture, romantic atmosphere, attention to detail and fine food. 'No trip to the UK is complete without a leisurely stop at Lewtrenchard,' say one smitten couple. The 17th-century house, embellished in Victorian times, has stuccoed ceilings, wood-panelled rooms and deep mullioned windows. Public rooms have large fireplaces, deep sofas, portraits of past owners and books in the library. 'Everywhere is immaculate,' guests report. Bedrooms are classic country house with lightly patterned or striped wallpapers, antiques, some with four-poster or sleigh bed and all but one with views of the gardens or surrounding hills. Bathrooms, most with bath and shower, are bright and modern. An 'impeccable' meal in the oak-panelled dining room starts with canapés and amuse-bouche and might be followed by cod with oyster and shrimp, or aged sirloin with celeriac and blue cheese. Simpler dishes are served in the bar, and fruit and vegetables come from the walled garden. Breakfast brings freshly squeezed juice and good-quality bacon and eggs. (GM, and others)

Lewdown
Okehampton EX20 4PN

T: 01566 783222
E: info@lewtrenchard.co.uk
W: lewtrenchard.co.uk

BEDROOMS: 14. 1 in folly, 4 with separate entrance, 1 suitable for disabled.
OPEN: all year.
FACILITIES: lounge, bar, library, restaurant, function facilities, in-room TV (Freeview), civil wedding licence, 12-acre gardens, public rooms wheelchair accessible, adapted toilet.
BACKGROUND MUSIC: none.
LOCATION: rural, 10 miles N of Tavistock.
CHILDREN: all ages welcomed, extra bed £25, no under-8s in restaurant in evening.
DOGS: allowed in bedrooms (£15 per stay, not unattended), in public rooms, not in restaurant.
CREDIT CARDS: Amex, MC, Visa.
PRICES: B&B doubles from £180, singles from £145. Set dinner £49.50, tasting menus £74. 1-night bookings sometimes refused Sat.

LIVERPOOL Merseyside

MAP 4:E2

2 BLACKBURNE TERRACE

For a bit of cool culture, look no further than Sarah and Glenn Whitter's chic B&B, in a Georgian town house on a tree-lined carriage drive. Convenient for performances of the Liverpool Philharmonic, and between the city's two cathedrals, it is adorned with art throughout, with a private gallery open to guests by appointment. In the sitting room, a stack of art books lies on a tangerine ottoman. The four bedrooms are seriously stylish. Each one comes with its own luxuries; three have views to the Anglican cathedral on St James Mount, the world's eighth largest church. Room 1 has tall Georgian windows, a deep-blue velvet sofa, a velvet sleigh bed, a freestanding bath on marble tiles and an en suite with power shower. An uplit corridor leads to Room 4, with works by Turkish artist Ayse Kucuk, a freestanding Victoria and Albert bath by a raw stone wall, and a Sonos music system to play your own choice of music (perhaps 'Splish, splash, I was taking a bath, long about a Saturday night' . . .). A breakfast of fresh fruit and artisan produce is served communally at a dining table laid with silverware, cut glass and fine china.

2 Blackburne Terrace
Liverpool L87 PJ

T: 0151 708 5474
E: info@2bbt.co.uk
W: 2blackburneterrace.com

BEDROOMS: 4.
OPEN: all year except 24 Dec–1 Jan.
FACILITIES: drawing room, dining room, in-room smart TV (Freeview), walled garden, unsuitable for disabled.
BACKGROUND MUSIC: classical at breakfast.
LOCATION: city centre.
CHILDREN: not under 12.
DOGS: not allowed.
CREDIT CARDS: MC, Visa.
PRICES: B&B doubles from £180.

SEE ALSO SHORTLIST

LODSWORTH Sussex   MAP 2:E3

THE HALFWAY BRIDGE

Halfway between historic Midhurst and the
antiques hot spot of Petworth, this 250-year-old
inn is owned by Janet and Sam Bakose, who also
have The Crab & Lobster in Sidlesham (see entry),
with Clyde Hollett skippering both kitchens.
And is it good? Not half, said our inspectors,
who found a 'near pitch-perfect Great British
inn experience'. Bedrooms in Cowdray Barns,
a converted stable block across a quiet country
road, are joined this year by a new shepherd's hut.
The 'barn' rooms are a mix of rustic features and
contemporary decor, perhaps a floor-to-ceiling
window. Our inspectors' 'very comfortable room'
would have been improved by a 'large-screen TV,
dressing table/desk and full-length mirror' but
was supplied with fresh milk. The 'comfortably
cosy' bar has inglenooks and beams. In dining
areas, under parasols on the lawn, and in the new
covered alfresco dining area, there is 'pub-style
grub' that is 'really well cooked with excellent
ingredients', such as braised lamb shank with
mint and orange gravy. You can expect a 'first-
class breakfast', too. The A272, which passes by, is
so scenic, it has inspired a book, Ode to a Road.

Lodsworth
Petworth GU28 9BP

T: 01798 861281
E: enquiries@halfwaybridge.co.uk
W: halfwaybridge.co.uk

BEDROOMS: 8. In converted stables,
165 yds from main building.
OPEN: all year.
FACILITIES: bar, restaurant, in-room
TV (Freeview), bar terrace, small beer
garden, unsuitable for disabled.
BACKGROUND MUSIC: 'quiet' in bar and
restaurant.
LOCATION: 3 miles W of Petworth,
on A272.
CHILDREN: all ages welcomed, extra
bed £30.
DOGS: allowed in bar area and garden
only.
CREDIT CARDS: Amex, MC, Visa.
PRICES: B&B doubles from £135, singles
from £95. Set lunch menu (Mon–Sat)
£22–£26, à la carte £32. 1-night
bookings refused Fri and Sat, when
single occupancy is charged at full
double rate.

LONG SUTTON Somerset

MAP 1:C6

THE DEVONSHIRE ARMS

From the outside, this 18th-century inn overlooking a green with a lime tree at each corner looks every inch the historic village pub, but within lies contemporary chic. From the Reformation until 1919 it was part of the Devonshire estate, but today all reforms at 'The Dev' are down to owners Sheila and Philip Mepham. Walls of deep blue, aubergine and charcoal are hung with lithograph caricatures and portraits of various Tudors and Stuarts. There is a log fire, padded banquettes, comfy armchairs, floral wallpaper. Bedrooms, in a neutral palette, may come with a modern four-poster or an oversized headboard. Two ground-floor rooms are in a cottage annexe, while another two are interconnecting. 'It is essentially a restaurant-with-rooms' but the rooms are 'well furnished' and the food 'good quality and enjoyable'. In the dining area, or in the walled garden, among the clipped box and lavender, the menu features local and home-grown produce in dishes such as confit duck leg with herb jus (deemed 'faultless' by one reader), the house burger, a vegetarian option. To drink, try Harry's cider, which is brewed in the village.

Long Sutton
Langport TA10 9LP

T: 01458 241271
E: info@thedevonshirearms.com
W: thedevonshirearms.com

BEDROOMS: 9. 2, on ground floor, in annexe behind main building.
OPEN: all year except 25/26 Dec.
FACILITIES: open-plan bar and restaurant, private dining room, in-room TV (Freeview), courtyard, garden (croquet lawn, vegetable garden), parking, public areas wheelchair accessible, no adapted toilet.
BACKGROUND MUSIC: in bar.
LOCATION: by the village green.
CHILDREN: all ages welcomed, extra bed £20, children's menus, free travel cot.
DOGS: allowed in bar only.
CREDIT CARDS: MC, Visa.
PRICES: B&B doubles from £105, singles from £95, Sun–Thurs, subject to availability. À la carte £32. 1-night bookings sometimes refused weekends.

LORTON Cumbria

MAP 4: inset C2

NEW HOUSE FARM

In the quieter north-western Lake District, against a backdrop of fields and fells, this whitewashed farmhouse B&B mixes rustic charm with romance. Dating from the 17th century, and enlarged in Georgian times, it retains original features of slate-flagged floors, open beams, sturdy oak doors and big fireplaces. With the stunning scenery and lawned garden, it's popular for weddings held either in the hayloft of the Victorian barn, above the tea room, or newly restored cart shed. (B&B and tea room availability fits around these bookings.) 'Wonderful' host Hazel Thompson, who greets guests with a cream tea, has furnished bedrooms to maintain their historic character – exposed-stone walls and beams – while adding touches of luxury. There are thick curtains, large brass beds and four-posters, country antiques, rich colours and huge bathrooms, most with a slipper bath or air bath. With those views, you won't mind the lack of TVs. Two rooms are separate from the farmhouse, with private entrances. Breakfast is a homely affair in the fire-warmed dining room, while supper options include the local pub or Kirkstile Inn, three miles away.

Lorton
Cockermouth CA13 9UU

T: 07841 159818
E: hazel@newhouse-farm.co.uk
W: newhouse-farm.com

BEDROOMS: 5. 1 in Stable, 1 in Old Dairy.
OPEN: all year except 23 Dec–2 Jan, and every Sat and most Tues (for weddings), tea room open April–Nov.
FACILITIES: entrance hall, 2 lounges, dining room, civil wedding licence, 17-acre grounds (garden, streams, woods, field, lake and river, safe bathing 2 miles), unsuitable for disabled.
BACKGROUND MUSIC: none.
LOCATION: on B5289, 2 miles S of Lorton.
CHILDREN: by arrangement.
DOGS: 'clean and dry' dogs with own bed allowed in bedrooms (£10 per night), not in public rooms.
CREDIT CARDS: MC, Visa.
PRICES: B&B doubles from £180, singles from £90. Min. 2-night stay.

LOWER BOCKHAMPTON Dorset

MAP 1:D6

YALBURY COTTAGE

Ⓥ Previous César winner

Ariane and Jamie Jones preside over a much-admired hotel and restaurant in this 300-year-old thatched cottage, once home to a local shepherd (Gabriel Oak, we like to think, for this is the very heart of Thomas Hardy country). 'It is one of our favourite places,' runs a typical report from a reader. 'Ariane served at all meals, and the warmth of her personality imbued Yalbury Cottage with an atmosphere that made me feel very much at home,' writes another. 'Simple country style' bedrooms are in a modern extension. 'Mine was warm, comfortable and well equipped, but a couple more pictures on the walls would have made it cosier.' After drinks in the lounge, dinner is served in the 'softly lit, smart but homely dining room'. Chef Jamie creates short but varied menus of 'fabulous food' such as brill Cordon Bleu, brown shrimp, mustard mash, with a 'very good wine list'. 'Breakfasts were superb, too.' After a full English, Bridport kipper with lemon butter, or brioche eggy bread with orange maple syrup, explore Hardy country – his old schoolhouse is over the road and you can walk to his birthplace. (Sara Price, Trevor Lockwood, and others)

Lower Bockhampton
Dorchester DT2 8PZ

T: 01305 262382
E: enquiries@yalburycottage.com
W: yalburycottage.com

BEDROOMS: 8. 6 on ground floor.
OPEN: all year except 23 Dec–14 Jan, closed Sun pm, Mon.
FACILITIES: lounge, restaurant, in-room TV (Freeview), garden with outdoor seating, EV charging.
BACKGROUND MUSIC: 'easy listening' in lounge in evening.
LOCATION: 2 miles E of Dorchester.
CHILDREN: all ages welcomed, extra bed free for under-12s, £20, 12 and over, no under-12s in restaurant after 8 pm.
DOGS: well-behaved dogs allowed in bedrooms (£8.50 per night), in lounge, not in restaurant.
CREDIT CARDS: MC, Visa.
PRICES: B&B doubles from £130, singles from £95. À la carte £47.50.

LUDLOW Shropshire

MAP 3:C4

OLD DOWNTON LODGE

♀ Previous César winner

'Pheasants scatter as you edge your way down
the lanes' to Pippa and Willem Vlok's restaurant-
with-rooms, occupying medieval and Georgian
farm buildings around a flower-filled courtyard.
It is a 'super-peaceful place, renovated and
furnished to a high standard', readers write. 'The
attention to detail is faultless.' Bedrooms, two
with oak four-poster, are a study in rustic chic.
A 'high-raftered' stables room had 'lighting so
elaborately digitised, it took most of the evening
to work out which switches to activate'. A log-
burner warms a sitting room in an old milking
barn, where local cheeses, including Remembered
Hills ('blue, of course') went down well with
a good bottle of wine. In the 'pseudo-baronial'
dining room, chef Nick Bennett's short market
menu might bring a choice of venison, squash
and chestnut, savoy; hake, saag aloo, lemongrass
and fennel; duck, chicory and orange. Most nights
there is also a tasting menu. Give them notice of
any dietary needs. 'We couldn't get enough of the
food,' another reader writes. As for the service,
'the entire team are the most genuine, lovely, kind
people'. (LH and JF, and others)

Downton on the Rock
Ludlow SY8 2HU

T: 01568 771826
E: bookings@olddowntonlodge.com
W: olddowntonlodge.com

BEDROOMS: 9. In buildings round
courtyard.
OPEN: all year, except Christmas,
dinner nightly, lunch Thurs–Sun.
FACILITIES: sitting room, dining room,
'museum' (function room), in-room
TV (Freeview), civil wedding licence,
1-acre courtyard, EV charging,
unsuitable for disabled.
BACKGROUND MUSIC: soft classical in
sitting and dining rooms.
LOCATION: 6 miles W of Ludlow.
CHILDREN: over-12s only.
DOGS: allowed in some bedrooms by
prior arrangement (£15 per dog), not
in public rooms.
CREDIT CARDS: Amex, MC, Visa.
PRICES: B&B doubles from £165.
Market menu (2–3 courses) £40–£50,
tasting menu (6 courses) Tues–Sat £65.

SEE ALSO SHORTLIST

LYME REGIS Dorset

MAP 1:C6

DORSET HOUSE

NEW

'A very strange stranger it must be, who does not see charms in the immediate environs of Lyme,' wrote Jane Austen, and only a very strange stranger would not see the charm in Lyn and Jason Martin's Regency-style, eco-friendly B&B. Urged by trusted readers to promote it from the Shortlist, we needed little persuasion. 'It is outstanding in every way,' they say. 'We were welcomed by Jason with tea, biscuits and an orientation chat.' Boutique bedrooms have 'an exceedingly comfortable bed', a minibar fridge, locally baked biscuits, fresh coffee, a walk-in rain shower, smart toiletries. A suite has a sofa bed in a separate living area. This is the only Guide hotel to prioritise gut health, with a daily-changing breakfast menu of local, organic produce, including home-made granola, a full Dorset, full veggie, daily specials (maybe 'Lyn's wonderful teff pancakes with roasted nectarines; black-rice porridge and kiwi fruit; lemon and garlic mushrooms on sourdough'). In fine weather you can eat on the veranda. There's an honesty bar, and if you want to dine in, they can order you a takeaway. (Hannah and Andrew Butterworth)

Pound Road
Lyme Regis DT7 3HX

T: 01297 442055
E: info@dorsethouselyme.com
W: dorsethouselyme.com

BEDROOMS: 5.
OPEN: all year except Christmas.
FACILITIES: snug, breakfast room, reception, in-room TV (Freeview), veranda, paid parking nearby.
BACKGROUND MUSIC: 'subtle' in breakfast room.
LOCATION: 300 yds from town centre.
CHILDREN: all ages welcomed, babies free, extra bed £30.
DOGS: not allowed.
CREDIT CARDS: Amex, MC, Visa.
PRICES: B&B doubles from £115, single occupancy from £105. 1-night bookings usually refused.

SEE ALSO SHORTLIST

LYMINGTON Hampshire

MAP 2:E2

BRITANNIA HOUSE

In a coastal town on the edge of the New Forest, with cosy pubs, cobbled back streets and fine Georgian architecture, this Victorian red brick house overlooking the marina is a much-loved B&B that half imagines it's a stately home. Rhineland-born owner Tobias Feilke is a natural host, as generous with local knowledge and conversation as he has been with fabrics and soft furnishings, swags and tassels, pictures and curios. New arrivals step into a hall displaying a jolly assortment of hats, a suit of armour and a collection of pipes. A dual-aspect first-floor drawing room has views of the marina with the Solent beyond. The Britannia Suite, styled in black and gold, has a bath and walk-in shower. The quietest is the Courtyard, a hand-painted bedroom overlooking the evergreen enclosed garden. There is also a duplex apartment in a town house opposite, with stairs to a lounge with a balcony and views to the Isle of Wight. The kitchen is the warm heart and social hub of the operation, just the place for a kaffeeklatsch, or breakfast cooked on the Aga by Tobias, before a stroll around the harbour. (GB)

Station Street
Lymington SO41 3BA

T: 01590 672091
E: enquiries@britannia-house.com
W: britannia-house.com

BEDROOMS: 5. 2 on ground floor, one 2-storey apartment.
OPEN: all year except over 'the festive season'.
FACILITIES: lounge, kitchen/breakfast room, in-room TV (Freeview), courtyard garden, parking, unsuitable for disabled.
BACKGROUND MUSIC: none.
LOCATION: 2 mins' walk from High Street/quayside, close to station.
CHILDREN: not under 8.
DOGS: not allowed.
CREDIT CARDS: MC, Visa.
PRICES: B&B doubles from £99, singles from £89. 1-night bookings refused weekends.

LYNDHURST Hampshire   MAP 2:E2

LIME WOOD

There's plenty of laid-back glamour at this
Georgian lodge in the heart of the New Forest,
with a relaxed, family-friendly vibe and well-
regarded spa. 'Everything is just so without being
strained,' says a Guide insider. Romantic, neutral-
tone rooms have a shabby-chic feel that is 'way
more chic than shabby'. They range from 'cosy'
main-house rooms with a bath by the window and
a walk-in shower, to hideaway suites, lodges and
cabins with open fires, and new-look pavilions.
Best of the public rooms is the glass-ceilinged
Courtyard bar, 'a hugely appealing place to sip
a drink'. In Hartnett and Holder restaurant,
Angela Hartnett and Luke Holder serve 'the best
of Italian and British food'. Short menus might
include Woolley Park guineafowl, confit leg
and nduja braised beans, and 'if you like truffle,
you're in for a treat'. Or go for alfresco grazing
from Raw & Cured, maybe Isle of Wight tomato
or spiced chickpea salad, butterbean hummus,
charcuterie from the smokehouse, local cheeses.
'The grounds are perfect for a wander' with forest
trails from the door. 'We took bikes and rode
to the Pig for lunch' (see The Pig in the Forest,
Brockenhurst).

Beaulieu Road
Lyndhurst SO43 7FZ

T: 02380 287177
E: info@limewood.co.uk
W: limewoodhotel.co.uk

BEDROOMS: 33. 5 on ground floor,
2 suitable for disabled, 16 in pavilions
and cottages in the grounds.
OPEN: all year.
FACILITIES: lifts, 2 bars, 3 lounges,
2 restaurants, private dining rooms,
in-room TV (Freeview), civil wedding
licence, spa (indoor pool), 14-acre
gardens, cookery school, public rooms
wheelchair accessible.
BACKGROUND MUSIC: all day in public
areas.
LOCATION: in New Forest, 12 miles
SW of Southampton.
CHILDREN: all ages welcomed, no
charge for extra bed.
DOGS: allowed in outside bedrooms
(£30 per stay), not main house.
CREDIT CARDS: MC, Visa.
PRICES: doubles from £395. Breakfast
from £18.50, à la carte £65. 1-night
bookings refused most weekends.

MARKET DRAYTON Shropshire   MAP 3:B5

GOLDSTONE HALL

There are many special things about John and Sue Cushing's red brick Georgian manor house in Shropshire dairy country, from the 'excellent food' to 'spotless, spacious and well-planned bedrooms', but the flower-filled borders and vast kitchen garden are truly remarkable. Open to the public from March to October under the Royal Horticultural Society Partner Garden scheme, they supply much of the produce for Liam Philbin's tasting menus. Garden-to-plate dishes might feature venison loin, faggot, parsnip, pine, cavolo nero, elderberry sauce; for vegetarians, beetroot, goat's cheese mousse, truffle honey, sourdough crackers. Of the wide choice of bedrooms, one has an impressive antique four-poster, while a garden room with a massive bath and power shower looks out over resplendent rose beds, through an ancient acacia. All have a fridge, milk and home-baked cookies. A 'delicious breakfast with freshly squeezed juices' is served in the orangery. 'The gardens are beautiful, but the overwhelming memory is of the proprietors and the friendly yet totally professional staff.' (Christopher Smith, and others)

Goldstone
Market Drayton TF9 2NA

T: 01630 661202
E: enquiries@goldstonehall.com
W: goldstonehall.com

BEDROOMS: 12. 2 on ground floor.
OPEN: all year.
FACILITIES: bar, lounge, drawing room, dining room, orangery, in-room TV (Sky, Freeview), function facilities, civil wedding licence, 5 acres of grounds (walled garden, kitchen garden, Great Lawn), public rooms and garden wheelchair accessible, adapted toilets.
BACKGROUND MUSIC: in bar and dining room.
LOCATION: 5 miles S of Market Drayton.
CHILDREN: all ages welcomed, extra bed £11.50–£28.
DOGS: not allowed.
CREDIT CARDS: Amex, MC, Visa.
PRICES: B&B doubles from £150, singles from £95. 7-course tasting menu £40.

MARTINHOE Devon   MAP 1:B4

THE OLD RECTORY HOTEL

❦ Previous César winner

The deliciously remote setting in a tiny Exmoor hamlet is as 'exceptional' as the food at this small hotel just 500 yards from the coast path, with views over hog-backed cliffs to the Bristol Channel. 'Attentive' hosts Huw Rees and Sam Prosser bought the hotel in 2008, chucked out the chintz and made it over in restrained good taste, with soft-hued paint finishes and wallpaper of the gentler kind. They took to hospitality as our readers took to them, praising everything from the 'friendly staff' to the 'attractive garden with waterfall and stream'. Dinner is a highlight, served after drinks and canapés, and cooked by Michael Caines alumnus Thomas Frost. He uses produce from surrounding land and sea with vegetables from the garden to create a short, nightly menu of dishes such as turbot with Noilly Prat sauce. Bedrooms, some in the coach house, have Noble Isle toiletries, spring water on tap, perhaps a roll-top bath and separate shower. A two-bedroom duplex suite should by now be ready, a perfect base from which to explore Exmoor's national park. Just be sure to return in time for tea – Huw's cakes get a special mention.

Berry's Ground Lane
Martinhoe EX31 4QT

T: 01598 763368
E: reception@oldrectoryhotel.co.uk
W: oldrectoryhotel.co.uk

BEDROOMS: 12. 2 on ground floor, 3 in coach house, 1 in cottage annexe.
OPEN: Mar–early Nov.
FACILITIES: 2 lounges, orangery, dining room, in-room TV (Freeview), 3-acre grounds, EV charging, public rooms including restaurant wheelchair accessible, toilet not adapted.
BACKGROUND MUSIC: 'very quiet' in dining room only.
LOCATION: 4 miles W of Lynton.
CHILDREN: not under 14.
DOGS: not allowed.
CREDIT CARDS: Amex, MC, Visa.
PRICES: B&B doubles from £190, singles from £175. À la carte £35, 1-night bookings refused at present (but check).

MAWGAN PORTH Cornwall

BEDRUTHAN HOTEL AND SPA

♔Previous César winner

'The location is stunning, the views as the sun sets truly magical' from this family-run, cliff-top hotel and spa, with acres of Scandi-style relaxation space and squashy sofas. There is plenty to do, from relaxing in a spa pool to surfing at the beach. A wide choice of accommodation suits everyone from the solo traveller to families and dogs. There are adults-only doubles, many with a sea view through a picture window, family apartments with a lounge, a coffee machine, and a terrace with sun loungers. A reader's country-facing room was 'smart and clean' but the lack of a sea view, he concedes, may have contributed to a sense that the hotel was slightly off form. However, 'I did have two reasonable evening meals, one in the Wild Café, one in The Herring', the former serving breakfast, deli lunches, dinner à la carte (including a vegan menu), the latter for dinner, with a choice of dishes such as roast cod, fregola, orange, lemongrass, basil, clams; one meat and one veggie option. Daytime alfresco dining is available in the dunes garden, or order packed lunches for a beach picnic. (See also sister hotel The Scarlet, next entry.)

Trenance
Mawgan Porth TR8 4BU

T: 01637 860860
E: stay@bedruthan.com
W: bedruthan.com

BEDROOMS: 101. 1 suitable for disabled, apartment suites in separate block.
OPEN: all year.
FACILITIES: lift, bar, terrace, 2 restaurants (vegan menu), lounge, in-room TV (Freeview), spa (indoor pool), shop, art gallery, civil wedding licence, 5-acre grounds (3 heated pools, tennis), EV charging, several areas wheelchair accessible.
BACKGROUND MUSIC: in restaurant, café and bar.
LOCATION: 4 miles NE of Newquay.
CHILDREN: all ages welcomed, family rooms but no extra beds.
DOGS: allowed in some bedrooms (£12 per dog), some public areas.
CREDIT CARDS: MC, Visa.
PRICES: B&B doubles from £165, singles from £95. Set-price dinner £40 (Herring), à la carte £26 (Wild Café).

MAWGAN PORTH Cornwall

MAP 1:D2

THE SCARLET

♀ Previous César winner

Serenity and space are the two words that crop up most in the wealth of praise we receive for this 'utterly relaxing' adults-only spa hotel with sublime views over beach and sea. 'It never feels crowded', so 'you can really relax', say guests, particularly with 'the sight and sound of the sea everywhere'. Bedrooms, with their light, Scandi styling of stripped-wood floors and floor-to-ceiling windows, have superb coastal views, all with outside space, whether terrace, balcony or courtyard garden. Readers had a 'Just Right' room and everything was 'just right, from the exquisite natural pool to the lobster rolls at lunch'. 'High-class' facilities include an art-filled library, relaxation terrace, an indoor as well as outdoor pool and Ayurvedic spa. The cliff-top hot tubs are 'a marvellous treat as the sun starts to descend'. There is a 'good and varied dinner menu' with inventive dishes such as lemongrass prawns followed by duck with blueberries and shiitake mushrooms, and 'excellent risotto'. Staff are 'discreet' but 'attentive when you need them'. 'Five stars is not enough for this hotel.' (Tessa Stuart, and many others)

Tredragon Road
Mawgan Porth TR8 4DQ

T: 01637 861800
E: stay@scarlethotel.co.uk
W: scarlethotel.co.uk

BEDROOMS: 37. 2 suitable for disabled.
OPEN: open all year.
FACILITIES: lift, 2 lounges, bar, library, restaurant (vegetarian/vegan menus), in-room TV (Freeview), civil wedding licence, spa, indoor pool, outdoor reed pool, terrace, meadow garden, EV charging, public areas wheelchair accessible, adapted toilet.
BACKGROUND MUSIC: all day in bar and restaurant.
LOCATION: 4 miles NE of Newquay.
CHILDREN: not allowed.
DOGS: allowed in 5 selected bedrooms (£15 per night), some public areas.
CREDIT CARDS: MC, Visa.
PRICES: B&B doubles from £245, singles from £225. Fixed-price dinner £52, tasting menu £70. 1-night bookings refused Fri/Sat.

MELLS Somerset

THE TALBOT INN

𝒬 Previous César winner

There's plenty of history in this 15th-century
coaching inn with its old arched carriageway, but
it's been brought bang up to date by a shabby-chic
make-over at no cost to its charm. It's the kind of
place you might find a suckling pig spit-roasting
over the open fire, but where you can be sure of
a comfortable night in the stylish, great-value
bedrooms. This was a second venture for Dan
Brod and Charlie Luxton, with Matt Greenlees
(see also The Beckford Arms, Tisbury; The Lord
Poulett Arms, Hinton St George; and The Bath
Arms, Horningsham). They have kitted out the
rooms with contemporary furniture, seagrass
flooring, a retro radio, Bramley toiletries, and
perhaps an emperor-size four-poster, with in-
room bath. Some rooms can sleep a family; two
can interconnect. Downstairs, the atmospheric bar
serves plenty of traditional tipples (try the Talbot
Ale), and in summer, the restaurant spills out into
the cobbled courtyard. Upgraded pub classics
include a very superior ploughman's with sausage
roll alongside more sophisticated dishes such as
sea bass with charred grelot, chanterelles and
sherry reduction, or herb polenta, pickled girolles,
kalettes, walnut pesto and tomato fondue.

Selwood Street
Mells BA11 3PN

T: 01373 812254
E: info@talbotinn.com
W: talbotinn.com

BEDROOMS: 8. 1 on ground floor.
OPEN: all year except 25 Dec.
FACILITIES: sitting room, bar,
restaurant, coach house grill room, in-
room smart TV (including Freeview),
cobbled courtyard, small garden,
parking.
BACKGROUND MUSIC: in public areas.
LOCATION: in village.
CHILDREN: all ages welcomed, cots
£10, extra bed £25.
DOGS: allowed in 1 bedroom (£10 one-
off charge), and in all public areas.
CREDIT CARDS: MC, Visa.
PRICES: B&B doubles from £105.
À la carte £35. 1-night bookings
refused weekends.

MILTON ABBOT Devon

MAP 1:D3

HOTEL ENDSLEIGH

♔ Previous César winner

Olga Polizzi's cottage-orné with tall chimneys, verandas, gables and dormers, in an Arcadian landscape on the River Tamar, is full of flair – and of history. Built as a fishing lodge for the 6th Duke of Bedford and Duchess Georgiana, it has a thatched dairy, and Grade I listed parkland created by Humphry Repton, who confessed 'I never so well pleased myself.' Readers share his sentiments: 'The grounds are simply spectacular, a valley of unreal natural beauty.' Guide trusties who had previously stayed only once were 'welcomed as though we were regulars'. A fire roars in the stylish, spacious drawing room, afternoon tea is laid out in the library, and bedrooms are chic and uncluttered. 'Our room, up two very steep sets of stairs, was welcoming and bright.' Dine in the panelled dining room, or outdoors, under a parasol. Tom Ewings' 'excellent' short menus include dishes such as John Dory, herb potato beignets, shrimp, caper and potato beurre noisette. However, the wine menu 'perhaps lacked choice for a hotel of this standard'. Breakfast brings organic porridge, free-range eggs, local sausages. (Chris and Erika Savory, SG}

Milton Abbot
Tavistock PL19 0PQ

T: 01822 870000
E: hotelendsleigh@
   thepolizzicollection.com
W: hotelendsleigh.com

BEDROOMS: 19. 1 on ground floor, 3 in stables, 1 in lodge (1 mile from main house), 1 suite suitable for disabled.
OPEN: all year.
FACILITIES: drawing room, library, card room, bar, 2 dining rooms, in-room TV (Freeview), civil wedding licence, 108-acre estate (fishing, ghillie), EV charging, public rooms wheelchair accessible, adapted toilet.
BACKGROUND MUSIC: none.
LOCATION: 7 miles NW of Tavistock.
CHILDREN: all ages welcomed, cots free, extra bed £40.
DOGS: allowed in bedrooms (£20 a night), lounges, not in restaurant or library at tea time.
CREDIT CARDS: MC, Visa.
PRICES: B&B doubles from £235. Set dinner £55. 1-night bookings refused Fri, Sat.

MOUSEHOLE Cornwall   MAP 1:E1

THE OLD COASTGUARD

♔ Previous César winner

'A haven of tranquillity from the moment you
arrive', this pub-with-rooms in a pretty Cornish
fishing village gets full marks from readers who
praise its 'amazing rooms, food and views'. The
Inkin brothers (see also The Gurnard's Head,
Zennor, and The Felin Fach Griffin, Felin Fach,
Wales) have created a relaxed family- and dog-
friendly vibe – 'they even have a doggie station,
with dog blankets, biscuits, poo bags'. The look is
of effortless, casual chic: bare floorboards, comfy
sofas, a blazing fire on cold days, lime-painted
walls hung with works by local artists. 'Spacious,
boutique-style' rooms have a Roberts radio,
cafetière coffee and books, but no TV to detract
from the sea view ('try to get a balcony room'). Eat
on the terrace in the 'beautiful gardens' or in the
Upper Deck, gazing out to St Clement's Island.
Chef Jamie Porter shares the owners' passion
for local, sustainable produce, which shines in
dishes such as wild sea bass with mussel velouté.
'The food is always great,' writes one reader.
'Our favourite place to stay in Cornwall,' writes
another. 'Breakfasts are to die for.' (CM, KB,
and others)

The Parade
Mousehole
Penzance TR19 6PR

T: 01736 731222
E: bookings@oldcoastguardhotel.
   co.uk
W: oldcoastguardhotel.co.uk

BEDROOMS: 14.
OPEN: all year except 24/25 Dec.
FACILITIES: bar, sun lounge, restaurant,
sea-facing garden with path to beach,
no in-room TV, parking, restaurant
and bar wheelchair accessible.
BACKGROUND MUSIC: Radio 4 at
breakfast, selected music at other
mealtimes.
LOCATION: 2-min. walk from village,
3 miles S of Newlyn.
CHILDREN: all ages welcomed, no
charge for under-5s, extra bed for 5
and over £25, children's menu.
DOGS: allowed in bedrooms (no charge,
treats, towels, bowls), in bar and on
sun deck, not in dining room.
CREDIT CARDS: MC, Visa.
PRICES: B&B doubles from £157.50,
singles from £115. Set dinner £27,
à la carte £32. 1-night bookings only
rarely refused.

MULLION COVE Cornwall

MAP 1:E2

MULLION COVE HOTEL

'In a glorious setting' on the cliff-top with 'spectacular views', this Edwardian cathedral of a hotel that opened its doors in 1898 after being built by the Great Western Railway also has a 'really nice, welcoming atmosphere'. Owned since 2006 by the Grose family, it has been thoroughly modernised, the most recent addition being a spa, with outdoor pool and hot tub and a wall of windows to show off the vista. That view is on offer from some of the bedrooms, decorated with a soft coastal palette and contemporary furniture. 'Our large room was lovely, with an excellent bathroom and very comfortable bed,' wrote a reader. You can eat in the bistro, outside, or in the more formal ambience of the Atlantic View restaurant. James Heath's menu caters to all tastes, from a burger, steak or fish and chips, to hot and cold seafood platters, and vegans have their own menu of dishes such as tofu and cashew curry, charred tenderstem, chickpea dhal, cucumber and mint salad. A varied breakfast featuring a full Cornish, smoked haddock, smashed avocado, sets you up to walk the Cornish Coast Path. 'Lovely staff, excellent food.' (PG, and others)

Cliff Road
Mullion Cove
Helston TR12 7EP

T: 01326 240328
E: enquiries@mullion-cove.co.uk
W: mullion-cove.co.uk

BEDROOMS: 30. Some on ground floor.
OPEN: all year.
FACILITIES: lift, 3 lounges, bar, restaurant (vegan menu), in-room TV (Freeview), 1-acre garden, 10-metre heated outdoor swimming pool, EV charging, public areas wheelchair accessible, adapted toilet.
BACKGROUND MUSIC: at mealtimes and in bar.
LOCATION: on edge of village.
CHILDREN: all ages welcomed, extra bed £35.
DOGS: allowed in some bedrooms (£9 a night) and in 1 lounge.
CREDIT CARDS: Amex, MC, Visa.
PRICES: B&B doubles from £110, singles from £95. Set-price dinner £40, à la carte £35. 1-night bookings sometimes refused bank holiday Sat.

NEAR SAWREY Cumbria

MAP 4: inset C2

EES WYKE COUNTRY HOUSE

Richard Lee often greets guests in his chef's uniform, which sets the tone for this personally run country house with views over Esthwaite Water and fells. The whitewashed Georgian house 'has the feel of a warm comfortable family home' with traditionally furnished rooms – floral-print sofas, lamps on side tables, dado panelling, open fires – and windows filled with classic Lakeland views. 'Good-sized bedrooms' have soft colours, pretty wallpapers and a sprinkling of antiques, with cosier, beamed rooms on the second floor. All enjoy those views plus decanters of sherry and luxurious Penhaligon amenities in the bright bathrooms; some are quite small and most shower only. 'Richard takes his food very seriously,' said one reader who enjoyed the set, short-choice menu which might include roast duckling with thyme, ginger and honey, or grilled salmon with crushed pink peppercorn sauce. (Vegan and vegetarian dishes upon request.) The 'consistently excellent' breakfast is a feast of freshly squeezed juices, home-made bread and marmalade, plus kippers, haddock and a Lakeland grill. 'Wonderfully helpful and friendly staff.' (Tony Hall, LH, AB)

Near Sawrey
Ambleside LA22 0JZ

T: 01539 436393
E: mail@eeswyke.co.uk
W: eeswyke.co.uk

BEDROOMS: 9. 1 on ground floor, 7 en suite, 2 with separate private bathroom.
OPEN: all year except 20–30 Dec.
FACILITIES: 2 lounges, restaurant, in-room TV (Freeview), veranda, ½-acre garden, unsuitable for disabled.
BACKGROUND MUSIC: none.
LOCATION: edge of village 2½ miles SE of Hawkshead on B5285.
CHILDREN: not under 12.
DOGS: not allowed.
CREDIT CARDS: MC, Visa.
PRICES: B&B doubles from £110, singles from £90. Set dinner £40. 1-night bookings sometimes refused weekends, bank holidays.

NETHER WESTCOTE Oxfordshire

MAP 3:D6

THE FEATHERED NEST

♥ Previous César winner

The lovely views across the Evenlode valley from the terrace or dining room could almost distract you from the exceptional food at this dining pub-with-rooms on the edge of a Cotswold village. A 300-year-old malthouse that was reincarnated as a boozer, it was elevated to gastronomic status by previous owners, and is now the pride and joy of Adam Taylor. You can join the locals and hop on a saddle stool in the beamed bar for a pint of Hooky, but this really is a place to eat. Matt Weedon has headed some formidable Michelin-starred kitchens, but the style here is simpler. Maybe Nest garden vegetable salad in miso aïoli; gnocchi with brassicas, truffled leeks and cauliflower; a burger, saddle of lamb, or soft-shell crab KFC style, surely finger-lickin' good. New this year are infrared heaters and a terrace canopy, a wood-fired pizza oven for alfresco dining. The four bedrooms are contemporary in style and supplied with a coffee machine, home-made cookies, a decanter of port, posh toiletries and fluffy robes. The largest, Cuckoo's Den, has a roll-top bath and separate drench shower, plus lovely valley views.

Nether Westcote
Chipping Norton OX7 6SD

T: 01993 833030
E: info@thefeatherednestinn.co.uk
W: thefeatherednestinn.co.uk

BEDROOMS: 4.
OPEN: closed Tues/Wed (except special trading days), open on Christmas Day.
FACILITIES: 2 bars, small lounge, dining room, in-room TV (Freeview), civil wedding licence, 2-acre garden, restaurant and bar wheelchair accessible, adapted toilet.
BACKGROUND MUSIC: all day in bar, restaurant and on terrace, occasionally live.
LOCATION: in hamlet, 5 miles S of Stow-on-the-Wold.
CHILDREN: all ages welcomed, no extra beds, children's menu.
DOGS: allowed in bar only.
CREDIT CARDS: Amex, MC, Visa.
PRICES: B&B doubles from £185. À la carte £50, 6-course tasting menu £65.

NEW MILTON Hampshire

MAP 2:E2

CHEWTON GLEN

Imagine a luxurious resort with spa, pools, tennis, kids' club – even a cookery school – at a quintessentially English country house, and you've captured the enduring appeal of Chewton Glen. Readers struggle for superlatives: 'Beautiful hotel, wonderful food, great cellar.' 'Chewton Glen is a gorgeous oasis in the New Forest with fantastic facilities.' With 130 acres of woodland, gardens and parkland as well, there's no need to leave this five-star cocoon. Relax in an elegant lounge or around the refurbished, gleaming-white spa pool – or outdoor pool, if you prefer. Bedrooms are elegant country house with marble bathrooms, many with balcony or terrace. Some have a contemporary edge – stripped-wood floor, shots of bold colour – while the 'amazing' treehouse suites are sharply modern, with hot tubs and log-burners, 'perfect in every way'. Both restaurants are 'superb': The Dining Room with traditional fine dining such as steaks and lobster, and the breezier Kitchen with gourmet burgers and fish platters. With 'outstanding' service throughout, it's 'the ultimate indulgent treat!' (Tim Mitchell, Stephanie Palfreeman, AH)

Christchurch Road
New Milton BH25 6QS

T: 01425 275341
E: reservations@chewtonglen.com
W: chewtonglen.com

BEDROOMS: 72. 14 on ground floor, 14 tree-house suites in grounds, 1 suitable for disabled.
OPEN: all year.
FACILITIES: lounges, bar, 2 restaurants, function rooms, in-room TV (Sky), civil wedding licence, cookery school, spa, indoor pool, 130-acre grounds (heated pool, tennis, golf), public rooms (not spa) wheelchair accessible, EV charging.
BACKGROUND MUSIC: 'subtle' in public areas.
LOCATION: on S edge of New Forest.
CHILDREN: all ages welcomed, no charge for extra bed.
DOGS: allowed in tree-house suites (£35 per stay), on terraces.
CREDIT CARDS: Amex, MC, Visa.
PRICES: B&B doubles from £370, singles from £350. À la carte £70 (Dining Room), £42 (Kitchen). 1-night stays sometimes refused Sat.

NEW ROMNEY Kent

MAP 2:E5

ROMNEY BAY HOUSE

Ω Previous César winner

Amid the evocative, sheep-grazed wetlands of
Romney Marsh, between golf course and shingle
beach, an Edwardian house built by Clough
Williams-Ellis is now 'a lovely, secluded hotel'.
Drive down a bumpy road to receive a warm
welcome from hosts Lisa and Clinton Lovell.
Bedrooms – two with four-poster, some sea facing,
with binoculars to train on France – are decorated
in soft tones, with wicker armchairs. On cold days
you might curl up by the fire in the first-floor
lounge with a good book (say Russell Thorndike's
Doctor Syn: A Smuggler Tale of Romney Marsh).
However, readers noted, 'before dinner it was lit
only by candles', which 'looked lovely' but made
reading tricky. Four nights a week, classically
trained chef Clinton cooks a four-course dinner,
maybe pan-fried skate cheeks; salt marsh lamb,
braised red cabbage, fondant potato, Madeira
jus. 'The food is as delicious as ever, and when
the young waiter noticed my hesitation, he asked
if I would like the duck cooked a little more.'
'Personal style, a kind hostess, delicious food, an
interesting building, good seaside walks. What
more could you want?' (M and JB, and others)

Coast Road
Littlestone
New Romney TN28 8QY

T: 01797 364747
E: enquiries@romneybayhousehotel.
co.uk
W: romneybayhousehotel.co.uk

BEDROOMS: 10.
OPEN: all year except Christmas and
New Year, dining room open Tues/
Wed/Fri/Sat for dinner only.
FACILITIES: bar, sitting room, first-
floor lounge with sea views, dining
room, in-room TV (Freeview), small
function facilities, 1-acre garden,
unsuitable for disabled.
BACKGROUND MUSIC: none.
LOCATION: 1½ miles from New
Romney.
CHILDREN: aged 14 and over
welcomed.
DOGS: only guide dogs allowed.
CREDIT CARDS: Amex, MC, Visa.
PRICES: B&B doubles from £95, singles
from £80. Set dinner £49. 1-night
advance bookings refused weekends.

NEWCASTLE UPON TYNE Tyne and Wear   MAP 4:B4

JESMOND DENE HOUSE

♺ Previous César winner

A city hotel with country house style, Jesmond
Dene House is a peaceful retreat 'in pretty
gardens on the edge of a beautiful valley', yet
only a ten-minute drive from Newcastle centre.
The Arts and Crafts mansion, once home to Sir
Andrew Noble, a partner in Lord Armstrong's
local shipping and armaments company, is
impressive, with towers, decorative chimneys and
tall, mullioned windows. Grand interiors of wood
panelling, inglenook fireplaces and stained glass
are softened with bold colours, contemporary
furniture, and modern art and photography:
'relaxed and inviting', reports a trusted reader,
with 'smiley and attentive staff'. Bedrooms are
'contemporary and understatedly elegant' – velvet
armchairs, muted colours, feature wallpapers.
One reader loved her 'large, immaculate, well-
decorated room' but found the 'lighting was
inadequate'. Metro-tiled bathrooms have under-
floor heating. Dinner from MasterChef: The
Professionals finalist Danny Parker could include
fishcakes with curry mayonnaise and confit
duck with spiced Puy lentils. There's a simpler
bar menu, popular afternoon tea and extensive
breakfast choice. (HP, and others)

Jesmond Dene Road
Newcastle upon Tyne NE2 2EY

T: 0191 212 3000
E: info@jesmonddenehouse.co.uk
W: jesmonddenehouse.co.uk

BEDROOMS: 40. 8 in adjacent New
House, 2 suitable for disabled.
OPEN: all year, Sun eve, Mon and Tues
restaurant for hotel guests only.
FACILITIES: lift, lounge, cocktail bar,
restaurant, conference/function
facilities, terrace, in-room TV (Sky),
civil wedding licence, parking, ¼-acre
garden, public areas wheelchair
accessible, adapted toilet.
BACKGROUND MUSIC: in public areas
and restaurant.
LOCATION: 2 miles from city centre.
CHILDREN: all ages welcomed, extra
bed £20.
DOGS: allowed on restaurant terrace
only.
CREDIT CARDS: Amex, MC, Visa.
PRICES: B&B doubles/singles from
£137. À la carte £45.

NEWTON ABBOT Devon

MAP 1:D4

THE ROCK INN

'The perfect place to stay for walking on Dartmoor', the Graves family's whitewashed inn may be 'difficult to find two miles along single-track roads' but it's worth it when you get there. It was built in the 1820s, amid a row of cottages for men working the quarry of Haytor, which would furnish the old London Bridge (now spanning the Colorado River in Arizona). Trusted readers 'feel very much at home there'. 'The friendliness of the staff, the comfort of the bedrooms and quality of cooking were all superb,' writes another reader. One important caveat: 'The bedrooms must be reached by steep stairs and a slightly difficult corner.' The bar is atmospheric with beams and brasses. Bedrooms, too, have exposed beams, perhaps a balcony with moorland views, or an antique four-poster. They are characterful with no boutique pretensions. Food is served in 'a very cosy section next to the bar', in a 'conservatory-style' area and in the pretty beer garden. Imaginative menus might include local pheasant with red wine jus or pumpkin risotto with goat's cheese. 'We always enjoy our visits.' (Dr Gerald Michael, DG)

Haytor Vale
Newton Abbot TQ13 9XP

T: 01364 661305
E: info@rock-inn.co.uk
W: rock-inn.co.uk

BEDROOMS: 9.
OPEN: all year except 25/26 Dec.
FACILITIES: bar, restaurant, snug bar, conservatory, in-room TV (Freeview), ½-acre garden, bar and restaurant wheelchair accessible, no adapted toilet.
BACKGROUND MUSIC: in bar, restaurant.
LOCATION: 3 miles W of Bovey Tracey.
CHILDREN: all ages welcomed, extra beds £20, no under-14s in main bar area, children's menu.
DOGS: allowed in 2 country-view bedrooms (£10 a night), bar, 1 dining room.
CREDIT CARDS: MC, Visa.
PRICES: B&B doubles from £120. À la carte £35. Sat night bookings must include dinner. 1-night bookings sometimes refused.

NORTH WALSHAM Norfolk

MAP 2:A6

BEECHWOOD HOTEL

Come for a whodunnit night at Emma and Hugh Asher's ivy-smothered hotel, 'well placed for touring north Norfolk', and murder by chocolate could be on the menu. South African nights bring dishes such as lamb bobotie, seafood potjiekos and ostrich kebabs. Agatha Christie memorabilia celebrate the fact that the author used to stay here with friends when the house was named The Shrubs. Bedrooms are old-fashioned, some with an antique four-poster, some with French doors to the garden, which is 'lovely to wander round'. Two garden rooms have a modern four-poster, a slipper bath and walk-in shower, sauna cabin and deck with hot tub. In the dining room, and now in a converted summer house, Steven Norgate's menus are sourced with the emphasis on quality, food miles, sustainability and animal welfare. Typical dishes include herb-crusted hake with caper beurre noisette; saddle of lamb with redcurrant jus; caramelised onion tart with three cheeses (maybe Binham Blue and Gurney's Gold, no mousetrap). Golfers' packages are available, but be wary: a 'golf stick' was the murder weapon in Spider's Web. (ML, SP)

20 Cromer Road
North Walsham NR28 0HD

T: 01692 403231
E: info@beechwood-hotel.co.uk
W: beechwood-hotel.co.uk

BEDROOMS: 20. 4 on ground floor, 2 garden spa rooms with deck, hot tub and sauna.
OPEN: all year except 27/28 Dec.
FACILITIES: bar, 2 lounges, restaurant (vegetarian/vegan menus), in-room TV (Freeview), 100-metre landscaped garden (croquet).
BACKGROUND MUSIC: all day in public rooms.
LOCATION: near town centre.
CHILDREN: all ages welcomed, extra bed £25 (under-12s).
DOGS: allowed in bedrooms by prior arrangement (£15 per night), public rooms, not in restaurant.
CREDIT CARDS: Amex, MC, Visa.
PRICES: B&B doubles from £110, singles from £70. À la carte £40, tasting menu £85.

NORWICH Norfolk

MAP 2:B5

THE ASSEMBLY HOUSE

A Georgian House of Assemblies, built over medieval footings, where Paganini played the violin and the Noverre family taught Norwich to polka, remains today a place for song and dance – an events venue with hotel, restaurant and cookery school. Bedrooms, in a separate building, have been beautifully styled by Annabel Grey in grand fashion, with splashes of bright, bold colours, and perhaps a modern four-poster, a display of Staffordshire dogs or Spode teapots, and eye-catching artwork. All have air conditioning, an espresso machine, under-floor bathroom heating. A panelled ground-floor room has a half-tester bed, a lounge, a terrace, a double-ended bath and drench shower. Four new rooms in the east wing are promised, in palatial style, with fine antiques and luxurious bathroom. You can have drinks by the fire under chandeliers in the Grand Hall. Meals are served by day in the restaurant. Maybe wake up to eggs Benedict, a vegetarian fry-up or Norfolk rarebit; lunch on a seafood platter, a bean burger or a meze platter, but it is afternoon tea that really takes the cake.

Theatre Street
Norwich NR2 1RQ

T: 01603 626402
E: admin@assemblyhousenorwich.co.uk
W: assemblyhousenorwich.co.uk

BEDROOMS: 15. All in St Mary's House extension, 6 with private garden, 2 suitable for disabled.
OPEN: all year.
FACILITIES: grand entrance hall, restaurant, 6 event rooms, civil wedding licence, in-room TV (Sky, Freeview), 1-acre courtyard garden, parking, public rooms wheelchair accessible, adapted toilet.
BACKGROUND MUSIC: none.
LOCATION: central, car park permits for pay-and-display.
CHILDREN: all ages welcomed, extra bed £25, daytime children's menu.
DOGS: not allowed.
CREDIT CARDS: Amex, MC, Visa.
PRICES: B&B doubles from £170. Fixed-price early supper £21–£25 (steak £3 supplement, side dishes £3.95).

NOTTINGHAM Nottinghamshire

MAP 2:A3

HART'S HOTEL

With its light footprint, floor-to-ceiling windows
and stainless steel roof, this sustainably built hotel
on the castle ramparts chimes with Nottingham's
ambition to be the UK's first carbon-neutral city.
Tim and Stefa Hart, who offer country luxury
par excellence at Hambleton Hall, Hambleton
(see entry), have created a chic urban counterpart
with all their values of service, good food and
local engagement. Rooms range from doubles
overlooking an internal courtyard, to family
suites, many with views over the gardens and
leafy neighbourhood. Dog owners do best to book
a room with outdoor seating and direct garden
access. None is huge ('You wouldn't come here
for spacious accommodation,' a Guide trusty has
advised), but you can take afternoon tea in the bar,
alfresco, or in your room via room service, with
snacks available all day. In the restaurant, Martin
Sludds's short menus might include grilled plaice
with burnt caper butter; gnocchi, wild garlic,
morels, miso butter. At breakfast there is freshly
squeezed orange juice, bread from Hambleton
Bakery, free-range eggs, Melton Mowbray
sausages and bacon. (RG)

Standard Hill
Park Row
Nottingham NG1 6GN

T: 0115 988 1900
E: reception@hartshotel.co.uk
w: hartsnottingham.co.uk

BEDROOMS: 32. 2 suitable for disabled.
OPEN: all year, restaurant closed 1 Jan.
FACILITIES: lift, bar, restaurant, in-
room TV (Sky, Freeview), exercise
room, meetings room, civil wedding
licence, courtyard, garden, car
park (£9.95), restaurant wheelchair
accessible, adapted toilet.
BACKGROUND MUSIC: in bar and
restaurant.
LOCATION: city centre.
CHILDREN: all ages welcomed, cot £19,
extra bed £29, children's menu.
DOGS: max. 2 in bedrooms (£10 per
night, no large/aggressive breeds), not
in restaurant or bar.
CREDIT CARDS: Amex, MC, Visa.
PRICES: room-only doubles from £139.
Breakfast £10 (cooked dishes from £5),
à la carte £38 (v/vg £32), (plus 12.5%
discretionary service charge).

OLD HUNSTANTON Norfolk

MAP 2:A5

THE NEPTUNE

Everything is shipshape at Jacki and Kevin
Mangeolles' Michelin-starred restaurant-with-
rooms, occupying a former coaching inn in
a quiet village bordering the busier resort of
'Hun'ston'. They are welcoming hosts ('Such
lovely people!'), Jacki front-of-house, Kevin in the
kitchen, although, as a reader says, he has been
known to come out in his chef's whites to help
serve. Bedrooms are light and bright, with walls
of the palest grey and white-painted furniture.
They are immaculate but fairly snug. Although
there is a bar area with an open fire, there isn't
a residents' lounge, which suggests more of a
gourmet overnight treat than a base for exploring
north Norfolk and returning with sand in your
shoes. It is foodie heaven, though, with 'amazing,
exquisite meals' served in the dining room with
tongue-and-groove and pale taupe walls. A
concise three-course menu brings locally landed
fish, and meat from local farms, or you can opt
for the tasting menu, which might include iced
tomato and mint tea, sweetbreads in maple syrup
and soy, deep-fried plaice with lobster salad and
toasted rice panna cotta.

85 Old Hunstanton Road
Old Hunstanton PE36 6HZ

T: 01485 532122
E: reservations@theneptune.co.uk
W: theneptune.co.uk

BEDROOMS: 4.
OPEN: all year, except Sun, Mon,
26 Dec, 3 weeks Jan, 1 week May,
1 week Nov.
FACILITIES: bar area, restaurant,
in-room TV (Freeview), parking,
unsuitable for disabled.
BACKGROUND MUSIC: in restaurant in
evening.
LOCATION: village centre, on A149.
CHILDREN: not under 10.
DOGS: not allowed.
CREDIT CARDS: Amex, MC, Visa.
PRICES: per room D,B&B from £295
(with tasting menu £335), single
occupancy rates on request. Set-price
dinner £49–£65, tasting menu £80
(to be taken by whole table). 1-night
bookings sometimes refused Sat in
high season.

OLDSTEAD Yorkshire

MAP 4:D4

THE BLACK SWAN AT OLDSTEAD

♔ Previous César winner

A sturdily built old drovers' inn on a sleepy country lane going nowhere in particular is the unlikely setting for this Michelin-starred restaurant-with-rooms. But location is everything. On the edge of the North York Moors, and overlooking the rich farmland which the Banks family have worked for generations, it has full access to the terroir that inspires chef Tommy's food (brother James is front-of-house). Using ingredients largely grown or foraged locally, including some from their kitchen garden, his dishes are about 'tradition and culture cut through with earthy exuberance'. You might start with a blackcurrant leaf martini in the flagged-floor bar before moving upstairs to the Scandi-light dining room to savour dishes such as onion and smoked egg yolk, salt-aged beef with truffle and young buck (cheese), lobster with green strawberries, and honey and yogurt paired with Jerusalem artichoke and chestnut. Bedrooms, in converted stables behind the inn or in a nearby Georgian village house, have a fresh country style with soft colours, solid wood furnishings, plaid wool fabrics and cottagey bathrooms. A peaceful night is pretty much guaranteed.

Oldstead
York YO61 4BL

T: 01347 868387
E: enquiries@blackswanoldstead.co.uk
W: blackswanoldstead.co.uk

BEDROOMS: 9. 4 on ground floor in annexe wing, 5 in Ashberry House, 50 yds away.
OPEN: all year except 24–26 Dec and 1–4 Jan, closed Mon/Tues.
FACILITIES: bar, restaurant (vegetarian menu), private dining room, in-room TV (Freeview), garden, 2-acre kitchen garden and orchard.
BACKGROUND MUSIC: in restaurant.
LOCATION: in village 7 miles E of Thirsk.
CHILDREN: no under-18s overnight, over-9s only in restaurant.
DOGS: not allowed.
CREDIT CARDS: MC, Visa.
PRICES: D,B&B doubles from £520. Tasting menu from £125 dinner and Sat lunch.

OSWESTRY Shropshire

MAP 3:B4

PEN-Y-DYFFRYN

We never want for glowing reports of this dog-friendly former Georgian rectory, 'set in a secluded and beautiful valley', with views to the Welsh hills. From tea and cakes on arrival to a morning newsletter, Miles and Audrey Hunter, with son Tommy and daughter Charlotte, care so well for their guests (sibling Henry has The Castle, Bishop's Castle – hospitality is in their DNA). Rooms range from cosy to suites, in main house, coach house and stables, some with a terrace, a double spa bath. The style is eclectic, nothing shouts 'designer', but so what? 'Our room was smallish but had everything we needed, and a stunning view across the valley,' a reader writes. A nightly-changing menu caters to all, with dishes such as saddle of Welsh lamb with braised salt marsh lamb shoulder, ratatouille and couscous, sea bass with herb gnocchi, and good veggie options. 'The food is absolutely superb,' our reader continues, only wishing there had been more wines by the glass. Breakfast is similarly varied, with smoked haddock, field mushrooms on granary toast, the full English. (R Freeman, SH, JB, and others)

Rhydycroesau
Oswestry SY10 7JD

T: 01691 653700
E: stay@peny.co.uk
W: peny.co.uk

BEDROOMS: 14. 4, each with patio, in coach house, 2 garden suites with patio, 1 on ground floor.
OPEN: all year except Christmas.
FACILITIES: 2 lounges, bar, restaurant, in-room TV (Freeview), 5-acre grounds (summer house, dog-walking area, fly-fishing pool).
BACKGROUND MUSIC: in evening in bar and restaurant.
LOCATION: 3 miles W of Oswestry.
CHILDREN: not under 3, extra bed £35.
DOGS: allowed in some bedrooms (no charge), not in public rooms after 6.30 pm.
CREDIT CARDS: MC, Visa.
PRICES: B&B doubles from £160, singles from £110. Set menu £45. 1-night bookings occasionally refused Sat.

OXFORD Oxfordshire

MAP 2:C3

OLD BANK HOTEL

Oxford alumni get a discount on rooms from Sunday to Thursday at Jeremy Mogford's smart hotel on the 'High', opposite the university church of St Mary's, and the Bodleian Library. Behind a unified stone facade of a former bank, with tall arched windows, three buildings of different vintage (one Tudor, two 18th century) have been made over in contemporary style. In the former banking hall, hung with modern works from the owner's art collection, tables are set for dining around a large horseshoe-shaped bar. This is Quod, serving food and drinks all day – steaks, burgers, pizza, maybe a lamb or aubergine curry, vegetable cassoulet, chicken schnitzel, spinach, wild garlic and ricotta ravioli. There is alfresco dining, too, on the garden terrace, overlooked by the residents' library. Rooms and suites have a handmade bed, a marble bathroom, more artwork, some with views of dreaming spires, others looking on to Merton College. The best view of all is from the rooftop suite with its cocktail-making station, a shower for two, and glass doors to a terrace. Guests get complimentary use of the hotel's bicycles. (See also next entry.)

92–94 High Street
Oxford OX1 4BJ

T: 01865 799599
E: reservations@oldbankhotel.co.uk
W: oldbankhotel.co.uk

BEDROOMS: 43. 1 suitable for disabled.
OPEN: all year.
FACILITIES: lift, residents' library/
bar, restaurant/bar, dining terrace,
2 meeting/private dining rooms,
in-room TV (Freeview), in-room
spa treatments, civil wedding
licence, small garden, use of bicycles,
parking, EV charging, restaurant, bar
wheelchair accessible, adapted toilet.
BACKGROUND MUSIC: in restaurant and
reception area.
LOCATION: central, car park.
CHILDREN: all ages welcomed, free
extra bed, children's menu.
DOGS: allowed on terrace only.
CREDIT CARDS: Amex, MC, Visa.
PRICES: B&B doubles from £320. À la
carte £35 (plus 12½% discretionary
service charge). 1-night bookings
refused weekends in peak season.

OXFORD Oxfordshire

OLD PARSONAGE HOTEL

Beyond the sturdy oak door of this handsome 17th-century stone dwelling, Jeremy Mogford's country-house-in-the-city hotel has a more bookish, bohemian, clubby feel than its sister enterprise (see previous entry). The walls of the Grill restaurant and bar are hung with oil portraits of writers and artists. You can dine here or in the walled garden, and enjoy 'very good food and wine' from Allan McLaughlin's eclectic menus. Typical dishes might include chicken, leek and morel pie or halibut, caramelised fennel, langoustine butter sauce. There is a library for guests' use, with glass doors to a small terrace. 'Good' modern bedrooms in this 'excellent hotel' range from small doubles with a handmade bed, air conditioning and a marble shower room, through deluxe doubles and junior suites to the two Churchill Suites, with an espresso machine, fresh fruit, a living and dining area, a walk-in rainfall shower and a freestanding bath. They are expensive but, to quote Oscar Wilde (who is said to have been a tenant in the house while temporarily suspended from Magdalen College), 'Anyone who lives within their means suffers from a lack of imagination.'

1 Banbury Road
Oxford OX2 6NN

T: 01865 310210
E: reservations@oldparsonage-hotel.co.uk
W: oldparsonagehotel.co.uk

BEDROOMS: 35. 10 on ground floor, 2 suitable for disabled.
OPEN: all year.
FACILITIES: lounge, library, bar/restaurant, in-room TV (Freeview), civil wedding licence, terrace, rear garden with summerhouse, parking, EV charging, restaurant wheelchair accessible.
BACKGROUND MUSIC: 'very light' in restaurant and bar.
LOCATION: NE end of St Giles, small car park.
CHILDREN: all ages welcomed, under-3s free, extra bed £65, all-day children's menu.
DOGS: allowed on terrace only.
CREDIT CARDS: Amex, MC, Visa.
PRICES: B&B doubles from £320. À la carte £45 (plus 12½% discretionary service charge). 1-night bookings sometimes refused peak weekends.

PADSTOW Cornwall   MAP 1:D2

PADSTOW TOWNHOUSE

The sybarite is like a kid in a sweetshop at Paul Ainsworth's Georgian town house B&B on a quiet back street, where each of the six suites is a lavish confection, with foodie references at every turn. Styled by Paul's wife Emma, they are the perfect accompaniment to the Michelin-starred Paul Ainsworth at No.6, where guests are whisked for dinner in an electric shuttle car (the couple also run a pub and cookery school). Toffee Apple has a double rain-head shower and a handmade double oak-and-copper bath, and a separate lounge/dining area, while Rhubarb & Custard has bedside tables made from restored flour bins, and a painting entitled Marzipan, by James Cullen. A kitchen pantry is run on an honesty basis, and breakfast arrives in a hamper. Or you can head out to the all-day sister venture Caffè Rojano for a sandwich of maple-cured bacon on sourdough, as well as pizzas, pasta and much more. Vegans will find options here, but can't be catered for at the eponymous No.6, where a limited-choice four-course menu includes dishes such as Anjou pigeon, umeboshi condiment, pain au pudding, or lobster, mashed potato and onion gravy.

16–18 High Street
Padstow PL28 8BB

T: 01841 550950
E: stay@padstowtownhouse.co.uk
W: paul-ainsworth.co.uk/padstow-townhouse

BEDROOMS: 6. 2 on ground floor.
OPEN: all year except 24–26 Dec, 2 weeks Jan, open at New Year.
FACILITIES: honesty pantry, in-room smart TV, in-room spa treatments, EV charging, parking, electric shuttle car for guest transport.
BACKGROUND MUSIC: in reception and kitchen pantry area.
LOCATION: in old town, 5 mins' walk from harbour.
CHILDREN: children over 4 welcomed, extra bed £40 for under-16s.
DOGS: allowed in 2 ground-floor bedrooms (max. 2, £25 per dog per night, plus deposit for damages/extra cleaning).
CREDIT CARDS: MC, Visa.
PRICES: B&B doubles from £245. Set menu (Paul Ainsworth at No.6) £105, à la carte (Caffè Rojano) £30.

PADSTOW Cornwall

MAP 1:D2

THE PIG AT HARLYN BAY [NEW]

'A superb new addition to Robin Hutson's Pig litter' comes in the form of an atmospheric mansion that is part Georgian, part Jacobean, part medieval, just minutes from the beach and the South West Coast Path. It is 'lovely in summer, but, we imagine, even better when waves are crashing against the Cornish shore', with a 'quiet, dark stillness' channelling Mark Rylance's Thomas Cromwell. 'From the moment you enter the Map Room, with its inky blue roof and panels, wood-burner and love seat, you can feel its moody magic.' The shabby-chic style blends House of Hackney wallpaper, reclaimed oak floors and Judy Hutson's quirky salvage finds. The bedrooms, some in a sympathetically built outhouse, range from tiny to generous, with a four-poster. 'Room 2 had olive walls, two window seats, views of Harlyn Bay, fresh milk in the fridge.' The 25-mile menus of kitchen garden and local produce include dishes such as ramrod spring onion risotto with Cornish blue, and there is outdoors dining at the Lobster Shed. 'Nothing quite beats sitting in the sun and feasting on the freshest seafood, which tasted even better with English wine.' (JK)

Harlyn Bay
Padstow PL28 8SQ

T: 01841 550240
E: reservations@thepighotel.com
W: thepighotel.com

BEDROOMS: 30. 15 in courtyard building, 4 in garden wagons.
OPEN: all year.
FACILITIES: bar, Map Room, 3 dining rooms, snug, civil wedding licence, Potting Shed treatment room, Lobster Shed (alfresco dining), kitchen garden, orchard, 8-acre grounds, public rooms wheelchair accessible, adapted toilet.
BACKGROUND MUSIC: all day in public areas.
LOCATION: 10-min. drive from Padstow.
CHILDREN: all ages welcomed, no charge for extra beds.
DOGS: not allowed.
CREDIT CARDS: Amex, MC, Visa.
PRICES: room-only doubles from £150. Breakfast £12, à la carte £40.

PADSTOW Cornwall

MAP 1:D2

THE SEAFOOD RESTAURANT

The words Padstow and Rick Stein go together like fish and chips, and his flagship restaurant offers stylish rooms so you can totter up to bed after your fill of the sea. Opened in 1975 by Rick and his former wife, Jill, and overlooking the Camel estuary, the restaurant, with its zinc-topped seafood bar and floor-to-ceiling windows, serves tip-top fresh seafood simply cooked. Perhaps kick off with langoustines or grilled scallops followed by bouillabaisse or lemon sole veronique. On sunny days, dine on the rooftop terrace. Bedrooms, styled by Jill, are fresh and uncluttered with milky-white walls, clean-lined contemporary furniture and pops of breezy colour in blanket throws and cushions. There are books, Roberts radios, simple pot plants and home-made biscuits while two have inviting terraces with wooden loungers and views over the river. Bathrooms are sharply modern with natural toiletries. Breakfast offers freshly squeezed juices, fruit compotes and home-made granola and hot dishes including kippers, smoked haddock kedgeree and smashed avocado on toast. If the food has fired you up, book in to the Cookery School.

Riverside
Padstow PL28 8BY

T: 01841 532700
E: reservations@rickstein.com
W: rickstein.com

BEDROOMS: 16.
OPEN: all year except 24–26 Dec.
FACILITIES: lift (to bedrooms), restaurant, in-room TV (Freeview), restaurant and toilet wheelchair accessible.
BACKGROUND MUSIC: in restaurant.
LOCATION: town centre.
CHILDREN: all ages welcomed, extra bed £30, no under-3s in restaurant.
DOGS: allowed in all but 4 bedrooms (£30 first night, £5 additional nights), in conservatory at breakfast.
CREDIT CARDS: Amex, MC, Visa.
PRICES: B&B doubles/singles from £170. À la carte £50. 1-night bookings refused Sat.

PAINSWICK Gloucestershire   MAP 3:D5

THE PAINSWICK

In a perfect Cotswold village, this 'charming' Palladian mansion with 'wonderful valley views' of Cider with Rosie country 'could not have been a more welcome find' for readers on a dismal day. 'Fires were burning in both sitting rooms, and the staff were equally warm.' The look is smart 'contemporary country house', say Guide insiders, whose 'Snug' room was 'really not so small', decorated in gentle pastel tones, with glorious views. 'A Roberts radio was playing soft classical music when we entered.' Other pleasing touches included 'good toiletries, fudge, biscuits, fresh milk in a minifridge'. You might take a room in the garden wing and have breakfast on the Italianate terrace. In the panelled, parqueted dining room and alfresco, 'first-rate chef' Jamie McCallum's menus are 'unpretentious, using good ingredients', with a 'sensibly short menu but good choice'. 'Broad bean and pea risotto was excellent, as were haddock soufflé and beef Wellington.' Breakfast brings 'delicious breads, pastries, perfectly poached eggs'. (See also Barnsley House, Barnsley; The Lord Crewe Arms, Blanchland; and Calcot & Spa, Tetbury.) (Sue Ockwell, Simon Tonking, and others)

Kemps Lane
Painswick GL6 6YB

T: 01452 813688
E: enquiries@thepainswick.co.uk
W: thepainswick.co.uk

BEDROOMS: 16. 7 in garden wing, 4 in chapel wing.
OPEN: all year.
FACILITIES: bar, lounge, restaurant, games room, private dining room, in-room TV (Sky, Freeview), civil wedding licence, terrace, treatment rooms, ¾-acre garden, unsuitable for disabled.
BACKGROUND MUSIC: all day in public areas.
LOCATION: in village, 4 miles NE of Stroud.
CHILDREN: all ages welcomed, cots £15, extra bed £20.
DOGS: allowed by arrangement in some garden rooms (£15 per night), on terrace, in lounge, not in restaurant.
CREDIT CARDS: Amex, MC, Visa.
PRICES: B&B doubles from £194. À la carte £43. 1-night bookings refused weekends.

PENRITH Cumbria

MAP 4: inset C2

⚲ASKHAM HALL

César award: country house hotel of the year
With topiary garden, 17th-century pele tower
and French drawing room, Askham Hall
sounds grand and formal; not a bit of it. The
ancestral home of the Lowthers, run by Charles
as a Michelin-starred restaurant-with-rooms, is
relaxed and unpretentious with dogs and children
mingling among family heirlooms. Comfortably
cluttered with books and modern art, one drawing
room has doors to a classic English country house
garden. This is a 'lovely building' in a 'wonderful
setting'. Main house bedrooms – some with
leaded windows and fireplace – mix antiques with
modern pieces, those in the courtyard have a rustic
style. Bathrooms may have marble washbasins
and roll-top bath. Most are spacious but one
couple found their standard room 'undersized'
for the price with 'limited hanging space'. Chef
Richard Swale is 'a real wizard' creating dishes
with produce from the kitchen garden and family
estate: beef fillet with cèpes, crab with lovage and
blackcurrant, and salt-baked celeriac with truffle.
Book dinner ahead, warns one reader. Overall,
it's a 'wonderful experience', with an honesty bar,
'affable' host and 'great breakfasts'.

Askham
Penrith CA10 2PF

T: 01931 712350
E: enquiries@askhamhall.co.uk
W: askhamhall.co.uk

BEDROOMS: 19. 2 suitable for disabled.
OPEN: all year excl. Christmas, 2 Jan–
mid-Feb, Sun/Mon.
FACILITIES: 2 drawing rooms, snug,
2 dining rooms (vegetarian menu),
in-room TV (Freeview), civil
wedding licence, 12-acre grounds,
outdoor swimming pool, hot tub,
function facilities, EV charging, main
restaurant wheelchair accessible,
adapted toilet.
BACKGROUND MUSIC: in reception
rooms in evening.
LOCATION: 10 mins from Penrith and
Jct 40 on M6.
CHILDREN: all ages welcomed, free
cots, extra bed £35, no under-10s in
restaurant in evening.
DOGS: allowed (£15 per night), not in
restaurant.
CREDIT CARDS: Amex, MC, Visa.
PRICES: B&B doubles from £160, singles
from £148. Tasting menu £75.

PENRITH Cumbria

MAP 4: inset C2

THE HOUSE AT
TEMPLE SOWERBY

In the oft-overlooked Eden valley, between the Lake District and north Pennines, this handsome country guest house offers 'high standards, a relaxed atmosphere' and fell views. Well placed for exploring both areas – the energetic can climb Cross Fell, the highest point on the Pennine Way – the Georgian-fronted house has a traditional elegance yet a laid-back charm. Owners Andi and Alison Sambrook's 'warm, friendly approach' helps guests 'relax straight away', as does the beautiful and extensive walled garden. 'Comfortable, quiet' bedrooms are smart but unfussy, with striped and patterned wallpapers, pretty fabrics, elegant furniture and a contemporary bathroom. Coach-house rooms are cosy with beams, while bigger bedrooms in the main house have a spa bath or hydrotherapy shower. Breakfast, taken in a red-panelled drawing room, includes own-grown smoothies, a grill of local produce and 'excellent' eggs Benedict. At weekends, the Sambrooks run a café in the conservatory-style dining room that overlooks the garden, but there is no longer a restaurant. For evening meals, local pubs include the Black Swan at Culgaith, two miles away.

Temple Sowerby
Penrith CA10 1RZ

T: 01768 361578
E: stay@templesowerby.com
W: templesowerby.com

BEDROOMS: 11. 2 on ground floor, 4 in coach house.
OPEN: all year, except Mon and Tues eves.
FACILITIES: 2 lounges, bar, coffee shop (Fri–Sun), conference/function facilities, in-room TV (Freeview), 1½-acre walled garden, EV charging, public rooms wheelchair accessible, adapted toilet.
BACKGROUND MUSIC: none.
LOCATION: village centre, 8 miles from Penrith.
CHILDREN: all ages welcomed, no extra beds.
DOGS: allowed in coach house rooms (£10 per night, not unattended), and all areas of main house plus garden.
CREDIT CARDS: MC, Visa.
PRICES: B&B doubles from £100, singles from £90.

PENRITH Cumbria

TEBAY SERVICES HOTEL

This location may surprise you! Tebay Services on the M6 motorway is a much-loved stop en route to Scotland for in-the-know readers who praise its 'quiet rooms overlooking the fell', excellent value, 'cheerful, friendly and helpful' staff, and tranquillity, with 'no hint of a busy motorway nearby'. Created by the resourceful Dunning family after the M6 carved up their hill farm, the chalet-style building has spacious, modern bedrooms and 'superb' king-size beds. One guest 'loved the heated bathroom floor'. There are home-made biscuits and locally produced Sedbergh Soap toiletries. Local sourcing features strongly in the homely, 'well-presented and delicious' food, served both in the fire-warmed lounge or in the restaurant with its panoramic windows. Dishes include home-made pies, gin-cured trout fishcakes and – 'a high spot' of one reader's stay – Dunning farm lamb with dauphinoise potatoes. More farm produce features at breakfast including 'one of the tastiest full English I've had for a long time'. 'We love coming here, the view gives a feeling of peace and well-being.' (Simon and Mithra Tonking, Richard Bright)

Orton
Penrith CA10 3SB

T: 01539 624351
E: reservations@tebayserviceshotel.
   com
W: tebayserviceshotel.com

BEDROOMS: 51. 1 suitable for disabled.
OPEN: all year except 24/25 Dec.
FACILITIES: lounge with log fire, bar, mezzanine, restaurant, in-room TV (Freeview), function/conference facilities, farm shop, restaurant, bar and lounge wheelchair accessible, adapted toilet.
BACKGROUND MUSIC: none.
LOCATION: 2½ miles SW of Orton.
CHILDREN: all ages welcomed, £15 per child in family rooms with bunk beds.
DOGS: allowed in some bedrooms (£15 per night), one area of lounge.
CREDIT CARDS: Amex, MC, Visa.
PRICES: B&B doubles from £111, singles from £79. À la carte £30.

PENSFORD Somerset

MAP 2:D1

THE PIG NEAR BATH

Everything proved to be hog heaven for Guide trusties on a winter weekend break at this Georgian country house in its own deer park. The Pigs are part of Robin Hutson's Home Grown group (see index), of which 'the enthusiastic staff remain the best element', says our aficionado. Interiors are in the signature style of dog-eared opulence, with bare floorboards and chandeliers, good antiques and distressed, faded, pre-loved finds. 'Snug' and 'comfy' rooms in the main house and coach house have a monsoon shower; trade up to 'comfy luxe' for a freestanding bath, or to 'big comfy luxe' for a four-poster. Most unusual is the two-storey Hide, within the largest of the Pigs' kitchen gardens, and with a wood-burning stove. Public rooms have 'plenty of seating areas' and 'a pleasant buzz'. Home-grown, foraged and local ingredients feature on the 25-mile menus in the conservatory, in dishes such as wild garlic pappardelle, whole roasted chicken to share, wild garlic potatoes; roasted plaice, trombone spinach and chicken butter sauce. 'Breakfast is outstanding', with 'freshly squeezed juices', new-laid eggs from the hens. (D and JB)

Hunstrete House
Pensford BS39 4NS

T: 01761 490490
E: info@thepighotel.com
W: thepighotel.com/near-bath

BEDROOMS: 29. 5 in gardens, some on ground floor, 1 with wheelchair access and wet room.
OPEN: all year.
FACILITIES: 2 lounges, bar, restaurant, snug, private dining room, in-room TV (Freeview), civil wedding licence, treatment room, kitchen garden, wild flower meadow, deer park, ground floor/garden areas wheelchair accessible.
BACKGROUND MUSIC: all day in public areas.
LOCATION: 7 miles SW of Bath.
CHILDREN: all ages welcomed, no charge for extra beds.
DOGS: only guide dogs.
CREDIT CARDS: Amex, MC, Visa.
PRICES: room-only doubles £170–£359. Breakfast (continental) £12, (cooked) £16, à la carte £35. 1-night bookings refused weekends, Christmas/New Year.

PENTON Cumbria   MAP 4:B2

PENTONBRIDGE INN

♀ Previous César winner

The lonely setting of this former coaching inn,
half a mile from the Scottish border, belies its
chic bedrooms and creative cooking. Gerald
and Margo Smith have created a stylish interior
– slate floors, tweedy fabrics, modern art – in
a traditional pub without eroding its character.
In the kitchen, Chris Archer, with The Cottage
in the Wood, Braithwaite, pedigree (see entry),
conjures beautiful flavours from seasonal produce.
Much comes from the Smiths' walled garden
at nearby Netherby Hall. Orkney scallop with
pickled kohlrabi and garden pea gazpacho could
be followed by Cartmel valley beef with roasted
carrot and bone-marrow sauce. Bedrooms – some
in the converted barn with high ceilings and
exposed beams, others up a swanky glass-banister
staircase – are contemporary country, with tartan
throws and headboards, rustic wooden cladding
and 'wonderful' designer bathroom. Thoughtful
touches include flowers and home-made
shortbread, while 'stunning views' stretch over
the countryside to Cumbria or Scotland. Breakfast
in the conservatory – with more views – includes
freshly squeezed juice, omelettes, and avocado and
'perfect' poached eggs. (SS)

Penton CA6 5QB

T: 01228 586636
E: info@pentonbridgeinn.co.uk
W: pentonbridgeinn.co.uk

BEDROOMS: 9. 3 in converted barn,
covered walkway from reception, 3 on
ground floor.
OPEN: all year, restaurant closed Mon,
Tues.
FACILITIES: bar, restaurant,
conservatory, in-room TV (Freeview),
EV charging, beer garden, bar and
conservatory wheelchair accessible,
adapted toilet.
BACKGROUND MUSIC: in bar and
restaurant.
LOCATION: rural, 10 mins from
Longtown.
CHILDREN: all ages welcomed, free cot.
DOGS: allowed in 6 bedrooms (£15 per
stay), bar and conservatory, not in
restaurant.
CREDIT CARDS: Amex, MC, Visa.
PRICES: B&B doubles from £150, singles
from £130. À la carte 2 courses £60,
3 courses £70, tasting menu £85.

PENZANCE Cornwall

MAP 1:E1

CHAPEL HOUSE

Susan Stuart's welcoming Georgian town house B&B is so beautiful, it might grace the pages of an interiors magazine. Light-filled rooms in soft greys, greens and blues are a gallery for works from Newlyn Art School. All bedrooms have a view over the harbour to St Michael's Mount, a bathroom with deep bath or monsoon shower and hand-made toiletries. Three at the top, one with in-room bath, share an open-plan landing under a sliding glass roof. Two self-catering suites in an adjoining building are ideal for longer stays. You can relax in the drawing room or on a sunny terrace. There is no bar, but tea, coffee, cakes and drinks can be had all day from the kitchen, where you breakfast on smoothies, locally smoked salmon, sourdough bread, hot dishes cooked to order, with tempting veggie options. Sunday brunch is served until midday. On Fridays and Saturdays guests can sit down to a supper of local ingredients – maybe Newlyn crab cakes, organic steak or wild mushroom risotto. Susan really makes the place, readers tell us: 'It's like staying with a close friend'; 'Susan has created a real treat.'

Chapel Street
Penzance TR18 4AQ

T: 01736 362024
E: hello@chapelhousepz.co.uk
W: chapelhousepz.co.uk

BEDROOMS: 6. Plus 2 self-catering suites in annexe.
OPEN: all year except 24–29 Dec, kitchen supper served Fri and Sat.
FACILITIES: double drawing room, open-plan kitchen/dining area, in-room TV (Freeview), function facilities, holistic treatments, terrace, garden, unsuitable for disabled, free street parking.
BACKGROUND MUSIC: none.
LOCATION: town centre.
CHILDREN: all ages welcomed, under-5s/cots free, extra bed £20 per night.
DOGS: allowed in bedrooms (no charge) and public areas with consent of other guests.
CREDIT CARDS: MC, Visa.
PRICES: B&B doubles from £170, singles from £140. Set dinner £30. 1-night bookings refused at bank holiday weekends.

SEE ALSO SHORTLIST

PENZANCE Cornwall

TREREIFE

With ancestral portraits gazing down from panelled walls, a Queen Anne facade overlooking a parterre, and extensive wooded grounds, the delightful Le Grice family's mansion 'feels more like a stately home than a B&B'. There is a relaxed feel within, with guests encouraged to treat the antique-filled sitting room as their own, and to wander freely on the 'small estate'. A magnificent staircase leads to four bedrooms, each named after a romantic poet, in honour of forebear Charles Valentine Le Grice, who counted Samuel Taylor Coleridge and Leigh Hunt as friends. Two self-catering apartments, across the courtyard, are named Arkle and Corbière, a nod to owner Tim Le Grice's sideline in horse breeding. Our reader, having booked a house room, was offered one of these at no extra charge. It was 'up some steep stairs, with a large kitchen, double bedroom, huge bathroom. The bed was perfection of comfort, the lighting was good.' A delicious breakfast is served in the elegant dining room, with jam from the medlars in the orchard. 'My wife ordered the full English on three consecutive mornings, and she's a notoriously light eater.' (MB)

Penzance TR20 8TJ

T: 01736 362750
E: trereifepark@btconnect.com
W: trereife.co.uk

BEDROOMS: 4. 2 on ground floor, plus 2 self-catering apartments, and bell tent for glamping.
OPEN: 1 Mar–end Nov.
FACILITIES: sitting room (honesty bar), dining room, in-room TV (Freeview), civil wedding licence, 5-acre grounds (parterres, walled garden, woodland), parking, unsuitable for disabled.
BACKGROUND MUSIC: none.
LOCATION: 1¼ miles SW of Penzance.
CHILDREN: all ages welcomed (no charge for extra bed).
DOGS: allowed in ground-floor bedrooms (£15 per stay) and in public rooms.
CREDIT CARDS: Amex, MC, Visa.
PRICES: B&B doubles from £100. Min. 2-night stay June–Sept and for self-catering.

SEE ALSO SHORTLIST

PETWORTH Sussex

MAP 2:E3

THE OLD RAILWAY STATION

'The best of a bygone railway age' is preserved at this 'totally authentic' Victorian station which, together with its railway carriages, is now run as a quirky and charming B&B by owners Jennie Hudson and Blair Humphry. Set in beautiful Sussex countryside, the station originally built in 1892 to enable the Prince of Wales to travel to Goodwood Racecourse has been beautifully restored, with tall sash windows, white-painted weatherboarding and decorative friezes. After checking in at the ticket window, guests are shown either to a room in the station house, decorated in restful shades of grey, with an en suite shower room, or to one of four Pullman carriages with beautiful mahogany fittings, colonial-style furniture and en suite bathroom. Recalling the golden age of steam travel, it is all so very romantic (think Brief Encounter or Dr Zhivago). It is fun, too, to sit down to a 'first-class breakfast' in the Waiting Room, or to take a cream tea or raise a glass of champagne under a parasol on the platform. 'The accommodation has been converted to a very high standard,' writes a reader, clearly chuffed. (BG-G, and others)

Station Road
Petworth GU28 0JF

T: 01798 342346
E: info@old-station.co.uk
W: old-station.co.uk

BEDROOMS: 10. 8 in Pullman carriages, 1 room suitable for guests with slightly restricted mobility.
OPEN: all year except 20–27 Dec.
FACILITIES: lounge/bar/breakfast room, in-room TV (Freeview), platform/terrace, 2-acre garden, public areas wheelchair accessible.
BACKGROUND MUSIC: 'soft '20s, '30s, '40s music' at breakfast and all day in the Waiting Room.
LOCATION: 1½ miles S of Petworth.
CHILDREN: not under 10.
DOGS: not allowed.
CREDIT CARDS: MC, Visa.
PRICES: B&B doubles from £150, reduced rates for single occupancy 'sometimes offered'.

PICKERING Yorkshire   MAP 4:D4

THE WHITE SWAN

Traditional pub features of local ales in a fire-warmed snug are mixed with a smarter dining room with candlesticks and polished tables at the Buchanan family's 16th-century coaching inn. Throughout, there is warm Yorkshire hospitality, with 'enthusiastic and helpful' staff. With a 'serious' approach to food, Darren Clemmit delivers classic dishes with creativity: perhaps 'very good king scallops, with charred cauliflower purée, capers for piquancy' or 'well-cooked herb-roasted chicken breast'. There are pub staples, too, and most items, including bread, black pudding and ice cream, are made in the kitchen. One reader was delighted with the 23-page wine list with '11 very reasonably priced St-Émilion wines' but another bewailed the 'limited' range of beer on draft. 'Excellent' breakfasts include home-made granola, kedgeree, mushrooms on brioche and a terrific Yorkshire grill. Rooms in the main building are the most characterful, with feature wallpapers, 'attractive fabrics' and the occasional antique. The modern bedrooms with slate floors in the converted stables at the back are more spacious. (DB, JS)

Market Place
Pickering YO18 7AA

T: 01751 472288
E: welcome@white-swan.co.uk
W: white-swan.co.uk

BEDROOMS: 21. 9 in annexe, 8 on ground floor.
OPEN: all year.
FACILITIES: lounge, bar, restaurant, private dining room, bothy bar, lounge, restaurant, event room, in-room TV (Freeview), small courtyard (alfresco meals), EV charging, bike storage, restaurant, bar and lounge wheelchair accessible, adapted toilet only in bothy/residents' lounge.
BACKGROUND MUSIC: in bar occasionally.
LOCATION: central.
CHILDREN: all ages welcomed, under-5s free, extra bed £20–£35.
DOGS: allowed in some bedrooms (£12.50 a night), bar and lounge, not in restaurant (owners may dine with dogs in snug).
CREDIT CARDS: Amex, MC, Visa.
PRICES: B&B doubles from £169, singles from £121. À la carte £38.

PORLOCK WEIR Somerset

MAP 1:B4

♕LOCANDA ON THE WEIR   **NEW**

César award: newcomer of the year
Italian foodie flair mixes with West Country
magic in this 'superb little restaurant-with-
rooms where Exmoor meets the sea', which is a
'real find', a Guide insider reports. 'The food is
outstanding', with everything possible made from
scratch, from the focaccia to the 'fluffiest ricotta
cheese', and meals including whatever is foraged
or plucked from the vegetable garden that day. 'I
would willingly drive the five-hour journey from
my home just to eat the celeriac with buttermilk
again, which was a prelude to perfectly cooked
cod with olives and capers' from chef/patron Pio
Catemario di Quadri. The food comes with a
hefty side serving of style created by co-owner
Cindy Siu: interiors are 'ornate but relaxed', a
blend of 'Italian and English antiques, classic and
contemporary art, flowers everywhere, divine Cire
Trudon scented candles'. San George bedroom
had 'a Cape Cod feel', comfy chairs, a table made
of old signposts, a small bathroom with electric
shower, Aromatherapy Associates toiletries. Santa
Maria has a four-poster, a bath and shower. 'The
owners are very much present, welcoming you
into their beautiful world.' (JK)

Porlock Weir
Minehead TA24 8PB

T: 01643 863300
E: czs@locandaontheweir.com
W: locandaontheweir.co.uk

BEDROOMS: 5.
OPEN: all year.
FACILITIES: bar/lounge, restaurant,
free Wi-Fi in reading room, in-room
TV (Freeview), gift boutique, civil
wedding licence, garden, public rooms
wheelchair accessible.
BACKGROUND MUSIC: none.
LOCATION: within Exmoor national
park, in a coastal hamlet on the South
West Coast Path.
CHILDREN: not under 12.
DOGS: allowed in 3 bedrooms (£10
a night), in lounge, restaurant if well
behaved.
CREDIT CARDS: MC, Visa.
PRICES: B&B doubles from £175, singles
from £165. Set menu £50. 2-night min.
stay, 1-night stays sometimes available
by phone booking, May–Sept.

PORTSCATHO Cornwall   MAP 1:E2

DRIFTWOOD HOTEL

Sink into a recliner on the terrace at this cliff-top
hotel, and you can gaze out at 'panoramic sea
views' over Gerrans Bay – or lie back and think
of New England, prompted by the seaside-chic
decor. Coastal-coloured interiors are home to
driftwood lamps, ornaments and artwork; some
rooms have a decked terrace with Adirondack
chairs. All but one of the bedrooms have an ocean
view. Families might opt for the 'rustic cabin' on
a path to the hotel's 'gorgeous secluded beach'
below the lawned gardens; large rooms have
plenty of space for an extra bed. Olly Pierrepont's
imaginative nightly-changing dinner menu
offers a choice of three dishes at each course,
with 'specials' charged extra. For instance, wild
turbot with grilled leek and salt-baked celeriac
is an extra £8.50. Veggies have separate menus.
Breakfast includes courgette fritter, cream cheese,
crispy bacon and honey. You can order a picnic
and spend a day on the sands, or stride out on the
South West Coast Path. 'Beautiful hotel, perfectly
placed for coastal walks,' one reader wrote. 'Our
second visit – we highly recommend it,' enthused
another. (John and Kay Patterson)'

Rosevine
Porthscatho TR2 5EW

T: 01872 580644
E: info@driftwoodhotel.co.uk
W: driftwoodhotel.co.uk

BEDROOMS: 15. 4 accessed via
courtyard, plus 2-bedroom cabin.
OPEN: all year except Jan.
FACILITIES: bar, restaurant (vegetarian
menu), drawing room, snug,
children's games room, in-room TV
(Freeview), 7-acre grounds (terraced
gardens, private beach, safe bathing),
EV charging, unsuitable for disabled.
BACKGROUND MUSIC: all day in
restaurant and bar.
LOCATION: 1½ miles N of Portscatho.
CHILDREN: all ages welcomed, extra
bed £15, children's supper menu (no
very young children at dinner).
DOGS: not allowed.
CREDIT CARDS: MC, Visa.
PRICES: B&B doubles from £190. Fixed-
price dinner £50–£60 (2/3 courses),
tasting menu £80. 1-night bookings
refused weekends.

RADNAGE Buckinghamshire

THE MASH INN

♕ Previous César winner

This village inn with its aged red brick and
bucolic surrounds has been reinvented as a
restaurant-with-rooms where the food is both
'delicious and original', cooked on a custom-
made wood-fired grill in the open kitchen.
There are still rustic features of an 18th-century
pub – cosy beamed bar, creaking wooden floors,
wood-burning stove – but they are clearly serious
about food here. Owner Nick Mash and chef Jon
Parry are passionate about 'connecting people
with nature'. The menu, including foraged
and kitchen-garden produce, reflects the inn's
terroir. Dishes might include local lamb with
purple sprouting broccoli and ewe's curd, truffled
chicken with wood-fired leeks and mushroom,
and Cornish mackerel (landed 24 hours earlier)
with horseradish. Natural and English wines
feature on the drinks list, plus local ales and
home-made infusions. Minimalist bedrooms in
milky-whites and greys have pale-wood furniture,
some with a roll-top bath in a jazzy-tiled
bathroom. A simple breakfast, including granola,
buttermilk yogurt and croissants with home-made
jams, is best taken in bed with views over the
Chiltern hills.

Horseshoe Road
Bennett End
Radnage HP14 4EB

T: 01494 482440
E: hello@themashinn.com
W: themashinn.com

BEDROOMS: 6.
OPEN: all year, Thurs–Sat dinner, Sat
lunch, planned for 2022 lunch also Fri
and Sun, Mar–Sept.
FACILITIES: snug bar and dining area,
semi-open-plan kitchen/dining room,
5-acre garden and grounds, restaurant
wheelchair accessible, adapted toilet.
BACKGROUND MUSIC: in public areas.
LOCATION: in hamlet 7 miles NW of
High Wycombe.
CHILDREN: not under 16.
DOGS: not allowed.
CREDIT CARDS: MC, Visa.
PRICES: D,B&B doubles from £300.
Set dinner Thurs–Sat, and Sat lunch,
from £85.

RAVENSTONEDALE Cumbria

MAP 4:C3

THE BLACK SWAN

⚜ Previous César winner

Between the Yorkshire Dales and the Lake
District, with views to the Howgill fells, this large
village inn offers classy food and bright bedrooms
for walkers and gentle explorers alike. The
Victorian building, with beer garden and stream,
is a hub of Ravenstonedale. Run by Louise Dinnes
for 15 years, together with her daughter and
'friendly' team, it's known for its cheery welcome
and tempting dishes. Chef Scott Fairweather
offers a creative twist on local produce – perhaps
cod with roasted cauliflower and fennel, or duck
with spiced red cabbage and blackcurrant sauce.
You can eat either in the elegant dining room with
dado panelling and ice-blue walls, or the jolly bar
with exposed-stone walls, open fire and collection
of stuffed animals. The 'high-quality' breakfast
includes smoked salmon with potato pancake,
avocado and poached egg as well as a full grill.
'Tasteful' bedrooms – several recently refurbished
– vary from the compact and cosy to an attic
suite, as well as dog-friendly annexe rooms and
glamping tents. With a contemporary cottage style
– pretty patterned wallpapers, breezy colours – all
have fresh milk and most have views.

Ravenstonedale
Kirkby Stephen CA17 4NG

T: 01539 623204
E: enquiries@blackswanhotel.com
W: blackswanhotel.com

BEDROOMS: 16. 6 in annexe, 4 on
ground floor, 1 suitable for disabled.
Plus 3 glamping tents.
OPEN: all year.
FACILITIES: 2 bars, lounge, 2 dining
rooms, free Wi-Fi in bars and lounge
only, Orange mobile network only,
in-room TV (Freeview), beer garden
in wooded grounds, tennis/golf in
village, public rooms wheelchair
accessible.
BACKGROUND MUSIC: in public areas all
day, but optional.
LOCATION: in village 5 miles SW of
Kirkby Stephen.
CHILDREN: all ages welcomed, extra
bed £30.
DOGS: in 4 ground-floor annexe rooms
(£15 per night), not in restaurant.
CREDIT CARDS: MC, Visa.
PRICES: B&B doubles/singles from
£125. À la carte £45. 1-night bookings
sometimes refused.

REEPHAM Norfolk

MAP 2:B5

THE DIAL HOUSE

You might fancy you are in a Parisian garret, in the mysterious east, on safari, or (mamma mia!) in a Venetian palazzo, when you book into Hannah Springham and Andrew Jones's hotel, with rooms themed on the Georgian Grand Tour and Victorian globetrotting. Each room has a marble bathroom with a roll-top bath and drench shower, a record player to give vinyl a spin. China room, styled in blue and white, with bamboo-pattern wallpaper, has 'a huge bed, two sash windows with working shutters'. Natural History has owl wallpaper, a bathroom concealed behind a cabinet of curiosities, glass doors to a decked terrace. The 'charming, attentive' staff are 'helpful from the moment you enter the front door'. In a restaurant set across three dining rooms, Andrew's menus reflect the principles of 'fine produce, not fine dining', with ingredients sourced direct from farmers, in dishes such as Swannington bavette steak cooked over sustainable charcoal, black garlic, kale, red wine jus; lentil and aubergine shepherd's pie. 'Breakfast, served in the spacious and airy Aga room, was of a similarly high standard.' (S and MT)

Market Place
Reepham
Norwich NR10 4JJ

T: 01603 879900
E: info@thedialhouse.org.uk
w: thedialhouse.org.uk

BEDROOMS: 8.
OPEN: all year, restaurant closed Sun night, Mon, Tues.
FACILITIES: lounge, 3 restaurant areas, private dining rooms, sun terrace, in-room TV (Sky), terrace, civil wedding licence, hairdresser's, vintage clothing shop, public rooms wheelchair accessible, no adapted toilet.
BACKGROUND MUSIC: 'retro classics' in public areas.
LOCATION: on main square.
CHILDREN: all ages welcomed, extra bed £40.
DOGS: allowed in 1 bedroom (£20 a night), some public rooms and in part of restaurant.
CREDIT CARDS: Amex, MC, Visa.
PRICES: B&B doubles from £140, singles from £130. À la carte £37. 1-night bookings refused Christmas week.

RICHMOND Yorkshire   MAP 4:C3

THE COACH HOUSE
AT MIDDLETON LODGE

♔ Previous César winner

Not so much a hotel as a grand country estate,
The Coach House has bedrooms in cottages,
former stables and outbuildings, a restaurant
and 200 acres to explore. The setting is glorious,
say readers of the gardens, woodland and
walled kitchen garden. James Allison and his
wife, Rebecca, have turned his family's estate
into a 21st-century retreat with relaxed but chic
bedrooms – beams, soft colours, vintage and rustic
furnishings. Some have a garden or patio, several
have hot tubs, one opens on to the potager. All
have modern bathrooms, most with a roll-top
bath. (The Palladian main house can also be
rented.) Georgian Richmond and the Yorkshire
Dales are nearby, or simply stay put and take a spa
treatment. The all-day Coach House restaurant,
in a double-height room, offers dishes such as
chalk-stream trout with wild garlic pasta, and
roast pork belly with smoked potato. Or you
can eat in the courtyard if sunny. Home-grown
produce guarantees plenty of vegetarian dishes. A
second tasting-menu restaurant opens in spring
2022. 'The food is so good, and the place itself is so
special.' (Polly Taylor)

Kneeton Lane
Middleton Tyas
Richmond DL10 6NJ

T: 01325 377977
E: stay@middletonlodge.co.uk
W: middletonlodge.co.uk

BEDROOMS: 29. 9 in coach house,
3 in Potting Shed, 11 in Dairy,
6 in farmhouse, 5 on ground floor,
1 suitable for disabled. Plus 16 rooms
in main house for exclusive hire only.
OPEN: all year.
FACILITIES: lounge, bar, snug, 2
restaurants, in-room TV (Sky),
function rooms, civil wedding licence,
treatment rooms, EV charging,
courtyard, 200-acre gardens and
grounds, public rooms wheelchair
accessible, adapted toilet.
BACKGROUND MUSIC: in public areas.
LOCATION: 1 mile N of village.
CHILDREN: all ages welcomed, under-
5s free, extra bed £25.
DOGS: allowed in 1 bedroom (£30 per
night), and courtyard.
CREDIT CARDS: MC, Visa.
PRICES: B&B doubles from £180, singles
from £165. À la carte £37.

RICHMOND Yorkshire

MAP 4:C3

THE FRENCHGATE
RESTAURANT & HOTEL

This Georgian town house, near the centre of a handsome Yorkshire Dales town, offers a personal welcome and good food in stylishly casual surroundings. Owner David Todd or one of his 'friendly and helpful' staff shows guests around the small but perfectly formed hotel. Public rooms are traditional and elegantly furnished, with modern art adding bold touches; there's a wood-burning stove in the lounge. David 'cares passionately' about food, so dinner is a highlight. Served in the Georgian dining room gleaming with candlelight and polished oak tables, 'excellent meals' kick off with an amuse-bouche and follow with dishes such as guineafowl with artichoke purée and truffle gnocchi, and sea bream with crispy squid and wood-fired peppers. Bedrooms, with a mix of contemporary and antique furniture, have large 'very comfortable' beds and views over the small terraced garden or the River Swale. Some are beamed, others have a fireplace, all have a 'hi-tech' bathroom and maybe a roll-top bath or Swedish shower. Breakfast includes freshly squeezed juice, home-made bread, smoked salmon and a full grill. (E and JG, and others)

59–61 Frenchgate
Richmond DL10 7AE

T: 01748 822087
E: info@thefrenchgate.co.uk
W: thefrenchgate.co.uk

BEDROOMS: 9, 1 on ground floor with 2 steps to en suite.
OPEN: all year.
FACILITIES: dining room, bar, lounge, terrace, in-room TV (Freeview), civil wedding licence, small garden, parking, public rooms wheelchair accessible, adapted toilet.
BACKGROUND MUSIC: soft jazz in public rooms.
LOCATION: 200 yds NE of town square.
CHILDREN: all ages welcomed, extra bed £35.
DOGS: not allowed.
CREDIT CARDS: Amex, MC, Visa.
PRICES: B&B doubles from £148, singles from £98. À la carte set-price menu £39.

RICHMOND Yorkshire

MAP 4:C3

THE HACK & SPADE

With sweeping Dales views, a peaceful setting
and set-you-up-for-the-day breakfasts after a
comfortably quiet night, this small but perfectly
formed B&B is a great little escape. Originally
a Georgian ale house, then Victorian 'parlour'
pub, it has a stout, no-nonsense exterior that
belies a warm and welcoming interior – tea and
home-made cakes at 4 pm – and friendly service
from owner Jane Ratcliffe. Simple but elegant
bedrooms are hotel standard, with a contemporary
style, rich fabrics and refreshing lack of clutter.
Some may be small for a lengthy stay, but all
have lovely views, plus bathroom with 'spotless
fittings', walk-in shower and Arran Aromatics
products. Zetland includes a sofa plus separate
bath and shower. Jane's breakfasts, served in the
beamed and flagged dining room, win praise for
their generosity, and include 'perfectly cooked
scrambled egg and sumptuous bacon, full of
flavour'. Come evening, it's a 15-minute walk to
the nearest pub, and Richmond is a five-minute
drive (see The Frenchgate, previous entry). With
walks from the doorstep, Georgian Richmond to
explore and the A1 just ten minutes away, it's an
attractive bolt-hole.

Whashton
Richmond DL11 7JL

T: 01748 823721
E: jane@hackandspade.com
W: hackandspade.com

BEDROOMS: 5.
OPEN: all year except Christmas/New
Year, last 2 weeks Jan.
FACILITIES: small lounge and bar,
breakfast room, in-room TV
(Freeview), garden, unsuitable for
disabled.
BACKGROUND MUSIC: 'quiet spa-type
music' in the mornings.
LOCATION: 4 miles NW of Richmond.
CHILDREN: over-7s only, by request.
DOGS: not allowed.
CREDIT CARDS: MC, Visa.
PRICES: B&B doubles from £125.

RICHMOND-UPON-THAMES Surrey

MAP 2:D3

BINGHAM RIVERHOUSE

A stroll from Richmond Park, with a verdant Thameside garden and terrace, this Georgian mansion is today an innovative hotel, wedding venue and members' club, run by mother and daughter Ruth and Samantha Trinder. It was once home to 'the Michaels', aunt-and-niece lovers Katherine Bradley and Edith Cooper, who wrote under the pen name Michael Field and fooled Victorian society until Robert Browning blew their cover. Bedrooms, each named after a Field novel, have designer chic, a bright palette and sustainable fitted furniture. Music was playing as Guide insiders entered their room, which had a copper bathtub and separate shower. 'My wife said it was the best bath she'd ever had – lovely and deep.' You can dine in the parlour or library, have a drink in the drawing room, which serves as a members' lounge/bar. Steven Edwards, of Etch in Hove, oversees the kitchen. At lunch and dinner, tasting menus bring dishes such as guinea hen and barbecued lettuce Caesar; for vegetarians, broccoli risotto with macadamia. Small plates are available from a bar menu, while breakfast choices include oak-smoked salmon with scrambled eggs, watercress and toasted sourdough.

61–63 Petersham Road
Richmond-upon-Thames TW10 6UT

T: 020 8940 0902
E: be@binghamriverhouse.com
W: binghamriverhouse.com

BEDROOMS: 15.
OPEN: all year, restaurant closed Sun evening from 5.30 pm.
FACILITIES: 3 drawing room/bar/restaurant rooms (vegan menus), function room, in-room TV, civil wedding licence, terrace, ½-acre garden, parking, nearby wellness centre, public rooms wheelchair accessible, adapted toilet.
BACKGROUND MUSIC: in bar and restaurant.
LOCATION: ½ mile S of centre.
CHILDREN: all ages welcomed, no charge for extra bed.
DOGS: allowed with prior permission in some bedrooms (charges apply) and public areas.
CREDIT CARDS: MC, Visa.
PRICES: B&B (continental) doubles from £170. Cooked breakfast from £9.50, tasting menu £55–£75 (5/7 courses). Check hotel website for latest offers/prices.

ROBERTSBRIDGE Sussex   MAP 2:E4

THE GEORGE INN   NEW

On the high street of a historic village on the main Hastings–London line, John and Jane Turner's Georgian coaching inn enters the Guide at the urging of a reader, with a nod from our inspectors. 'It has four comfortable bedrooms, done up to a high standard, above a very convivial restaurant and bar.' The welcome was 'friendly and effusive from Jane and a member of staff'. Bamfylde bedroom was 'a decent size', with 'a super-king bed with faux-fur cover, fitted carpet, an old wooden chest of drawers and dressing table, tub chairs, a useful laptop table', an inset shower room. The hospitality tray was basic, but fresh milk was offered. All rooms have distinctive styling. You dine in the open-plan bar/restaurant, from a 'carefully sourced' 30-mile menu. 'We opted for a generous fishy sharing board with wonderful warm, home-baked bread, then a free-range beef burger and a veggie stack. The lightest sponge I've ever eaten came with compote, Devon cream and ice cream.' Breakfast passed the scrambled eggs test with honours. Verdict: 'A very doggy, cosy, jolly place for an overnight stay.' (Maggie Hodges, and others)

High Street
Robertsbridge
Hastings TN32 5AW

T: 01580 880315
E: info@thegeorgerobertsbridge.co.uk
W: thegeorgerobertsbridge.co.uk

BEDROOMS: 4.
OPEN: all year, except Mon, 25/26 Dec, New Year's Day.
FACILITIES: bar/dining area, in-room TV, courtyard garden (covered, heated area for alfresco dining), parking, public areas wheelchair accessible, adapted toilet.
BACKGROUND MUSIC: soft background music.
LOCATION: in village, 11 miles N of Hastings.
CHILDREN: all ages welcomed, extra bed £30–£45 a night, depending on age.
DOGS: allowed in bar, dining room, courtyard, not in bedrooms.
CREDIT CARDS: MC, Visa.
PRICES: B&B doubles from £99, singles from £94. À la carte £30.

ROMALDKIRK Co. Durham

MAP 4:C3

THE ROSE & CROWN

Overlooking the green in a 'beautiful village with lots of country walks', this local inn strikes exactly the right balance between old-world charm and modern comforts. Flagged floors, 'a welcoming bar with a roaring fire' and panelled dining room await guests after a day's exploring. Rooms are divided between more characterful ones in the main building (with window seats and exposed stone) and more contemporary, 'spacious and well-appointed' dog-friendly mews cottages with patio. One couple, on their fourth visit, enjoyed their suite with 'comfy bed, lots of storage space, decent shower above the bath'. Thomas Robinson, co-owner with wife, Cheryl, comes from a long-established local farming family, and the inn has a good reputation for its food, served either in the candlelit dining room or buzzier bar. Readers enjoyed an 'excellent grilled sea bass with a light curry sauce' and 'tasty and generous' beef bourguignon, though desserts were less successful. Staff are 'friendly and professional' and can advise on local walks. 'Beautiful hotel, great location for a relaxing break.' (Peter Anderson, John and Elspeth Gibbon, and others)

Romaldkirk
Barnard Castle DL12 9EB

T: 01833 650213
E: info@rose-and-crown.co.uk
W: rose-and-crown.co.uk

BEDROOMS: 14. 2 in Monk's Cottage, 5 in rear courtyard, some on ground floor, 1 suitable for disabled.
OPEN: all year except 23–28 Dec.
FACILITIES: lounge, bar, restaurant, front terrace, in-room TV (Freeview), boot room, EV charging, public rooms wheelchair accessible, no adapted toilet.
BACKGROUND MUSIC: in restaurant.
LOCATION: village centre, 6 miles W of Barnard Castle.
CHILDREN: all ages welcomed, extra bed £25, no under-8s in restaurant after 8 pm.
DOGS: allowed in most bedrooms (no charge) plus public rooms, except restaurant.
CREDIT CARDS: Amex, MC, Visa.
PRICES: B&B doubles from £135, singles from £120. À la carte £35.

ROWSLEY Derbyshire   MAP 3:A6

THE PEACOCK AT ROWSLEY

Foodies and fishing folk, hikers and bikers flock
to this 17th-century manor house in the Peak
District national park. Owned by Lord and Lady
Edward Manners of Haddon Hall, the hotel is full
of tradition, with a beamed bar, four-posters in
some of the bedrooms and paintings of aristocrats
hanging on the walls. Readers returning after
four years declare it 'better than ever'. While
some come to fish for wild trout in the Derbyshire
Wye, others are more interested in the seafood
on their plate – 'the best fish and chips in a long
time'. Dan Smith's dishes get a huge thumbs up,
whether you go for gourmet or cheaper options in
the bar, where a reader enjoyed 'extremely tender
shoulder of lamb, sublime lemon tart'. 'The big
bonus was dinner – an interesting selection, well
cooked and presented,' another reader writes.
There are minor niggles about the 'comfortable,
country style' bedrooms ('a bit old style … very
small bathroom'), but they're classy, clean and, in
a heatwave, thank goodness for air conditioning!
'Staff are warm and efficient.' There are lovely
walks from the door. (Peter Anderson, Peter and
Anne Davies, F and IW)

Bakewell Road
Rowsley DE4 2EB

T: 01629 733518
E: reception@thepeacockatrowsley.
   com
W: thepeacockatrowsley.co.uk

BEDROOMS: 15.
OPEN: all year except 24–26 Dec,
2 weeks in Jan.
FACILITIES: lounge, bar, 2 dining
rooms, private dining room, in-room
TV (Freeview, Apple), ½-acre garden
on river, fishing rights, public areas
wheelchair accessible.
BACKGROUND MUSIC: in public rooms.
LOCATION: village centre.
CHILDREN: not under 10 at weekends.
DOGS: allowed in bedrooms only ('for
small supplement').
CREDIT CARDS: Amex, MC, Visa.
PRICES: B&B doubles from £215,
singles from £150. À la carte in bar
£34, restaurant (Mon–Sat) £65, tasting
menu (Fri and Sat) £80. 1-night
bookings sometimes refused.

RYE Sussex

MAP 2:E5

JEAKE'S HOUSE

'Beautiful Rye, cobbled hilly streets, higgledy-piggledy alleyways – enchanting, and so was Jeake's House,' writes a trusted reader about Jenny Hadfield's beguiling B&B. The creeper-swathed property brings together 17th-century buildings that have served as a wool store, school, chapel and Quaker Meeting House. This was once home to American novelist Conrad Aiken, who wrote for The New Yorker as 'Samuel Jeake Jr.'; four-poster bedrooms up 'creaking staircases' are named after him and some of the luminaries he entertained here. Radclyffe Hall is pretty, with toile fabrics, Malcolm Lowry light and airy, with a roll-top bath and walk-in shower. A 'tight double' was 'very traditional (no boutique funk here), clean, but with the smallest cupboard of a shower room'. Another Guide trusty loved the atmospheric honesty bar, 'the deep red walls' of the galleried breakfast room, hung with portraits. Breakfast brings 'a delicious choice of traditional (bacon and eggs) and modern (avocado on sourdough)', smoked haddock and devilled kidneys. Medieval Rye is a touristic honeypot, so access to parking is a boon. (Joanna Gibbon, RB)

Mermaid Street
Rye TN31 7ET

T: 01797 222828
E: stay@jeakeshouse.com
W: jeakeshouse.com

BEDROOMS: 11.
OPEN: all year.
FACILITIES: parlour, bar/library, breakfast room, in-room TV (Freeview), parking permit, unsuitable for disabled.
BACKGROUND MUSIC: chamber music in breakfast room.
LOCATION: central, private car park 6 mins' walk away (charge for parking permit, advance booking).
CHILDREN: not under 8.
DOGS: allowed in bedrooms (£5 a night), public rooms, on leads and 'always supervised', not in breakfast room.
CREDIT CARDS: MC, Visa.
PRICES: B&B doubles from £100 (private bathroom), £128 en suite, triple from £160, 4 guests £225. 1-night bookings sometimes refused Fri/Sat.

ST IVES Cornwall

MAP 1:D1

BLUE HAYES

Perched on the hill above teeming St Ives, in sub-tropical gardens, Malcolm Herring's exclusive small hotel is 'aimed at those who can afford it, and it really does deliver'. It is decorated throughout in a coastal palette of white and blue, with potted palms and modern artwork. Every bedroom has a bath and walk-in shower with body jets. Molton Brown bath products, 'luxury fabrics, bone china, a teapot, mini-cafetière and fresh milk' are nice touches. A four-poster room has a sea-facing balcony. The Garden Suite has French doors to a private patio. You can have breakfast in the dining room or on the sea-facing terrace, maybe Cornish gammon steak with eggs, kedgeree or grilled mackerel, berry pancakes and croissants. Order ahead if you want to eat in at night. New chef Nancy Osborne prepares cold dishes such as tian of smoked salmon and Cornish crab, and chargrilled Cornish beef fillet, served in the dining room or alfresco. You could, of course, head down to town and take your pick of restaurants, but why tear yourself away? 'One could have a very enjoyable couple of days without stirring anywhere.'

Trelyon Avenue
St Ives TR26 2AD

T: 01736 797129
E: bluehayes@btconnect.com
W: bluehayes.co.uk

BEDROOMS: 6.
OPEN: Mar–Oct.
FACILITIES: 2 lounges, bar, dining room, in-room TV (Freeview), small function facilities, room service, terrace, garden, parking.
BACKGROUND MUSIC: in bar and dining room only, at breakfast and supper.
LOCATION: ½ mile from centre of St Ives.
CHILDREN: no under-10s, extra bed for ages 10–15 40% of room rate per night.
DOGS: not allowed.
CREDIT CARDS: Amex, MC, Visa.
PRICES: B&B doubles from £235, singles from £160. Supper from £17. Min. 2-night stay, but check availability.

SEE ALSO SHORTLIST

ST IVES Cornwall

MAP 1:D1

BOSKERRIS HOTEL

Panoramic views over the blue waters and Blue Flag beach of Carbis Bay, a cream tea on the terrace, friendly service . . . Although there has been change afoot at this boutique hotel, the good things remain. Previous owners Jonathan and Marianne Bassett have moved on, but it seems their standards and values have been upheld. 'It is extremely professionally run,' writes a recent guest. 'The staff were helpful, charming and enthusiastic.' This 1930s house is decorated throughout in gleaming shades of blue and white, shell pink and teal. Bedrooms range from 'classic compact' with a shower over bath, to the sea-view 'celebration room', with a sunken bath and a wet room with rain shower. All have a bright, airy aspect, designer fabrics, coffee machine, botanical toiletries, and beds that are 'extremely comfortable'. A new chef continues the Boskerris tradition for using small, local suppliers – from Newlyn-landed crab to artisan bread. 'As well as excellent breakfasts, we had two marvellous dinners (scallops a real speciality)'. An interesting wine list was reasonably priced. 'All told, our visit was a great pleasure.' (Andrew Warren)

Boskerris Road
Carbis Bay
St Ives TR26 2NQ

T: 01736 795295
E: reservations@boskerrishotel.co.uk
W: boskerrishotel.co.uk

BEDROOMS: 15. 1, on ground floor, suitable for disabled.
OPEN: mid-Feb–Nov, restaurant closed Sun, Mon.
FACILITIES: lounge, bar, breakfast room, supper room, in-room TV (Freeview), decked terrace, massage and reflexology treatment room, 1½-acre garden, parking, EV charging, public rooms wheelchair accessible.
BACKGROUND MUSIC: 'chilled', in public rooms.
LOCATION: 1½ miles from centre (20 mins' walk), close to station.
CHILDREN: not allowed.
DOGS: not allowed.
CREDIT CARDS: Amex, MC, Visa.
PRICES: B&B doubles from £200. À la carte £30. 1-night bookings usually refused in high season.

SEE ALSO SHORTLIST

ST MARY'S Isles of Scilly

STAR CASTLE

You can take tea on the ramparts or imbibe history along with a St Agnes gin in the Dungeon Bar at the Francis family's hotel, occupying an Elizabethan artillery castle within star-shaped fortress walls. 'Back from ten idyllic days – just blissful,' writes a trusted reader. There is a wide choice of bedrooms, including characterful singles and beamed superior sea-view doubles with a half-tester bed. Dog-friendly rooms and suites in a garden annexe, some recently refurbished, have a private entrance, a veranda or private lawn area. The styling is neutral and contemporary, with seaside colours, some with impressive sea views. From March, guests can dine under a vine in the conservatory, or in a stone-walled dining room. 'Four-course dinners were stupendous. Quite small portions, but they all added up to a super meal, with lots of fish and meat, venison especially good, and most ingredients from the Islands.' With notice they will adapt dishes for vegans. 'Residents have access to the golf course, and the driver will drop you somewhere on the island for you to walk home if you fancy.' (Abigail Kirby-Harris, and others)

The Garrison
St Mary's TR21 0JA

T: 01720 422317
E: info@star-castle.co.uk
W: star-castle.co.uk

BEDROOMS: 38. 27 in 2 garden wings.
OPEN: all year, B&B only Nov–early Mar, closed Christmas and New Year.
FACILITIES: lounge, bar, 2 restaurants, in-room TV (Freeview), civil wedding licence, sun deck, 2-acre gardens, covered swimming pool (12 by 4 metres), tennis, EV charging, unsuitable for disabled.
BACKGROUND MUSIC: none.
LOCATION: ¼ mile from town centre.
CHILDREN: all ages welcomed, no charge for extra beds, under-5s must eat before 6.30 pm.
DOGS: allowed in garden rooms (£15 a night), lounge, bar, not in restaurants.
CREDIT CARDS: Amex, MC, Visa.
PRICES: B&B doubles from £153, singles from £89. Set-price menu £37–£45. 1-night bookings usually refused (but call to check).

SEE ALSO SHORTLIST

ST MAWES Cornwall

MAP 1:E2

THE IDLE ROCKS

A 25-seat cinema is a novelty at Karen and David Richards' hotel in a village of white-painted houses on the Roseland peninsula, but no film can rival the wide-screen views over the Fal estuary from the waterside terrace. It makes the perfect backdrop to a meal at this Relais & Châteaux property, which has been known for great food since the 1950s, when it touted its 'French cuisine' and 'staff engaged on the Continent'. Today, classic French techniques, honed at Le Manoir aux Quat'Saisons, Great Milton (see entry), along with a passion for Cornish produce, still inform Dorian Janmaat's modern British dishes. You might have an alfresco lunch of wild garlic soup, spring lamb or bouillabaisse, then dine in the restaurant with its floor-to-ceiling windows on Fowey mussels or parsley farfalle with morel cream, sea herbs, ricotta and lemon. Bedrooms, styled by Karen in soft seaside shades, have hand-picked artwork, the odd piece of period or artfully distressed furniture, a Roberts radio. In a seaview room, you can fall asleep to the sound of the waves, then enjoy a full Cornish breakfast as you watch people messing about in boats.

Harbourside
St Mawes TR2 5AN

T: 01326 270270
E: info@idlerocks.com
W: idlerocks.com

BEDROOMS: 19. 4 in adjacent cottage, 1 suitable for disabled.
OPEN: all year.
FACILITIES: lounge, restaurant (vegetarian/vegan menus), kids' room, boot room, in-room TV (Sky), terrace, civil wedding licence, parking, EV charging, public areas wheelchair accessible, adapted toilet.
BACKGROUND MUSIC: all day in public areas, except lounge.
LOCATION: central, on the harbour.
CHILDREN: all ages welcomed, family room, under-10s not encouraged in restaurant after 8 pm.
DOGS: allowed in 2 cottage bedrooms (£30 per stay), not in hotel.
CREDIT CARDS: Amex, MC, Visa.
PRICES: B&B doubles from £355. Set-price dinner £70. Min. 2-night stay weekends, 3 nights in high season, 1 on D,B&B.

ST MAWES Cornwall   MAP 1:E2

TRESANTON

A seaside hotel with serious style, Olga Polizzi's
glowing white collection of cottages and former
yacht clubhouse cascading down the hillside is a
cross between New England and Mediterranean
Riviera. Buildings are linked by terraces and
gardens with lots of steps; one reader bewailed
the fact that 'the car park is up the hill' despite
valet parking. The setting does, though, make
the most of the 'splendid sea views', from the
restaurant terrace and beach club and from the
'homely' bedrooms. These are furnished with an
easy elegance, some with terraces, and range in
style from understated country house to breezier
beach chalet. Modern bathrooms might have twin
monsoon showers. At night, the only sound is the
sea. Menus are the same in both the restaurant
and the dog-friendly bar. Seafood is the obvious
choice, perhaps Porthilly oysters, a seafood platter
or fishcake with clams. In summer, try the lobster
barbecue. Breakfasts feature freshly squeezed
juices and cooked items such as mushroom
rarebit, and poached eggs and ham on brioche.
Service is 'informal' but 'slick'. It's not cheap, 'but
it's worth paying for quality'.

27 Lower Castle Road
St Mawes TR2 5DR

T: 01326 270055
E: hoteltresanton@
   thepolizzicollection.com
W: tresanton.com

BEDROOMS: 30. In 5 houses.
OPEN: all year.
FACILITIES: lounge, lounge/bar,
restaurant, cinema, playroom,
conference facilities, in-room TV
(Freeview), civil wedding licence,
terrace, ¼-acre garden, beach club
(May–Sept), 48-foot yacht, EV
charging, restaurant wheelchair
accessible, adapted toilet.
BACKGROUND MUSIC: none.
LOCATION: on seafront, valet parking
(car park up hill).
CHILDREN: all ages welcomed, extra
bed £40, family rooms.
DOGS: allowed in some bedrooms
(£25 a night) and in dogs' bar.
CREDIT CARDS: MC, Visa.
PRICES: B&B doubles from £270.
À la carte £48. Min. 2-night bookings
at weekends, 3-night bookings on
bank holidays.

SALCOMBE Devon

MAP 1:E4

SOAR MILL COVE HOTEL

ⓆPrevious César winner

It's just a ten-minute walk to a beautifully uncrowded beach through National Trust land from this ocean-facing hotel, purpose built for families and fun. Spectacular cove and countryside views are framed by floor-to-ceiling windows in the smart, contemporary bedrooms, which open on to patios and the garden (dogs are welcome). Long-time owners Keith and Jenny Makepeace know how to make their visitors happy, offering extras such as a complimentary cream tea for people booking direct, with books and board games in the bedrooms. Returning guests who are disabled reported that staff 'went out of their way to help'. Lunch might be a crab sandwich in the sunshine on the new dining deck with pirate ship play. At dinner, Ian MacDonald, in his 21st year here, uses prime local produce in his short, tempting menus, including kids' portions and a vegan option. 'The fishcake with salsa verde was all fish' in a 'light, thin, crispy' coating. 'The shin of West Country beef was tender and moist.' Nor does the full Devonshire breakfast disappoint: 'In particular the bacon and the creamy scrambled egg went down well.' (Stephen Rees, and others)

Soar Mill Cove
Salcombe TQ7 3DS

T: 01548 561566
E: info@soarmillcove.co.uk
W: soarmillcove.co.uk

BEDROOMS: 22. 21 on ground floor.
OPEN: all year.
FACILITIES: lounge, bar, restaurant, coffee shop, in-room TV (Freeview), indoor swimming pool, spa, gym, civil wedding licence, 10-acre grounds, EV charging, public rooms wheelchair accessible, adapted toilet.
BACKGROUND MUSIC: in restaurant and bar.
LOCATION: 3 miles SW of Salcombe.
CHILDREN: all ages welcomed, no under-7s in restaurant after 8.45 pm.
DOGS: allowed in bedrooms (£15 per night), bar, coffee shop.
CREDIT CARDS: Amex, MC, Visa.
PRICES: B&B doubles from £219, singles from £175, family from £319. À la carte £39. 1-night bookings refused Fri, Sat and holiday weekends.

SEE ALSO SHORTLIST

SEAHAM Co. Durham   MAP 4:B4

SEAHAM HALL

A striking sculptural fountain in front of a white
classical porticoed facade is a clue that this spa
hotel offers luxury with a contemporary edge.
Ten minutes' walk from the cliffs of County
Durham, the Georgian hall – where poet Byron
married – has startling interiors of bright colours,
dark-wood floors and huge velvet sofas. To
some guests the style is 'bizarre', to others it's
'amazing'. With its Asian-themed spa – accessed
by an underground boardwalk over trickling
water – most guests rarely leave the hotel. 'The
spa facilities are the best ever,' enthused one.
Bedrooms are huge affairs with a contemporary
country house style of bold feature wallpapers,
oversized headboards and zinging colours. Rooms
in the original hall have sea views, those in the
newer wing overlook gardens; some with hot tub.
All have a 'very comfortable' bed and a bathroom
with 'excellent fittings'. Dine under gleaming
chandeliers in the main restaurant on dishes such
as sea bass with artichoke, beef with glazed cheek
and mushroom gratin, or more casually on 'very
competent' Asian food in the spa. The service is
enthusiastic and attentive, too.

Lord Byron's Walk
Seaham SR7 7AG

T: 0191 516 1400
E: reservations@seaham-hall.com
W: seaham-hall.co.uk

BEDROOMS: 21. 1 suitable for disabled.
OPEN: all year.
FACILITIES: lift, lounge, lounge/bar,
2 restaurants, private dining room,
conference facilities, in-room TV
(Sky, BT), civil wedding licence, spa
(treatment rooms, outdoor hot tubs,
sun terrace, fitness suite, 20-metre
heated swimming pool), 37-acre
grounds (terraces, putting green),
public areas wheelchair accessible,
adapted toilet.
BACKGROUND MUSIC: all day in public
areas.
LOCATION: 5 miles S of Sunderland.
CHILDREN: all ages welcomed, extra
bed £50.
DOGS: not allowed.
CREDIT CARDS: Amex, MC, Visa.
PRICES: B&B doubles from £315.
À la carte (in restaurant) £50, (in
Ozone in spa) £31.

SEAHOUSES Northumberland   MAP 4:A4

ST AIDAN HOTEL & BISTRO

You could spend all day gazing at the sea views from this bright and friendly, modern little hotel with its buzzing bistro on Northumberland's majestic coast. Practically all the bedrooms have good views – Bamburgh Castle, the Farne Islands or Seahouses harbour – and are done out in breezy seaside colours with a simple unfussy style. Some are on the cosy side, but all have nice touches such as local artwork, blanket throws and binoculars to scan the horizon. Rob and Tegan Tait and their staff are 'very friendly and helpful' with plenty of suggestions for walks and day-trips, plus eating options when the bistro is closed. For a small operation, the latter has a surprisingly sophisticated choice: starters could include fresh crab and fennel crostini with avocado mayonnaise, followed by roast pork loin with colcannon mash or baked sea trout with roasted garlic and rosemary potatoes, hollandaise sauce. The interesting wine list reflects Rob's earlier career at Hotel du Vin. Breakfast is equally well above average with 'delicious' treats such as home-made banana bread, as well as eggs Benedict and the full Northumbrian.

1 St Aidan's
Seahouses NE68 7SR

T: 01665 720355
E: info@staidanhotel.co.uk
W: staidanhotel.co.uk

BEDROOMS: 9. 3 on ground floor, 2 in annexe.
OPEN: all year except 21–25 Dec, 3 Jan–10 Feb, bistro open Thurs–Sat dinner.
FACILITIES: breakfast room/bistro, bar area (honesty bar), in-room TV (Freeview), front lawn (picnic tables), unsuitable for disabled.
BACKGROUND MUSIC: chilled acoustic in public rooms.
LOCATION: 300 yds from harbour, on north side of village, with views towards Bamburgh.
CHILDREN: not under 12.
DOGS: allowed in annexe rooms (no charge), 1 area of breakfast room, not in bistro.
CREDIT CARDS: MC, Visa.
PRICES: B&B doubles from £115. À la carte £35. 1-night bookings may be refused in summer.

SHAFTESBURY Dorset

MAP 2:D1

LA FLEUR DE LYS

The hilltop town immortalised by Ridley Scott's classic Hovis ad is home to this well-liked restaurant-with-rooms. Owners David and Mary Griffin-Shepherd and Marc Preston met when working at Lewtrenchard Manor, Lewdown (see entry), and opened their first Shaftesbury venture in 1991, before relocating to what was then the Sunridge Hotel. Mark and David cook 'outstanding food', while 'lovely proprietress' Mary is front-of-house. A party on a celebratory night out felt 'well taken care of'; staff are 'excellent'. There is nothing designer or chichi about it: the look is quite old-fashioned. Wide double doors open from the restaurant on to a courtyard garden, there's a comfy lounge with a piano, and bedrooms with muted paint finishes are home to a mix of furniture. Half have both a bath and a separate shower while the remainder have only showers. All have a mini-fridge, fresh milk, coffee and home-made biscuits. Local produce features in dishes such as fillet of brill on a tomato, red pepper and marjoram salsa, with mussels in creamy garlic sauce. Year-round events include wine tastings, music nights and cookery demonstrations. (KM, and others)

Bleke Street
Shaftesbury SP7 8AW

T: 01747 853717
E: info@lafleurdelys.co.uk
W: lafleurdelys.co.uk

BEDROOMS: 8. 1, on ground floor, suitable for disabled.
OPEN: all year, restaurant closed Sun.
FACILITIES: lounge, bar, dining room, conference room, in-room TV (Freeview), courtyard garden, parking, bar and restaurant wheelchair accessible, adapted toilet.
BACKGROUND MUSIC: none, but some live music events.
LOCATION: N edge of historic town centre.
CHILDREN: all ages welcomed.
DOGS: not allowed.
CREDIT CARDS: Amex, MC, Visa.
PRICES: B&B doubles from £100, singles from £90, triples from £170. À la carte (2 courses) £35, (3 courses) £42. 1-night bookings sometimes refused weekends in summer.

SEE ALSO SHORTLIST

SHEFFIELD Yorkshire

MAP 4:E4

BROCCO ON THE PARK

♟ Previous César winner

This Edwardian suburban villa, on the Peak District side of the city, surprises with Scandichic rooms, a buzzing restaurant and relaxed vibe. 'Everything about this smart, cosmopolitan, sophisticated establishment impressed,' reports a reader. Yorkshire-born owner Tiina Carr has now moved on, leaving behind her uncluttered style, both in the restaurant with its white walls and open kitchen and in the light-filled bedrooms. Furnished with 'an air of flair', rooms make the most of their space with wooden floors, open wardrobes and white-shuttered windows. Bathrooms are sharply modern, some with rolltop baths, all with posh products. The 'attention to detail' includes home-made brownies and fresh milk. Food is small-plates style with a Nordic influence, such as roasted cod with charred leeks, and pork belly with roasted pear purée. An excellent vegetarian choice, too. Breakfast draws universal praise, 'one of the best I've ever had', with a spoiling menu from smoothies and home-made granola to smashed avocado, hash browns and eggs Benedict. With 'most welcoming' staff this is 'an excellent little hotel'. Reports, please. (D and JB)

92 Brocco Bank
Sheffield S11 8RS

T: 0114 266 1233
E: hello@brocco.co.uk
W: brocco.co.uk

BEDROOMS: 8. 1, on ground floor, suitable for disabled.
OPEN: all year, restaurant closed Mon/Tues and Sun pm and Christmas Day.
FACILITIES: reception area with sofas, restaurant with bar, terrace (al fresco dining), in-room TV (Freeview), parking, restaurant wheelchair accessible, adapted toilet.
BACKGROUND MUSIC: in restaurant, Sunday jazz afternoons.
LOCATION: 1½ miles W of city centre.
CHILDREN: all ages welcomed, under-3s free, extra bed £35.
DOGS: allowed only on terrace.
CREDIT CARDS: Amex, MC, Visa.
PRICES: Room-only doubles from £125. Breakfast items from £4, full English £12, 2-course lunch/dinner from £25. Min. 2-night stay at Christmas.

SIDLESHAM Sussex   MAP 2:E3

THE CRAB & LOBSTER

This 'little gem' of a 17th-century pub, run as a
restaurant-with-rooms on the harbour, overlooks
Pagham Harbour Local Nature Reserve with its
black-tailed godwits, little egrets and spoonbills.
Proprietors Sam and Janet Bakose also own The
Halfway Bridge, Lodsworth (see entry). Cottage-
style bedrooms with soft pastel walls and fresh
flowers also have some structural idiosyncrasies. A
spacious deluxe room with 'plenty of storage and
a view over the salt marsh' has 'a floor-to-ceiling
beam in the middle', great for pole dancing but it
could make 'night-time visits to the loo a painful
proposition', while a room under the eaves is a
bit short on head room. A stalwart reader, on his
third visit, reaffirms his advice to choose Room
1. 'Fish predominates' on a varied menu with
plenty of other choices. This year, 'squid tempura
and chicken croquette, curried cod loin, baked
crab and duck were all very good'; a haddock
fishcake was heavy on potato. Breakfast brings
porridge and 'perfect scrambled egg' but sadly,
for one reader, no Frosted Flakes to bring out the
tiger in him ('I'd have liked some cereal'). (Peter
Anderson, and others)

Mill Lane
Sidlesham PO20 7NB

T: 01243 641233
E: enquiries@crab-lobster.co.uk
W: crab-lobster.co.uk

BEDROOMS: 4. 2 in adjacent self-
catering Crab Cottage.
OPEN: all year.
FACILITIES: bar/dining room/snug,
in-room TV (Freeview), terrace,
small beer garden, bar and restaurant
wheelchair accessible, adapted toilet.
BACKGROUND MUSIC: 'quiet' music in
restaurant and bar.
LOCATION: 6 miles S of Chichester.
CHILDREN: all ages welcomed, under-
9s on extra bed £30.
DOGS: allowed in garden area.
CREDIT CARDS: Amex, MC, Visa.
PRICES: B&B doubles from £200, singles
from £125 (full rates apply Fri–Sun),
extra child/adult guest (Crab Cottage)
£30. À la carte £42. Min. 2-night stay
at weekends.

SIDMOUTH Devon

MAP 1:C5

HOTEL RIVIERA

On the esplanade, overlooking the pink-pebble beach, Peter Wharton's stuccoed Regency hotel is loved by many readers for its old-style values. 'I last stayed in 2014, but was welcomed back by the concierge, who collected my bags from the taxi and showed me to my room,' writes one. 'We have not had such a wonderful reception since we stayed at the Savoy,' declares another. A bow-windowed sea-view room is top choice, but town-facing rooms are perfectly fine. 'My room was clean, comfortable and well appointed, with Molton Brown toiletries, shortbread, a well-stocked hospitality tray.' A resident pianist sometimes plays in the refurbished cocktail bar. In the restaurant, dinner is a 'delightful ritual' with 'consistently imaginative but unpretentious cooking' including dishes such as Dover sole with chive butter or mushroom stroganoff. 'The arancini is standout.' Like Sidmouth itself, the Riviera has resisted modernisation, but that's part of its charm. 'It is slightly dated but it has a wonderful feel about it and very attentive, well-trained staff.' (Ian Marshall, Michael Lewis, Richard Bright, and others)

The Esplanade
Sidmouth EX10 8AY

T: 01395 515201
E: enquiries@hotelriviera.co.uk
W: hotelriviera.co.uk

BEDROOMS: 26. None on ground floor.
OPEN: all year.
FACILITIES: small lift, foyer, lounge, bar, restaurant, function rooms, in-room TV (Freeview), terrace, parking (£7.50 a day), public rooms wheelchair accessible.
BACKGROUND MUSIC: in bar and restaurant, occasional pianist in bar.
LOCATION: central, on the esplanade.
CHILDREN: all ages welcomed, under-3s free, extra bed 25%–75% of per-person adult rate.
DOGS: small dogs allowed in some bedrooms (£16.50 a night, by arrangement, not in public rooms.
CREDIT CARDS: Amex, MC, Visa.
PRICES: B&B doubles from £258, singles from £142. Set-price dinner £43–£47, à la carte £60.

SNETTISHAM Norfolk

MAP 2:A4

THE ROSE & CROWN

There is a warm-hearted sense of fun about Jeannette and Anthony Goodrich's 'very welcoming' child-friendly, dog-friendly, rose-covered 14th-century pub (a reader loved the way they had pinned up a bad review alongside a good one 'as if to say "please make up your own minds"'). It is a social hub, sponsoring the village cricket team, which plays on the green opposite. Our reader's bedroom was 'cosy and spotlessly clean'; the bathrooms have walk-in power showers and luxury toiletries. Two bedrooms with garden access have a daybed for a child, a new shower room, wood-effect flooring for sandy feet and muddy paws. Most double beds have been upgraded to super-kings. You can drink in the beamed bar and eat 'delicious food' indoors or in the walled garden, where the Beach Hut bar now dispenses drinks while children scale the Merry Rose climbing ship. The kitchen uses fish from the Norfolk coast, produce from local farms and allotments, in pub classics and more adventurous dishes such as lobster and mussel Thai broth. 'No wonder this place is consistently so highly rated.' (Tessa Stuart, and others)

Old Church Road
Snettisham PE31 7LX

T: 01485 541382
E: info@roseandcrownsnettisham.co.uk
W: roseandcrownsnettisham.co.uk

BEDROOMS: 16. 2 on ground floor, 1 suitable for disabled.
OPEN: all year.
FACILITIES: 3 bar areas, 2 restaurant rooms, in-room TV (Freeview), large walled garden (children's play area, climbing ship), EV charging, Garden Room restaurant wheelchair accessible, adapted toilet.
BACKGROUND MUSIC: low-key, mainly soft jazz in dining areas.
LOCATION: in village centre, 5 miles S of Hunstanton.
CHILDREN: all ages welcomed, cots £10, extra bed £20, children's menu.
DOGS: well-behaved dogs allowed in bedrooms (£15 per night), bars and garden room, not in dining areas.
CREDIT CARDS: Amex, MC, Visa.
PRICES: B&B doubles from £140, singles from £110. À la carte £36.

SOMERTON Somerset   MAP 1:C6

THE LYNCH COUNTRY HOUSE

Guests can ascend to the belvedere atop jazz musician Roy Copeland's classical late Georgian mansion B&B for views across the countryside and grounds, the lake and specimen trees. Mr Copeland and 'delightful, helpful' manager Lynne Vincent are welcoming hosts. Period furniture, artwork and jazz memorabilia lend a home-from-home character. Bedrooms may be a bit dated, but they are attractive, with a comfy bed. Goldington has an antique oak four-poster. Kendal, under the eaves, has a double and single bed plus a campaign couch for a little soldier, a bathroom across the landing. Breakfast in the orangery includes freshly squeezed orange juice, French yogurts, Wiltshire bacon, scrambled eggs, Loch Fyne smoked salmon with a toasted muffin. You are free to wander outside, admire the topiary and explore woodland planted 20-odd years ago. If you care to sit out with a drink, the Lynch's iconic black swans, native to Australia, might come to say 'G'day'. For dinner, readers have praised The White Hart in Somerton (see Shortlist) and it is a short drive to both The Devonshire Arms, Long Sutton, and The Red Lion, Babcary (see main entries).

4 Behind Berry
Somerton TA11 7PD

T: 01458 272316
E: enquiries@thelynchcountryhouse.co.uk
W: thelynchcountryhouse.co.uk

BEDROOMS: 5. Self-catering annexe in coach house.
OPEN: all year, only coach house rooms at Christmas and New Year, no breakfast 25/26 Dec, 1 Jan.
FACILITIES: breakfast room, small sitting area, in-room TV (Freeview), ¾-acre grounds (lake), unsuitable for disabled.
BACKGROUND MUSIC: none.
LOCATION: edge of town.
CHILDREN: all ages welcomed, extra bed £20–£35.
DOGS: not allowed.
CREDIT CARDS: Amex, MC, Visa.
PRICES: B&B doubles from £80, singles from £70.

SEE ALSO SHORTLIST

SOUTH BRENT Devon   MAP 1:D4

GLAZEBROOK HOUSE

Oh, my fur and whiskers, here's Wonderland
for adults, an Alice-themed hotel on the edge
of Dartmoor national park. Public rooms pay
homage to British eccentricity, evoking the home
of a 19th-century collector and bon vivant, with
a red marble bar, leather armchairs, a cigar-
smoking room dedicated to Winston Churchill,
here a pith helmet, there a wall of china plates, a
line of bowler hats, a flamingo skeleton. Bedrooms
drip with chandeliers. High-spec bathrooms have
under-floor heating, with perhaps a wet-room
shower or an egg-shaped bath. The Mad Hatter
room has a wall-mounted doll's house. Tweedle
Deez has twin four-posters. All rooms have a
minibar with complimentary snacks, White
Company toiletries – and daily housekeeping by
seven maids with seven mops, we like to think.
Chefs Ben Palmer and Josh Ackland's locally
sourced menus include dishes such as braised beef
cheek with horseradish mash, market fish, and
confit duck leg with braised red cabbage. You can
breakfast on eggs Benedict or American pancakes
with crispy bacon, then head out to hunt the snark
or explore Dartmoor's mustard mines.

Glazebrook
South Brent
Totnes TQ10 9JE

T: 01364 73322
E: enquiries@glazebrookhouse.com
W: glazebrookhouse.com

BEDROOMS: 8. 1, on ground floor,
suitable for disabled.
OPEN: all year, Wed–Sun, except
22–31 Dec 2021.
FACILITIES: reception lobby, drawing
room, bar/library, whisky/gin tasting
room, restaurant, chef's kitchen patio,
in-room TV (Freeview), civil wedding
licence, 3½-acre garden, EV charging,
public rooms wheelchair accessible,
adapted toilet.
BACKGROUND MUSIC: in public areas,
not library or tasting room.
LOCATION: 1 mile SW of town centre.
CHILDREN: over-16s welcomed,
supervised children over 6 in
restaurant only.
DOGS: not allowed.
CREDIT CARDS: Amex, MC, Visa.
PRICES: B&B doubles from £199, singles
from £164. À la carte £40.

SOUTH DALTON Yorkshire

MAP 4:D5

THE PIPE AND GLASS INN

♕ Previous César winner

The winning formula of Michelin-starred food plus spoiling bedrooms in James and Kate Mackenzie's classic coaching inn prompted one fan to make a 60-mile detour to spend the night there. 'We were not disappointed. This remains a top-notch venue.' In an 'enchantingly beautiful' estate village, the traditional pub still features exposed brick, beams and gleaming copper alongside its graceful dining room, where James showcases his creative cooking. Meals might include duck three ways with pickled brambles and Parkin crumb or 'excellent' grilled halibut with lobster bisque. Bedrooms are equally indulgent, with statement wallpapers, bold colours, velvet fabrics and sleigh or four-poster beds. Five overlook the garden – a treat of quirky sculpture, hidden arbours and kitchen produce – while four are in outbuildings. Even the smallest room 'doesn't feel cramped' and holds a king-size bed, although its bathroom is 'compact'. Breakfasts are impressive, 'with generous portions'. One night is not enough, concludes our reader, whose only problem was 'choosing between the grouse and the very tender, traditionally garnished halibut'. (Peter Anderson)

West End
South Dalton HU17 7PN

T: 01430 810246
E: email@pipeandglass.co.uk
W: pipeandglass.co.uk

BEDROOMS: 9. 5 in main building, 4, in converted buildings, all on ground floor, 1 suitable for disabled.
OPEN: all year except 2 weeks in Jan, no room reservations Sun and Mon.
FACILITIES: lounge, conservatory, bar, restaurant (vegetarian/vegan menus), in-room TV (Freeview), patio (alfresco dining), garden, EV charging, public rooms wheelchair accessible, adapted toilet.
BACKGROUND MUSIC: in bar and restaurant.
LOCATION: 7 miles NW of Beverley.
CHILDREN: all ages welcomed, under-3s free, extra bed for under-16s £30.
DOGS: not allowed.
CREDIT CARDS: Amex, MC, Visa.
PRICES: B&B doubles from £200, singles from £170. À la carte £55. Dinner usually required as part of booking.

SOUTH LEIGH Oxfordshire   MAP 3:E6

ARTIST RESIDENCE OXFORDSHIRE

When you step into this olde-worlde, thatched Cotswold village farmhouse-turned-pub, prepare to do a double take when you see the offbeat interior. Yes, here are the expected flagstone floors, the beams, the blazing log fires, but here, too, over an inglenook, is a battered sign reading 'Casino', vintage photos of pugilists, the words 'What did I do last night?' spelt out in pink neon. Like all of Justin and Charlotte Salisbury's Artist Residence properties (see index), this hotel with a downstairs pub, the Mason Arms, is infused with wit. Your rustic-chic bedroom might have bare floorboards, an upcycled tea crate for a bedside table, vintage armchairs, along with a roll-top bath and rainfall shower, espresso machine, minibar and organic toiletries. Two suites and one bedroom are in outbuildings with their own entrance. The best has a crazy statement four-poster, Beatles Sgt Pepper cushions, comfy seating by a log-burner, a private terrace. There is good pub grub in the bar, summer barbecues in the garden with an open marquee for alfresco dining. Lobster and margaritas in the sunshine; freshly squeezed OJ and eggs Benedict for breakfast.

Station Road
South Leigh OX29 6XN

T: 01993 656220
E: oxford@artistresidence.co.uk
W: artistresidence.co.uk/our-hotels/
   oxford

BEDROOMS: 9. 1 bedroom and 2 suites in outbuildings, Shepherd's Hut in garden.
OPEN: all year.
FACILITIES: bar, restaurant (2 dining areas, closed Sun eve), in-room TV (Freeview), large beer garden, EV charging, unsuitable for disabled.
BACKGROUND MUSIC: in pub and restaurant.
LOCATION: countryside, 10 miles from Oxford, 3 miles from Witney centre.
CHILDREN: all ages welcomed, free cots, extra bed £30.
DOGS: allowed in some bedrooms (£20 per dog per night, dog beds provided), and public rooms.
CREDIT CARDS: Amex, MC, Visa.
PRICES: room from £165. Breakfast full English £13, à la carte £30. Min. 2-night stay at weekends.

SOUTHAMPTON Hampshire

MAP 2:E2

THE PIG IN THE WALL

The Babe of the litter, this crenellated Georgian house set into the 14th-century city wall is unique among Robin Hutson's Pig collection (see index) in having no restaurant, nor a vast, prolific kitchen garden. You simply step inside and check in at the counter of a bar/lounge/deli with scuffed floorboards, mix-and-match furniture, a big dresser, and pot herbs on bare wooden tables, reflecting designer Judy Hutson's penchant for shabby-chic. There are only a dozen bedrooms, the smallest of which is tucked away under the eaves, with sloping ceilings, exposed timbers and a monsoon shower. The most spacious have a freestanding roll-top bath, a walk-in monsoon shower, perhaps a white-painted, barley-sugar-twist four-poster. Food is served from noon until 8 pm, with some tables on the front terrace when the sun shines. You can just swing by to graze on veggie, fish and meat plates, home-made pork, sage and cranberry sausage rolls, soup, quiches, cheeses. Breakfast brings a choice of a 'Piggy Pan' cooked breakfast and continental options. If you want a proper dinner, the Pig in the Forest at Brockenhurst is a 30-minute drive away.

8 Western Esplanade
Southampton SO14 2AZ

T: 02380 636900
E: info@thepighotel.com
W: thepighotel.com

BEDROOMS: 12. 2 on ground floor, 1 with wet room and wheelchair access via side door from car park (not suitable for wider wheelchairs).
OPEN: all year.
FACILITIES: open-plan lounge/bar/deli counter, in-room TV (Freeview), car park (free if you're dining; £10 overnight), public rooms wheelchair accessible.
BACKGROUND MUSIC: in public areas.
LOCATION: close to city centre.
CHILDREN: all ages welcomed, no charge for extra beds.
DOGS: not allowed.
CREDIT CARDS: Amex, MC, Visa.
PRICES: room-only doubles from £140. Breakfast £10–£15.

SOUTHROP Gloucestershire

MAP 2:C2

THYME

The collection of honeyed buildings on Caryn
Hibbert's restored Cotswold manor and farm are
home to chic bedrooms, a cookery school, pub
and spa, interspersed with quintessential English
gardens. Everything has been 'beautifully thought
out' with some fun farm theming – the cool
Baa bar has life-size sheep seats – though it can
feel 'a little too perfectly designed'. 'Top-notch'
bedrooms, in the main building and grounds, are
country chic with soft colours, feature wallpapers,
antique and modern furniture. 'Ours had exposed
beams and lopsided walls.' 'Nice touches' include
complimentary vermouth in larger rooms, and
hot-water bottles. In the enormous, beamed Ox
Barn, 'warm and inviting with twinkly lights',
Caryn's son, Charlie, creates a short-choice menu
of modern dishes. The brill, in a pale oyster
and salsify sauce, was 'creamy and succulent'
though one reader thought the breakfast, with
its juice 'from whatever was fresh in the garden',
was much better than dinner. With a natural
spring water pool, bikes to hire, a shop to browse
and 'friendly, warm and helpful' staff, it's an
'expensive, but special treat'. (SG, and others)

Southrop Manor Estate
Southrop
Lechlade GL7 3NX

T: 01367 850174
E: info@thyme.co.uk
W: thyme.co.uk

BEDROOMS: 32. 8 in main building,
others in a lodge, outbuildings and
cottages.
OPEN: all year.
FACILITIES: drawing room, cocktail
bar, restaurant, pub, in-room TV
(Freeview), civil wedding licence,
event space, 150-acre estate (farm,
gardens, swimming pool, spa), EV
charging, unsuitable for disabled.
BACKGROUND MUSIC: in public spaces.
LOCATION: on large Cotswold estate
N of Lechlade.
CHILDREN: not under 12, except in 1
cottage and Ox Barn at lunchtime.
DOGS: only in 1 cottage (no charge)
and pub.
CREDIT CARDS: Amex, MC, Visa.
PRICES: B&B doubles from £335. À la
carte (3 courses) £50. 1-night bookings
refused weekends and bank holidays.

STAMFORD Lincolnshire
MAP 2:B3

THE GEORGE OF STAMFORD

For Walter Scott, the view of Stamford from this historic coaching inn was 'the finest twixt Edinburgh and London'. Our readers' appreciation extends beyond the view. 'The staff are lovely, the hotel is lovely and the town is lovely,' they say. 'Splendid hotel, staff very friendly, personable and well trained.' Owned for 50 years by Lawrence Hoskins, and in the care of chef/patron Paul Reseigh, The George cleaves to traditional values. Accommodation ranges from singles to four-poster rooms. 'Our bedroom and bathroom were spacious and up to date; the lighting was very good. The bathroom had the best shaving mirror I've ever used.' You can have a cream tea by the fire or in the courtyard, drink bubbly in the Champagne Bar, or don best bib and tucker to dine in the Oak Room, where the signature roast sirloin arrives on a silver-domed carving wagon, and desserts are served from a trolley. The food in the Garden Room is more modern, with pasta, steaks, a shellfish platter and a plant-based menu. In summer, food is served all day in a tented area in the former monastery garden. (John and Elspeth Gibbon, David Sefton, and others)

71 St Martins
Stamford PE9 2LB

T: 01780 750750
E: reservations@
   georgehotelofstamford.com
W: georgehotelofstamford.com

BEDROOMS: 45.
OPEN: all year.
FACILITIES: 2 lounges, 2 bars, 2 restaurants (vegetarian and vegan menu), 3 private dining rooms, business centre, in-room TV (Sky, Freeview), civil wedding licence, 2-acre grounds (courtyard, gardens). parking, public rooms wheelchair accessible, adapted toilet.
BACKGROUND MUSIC: quiet, in summer in garden covered area.
LOCATION: ¼ mile from centre.
CHILDREN: all ages welcomed, extra bed £60.
DOGS: small dogs allowed with prior notice, not unattended in bedrooms (£10 per night), not in restaurants.
CREDIT CARDS: Amex, MC, Visa.
PRICES: B&B doubles from £270, singles from £150. À la carte £75 (Oak Room), £55 (Garden Room).

STANTON HARCOURT Oxfordshire   MAP 2:C2

THE HARCOURT ARMS

Among the neat rows of Cotswold houses, this
'equally pristine' 17th-century pub with extensions
sideways and upwards offers a 'really pleasant
place to stay' as well as acting as a village social
hub, with bar, restaurant and even a deli selling
bread, cakes, coffee and local produce. After
a four-year make-over, there is still plenty of
tradition in the beamed bar with rugs on flagstone
floors and lots of comfy leather seating – on
cold days 'wood-burning stoves, all lit and cosy'.
Bedrooms blend modern comforts with vintage
pieces, bold patterned headboards, original
artwork, a coffee machine and posh toiletries.
The dual-aspect Blenheim Suite has a bespoke
four-poster, a stand-alone copper bathtub and a
lounge area. Staff are 'terrific and unjaded'. In
the restaurant, the short menu ranges from pub
classics to more unusual dishes. Grilled butternut
squash with cavolo nero, goat's curd and apple
syrup, and a venison 'Barnsley chop' were 'greatly
enjoyed'. Sadly, trusted readers this year had a
disappointing meal, and wondered if the chef was
having a day off, or an off day: 'What a pity! This
is otherwise a pleasant place.'

Stanton Harcourt
Witney OX29 5RJ

T: 01865 416516
E: theharcourtarms@barkbygroup.
  com
W: www.theharcourtarms.com

BEDROOMS: 10. 1 garden room across
small rear courtyard suitable for
disabled.
OPEN: all year, kitchen closed Sun
evening.
FACILITIES: snug bar, dining bar,
restaurant, ½-acre garden, in-room
TV (Freeview), all ground floor
wheelchair accessible from parking
bays to rear, adapted toilet.
BACKGROUND MUSIC: in all public areas.
LOCATION: 6 miles SE of Witney,
4 miles SW of Eynsham.
CHILDREN: all ages welcomed, family
rooms.
DOGS: allowed in bar only.
CREDIT CARDS: Amex, MC, Visa.
PRICES: B&B (continental breakfast)
doubles from £111, singles from £105,
family from £125. Cooked breakfast
charged per item, full English £14,
à la carte £30.

STANTON WICK Somerset

MAP 1:B6

THE CARPENTERS ARMS

Flower-bedecked without, warm and buzzy within, this pub-with-rooms in a Chew valley hamlet occupies three old, knocked-through miners' cottages. It has been run for many years by Simon Pledge for small pub group Buccaneer Holdings and, say ex-hotelier readers, is a pleasing blend of 'the personal and professional'. It's perfect for all seasons, with picnic tables at the front, a no-smoking terrace at the side, and plenty of atmosphere within, with stone walls, beams, settles, log-burners and comfy seating. Food is served in the bar and two dining rooms by 'obliging and helpful' staff. Attractive bedrooms are 'modern without being drab', with a big, padded headboard and jolly, modern artwork clearly chosen with thought and not bought as a job lot. Five have a walk-in shower, the rest a bath with shower over. 'Housekeeping and decor were in excellent condition.' Good-quality pub grub includes Brixham fish from the day boats and Thai green vegetable curry, while Sunday roasts come with 'gigantic portions of vegetables and potatoes'. Breakfast gets a thumbs-up for good hot toast served with the cooked dishes. (S and JJ)

Wick Lane
Stanton Wick
Pensford BS39 4BX

T: 01761 490202
E: carpenters@buccaneer.co.uk
W: the-carpenters-arms.co.uk

BEDROOMS: 13.
OPEN: all year except evenings 25/26 Dec, 1 Jan.
FACILITIES: bar, snug, lounge, 2 restaurants, function room, in-room TV (Freeview), patio, secure parking, public areas wheelchair accessible, adapted toilet.
BACKGROUND MUSIC: in some areas.
LOCATION: 8 miles S of Bristol, 8 miles W of Bath.
CHILDREN: all ages welcomed, under-12s stay free, children's menu, high chairs, changing facilities.
DOGS: allowed in bar, snug and outside areas.
CREDIT CARDS: Amex, MC, Visa.
PRICES: B&B doubles from £140, singles from £90. À la carte £37.

STUDLAND Dorset

MAP 2:E2

THE PIG ON THE BEACH

♀ Previous César winner

Robin Hutson put the Pig in higgledy-piggledy with the most fanciful of his litter of porcine hotels (see index), set in a yellow seaside villa built in 1820 in romantic picturesque style, with gabled dormers, a turret and random roof line. It stands on the reputed site of vanished Studland Castle, with views across Studland Bay to Old Harry Rocks, and the fairy-tale fantasy extends to two thatched dovecotes in the kitchen garden, each with a four-poster, one with its own beach hut. House bedrooms – from very snug, with countryside views, to 'generous', with a sea view, perhaps French doors to the grounds – are all in the group's signature shabby-chic style, with bare floorboards and soft paint finishes. You can dine in the conservatory on dishes such as Dorset Horn hogget loin, wood-oven-roasted carrots, garden nettle and mint sauce, or go for wood-fired flatbreads on the terrace. On a sunny day, Guide insiders found the place thronged. 'They were so busy we had a long wait for our lunch. When it came, the food was fine – fresh fish simply cooked, rich puddings.' And, as ever, 'friendly young staff keep things going'. (C and AR)

Manor House
Manor Road
Studland BH19 3AU

T: 01929 450288
E: info@thepighotel.com
W: thepighotel.com

BEDROOMS: 28. Some on ground floor, 2 dovecote hideaways, Harry's Hut and Pig Hut in grounds, 1 suitable for disabled.
OPEN: all year.
FACILITIES: bar, lounge, snug, restaurant, private dining room, in-room TV (Freeview), civil wedding licence, 2 treatment cabins, garden, ground-floor public rooms and part of gardens wheelchair accessible, adapted toilet.
BACKGROUND MUSIC: all day in public areas.
LOCATION: above Studland beach.
CHILDREN: all ages welcomed, no charge for extra beds.
DOGS: not allowed.
CREDIT CARDS: Amex, MC, Visa.
PRICES: room-only doubles £145–£389. Breakfast £10–£15, à la carte £35. 1-night bookings refused weekends, Christmas, New Year.

STURMINSTER NEWTON Dorset

MAP 2:E1

PLUMBER MANOR

In the same family since it was built in the early 17th century, this manor house in Thomas Hardy's 'vale of little dairies' has a timeless appeal – but change has been afoot. Bedrooms, in the main house and a converted barn, have been updated, as avocado bathrooms fade from memory, and some now have a bath and super walk-in shower. Not that loyal fans should fear: the look remains traditional, the welcome warm as ever, from Alison and Richard Prideaux-Brune and their Labradors, with the ambience of a much-loved home. Interiors are furnished with antiques, the gallery is still hung with ancestral portraits. Richard's brother Brian continues to cook alongside head chef Louis Haskell, serving traditional British fare. At night Richard tours the dining rooms, making sure that diners – including 'lots of locals' – are enjoying their wild mushroom millefeuille, lemon and rosemary chicken, or brill with orange and chives, from a short but varied menu. 'Wine very reasonably priced,' writes a reader. The waiting staff are 'lovely and very efficient'. In all, a 'very pretty house, nice gardens, lovely planting'.

Sturminster Newton DT10 2AF

T: 01258 472507
E: book@plumbermanor.com
W: plumbermanor.com

BEDROOMS: 16. 10 on ground floor in courtyard, 2 suitable for disabled.
OPEN: all year except Feb.
FACILITIES: snug, bar/lounge, dining room, gallery, in-room TV (Freeview), civil wedding licence, 14-acre grounds (3-acre garden, tennis, croquet, stream), EV charging, restaurant, lounge and toilet wheelchair accessible.
BACKGROUND MUSIC: none.
LOCATION: 2½ miles SW of Sturminster Newton.
CHILDREN: all ages welcomed, cots £10, extra bed £20.
DOGS: allowed in 4 courtyard bedrooms (no charge), not in main house bedrooms or public rooms.
CREDIT CARDS: Amex, MC, Visa.
PRICES: B&B doubles from £170, singles from £130. Fixed-price dinner £36–£40.

SWAFFHAM Norfolk   MAP 2:B5

STRATTONS

Tucked away behind a shopping street in a market town, Vanessa and Les Scott's dog-friendly, child-friendly hotel occupies a Palladian villa in gardens. Walk up a narrow lane and you will pass the hotel's 'happy, bustling' deli, the place for all-day breakfast, cakes (including 'rightly famous' fishcakes with fennel slaw), quiches, tapas, rare breed and vegetarian sausage rolls. Each bedroom, in the main house and annexes, is one of a kind, with perhaps a cinema screen, a woodland mural on the walls, or a mermaid mosaic in the bathroom. Opium has a large bath at the foot of an oriental-style four-poster. The opulent dual-aspect Red Room includes a large lounge area, a Jacobean four-poster on a plinth, and access via its own courtyard garden. You might find resident cats snoozing in the lounge. In Afterfive restaurant, a spiffy, flint-walled barn conversion, ethically sourced, organic, artisan, home-grown and foraged produce appears on a seasonal menu of dishes devised by Vanessa. They might include seafood lasagne, wild mushroom risotto with carpaccio of beetroot, or rack of lamb with jus and Binham Blue bubble and squeak.

4 Ash Close
Swaffham PE37 7NH

T: 01760 723845
E: enquiries@strattonshotel.com
W: strattonshotel.com

BEDROOMS: 14. 6 in annexes, 1 on ground floor (via entrance steps), 2 with self-catering facilities.
OPEN: all year except 1 week at Christmas.
FACILITIES: drawing room, reading room, restaurant, in-room TV (Freeview), terrace, café/deli, 1-acre garden, limited guest parking, EV charging, café wheelchair accessible.
BACKGROUND MUSIC: all day in public areas.
LOCATION: central, parking.
CHILDREN: all ages welcomed, cot £10, extra bed £25.
DOGS: allowed in some bedrooms (£10 per night), public rooms.
CREDIT CARDS: Amex, MC, Visa.
PRICES: B&B doubles from £159, singles from £94. Set-price menu £49. 1-night bookings refused weekends, 3-night min. bank holidays.

SWALLOWCLIFFE Wiltshire

MAP 2:D1

THE ROYAL OAK

NEW

'Rescued from dilapidation', by locals, this 'charming, white-painted, part-thatched' former 18th-century tannery-turned-inn stands on a quiet country lane, in a village buried in the Nadder valley. Our inspectors approached 'through the truly beautiful parkland' of the Fonthill Estate, on a largely single-track road, 'ironic as James (Top Gear) May owns 50 per cent of the pub'. The greeting was 'warm and welcoming', though a request for payment up front felt less friendly. The bedrooms are 'spacious, with a stylish contemporary rustic simplicity, oak furniture, a Lloyd Loom chair'. Occupying the entire top floor, Ashcombe is 'almost a suite, with a super-king bed'. The bathroom 'looked stunning', but an egg-shaped bath on a plinth was for the more limber. At dinner, in a light-filled, beamed extension, a pea and wild garlic soup with garlic flower garnish was 'up to best expectations', while an 'aubergine tartlet with glazed onion, romesco sauce and tempura onion' was much enjoyed; a cheeseburger, less so. A 'really well-cooked breakfast' included 'delicious granola' and 'the yellowest eggs ever seen'.

Common Lane
Swallowcliffe SP3 5PA

T: 01747 870211
E: hello@royaloakswallowcliffe.com
W: royaloakswallowcliffe.com

BEDROOMS: 6. 1 suitable for disabled.
OPEN: all year, but no accommodation 25 Dec evening.
FACILITIES: lift, bar, dining room, Oak Room, in-room TV (Freeview), garden with outdoor seating, public rooms wheelchair accessible, adapted toilet.
BACKGROUND MUSIC: none.
LOCATION: 2 miles SE of Tisbury.
CHILDREN: all ages welcomed, extra bed £15.
DOGS: 'friendly, well-behaved' dogs allowed in 1 bedroom (£15 a night, treats, towels provided), public rooms except Oak Room.
CREDIT CARDS: Amex, MC, Visa.
PRICES: B&B doubles from £100. À la carte £33.

TALLAND-BY-LOOE Cornwall

MAP 1:D3

TALLAND BAY HOTEL

Sub-tropical gardens with spectacular sea views are lent an extra touch of magic by the witty artwork that fills them at this quirky hotel, which also features unusual furnishings within. Look out for a stone cat on a wall, a human-sized fairy, and a zebra-striped sofa beneath a bull in a top hat. Interior decoration is 'vibrant', comments a reader, occasionally 'kitsch' but this doesn't detract from the 'simply excellent service'. You could spend all day gazing at the 'lovely sea view' and 'interesting grounds', although the South West Coast Path skirts the gardens. Return to drinks on the terrace – perhaps their own-label gin – and 'brilliantly cooked meals' such as fillet with truffle butter or local salt hake with prawn dumplings. 'The food is absolutely delicious.' Rooms are themed with colourful wallpapers and fabrics; perhaps nautical stripes, wood panelling, decadent golds or a woodland theme, and are 'luxurious without being heavy or old-fashioned'. Some have a private garden or patio, one has a balcony and hot tub. 'Generous' breakfasts include smoked haddock and eggs how you want. (Martin and Emma Leuw, MC, and others)

Porthallow
Talland-by-Looe PL13 2JB

T: 01503 272667
E: info@tallandbayhotel.com
W: tallandbayhotel.co.uk

BEDROOMS: 21. 3 in cottages, 6 on ground floor, 1 suitable for disabled. Plus 2-bed self-catering bungalow.
OPEN: all year, except Jan.
FACILITIES: lounge, bar, restaurant, brasserie/conservatory, in-room TV (Freeview), civil wedding licence, terrace, outside seating, 2-acre garden, public rooms wheelchair accessible.
BACKGROUND MUSIC: in bar and restaurant.
LOCATION: 2½ miles SW of Looe.
CHILDREN: all ages welcomed, extra bed £45.
DOGS: in bedrooms (£15 per night) and brasserie, not in restaurant.
CREDIT CARDS: Amex, MC, Visa.
PRICES: B&B doubles from £240, singles from £230. À la carte £52. 1-night bookings refused weekends in peak season.

TAPLOW Berkshire

MAP 2:D3

CLIVEDEN HOUSE

Standing grandly above the Thames, in National Trust gardens and pleasure grounds, an Italianate mansion built by Charles Barry for the Duke of Sutherland 'seems to have hosted everyone who is anyone', from Winston Churchill to Lawrence of Arabia. A Relais & Châteaux hotel, it has 'bedrooms filled with antiques and named after famous past guests', of whom there have been many, from Lord Curzon and Mahatma Gandhi, when Nancy Astor held court here, to Meghan Markle on the night before her wedding. John Singer Sargent's portrait of Lady Astor hangs in the Great Hall by a monumental Italian Renaissance fireplace, amid a sea of sofas. Bedrooms range from 'club' doubles to the Lady Astor Suite, with a private terrace and views over the spectacular parterre to the river. Some 'classic' rooms overlooking the spa garden have a terrace with a hot tub. You can take tea alfresco, address yourself to Cliveden fish stew, English rose veal or black truffle risotto under chandeliers in the dining room, or settle into a blue-painted banquette in the Astor Grill, in former stables, for a sharing platter, rib-eye steak or fish and chips. (JK)

Cliveden Road
Taplow SL6 0JF

T: 01628 668561
E: reservations@clivedenhouse.co.uk
W: clivedenhouse.co.uk

BEDROOMS: 47. Some on ground floor, 1 suitable for disabled.
OPEN: all year.
FACILITIES: Great Hall, bar/lounge, library, 2 restaurants (vegetarian/vegan menus), private dining rooms, in-room TV (Sky), civil wedding licence, spa, swimming pools, 376-acre estate, EV charging, public areas wheelchair accessible, adapted toilet.
BACKGROUND MUSIC: all day in public areas.
LOCATION: 20 mins from Heathrow, 40 mins central London.
CHILDREN: all ages, extra bed free in school holidays.
DOGS: allowed in bedrooms (£35 a night), most public areas.
CREDIT CARDS: Amex, MC, Visa.
PRICES: B&B doubles from £445. Tasting menu £97.50, à la carte £73 (dining room). 1-night bookings sometimes refused.

TAVISTOCK Devon

MAP 1:D4

THE HORN OF PLENTY

The name promises all manner of good things, and they certainly deliver at this dog-friendly hotel in a former Victorian mine captain's house with glorious views over the 'dramatic sweep of the Tamar valley' and a long reputation for foodie excellence. Inside, it's a mixture of traditional bedrooms in the main house, where a reader had a 'comfortable bed, a sunken bath and separate shower', and more stylish and contemporary in the coach house, with splashes of colour. Most bedrooms have a balcony or terrace, some with folding glass doors in a newer annexe. New chef Ashley Lewis's menus showcase West Country ingredients in 'top-notch' dishes such as Brixham skate, wild mushrooms, black garlic and gnocchi, complemented by the sweeping views through floor-to-ceiling windows. 'I had salmon, hake, and a cauliflower risotto, all excellent,' reports a repeat visitor. 'One of my favourite hotels.' A word of praise this year from a reader who commends the management for declining his offer of payment when he cancelled his booking: 'That speaks of a hotel that puts its customers first.' (Peter Anderson, Sir Frank Berman, and others)

Gulworthy
Tavistock PL19 8JD

T: 01822 832528
E: enquiries@thehornofplenty.co.uk
W: thehornofplenty.co.uk

BEDROOMS: 16. 12 in old and new coach houses (1–2 mins' walk), 7 on ground floor, 1 suitable for disabled.
OPEN: all year.
FACILITIES: lounge/bar, library, drawing room, restaurant, in-room TV (Freeview), civil wedding licence, 5-acre grounds, ground-floor public areas wheelchair accessible.
BACKGROUND MUSIC: occasional background music in restaurant only, 'when it's quiet'.
LOCATION: 3 miles SW of Tavistock.
CHILDREN: all ages welcomed, extra bed £25.
DOGS: allowed in 12 bedrooms (£10 per night) and library, not in restaurant or drawing room.
CREDIT CARDS: MC, Visa.
PRICES: B&B doubles from £150, singles from £140. Set-price dinner £52.50, tasting menu £70.

TEFFONT EVIAS Wiltshire

MAP 2:D1

HOWARD'S HOUSE

The Teff brook runs by this 17th-century limestone small hotel and former dower house in a Nadder valley village, with views of green fields and gardens. Here are roaring fires, fresh-cut flowers, 'plenty of comfy seating areas, and a lovely outside terrace' for a cream tea or lunch alfresco. Bedrooms, ranging from cosy to a four-poster room, have a restrained country house feel, a coffee machine, bathrobes and smart toiletries. 'Our smallish twin double-aspect on the first floor had extremely comfortable beds with a decent-sized shower room.' Andy Britton, who joined in 2017 having worked under stellar chefs such as Albert Roux and Michael Caines, is a key part of the operation. He will stop to chat with guests on his way to collect produce from the prolific kitchen garden that he has helped to develop. Farm-to-fork menus feature game from the Teffont shoot, trout from the Nadder. A typical dish: breast of guineafowl, confit leg, pommes Anna, carrot purée and confit shallot. The Legbar hens in a custom-built reserve lay beautiful blue-shelled eggs for breakfast. 'A lovely atmosphere. We will be back.' (IGC Farman, CH, SS)

Teffont Evias
Salisbury SP3 5RJ

T: 01722 716392
E: enq@howardshousehotel.co.uk
W: howardshousehotel.co.uk

BEDROOMS: 9.
OPEN: all year except 23–27 Dec.
FACILITIES: lounge, snug, restaurant, function facilities in coach house, in-room TV (Freeview), 2-acre grounds, coach house (private function room) wheelchair accessible, adapted toilet.
BACKGROUND MUSIC: in dining room.
LOCATION: 10 miles W of Salisbury.
CHILDREN: all ages welcomed, cot, high chair, extra bed £35.
DOGS: allowed in bedrooms (£15 charge), in public rooms except restaurant.
CREDIT CARDS: Amex, MC, Visa.
PRICES: B&B doubles from £150, singles from £95. Tasting menu £80, à la carte £38–£48.50, seasonal menu £28.50–£35.

TETBURY Gloucestershire   MAP 3:E5

CALCOT & SPA

Country house luxury and child-friendliness are
a happy combination at this spa hotel, occupying
a 16th-century Cotswold manor house in 'lovely,
manicured grounds'. Flagship of the Calcot
Collection (see Barnsley House, Barnsley; The
Painswick, Painswick; and The Lord Crewe
Arms, Blanchland), it has everything to keep
young guests amused, from a crèche, play barn
and cinema to a pirate ship and mini-football.
The ambience is 'easy, informal, relaxed'. Smart
bedrooms, some in outbuildings, range from 'cosy'
to 'family', and even the smallest have a coffee
machine, fresh fruit, home-made shortbread, a
mini-fridge, pantry and aromatherapy toiletries.
Duplex family pads, some with private garden
and side-by-side baths, have bunks, mini-beds,
baby-listening. You can dine in the Conservatory
restaurant ('with an endless view of rolling hills'),
in the more informal Gumstool Inn or alfresco,
on fish and chips, burger, maybe rump of
Wiltshire lamb, roasted squash, salsa verde,
gnocchi; smoked tomato and five-bean cassoulet.
At breakfast there is bread from the on-site
bakery, a house smoothie, 'tasty egg dishes, as
many as you like'. (JB)

Tetbury GL8 8YJ

T: 01666 890391
E: sally.barker@calcot.co
W: calcot.co

BEDROOMS: 35. 10 (for families) in
cottage, 13 around courtyard, on
ground floor, some suitable for
disabled.
OPEN: all year.
FACILITIES: lounge, 2 bars,
2 restaurants, crèche, in-room TV
(Sky, Freeview), civil wedding licence,
220-acre grounds (tennis, heated
swimming pool), spa (with pool), EV
charging, public areas wheelchair
accessible, adapted toilet.
BACKGROUND MUSIC: in restaurants.
LOCATION: 3 miles W of Tetbury.
CHILDREN: all ages welcomed, extra
bed £40.
DOGS: allowed in courtyard bedrooms
(no charge), not in public rooms.
CREDIT CARDS: Amex, MC, Visa.
PRICES: B&B doubles from £239.
À la carte (Conservatory) £50,
(Gumstool Inn) £38.

TETBURY Gloucestershire

MAP 3:E5

THE HARE AND HOUNDS

This Cotswold stone country house hotel, now under the ownership of Fuller's, retains both its charm and its hare motifs, which crop up everywhere, from pillowcases to prints. It's thoughtful rather than twee, and hounds get a look in, too, in Jack Hare's bar, where you can dine with your dog at your side in sight of an enormous canine mural. Bedrooms in the main house – built in the 1860s in the neo-Renaissance style, by Robert Stayner Holford, founder of the wonderful neighbouring Westonbirt National Arboretum – retain pleasing original features. Further rooms, a stroll away in the Silkwood Court annexe, have a more contemporary feel, some with wheelchair access, others with their own garden terrace. Magnolia Suite has an outdoor hot tub, as does the hideaway Game Keeper's cottage, with its private garden. If you prefer something more formal than the bar for dinner, the stylish Beaufort restaurant (with, yes, a hare ornament over the fireplace) has an à la carte menu with dishes such as rack of lamb, glazed artichokes, spinach, anchovy and nettle butter, jus; fruits of the sea ragout or gnocchi with wild garlic pesto.

Bath Road
Westonbirt
Tetbury GL8 8QL

T: 01666 881000
E: reception@hareandhoundshotel.com
W: cotswold-inns-hotels.co.uk

BEDROOMS: 42. 2 suitable for disabled, 3 in coach house, 5 in garden cottage, 12 in Silkwood Court, 1 in Game Keeper's Cottage.
OPEN: all year.
FACILITIES: drawing room, lounges, library, bar, restaurant, private dining room, in-room TV (Freeview), civil wedding licence, gardens, woodland.
BACKGROUND MUSIC: in lounge and bar.
LOCATION: 3 miles SW of Tetbury.
CHILDREN: all ages welcomed, extra bed £20.
DOGS: allowed by arrangement in some bedrooms (£20 per night), bar, garden, not in restaurant.
CREDIT CARDS: Amex, MC, Visa.
PRICES: B&B doubles from £140, singles from £105. À la carte £40.

TETBURY Gloucestershire   MAP 3:E5

THE ROYAL OAK

Give Django Reinhardt a spin on the vintage
jukebox and drop in for a quiz night or for a
Sunday-night session on the 1920s Art Deco
piano at this fun local hang-out handy for the
chic boutiques of Tetbury. Rooms, with wooden
floors and a stripped-back chic, are in an annexe
across a cobbled courtyard. Some are dog-friendly,
several have comfy seating areas, all have luxury
toiletries along with serious style. They range
from a very snug space with a shower over the
bath in the bathroom to a showstopper suite with
beams, a mezzanine, an in-room roll-top bath,
walk-in rain shower, log-burner and balcony. You
can dine in the bar or outside with your dog, or
dogless upstairs under the rafters. Chef Stergios
Pikos's menus have 'a firm vegan theme': choose
a beef burger or superfood burger, smoked tofish
or beer-battered fish and chips, a one-pot stew
of the day. New this year is the covered, heated
'Tavern on the Green' for outdoor drinking. In
summer, world street food is dispensed from a
silver Airstream trailer. 'The cheerful young staff,
the hubbub of a busy pub and some excellent food
made for a very enjoyable stay.' (DB)

1 Cirencester Road
Tetbury GL8 8EY

T: 01666 500021
E: stay@theroyaloaktetbury.co.uk
W: theroyaloaktetbury.co.uk

BEDROOMS: 6. 3 on ground floor,
1 suitable for disabled.
OPEN: all year except 1 week Jan,
kitchen closed Sun pm.
FACILITIES: bar, restaurant, private
dining/meeting room, in-room TV
(Freeview), large garden, bar and
garden wheelchair accessible, adapted
toilet.
BACKGROUND MUSIC: in bar and
restaurant, free jukebox, monthly live
music sessions.
LOCATION: a few mins' walk up the hill
from the town centre.
CHILDREN: all ages welcomed, extra
bed £30, children's menu.
DOGS: allowed in ground-floor
bedrooms (no charge), bar.
CREDIT CARDS: Amex, MC, Visa.
PRICES: B&B doubles from £90.
À la carte £32. 1-night bookings
usually refused Fri and Sat.

THORNBURY Gloucestershire

MAP 3:E5

THORNBURY CASTLE   NEW

'It feels like you're walking through the pages of a history book' at this 16th-century castle, where everything from the bee skeps in the goodly garden to canopied four-posters is redolent of Tudor England. Built for Edward Stafford, 3rd Duke of Buckingham, it has 'some truly palatial parts', with oriel windows, acres of wood panelling and enormous fireplaces. Henry VIII stayed in 1535 with Anne Boleyn after he had sent Buckingham to the scaffold and swiped the property. Fresh from a multi-million pound facelift it 'now adds contemporary comfort to a historic stay'. Your 'bedchamber' might have arrow-slit windows in the bathroom along with a walk-in power shower. The 77-step spiral staircase to the Catherine of Aragon suite is 'worth the climb for a magnificent bed big enough for Henry and several wives, and enormous bathroom, but even standard rooms are special'. Pre-dinner drinks are served in the double-height drawing room before an 'elaborate dinner' in the 'atmospheric restaurant'. There was 'good pea and wild garlic risotto, perfectly cooked fillet of beef' but 'you'll need Henry's appetite to finish six courses'. (JK)

Castle Street
Thornbury BS35 1HH

T: 01454 281182
E: reception@thornburycastle.co.uk
W: thornburycastle.co.uk

BEDROOMS: 27. Some across courtyard. 2 on ground floor suitable for disabled.
OPEN: all year.
FACILITIES: lounge, library, dining rooms (vegetarian menu), in-room TV, treatment room, civil wedding licence, 15-acre grounds, helipad, partially wheelchair accessible, adapted toilets.
BACKGROUND MUSIC: classical in public rooms.
LOCATION: 15 miles N of Bristol.
CHILDREN: aged 8 and over welcomed, no charge for extra bed.
DOGS: allowed in some bedrooms (£15 per night), public areas, not dining rooms.
CREDIT CARDS: Amex, MC, Visa.
PRICES: B&B doubles from £229, singles from £214. À la carte £62, tasting menus £72. 1-night stays sometimes refused at peak times.

THORPE MARKET Norfolk

MAP 2:A5

THE GUNTON ARMS

Oozing bonhomie and good cheer, this country pub with its robust food, flamboyant art and country house-style bedrooms is a memorable place to stay. 'Unique and fascinating; we enjoyed it tremendously,' said inspectors of this 19th-century brick-and-flint lodge house set in a 1,000-acre deer park. Country inn essentials – open fires, stripped-wood floors, scrubbed tables, snooker room – are vamped up with a London-gallery collection of art (the owner is art dealer Ivor Braka) including Lucian Freud, Anthony Caro and Tracey Emin. Expect David Bailey photographs in the loos, and Gilbert & George in the dining room. Stuart Tattersall (Mark Hix-trained) serves up punchy food such as deer rump with goose-fat roast potatoes and crab pasta with chilli and coriander; beef and venison are cooked over the fire in one dining room. Bedrooms have an Edwardian elegance with William Morris wallpapers, antiques, rich fabrics and marbled bathrooms. There are blankets, not duvets; Roberts radios, not TVs. Gaze over the deer park from the clubby sitting rooms with more fires and art as well as books. A rock'n'roll adventure.

Cromer Road
Thorpe Market NR11 8TZ

T: 01263 832010
E: office@theguntonarms.co.uk
W: theguntonarms.co.uk

BEDROOMS: 16. 4 in coach house on ground floor, 4 suites in converted barn house, 1 suitable for disabled.
OPEN: all year except 25 Dec.
FACILITIES: 3 restaurants, 3 lounges, bar, TVs in bar and lounges, set in privately owned 1,000-acre game estate, public rooms wheelchair accessible, adapted toilet.
BACKGROUND MUSIC: in bar area.
LOCATION: 5 miles from Cromer, 4 miles from North Walsham.
CHILDREN: all ages welcomed, free cots, extra bed £7, plus 2 family rooms.
DOGS: allowed in some bedrooms (£10 per stay), public rooms, not in Elk Room.
CREDIT CARDS: Amex, MC, Visa.
PRICES: B&B doubles from £95.
À la carte £32–£40. Min. 2-night stays on Sat.

TISBURY Wiltshire
MAP 2:D1

THE BECKFORD ARMS

A hubbub of happy drinkers and diners, house ale on tap and laid-back casual-chic style greet visitors at this Georgian dining pub-with-rooms on the edge of the Fonthill Estate. It was a first venture for Dan Brod and Charlie Luxton, using a successful formula blending traditional and contemporary style that has since been applied to The Talbot Inn, Mells; The Lord Poulett Arms, Hinton St George; and The Bath Arms, Horningsham (see entries). Bedrooms have a mix of retro and contemporary furniture and Bramley toiletries. Fresh milk with a treat of chocolate cake delighted readers, whose large double had a 'writing table/desk that opened to reveal a mirror', 'a comfortable armchair', but no wardrobe. Two adults-only lodges are a stroll away. Richie Peacock uses local produce to create classy pub fare – burger, cider-battered haddock, game from the estate, maybe 'excellent lemon polenta, baked celeriac, asparagus'. 'The dishes were all excellent, and choice is plentiful.' In the summer they light the barbecue and pizza oven. Breakfast on home-smoked salmon and eggs from happy hens, then drive to nearby Salisbury, Longleat or Stourhead, or explore the Fonthill Estate.

Fonthill Gifford
Tisbury SP3 6PX

T: 01747 870385
E: info@beckfordarms.com
W: www.beckfordarms.com

BEDROOMS: 10. 2 in lodges on the Fonthill Estate.
OPEN: all year except 25 Dec.
FACILITIES: sitting room (sometimes Sunday classic-movie nights), bar, restaurant, private dining room, in-room TV (Freeview), function facilities, 1-acre garden, parking.
BACKGROUND MUSIC: in public areas all day.
LOCATION: in village, 1 mile N of Tisbury.
CHILDREN: all ages welcomed, travel cot £10, family room, no children in lodges.
DOGS: allowed in 1 bedroom (£10 fee) and public areas.
CREDIT CARDS: MC, Visa.
PRICES: B&B doubles from £105, family room from £135 (lodges £195). À la carte £40. 1-night bookings usually refused weekends (but check).

SEE ALSO SHORTLIST

TITCHWELL Norfolk

MAP 2:A5

TITCHWELL MANOR

With views to the north Norfolk coast and the reed beds and lagoons of Titchwell Marsh RSPB nature reserve nearby, this characterful family-friendly, dog-friendly hotel is set in a Victorian farmhouse. Chef/proprietor Eric Snaith has lived here since he was nine, when his parents took it on in 1988, and his enthusiasm for the manor is undoubted. The razzle-dazzle designer decor of public rooms spills over into some main-house bedrooms. Others, in the herb-garden courtyard and converted outbuildings, have a more subtle palette, maybe an espresso machine, a private terrace with hot tub. Two new shepherd huts have a terrace, hot tub and outdoor dining facilities. 'Our rooms in the main house were spacious and comfortable, with views over the road to the sea,' writes a reader. You can dine in the Eating Rooms or in the Conservatory, 'a lovely place to spend time'. Eric and head chef Chris Mann cook varied menus of carefully sourced produce. 'The food was interesting and had touches of brilliance: the consommé with mussels looked beautiful and tasted wonderful. The staff were helpful. We enjoyed our stay.' (Sara Price)

Titchwell
Brancaster PE31 8BB

T: 01485 210221
E: info@titchwellmanor.com
W: titchwellmanor.com

BEDROOMS: 28. 12 in herb garden, 3 in stables, 1 in Potting Shed, 18 on ground floor, 2 suitable for disabled.
OPEN: all year.
FACILITIES: lounge, bar, conservatory, restaurant, in-room TV (Freeview), civil wedding licence, in-room treatments, ¼-acre walled garden, public rooms wheelchair accessible, adapted toilet.
BACKGROUND MUSIC: in restaurant and bar.
LOCATION: off A149 between Burnham Market and Hunstanton.
CHILDREN: all ages welcomed, extra bed £25.
DOGS: allowed in some rooms (£15 per night), bar, not lounge or restaurant.
CREDIT CARDS: Amex, MC, Visa.
PRICES: B&B doubles from £113. À la carte £42. 1-night bookings occasionally refused.

TITLEY Herefordshire

MAP 3:C4

THE STAGG INN

♦ Previous César winner

An ancient inn at the meeting of two drovers' roads where farmers came to weigh wool has won awards aplenty as a dining pub-with-rooms since Steve and Nicola Reynolds took it over more than 20 years ago. Steve trained at Le Gavroche, and in 2001 was one of the first pub chefs in Britain to hold a Michelin star, but the food today is more in keeping with the ethos of a rustic village local, complete with beams and novelty jugs. There are four small bedrooms with exposed timbers in the pub itself, three larger, homier rooms in the Grade II listed, Georgian/Victorian Old Vicarage five minutes' walk away. Pub rooms are dog-friendly, while the vicarage benefits from a garden. All are supplied with fresh milk, tea and ground coffee, and if you want a beer in the afternoon when the pub is closed, there will be someone to pull you a pint. Locally sourced seasonal menus include pub classics such as fish and chips and Herefordshire steak Béarnaise, as well as more inventive dishes – maybe chaat roasted cauliflower, cauliflower purée and couscous, spiced chickpeas, sultanas and coriander, or herb-crumbed, pan-fried sea bass.

Titley
Kington HR5 3RL

T: 01544 230221
E: reservations@thestagg.co.uk
W: thestagg.co.uk

BEDROOMS: 7. 3 at The Old Vicarage (300 yds).
OPEN: all year except 24–26 Dec, 1 Jan, 1 week Jan/Feb, 1 week June, 2 weeks Nov, every Sun eve, Mon, Tues.
FACILITIES: sitting room (Vicarage), bar, dining room (vegetarian/vegan menus), small outside seating area (pub), in-room TV (Freeview), 1½-acre garden (Vicarage).
BACKGROUND MUSIC: none.
LOCATION: on B4355 between Kington and Presteigne.
CHILDREN: all ages welcomed, extra bed £15.
DOGS: allowed in pub bedrooms (no charge), public rooms.
CREDIT CARDS: Amex, MC, Visa.
PRICES: B&B doubles from £100. À la carte £37. 1-night bookings occasionally refused bank holiday weekends.

TORQUAY Devon

MAP 1:D5

THE 25 BOUTIQUE B&B

Hosts Andy and Julian Banner-Price love to make their guests smile, and there is much to smile about at their award-winning boutique B&B, stylish yet infused with wit and warmth. In 2015 they bought what was then a rather mushroom-soupy ten-room guest house on the English Riviera and reinvented it as the six-room jeu d'esprit we see today. Rooms may feature a giant orange gerbera mural, a black and white feature wall with the head of Frank the (fake) zebra, or an oversized silver headboard. Shoalstone has a separate sitting room as well as a lamp contrived from a male mannequin spray-painted by Andy and wired by Julian. All have an espresso machine, mood lighting, a power shower, a fridge and a daily home-made treat (maybe Viennese whirls). There is an honesty bar in the Edwardian-style drawing room if you fancy a drink by the fire or alfresco. Breakfast is a feast, with kippers, and eggs from happy hens, scrambled with butter and cream. The warm croissants with herby mushroom and melted goat's cheese were pronounced 'absolutely fabulous' by Joanna Lumley when she stayed. Now meet resident miniature schnauzer Patsy.

25 Avenue Road
Torquay TQ2 5LB

T: 01803 297517
E: stay@the25.uk
W: the25.uk

BEDROOMS: 6.
OPEN: Feb–end Oct.
FACILITIES: drawing room, dining room, in-room smart TV (movies on demand), patio, parking.
BACKGROUND MUSIC: at breakfast.
LOCATION: 5 mins' walk from the sea, 20 mins' walk from town.
CHILDREN: not under 17.
DOGS: not allowed.
CREDIT CARDS: Amex, MC, Visa.
PRICES: B&B doubles from £139, singles from £129. Min. stay of 2 or 3 nights may apply in high season.

SEE ALSO SHORTLIST

TUDDENHAM Suffolk

MAP 2:B5

TUDDENHAM MILL

Surrounded by water meadows, this 18th-century watermill offers unexpectedly modern bedrooms and a metropolitan-smart restaurant in a soothing location. The 'idyllic' setting ensures a 'very peaceful night's sleep'. Bedrooms are spread between the mill building, modern lodges and cute 'hobbit house' chalets, all in airy whites and greys, with Italian designer furniture; some with white-painted floorboards and open beams. Walk-in showers, double-ended baths (in larger rooms), high-tech sound systems and 'dreamy' views ensure these are classy affairs. The food in the first-floor restaurant, with its great oak beams, old mill machinery and views of 'ducks, haughty swans and a weeping willow', is highly praised, but one reader was unhappy with a 'very limited' à la carte menu. He ate instead in Tipi, an open-sided wigwam, in the garden, which was too cold in inclement weather, and where he found the service was poor. Breakfast, however, was 'great, the best porridge ever'. The smoothies, bircher muesli, French toast and local sausages will keep you fuelled all day to explore the 12-acre grounds. (DV, and others)

High Street
Tuddenham
Newmarket IP28 6SQ

T: 01638 713552
E: info@tuddenhammill.co.uk
W: tuddenhammill.co.uk

BEDROOMS: 21. 18 in 2 separate buildings, 8 on ground floor, 6 in pods in meadow, 2 with hot tub, 1 suitable for disabled.
OPEN: all year.
FACILITIES: bar/snug, restaurant, tipi dining area, function rooms, in-room TV (Freeview), civil wedding licence, 12-acre meadow, bar area wheelchair accessible.
BACKGROUND MUSIC: in bar, reception and restaurant.
LOCATION: in village, 8 miles NE of Newmarket.
CHILDREN: all ages welcomed, extra bed £25, children's menu and half portions.
DOGS: allowed in some bedrooms (£25 a night), bar.
CREDIT CARDS: MC, Visa.
PRICES: B&B doubles from £195. À la carte £45, tasting menu £75. Min. 2-night stay at weekends.

ULLSWATER Cumbria

MAP 4: inset C2

HOWTOWN HOTEL

Guests were 'intrigued by the old-style hospitality' of this Ullswater institution, a creeper-covered lakeside farmhouse that maintains the traditions of a bygone age. Owned by the Baldry family for over 120 years, it has no bedroom TVs (or door locks), limited Wi-Fi and a gong for dinner. 'Numerous' lounges are comfortable with fires, chintzy sofas, warming pans and country antiques. The style is very much that of Mrs Baldry, who balances traditional standards with a 'personal touch'. Red-carpeted landings lined with pictures lead to large, comfortable bedrooms. Expect blankets, not duvets, and Imperial Leather in the bathroom; no shampoo but plenty of hot water for a soak after a day's walking. There are hikes from the door and lakeside strolls. At the dinner gong, guests gather in the red-velvet and stained-glass bar before a four-course meal of dishes such as fillet of plaice with tomato and herb topping, and venison with red cabbage. The duck egg-blue dining room is a treat of silver cutlery and polished-wood tables. Next morning, tea is brought to your room. 'A glorious setting; we loved it.' (Tom and Sybille Raphael)

Ullswater
Penrith CA10 2ND

T: 01768 486514
E: david@howtown-hotel.com
W: howtown-hotel.com

BEDROOMS: 15. 2 in annexe, plus 4 self-catering cottages.
OPEN: end Mar–beginning Nov.
FACILITIES: 3 lounges, TV room, 2 bars, dining room, tea room, Wi-Fi (bedrooms, 1 lounge, cottages and tea room), 2-acre grounds, 200 yds from lake (private foreshore, fishing), restaurant wheelchair accessible, toilet not adapted.
BACKGROUND MUSIC: none.
LOCATION: 4 miles S of Pooley Bridge, bus from Penrith station 9 miles.
CHILDREN: all ages welcomed, call for prices.
DOGS: allowed in some bedrooms (£7 per night), not in public rooms.
CREDIT CARDS: MC, Visa.
PRICES: D,B&B doubles from £260, B&B prices on request. Dinner £41.

UPPER SLAUGHTER Gloucestershire   MAP 3:D6

LORDS OF THE MANOR

♔ Previous César winner

The River Eye drifts through the gardens of this Cotswold stone former rectory, once home to the Witts family, rectors and then lords of Upper Slaughter, run as a hotel for the past 50 years. It is luxurious but unstuffy ('welcoming, comfortable and relaxing', said one reader), with a wide choice of bedrooms in the main building, converted barn and granary. Suites have a separate lounge, some with a sofa bed. The style is easy on the eye, blending a traditional country house feel with contemporary furnishings and carefully chosen artwork. You can have a light lunch in the bar, take afternoon tea in the lounge or on the lawn, discover the walled garden, the lake, and the bog garden with giant rhubarb. Head chef Charles Smith sources the finest ingredients, whether on the doorstep or from farther afield, for his tasting and à la carte menus, with separate choices for vegans. Typical dishes might include grilled Herdwick lamb rump, spiced aubergine purée, carrots, chickpeas, minted yogurt; gnocchi with confit garlic, crushed peas, seared lettuce. Home-made biscuits and country walks await your four-legged friend. (RM)

Upper Slaughter GL54 2JD

т: 01451 820243
е: reservations@lordsofthemanor.com
w: lordsofthemanor.com

BEDROOMS: 26. 16 in granary and stables.
OPEN: all year.
FACILITIES: lounges, bar, 2 restaurants (vegan menu), library, games room, in-room TV (Freeview), civil wedding licence, 8-acre grounds, EV charging, some public rooms wheelchair accessible, no adapted toilet.
BACKGROUND MUSIC: in lounge bar and restaurant.
LOCATION: in village, 2 miles N of Bourton-on-the-Water.
CHILDREN: all ages welcomed, no charge for extra bed in junior suite.
DOGS: allowed in some bedrooms (no charge), public rooms, not restaurant.
CREDIT CARDS: Amex, MC, Visa.
PRICES: B&B doubles from £155. À la carte £40, tasting menu £95. 1-night bookings refused mid-summer Sat.

UPPINGHAM Rutland   MAP 2:B3

LAKE ISLE

There is neither lake nor isle at Richard and
Janine Burton's listed 18th-century whitewashed
restaurant-with-rooms, behind a shopfront in the
oldest part of town. It had been a draper's, barber's
and baker's before being opened as a restaurant
in the 1970s by people who clearly had a feeling
for Yeats. Bedrooms are a mix of the traditional
and the contemporary, with bold wallpaper but
with a muted palette. Larger ones have a spa
bath; there are two cottages for a family within
the courtyard. All are reasonably priced and
supplied with home-baked biscuits, though they
may be on the cosy side. No matter, say readers,
because the reason you go is 'definitely for the
food'. Stuart Mead's locally sourced dishes might
include monkfish, beef fillet with triple-cooked
chips, breast of chicken with a mini-chicken-and-
mushroom pie and veg, black bean balti. 'Our
meal was excellent, well cooked and efficiently
served.' A 'wide and appealing choice' at breakfast
includes fresh orange juice, just-baked croissants,
salmon and smoked haddock fishcakes, kipper,
cheese omelette and the full English. (J and EG,
and others)

16 High Street East
Uppingham LE15 9PZ

T: 01572 822951
E: info@lakeisle.co.uk
W: lakeisle.co.uk

BEDROOMS: 11. 2 in cottages sleeping
3/4.
OPEN: all year, restaurant closed Mon
and bank holidays.
FACILITIES: bar, restaurant, in-room
TV (Freeview), small car park,
unsuitable for disabled.
BACKGROUND MUSIC: in restaurant.
LOCATION: town centre.
CHILDREN: all ages welcomed, extra
bed £15, children's portions.
DOGS: allowed in courtyard bedrooms
(£15 a night), not in public areas.
CREDIT CARDS: Amex, MC, Visa.
PRICES: B&B doubles from £95,
cottages (3/4 guests) from £125.
À la carte £40.

VENTNOR Isle of Wight

MAP 2:E2

⚘HILLSIDE

César award: island hotel of the year

'At the top of the town, below St Boniface
Down, a thatched cottage exterior belies the
uber-cool interior' of a hotel run by 'charismatic,
omnipresent Danish owner' Gert Bach. Despite a
road running by, the situation is 'suitably bucolic',
with 'impressive vegetable gardens, chickens,
ducks on the lawn, grounds home to black sheep,
doves and beehives'. Interiors, filled with fresh
flowers, are 'Scandi chic – wherever you go,
white walls act as a backdrop for huge canvases
of abstract art'. A compact twin bedroom was
'almost stark in its simplicity' (more white paint,
more flowers, more art). 'Eight rooms have a
view of the sea, which can also be seen through
a huge triple window in the downstairs room.'
Tea and coffee are served downstairs and charged
for. Home-grown and local produce appear on 'a
short menu of delectable artisan dishes that zing
with flavour – fresh garden soup, crab ramekin,
fish pie.' Breakfast brings 'excellent sausages
and bacon, meat and cheese to go with the lovely
bread'. 'Sitting in the gardens sipping a glass of
rosé and looking out to sea felt like the perfect
summer moment.' (JK)

151 Mitchell Avenue
Ventnor PO38 1DR

T: 01983 852271
E: mail@hillsideventnor.co.uk
W: hillsideventnor.co.uk

BEDROOMS: 12. Plus self-catering
apartment.
OPEN: all year.
FACILITIES: restaurant, 2 lounges,
conservatory, in-room TV (Freeview),
terrace, 5-acre garden (vegetable
garden, sheep, beehives), EV charging,
close to tennis club, golf, unsuitable
for disabled.
BACKGROUND MUSIC: in restaurant in
evening but 'not if not wished'.
LOCATION: above village centre.
CHILDREN: not under 12.
DOGS: not allowed.
CREDIT CARDS: MC, Visa.
PRICES: B&B doubles from £133, singles
from £98, apartment doubles from
£206. Brasserie 2 courses £15. Min.
2-night bookings preferred.

VENTNOR Isle of Wight

MAP 2:E2

THE ROYAL HOTEL

'Beautiful views of the bay', 'outstanding staff' and lovely sub-tropical gardens see guests returning to book their favourite room year after year at this 'wonderful hotel' whose afternoon teas were once enjoyed by Queen Victoria. Regulars were charmed when someone took cushions to them in the garden 'to make us comfortable!' Special mention goes to head gardener Gary Steptoe who 'gives advice and cuttings of his famous pink geraniums'. Public rooms have an 'understated elegance' with pale panelling and classic striped wallpapers, and the conservatory or Geranium Terrace is the place for tea. Food is 'amazingly tasty' and dinner an event among starched linen. Classic dishes with a modern twist might include pan-fried trout fillet with smoked mussel sauce. Breakfasts, too, are 'outstanding' and can be eaten in the garden. The best bedrooms have sea views and are either classic country house with pretty wallpapers and fabrics, or more contemporary. 'Ours was well equipped, with more than enough space,' said delighted first-time visitors. The best room? It's room 20, say our returning guests. (Alice Sennett, Mary Woods, and others)

Belgrave Road
Ventnor PO38 1JJ

T: 01983 852186
E: enquiries@royalhoteliow.co.uk
W: royalhoteliow.co.uk

BEDROOMS: 51. 1 suitable for disabled.
OPEN: all year.
FACILITIES: lift, lounge, bar,
2 restaurants (vegetarian/vegan menu), conservatory, function rooms, in-room TV, civil wedding licence, spa treatment rooms, terrace, 2-acre grounds, outdoor heated pool, EV charging, public areas/toilet wheelchair accessible.
BACKGROUND MUSIC: in public areas, pianist on peak-season weekends.
LOCATION: short walk from centre.
CHILDREN: all ages welcomed, family rooms, no under-4s at dinner.
DOGS: allowed in some bedrooms (£25 a night), not in restaurants.
CREDIT CARDS: Amex, MC, Visa.
PRICES: B&B doubles from £210, singles from £105. Dinner £40. Min. 2-night stays on peak weekends.

VERYAN-IN-ROSELAND Cornwall

MAP 1:D2

THE NARE

☘ Previous César winner

The prices might look 'eye-watering' at Toby Ashworth's family-friendly, dog-loving Edwardian hotel in a fantastic position above Carne beach, but they are 'great value for this level of luxury'. 'Breathtaking views of the wonderful beach' can be seen from many rooms, with a balcony or terrace. Extras include fresh flowers, posh toiletries, 'a generous bowl of fruit, a small decanter of sherry', valet, shoe cleaning and 24-hour room service. 'The design is traditional country house,' writes a Guide stalwart, 'but with many modern twists, outstanding soft furnishings and well-cared-for antiques.' A complimentary cream tea is offered, and the under-sevens can have an early supper. In the dining room, with hors d'oeuvre trolley and tableside flame grilling, a typical dish might feature smoked haddock, poached egg, cauliflower tempura, wilted spinach, Bombay potatoes. 'The staff are delightful, very polite and wholly obliging,' writes a reader whose complaint about a steak was handled with real grace. Breakfast brings 'delicious kedgeree, an amazing full English'. (Abigail Kirby-Harris, Ian White)

Carne Beach
Veryan-in-Roseland TR2 5PF

T: 01872 501111
E: stay@narehotel.co.uk
W: narehotel.co.uk

BEDROOMS: 40. Some on ground floor, 1 in cottage, 5 suitable for disabled.
OPEN: all year.
FACILITIES: lift, lounge, drawing room, sun lounge, gallery, study, bar, library, light lunch room, 2 restaurants, conservatory, in-room TV (Freeview), gym, indoor and outdoor swimming pools, 2-acre grounds, 2 boats, tennis, public rooms wheelchair accessible, adapted toilet.
BACKGROUND MUSIC: none.
LOCATION: 1 mile SW of Veryan.
CHILDREN: all ages welcomed, extra bed £65–£99.
DOGS: allowed in bedrooms (£19–£28 a night), not in public areas.
CREDIT CARDS: Amex, MC, Visa.
PRICES: B&B doubles from £328, singles from £174. Fixed-price dinner £50, tasting menu £60, à la carte £50.

WADEBRIDGE Cornwall   MAP 1:D2

TREWORNAN MANOR

'This really is a brilliant B&B establishment,'
writes a reader this year, joining a chorus of
approval for Paul and Lesley Stapleton's Grade II
listed manor house amid gardens and pastureland
near the Camel estuary. 'The property and
grounds are at once stunning and homely,' says a
Guide regular, who enjoyed the complimentary
cream tea. 'It's a very relaxing place.' Smart
bedrooms have an emperor-size bed, and even
Lundy, which is described as cosy, is a decent
size. Dual-aspect Porthilly is 'very large, with
a vast bathroom' with freestanding bath and
walk-in shower. Extras include a cafetière, fresh
milk, home-made flapjacks – 'far more than
you'd expect at this price'. There is high praise
for the host. 'Paul did a fantastic job, carrying
luggage, bringing tea and cake, recommending
and booking dinner, gossiping and giving life
advice, serving at breakfast . . .' The last is 'in a
class of its own', with 'a wonderful array of fruit',
'brilliant bread for toast, well-sourced sausages
and hog's pudding'. In sum: 'An example of the
results when the owner is personally present and
committed.' (David Hampshire, SH, K and VS)

Trewornan Bridge
Wadebridge PL27 6EX

T: 01208 812359
E: info@trewornanmanor.co.uk
W: trewornanmanor.co.uk

BEDROOMS: 7. 2 in courtyard annexe,
1 on ground floor.
OPEN: all year.
FACILITIES: lounge, snug, dining room,
in-room TV (Freeview), civil wedding
licence, 25-acre grounds with 8-acre
gardens.
BACKGROUND MUSIC: in dining room,
lounge at breakfast and evening.
LOCATION: 1 mile N of Wadebridge.
CHILDREN: not under 14.
DOGS: not allowed.
CREDIT CARDS: MC, Visa.
PRICES: B&B doubles from £150, singles
from £135.

WAREHAM Dorset

MAP 2:E1

THE PRIORY

Idyllically situated by a Saxon church with
gardens bordered by the River Frome, this
16th-century priory has cast off its monk's habit
to become a characterful hotel. Each beautifully
styled bedroom has its own charm, some with
beams, sloping ceilings, and antiques, perhaps
up steep staircases tucked in the eaves with
river views, others looking on to the garden or
courtyard. All have binoculars, fresh fruit and
milk. The most opulent are in the waterside Boat
House, where Mallard mini-suite has a four-
poster, a balcony, a spa bath and walk-in shower,
and Swan has a lounge with French doors to a
riverside veranda. 'Even in February, walking the
short distance to the restaurant was not a chore,'
writes a trusted reader. Dinner is no longer served
in the 'rather gloomy' Abbot's Cellar, but in the
'light, modern' garden restaurant, where Stephan
Guinebault's menus include dishes such as loin of
Purbeck venison with thyme jus or beetroot and
goat's cheese risotto. 'Dinner was excellent, and
breakfast equally good' with freshly squeezed
juices, grilled kipper, smoked fish, crushed
avocado on sourdough toast. (ML, and others)

Church Green
Wareham BH20 4ND

T: 01929 551666
E: admin@theprioryhotel.co.uk
W: theprioryhotel.co.uk

BEDROOMS: 17. Some on ground floor,
4 suites in Boat House, 1 suitable for
disabled.
OPEN: all year.
FACILITIES: sitting room, drawing
room, snug bar, 2 dining rooms, in-
room TV (Freeview), spa treatments,
4½-acre gardens (croquet, river
frontage, moorings, fishing), parking,
EV charging, restaurant wheelchair
accessible.
BACKGROUND MUSIC: in public rooms;
pianist in drawing room Sat evenings
'and special occasions'.
LOCATION: town centre.
CHILDREN: not under 14.
DOGS: not allowed.
CREDIT CARDS: Amex, MC, Visa.
PRICES: B&B doubles from £220, singles
from £176. Fixed-price dinner £57.50.
1-night bookings refused high season,
peak weekends.

WELLS-NEXT-THE-SEA Norfolk

MAP 2:A5

THE CROWN

NEW

'A former coaching inn overlooking a tree-lined oval green' is today 'a welcoming, warm, laid-back pub and hotel'. Alerted to it by a reader ('all four of us loved it'), our inspectors checked in and were shown to a suite in a converted barn, 'through an archway, down a sweet little lane'. It had a super-king bed with kids' beds on a mezzanine, a coffee machine, 'exposed-stone wall, pretty, glass-domed lights, prints and etchings', a bath and power shower. An accessible room in old living quarters has a four-poster, an espresso machine, a wet-room shower, a copper bath on a decked patio. 'The main building is a warren of rooms with flagstone floors, bar, dining areas, slouchy sofa areas and crannies.' Chef/proprietor Chris Coubrough was 'working hard alongside his staff, chatting to guests and regulars'. A short, good menu brought Brancaster rock oysters with lemon and tabasco, fishcakes, grilled goat's cheese on walnut and caramelised shallot couscous. At breakfast, 'freshly squeezed orange juice and a full English to last you the day' were served by 'young, friendly, fleet staff – a lovely team'. (Karen Hillier, and others)

The Buttlands
Wells-next-the-Sea NR23 1EX

T: 01328 710209
E: info@crownhotelnorfolk.co.uk
W: crownhotelnorfolk.co.uk

BEDROOMS: 20. 5 in annexe, 2 in barn, 3 on ground floor, 1 suitable for wheelchair-user (wet-room shower, terrace).
OPEN: all year.
FACILITIES: bar, 3 dining rooms, terrace, in-room TV, parking, orangery wheelchair accessible, adapted toilet.
BACKGROUND MUSIC: none.
LOCATION: central, on the Buttlands.
CHILDREN: all ages welcomed, extra bed £35.
DOGS: allowed in most bedrooms (£10 per night), some public rooms.
CREDIT CARDS: Amex, MC, Visa.
PRICES: B&B doubles from £150, singles from £125. À la carte £35.

WEST HOATHLY Sussex   MAP 2:E4

THE CAT INN

♔Previous César winner

A timber-framed and tile-hung dining pub-with-rooms in a hilltop High Weald village is the veritable cat's whiskers, say many of our readers. 'This really is something special,' affirms a Guide trusty. Owner Andrew Russell held a senior role at Gravetye Manor, East Grinstead (see entry), and is 'a consummate host who rightly deserves all the awards he has received'. The bedrooms are fairly simple, in keeping with the pub ethos, with good fabrics, an espresso machine, fresh milk, Bramley toiletries. A split-level suite has a separate seating area. On cold days log fires burn in the inglenooks in the beamed 16th-century bar, which serves real ale and English sparkling wine. You can eat here with your dog, in the dining room or, in warm weather, on the terrace. Alex Jacquemin cooks superior pub grub with produce from The Cat's own market garden. Typical dishes might include Brighton day-boat plaice, marinated heritage cherry tomatoes, basil and almond pesto, or wild mushroom and truffle tart. 'Our fifth time here. Staff are terrific.' 'After an excellent lunch we decided to stay for a few days. Fabulous!' (Chris and Erika Savory, ER, SR, and others)

North Lane
West Hoathly RH19 4PP

T: 01342 810369
E: thecatinn@googlemail.com
W: catinn.co.uk

BEDROOMS: 4.
OPEN: all year except Mon, Tues, 24–26 Dec, 1 Jan, restaurant open lunch 26 Dec, 1 Jan.
FACILITIES: bar, 3 dining areas, in-room TV (Freeview), terrace (alfresco meals), parking, restaurant wheelchair accessible, adapted toilet.
BACKGROUND MUSIC: none.
LOCATION: in village.
CHILDREN: not under 7 (unless 'well-behaved').
DOGS: allowed in bedrooms (£10 a night), bar, specific dining area.
CREDIT CARDS: Amex, MC, Visa.
PRICES: B&B doubles from £140, singles from £95. À la carte £28.

WHITEWELL Lancashire

MAP 4:D3

THE INN AT WHITEWELL

On the banks of the River Hodder in the Forest of
Bowland, this 'cheerful, doggy' inn is chock-full
of tradition, with stone-flagged floors, open fires,
oak furniture and walls bedecked with paintings
and hunting cartoons. Run by third-generation
Bowmans with a team of 'extremely friendly and
helpful staff', it serves local ales in the bar and
has a good reputation for its food. Chef Jamie
Cadman turns out 'outstanding' dishes such as
slow-roast belly pork, whole roast grouse (in
season) and a famed fish pie. Although carnivore
heavy, the menu has 'good vegetarian and vegan
options'. There's an 'excellent' wine list, too –
and a wine shop if something takes your fancy.
Bedrooms, including four outside rooms up a
steep slope, are furnished with antiques, country-
print fabrics and handsome artwork. Many have
working fires, some have Victorian cabinet baths,
four-posters, and restful river views. If you want
to take full advantage of the waterside setting,
there are seven miles of riverbank fishing, with
the services of a ghillie should you need them.
'We couldn't recommend it more highly.'
(JS, R and MM-D)

Whitewell
Clitheroe BB7 3AT

T: 01200 448222
E: reception@innatwhitewell.com
W: innatwhitewell.com

BEDROOMS: 23. 4 in coach house,
150 yds, 2 on ground floor.
OPEN: all year.
FACILITIES: 3 bars, restaurant,
boardroom, private dining room,
in-house wine shop, spa treatments,
in-room TV (Freeview), civil wedding
licence, 5-acre grounds, terrace
with tables, 7 miles' fishing (ghillie
available), main bar, hall, reception
wheelchair accessible, adapted toilet.
BACKGROUND MUSIC: none.
LOCATION: 6 miles NW of Clitheroe.
CHILDREN: all ages welcomed, cots £6,
extra bed £35.
DOGS: allowed in bedrooms (no
charge), public rooms, not in main
dining room.
CREDIT CARDS: MC, Visa.
PRICES: B&B doubles from £140, singles
from £100. À la carte £40.

WHITLEY Wiltshire   MAP 2:D1

THE PEAR TREE INN

This 17th-century pub complete with vintage
Usher sign is no ordinary village inn, but its
restaurant and rooms are 'perfect for a secluded
weekend getaway', offering all the values that this
Guide champions. It is owned by hostess Jackie
Cosens and chef Adrian Jenkins, with both real
ales and humour on tap. Bedrooms, each named
after a pear variety (what, no Conference room?),
are comfy and quirky. Accessible Seckel, in a
converted barn, has a wet room with waterfall
shower; Taylor's Gold has a king-size bed, twin
beds on a mezzanine, a private patio. Each has
home-baked biscuits, fresh milk on request.
In the dining rooms or lovely garden, seasonal
menus of ethically raised, local and home-grown
ingredients include dishes such as twice-cooked
chicken with wild mushroom and sage sauce;
or grilled cauliflower on white bean mash with
Bromham greens and kale pesto. 'If a quiet pint is
preferred the farmhouse has a small but perfectly
formed traditional bar.' Breakfast brings surprises
– dukka and garden shoots with the smashed
avocado on sourdough toast; a full vegan with
dhal and sautéed potatoes. (NG)

Top Lane
Whitley
Melksham SN12 8QX

T: 01225 704966
E: hello@peartreewhitley.co.uk
W: peartreewhitley.co.uk

BEDROOMS: 8. 4 in converted barn,
1 suitable for disabled.
OPEN: all year.
FACILITIES: bar/snug, 2 dining rooms,
garden (alfresco dining), in-room TV
(terrestrial), parking, EV charging,
restaurant wheelchair accessible,
adapted toilet.
BACKGROUND MUSIC: in restaurants
and bar.
LOCATION: in the heart of the village.
CHILDREN: all ages welcomed, cot free,
extra bed for under-12s £15, £25 for
12s and over), high chairs, children's
menu.
DOGS: allowed in barn annexe
bedrooms (£12.50 per night), bar and
Garden Room restaurant (not Sun
Room).
CREDIT CARDS: Amex, MC, Visa.
PRICES: B&B doubles from £125.
À la carte £35. 1-night bookings
refused Fri and Sat.

WINCHESTER Hampshire

THE OLD VINE

Around the corner from Winchester's Gothic
cathedral, The Old Vine mixes old-world charm
with designer sharpness, spiced up with robust
pub food. Behind the mellow brick facade of the
18th-century inn, with its window boxes and vine,
you'll find a warm welcome, with a convivial bar
and dining room of stripped-wood floors, exposed
brickwork, beams and timber posts. 'Beautifully
decorated', spacious bedrooms are named after
designers, such as Nina Campbell, and Osborne
& Little, whose fabrics and wallpapers make
colourful features. Furniture is a mix of antique
and contemporary. Several rooms have large sash
windows, one has Georgian panelling, all have
views over the town or rear patio. 'The cathedral
view from our suite was a delight.' Designers
Guild is an apartment for those who prefer to
self-cater. Otherwise, dinner offers pub favourites
such as steak-and-ale pie plus bistro classics such
as lamb tagine, and fishcakes with salsa. Staff are
'friendly and efficient' and room-service breakfast
at no extra charge delighted guests. Parking
permits are a bonus. 'Highly recommended, and
not expensive.' (Andrew Warren)

8 Great Minster Street
Winchester SO23 9HA

T: 01962 854616
E: reservations@oldvinewinchester.
    com
W: oldvinewinchester.com

BEDROOMS: 6. Self-contained 2-bed
apartment, with garage, in annexe.
OPEN: all year except 24/25 Dec.
FACILITIES: bar, restaurant, in-room
TV (Freeview), courtyard with
tables and chairs, parking permits,
restaurant and bar wheelchair
accessible, but not toilets.
BACKGROUND MUSIC: in bar.
LOCATION: town centre, permits
supplied for on-street parking.
CHILDREN: all ages welcomed, under-
3s free, extra bed £30, no under-6s in
restaurant or in bar at night.
DOGS: only in bar.
CREDIT CARDS: Amex, MC, Visa.
PRICES: B&B doubles from £125, singles
from £110. À la carte £30.

WINDERMERE Cumbria

MAP 4: inset C2

CEDAR MANOR

The praises keep showering down on Cedar Manor, a 'delightful' and 'intimate' hotel, close to Lake Windermere, with luxurious bedrooms, thoughtful comforts and faultless yet friendly service. 'Wonderful hosts' Jonathan and Caroline Kaye provide 'a five-star service' and 'excellent standards of decoration' in their large Victorian house. Bedrooms have a contemporary country house style with striking wallpapers and fabrics, Herdwick wool carpets, bespoke wood furniture and great attention to detail. Readers love the thick towels, bathrobes, fresh milk and chocolates, plus REN products in the ultra-modern bathroom, some with spa bath; only one is shower only. 'Our room was perfect with a most comfortable bed.' Afternoon tea, with home-made scones and cakes, is a 'great feature' and can be followed later by a short evening menu of home-made soup, cheese and meat platters. Alternatively, the Kayes advise on 'good eateries nearby'. Staff are 'highly efficient, knowledgeable and helpful'. 'Delicious' breakfasts include smoked haddock, Cumbrian grill and vegetarian alternative. 'We will be back soon.' (S and SR, and others)

Ambleside Road
Windermere LA23 1AX

T: 01539 443192
E: info@cedarmanor.co.uk
W: cedarmanor.co.uk

BEDROOMS: 10. 1 split-level suite in coach house.
OPEN: all year except 13–26 Dec, 3–20 Jan.
FACILITIES: lounge, lounge/bar, restaurant, in-room TV (Freeview), patio, ¼-acre garden, EV charging, unsuitable for disabled.
BACKGROUND MUSIC: 'very quiet', at mealtimes, in lounge and restaurant.
LOCATION: 5-min. walk from town centre.
CHILDREN: not under 10, extra bed £70.
DOGS: not allowed.
CREDIT CARDS: Amex, MC, Visa.
PRICES: B&B doubles from £145, singles from £125. Afternoon tea £25, supper dishes from £7. Min. 2-night stay at weekends and bank holidays.

WINDERMERE Cumbria

MAP 4: inset C2

GILPIN HOTEL AND LAKE HOUSE

By many standards, Gilpin is the Lake District's most luxurious hotel with no-expense-spared rooms, Michelin-starred dining, numerous staff, and acres of space. Last year it upped its game again with five extravagantly large glass-cube spa suites with private garden, spa and circular bath. The Cunliffe family, who have owned this 'exceptional hotel' since 1988, know their loyal guests well. Other faultlessly comfortable rooms include smaller spa lodges overlooking a pond, Scandi-style garden suites with hot tub and sauna, and smart country house rooms in the main Edwardian building. Six Lake House rooms, in a lodge on a 100-acre estate half-a-mile away, have a period charm and exclusive access to an indoor pool and woodland spa. Dining is a choice between Michelin-starred HRiSHi, which offers Modern British cuisine with an Asian twist, such as masala-braised lamb with caramelised onion, and the colourful Gilpin Spice with its Pan-Asian small and large plates. Everything, from the blingy cocktail bar and sheltered terrace to the restful sitting room, is designed for indulgence. The hotel is a member of Relais & Châteaux.

Crook Road
Windermere LA23 3NE

T: 01539 488818
E: hotel@thegilpin.co.uk
W: thegilpin.co.uk

BEDROOMS: 36. 6 garden suites, 10 spa lodges/suites, 6 in Lake House, 1 suitable for disabled.
OPEN: all year.
FACILITIES: Gilpin Hotel: bar, lounge, 2 restaurants, patio, 22-acre grounds, public rooms wheelchair accessible, adapted toilet. Lake House: lounge, conservatory, spa (pool), 100-acre grounds; in-room TV, civil wedding licence, EV charging (spa suites).
BACKGROUND MUSIC: in restaurants.
LOCATION: on B5284, 2 miles SE of Windermere.
CHILDREN: no under-7s, extra bed £70.
DOGS: allowed in 2 bedrooms (£30 a night), not in public rooms.
CREDIT CARDS: Amex, MC, Visa.
PRICES: B&B doubles from £295. Set dinner £75, tasting menu £95 (HRiSHi), à la carte £35 (Gilpin Spice). Min. 2-night stay at weekends.

WINGHAM Kent

MAP 2:D5

THE DOG AT WINGHAM

A passion for Kent produce, a monthly dining club, tee times and transport to nearby golf clubs, including Royal St George's, are among many reasons to commend Marc Bridgen's village gastropub. 'The service,' says a reader, 'really is second to none.' Bedrooms, styled by Marc's mother, Marilyn, have plain walls, rustic original features and touches of pizzazz (bright fabrics, a statement headboard). The bridal suite has exposed timbers and a four-poster; a family room has bunks for kids. The pub interior is stripped out and airy. Dine indoors, in the conservatory, or alfresco. Samuel McClurkin sources as much produce as possible from local farmers, growers and fishermen for his regularly changing menus (though smoked salmon and small-batch hand-made black pudding are from the Isle of Lewis). Typical dishes might include caramelised onion tart with asparagus from Sevenscore Farm; classic fish and chips; herb-fed chicken with polenta; or Moroccan spiced lamb with smoked chickpea and black quinoa. 'I can't stress enough how delicious the food is.' Wingham Wildlife Park is almost on the doorstep. (JC, VC, and others)

Canterbury Road
Wingham
Canterbury CT3 1BB

T: 01227 720339
E: info@thedog.co.uk
W: thedog.co.uk

BEDROOMS: 8.
OPEN: all year, kitchen closes 5 pm Sun.
FACILITIES: lounge bar, restaurant bar, dining room, garden room, terrace (alfresco dining), in-room TV (Freeview), civil wedding licence, golf packages, monthly dining club, unsuitable for disabled.
BACKGROUND MUSIC: in bar and restaurant, live music events.
LOCATION: in village, 7 miles E of Canterbury.
CHILDREN: all ages welcomed.
DOGS: welcomed throughout.
CREDIT CARDS: Amex, MC, Visa.
PRICES: B&B doubles from £140, singles from £100. À la carte £40 (vegan £38, 24 hours' notice).

WOLD NEWTON Yorkshire

MAP 4:D5

THE WOLD COTTAGE

This 'cottage' is a handsome Georgian manor house with elegant rooms and peaceful views over landscaped gardens and surrounding farmland. While certainly gracious, with high-ceilinged rooms, large sash windows and high-quality paintings and furnishings, it has a warm and welcoming air. Katrina and Derek Gray emphasise it's their home and greet guests with tea in the fire-warmed sitting room. Bedrooms, divided between the main house and a converted barn, range from traditional, with antiques and silky drapes – one has a four-poster – to more contemporary, where neutral colours are jazzed up with a tartan-covered armchair or a bold throw. All but one are spacious, with armchairs and sofas, and most have a bath and shower; all have robes and fresh milk. Breakfast in the large dining room, with its Georgian-red walls and garden views, is a handsome affair served at a large, smartly laid table. The menu is a feast of local produce including Yorkshire ham and cheese, kippers, Filey Bay crab and boiled egg, as well as home-made bread and preserves. It's enough to set you up for a day exploring the coast and Wolds.

Wold Newton
Driffield YO25 3HL

T: 01262 470696
E: katrina@woldcottage.com
W: woldcottage.com

BEDROOMS: 6. 2 in converted barn, 1 on ground floor, 1 has option of self-catering apartment. 3 self-catering cottages.
OPEN: closed Dec and Jan.
FACILITIES: lounge, dining room, in-room TV (Freeview), 3-acre gardens (croquet) in 240-acre grounds (farmland, woodland), public rooms wheelchair accessible.
BACKGROUND MUSIC: at breakfast in dining room.
LOCATION: just outside village.
CHILDREN: all ages welcomed, only in family room.
DOGS: not allowed.
CREDIT CARDS: MC, Visa.
PRICES: B&B doubles from £110, singles from £80, family room £145. 2-course suppers occasionally offered, £24. Min. 2-night bookings.

WOODDITTON Cambridgeshire

MAP 2:B4

THE THREE BLACKBIRDS `NEW`

A 17th-century thatched pub on a residential village street has risen Phoenix-like from the ashes after a fire in 2018. 'It has been beautifully spruced up,' writes a Guide insider, 'maintaining a certain olde-worlde charm, with wooden benches, rustic furniture, old farm implements on the walls, yet with a thoroughly modern twist.' Bedrooms are in a newbuilt barn. 'Ours felt like it was straight out of a posh boutique hotel, with its oversized fabric headboard and battleship-grey tongue-and-groove wall panels.' It had pale wood furniture, a plush blue armchair with matching throws and cushions, cowhide stools, fresh milk – no fridge and no bathrobes. 'Wood-burners glow in both the bar and restaurant, and no one bats an eyelid if muddy boots or paws pad over the flagstones or parquet.' There are pub standards such as fish and chips, but the food is 'a cut above your normal pub grub – partridge, with celeriac mash and kale that was cooked so beautifully, I had to ask how they did it'. We await reports from discerning canine diners as to the quality of the pooch's venison jerky and Bottom-Sniffer beer. (JK)

Woodditton
Newmarket CB8 9SQ

T: 01638 731100
E: info@threeblackbirds.co.uk
W: threeblackbirds.co.uk

BEDROOMS: 9. All in self-contained barns, 1 suitable for disabled.
OPEN: all year, closed Mon and Tues except bank holidays.
FACILITIES: 2 restaurants, bar, private dining room, in-room TV, garden (outdoor dining), EV charging, 'some challenges for ease of wheelchair access'.
BACKGROUND MUSIC: all day in public spaces.
LOCATION: 4 miles SE of Newmarket.
CHILDREN: all ages welcomed, extra bed £15, children's menu.
DOGS: well-behaved dogs welcomed (£15 per night) except in 3 dog-free bedrooms.
CREDIT CARDS: Amex, MC, Visa.
PRICES: B&B doubles from £100. À la carte £32.

WOOTTON COURTENAY Somerset

MAP 1:B5

DUNKERY BEACON COUNTRY HOUSE

Built at the dawn of the Edwardian era as a men-only hunting lodge, and with views to the beacon after which it was named, this smart but unstuffy hotel is an ideal base from which to explore Exmoor. It is 'a consistent beacon of excellence', writes a reader whose walking group stays annually. 'We had a super room with a four-poster and a big bathroom,' relates a trusted Guide regular. Styling is a pleasing blend of traditional and contemporary. Some suites have a separate sitting room. Thoughtful extras include fresh milk, a coffee machine or cafetière, Keiji toiletries. Hosts John and Jane Bradley garner high praise, he as chef, she the wine expert and a warm presence front-of-house. Menus are devised around local and home-grown produce. 'The cooking is top-notch. I had sea trout in a mussel and saffron sauce – so good I had it twice!' And for dessert? 'I mentioned that I didn't really eat pudding, apart from summer pudding, so they made one specially for me.' Great breakfasts, a star-spangled dark sky (the hotel has a Newtonian telescope), and deer safaris are among the many attractions. (Andrew and Hannah Butterworth, Peter Anderson)

Wootton Courtenay TA24 8RH

T: 01643 841241
E: info@dunkerybeaconaccommodation.co.uk
W: dunkerybeaconaccommodation.co.uk

BEDROOMS: 8. 1 on ground floor.
OPEN: 11 Feb–27 Dec, restaurant Wed–Sun pm.
FACILITIES: lounge, restaurant, breakfast room, in-room TV (Freeview), limited mobile phone reception, ¾-acre garden, unsuitable for disabled.
BACKGROUND MUSIC: in restaurant in evening.
LOCATION: 4 miles SW of Dunster.
CHILDREN: not under 10.
DOGS: allowed in 2 suites (£5 per night, max. 2 dogs), not in public rooms.
CREDIT CARDS: MC, Visa.
PRICES: B&B doubles from £115, singles from £85. À la carte £37. 1-night bookings refused Fri/Sat and on all stays in peak season (but check for late availability).

YARM Yorkshire

MAP 4:C4

JUDGES

♀ Previous César winner

A circular drive, creeper-covered facade, rolling lawns and woodland are as you would expect of a country home that was once a retreat for circuit judges. Today's guests at this Victorian country house feel the same relaxation on arrival: 'a warm welcome, excellent hospitality and service'. 'In no time at all we were whisked to our room', report readers. Bedrooms are comfortably traditional with striped and toile du Jouy wallpapers and upholstered armchairs and include a 'lovely large room overlooking the garden with four-poster bed'. The fresh fruit, flowers, chocolates and sherry go down well, while bathrooms are surprisingly modern, some with televisions or air baths. Before dining, take a drink and canapés in the clubby bar or beside the 'blazing' fire in the elegant drawing room. Dinner in the conservatory dining room, with its 'excellent' garden views, offers sophisticated dishes such as lamb with pommes Anna and mint emulsion, sea trout with potato rösti and clam velouté. There's an impressive wine list, too. 'The grounds are gorgeous,' reports a reader who married here, 'the staff couldn't do enough for us.' (Melvin Gold, JV, AB)

Kirklevington Hall
Kirklevington
Yarm TS15 9LW

T: 01642 789000
E: reception@judgeshotel.co.uk
W: judgeshotel.co.uk

BEDROOMS: 21. Some on ground floor.
OPEN: all year.
FACILITIES: lounge, bar, restaurant, private dining room, in-room TV (Freeview), function facilities, business centre, EV charging, civil wedding licence, 36-acre grounds (paths, running routes), access to local spa and sports club, unsuitable for disabled.
BACKGROUND MUSIC: Radio 4 at breakfast, classical background music in restaurant.
LOCATION: 1½ miles S of centre.
CHILDREN: all ages welcomed, under-4s free, cots £20, extra bed £39.50.
DOGS: guide dogs only.
CREDIT CARDS: Amex, MC, Visa.
PRICES: B&B doubles from £145, singles from £105. À la carte (Sun–Thurs) £45, set-price meal (incl. cocktail, house wine, coffee) £80 per couple (Fri, Sat).

YORK Yorkshire

MIDDLETHORPE HALL & SPA

Arrive at this William and Mary house, with its lovely facade and 20 acres of gardens and parkland, and you'd think you were deep in the country – York, however, is just over a mile away. (The racecourse is handily opposite.) Step inside to elegant rooms of shuttered sash windows and wood-panelling, furnished with deep sofas, paintings and glowing table lamps. The house was given to the National Trust in 2008, but it's not precious; there are newspapers to browse, and fires generously stoked, plus a charming, slightly dated spa in converted cottages. Bedrooms, split between the main hall and converted stable block and cottages, are traditional country house with antiques, patterned wallpapers, blankets and eiderdowns. Some have window seats, all have books, fresh flowers, fruit and home-made biscuits. Bathrooms are small but 'spotless'. After canapés and drinks in the vast drawing room, dine on Modern British dishes such as chicken with spiced plum, or sea bream with scallop and sea aster. Breakfast offers freshly squeezed juice, leaf tea and cooked dishes such as poached haddock and a full grill.

Bishopthorpe Road
York YO23 2GB

T: 01904 641241
E: info@middlethorpe.com
W: middlethorpe.com

BEDROOMS: 29. 17 in courtyard, 2 in cottage, 1 suite suitable for disabled.
OPEN: all year.
FACILITIES: hall, drawing room, library, 2 dining rooms, 2 private dining rooms, in-room TV, civil wedding licence, 20-acre grounds, spa (10 by 6 metre indoor swimming pool), EV charging, public rooms wheelchair accessible, no adapted toilet.
BACKGROUND MUSIC: none.
LOCATION: 1½ miles S of centre.
CHILDREN: not under 6, extra bed £55.
DOGS: allowed in garden suites and cottage, by prior arrangement (no charge).
CREDIT CARDS: Amex, MC, Visa.
PRICES: B&B doubles from £230, singles from £155. Tasting menu £85, à la carte 3-course £60. 1-night bookings refused summer weekends.

SEE ALSO SHORTLIST

ZENNOR Cornwall

MAP 1:D1

THE GURNARD'S HEAD

'There is a Celtic feel' to Charles and Edmund Inkin's pub and its surrounds, 'with views of the Atlantic and the moors and tors of Penwith', writes a reader on a return visit. Like sister pubs The Old Coastguard, Mousehole, and The Felin Fach Griffin, Felin Fach, Wales (see entries), it is rooted in the community, employing local staff, featuring works by local artists and sourcing as much as possible on the doorstep. It is also an 'ideal base for walking the coastal path'. 'Smart and practical' bedrooms have a Roberts radio, flowers, books, Welsh blankets, good toiletries, fresh milk. Downstairs you find real ales, open fires, comfy sofas, no starched napery or crystal glass. The nightly-changing menu is short, with tempting plant-based options and day-boat fish. Maybe St Austell mussels, white wine, garlic, parsley or courgette, pepper and goat's cheese tart with nettle pesto. 'I had some superb hake, plaice and lemon sole, some of the nicest ice cream I ever tasted.' 'Breakfast is a treat too' with 'delicious home-made breads, bacon, sausage and vine tomatoes'. One niggle: 'They don't do cream teas!' (Mike Craddock)

Treen
Zennor
St Ives TR26 3DE

T: 01736 796928
E: enquiries@gurnardshead.co.uk
W: gurnardshead.co.uk

BEDROOMS: 7.
OPEN: all year except 24/25 Dec.
FACILITIES: bar, restaurant, lounge area, 3-acre garden (alfresco dining), EV charging, public areas wheelchair accessible.
BACKGROUND MUSIC: Radio 4 at breakfast, selected music at other times, in bar and restaurant.
LOCATION: 7 miles SW of St Ives, on B3306.
CHILDREN: all ages welcomed, extra bed £25.
DOGS: allowed (no charge, water bowls, towels and biscuits provided).
CREDIT CARDS: MC, Visa.
PRICES: B&B doubles from £140, singles from £110. Set supper £29.50–£35. 1-night bookings refused weekends occasionally.

SCOTLAND

Kilchurn Castle and Loch Awe, Argyll and Bute

ARDUAINE Argyll and Bute   MAP 5:D1

LOCH MELFORT HOTEL

It's all about the views at this lochside hotel, with panoramic seascapes from many of its rooms across Asknish Bay to the Sound of Jura and the Inner Hebrides. In 17-acre grounds, it is a place for outdoor pursuits, with wild swimming and a wealth of furred and feathered wildlife. Goats and Highland cattle keep the grass in check. The Victorian mansion was built for James Arthur Campbell, who started the adjacent Arduaine Garden, now owned by the National Trust for Scotland, 'which has a number of fine walks'. The hotel has a relaxed, welcoming feel. A reader reported that the style was contemporary and comfortable, with the main luxury being the 'lovely views from an annexe room'; ground-floor rooms are dog-friendly. In the restaurant, Richard Young's locally sourced menus feature dishes such as hand-dived scallops, Argyll venison burger, halibut with mushroom duxelles, and vegetarian options. The Garden Bistro opens all day for light snacks, you can request a packed lunch, and there is a newly expanded decking area so you can sit as long as you like and drink in those vistas. (TH)

Arduaine
Oban PA34 4XG

T: 01852 200233
E: reception@lochmelfort.co.uk
W: lochmelfort.co.uk

BEDROOMS: 30. 20 in annexe, 10 on ground floor, 2 suitable for disabled.
OPEN: all year except Mon–Wed Nov–Mar, 3 weeks Dec/Jan, open Christmas/New Year.
FACILITIES: sitting room, library, bar/bistro, restaurant, in-room TV (terrestrial), wedding facilities, 17-acre grounds, E.V charging, public rooms wheelchair accessible.
BACKGROUND MUSIC: in restaurant and bistro.
LOCATION: 19 miles S of Oban.
CHILDREN: all ages welcomed, under-2s/cots free, extra bed £30.
DOGS: allowed in 6 bedrooms (£10 per night), not in public rooms, except bistro in summer.
CREDIT CARDS: Amex, MC, Visa.
PRICES: B&B doubles from £70. À la carte £40.

ARINAGOUR Argyll and Bute

MAP 5:C1

COLL HOTEL

'Run by generations of the Oliphant family since 1963', Coll's welcoming social hub and only hotel sits at the head of Loch Eatharna, close to the ferry terminal. There are six first-floor bedrooms in the main hotel, with views across the bay to the Treshnish Isles, Staffa, Iona and Jura. Four ground-floor rooms, two with patio doors, in a recent sympathetic extension, overlook the garden. All are contemporary and unfussy, with sweet treats and Sea Kelp toiletries. Dine in the 'excellent, modern and spacious restaurant' or alfresco. Menus showcase locally raised, grown and fished produce. Maybe langoustine bisque, crab cakes, Hebridean lamb, smoked meat and fish from Loch Fyne and Inverawe. There is 'a reasonable wine list with two whites and two reds by the glass; nothing expensive'. Breakfast brings home-baked bread and new-laid free-range eggs. 'Many congratulations to the Oliphants,' writes an impressed trusted reader. The island is a dark-sky park known for its sandy beaches and dunes, lochs and lochans, and there is an RSPB reserve on the west side – 'Think corncrakes, among others.' (Tony Hall, DB)

Arinagour
Isle of Coll PA78 6SZ

T: 01879 230334
E: info@collhotel.com
W: collhotel.com

BEDROOMS: 10. 1 suitable for disabled (wet room, Blue Badge parking).
OPEN: all year.
FACILITIES: lounge bar, public bar, restaurant, residents' lounge and dining room, in-room TV (Freeview), garden, helipad, bicycles, extension room wheelchair accessible, adapted toilet, parking.
BACKGROUND MUSIC: none.
LOCATION: village centre.
CHILDREN: all ages welcomed (children stay free, except for food).
DOGS: allowed in bar areas, not in restaurant or bedrooms.
CREDIT CARDS: MC, Visa.
PRICES: B&B doubles from £110, singles from £80. À la carte from £25.

BOATH HOUSE

♞ Previous César winner

The Matheson family's classical Regency mansion stands in 22 acres of spectacular walled and woodland gardens, so 'the rustle of the leaves in the trees' drowns out any traffic noise from the Aberdeen–Inverness road. 'It is certainly a beautiful location,' relate trusted readers. Bedrooms have period furniture, perhaps a four-poster or French antique double bed, twin slipper baths in a tall window. 'Speciality teas, an espresso machine and delicious shortbread biscuits settled us in.' A short walk away, the old gamekeeper's bothy contains a suite with a lounge area, a wood-burner and sofa bed, a king-size/twin bed, a freestanding bath, walk-in shower and views of the lake. In the 'attractive bow-fronted dining room', two 'smartly dressed waitresses' were charming and knowledgeable. 'Canapés were beautiful, smoked lamb and carrot chutney on a wafer.' A heritage tomato salad and gnocchi 'met with approval'. You can eat more informally from garden-to-plate menus inside or alfresco at the Kale Yard café, with wood-fired pizza oven. Freshly squeezed orange juice comes with a 'lovely breakfast'.

Auldearn
Nairn IV12 5TE

T: 01667 454896
E: info@boath-house.com
W: boath-house.com

BEDROOMS: 11. 2 in cottages (50 yds), 1 suitable for disabled, 2 self-catering eco lodges. Plus 2 in separate B&B at owners' house.
OPEN: all year.
FACILITIES: 2 lounges, whisky bar/library, restaurant with private dining annexe, in-room TV (Freeview), wedding facilities, 22-acre parkland, public rooms and café wheelchair accessible, step up to toilet.
BACKGROUND MUSIC: soft in dining room.
LOCATION: 2 miles E of Nairn.
CHILDREN: all ages welcomed, extra bed for under-16s £55, no under-8s at dinner.
DOGS: allowed in some bedrooms, not in public rooms.
CREDIT CARDS: Amex, MC, Visa.
PRICES: B&B doubles from £220. Set dinner £45.

BALLANTRAE Ayrshire

MAP 5:E1

GLENAPP CASTLE

Gazing out over the Ayrshire coast to the Isle of Arran, Glenapp may be towered and turreted, but the Scottish Baronial-style hotel (Relais & Châteaux) is more luxury country house than castle. Imposing public rooms come with stucco ceilings, Corinthian columns and wood panelling. Spacious bedrooms and opulent suites have antiques, paintings, perhaps a four-poster, comfy seating, a sea or garden view, or both. 'Our large garden-view room had a bathroom with a sea view to Ailsa Craig.' In the dining room, head chef Ian Bennett's menus of local and home-grown produce offer choices that might include roast loin of roe deer, celeriac purée, girolles, haggis bonbon, blackberry and port reduction. 'Every bite was delicious.' The staff are 'professional but warm and friendly'. When a guest suffered a coughing fit, she was brought 'a silver teapot of hot water, lemon slices and a little dish of honey'. Breakfast is 'freshly prepared and beautifully presented'. In season, cream teas are served in the walled garden in 'wonderful grounds overlooking the sea', with glorious walks, tennis, croquet, picnic spots and a deer park. (CB)

Ballantrae KA26 0NZ

T: 01465 831212
E: info@glenappcastle.com
W: glenappcastle.com

BEDROOMS: 17. 7 on ground floor, 1 suitable for disabled, lift to public rooms on first floor.
OPEN: all year.
FACILITIES: lift, drawing room, library, 2 dining rooms, wedding facilities, in-room TV (Freeview), 36-acre grounds (walled gardens, woodland, lake, tennis, croquet), boat for charter, access to local spa, EV charging, public rooms wheelchair accessible.
BACKGROUND MUSIC: occasional pianist during meals.
LOCATION: 2 miles S of Ballantrae.
CHILDREN: all ages welcomed, under-7s free, extra bed 7–15s, £65.
DOGS: allowed in some bedrooms (£25 per night), not in public rooms.
CREDIT CARDS: Amex, MC, Visa.
PRICES: B&B doubles from £465. Set 3-course dinner £55, 6-course £75.

BALQUHIDDER Stirlingshire   MAP 5:D2

MONACHYLE MHOR

It feels wild and remote at this farmhouse turned restaurant-with-rooms overlooking lochs and hills, but, inside, it is surprisingly glamorous. It may be a 'thousand times more peaceful' than nearby Loch Lomond, with wild walks from the doorstep, yet it has a bar with colourful Italian stools, a white lounge with vintage chairs and a glass-and-wood, three-storey bedroom 'pod' in the trees. Tom Lewis, who grew up here, runs the property with wife Lisa May; both have an eye for design. Main bedrooms range from cosily rustic with blanket throws, exposed-stone walls and bright colours, to sprawling affairs with designer lighting and egg-shaped bath. (One couple found the bathroom, with shuttered window to bedroom, a bit too bold.) Quirky options in the grounds, apart from the pod, include a 1950s wagon, a ferry cabin and yurts. Relax in the candle-lit lounge before a 'superb' dinner – much sourced from their farm – offering dishes such as Shetland salmon with pink grapefruit ceviche, and local venison with chanterelles. Breakfast on smoked haddock, or poached egg and mushrooms, among other dishes, and enjoy the 'stunning views'. (BW, and others)

Balquhidder
Lochearnhead FK19 8PQ

T: 01877 384622
E: monachyle@mhor.net
W: monachylemhor.net

BEDROOMS: 18. 5 on ground floor, 11 in courtyard, 1 in modular three-storey 'pod', 1 suitable for disabled. Plus 3 yurts and self-catering wagon, cabin and lodge.
OPEN: all year.
FACILITIES: lounge, living room, bar, conservatory restaurant, in-room TV, wedding facilities, function facilities, garden, 2,000-acre estate (foraging, wild swimming, water sports), EV charging, public rooms wheelchair accessible.
BACKGROUND MUSIC: all day in public areas.
LOCATION: 4 miles off A84, down a single-track lane skirting Loch Voil.
CHILDREN: all ages welcomed, under-3s free, extra bed from £30.
DOGS: allowed in 3 bedrooms (£10 per stay), bar and lounge.
CREDIT CARDS: Amex, MC, Visa.
PRICES: B&B doubles from £250 (hotel), £200 (yurt). Set menu £70, seasonal tasting menu £90.

BLAIRGOWRIE Perth and Kinross
MAP 5:D2

KINLOCH HOUSE

'After touring Scotland this was our favourite place, and we can't wait to return,' a trusted reader writes of the Allen family's Victorian mansion, in woodland and parkland, with views over rolling fields to Marlee Loch. Country house luxury abounds in this Relais & Châteaux property; guests can relax in a pretty, raspberry-coloured drawing room, or settle in by a log fire in the impressive oak-panelled hall, perhaps with a book from the library. Everywhere there are paintings, ornaments, china, antlers, while some past owner has kept a taxidermist busy. Bedrooms range from tolerably large to positively huge suites, two of which have an extra seated area in a turreted section where you can sit and soak up the blissful views. Bathrooms are also spacious. In the dining room, chef Steve MacCallum uses Scottish game, beef, fish and shellfish, home-grown produce from the walled garden and fruit from Perthshire's orchards, in his nightly-changing menus. 'The meals were absolutely delicious.' Breakfast brings home-baked bread, home-made sausages and jam. 'Faultless in every respect.' (Lynn Middleton, and others)

Dunkeld Road
Blairgowrie PH10 6SG

T: 01250 884237
E: reception@kinlochhouse.com
W: kinlochhouse.com

BEDROOMS: 15. 4 on ground floor.
OPEN: all year except 2 weeks from mid-Dec, open for New Year.
FACILITIES: bar, lounge, drawing room, conservatory, dining room, private dining room, in-room TV (Freeview), wedding facilities, 20-acre grounds, public areas on ground floor wheelchair accessible, toilet not adapted.
BACKGROUND MUSIC: none.
LOCATION: 3 miles W of Blairgowrie, on A923.
CHILDREN: all ages welcomed, extra bed £40, no under-6s in restaurant at dinner.
DOGS: not allowed.
CREDIT CARDS: Amex, MC, Visa.
PRICES: B&B doubles from £250. Set dinner £58. 1-night bookings refused busy periods.

THE FIFE ARMS

Never was a hotel more thoroughly transformed than this landmark Victorian coaching inn, curated by its owners, the Swiss gallerists behind Hauser and Wirth. With works by Picasso, Lucien Freud, Queen Victoria and Prince Charles, a bespoke house tartan, a cocktail bar homage to fashion designer Elsa Schiaparelli, and an ossuary of stuffed and mounted birds and animals, it is pure theatre. 'Quirky' rooms range from snug croft rooms with a cabin bed to suites, with maybe a carved four-poster, antiques and artwork. Most fun are the Scottish Culture rooms inspired by leading figures of science and the arts. 'The reception was welcoming,' writes a trusted reader, who enjoyed a 'very good and reasonably priced' lunch in the Flying Stag bar with commendable 'prompt service'. But a set three-course dinner in the Clunie dining room was 'a disappointment'. If you want choice, dine à la carte on dishes such as loin of Highland venison with wood-roasted pumpkin and Castelluccio lentils; birch-seared salmon, lemon and fennel. Breakfast of perhaps game sausage or wood-fired kipper sets you up to explore the Cairngorms national park.

Mar Road
Braemar AB35 5YN

T: 01339 720200
E: mail@thefifearms.com
W: thefifearms.com

BEDROOMS: 46.
OPEN: all year.
FACILITIES: pub, restaurant, cocktail bar, drawing room, dining room, 2 meeting rooms, wedding facilities, in-room TV (terrestrial), 2-acre gardens, spa, public areas wheelchair accessible, adapted toilet.
BACKGROUND MUSIC: in public spaces.
LOCATION: in town centre.
CHILDREN: all ages welcomed, children's menus, family and interconnecting rooms.
DOGS: in some bedrooms (£25 per stay), in pub, by prior arrangement.
CREDIT CARDS: Amex, MC, Visa.
PRICES: B&B doubles from £250. À la carte £55 (Clunie restaurant), £38 (Flying Stag), tasting menu (restaurant) £95.

CHIRNSIDE Scottish Borders   MAP 5:E3

CHIRNSIDE HALL

Pack your walking boots, waxed jacket, waders, guns, camera, binoculars – Christian Korsten's pink-sandstone Borders mansion is very much about the great outdoors. Spin in through a glazed revolving door to find, beyond the impressive hallway, multiple sofas around roaring log fires. Spin out to find mature gardens with dreamy views to the Cheviot hills. Stags' heads look over the staircase, which leads to large first-floor bedrooms with tall windows, maybe a modern four-poster. Attic-floor rooms are more compact, but trusted readers were happy with theirs. 'The large bed was very comfortable. There was plenty of storage space and a sofa. The bathroom was large and well appointed' with bath and walk-in shower. At night, a short, fixed-price menu showcases local produce – perhaps home-smoked pigeon, roe deer from the estate, salmon with tomato and coriander couscous and Mediterranean vegetable filo parcels. A substantial breakfast with porridge, haggis, Eyemouth kippers or the full Scottish sets you up for a day of shooting, fishing or 'photo-stalking' otters and hares. (E and JG)

Chirnside
Duns TD11 3LD

T: 01890 818219
E: reception@chirnsidehallhotel.com
W: chirnsidehallhotel.com

BEDROOMS: 10.
OPEN: all year.
FACILITIES: 2 lounges, dining room, private dining room/library/conference rooms, in-room TV (Freeview), billiard room, wedding facilities, 1½-acre grounds, lounges and restaurant wheelchair accessible.
BACKGROUND MUSIC: 'easy listening' in public areas.
LOCATION: 1½ miles E of Chirnside, NE of Duns.
CHILDREN: all ages welcomed, under-5s free, extra bed £50.
DOGS: allowed in some bedrooms (£15 per dog per night), not in public rooms.
CREDIT CARDS: Amex, MC, Visa.
PRICES: B&B doubles from £200, singles from £105. À la carte £45.

COLINTRAIVE Argyll and Bute

MAP 5:D1

THE COLINTRAIVE HOTEL

With mesmerising sea views to the Isle of Bute, this quietly situated village hotel offers excellent seafood and a friendly welcome from the owners and locals. Owners Clare Banner and Joe Burnett have refreshed the bedrooms but kept the Colintraive's much-loved homeliness. With sea or fell views, rooms are light and airy with Scottish artwork, simple contemporary furnishings and the occasional vintage piece. Some have feature wallpapers; all have fresh milk and smart bathrooms with under-floor heating. Leave plenty of time for a drink in the bar before dinner; you'll probably meet most of the locals who use it regularly, lending the place a warm, buzzy atmosphere. Joe's meals are a treat of local produce (he worked in London under Angela Hartnett); perhaps Barra scallops with foraged girolles followed by Isle of Bute rump with garlic butter, or Gigha halibut with fennel and samphire. Desserts include a Scottish cheeseboard. Days can be filled with walking, kayaking and cycling, or spotting wildlife such as seals, basking sharks and eagles. The road stops after the next village, so you're assured a peaceful night's sleep.

Colintraive PA22 3AS

T: 01700 841207
E: enquiries@colintraivehotel.com
W: colintraivehotel.com

BEDROOMS: 4.
OPEN: all year except 25 Dec, restaurant closed Mon lunch.
FACILITIES: lounge, bar, restaurant, in-room TV (Freeview), wedding facilities, small beer garden, yacht moorings, public rooms on ground floor wheelchair accessible, no adapted toilet.
BACKGROUND MUSIC: in public areas; occasional live music.
LOCATION: in village, 20 miles W of Dunoon.
CHILDREN: all ages welcomed, extra bed £20.
DOGS: allowed in bedrooms (£10 per night), public rooms, not in restaurant.
CREDIT CARDS: Amex, MC, Visa.
PRICES: B&B doubles from £100, singles from £85. À la carte £35.

COLONSAY Argyll and Bute   MAP 5:D1

THE COLONSAY

It's a scenic crossing from Oban to this island of white-sand beaches, where the one hotel stands on a hillside overlooking the harbour, with views to neighbouring Jura. Built in 1750, it is at the heart of social life for the 135 islanders, and welcomes visitors drawn by the beauty, the peace and abundant wildlife. 'I cannot recommend it highly enough,' writes a trusted reader, charmed by the 'friendly, welcoming' staff. 'The young man in the bar worked his socks off to please everyone.' There are plenty of spaces to relax in the stylish bar and lounges, with log-burner and comfy sofas. The bedrooms have plain paintwork, artwork, designer fabrics, oak furniture. Pig's Paradise, a double with adjoining single, is named after dramatic cliffs where guillemots nest in their thousands (paradise for birdwatchers, less so for Gadarene swine). Gastropub-style food is served in the bar, old dining room or more formal restaurant, from a seasonally changing menu big on locally landed seafood – fish pie, lobster, rib-eye steak, burger. 'Breakfast and dinner were delicious. We will definitely be back.' (Caroline Hands)

Isle of Colonsay PA61 7YU

T: 01951 200316
E: manager@colonsayholidays.co.uk
W: colonsayholidays.co.uk

BEDROOMS: 9.
OPEN: mid-Mar–Nov, Christmas, New Year.
FACILITIES: conservatory, 2 lounges, log room, bar, restaurant, Wi-Fi on ground floor only, in-room TV (Sky), 1-acre grounds, EV charging, ground-floor public rooms wheelchair accessible, adapted toilet.
BACKGROUND MUSIC: in bar sometimes.
LOCATION: 400 yds W of harbour.
CHILDREN: all ages welcomed, under-12s sharing Pig's Paradise stay free, children's menu.
DOGS: allowed in 2 bedrooms (£10 per night), public rooms except restaurant.
CREDIT CARDS: MC, Visa.
PRICES: B&B doubles from £115, singles from £85, family from £130. Pre-ferry set menus £22–£35 Mon, Thurs, Fri, Sat, à la carte £30.

CONTIN Highland

MAP 5:C2

COUL HOUSE

Set amid gardens and woodlands, this Georgian
country house has been a labour of love for
Susannah and Stuart Macpherson since they first
opened to guests in 2003. Our inspectors have
found much to like, from the 'warm, inviting'
atmosphere, to a 'large bed with crisp sheets' in a
'lovely room'. Public rooms have striking original
features, antiques, paintings, a grandfather clock,
a stag's head above a carved fireplace. Bedrooms
are all dog-friendly, and range from small but
adequate doubles to master rooms with perhaps
a modern four-poster, an espresso machine,
a double-ended bath and walk-in shower,
with views to the mountains of Strathconon.
The showpiece is the octagonal dining room
(astonishingly, the splendid mansion was once
split into two competing guest houses). Garry
Kenley's seasonally changing menus are long on
meat – slow-roast pork belly, venison, coq au vin –
but there are veggie options and a fish of the day.
After breakfast, wander the grounds to admire
the 'beautiful mature trees', notably 'two giant
sequoia and a huge Douglas fir'. Children love
the fairy trail.

Contin
Strathpeffer IV14 9ES

T: 01997 421487
E: stay@coulhouse.com
W: coulhousehotel.com

BEDROOMS: 21. 4 on ground floor, 1
suitable for disabled.
OPEN: all year except 23–26 Dec.
FACILITIES: lounge bar, drawing
room, hall, restaurant, in-room TV,
wedding/conference facilities, 8-acre
grounds (9-hole golf practice area),
EV charging, ground floor wheelchair
accessible, adapted toilet.
BACKGROUND MUSIC: in lounge bar and
restaurant.
LOCATION: 17 miles NW of Inverness.
CHILDREN: all ages welcomed, no
charge for under-5s, extra bed 5–15
£25, over-15s £35 on extra beds.
DOGS: allowed in some bedrooms
(£9.50 per night), all public rooms
except restaurant.
CREDIT CARDS: Amex, MC, Visa.
PRICES: B&B doubles from £150 (single
occupancy rates on application). À la
carte £45. 1-night bookings refused
New Year.

JURA HOTEL

The only hotel in Jura's sole village is part of the appeal of this modest yet hospitable, family-run affair; the rest is the peace, remoteness, views, wildlife and fresh, island-sourced food. And whisky; the hotel, overlooking the Sound of Jura, is yards from the Jura Distillery. The best bedrooms share this view – guests report seeing grey seals, deer and 'an otter fishing in the bay' – and are comfortably if plainly styled with creamy walls, chunky wooden furniture and a splash of colour in tartan throws and cushions. There are no TVs but 'switching off' is the point of staying here (if desperate, one of the lounges has one). Most have 'good storage', an armchair; a sofa in the largest. Bathrooms are modern, about half with bath as well as shower. After a day of walking, cycling or wildlife watching, relax in the cheery and 'friendly' lounge bar, a focal point for locals, before tucking in to a 'delicious' meal which makes excellent use of local produce: langoustines with garlic mayonnaise, Loch Gruinart oysters, and roast venison with strawberry and chilli jus. A varied, 'imaginative' breakfast sets you up for a day's exploring.

Craighouse
Isle of Jura PA60 7XU

T: 01496 820243
E: hello@jurahotel.co.uk
W: jurahotel.co.uk

BEDROOMS: 17. 15 en suite, 2 with private bathroom, unsuitable for disabled.
OPEN: all year except Christmas and New Year.
FACILITIES: bar, lounge, restaurant, outdoor eating area, picnic benches, wedding facilities (events shack), public areas wheelchair accessible, no adapted toilet.
BACKGROUND MUSIC: all day in bar, restaurant.
LOCATION: in village, opposite Small Isles Bay, 300 yds from passenger ferry terminal, 7 miles from car ferry terminal.
CHILDREN: all ages welcomed, free cots, 5–12s £7.50/over-12s £35 on extra bed.
DOGS: allowed in pub only.
CREDIT CARDS: MC, Visa.
PRICES: B&B doubles from £115, singles from £70. À la carte £36. Min. 2-night stay except in winter.

DUNVEGAN Highland

MAP 5:C1

THE THREE CHIMNEYS
AND THE HOUSE OVER-BY

In a scattered hamlet on the western shore of
Loch Dunvegan, in the far north of Skye, a
whitewashed stone crofter's cottage is the setting
for this fine-dining restaurant-with-rooms. In
2019 it was acquired from long-time owners
Shirley and Eddie Spear, by Gordon Campbell
Gray's new Wee Hotel Company (see also The
Pierhouse, Port Appin), whose motto is 'Where
small is beautiful'. There is nothing small about
the views across the loch and over the Minch
to the peaks of Harris and North Uist nor, it
must be said, the prices, but, then, this is an
internationally renowned destination. Chef Scott
Davies is committed to the use of island produce
from land, sea and Skye, and whatever possible
is made in-house. In the dining room, with bare
stone walls and jolly artwork, you can dine from a
short menu of dishes such as Gigha halibut, wild
mushroom, leek, potato terrine; Soay lamb with
bramble sauce; red deer, faggot, black cabbage.
New arrivals are greeted with tea and cakes and
shown to a swish, sea-facing room in the House
Over-By, with restful decor, garden access, a
king-size bed and a new bathroom with walk-in
rain shower.

Colbost
Dunvegan
Isle of Skye IV55 8ZT

T: 01470 511258
E: eatandstay@threechimneys.co.uk
W: threechimneys.co.uk

BEDROOMS: 6. All on ground floor
(5 split-level) in separate building,
1 suitable for disabled.
OPEN: all year except mid-Dec–end
Jan.
FACILITIES: lounge/breakfast room,
restaurant, in-room TV (Freeview),
wedding facilities, garden, EV
charging, restaurant and lounge
wheelchair accessible, adapted toilet.
BACKGROUND MUSIC: in lounge and
restaurant.
LOCATION: 5 miles W of Dunvegan.
CHILDREN: all ages welcomed, extra
bed free for under-8s.
DOGS: allowed in 1 bedroom (max.
1 dog, no charge unless for damage or
extra cleaning), not in public spaces.
CREDIT CARDS: Amex, MC, Visa.
PRICES: B&B doubles from £365, triple
£465. À la carte £65.

EDINBURGH

MAP 5:D2

PRESTONFIELD

'Neatness and sweetness all around, These at Prestonfield are found,' wrote Benjamin Franklin after a stay at this 17th-century mansion in parkland under Arthur's Seat. 'This hotel was wonderful,' a trusted reader waxes no less lyrical. For James Thomson OBE, who bought it in 2003, it was the fulfilment of a long-held dream, and a dream it is, a vision of lavishness, with paintings, tapestries, gilded mirrors, carved four-posters, chinoiserie lacquered cabinets, tooled and gilded leather wall coverings in the principal bedchamber ... The atmosphere is so rich you could bottle it. 'When we arrived, the remnants of a wedding were in progress. Pipers and pretty maidens abounded.' Bedrooms have a minibar, mood lighting, perhaps a view of Craigmillar Castle ruins. In Rhubarb restaurant 'dinner was superb', from 'a leek thing and duck pâté' to 'rack of lamb and a gorgeous strawberry concoction'. Introduced to Scotland by former resident Sir Alexander Dick, rhubarb appears at breakfast in compote and porridge, along with a full Scottish, full vegan, house-smoked salmon and much more, all just ten minutes from the city centre. (JB)

Priestfield Road
Edinburgh EH16 5UT

T: 0131 225 7800
E: reservations@prestonfield.com
W: prestonfield.com

BEDROOMS: 23. 1, on ground floor, suitable for disabled.
OPEN: all year.
FACILITIES: lift, 2 drawing rooms, sitting room, library, whisky bar, restaurant (vegetarian /vegan menus), private dining rooms, in-room TV (Sky), wedding facilities, terraces, tea house, 20-acre grounds, EV charging, public rooms wheelchair accessible, adapted toilet.
BACKGROUND MUSIC: 'as suitable' in public areas.
LOCATION: next to Royal Holyrood Park.
CHILDREN: all ages welcomed, extra bed £25.
DOGS: allowed in bedrooms (no charge), public rooms and park, not in restaurant.
CREDIT CARDS: Amex, MC, Visa.
PRICES: B&B doubles from £375. Set 3-course dinner £44, à la carte £70.

SEE ALSO SHORTLIST

EDINBURGH

24 ROYAL TERRACE

After you have stepped back to admire the colonnaded, balustraded front of William Playfair's showpiece terrace, cross the road and step inside this boutique hotel, bar and gallery to admire the art. The owner had run out of space for his collection of contemporary artwork, so he bought this sublime Georgian town house, replete with original features, equipped it with every modern comfort, and opened it to guests so that all could share an ever-changing exhibition. You don't have to stay here to have a glass of house champagne or a cappuccino with a Kandinsky, breakfast or brunch in the bar or walled garden. It's a welcoming, social place, with enthusiastic young staff, and always something on the go, from the latest cocktail to competitions. Luxurious bedrooms have a mix of contemporary and period furniture, perhaps an original John Bellany, an in-room roll-top bath, a view of the Firth of Forth. In the past year many have been fitted with a distinctive new carpet, a Murano glass chandelier. In the morning, enjoy a full Scottish, full vegan, or waffles with bacon and maple syrup, downstairs or delivered to your room.

24 Royal Terrace
Edinburgh EH7 5AH

T: 0131 297 2424
E: reservations@24royalterrace.co.uk
W: 24royalterrace.co.uk

BEDROOMS: 15. Plus 2 studio apartments.
OPEN: all year.
FACILITIES: bar, lounge, in-room smart TV, terrace, garden (outdoor tables), street parking (fee), car park (discounted fee) 10-min. walk, unsuitable for disabled.
BACKGROUND MUSIC: in public areas.
LOCATION: E of city centre.
CHILDREN: all ages welcomed, extra bed £25.
DOGS: allowed in public rooms and garden.
CREDIT CARDS: Amex, MC, Visa.
PRICES: room-only doubles from £159. Continental breakfast £9, cooked breakfast £15. 1-night bookings refused Aug, New Year, special events.

SEE ALSO SHORTLIST

23 MAYFIELD

Guests are entrusted with a key to Ross and
Kathleen Birnie's Victorian house, a period gem
a mile from the city centre, beautifully presented
with antique furniture and many original
features. The hosts 'make a strong team', clearly
love what they do, and provide many novel
touches, from the vintage Punch cartoons in one
bedroom, to a Georgian chessboard in the Club
Room. 'Ross revealed he had rescued the globe in
the dining room from scrap.' The bedrooms, two
with a four-poster, one with a half-tester bed, have
mahogany antique furniture, Border biscuits and
smart toiletries. A 'tastefully appointed' double
had a 'modern bathroom with glitzy illuminated
mirror and a capacious monsoon and hand-held
shower'. A family room sleeps five. Guests can sit
out in the front garden with the monkey puzzle
tree and topiary. An award-winning breakfast,
ordered the night before, tick-box fashion, brings
many tempting choices, including rare breed
pork sausages, tomatoes slow-roasted with thyme,
clootie dumpling, peat-smoked haddock, a full
vegan, tattie scones, brioche, and much more.
'Kathleen was a cheerful waitress.' (RG)

23 Mayfield Gardens
Edinburgh EH9 2BX

T: 0131 667 5806
E: info@23mayfield.co.uk
W: 23mayfield.co.uk

BEDROOMS: 7. 1 on ground floor.
OPEN: all year except Christmas.
FACILITIES: club room, breakfast room,
in-room smart TV (Freeview), terrace,
garden, parking.
BACKGROUND MUSIC: at breakfast.
LOCATION: 1 mile S of city centre.
CHILDREN: aged 3 and over welcomed,
family room.
DOGS: not allowed.
CREDIT CARDS: MC, Visa.
PRICES: B&B doubles/singles from
£130. Usually 2-night min. stay but
check availability.

SEE ALSO SHORTLIST

ELIE Fife

THE SHIP INN

With its own beach cricket team, Rachel and
Graham Bucknall's white-and-blue friendly
gastropub on a no-through road to the sailing
club overlooks a sandy bay on the Firth of
Forth. When the tide stops play, you might eat
fish and chips or a barbecued burger on the
sea-view terrace, or have a drink by the fire in
the dog-friendly bar. The Captain rooms are
styled in colours of sky, sea and surf, with white
shutters framing glorious sunsets. A ground-
floor, street-facing Sea Dog room was 'simple
but all we would want for a comfortable stay
– warmth, quiet and a huge, cosy bed', a coffee
machine and good Scottish toiletries. Best is the
top-floor Admiral room, with a slipper bath and
walk-in shower, and a seat in the bay window
from which to admire the vista. In the restaurant,
with wooden floors and furniture, Mat Majer's
menus of Scottish produce include dishes such as
lamb rump and braised shoulder with lyonnaise
potatoes or tagliatelle, mushroom and hazelnut
ragù. 'We loved the atmosphere and welcome and
will certainly go back.' (See also sister property
The Bridge Inn at Ratho, Shortlist.)

The Toft
Elie KY9 1DT

T: 01333 330246
E: info@shipinn.scot
W: shipinn.scot

BEDROOMS: 6. 1 partially accessible on
ground floor.
OPEN: all year, except Christmas Day.
FACILITIES: bar, restaurant, in-room
TV (Sky, Freeview), wedding
facilities, private function room/
cricket pavilion, terrace (beach bar,
alfresco dining), restaurant, bar,
terrace wheelchair accessible, adapted
toilet.
BACKGROUND MUSIC: in public areas.
LOCATION: in town, on the bay.
CHILDREN: all ages welcomed, extra
bed £50, children's menu.
DOGS: in 2 bedrooms (£25 per dog per
stay), bar, downstairs restaurant.
CREDIT CARDS: MC, Visa.
PRICES: B&B doubles from £120.
À la carte £35. 1-night bookings
refused at New Year.

GAIRLOCH Highland

MAP 5:B1

SHIELDAIG LODGE

With 'wonderful views' of Loch Gairloch, this Victorian hunting lodge on a wooded estate where falconry, fishing and deer stalking can all be laid on for guests now accepts dogs in its bedrooms and bar. A sister hotel to Widbrook Grange, Bradford-on-Avon (see entry), it ticks every box for a sporty Highland retreat, from the blazing log fires, deep leather sofas and tartan and tweed furnishings to the 250 whiskies in the bar. Antique-furnished bedrooms range from cosy to a suite with a four-poster, separate lounge, in-room roll-top bath and loch-facing bay window. 'The lawn runs down to the shore and we saw seals, an otter, heron and curlew, all from our room.' Several bathrooms have been upgraded, and a new mains water system means more powerful showers. Jerome Prodanu uses estate and home-grown produce, with shellfish from the loch, to compose each night's menu. 'We enjoyed cod fillet with cauliflower risotto and beetroot cream with lobster sauce; duck with braised Brussels sprouts, mushroom duxelles and Provençal sauce.' In all, 'fantastic location, unpretentious hotel, excellent staff and very good food'. (Bruce Wilson, DB)

Badachro
Gairloch IV21 2AN

T: 01445 741333
E: reservations@shieldaiglodge.com
W: shieldaiglodge.com

BEDROOMS: 12.
OPEN: all year.
FACILITIES: lounge, library, bar, restaurant, snooker/private dining room, in-room TV (Freeview), wedding facilities, garden, 26,000-acre estate (fishing, red deer stalking, falconry centre, motor boat for charter), public areas wheelchair accessible.
BACKGROUND MUSIC: in lounge, bar and restaurant.
LOCATION: 4¼ miles S of Gairloch.
CHILDREN: all ages welcomed, family room.
DOGS: allowed in 2 bedrooms (£20 a night) and bar only.
CREDIT CARDS: Amex, MC, Visa.
PRICES: B&B doubles from £130, singles from £95, family from £190. Set-price menu £49, 5-course tasting menu (on request) £69.

GLASGOW

GRASSHOPPERS

An Edwardian railway office building seems an unlikely place for a hotel – but buzz an intercom and take the lift to the sixth floor, where a warm reception, cupcakes and affordable Scandi-style comfort await. This penthouse enterprise was the brainchild of owner Barrie Munn, and designed to strike a perfect balance between character and efficiency, to be well run and welcoming, spotless but not clinical. Bedrooms – some overlooking the station's 48,000-pane glass roof – have a handmade king-size divan bed, a handmade desk, a Caledonian oak floor, Italian lighting, a Grohe power shower in a pod-like bathroom, Arran Aromatics toiletries and blackout blinds. There is a small bar in the sitting room, but the beating heart of the operation is the kitchen, where tea, coffee, home-made cakes and other treats are on offer. Breakfast includes porridge, freshly baked breads, eggs and bacon from local delis, with kedgeree on certain days. You can have supper here too (soups, salad, perhaps lamb curry), but it's best to book. Parking for guests costs just £8 for 24 hours at a nearby Q-Park.

87 Union Street
Glasgow G1 3TA

T: 0141 222 2666
E: info@grasshoppersglasgow.com
W: grasshoppersglasgow.com

BEDROOMS: 29.
OPEN: all year except 4 days at Christmas.
FACILITIES: breakfast/supper room, sitting room with small bar, in-room TV (Freeview), unsuitable for disabled.
BACKGROUND MUSIC: none.
LOCATION: by Central Station.
CHILDREN: all ages welcomed, no charge for cot or extra bed for under-12s if space allows (request at time of booking).
DOGS: allowed (no charge).
CREDIT CARDS: Amex, MC, Visa.
PRICES: B&B doubles from £85, singles from £75, triples from £115. À la carte £17.

SEE ALSO SHORTLIST

GLENFINNAN Highland

MAP 5:C1

GLENFINNAN HOUSE HOTEL

Peacefully set beside Loch Shiel, opposite the Glenfinnan Monument and with distant views of Ben Nevis, this handsome country house with tartan fabrics and four-poster bedrooms is a great Highland hideaway. Owned by the MacFarlane family for 40 years, and 'courteously' run by chef Duncan Gibson and his wife, Manja, with the help of 'efficient and friendly staff', it feels like a private home. There are no keys for the cream- and gold-coloured bedrooms, styled with mahogany and oak furniture and traditionally tiled bathrooms. No TVs either; instead nearly all have loch or mountain views. The walking is glorious, 'we didn't use our car until we left', while the drawing room, with warm colours and velvet-covered armchairs, is wonderfully relaxing. Indulge in afternoon tea or save yourself for the 'really excellent' dinner, which mixes simpler fare – fish and chips or home-made venison sausage and mash – with classier dishes such as rib of Scotch beef, and pan-fried trout with parsley-crushed potatoes. Leave room for home-made dessert, urges a reader, 'I highly recommend the sticky toffee pudding.' (Jeremy Bonnett, JR)

Glenfinnan
Fort William PH37 4LT

T: 01397 722235
E: availability@glenfinnanhouse.com
W: glenfinnanhouse.com

BEDROOMS: 14.
OPEN: 1 Apr–30 Oct.
FACILITIES: drawing room, bar/lounge, playroom, restaurant, wedding facilities, 1-acre grounds (play area), unsuitable for disabled.
BACKGROUND MUSIC: Scottish in bar and restaurant.
LOCATION: 15 miles NW of Fort William.
CHILDREN: all ages welcomed, under-12s free, extra bed £15.
DOGS: allowed in bedrooms (£15 per night, max. £45 per stay), in some public rooms, not in restaurant or drawing room.
CREDIT CARDS: Amex, MC, Visa.
PRICES: B&B doubles from £150, singles from £130. À la carte (3 courses) £33.

SEE ALSO SHORTLIST

GRANTOWN-ON-SPEY Highland   MAP 5:C2

CULDEARN HOUSE

Guests can follow the Speyside whisky trail from
the Marshall family's bay-fronted Victorian house,
then return to sit by the fire with a dram from
a list of fine malts and rare single-barrel casks.
The atmosphere is warm and informal; Sonia
and William have distilled the essence of Scottish
hospitality with 'the enjoyment of their guests at
heart', and are a mine of local information. Of
the six bedrooms, in eclectic country house style,
'lovely, well-furnished' Dunnottar looks out to
one of the ancient woodlands encircling the town.
Dual-aspect Craigievar has a bathroom with
double-ended bath and walk-in shower, views
of woods and the Cromdale hills. Guests gather
for drinks in the drawing room, with 'little treats
on savoury biscuits', before a 'simply served'
but delicious four-course dinner, cooked from
locally sourced produce by Sonia. Dishes include
the Culdearn steak, 'so tender it melted in your
mouth', with a Drambuie sauce, or monkfish tail
with crayfish and Parmesan sauce. Breakfast, with
free-range eggs, is 'all one could wish for' before a
day that might be spent fishing, birdwatching, or
on a whisky tour.

Woodlands Terrace
Grantown-on-Spey PH26 3JU

T: 01479 872106
E: enquiries@culdearn.com
W: culdearn.com

BEDROOMS: 6. 1, on ground floor, with
wet room, suitable for disabled.
OPEN: all year except Feb, Mar,
Christmas (open New Year).
FACILITIES: drawing room, dining
room, in-room TV (Freeview), ¾-acre
garden, public rooms wheelchair
accessible, parking.
BACKGROUND MUSIC: none.
LOCATION: edge of town (within
walking distance).
CHILDREN: aged 10 and upwards
welcomed, younger children by
arrangement.
DOGS: only guide dogs.
CREDIT CARDS: Amex, MC, Visa.
PRICES: B&B doubles from £160. Fixed-
price dinner £48.

GRANTOWN-ON-SPEY Highland

MAP 5:C2

THE DULAIG

Warm Scottish hospitality is the hallmark of this Edwardian country house B&B, from the home-made cakes and whisky-fuelled porridge to the beautifully tended garden and comfortable bedrooms. Carol and Gordon Bulloch treat guests as friends; there are tea and scones to welcome you in the drawing room, with its log fire, antiques and plump sofas, and fresh flowers and chocolates in the large bedrooms. All rooms overlook the garden and are filled with a mix of Arts and Crafts (reflecting the house's history) and contemporary furniture. Fabrics are prettily patterned country house style, beds are praised for their comfort while bathrooms have under-floor heating, luxury Scottish products and a choice of slipper bath, whirlpool bath or shower with body-jets. 'Home-made and delicious' breakfasts are 'second to none' according to one happy reader, with fishcakes and potato cakes adding to the spread of granola, scrambled eggs (from the owners' hens) and porridge (with a nip of the good stuff). After a day's walking, guests look forward to home-made cake while spotting squirrels, pheasants, woodpeckers and hens in the garden. (VA)

Seafield Avenue
Grantown-on-Spey PH26 3JF

T: 01479 872065
E: enquiries@thedulaig.com
W: thedulaig.com

BEDROOMS: 3.
OPEN: all year except Christmas, New Year.
FACILITIES: drawing room, dining room, in-room TV (Freesat), 1½-acre garden (pond, summer house), veranda, parking (garage for motorbikes and bicycles), not suitable for disabled.
BACKGROUND MUSIC: quiet Scottish music at breakfast 'with guests' permission'.
LOCATION: 600 yds from Grantown-on-Spey.
CHILDREN: not under 12.
DOGS: only assistance dogs allowed.
CREDIT CARDS: Amex, MC, Visa.
PRICES: B&B doubles from £190, singles from £150.

GULLANE East Lothian

MAP 5:D3

THE BONNIE BADGER

There's a definite Scandi-Scottish style at Tom
and Michaela Kitchin's gastropub-with-rooms.
The impressive beamed restaurant in the former
village inn's horse stables has a stripped-back look,
with designer lighting, original stone walls and a
massive fireplace, while bedrooms might feature
wallpaper with a thistle design or Nordic birch
forests. Michaela's Swedish heritage is clearly
reflected in the interiors while Tom has been busy
in the kitchen, devising menus with his team.
They aren't as fancy as at Kitchin's Michelin-
starred Edinburgh restaurant – more fun dining
than fine dining – but dishes such as spelt-and-
lentil burger, Orkney scallops, and Borders
venison with celeriac fondant are true to his
nature-to-plate values. In fine weather, you can eat
in the garden. Here, five rooms are set in cottages,
where sliding glass doors open to a patio, with
the rest in the main building, featuring perhaps
a four-poster and in-room bath. Downstairs is
an inky-blue bar with leather seats and a lounge
where hungry golfers can tuck into afternoon tea
having played on the world-class courses nearby.

Main Street
Gullane EH31 2AB

T: 01620 621111
E: info@bonniebadger.com
W: bonniebadger.com

BEDROOMS: 13. 5 in adjacent cottages.
OPEN: all year.
FACILITIES: bar, restaurant, outside
dining room, garden room, private
dining room, garden area, in-room
TV (Sky), wedding facilities, bar
and restaurant wheelchair accessible,
adapted toilet.
BACKGROUND MUSIC: in public areas.
LOCATION: centre of village.
CHILDREN: all ages welcomed, cots free,
extra bed £50, children's menu.
DOGS: allowed in specific bedrooms
(£25 a night), in restaurant and pub
area.
CREDIT CARDS: Amex, MC, Visa.
PRICES: B&B doubles from £195
(£300 around key golf event days).
À la carte £40, early set dinner
(5–6.30 pm) £19–£26.

GULLANE East Lothian

MAP 5:D3

GREYWALLS

One of just two Scottish buildings designed by Edwin Lutyens, this crescent-shaped house by Muirfield golf course is the epitome of Edwardian Arts and Crafts comfort. From gardens designed by Gertrude Jekyll, you look across the 18th green to the Firth of Forth. 'The location is superb,' writes a reader, 'the food, comfort and staff were all excellent.' Bedrooms, some in cottages, range from singles to generous doubles with a roll-top bath and walk-in shower. Other readers this year were pleased to be upgraded to a premium room with 'wonderful views over the gardens, golf course and firth'. On cold days a fire burns in a panelled, book-lined drawing room with a grand piano. In Chez Roux restaurant, across four dining rooms, 'classic, perfectly cooked' dishes might include truffled chicken, cauliflower, watercress pesto; chickpea pancakes, ratatouille, caponata dressing. Imaginative breakfasts include Balvenie cured smoked salmon with scrambled egg and herring caviar. 'I had porridge brûlée and will try to recreate the crisp toffee topping over creamy oats.' (Clive Ringrose, Frances Thomas)

Muirfield
Gullane EH31 2EG

T: 01620 842144
E: gm@greywalls.co.uk
W: greywalls.co.uk

BEDROOMS: 23. 4 on ground floor, 6 in cottages 100 yds from main house.
OPEN: all year.
FACILITIES: bar/lounge, drawing room, library, restaurant, in-room TV (Freeview), wedding facilities, function facilities, spa treatments, 6-acre garden, Summer House Tea Room.
BACKGROUND MUSIC: none, pianist on Fri, Sat pm.
LOCATION: 20 miles E of Edinburgh.
CHILDREN: all ages welcomed, free travel cots, extra bed £85.
DOGS: allowed in cottage bedrooms, not unattended, not in public rooms.
CREDIT CARDS: Amex, MC, Visa.
PRICES: B&B doubles from £335. Set-price dinner £45, market menu £45, vegetarian £40, à la carte £55.

INVERGARRY Highland

GLENGARRY CASTLE

A rambling Victorian baronial pile on the shore
of Loch Oich, at the heart of the Great Glen,
with the history-freighted ruins of Invergarry
Castle in its grounds, has been run as a hotel by
the MacCallum family for more than 60 years. A
trusted reader who picked it pin-in-map fashion
was not disappointed: 'It was wonderful.' Within
you will find blazing log fires, patterned carpet,
gilt-framed landscape paintings and stag heads –
the authentic Scottish country house experience.
Some bedrooms are huge, with loch views, lots
of comfy seating, perhaps a four-poster or half-
tester bed. 'Ours was magnificent, with sheets
and blankets rather than horrid duvets, and an
amazing, long bath.' You can relax in 'large and
wonderful lounges' over a drink. 'There is no bar,
so all requests have to be to the reception desk, but
it seems to work.' At dinner, short menus bring a
choice of dishes such as polenta, watercress purée,
roasted garlic; confit Wester Ross salmon; Puy
lentil, potato and vegetable pie. 'We asked the
waiter how long he had been there. It turned out
he was one of the family.' (JB)

Invergarry PH35 4HW

T: 01809 501254
E: castle@glengarry.net
W: glengarry.net

BEDROOMS: 26.
OPEN: 8 Apr–31 Oct.
FACILITIES: library, lounge with bar
service, in-room TV (Freeview),
60-acre grounds (gardens, woodlands,
tennis, rowing boats).
BACKGROUND MUSIC: none.
LOCATION: on A82, 1 mile S of A87
junction in Invergarry.
CHILDREN: all ages welcomed, not in
deluxe bedrooms (ages 3–12 £25, over-
12s £50 on extra bed, children's supper
by arrangement).
DOGS: allowed by arrangement in some
bedrooms (no charge), and hall, not in
deluxe rooms, lounge or library.
CREDIT CARDS: Amex, MC, Visa.
PRICES: B&B doubles from £150, singles
from £100. Fixed-price dinner £38.

IONA Argyll and Bute   MAP 5:D1

ARGYLL HOTEL

You can take a cream tea on the grass in front of this homely hotel on a small, rugged island and spot dolphins in the Sound of Iona. Hands-on owners Wendy and Rob MacManaway and Dafydd and Katy Russon are 'constantly present and available', a reader writes. Within the 19th-century building, bedrooms range from singles to a luxury sea-view room with a wood-burner, armchairs, a bath and walk-in shower. Styling is contemporary with rustic touches. On cold days a fire burns in one of the lounges. 'Soup lunches in the conservatory made a pleasant break to the day.' Chef Tom Morley devises menus of produce from local crofts, sustainably landed fish and abundant fruit and vegetables from the organic garden behind the hotel, beside nunnery ruins. A typical dish: braised beef cheeks, blue cheese mash, garden kale pesto, greens. 'The food was absolutely delicious. Vegetarian options were a visual delight (decorated for example with borage).' St Columba sailed to Iona in 563 in a hide-covered wicker boat. Today's traveller disembarks on foot from the ferry just a stroll from the hotel door. (Alison Forrester)

Isle of Iona PA76 6SJ

T: 01681 700334
E: reception@argyllhoteliona.co.uk
W: argyllhoteliona.co.uk

BEDROOMS: 17. 7 in linked extension.
OPEN: late Mar–late Oct.
FACILITIES: 3 lounges, conservatory, dining room, patchy Wi-Fi in public areas, wedding facilities, seafront lawn, lounges/dining room wheelchair accessible, unadapted toilet, step.
BACKGROUND MUSIC: modern Scottish, 'gentle' jazz, country music in dining room.
LOCATION: village centre.
CHILDREN: all ages welcomed, under-4s free, extra bed £20–£40.
DOGS: max. 2 allowed in bedrooms (£15 per stay), not in dining room or 2 lounges.
CREDIT CARDS: Amex, MC, Visa.
PRICES: B&B doubles from £100, singles from £77. À la carte £35. 1-night bookings often refused.

KILBERRY Argyll and Bute

MAP 5:D1

KILBERRY INN

'Wonderfully remote', this delightful restaurant-with-rooms is reached down a winding, scenic single-track road with views to the Inner Hebrides. David Wilson and Clare Johnson's whitewashed former croft under a corrugated red tin roof has simple rooms, with a walk-in shower and direct access to a courtyard of raised beds planted with herbs and flowers. The star attraction is the 'tremendous food, which thoroughly lived up to expectations', with three-course menus created by 'fantastic' cook Clare and served in the rustic dining room, with its low, beamed ceilings and stone walls. A typical meal might include shellfish bisque; Gigha halibut with white beans, olives and parsley; rhubarb frangipane tart, crème fraîche. Breakfast brings home-made granola and preserves, Auchinbreck dry-cured bacon, Skipness smoked salmon, Kintyre eggs. The isolated location has its drawbacks. Wi-Fi is patchy, you might have to step outside to get a mobile signal, and the red telephone box outside is defunct. With typical humour, David bought it from BT for a princely pound and established it as perhaps the world's smallest bar. (TH, and others)

Kilberry
Tarbert PA29 6YD

T: 01880 770223
E: relax@kilberryinn.com
W: kilberryinn.com

BEDROOMS: 5. All on ground floor.
OPEN: Tues–Sun mid-Mar–end Sept, Tues–Sat Oct, Fri/Sat Nov/Dec, New Year (closed Christmas).
FACILITIES: restaurant, snug (wood-burning stove), variable Wi-Fi, 4G signal in car park, in-room TV (Freeview), small garden.
BACKGROUND MUSIC: in restaurant at dinner.
LOCATION: 16 miles NW of Tarbert, on B8024.
CHILDREN: not under 12.
DOGS: allowed by arrangement in 2 bedrooms (no charge), not in public rooms.
CREDIT CARDS: MC, Visa.
PRICES: D,B&B doubles £250, singles £160. À la carte £37. 1-night bookings refused Fri and Sat in busier months.

KINGUSSIE Highland

MAP 5:C2

THE CROSS AT KINGUSSIE

♕ Previous César winner

'Wonderful, innovative and perfectly cooked food' combine with 'charming and sociable hosts' in this 'sensational' restaurant-with-rooms by a bubbling burn in the Cairngorms national park. Celia and Derek Kitchingman's former Victorian tweed mill attracts high praise from readers. 'We are foodies and this is some of the best we have ever eaten.' 'We have stayed many times and it has never let us down.' In the beamed, stone-walled dining room, David Skiggs's nightly three-course menu includes dishes such as venison, creamed cabbage, braised oxtail, pickled beets, celeriac, accompanied by a 'very good and reasonable wine list'. After dinner, retire to one of the larger rooms which overlook the burn as it rushes by. 'The only noise was the wind in the trees and the shimmer of running water.' All the bedrooms have a cottagey feel, soft-hued decor, and now a large walk-in power shower. There are cosy lounges with books and a terrace by the burn, frequented by herons, red squirrel and roe deer. Or head out to work off those calories with a hike in the national park – after an amazing breakfast, of course. (Peter Scott, CB, JH)

Ardbroilach Road
Kingussie PH21 1LB

T: 01540 661166
E: relax@thecross.co.uk
W: thecross.co.uk

BEDROOMS: 8.
OPEN: Tues–Sat, Feb–early Jan, closed Christmas but open for New Year.
FACILITIES: 2 lounges, restaurant, in-room TV (Freeview), 4-acre grounds (terraced garden, woodland), restaurant wheelchair accessible.
BACKGROUND MUSIC: none.
LOCATION: 440 yds from village centre.
CHILDREN: all ages welcomed.
DOGS: not allowed.
CREDIT CARDS: Amex, MC, Visa.
PRICES: D,B&B doubles from £200 (B&B sometimes available by arrangement). Fixed-price 3-course dinner £55, 6-course tasting menu £65.

KIRKBEAN Dumfries and Galloway   MAP 5:E2

CAVENS

Guests feel 'very cared for' at Jane and Angus Fordyce's Georgian country house, which stands in mature grounds close to the empty beaches of the Solway coast. 'It is a genuine oasis of tranquillity.' Public rooms are filled with antiques, portraits, clocks, ornaments … all the trappings of an elegant but lived-in private home. 'We had a lovely stay in this fabulous hotel,' wrote readers who had probably the grandest room, Criffel. Light-filled Oswald room has toile de Jouy wallpaper and a separate sitting room. Both of these rooms have a sofa that converts to a bed for a child. If you would like direct garden access, go for ground-floor Solway, with bath and wet-room shower. All rooms are supplied with locally made biscuits and good china for tea and coffee. Angus's 'very tasty', nightly, no-choice menu (let them know if you have dietary requirements) might include hand-dived scallops, venison, wild Solway salmon or a terrific steak. At breakfast there are local sausages and black pudding, locally smoked fish, organic eggs from Mrs McMyn's Lohmann browns – or from happy hens at the bottom of the garden. (David Sowden, CA)

Kirkbean
Dumfries DG2 8AA

T: 01387 880234
E: enquiries@cavens.com
W: cavens.com

BEDROOMS: 6. 1 on ground floor.
OPEN: Mar–Nov, exclusive use by groups at New Year.
FACILITIES: 2 sitting rooms, dining room, wine cellar, meeting facilities, in-room TV (Freeview), 10-acre grounds.
BACKGROUND MUSIC: light classical all day in 1 sitting room, dining room.
LOCATION: in village, 12 miles S of Dumfries.
CHILDREN: all ages welcomed, free cots, sofa beds in some rooms.
DOGS: allowed by arrangement, not in public rooms or unattended in bedrooms.
CREDIT CARDS: MC, Visa.
PRICES: D,B&B doubles from £290, singles from £232, family from £425. Dinner £35 for non-residents. 1-night bookings may be refused Easter, bank holidays.

KYLESKU Highland

KYLESKU HOTEL

♥Previous César winner

In a 'very beautiful spot' on the remote, rocky shores of Loch Glendhu, an old coaching inn has been transformed into a modern hotel that takes full advantage of the beauty of its setting. Former owners Tanja Lister and Sonia Virechauveix have just sold to Highland Coast Hotels, but we are assured that no major changes are planned. 'The relaxed hospitality is the ideal match for the natural beauty outside,' writes one reader. 'All the staff we met were very good indeed,' adds another. Bedrooms have a chic simplicity. Most desired are the loch-facing rooms from which to spy otters, dolphins, golden eagles – and the best are in the annexe, two with balcony. Guests enjoy the views from the terrace, bar and restaurant, where 25-mile menus specialise in the catch you might see landed on the old ferry slipway. 'Food was first rate. They have much fresh seafood and understand the need to keep recipes simple.' Typical dishes include hand-dived scallops, fish supper, venison. Veggies have their own menu. Breakfast brings the full Highland, whisky-cured hot smoked salmon, kedgeree, oysters. Walkers can take a picnic and be glad of laundry and drying facilities on their return. (SJ, and others)

Kylesku IV27 4HW

T: 01971 502231
E: info@kyleskuhotel.co.uk
W: kyleskuhotel.co.uk

BEDROOMS: 11. 4 in annexe, 1 suitable for disabled.
OPEN: all year except 20 Dec–11 Feb, ring to enquire about Christmas and New Year.
FACILITIES: lounge, bar, restaurant (vegetarian/vegan menus), in-room TV (Freeview), small garden (tables for outside eating), area of lounge and dining room wheelchair accessible, toilet not adapted.
BACKGROUND MUSIC: from 10 am, in bar and half the dining area.
LOCATION: 10 miles S of Scourie.
CHILDREN: all ages welcomed, cot £15, extra bed £40.
DOGS: allowed in bedrooms (£15 a night to max. £60 a stay), and in public rooms.
CREDIT CARDS: MC, Visa.
PRICES: B&B doubles from £137.50, singles from £100, family from £170. À la carte £50.

MUTHILL Perth and Kinross

BARLEY BREE

At the heart of the conservation village of 'Mew-thil', with views of the Earn valley and the Grampians, this former inn is run by Fabrice and Alison Bouteloup as a 'delightful restaurant-with-rooms'. Fabrice spent boyhood summers on his grandmother's farm in Mayenne, and cooks prime Scottish produce with a French accent. You can eat in the beamed dining room, its walls adorned with scintillating fishy artwork by sculptor Sam MacDonald, or in the sunshine, alfresco. Short daily-changing 'delicious menus' might include hand-dived West Coast scallops, slow-cooked pork cheek, and Fabrice's signature tarte Tatin. Children have their own menu; a family room sleeps four. Contemporary double rooms have a walk-in shower, bottled water, a miniature of own-label whisky. One dual-aspect superior double has a roll-top bath and a view of a ruined medieval church tower. Breakfast brings home-baked bread, free-range eggs, sausages from Simon Howie. Walkers and shooting parties can take a packed lunch, then return for a dram by a blazing fire. Returning guests say it is their 'most eagerly anticipated stay' in Scotland. (SJ, and others)

6 Willoughby Street
Muthill PH5 2AB

T: 01764 681451
E: info@barleybree.com
W: barleybree.com

BEDROOMS: 6.
OPEN: all year except 24–26 Dec, various dates throughout year (see website), restaurant closed Mon, Tues.
FACILITIES: lounge bar, restaurant (vegetarian menu), in-room TV (Freeview), variable Wi-Fi, small terrace and lawn, drying facilities, gun cupboard, restaurant wheelchair accessible, toilet not adapted.
BACKGROUND MUSIC: none.
LOCATION: village centre.
CHILDREN: all ages welcomed, cot, baby-changing, children's menu, family room.
DOGS: assistance dogs only.
CREDIT CARDS: Amex, MC, Visa.
PRICES: B&B doubles from £99, singles from £80. À la carte £45.

PEAT INN Fife   MAP 5:D3

THE PEAT INN

♔ Previous César winner

Amid rolling countryside, this unassuming roadside inn is so renowned for its outstanding food that it gave its name to the hamlet that grew up around it. Owned by chef Geoffrey Smeddle and his wife, Katherine, it regained its Michelin star (first won in 1987) in 2010, and has held it ever since. Original features of the 18th-century building – raftered ceiling, exposed-stone walls – form the backdrop to a modern elegance of white walls, soft-grey and teal-blue furnishings, and contemporary art. Bedrooms, in a separate building and all split-level bar one, are 'light and comfortable' with views over fields. In calm colours, they're restful spaces, 'even on a rainy evening, a lovely light place to sit'. Bathrooms, most shower only, are big and modern. Drinks are served in the lounge before a 'fantastic' dinner in one of three dining rooms. When our inspectors called, they enjoyed 'perfect fresh asparagus with lemon en croûte' from the tasting menu. Or you can pick inspired dishes such as home-cured sea trout pastrami with cucumber and grapefruit, and roe deer with butternut squash and passion fruit purée from the à la carte menu.

Peat Inn
Cupar KY15 5LH

T: 01334 840206
E: stay@thepeatinn.co.uk
W: thepeatinn.co.uk

BEDROOMS: 8. All suites, on ground floor in annexe, 7 split-level, 1 suitable for disabled.
OPEN: all year except 24–26 Dec and 1–6 Jan, restaurant closed Sun/Mon.
FACILITIES: lounge in restaurant, in-room TV (terrestrial), ½-acre garden, EV charging, restaurant wheelchair accessible, adapted toilet.
BACKGROUND MUSIC: in restaurant.
LOCATION: in hamlet, 7 miles SE of Cupar and 6 miles SW of St Andrews.
CHILDREN: all ages welcomed, extra bed for under-12s £65, no under-7s at dinner.
DOGS: not allowed.
CREDIT CARDS: Amex, MC, Visa.
PRICES: B&B doubles from £245, singles from £225. À la carte £65, tasting menu £78.

PERTH Perth and Kinross

MAP 5:D2

⚜ WOODCROFT HOUSE

NEW

César award: Scottish guest house of the year

On a private no-through road, with views from its elevated position over the pointy roofscape of Perth to the mountains, Claire Dingwall Slater and Alick Slater's Arts and Crafts-style Victorian guest house enters the Guide this year with lavish praise from our inspectors. 'Claire's lively, friendly personality and enthusiasm are refreshing to experience.' Smart bedrooms have contemporary decor, antiques, a coffee machine, mini-fridge and home-made treats. 'A sizeable room had a small integral lounge, a beautifully tiled and fitted bathroom.' The pièce de résistance is a suite with emperor bed, a bathroom with cast iron slipper bath and walk-in shower, a seating area in the turret. Dinner, served in the candlelit dining room, must be ordered 48 hours in advance, from extensive menus. 'Pea velouté, a grilled scallop, roast salmon and duck did not disappoint, and led to wonderful cranachan.' Venison is sourced from the owners' deer park. Bring your own wine; they don't charge corkage. Eggs for breakfast are laid by the hens that forage in a garden with 'lush lawns, vibrant flower borders and majestic monkey puzzle tree'.

Bellwood Park
Perth PH2 7AJ

T: 07468 606363
E: claire@woodcroft-house.com
W: woodcroft-house.com

BEDROOMS: 3.
OPEN: all year.
FACILITIES: lounge, dining room, in-room smart TV (Freeview), large garden.
BACKGROUND MUSIC: in lounge and dining room.
LOCATION: 15 mins' walk, across the River Tay, from the centre.
CHILDREN: not under 18.
DOGS: not allowed.
CREDIT CARDS: Amex, MC, Visa.
PRICES: B&B doubles from £190.
À la carte £50, plant-based menu £37.

PITLOCHRY Perth and Kinross

MAP 5:D2

THE GREEN PARK

Ω Previous César winner

In lawned gardens lapped by Loch Faskally, the
McMenemie family's Victorian country house
hotel caters especially to evergreen guests who
enjoy a gentler pace of life. Year-round activity
breaks include painting, creative writing,
crosswords and photography. Binoculars are on
hand for wildlife spotters, and when it's time
for a little something, biscuits are laid out on
the sideboard, with tea and coffee in vacuum
flasks, and home-baked cakes in the afternoon.
There are books and nooks for a quiet read, and
a jigsaw always a work in progress. Bedrooms
(16 on the ground floor, most with loch view
and four with balcony) are in the main house,
the sympathetically designed Tower Wing and
modern Garden Wing. All have bright fabrics,
modern artwork and a fridge. Sherry is served ad
lib before a dinner cooked by long-serving chef
Richard Murray – maybe roast sirloin of Speyside
beef, cold gammon salad, pancetta-wrapped
guineafowl in whisky cream sauce, or haddock
and chips. Give them notice if you have special
dietary needs. After breakfast you might sit out by
the loch, go walking – or even make a splash with
some wild swimming.

Clunie Bridge Road
Pitlochry PH16 5JY

T: 01796 473248
E: bookings@thegreenpark.co.uk
W: thegreenpark.co.uk

BEDROOMS: 51. 16 on ground floor,
1 suitable for disabled.
OPEN: all year except Christmas.
FACILITIES: 2 lifts, lounge bar, main
lounge, sun lounge, in-room TV
(BT, Freeview), 3-acre garden,
EV charging, public areas wheelchair
accessible, adapted toilet.
BACKGROUND MUSIC: none.
LOCATION: ½ mile N of town centre.
CHILDREN: all ages welcomed, under-
3s free, extra bed £20–£30.
DOGS: allowed in bedrooms (no
charge), not in public rooms.
CREDIT CARDS: MC, Visa.
PRICES: per person B&B from £94 (no
supplement for singles). Set-price
dinner £30–£35 (3/4 courses).

SEE ALSO SHORTLIST

PITLOCHRY Perth and Kinross   MAP 5:D2

KNOCKENDARROCH HOTEL

♘ Previous César winner

'A stately house with a fairly large garden, quite close to town' is how John Stewart, founder of Pitlochry Festival Theatre, described this Victorian baronial mansion which in 1951 hosted the first performances in a marquee. Now the festival has moved to the other side of the river, but Struan and Louise Lothian's small hotel makes a good base for those attending, as well as for hiking and biking. This year they launch new dog-friendly bedrooms in a timber annexe, with under-floor heating and private patio; plus a huge suite with epic views. Main-house rooms are more traditional, some with a balcony from which to enjoy mountain vistas; binoculars are provided. Log fires burn in lounges with 'very comfortable seating' and malt whisky galore. Here, 'mouth-watering canapés were served before the delicious three-course dinner'. You can dine to the sound of music in the restaurant or in the new orangery. Nick Imrie's short menu might include guineafowl with Cheddar mustard dauphinoise, assiette of seafood, Highland beef, a vegan option. At breakfast a 'wide choice includes top-class smoked salmon and scrambled eggs'. (RG, and others)

Higher Oakfield
Pitlochry PH16 5HT

T: 01796 473473
E: bookings@knockendarroch.co.uk
W: knockendarroch.co.uk

BEDROOMS: 18. 2 on ground floor, 4 in annexe.
OPEN: Feb–early Dec.
FACILITIES: 2 lounges, dining room with orangery extension, in-room TV (Freeview), 2-acre wooded garden, bicycle storage, EV charging, unsuitable for disabled.
BACKGROUND MUSIC: at dinner.
LOCATION: central.
CHILDREN: not under 10.
DOGS: allowed in some annexe rooms by arrangement (£15 a night up to max. £60), not in main house.
CREDIT CARDS: Amex, MC, Visa.
PRICES: B&B doubles from £185. Set-price dinner £49. 1-night bookings sometimes refused Sat.

SEE ALSO SHORTLIST

PORT APPIN Argyll and Bute

THE AIRDS HOTEL

✪ Previous César winner

'Spectacular views' across Loch Linnhe to the Morvern mountains are available from some of the rooms, from the fine-dining restaurant (Relais & Châteaux), and from the waterside gardens just across the road from this former ferry inn. 'The fairly simple exterior belies the warm, comfortable interior,' write trusted Guide hoteliers on a busman's holiday. Bedrooms have traditional and contemporary furnishings, designer fabrics and complimentary whisky mac. Prices are high, and a reader felt unforgiving after a chaotic night, when the ship seemed rudderless, but owners Shaun and Jenny McKivragan really care. Lounges and suites have been upgraded and, in the kitchen, Calum Innes creates dishes such as lemon and basil-crusted brill, linguine, cucumber, oyster, caviar beurre blanc, as well as tempting plant-based options. One guest felt it was 'a little elaborate when staying four nights' and was very fish heavy, another relished 'every beautifully presented bite'. Breakfast proved 'equally delicious, from freshly squeezed fruit juices to the bannocks, smoked haddock to free-range eggs'. (Carol Bulloch, and others)

Port Appin PA38 4DF

T: 01631 730236
E: airds@airds-hotel.com
W: airds-hotel.com

BEDROOMS: 11. 2 on ground floor, plus 2 self-catering cottages.
OPEN: all year, restaurant closed Mon/ Tues Nov–end Jan (open Christmas and New Year).
FACILITIES: 2 lounges, conservatory, whisky bar, restaurant (vegetarian menu), wedding facilities, in-room TV (Freeview), spa treatments, ½-acre garden, unsuitable for disabled.
BACKGROUND MUSIC: none.
LOCATION: 20 miles N of Oban.
CHILDREN: all ages welcomed, under-2s free, extra bed £85 a night with high tea, no under-8s at dinner.
DOGS: allowed in bedrooms by arrangement (£10 per night, not unattended) and conservatory.
CREDIT CARDS: Amex, MC, Visa.
PRICES: D,B&B doubles from £370, singles from £335. Set-priced dinner £70.

PORT APPIN Argyll and Bute   MAP 5:D1

THE PIERHOUSE

There are glorious views to Lismore and Mull
across Loch Linnhe from the dining room and
sun terraces of this hotel in a 'magic, peaceful
place', once a drop-off point for steamships.
Today, lobsters come fresh from the creels at
the end of the pier, which is overlooked by the
newly furnished Ferry bar. The owner, Gordon
Campbell Gray (see also The Three Chimneys,
Dunvegan), came aboard two years ago without
rocking the boat; public rooms are hung with
works from his art collection. Four cliff-facing
king-size/twin rooms look into a rockery; others
have 'wonderful sea views'. All are simple and
pleasing with a super-comfy bed. Superior loch-
facing rooms have lounge seating, a combined
bath and shower. All now have smart TV. Chef
Michael Leathley sources ingredients from
within 50 miles – if not 50 feet – and pescatarian
dishes include a shellfish platter, Loch Leven
mussels, roast monkfish and Loch Linnhe
langoustine stew. There is game in season, too,
and imaginative vegan options, 'good and helpful'
service. After a breakfast of Inverawe kipper, be
sure to see 'the amazing Castle Stalker from the
Monty Python film'. (DG, and others)

Port Appin PA38 4DE

T: 01631 730302
E: reservations@pierhousehotel.co.uk
W: pierhousehotel.co.uk

BEDROOMS: 12.
OPEN: all year except 24–26 Dec.
FACILITIES: snug, lounge, bar,
restaurant (vegan menu), private
dining room, in-room TV (Freeview),
wedding facilities, sauna, spa
treatments, sun terraces, moorings,
unsuitable for disabled.
BACKGROUND MUSIC: in bar and
restaurant.
LOCATION: in village, 20 miles N of
Oban.
CHILDREN: all ages welcomed, extra
bed for under-13s £30, cots and high
chairs available.
DOGS: well-behaved dogs allowed in
2 bedrooms (not unattended, £15 per
night), bar and dining room, not in
main restaurant.
CREDIT CARDS: Amex, MC, Visa.
PRICES: B&B doubles from £125 (single
occupancy of cliff-facing room, Sun–
Thurs, Nov–Mar, £85). À la carte £45.

PORTPATRICK Dumfries and Galloway   MAP 5:E1

KNOCKINAAM LODGE

A 'wonderful country house hotel in a peaceful location by the sea', this former Victorian hunting lodge comes with panelled walls, log fires, period furniture, the obligatory stag's head, a dazzling array of malt whiskies, and views across the water to Northern Ireland. It is said that Churchill and Eisenhower met here to plan the D-Day landings (a claim also made by Glenapp Castle, see Ballantrae). True or not, Churchill did stay as a guest of the Orr-Ewing family, and you can book his room, with its sleigh bed and the concrete soaking tub in which the great man would rehearse his speeches as he wallowed. Other rooms may have a lounge area, a half-tester, and either sea view or garden views. Chef Tony Pierce cooks a daily-changing five-course dinner, using local and home-grown ingredients in dishes such as slow-roast Gressingham duck, salt-baked celeriac, sweet-and-sour red cabbage, thyme jus. 'The food and wine were excellent and imaginative.' Readers praise owners Sian and David Ibbotson and their 'professional staff' who 'do all they can to ensure that all guests enjoy their stay'. (William Reid, PF, and others)

Portpatrick DG9 9AD

T: 01776 810471
E: reservations@knockinaamlodge. com
W: knockinaamlodge.com

BEDROOMS: 12. 2 in self-catering lodge overlooking beach.
OPEN: all year.
FACILITIES: 2 lounges, bar, restaurant, in-room TV (Freeview), wedding facilities, 20-acre grounds (garden, beach), public areas wheelchair accessible.
BACKGROUND MUSIC: in restaurant in evening.
LOCATION: 3 miles S of Portpatrick.
CHILDREN: all ages welcomed, extra bed £55 including high tea, no under-12s in dining room.
DOGS: max. 1 allowed in some bedrooms (£30 per stay), in grounds, not in public rooms.
CREDIT CARDS: Amex, MC, Visa.
PRICES: D,B&B doubles from £350, singles from £195. Set lunch £40 (Sun £35). 1-night bookings refused certain weekends, Christmas, New Year.

PORTREE Highland

MAP 5:C1

VIEWFIELD HOUSE

A bravura Victorian rebuild of a Georgian country house in wooded grounds above Portree Bay and the Sound of Raasay, Viewfield has been home to generations of Macdonalds, and is filled with family possessions and mementos. The grand entrance hall is a Who's Zoo of trophies, fair game and foul. Affable host Hugh may now be 'the lesser spotted' Macdonald, while his daughter Iona, and her husband, Jasper Buxton, welcome guests, but he will still share his local knowledge over a glass of single malt by the drawing-room fire. Each traditionally furnished bedroom has its own special character. Two, with shower room, are in the old stables block. None has a TV. The impressive dual-aspect master bedroom is huge, with fine antiques, and can sleep a family. Breakfast on porridge and a full Scottish with haggis, black pudding and tattie scone, under the gaze of ancestors. At night you can opt for a supper of soup and cheese, or head into wonderfully quaint Portree. The friendly staff can show you a shortcut through the woods (not recommended after dark or if you're oot yer tree). Sailing trips can be arranged aboard the family yacht, Breeze.

Viewfield Road
Portree
Isle of Skye IV51 9EU

T: 01478 612217
E: info@viewfieldhouse.com
W: viewfieldhouse.com

BEDROOMS: 13. 1 on ground floor (suitable for disabled), 2 in adjacent converted stables.
OPEN: Apr–Oct.
FACILITIES: drawing room, morning/TV room, dining room, 20-acre grounds (croquet, swings), public rooms wheelchair accessible.
BACKGROUND MUSIC: none.
LOCATION: S side of Portree.
CHILDREN: all ages welcomed, extra bed for under-12s £10.
DOGS: allowed in bedrooms (no charge), drawing room if other guests don't object, not in dining room.
CREDIT CARDS: MC, Visa.
PRICES: B&B doubles from £164, singles from £82. Supper (soup, cheese, charcuterie) £15.50. 1-night bookings only on application in high season.

SEE ALSO SHORTLIST

RANNOCH STATION Perth and Kinross   MAP 5:D2

MOOR OF RANNOCH – RESTAURANT & ROOMS

♥ Previous César winner

Alight from the Caledonian sleeper from London in time for breakfast at Stephanie and Scott Meikle's dog-friendly restaurant-with-rooms and you find yourself in a wilderness landscape of lochs and lochans. If you think 'remote' is what you use to switch channels, know that here there is no TV or radio signal, and no Wi-Fi. What you will find are comfy lounges with a blazing fire, and a 'well-stocked bar' with 110 Scottish malts. Bedrooms in shades of heather or peat are smart-functional, with thoughtful extras such as 'powerful binoculars, a decanter of local malt whisky, truffle chocolates and oatmeal biscuits'. The Meikles are passionate about provenance, using locally reared and artisan produce, home-grown leaves and foraged ingredients. The nightly-changing menu might include whisky-, muscovado- and orange-cured salmon; slow-cooked goat shoulder, aubergine, courgette, pistachio crumb. 'Steph's cooking is amazing.' People come here for the dark skies and wild beauty and they're not disappointed in this 'special stay in a special place'. 'This is comfortable isolation at its very best.' (AB, and others)

Rannoch Station PH17 2QA

T: 01882 633238
E: info@moorofrannoch.co.uk
W: moorofrannoch.co.uk

BEDROOMS: 5.
OPEN: Thurs–Mon until 23 Nov 2021, 10 Feb–22 Nov 2022.
FACILITIES: lounge, bar, conservatory dining room, no Wi-Fi or TV, unsuitable for disabled.
BACKGROUND MUSIC: none.
LOCATION: on a single-track, dead-end road, 40 miles W of Pitlochry.
CHILDREN: all ages welcomed, extra bed £40.
DOGS: welcomed in all areas of the hotel (no charge), max. 2 per room.
CREDIT CARDS: Amex, MC, Visa.
PRICES: D,B&B doubles £320, singles £260. Fixed-price dinner non-res £60.

ST OLA Orkney Islands   MAP 5:A3

THE FOVERAN

It's a family affair in this restaurant-with-rooms with glorious views across the sheltered natural harbour of Scapa Flow to the southern Orkney islands. Paul Doull is the chef, his wife, Helen, front-of-house, while Paul's brother Hamish, and Hamish's wife, Shirley, take care of day-to-day operations. The many-windowed, light-drenched dining room (in the 'simmer dim' around the solstice it is never really dark) features a tapestry woven by cousin Leila Thomson as well as photographs by Leila's daughter Johan. It is here that Paul's farm-to-fork (or boat-to-plate) menus showcase the best island produce: maybe pan-seared scallops; loin of lamb with plum and rhubarb sauce, or a steak flamed in peaty Highland Park whisky. While food is the main event, the ground-level bedrooms are comfortable, with natural Scottish fabrics and paraben-free toiletries. Breakfast includes porridge, local free-range eggs, sausages and black pudding, smoked salmon, the full Orcadian, home-baked bread, bannocks and home-made preserves. A visit to Britain's most northerly cathedral on this island of myth and abundant wildlife is not to be missed.

Kirkwall
St Ola KW15 1SF

T: 01856 872389
E: info@thefoveran.com
W: thefoveran.com

BEDROOMS: 8. All on ground floor, 1 single with private bathroom across hall.
OPEN: Apr–early Oct, by arrangement at other times, restaurant closed variable times Apr, Oct.
FACILITIES: lounge, restaurant, in-room TV, 12-acre grounds (private rock beach), restaurant wheelchair accessible, adapted toilet.
BACKGROUND MUSIC: local/Scottish traditional in restaurant.
LOCATION: 3 miles SW of Kirkwall.
CHILDREN: all ages welcomed, ask for details when booking.
DOGS: not allowed.
CREDIT CARDS: MC, Visa.
PRICES: B&B doubles from £130, singles from £95. À la carte £37. 1-night bookings refused May–Sept (phone to check).

SANQUHAR Dumfries and Galloway

MAP 5:E2

BLACKADDIE HOUSE

Traditional hospitality, home comforts and creative modern cooking are a winning combination at this mellow-stone manse with the River Nith surging past the garden. On arrival you'll find home-made shortbread, Scottish mineral water and a fruit basket in your bedroom, with maybe grapes from the greenhouse. The River Suite has a king-size bed, its own small kitchen and a lounge with French doors to a waterside patio. Dual-aspect Grouse has an antique four-poster. One reader found the 'beige, khaki and eau de nil' decor made her room with 'large beige bathroom' seem 'awfully dingy'. Her spirits were restored with the set dinner, 'excellent on both nights'. Ian McAndrew's nightly-changing menu offers either/or choices such as slow-braised then roast pork belly, pulled pork, roast apple purée. One reader's beetroot sorbet was the 'first star of the show', followed by 'extremely fresh and delicious' trout with pea purée. Produce is locally sourced or home grown. The hotel is very dog-friendly,. You can fish for salmon or take a 20-minute drive to Drumlanrig Castle. NOTE: As the Guide went to press, the hotel was in the process of being sold.

Blackaddie Road
Sanquhar DG4 6JJ

T: 01659 50270
E: ian@blackaddiehotel.co.uk
W: www.blackaddiehotel.co.uk

BEDROOMS: 7. Plus two 2-bed self-catering cottages, 1 suitable for disabled.
OPEN: all year except 24–27 Dec.
FACILITIES: bar, restaurant, breakfast/function room, library, conservatory, in-room TV (Freeview), wedding facilities, 2-acre grounds, cookery school, fishing, EV charging, public rooms wheelchair accessible.
BACKGROUND MUSIC: in public areas.
LOCATION: outskirts of village.
CHILDREN: all ages welcomed, under-5s/cots free.
DOGS: allowed in most bedrooms (£10 per night), public rooms, not in restaurant.
CREDIT CARDS: Amex, MC, Visa.
PRICES: B&B doubles from £135, singles from £115. Fixed-price menu £65, tasting menus £75/£90.

SCARISTA Western Isles   MAP 5:B1

SCARISTA HOUSE

♵ Previous César winner

The only sounds are the soughing of the sea and the cry of gulls at this remote Georgian manse in an 'extraordinary setting' between a three-mile sandy beach and heather-clad mountains. Patricia and Tim Martin are good, hands-on hosts. The house feels 'a bit lived in', with 'a homely atmosphere' and comfy sitting room, just the place for an indulgent afternoon tea by the fire. Bedrooms – three in an annexe with picture windows to frame the spectacular sea view – are entirely traditional. Elsa has antique furniture, views over the garden to the beach, and from the bathroom to Taransay and the North Harris hills. Families opt for Flora, with king-size bed, a single bed, a sofa bed in the sitting room, and a galley kitchen for self-catering. But Patricia's cooking is too good to miss. Everything from bread and biscuits to cakes and ice cream are home-made and the Martins are praised for their 'noble insistence on high-quality, largely organic ingredients'. A nightly-changing no-choice menu might include navarin of Lewis lamb or marmalade frangipane tart. Given notice, they catered royally for a vegan Guide insider.

Scarista
Isle of Harris HS3 3HX

T: 01859 550238
E: bookings@scaristahouse.com
W: scaristahouse.com

BEDROOMS: 6. 3 in annexe.
OPEN: 1 Mar–30 Nov.
FACILITIES: drawing room, library, 2 dining rooms, Wi-Fi not available in some bedrooms, wedding facilities, 1-acre garden, unsuitable for disabled.
BACKGROUND MUSIC: none.
LOCATION: 15 miles SW of Tarbert.
CHILDREN: all ages welcomed, extra bed £20.
DOGS: allowed in bedrooms (no charge) and 1 public room.
CREDIT CARDS: Amex, MC, Visa.
PRICES: B&B doubles from £246, singles from £190. Set dinner £49.50–£57. Advance 1-night bookings refused.

EDDRACHILLES HOTEL

The breathtakingly scenic North Coast 500 road passes the driveway to this 18th-century manse, now a small, friendly hotel, gazing over Badcall Bay. Owners Fiona and Richard Trevor are welcoming hosts: 'Fantastic hospitality from the moment we arrived,' runs a typical comment. There is not much of a mobile signal, but a gentle programme of improvements this year sees Wi-Fi throughout, and new paths, plantings and seats in the grounds. Bedrooms are more about comfort than high style. Most have views over moorland, mountain and across the water to Assynt. All guests can enjoy glorious vistas from a 'lovely conservatory where afternoon cakes were served at no extra charge'. There are 60-odd malt whiskies in a lounge/bar hung with works by local artists. Chef Trevor Williams, who left in 2017, is back, cooking a short menu of dishes such as Highland rib-eye steak, pan-seared hake, and always a vegetarian option. 'The food is excellent and the menu changes daily.' Another reader writes: '"Efficient informality" may seem like an oxymoron, but the Trevors and their team have mastered the art.' (Jacqui Baker, John Arbuckle, and others)

Badcall Bay
Scourie IV27 4TH

T: 01971 502080
E: info@eddrachilles.com
W: eddrachilles.com

BEDROOMS: 10. 4 on ground floor.
OPEN: 28 Mar–18 Oct.
FACILITIES: large reception, bar/lounge, sun lounge, restaurant, in-room TV (Freeview), wedding facilities, 3-acre grounds, public rooms wheelchair accessible.
BACKGROUND MUSIC: none.
LOCATION: 2 miles S of Scourie, on the North Coast 500 route.
CHILDREN: all ages welcomed, 2 rooms can accommodate cot or bed for toddler (max. 23 months, no charge).
DOGS: well-behaved dogs allowed in bedrooms (£10 per stay), public rooms (part of restaurant, subject to 'three barks' rule).
CREDIT CARDS: MC, Visa.
PRICES: B&B doubles from £105, singles from £87.50. Set-price dinner £35–£40.

SEE ALSO SHORTLIST

KINLOCH LODGE

🏵 Previous César winner

'A great place to stay if you're after excellent food and high standards of comfort', the family home of Lord Macdonald and his wife, cookery writer Lady Claire Macdonald, is 'in a beautiful position' on the shores of Loch Na Dal. A former hunting lodge, it is filled with portraits and memorabilia and is run by daughter Isabella. Main-house bedrooms and suites, many with a loch view and a bath and walk-in shower, have fine antiques. Those in a newer extension are more contemporary. 'Our ground-floor room had its own entrance, so was ideal for our border terrier,' writes a Guide trusty. Chef Jordan Webb shares Lady Macdonald's passion for seasonal food sourced locally. A short nightly menu (one fish, one meat, one veggie dish) might include rolled saddle of lamb, wild garlic potatoes, port and rosemary. Our reader points out that a £58 bottle of red was 'very much at the cheaper end of an extensive list'. 'The staff were all courteous, friendly and helpful,' another reader writes. There is a 'gracious lounge', a small bar, with a grazing menu. Foraging, fishing and deer stalking can be arranged. (Robert Gower, Christine Hughes)

Sleat
Isle of Skye IV43 8QY

T: 01471 833333
E: reservations@kinloch-lodge.co.uk
W: kinloch-lodge.co.uk

BEDROOMS: 19. 10 in North Lodge, 9 in South Lodge, 3 on ground floor, 1 suitable for disabled.
OPEN: all year.
FACILITIES: 3 drawing rooms, whisky bar, dining room, in-room TV (Sky), wedding facilities, cookery courses, 'huge' grounds on edge of loch, public rooms wheelchair accessible.
BACKGROUND MUSIC: in dining room.
LOCATION: on shore of Loch Na Dal on E coast of Skye, not far off A851.
CHILDREN: all ages welcomed, extra bed £45.
DOGS: in bedrooms only (£20 per night, not unattended).
CREDIT CARDS: MC, Visa.
PRICES: B&B doubles from £280. Set dinner (5 courses) £75.

SPEAN BRIDGE Highland

MAP 5:C2

SMIDDY HOUSE

Whichever way you approach, it is a scenic drive to Robert Bryson and Glen Russell's restaurant-with-rooms, at a crossroads in a south Highlands village. Head north for Inverness and Skye, east for the Cairngorms, or just stay and enjoy the 'warm welcome, excellent draught beer, comfortable room and, of course, the food'. Guide inspectors, who were treated to tea and cakes in the lounge on arrival, assure us that double glazing cuts out traffic noise. The four bedrooms have pretty, cottage-cum-contemporary decor; one at the rear has distant views of Aonach Mòr in the Nevis range. A suite in the old smithy workshop has a lounge and double bedroom, spiral stairs to a mezzanine with twin beds; a shower room. Robert is the perfect host, 'charming and full of information'. At night, Glen's menus are a showcase for Scottish produce, maybe Mull scallops, herb-roasted chicken, Wester Ross salmon with crab ravioli, lemongrass and ginger velouté. 'The evening meal was delicious. Robert even provided us with a breakfast for the following morning, as we had to be away early – how thoughtful.' (Lynn Middleton, PB)

Roy Bridge Road
Spean Bridge PH34 4EU

T: 01397 712335
E: enquiry@smiddyhouse.com
W: smiddyhouse.com

BEDROOMS: 5. 1 suite in adjacent cottage.
OPEN: all year except 25/26, 31 Dec, restaurant closed Mon all year, Sun, Tues, Wed, Jan–Mar.
FACILITIES: garden room, restaurant, in-room TV (Freeview), parking.
BACKGROUND MUSIC: in restaurant.
LOCATION: 9 miles N of Fort William.
CHILDREN: not under 7.
DOGS: not allowed.
CREDIT CARDS: MC, Visa.
PRICES: B&B doubles from £125, singles from £115, suite (sleeps 2–4) from £195. À la carte, min 2 courses, £35–£40.

STRACHUR Argyll and Bute

THE CREGGANS INN

The steamboat from Glasgow no longer docks at Creggans Point, but it is just an 80-minute drive from the city to this whitewashed inn with breathtaking views over Loch Fyne, and there are moorings if you wish to come by water. A hotel since Victorian times, it is run today by Gill and Archie MacLellan. Bedrooms have traditional furnishings, soft paint hues or pretty wallpaper with Fine Soaps Sea Kelp toiletries. The ones to go for are those which share the same loch views as the dining room below. The inn was once owned by soldier-diplomat Sir Fitzroy Maclean, said to have been Ian Fleming's model for James Bond. You can sit by the fire with a shot of MacPhunn single malt, which Sir Fitzroy developed, or a vodka martini, shaken, not stirred, before dining in the bistro on such unpretentious fare as haddock and chips, steak-and-ale pie, butternut squash risotto. Alternatively, eat in the dog-friendly bar, or alfresco, and watch the sunset. A hearty breakfast brings porridge with thick cream and a wee dram, free-range eggs, Loch Fyne smoked fish, Ayrshire bacon, and more.

Strachur PA27 8BX

T: 01369 860279
E: info@creggans-inn.co.uk
W: creggans-inn.co.uk

BEDROOMS: 14.
OPEN: all year, except Christmas.
FACILITIES: 2 lounges, bar, dining room, bistro, in-room TV (Freeview), 2-acre grounds, moorings for guests arriving by boat.
BACKGROUND MUSIC: all day in bar.
LOCATION: in village.
CHILDREN: all ages welcomed, under-14s on extra bed £15.
DOGS: allowed in bedrooms (not unattended, £10 per night) and in bar, not in other public rooms.
CREDIT CARDS: Amex, MC, Visa.
PRICES: B&B doubles from £140. À la carte £30.

THE INN AT LOCH TUMMEL

'A wonderful setting beside the loch' with views across the water to Schiehallion, the local Munro, makes Jade and Alice Calliva's former coaching inn a superbly relaxing place to stay. The bar and snug oozes rustic-chic charm, with an open fire and white-painted beams, while the first-floor dining and sitting room is breezy with blue-painted beams, velvet-covered sofas and leather armchairs. There are plenty of books if you can pull yourself away from the stunning loch views. Bedrooms are uncluttered havens with muted colours, goatskin rugs on well-worn floorboards, a mix of contemporary and vintage furniture, and perhaps a simple hanging rail. Colourful artwork is a nice touch along with 'luxurious' extras including robes, home-made shortbread, a coffee machine and complimentary whisky. All but one room has a bath as well as shower. The 'very good' dinner offers dishes such as herb-crusted Perthshire lamb with salsa verde, and home-made ravioli filled with butternut squash pesto. Generous breakfasts include freshly squeezed juice, omelette, smoked salmon and a full grill.

Queens View
Strathtummel
Pitlochry PH16 5RP

T: 01882 634317
E: info@theinnatlochtummel.com
W: theinnatlochtummel.com

BEDROOMS: 6. 2, on ground floor, suitable for disabled.
OPEN: all year, but closed Christmas and Jan (except the few days before New Year), Mon, Tues.
FACILITIES: snug, bar, library, breakfast room, large garden and patio, wedding facilities, ground-floor bar and snug wheelchair accessible, no adapted toilet.
BACKGROUND MUSIC: in bar/restaurant and library.
LOCATION: 10 miles W of Pitlochry.
CHILDREN: usually not under 5.
DOGS: allowed (£10 per night).
CREDIT CARDS: MC, Visa.
PRICES: B&B doubles from £160. À la carte £35. 1-night bookings refused peak weekends.

KILCAMB LODGE

'The situation is absolutely beautiful; perfect for wild swimmers,' write readers this year, in praise of this remote hideaway hotel on the shores of Loch Sunart. Within a Georgian house bookended by Victorian wings, bedrooms have contemporary or more traditional styling, home-made shortbread, good toiletries. Choose carefully: some rooms are snug, and light sleepers should check if close to the kitchens. A dual-aspect loch suite has a roll-top bath and walk-in shower. Some readers feel the prices are high, and there is a minor grumble about 'tired decor', but refurbishment is ongoing. You can eat by candlelight in the dining room, or in the less formal brasserie. In either, Gary Phillips's daily-changing, no-choice menu features local produce in dishes such as wild halibut with crayfish and spring onion butter, oriental glazed pork belly. Staff are 'attentive and very responsive'. Breakfast brings free-range eggs, smoked salmon, kippers, superior sausages, and much more. 'It is quiet, peaceful – the loch is exceptional.' NOTE: As the Guide went to press, Kilcamb Lodge was sold to Barbara Grzeda and Raymond Sterpaio. (Tessa Stuart, JS)

Strontian PH36 4HY

T: 01967 402257
E: enquiries@kilcamblodge.co.uk
W: kilcamblodge.co.uk

BEDROOMS: 11.
OPEN: all year, 'some closures in Nov, Dec, Jan', restaurant closed Mon/Tues Nov–Jan.
FACILITIES: drawing room, lounge/bar, restaurant, brasserie, in-room TV (Freeview), wedding facilities, 22-acre grounds, EV charging, bar, brasserie, restaurant wheelchair accessible, toilet not adapted.
BACKGROUND MUSIC: at dinner.
LOCATION: edge of village.
CHILDREN: all ages welcomed, under-5s free, 5–12s on extra bed £95, with child meal.
DOGS: allowed in 5 bedrooms (£14 a night), not in public rooms.
CREDIT CARDS: MC, Visa.
PRICES: B&B doubles from £255, singles from £225. Set 5-course dinner £60. 1-night bookings refused Christmas, New Year, Easter.

DOUNESIDE HOUSE

An Edwardian Scottish Baronial fantasy mansion, with crow-stepped gables and castellation, stands on the edge of the Cairngorms national park with views over the Howe of Cromar. Created for Sir Alexander MacRobert, it retains the feel of a family home, and is filled with antiques, paintings, photos and touching mementos of three sons lost in flying tragedies, two in WW2. Military guests get a discount, and all can use the health club, tennis court and croquet lawn, or wander the 'stunning, meticulously maintained grounds', with arboretum and luxuriant borders. House bedrooms range from snug to the sumptuous Lady MacRobert suite. One has a roof terrace, and there are characterful dog-friendly apartments in annexes. In the conservatory, new head chef Matthew Price's short menus feature locally farmed and fished produce, with fruit and vegetables from the kitchen garden. Typical dishes: roast partridge with truffle linguine; sea bass with wild mushroom foam; pumpkin risotto. An amazing breakfast brings peat-smoked haddock, duck eggs Benedict. 'Quality in every respect – accommodation, location, views, walks … and the food!'

Tarland AB34 4UL

T: 01339 881230
E: manager@dounesidehouse.co.uk
W: dounesidehouse.co.uk

BEDROOMS: 23. 9 in cottages, 4 apartments, 2 cottages suitable for disabled.
OPEN: all year.
FACILITIES: bar, wine bar, piano lounge, library, conservatory restaurant, in-room TV (Freeview), wedding facilities, health centre (indoor pool, tennis court), 17-acre grounds, public areas wheelchair accessible, adapted toilet.
BACKGROUND MUSIC: in bar and restaurant.
LOCATION: 7 miles NW of Aboyne.
CHILDREN: all ages welcomed, cots free, extra bed £35, children's menu, play park.
DOGS: allowed in cottages and apartments (£25 charge), not main building.
CREDIT CARDS: MC, Visa.
PRICES: B&B doubles from £200, singles from £183. Set-price dinner £35–£45, tasting menu (Thurs–Sat) £80.

FORSS HOUSE

The Forss river curves around the wooded grounds of this late Georgian country house, run today as a 'wonderful hotel' with salmon fishing at the bottom of the garden. It is 'Scottish country house living on a grand scale – faded elegance but with modern fittings', writes a reader. Public rooms are a sea of tartan carpet. Main-house bedrooms, with a newly refurbished bathroom, are traditional in style, with antique pieces. The two largest bedrooms are named after renowned hunter and falconer Major Radclyffe, who, in 1930, built the crenellated extension to display his trophies. There are also dog-friendly rooms with garden access in the annexes. In a dining room hung with portraits of bewigged men, a locally sourced dinner might bring lamb rump and flank, polenta, mint and jus; orzo with spring onions and white truffle oil; Scrabster-landed fish. At breakfast there is porridge, smoked haddock, the full Forss with 'very nice local bacon and sausages, tasty mushrooms', free-range eggs. The coast is but a short drive: if you want to go far north from here, it will have to be by ferry from Scrabster to Orkney and Shetland.

Forss
Thurso KW14 7XY

T: 01847 861201
E: stay@forsshousehotel.co.uk
W: forsshousehotel.co.uk

BEDROOMS: 14. 3 on ground floor, 6 in neighbouring annexes, 1 suitable for disabled.
OPEN: all year.
FACILITIES: bar, dining room, breakfast room, lounge, in-room TV (Freeview), meeting room, wedding facilities, 19-acre grounds with river and waterfall.
BACKGROUND MUSIC: in public areas breakfast and evening.
LOCATION: 5 miles W of Thurso.
CHILDREN: all ages welcomed, no charge for under-5s, extra bed £25.
DOGS: allowed in sportsmen's lodge bedrooms (£15 a night) and in bar.
CREDIT CARDS: Amex, MC, Visa.
PRICES: B&B doubles from £215. Fixed-price 3-course dinner £49.50, 6-course tasting menu £70.

TORRIDON Highland
MAP 5:C1

THE TORRIDON

It's hard to beat the setting of this Victorian
baronial-style hunting lodge, in a wooded estate
at the head of Loch Torridon. You arrive via a
single-track road to stunning loch and mountain
views and 'a warm and personal welcome'. The
most expensive rooms are in the main house, some
with in-room roll-top bath, others with bright,
even garish colours but 'everything you could
need'. There are cheaper, simpler rooms, some for
a family, in former stables, shed and buttery, with
a pub restaurant, Bo & Muc, serving breakfast,
lunch and dinner (think Highland beef burger or
macaroni cheese). Fires blaze in richly panelled,
'spacious and comfortable' public rooms. There
is a whisky bar, as well as a lounge with a Zodiac
ceiling. In 1887 restaurant, chef Paul Green
uses produce from the home farm and two-acre
kitchen garden to create 'good, sometimes very
good' dishes on tasting menus which might
feature pheasant ravioli; beef rib, asparagus and
wild garlic; Talisker-cured sea trout, cucumber
and lovage. From archery to mountain biking,
wildlife watching to Munro bagging, there is
plenty to do here. Stargazers are bedazzled by the
night sky. (SP)

Annat
by Achnasheen
Torridon IV22 2EY

T: 01445 791242
E: info@thetorridon.com
W: thetorridon.com

BEDROOMS: 18 in main hotel. Plus 12 in
Stables, some adapted for disabled.
OPEN: Feb–Dec (resort); Feb–Nov
(Stables and Bo & Muc), may close
Mon, Tues off-season.
FACILITIES: ramp, lift, drawing room,
library, whisky bar, dining room,
wedding facilities, 48-acre estate, EV
charging.
BACKGROUND MUSIC: classical at night
in dining room.
LOCATION: on W coast, 10 miles SW of
Kinlochewe.
CHILDREN: all ages welcomed, extra
bed in suites £45.
DOGS: allowed in 1 house room,
ground-floor Stables rooms (no
charge), Bo & Muc bar area.
CREDIT CARDS: Amex, MC, Visa.
PRICES: B&B doubles from £155
(Stables), £295 (main house). Tasting
menus £80 (1887). 1-night bookings
sometimes refused.

ULLAPOOL Highland

MAP 5:B1

THE CEILIDH PLACE

Whether you want a ceilidh, a hooley or a quiet read, a drink or bistro meal, a bed or bunk, the Urquhart family's hotel, in a fishing village set amid rugged mountains on the east shore of Loch Broom, can accommodate you. It is more than 50 years since actor Robert Urquhart opened a café in a boatshed and invited musicians to play in exchange for a meal. This lively social hub is still a place for music gigs, but now with gallery space, bookshop, restaurant and bar, having spread itself across adjoining whitewashed cottages. Bedrooms have a pleasing simplicity, no TV but a retro radio, and an eclectic mix of books chosen by customers. There is a first-floor guest lounge with a balcony, pantry, tea and coffee facilities, and an honesty bar if you don't want to scrum down with the punters on a busy night. For 16 years chef Scott Morrison has been serving up dishes such as Loch Broom langoustine, venison burger, steak pie with rumblethumps (bubble and squeak), and veggie options. If you're on a shoestring, you can sleep in the Clubhouse. Breakfast brings kippers, smoked haddock, a full Scottish or vegan.

12–14 West Argyle Street
Ullapool IV26 2TY

T: 01854 612103
E: stay@theceilidhplace.com
W: theceilidhplace.com

BEDROOMS: 13. 10 with facilities en suite, 3 sharing bathroom and shower room, plus 11 in Clubhouse (max. 32 guests).
OPEN: all year except from 5 Jan for 3 weeks.
FACILITIES: bar, lounge, café/restaurant, bookshop, conference/function facilities, wedding facilities, 2-acre garden, parking, public areas wheelchair accessible.
BACKGROUND MUSIC: in public areas.
LOCATION: village centre (car park).
CHILDREN: all ages welcomed, under-5s free, £30 a night for 5–10s.
DOGS: allowed in bedrooms (£12 per dog per stay, not unattended) and throughout.
CREDIT CARDS: MC, Visa.
PRICES: B&B doubles from £132, singles from £100 (bunk-beds in Clubhouse £24–£32 per person). À la carte £30.

WALKERBURN Scottish Borders

WINDLESTRAW

An Edwardian manor house built in the Tweed valley as a wedding gift for the future wife of a cashmere mill owner is today a small, elegant hotel with a serious emphasis on food. Arts and Crafts details include wood panelling in the light sitting room and 'exquisitely carved' grotesque birds on the newel posts of the oak staircase, leading to individually styled bedrooms. Deluxe rooms have a slipper bath and walk-in shower; the best room has a lounge area and original cast iron bathtub. Owners John and Sylvia Matthews are natural hosts – one reader felt 'looked after with care'. But it's at mealtimes that this place really shines, with Stu Waterston's menus showcasing home-grown and local produce. 'On a six-night stay, all our dinner courses were different. All the food was good and imaginative.' There is special mention for 'meltingly tender' Borders roe deer with blackcurrants and beet leaves – 'and I'm going to try to recreate the Asian-spiced pulled pork'. Breakfast brings home-baked soda bread and the full Scottish. 'Luckily we were able to do plenty of long walks to burn off the calories.' (Frances Thomas)

Galashiels Road
Walkerburn EH43 6AA

T: 01896 870636
E: stay@windlestraw.co.uk
W: windlestraw.co.uk

BEDROOMS: 6.
OPEN: all year except 20 Dec–22 Feb.
FACILITIES: bar, sunroom, lounge/restaurant, in-room TV (Freeview), wedding facilities, 3-acre landscaped gardens, parking.
BACKGROUND MUSIC: none.
LOCATION: in Walkerburn, 8 miles E of Peebles.
CHILDREN: all ages welcomed, under-4s free, additional bed for under-12s £50, in own room £140.
DOGS: allowed in bedrooms (max. 2, not unattended, £10 per dog per night), public rooms, not restaurant.
CREDIT CARDS: Amex, MC, Visa.
PRICES: B&B doubles from £190. 5-course set menu £80.

WALES

Tryfan, Snowdonia

HARBOURMASTER HOTEL

Light, colour and fishy fun are the key ingredients of this periwinkle-blue building in prime position on cheery Aberaeron's harbourside. Run with enthusiasm by locally born Glyn and Menna Heulyn, it feels like 'the hub of the town', with people coming there as much for the atmosphere as the food and bedrooms. Spread between the original harbourmaster's house and adjoining warehouse, 'first-class' rooms (some quirkily shaped) are 'stylish and calm' in breezy shades with crisp, contemporary furnishings, Welsh rugs and designer lighting; most with sea views. Bathrooms are generous, some with roll-top bath. For more privacy, choose the two-bedroom cottage. After drinks on the harbourside terrace, dine in the smart, blue-panelled restaurant or more rustic warehouse (both with boat-bobbing views) on food brimming with Welshness – Carlingford Bay crabs and oysters, Welsh rib of beef and sirloin steak, home-made burger with Welsh Cheddar. Decent vegetarian choices, too, including Welsh rarebit at breakfast. The hard-working, friendly staff, who ensure everything is 'running smoothly', add to the 'wonderful' experience. (Frances Thomas)

Pen Cei
Aberaeron SA46 0BT

T: 01545 570755
E: info@harbour-master.com
W: harbour-master.com

BEDROOMS: 13. 4 in warehouse, 2 in cottage, 1 suitable for disabled.
OPEN: all year except 24–26 Dec, drinks only (from 2 pm) on Boxing Day.
FACILITIES: lift (in warehouse), bar, restaurant, in-room TV (Freeview), small terrace, restaurant and bar wheelchair accessible, adapted toilet, EV charging, limited parking.
BACKGROUND MUSIC: all day in bar and restaurant.
LOCATION: central, on the harbour.
CHILDREN: aged 5 and upwards welcomed, no additional beds, or book cottage.
DOGS: only guide dogs.
CREDIT CARDS: Amex, MC, Visa.
PRICES: B&B doubles from £145, singles from £95. À la carte dinner £38. 1-night bookings refused most weekends.

TREFEDDIAN HOTEL

For a century, generations of Cave-Browne-Caves
have welcomed families and four-legged friends
to their hotel on a hillside above Cardigan Bay,
across road and railway line from golf links and
white-sand beaches. 'It keeps up high standards,'
says a reader who praises the 'well-appointed
rooms' and 'friendly staff'. Bedrooms are
decorated in coastal colours, and more than half
have a sea view, perhaps with a balcony. Some
can sleep up to two adults and four children.
Activities include tennis and putting, with sailing
and pony trekking to hand. On rainy days the
playroom, library and indoor pool come into
their own. An all-day menu has fish fingers for
the kids, a fish platter for grown-ups. A baby-
listening service gives peace of mind, as parents
tuck into duck-liver pâté and slow-roasted belly
pork on braised red cabbage with sauce Albert.
'The food was plentiful, five courses with several
good choices, extremely quickly served.' It may
not be fine dining, but a smart-casual dress code
confers a sense of occasion. 'When you call it an
institution, you are right. Everything seemed to
work smoothly.' (DB, and others)

Tywyn Road
Aberdovey LL35 0SB

T: 01654 767213
E: info@trefwales.com
W: trefwales.com

BEDROOMS: 59. 1 suitable for disabled.
OPEN: all year except 11 Dec–16 Jan.
FACILITIES: lift, lounge bar, study,
family lounge, adult lounge,
restaurant, games room (snooker,
table tennis), in-room TV (Freeview),
indoor swimming pool, beauty salon,
15-acre grounds (tennis, putting
green), most public rooms wheelchair
accessible, adapted toilet.
BACKGROUND MUSIC: none.
LOCATION: ¼ mile N of Aberdovey.
CHILDREN: all ages welcomed, under-
10s free, extra bed (aged 10–16)
£35–£45, with dinner.
DOGS: allowed in some bedrooms
(£12 per night), library.
CREDIT CARDS: MC, Visa.
PRICES: D,B&B from £116 per person
(per night for min. 2-night stay; longer
stay discounts).

THE ANGEL HOTEL

♀ Previous César winner

At the heart of a market town on the edge of the
Brecon Beacons, William Griffiths's Georgian
coaching inn is today a stylish contemporary hotel.
Sister ventures include the next-door bakery,
which provides cakes for afternoon tea, the Art
Shop, which supplies works to adorn Farrow &
Ball-painted walls, and the nearby Walnut Tree
Inn, where Shaun Hill holds a Michelin star.
Smart bedrooms are decorated in restful shades,
with bathroom fittings by Villeroy & Boch or
Fired Earth, and designer fabrics. 'All was very
nice and efficient, and the staff were lovely,' writes
a reader. 'Blankets and sheets were provided on
request' for Guide insiders who think duvets
are the work of the devil. You can eat in the
Foxhunter bar or the Oak Room, from a menu for
all tastes, with children's dishes and good veggie
options. Maybe butternut squash and aubergine
curry with coconut rice, or dry-aged Welsh beef
rib-eye steak. At breakfast there is 'good OJ,
delicious granola', smoked salmon, local
sausages. 'Even my sister, who doesn't like
hotels, said how much she liked the Angel.'
(Josie Mayers, and others)

15 Cross Street
Abergavenny NP7 5EN

T: 01873 857121
E: info@angelabergavenny.com
W: angelabergavenny.com

BEDROOMS: 31. 2 in adjacent mews.
OPEN: all year except 24–27 Dec.
FACILITIES: lift, lounge, bar, tea room,
restaurant, private function rooms,
bakery, in-room TV (Freeview), civil
wedding licence, courtyard, parking,
EV charging, public rooms wheelchair
accessible, adapted toilet.
BACKGROUND MUSIC: in restaurant and
tea room, pianist in restaurant Fri and
Sat dinner.
LOCATION: town centre.
CHILDREN: all ages welcomed, extra
bed £26.
DOGS: allowed in the Foxhunter bar
and courtyard.
CREDIT CARDS: Amex, MC, Visa.
PRICES: B&B doubles from £145.
À la carte £50. 1-night bookings
sometimes refused.

ABERSOCH Gwynedd

MAP 3:B2

☽PORTH TOCYN HOTEL

César award: family friendly hotel of the year

This homely, family-friendly hotel, just outside Abersoch, with glorious views of Cardigan Bay, continues to get things right year after year, which is why its loyal guests keep on returning. Some, who first came as children and now have their own brood, are delighted to find it run by the fourth generation of the Fletcher-Brewer family. 'Very friendly and efficient staff' help create a 'warm and inviting' atmosphere while the facilities for children, including a 'lovely warm pool' and high tea, help parents relax. Bedrooms are traditional, with light colours, pretty feature wallpapers and country antiques. Most have sea views and super-king-size beds. Modern bathrooms have a bath as well as a shower. Mealtimes are a highlight, especially dinner – either a full affair with canapés and petits fours, or lighter à la carte. The latter might include fish pie and vegetable ravioli while the former has options such as roast monkfish tail with charred fennel and chicory. On warmer days, lunch and afternoon tea are served on the terrace overlooking the gardens to the sea. 'Already planning another trip,' enthuses a reader. (AC, A and EW)

Bwlchtocyn
Abersoch LL53 7BU

T: 01758 713303
E: bookings@porthtocynhotel.co.uk
W: porthtocynhotel.co.uk

BEDROOMS: 17. 3 on ground floor. 1 shepherd's hut, 1 self-catering cottage.
OPEN: 2 weeks before Easter–end Oct.
FACILITIES: sitting rooms, children's snug, small bar, dining room, in-room TV (Freeview), terrace, 20-acre grounds (outdoor swimming pool heated May–Sept, tennis), EV charging, call to discuss wheelchair access.
BACKGROUND MUSIC: none.
LOCATION: 2 miles outside village.
CHILDREN: all ages welcomed, free cots/extra beds, no under-6s at dinner.
DOGS: allowed in bedrooms (no charge), not in restaurant or some public rooms.
CREDIT CARDS: MC, Visa.
PRICES: B&B doubles from £130, singles from £92. À la carte £38, fixed-price dinner £42–£49. 1-night bookings occasionally refused at weekends.

TY MAWR

With the vast Brechfa Forest on its margins, this 'gorgeous, lovely hotel' whose gardens are bordered by the River Marlais is perfect for hikers and bikers. Dogs stay free; biscuits, bowls and information on local walks are provided by owners Paul Bennett and Melissa Hurley as well as a 'wonderful warm welcome'. Since arriving in 2019 they have been updating interiors in the 16th-century country house, and have plans for the gardens. 'Spacious, clean and comfortable' bedrooms are beautifully styled, with antiques, perhaps a sleigh bed, beams, bare stone, and Myddfai toiletries. Dryslwyn was once the loom room. Coedwig Brechfa, with its own front door, super-king-size bed, separate seating area and sofa bed, has been a stable and bakery. Or when it's night above the dingle starry, retire to Dylan Thomas-inspired ground-floor, Laugharne. Paul's scrupulously sourced nightly menu might include North Sea cod, creamed borlotti beans, lime and herb crust. 'Meals were tasty and always served with a smile.' At breakfast there is porridge with local honey and Penderyn whisky, free-range eggs, maybe juiced garden apples. (Nicky Noble, Ian Jervis)

Brechfa SA32 7RA

T: 01267 202332
E: info@wales-country-hotel.co.uk
W: wales-country-hotel.co.uk

BEDROOMS: 6. 2 on ground floor, 1 with private access.
OPEN: all year.
FACILITIES: sitting room, bar, breakfast room, restaurant, in-room TV (Freeview), EV charging, 1-acre grounds.
BACKGROUND MUSIC: classical in restaurant during dinner.
LOCATION: village centre.
CHILDREN: aged 10 and over welcomed.
DOGS: allowed in some bedrooms (no charge), sitting room and bar, not in restaurant or breakfast room (biscuits, bowls, and information on local walks provided).
CREDIT CARDS: Amex, MC, Visa.
PRICES: B&B doubles from £130, singles from £85, À la carte £42. 1-night bookings occasionally refused.

THE COACH HOUSE

In a market town home to an August Jazz Festival and October Baroque Music Festival, Kayt and Hugh Cooper run their former 19th-century coaching inn as a smart and welcoming, fully licensed B&B. The Baroque Festival was online in 2020 (so no live Bach, bach), and trusted readers were disappointed not to be able to enjoy their annual trip to enjoy 'the best accommodation in town'. Bedrooms are contemporary in style and painted in restful hues. Most have a walk-in shower, and all are supplied with posh toiletries and fresh milk on request. A mini-suite has a lounge area, coffee machine, small fridge, and a bathroom with a roll-top bath and walk-in shower. If you have special dietary requirements, your hosts will go out of their way to cater for you. An extensive breakfast menu includes Welsh rarebit, omelettes, a full Welsh or vegetarian, and the house speciality: free-range eggs, smoked salmon and laver bread. You can sit in the secluded garden with a drink and order a picnic to take with you when you set out to roam the Brecon Beacons national park. (J and MB)

12 Orchard Street
Brecon LD3 8AN

T: 01874 640089
E: reservations@coachhousebrecon.com
W: coachhousebrecon.com

BEDROOMS: 6.
OPEN: all year except 1 week over Christmas (open New Year).
FACILITIES: reading room, breakfast room, lounge (with drink service), in-room TV (Freeview), garden, drying room, parking, secure bicycle storage, unsuitable for disabled.
BACKGROUND MUSIC: classical or Welsh harp music in breakfast room.
LOCATION: ½ mile from town centre.
CHILDREN: 15 and upwards welcomed.
DOGS: not allowed.
CREDIT CARDS: MC, Visa.
PRICES: B&B doubles from £109, single occupancy from £84. 2-night min. stay.

CAERNARFON Gwynedd

PLAS DINAS COUNTRY HOUSE

Guests are dazzled by the views of Snowdonia and the Menai Strait at the former home of the Armstrong-Joneses, a trove of memorabilia. 'Incredible place,' a reader writes. 'This is the place for relaxation and romance,' writes another. Since buying the 17th-century-cum-Victorian house in 2019, Annie and Daniel Perks have updated the bedrooms, while preserving the history of the love story of Princess Margaret and Lord Snowdon, who regularly spent weekends here. The dual-aspect Princess Margaret room retains an antique four-poster. Original signed photographs hang in the corridor outside Snowdon, with its carved French bed. In a cabinet in Judges is the QC wig that once blanketed the head of Snowdon's father, Ronald. Daniel ap Geraint cooks a monthly-changing menu of 'absolutely divine' dishes that might include treacle-soaked venison, roast salsify, Orme beer-braised onions and horseradish, or beetroot tarte Tatin with Perl Las blue cheese. Guests gather for drinks before one of the two sittings in the Gunroom, with its ancient fireplace and portraits in gilded frames. 'Rave reviews are all deserved.' (Trevor Chenery, TB, DM)

Bontnewydd
Caernarfon LL54 7YF

T: 01286 830214
E: info@plasdinas.co.uk
W: plasdinas.co.uk

BEDROOMS: 10. 1 on ground floor.
OPEN: all year except Christmas, restaurant closed Sun, Mon.
FACILITIES: drawing room, restaurant, private dining room, in-room TV (Freeview), civil wedding licence, 15-acre grounds.
BACKGROUND MUSIC: in drawing room and dining room.
LOCATION: 5-min. drive S of town.
CHILDREN: over-10s welcomed.
DOGS: pets allowed in bedrooms and in drawing room (not food service areas) at additional charge by arrangement.
CREDIT CARDS: Amex, MC, Visa.
PRICES: B&B doubles from £139. Set dinner £54. 1-night bookings refused New Year's Eve.

CRICKHOWELL Powys

MAP 3:D4

GLIFFAES

There are sublime views from this eccentric
Victorian country house with Italianate
campaniles and 20th-century porte cochère, in
wooded grounds overlooking the River Usk. Built
for a Revd West and his father, who planted the
arboretum, it has been in the same family since
1948 and is today owned by Susie and James
Suter. 'We love it,' wrote readers who relish the
old-fashioned look and hospitality, the comfy
lounges with 'an array of magazines and papers',
the 'shoe cleaner on the landing', the 'professional
housekeeping'. Bedrooms, with spring water
on tap, range from cosy to two large river-view
rooms with French doors to a wisteria-festooned
balcony. One room has an antique four-poster
with embroidered canopy. Chef Karl Cheetham
works with local produce, fruit, herbs – and
nettles – from the garden, to create short menus
of dishes such as venison with pancetta, orange
bread-and-butter pudding, smoked chestnuts,
blackberry jus. Unusual breakfast dishes include
twice-baked Welsh Cheddar soufflé, vegan tofu
scramble, kippers with laver bread, and pork-
and-leek sausages to set you up for a day's fly-
fishing. (FK)

Gliffaes Road
Crickhowell NP8 1RH

T: 01874 730371
E: calls@gliffaes.com
W: gliffaeshotel.com

BEDROOMS: 23. 4 in cottage, 1, on
ground floor, suitable for disabled.
OPEN: all year except Christmas, open
for New Year.
FACILITIES: 2 sitting rooms,
conservatory, bar, dining room, in-
room TV, civil wedding licence,
33-acre garden (tennis, croquet,
private fishing on River Usk), EV
charging, public rooms wheelchair
accessible.
BACKGROUND MUSIC: in bar in the
evening.
LOCATION: 3 miles W of Crickhowell.
CHILDREN: all ages welcomed, cots
free, extra bed £30.
DOGS: not allowed indoors (free
kennels available).
CREDIT CARDS: Amex, MC, Visa.
PRICES: B&B doubles from £159.
À la carte £45. 1-night bookings
refused high-season weekends.

THE OLD VICARAGE

The red brick exterior of this former Victorian vicarage set back from the A483 in the Welsh marches might look 'somewhat gaunt' but inside are light-filled rooms, a 'very pleasant lounge' and a warm welcome. Tim and Helen Withers are 'good hosts', welcoming guests with tea, and happy to help with planning days out. Bedrooms, including a family room, have a light-touch country house look with pretty wallpaper, botanical prints and perhaps a cast iron bed or sloping ceiling. 'A lovely view from the bathroom,' noted one reader. 'Our room, Mule, though not huge was perfectly big enough, with an extremely comfortable bed.' With notice, Tim cooks a set evening meal which might include a meze starter followed by roast Welsh lamb with dauphinoise potatoes. The salmon en croûte is 'outstanding, restaurant standard, and a lot of it!'. Wine is available by the glass or bottle; the property is licensed. Breakfast can kick off with 'fabulous' porridge with Welsh honey followed by a wide range of cooked dishes including omelettes, with eggs from their own hens. 'The simply superb kipper was the best I've ever had.' (Andrew and Moira Kleissner)

Dolfor
Newtown SY16 4BN

T: 07753 760054
E: mail@theoldvicaragedolfor.co.uk
W: theoldvicaragedolfor.co.uk

BEDROOMS: 4.
OPEN: all year except last 3 weeks Dec and New Year, reopens 5 Jan, dining room closed Sun.
FACILITIES: drawing room, dining room, in-room TV (Freeview), 1½-acre garden, EV charging, unsuitable for disabled.
BACKGROUND MUSIC: none.
LOCATION: 3 miles S of Newtown.
CHILDREN: all ages welcomed, family room, cot £10, extra bed £20.
DOGS: not allowed.
CREDIT CARDS: Amex, MC, Visa.
PRICES: B&B doubles from £95, singles from £70. Set 3-course dinner £25. 1-night bookings refused bank holidays and Royal Welsh Show week.

DOLYDD Gwynedd   MAP 3:A3

Y GOEDEN EIRIN

Views of Snowdonia and the Menai Strait are on offer at Eluned Rowlands' rustic but comfortable B&B, as well as books, artwork and some true Welsh hospitality. Named after the plum trees that grow in the garden – also the name of a book by local author John Gwilym Jones whose portrait hangs in the dining room – the house is a colourfully converted granite cowshed with exposed-stone walls, beamed ceilings and slate floors. It is a very eco-friendly place, with an electric car charging point, solar panels and in-room recycling instructions. Guests are welcomed with tea and biscuits or Welsh cakes, and there's fruit, sherry and fresh milk in the bedrooms. These are large and brightly furnished, with colourful bedspreads, heated slate floors in the two outbuilding rooms, Fired Earth tiles in the bathroom, and masses of books. All have far-reaching countryside views; you can even enjoy them from the bath in the larger room in the house. Eluned's Aga-cooked breakfasts are generous affairs with freshly squeezed juice, kippers, omelettes and a huge grill, plus home-made preserves.

Dolydd
Caernarfon LL54 7EF

T: 01286 830942
E: eluned.rowlands@tiscali.co.uk
W: ygoedeneirin.co.uk

BEDROOMS: 3. 2 on ground floor in annexe 3 yds from house.
OPEN: all year except Christmas/New Year.
FACILITIES: breakfast-room-lounge, in-room TV (Freeview), 20-acre pastureland, Wi-Fi in house only, EV charging, unsuitable for disabled.
BACKGROUND MUSIC: none.
LOCATION: 3 miles S of Caernarfon.
CHILDREN: not under 10.
DOGS: well-behaved dogs in annexe bedrooms and public rooms by prior arrangement.
CREDIT CARDS: none, cash or cheque payment requested on arrival.
PRICES: B&B doubles from £90, singles from £65. 1-night bookings refused in peak summer.

AEL Y BRYN

♀ Previous César winner

One of Wales's best-loved B&Bs stands in beautiful gardens, with a wildlife pond, a courtyard with a fountain, and glorious views to the Preseli hills. It is the creation of Robert Smith and Arwel Hughes, who in 2000 bought a wartime hostel that once housed land girls and transformed it into the light-filled 'peaceful haven of luxury' we see today. 'It is always a joy to return,' one reader reports. 'Robert and Arwel immediately made us feel welcome,' writes another, comparing the experience to visiting 'much-loved relatives and friends'. Everyone commends the attention to detail, which includes fresh milk in a mini-fridge in each of the modern, spacious bedrooms. One twin/super-king suite has a lounge and patio, and a big, powerful walk-in shower. Guests have use of the lounge/music room, library, conservatory and grounds. At night, by prior arrangement, the hosts serve a locally sourced dinner in the beamed dining hall. They charge no corkage if you bring wine. Breakfast includes a generous buffet, the full Welsh, porridge and smoked haddock on request. 'Truly exceptional,' readers conclude. (B and JH, R and MG, and others)

Eglwyswrw
Crymych SA41 3UL

T: 01239 891411
E: stay@aelybrynpembrokeshire.
  co.uk
W: aelybrynpembrokeshire.co.uk

BEDROOMS: 4. All on ground floor.
OPEN: all year except Christmas/New Year.
FACILITIES: library, music room, dining room, conservatory (telescope), in-room TV (Freeview), courtyard, 2½-acre garden (wildlife pond, stream, bowls court), public rooms wheelchair accessible.
BACKGROUND MUSIC: none.
LOCATION: ½ mile N of Eglwyswrw.
CHILDREN: not under 16.
DOGS: not allowed.
CREDIT CARDS: Amex, MC, Visa.
PRICES: B&B doubles from £110, singles from £90. Set dinner £26–£30 (2/3 courses). 1-night bookings refused bank holidays.

FELIN FACH Powys

THE FELIN FACH GRIFFIN

♔ Previous César winner

Brothers Charles and Edmund Inkin keep a welcome in the vales at their relaxed, brick-red dining pub-with-rooms, amid sheep-grazed pastures just outside the Brecon Beacons national park. The style – as at sister properties The Gurnard's Head, Zennor, and The Old Coastguard, Mousehole (see entries) – is one of casual chic, with blazing fires, squashy sofas, mismatched chairs and tables. You won't find a TV in your bedrooms, but you will find Welsh blankets, a Roberts radio, cut flowers, home-made biscuits, fresh milk, local artwork and botanical toiletries. In clement weather you can eat outside on perhaps garden vegetable risotto or a seafood grill; later, have supper in the Library or Aga Room or, if your dog is with you, in the bar or Tack Room (dogs stay at the pub free of charge). A short, nightly-changing menu of vegetables from the kitchen garden, fish from Cornwall, local meat and game includes dishes such as halibut, broad bean, pine nut and hazelnut fricassée; farro risotto, or duck breast, sweet potato, beetroot. Shooting and salmon and trout fishing can be organised, and you can play golf at Llandrindod Wells, Cradoc or Kington.

Felin Fach
Brecon LD3 0UB

T: 01874 620111
E: enquiries@felinfachgriffin.co.uk
W: eatdrinksleep.ltd.uk

BEDROOMS: 7.
OPEN: all year except 24/25 Dec.
FACILITIES: bar, dining rooms, limited mobile signal, 3-acre garden (kitchen garden, alfresco dining), bar/dining room wheelchair accessible, adapted toilet.
BACKGROUND MUSIC: Radio 4 at breakfast, 'selected music' afternoon and evening.
LOCATION: 4 miles NE of Brecon, in village on A470.
CHILDREN: all ages welcomed, travel cot no charge, extra bed £15, children's menu.
DOGS: allowed in bedrooms (no charge, bowls, towels, biscuits supplied), in bar and Tack Room, but not in restaurant.
CREDIT CARDS: MC, Visa.
PRICES: B&B doubles from £145, singles from £115. Set supper £38.

THE MANOR TOWN HOUSE

Behind a powder-blue facade, Helen and
Chris Sheldon's Georgian town house B&B
has the welcoming feel of a private home, and
unexpected, spectacular views from the rear
terrace, across Cardigan Bay to the Preseli hills.
Bedrooms have contemporary decor, with perhaps
bright fabric headboards or an accent wall of deep
blue, and the occasional well-chosen antique.
Four out of six rooms have a sea view, with the
two largest big enough for a family. Downstairs
you'll find lots of comfy seating, books, magazines
and an honesty bar. Let them know ahead of
time if you would like a cream tea to enjoy by
the log-burning stove or alfresco, where you can
toast the fishing-boat-bobbing harbour view with
accompanying bubbles. A continental breakfast
includes home-baked bread and granola, and
you can order packed lunches. One regular guest
regrets that they don't do dinner, but Helen and
Chris can suggest places to eat, while Llys Meddyg
in Newport (see entry) is a ten-minute drive or
taxi ride away. Bike hire can be arranged, or you
can walk the Pembrokeshire Coast Path that runs
below or hop on a Poppit Rocket coastal bus.

11 Main Street
Fishguard SA65 9HG

T: 01348 873260
E: info@manortownhouse.com
W: manortownhouse.com

BEDROOMS: 6.
OPEN: all year except 23–28 Dec.
FACILITIES: 2 lounges, breakfast room,
in-room TV (Freeview), small walled
garden, bicycle storage, parking
in public car park, unsuitable for
disabled.
BACKGROUND MUSIC: classical in
breakfast room.
LOCATION: town centre.
CHILDREN: all ages welcomed, cots
free, extra bed £25.
DOGS: not allowed.
CREDIT CARDS: Amex, MC, Visa.
PRICES: B&B doubles from £120, singles
from £90. 1-night bookings sometimes
refused peak weekends.

GLYNARTHEN Ceredigion

MAP 3:D2

PENBONTBREN

♊ Previous César winner

Guests enjoy the warmth and friendliness of a traditional guest house combined with all the space and privacy they could wish for at this unusual rural B&B which 'couldn't be better'. In gentle countryside, a short drive from sandy beaches, it centres on a pretty Victorian farmhouse, with smart contemporary accommodation in converted stables, granary, mill and threshing barn. Now the Garden Room has been upgraded to a suite, all have a separate sitting room, a kitchenette with espresso machine, fridge, mini bar and microwave, and their own outdoor space. Richard Morgan-Price and Huw Thomas have handed over the reins to Kathryn and Richard Jones, who plan to maintain their excellent standards. In the morning, tables are set with starched linen and fine china for breakfast. Help yourself to freshly squeezed orange juice, organic yogurt, and Agen prunes steeped in triple sec. Hot dishes include cockles, bacon and laver bread, locally smoked salmon, haddock, kipper, free-range farm eggs, the full Welsh or vegetarian. 'For such an excellent place, the prices are amazing.' (Dr John D. Lee)

Glynarthen
Llandysul SA44 6PE

T: 01239 810248
E: contact@penbontbren.com
W: penbontbren.com

BEDROOMS: 6. 5 in annexe, 1 in garden, 3 on ground floor, 1 family suite, 1 suitable for disabled.
OPEN: all year except 24–26 Dec.
FACILITIES: breakfast room, in-room TV (Freeview), 7-acre grounds (croquet lawn), bike storage, public rooms wheelchair accessible, adapted toilet.
BACKGROUND MUSIC: none.
LOCATION: 5 miles N of Newcastle Emlyn.
CHILDREN: all ages welcomed.
DOGS: allowed in some bedrooms by prior agreement (no charge), not in breakfast room.
CREDIT CARDS: Amex, MC, Visa.
PRICES: B&B doubles from £100, singles from £89, family suite from £140. 1-night bookings sometimes refused weekends.

THE FALCONDALE

In 'most beautiful surroundings' on a bluff overlooking the Teifi valley, this Victorian Italianate villa, designed by Thomas Talbot Bury, an associate of Pugin's, is a very dog-friendly hotel and popular wedding venue. It has a 'cosy' feel to it, with 'professional, competent and warm' staff. Bedroom styling is a little démodé, with patterned carpet and a lot of peach, but two rooms, one with a four-poster, have French windows to a Juliet balcony. Nice touches include a cafetière and teapot, home-made shortbread and Temple Spa toiletries (noted by a reader, with approval, in the ground-floor cloakroom). In the attractive restaurant, a fixed-price menu might include boeuf bourguignon or from the à la carte, Welsh steaks, bean burger, or BBQ pulled pork burger. Breakfast choices are more adventurous, with cockles and laver bread, sautéed potatoes, and mushroom fricassée. In what remains of former pleasure grounds – a lawned garden with flower borders, some rockwork, some parasol walks – Victorian conifers survive, while azaleas blaze. There are wonderful walks along the Ceredigion Coast Path or in the Cambrian mountains.

Falcondale Drive
Lampeter SA48 7RX

T: 01570 422910
E: info@thefalcondale.co.uk
W: thefalcondale.co.uk

BEDROOMS: 17.
OPEN: all year.
FACILITIES: lift (to some bedrooms), bar, 3 lounges, conservatory, restaurant, in-room TV (Freeview), civil wedding licence, beauty treatment room, terrace, 14-acre grounds, EV charging, restaurant and ground floor wheelchair accessible, adapted toilet.
BACKGROUND MUSIC: in restaurant and lounges.
LOCATION: 1 mile N of Lampeter.
CHILDREN: all ages welcomed, cots £10, extra bed £30.
DOGS: allowed in bedrooms (£10 per night), public areas, not restaurant.
CREDIT CARDS: MC, Visa.
PRICES: B&B doubles from £135, singles from £110. À la carte £35, fixed-price 3-course menu £32.

LLANDRILLO Denbighshire

MAP 3:B4

TYDDYN LLAN

Foodies flock to Susan and Bryan Webb's restaurant-with-rooms with views over the Vale of Edeyrnion for good reason – Bryan has been cooking up a storm for 45 years and Susan is the consummate hostess. Menus feature prime Welsh produce and freshly landed fish in dishes such as turbot with coco beans and Morteau sausage, grain mustard sauce; chicken breast, potato pancake, morels and tarragon. 'We ate from the three-course à la carte on one night and the tasting menu the next. All excellent.' The wine list was 'all you would expect', with 'an excellent range by the glass'. Vegetarians, give them notice and they'll fix you something special. Bedrooms in the extended Georgian property are traditionally styled, 'well furnished and comfortable', with Gilchrist & Soames toiletries and home-made biscuits. One has an ornate Victorian four-poster, a slipper bath and walk-in shower; the Garden Suite has a private garden area. For breakfast, there's freshly squeezed orange juice, farm apple juice, lavender honey, dry-cured Welsh bacon, smoked salmon. Packed lunches and a drying room are ideal for walkers heading out in capricious weather.

Tyddyn Llan
Llandrillo
Corwen LL21 0ST

T: 01490 440264
E: info@tyddynllan.co.uk
W: tyddynllan.co.uk

BEDROOMS: 13. 3 with separate entrance, 1, on ground floor, suitable for disabled.
OPEN: all year except Mon/Tues, and last 2 weeks of Jan.
FACILITIES: 2 lounges, bar, 2 dining rooms, in-room TV (Freeview), no mobile signal, civil wedding licence, 3-acre garden, public rooms wheelchair accessible, adapted toilet.
BACKGROUND MUSIC: none.
LOCATION: 5 miles SW of Corwen.
CHILDREN: all ages welcomed, extra bed £30.
DOGS: allowed in some bedrooms (£10 per night), not in public rooms.
CREDIT CARDS: Amex, MC, Visa.
PRICES: room-only doubles from £110, cooked breakfast £25, continental £14. Fixed-price dinner, 3 courses £75, tasting menu £95. 1-night bookings refused Christmas.

LLANDUDNO Conwy   MAP 3:A3

BODYSGALLEN HALL AND SPA

On the slopes of Pydew mountain, with views
to Conwy Castle and the Snowdonia mountains,
a 17th-century mansion in parkland and Arts
and Crafts gardens, extended over centuries,
is today a luxury hotel and spa. Owned by the
National Trust, it is part of the Historic House
Hotels group (see Hartwell House, Aylesbury,
and Middlethorpe Hall & Spa, York). In comfy
public rooms you will find blazing fires, 'plenty
of seating, nooks and crannies', antiques and
ancestral portraits. Some bedrooms have a four-
poster. All have home-made biscuits and posh
toiletries. If you bring your dog, go for one in the
stone cottages above the parterre. 'The grounds
are lovely, with good walks along the terrace and
up to an obelisk.' Abdalla El Shershaby has now
been promoted to head chef. In the beautiful
dining room, his menus include dishes such as
slow-cooked loin of Welsh lamb, herb gnocchi,
broccoli, cream, Madeira sauce; herb risotto,
glazed estate carrots, baby leek and asparagus.
After a Welsh breakfast with local sausages, or a
Loch Fyne kipper, you can zip down the Royal
Welsh Way to Victorian Llandudno for a breath
of sea air. (AB)

The Royal Welsh Way
Llandudno LL30 1RS

T: 01492 584466
E: info@bodysgallen.com
W: bodysgallen.com

BEDROOMS: 31. 16 in cottages, 1 suitable
for disabled.
OPEN: all year, restaurant closed
weekday lunch, house parties at
Christmas, New Year.
FACILITIES: hall, drawing room, library,
bar, dining room (vegetarian/vegan
menus), in-room TV (Freeview),
civil wedding licence, 220-acre park,
spa (swimming pool), EV charging,
ground floor wheelchair accessible.
BACKGROUND MUSIC: none.
LOCATION: 2 miles S of Llandudno
and Conwy.
CHILDREN: no under-6s in hotel, or
under-8s in spa.
DOGS: allowed in some cottages by
request (no charge).
CREDIT CARDS: Amex, MC, Visa.
PRICES: B&B doubles from £225,
singles from £200. Set-price menu
£54.60–£69.30. 1-night bookings
refused bank holidays.

SEE ALSO SHORTLIST

LLANGAMMARCH WELLS Powys

MAP 3:D3

LAKE COUNTRY HOUSE HOTEL & SPA

Anne Hathaway meets Heidi in the hybrid architecture of Pierre Mifsud's former hunting and fishing lodge, beautifully situated in the foothills of Mynydd Epynt, with a trout lake and the River Irfon running through. You can no longer take the barium waters here as Kaiser Wilhelm II did (recommended dose, two pints a day), but you can have a drink in the Oak Room, a sandwich lunch or afternoon tea by the log-burner in the Grand Lounge, with its plum-velvet Knole sofas, oil paintings and grandfather clock. Bedrooms in the main house are traditionally furnished, with the occasional antique. State rooms have a spa bath or four-poster. Dogs with well-behaved owners are welcome in the lodge suites that open on to the grounds. All have home-made biscuits and good toiletries. At dinner, a short menu might include roast loin of Welsh venison with blackberries, game chips, onion bread sauce, port and juniper jus – from the vegetarian menu, roasted vegetables, onion purée, Swiss chard, red wine essence. You can breakfast on smoked haddock, a kipper or a full Welsh before playing a round on the 9-hole golf course or visiting the spa.

Llangammarch Wells LD4 4BS

T: 01591 620202
E: info@lakecountryhouse.co.uk
W: lakecountryhouse.co.uk

BEDROOMS: 32. 12 suites in adjacent lodge, 7 on ground floor, 1 suitable for disabled.
OPEN: all year.
FACILITIES: lounge, bar, restaurant (vegetarian menu), breakfast room, in-room TV (Freeview), spa (15-metre swimming pool), civil wedding licence, 50-acre grounds (tennis, trout lake, 9-hole golf course), public rooms wheelchair accessible, adapted toilet.
BACKGROUND MUSIC: none.
LOCATION: 8 miles SW of Builth Wells.
CHILDREN: all ages welcomed, extra bed £25, no under-8s in spa.
DOGS: allowed (£15 per night), not in main lounge, dining room, spa.
CREDIT CARDS: Amex, MC, Visa.
PRICES: B&B doubles from £205, singles from £155. Fixed-price dinner £47.50.

LLANTHONY PRIORY HOTEL

Far up the Vale of Ewyas in the Welsh Black mountains, and just before the road becomes a narrow track, is where you'll find the wild and remote setting of Llanthony Priory Hotel. You won't find a mobile signal, Wi-Fi, or television here. What you will find are comfort, simplicity and peace. The hotel is in the original prior's quarters for the adjoining 12th-century Augustinian priory, the latter now a roofless but impressive ruin. Rooms are not monastic, but they are simple with whitewashed walls, sparse but solid Victorian furniture – perhaps a marble-topped washstand or four-poster bed – and colourful bedspreads. Four are in the tower, up a spiral staircase, and share two modern shower rooms. The other three share a bathroom. There's a large lounge, with fire, that overlooks the priory interior while you can enjoy a drink before supper in the tiny, stone-flagged and vaulted bar. The dining room, also vaulted, is equally cosy with large black range, gleaming brass and copper and a carved oak sideboard. Food is homely pub style with a surprisingly large choice that could include beef casserole, fish pie and spicy bean goulash.

Llanthony
Abergavenny NP7 7NN

T: 01873 890487
E: llanthonypriory@btconnect.com
W: llanthonyprioryhotel.co.uk

BEDROOMS: 7. All with shared showers/bathrooms.
OPEN: Fri–Sun (Nov–Mar), Tues–Sun (Apr–Oct), 27 Dec–1 Jan, closed Mon except bank holidays.
FACILITIES: lounge, bar, dining room, no Wi-Fi, mobile phone signal or TV, extensive grounds (including priory ruins), unsuitable for disabled.
BACKGROUND MUSIC: none.
LOCATION: 10 miles N of Abergavenny.
CHILDREN: over-10s, ring for pricing.
DOGS: not allowed.
CREDIT CARDS: MC, Visa.
PRICES: B&B doubles from £100, singles from £80. À la carte 3 courses £21.

LLYSWEN Powys

MAP 3:D4

LLANGOED HALL

The picturesque Wye valley is the setting for this 17th-century manor house that opened as a hotel in 1990 under the late Sir Bernard Ashley, of the Laura Ashley fashion and textiles empire. The aim was to recreate the Edwardian country house experience in a historic building that had been remodelled by Clough Williams-Ellis in 1912 in the Lutyensesque style for a London bowler hat-maker. Hats off to all concerned! This is a luxurious place, still hung with Sir Bernard's Sickerts and Augustus Johns. Whether you book a 'bijou' bedroom, suite or four-poster state room, you will find antiques, a decanter of Madeira, home-made shortbread. Afternoon tea is served on bespoke 'Gold Rose and Butterfly' bone china. Fires burn, floors gleam, deep sofas invite you to sink in and relax. Head chef Sam Bowser creates menus inspired by produce from the prolific kitchen garden and foraged in the grounds. Dress smartly (no T-shirts or trainers) to enjoy dishes of venison with artichoke molasses and kohlrabi – for vegans maybe mung bean dhal, vadouvan masala and kaffir lime. A full Welsh breakfast includes laver bread, eggs from the Llangoed hens.

Llyswen
Brecon LD3 0YP

T: 01874 754525
E: reception@llangoedhall.com
W: llangoedhall.co.uk

BEDROOMS: 23.
OPEN: all year, Thurs–Sun.
FACILITIES: great hall, morning room, library, bar/lounge, restaurant (vegetarian menu), billiard room, function rooms, in-room TV (Freeview), civil wedding licence, 17-acre gardens, EV charging, public areas wheelchair accessible.
BACKGROUND MUSIC: in restaurant, during functions, pianist on special occasions.
LOCATION: 12 miles NE of Brecon.
CHILDREN: all ages welcomed, extra bed (under-12s) £65 per night.
DOGS: allowed in 2 bedrooms (call to check availability, £25 per dog per night), not in public rooms. Heated kennels (no charge) available.
CREDIT CARDS: MC, Visa.
PRICES: B&B doubles from £215. À la carte £55, tasting menu £55, £75, £95.

THE GROVE OF NARBERTH

♔ Previous César winner

Described in 1811 as the 'respectable old house of Grove, embosomed in trees', the ancient seat of the Poyer family is today a luxurious country house hotel, embosomed in verdant grounds. Neil and Zoë Kedward have lavished love and money on the 17th-cum-19th-century mansion since buying it in 2007. Interiors mix designer chic and solid tradition, with the use of local stone, hand-made furniture, Welsh textiles, ceramics and fine antiques. Newly refurbished bathrooms now have a freestanding bath and monsoon shower and this year, six bedrooms are being updated in a 15th-century longhouse with exposed stone walls, beams and arrow slits. In the main building, a triple-aspect, top-floor four-poster suite has a lounge and views to the Preseli hills. You can take tea in a sitting room or outside, dine in the Fernery, from Douglas Balish's creative tasting menus, or more casually, with your dog in tow, in the Artisan Rooms. Dishes might include sea bream, with seaweed broth and noodles, or pumpkin risotto, with duck egg and sage. Order a picnic and tootle down to the nearby coast, or simply relax in the 17th-century flower-filled walled garden.

Molleston
Narberth SA67 8BX

T: 01834 860915
E: reservations@grovenarberth.co.uk
W: thegrove-narberth.co.uk

BEDROOMS: 25. 12 in cottages in grounds, 1 suitable for disabled.
OPEN: all year, Fernery closed Sun and Mon.
FACILITIES: 3 lounges, bar, 2 restaurants (veg/vegan menus), in-room TV (Sky), in-room spa treatments, civil wedding licence, 26-acre grounds, EV charging, ground floor wheelchair accessible, adapted toilet.
BACKGROUND MUSIC: in public areas.
LOCATION: 1 mile S of Narberth.
CHILDREN: all ages welcomed, extra bed £45, no under-12s in Fernery.
DOGS: allowed in some bedrooms (£20 a night) and lounge, the Snug dining room.
CREDIT CARDS: MC, Visa.
PRICES: B&B doubles from £260. Tasting menus £74–£105, à la carte (Artisan Rooms) £42. 1-night bookings refused at peak times.

SEE ALSO SHORTLIST

NEWPORT Pembrokeshire

MAP 3:D1

CNAPAN

Third-generation hosts Judith and Michael Cooper welcome new arrivals with tea and Welsh cakes in the lounge or the 'lovely garden, complete with stream', at their pink-washed Georgian house on the bustling main street of this small town on the Nevern estuary. It has a home-from-home feel. 'Everywhere is comfy and cosy and, to me, very familiar,' writes a reader who first stayed as a child and now drives out from London with her own family. Bedrooms are 'nothing too grand' but 'pretty and well equipped', with contemporary furniture, bright fabrics, Welsh wool blankets, art by local artists, books, local information and Mason & Miller toiletries. A family of three can book a double with adjoining single. En suite shower rooms have been recently renovated, with a bigger, better shower, and if you fancy a good soak, there is a bathroom for guests to enjoy. A varied breakfast menu includes Glamorgan sausages, kippers and smoked salmon, as well as the full Cnapan. 'It will set you up for the rest of the day' to explore the spectacular coastline or the footpaths and bridleways of the Preseli hills. (HH, RG)

East Street
Newport SA42 0SY

T: 01239 820575
E: enquiry@cnapan.co.uk
W: cnapan.co.uk

BEDROOMS: 5. Includes 1 family room. Plus self-catering cottage.
OPEN: all year except Christmas and holiday in Feb and early March (ring or check website for dates).
FACILITIES: sitting room, bar, in-room TV (Freeview), small garden, parking, electric bikes to hire.
BACKGROUND MUSIC: none.
LOCATION: town centre.
CHILDREN: all ages welcomed, family room, cots.
DOGS: not allowed.
CREDIT CARDS: MC, Visa.
PRICES: B&B doubles from £85, singles from £67, family room (sleeps 3) from £105. Dinner for parties of 18 or more by arrangement. 1-night bookings sometimes refused at busy times.

LLYS MEDDYG

♦ Previous César winner

In a small town on the glorious Pembrokeshire coast, Ed and Lou Sykes run their Georgian stone house as a smart restaurant-with-rooms, successfully blending character with cool contemporary design. Work from local artists hangs on bold-coloured walls, reclaimed wood features are everywhere, and there is bags of personality in this 'well-run family business' with 'friendly staff' – there's even a dog-friendly yurt, with under-floor heating. Some of the chic bedrooms have a view of Carnigli (Mountain of the Angels), others look out to Newport Bay; three are in a mews annexe. All have a minibar with fresh milk, Welsh blankets and a stylish bathroom. You can dine in the traditional flagstone cellar bar or in a modern pod in the garden as well as in the main restaurant. Wherever you eat, menus feature local, organic produce, with dishes such as cod, peas, cockles and kohlrabi, or shoulder of lamb with squash, beetroot, goat's cheese and sea vegetables. Ed, a dedicated forager, occasionally gives short courses on hunting for wild food. At breakfast, don't miss the salmon smoked in the brick kiln they built out the back. (M and PB)

East Street
Newport SA42 0SY

T: 01239 820008
E: info@llysmeddyg.com
W: llysmeddyg.com

BEDROOMS: 8. 1 on ground floor, 3 in mews annexe, plus a yurt.
OPEN: all year.
FACILITIES: bar, lounge, restaurant, kitchen garden dining area (open in summer holidays), in-room TV (Freeview), civil wedding licence, garden, unsuitable for disabled, limited on-site parking.
BACKGROUND MUSIC: in bar and dining room.
LOCATION: central.
CHILDREN: all ages welcomed, family room.
DOGS: allowed in 3 annexe bedrooms (£15 charge), in the bar, on lead in the garden.
CREDIT CARDS: MC, Visa.
PRICES: B&B doubles from £130, family from £210. À la carte £35. 1-night bookings refused some Saturdays.

PENALLY Pembrokeshire

MAP 3:E1

PENALLY ABBEY

A 'good base for exploring the Pembrokeshire coast', the Boissevain family's 'Strawberry Hill Gothic' house in a 'beautiful location with outstanding rooms and dinner' proves hard to leave, say readers. It's an idyllic bolt-hole with views from the terrace and through romantic cusped windows over Carmarthen Bay to Caldey Island. Melanie Boissevain is an interior designer – and it shows. Rooms, refurbished after a fire, are beautifully decorated in soft pastels, with chic furniture and comfy seating. One sea-facing room has floor-to-ceiling Gothic windows and toile de Jouy wallpaper. Those in the coach house are more Scandi in style, and dog-friendly, with a balcony or terrace. On cold days a fire blazes in an Adam-style fireplace in the sitting room with the subtle 'gloomth' that Horace Walpole sought at Strawberry Hill to show off artwork and antiques. The sea-facing dining room impresses as much for its style, with parquet floors and wooden furniture, as it does with its short menu of Welsh produce, including dishes such as pan-fried hake with parsley risotto. 'We were very happy with our stay.' (Max Licktold, SM, and others)

Penally
Tenby SA70 7PY

T: 01834 843033
E: info@penally-abbey.com
W: penally-abbey.com

BEDROOMS: 12. 4 in coach house, 2 on ground floor.
OPEN: all year.
FACILITIES: drawing room, bar, sunroom, restaurant (vegetarian menu), function room, in-room TV (Freeview), civil wedding licence, in-room treatments, terrace, 1-acre lawns.
BACKGROUND MUSIC: 'very gentle' in bar and restaurant.
LOCATION: 1½ miles SW of Tenby.
CHILDREN: all ages welcomed, over-3s on extra bed £25.
DOGS: allowed in coach house bedrooms (not unattended, £15 a night), bar, sunroom, not in restaurant.
CREDIT CARDS: MC, Visa.
PRICES: B&B doubles from £155. À la carte £45 (vegetarian £35). 1-night bookings refused only at Christmas and major sporting event weekends.

TWR Y FELIN HOTEL

Modern art and minimalist bedrooms rub shoulders with a Georgian windmill in Wales's first contemporary arts hotel, with views of the Pembrokeshire coast. Buildings from the early 1900s surround the windmill but interiors throughout are strikingly contemporary: monochrome colours, sleek furniture and hardwood floors. Of more than 100 artworks, some are provocative; the most fun are portraits of well-known Welsh actors. Dinner features 'fine-dining' dishes such as curried crab with coriander and confit duck with lime, or a deconstructed lemon meringue pie, while breakfast's extensive menu has a Welsh flavour, including potato and laver bread hash, and freshly squeezed juice. 'Immaculately furnished' bedrooms with 'great attention to detail' have a masculine feel – sober colours, clean-lined furniture, wooden floors, and 'the best' limestone-tiled bathroom. Some rooms have terraces, and the windmill's Tower Suite commands superb views of the St Davids peninsula. There are 'beautifully landscaped grounds' and, even better, 'exceptionally friendly staff who went to great lengths to ensure we were happy with everything'. (Mary Coles)

Caerfai Road
St Davids SA62 6QT

T: 01437 725555
E: stay@twryfelinhotel.com
W: twryfelinhotel.com

BEDROOMS: 21. Some on ground floor, some in separate wing, 1 suitable for disabled, 20 more in purpose-built annexe scheduled to be available soon.
OPEN: all year.
FACILITIES: bar, restaurant, lounge, in-room TV (Sky), landscaped grounds, civil wedding licence, EV charging, public areas wheelchair accessible, adapted toilet.
BACKGROUND MUSIC: in public areas.
LOCATION: a few hundred yards from centre of St Davids.
CHILDREN: not under 12.
DOGS: not allowed.
CREDIT CARDS: Amex, MC, Visa.
PRICES: B&B doubles from £230. À la carte £45. Normally 2-night min. stay Fri and Sat, but check for 1-night availability.

SEE ALSO SHORTLIST

SKENFRITH Monmouthshire

MAP 3:D4

❧THE BELL AT SKENFRITH

César award: Welsh inn of the year

The River Monnow flows just in front of the door of Sarah Hudson's former coaching inn and well-liked pub-with-rooms. Last year it even flowed right through it, so the ground floor has had a thorough refurb, and 'how smart and fresh the place looks!' Bedrooms, named after fishing flies, range from Marsh Brown, with garden views and a shower over the bath, to Heckham Peckham, with modern four-poster, river views, a bath and walk-in shower. All have Welsh blankets, ground coffee, fresh milk and shortbread. Staff are 'young, attentive and smiling'. Joseph Colman's locally sourced menus are served in the 'bright extended dining area' and outside, maybe Brecon beef fillet, ox cheek, red wine jus; roasted beetroot, goat's cheese and spinach risotto. 'A passion-fruit parfait had my wife cheering it on.' Westies, whippets and wellies are all welcome in the Dog and Boot bar for a pint with Scotch egg and piccalilli. Order a picnic for a day's fishing, to eat in the riverside orchard, or to take on one of the walks starting from the pub. 'Unsinkable, that's The Bell. We'll be back.' (Richard Barrett, and others)

Skenfrith NP7 8UH

T: 01600 750235
E: reception@skenfrith.co.uk
W: thebellatskenfrith.co.uk

BEDROOMS: 11.
OPEN: all year.
FACILITIES: 2 bars, restaurant (vegan menu), Wine Room (lounge/private dining), in-room TV (BT, Freeview), 2-acre grounds (terrace, garden), restaurant, bar and terrace wheelchair accessible, adapted toilet.
BACKGROUND MUSIC: 'intermittently' in bar and restaurant.
LOCATION: 9 miles W of Ross-on-Wye.
CHILDREN: all ages welcomed, extra bed £20 (£24.95 incl. early supper), no under-8s in restaurant after 7 pm.
DOGS: well-behaved dogs allowed in bedrooms (£20 charge) and 1 bar, dog shower in garden with towels.
CREDIT CARDS: MC, Visa.
PRICES: B&B doubles from £150. Set-price dinner £43. À la carte from £35. 1-night bookings refused Sat.

TREMADOG Gwynedd

PLAS TAN-YR-ALLT

'A bit of luxury in the middle of Snowdonia', with views over the Glaslyn estuary, this B&B in a late Georgian villa comes with an interesting history, told through its bedroom names. Beamed Shelley's Theatre recalls the year that the budding romantic poet lived here and completed his utopian epic Queen Mab. It has a four-poster, antiques, night-time views of 'studded heaven's dark blue vault'. William Madocks, with sea and mountain views, celebrates a former owner who oversaw the construction of Porthmadog's sea wall, which ushered in the development of the Ffestiniog Railway that runs nearby. The third, with half-tester bed, recalls Hilda Greaves, born here in 1855, who engaged nephew Clough Williams-Ellis to restore the 'Triumph of Neptune' mural. Each has a coffee machine, fresh milk, a mini-fridge, cut flowers, a heated bathroom floor, luxury toiletries. Howard Mattingley and Mark White are 'great hosts' and serve afternoon tea in the drawing room. 'Breakfast is plentiful and cooked to order.' 'A beautiful hotel in a beautiful location with great service' runs a typical report. (Helen Hume, Mick Huddlestone, and many others)

Tremadog
Porthmadog LL49 9RG

T: 01766 514591
E: info@plastanyrallt.co.uk
W: plastanyrallt.co.uk

BEDROOMS: 3.
OPEN: all year except 3rd week of Dec to 1 Feb.
FACILITIES: drawing room, dining room, 40-acre grounds, in-room TV (Freeview), unsuitable for disabled.
BACKGROUND MUSIC: in drawing room and dining room.
LOCATION: just above the village of Tremadog.
CHILDREN: not under 18.
DOGS: not allowed.
CREDIT CARDS: MC, Visa.
PRICES: B&B doubles from £155. 1-night bookings refused bank holidays, weekends and at peak times.

TYWYN Gwynedd

MAP 3:B3

DOLFFANOG FAWR

Against the backdrop of Cader Idris, with views across sheep-grazed pastures to Tal-y-llyn lake and the Dyfi and Tarren hills, this 18th-century farmhouse-turned-B&B is beautifully situated, even by Snowdonia's standards. The simple, traditional bedrooms have a pocket-sprung mattress, a Welsh wool throw, a shower, or bath with shower over, and L'Occitane toiletries. Wi-Fi is temperamental at best, so forget your devices and go walking, biking or fishing. Breakfast at the oak dining table brings award-winning sausages, free-range eggs, home-baked organic bread and home-made preserves, with fish options if you prefer. Three nights a week, guests can sit down to a convivial dinner of local produce – perhaps Welsh Black beef, salt marsh lamb or wild sea trout. Your hosts Alex Yorke and Lorraine Hinkins really want you to relax and have fun. Let them know your dietary needs. There's a comfortable lounge with log-burner, leather sofas, books and maps, and if you want to steep in the hot tub under a star-filled dark sky, only the owls will give two hoots.

Tal-y-llyn
Tywyn LL36 9AJ

T: 01654 761247
E: info@dolffanogfawr.co.uk
W: dolffanogfawr.co.uk

BEDROOMS: 4. 1 reached by covered walkway.
OPEN: Mar–Oct, dinner served Thurs–Sat.
FACILITIES: lounge, dining room, in-room TV (Freeview), variable Wi-Fi, 1-acre garden (hot tub), unsuitable for disabled.
BACKGROUND MUSIC: background during evening meals.
LOCATION: by lake, 10 miles E of Tywyn.
CHILDREN: not under 10.
DOGS: allowed by arrangement with own bed (£10 per night), in bedrooms (not unattended) and lounge 'if other guests don't mind', not in dining room.
CREDIT CARDS: MC, Visa.
PRICES: B&B doubles from £110, singles from £90. Set dinner £25–£28 (2% surcharge if paying by credit card). 1-night bookings often refused.

THE WHITEBROOK

Hedge bedstraw, lamb's sorrel, mugwort and estuary greens appear on the plate at Chris and Kirsty Harrod's Michelin-starred 'super, small restaurant-with-rooms', on a single-track road in a Wye valley hamlet. 'The concepts are brilliant,' a reader enthused. 'Mr Harrod forages for ingredients, he highlights the best of local produce' with fruit and vegetables from the kitchen garden. The four years that he spent honing his skills in his hero Raymond Blanc's kitchen at Le Manoir aux Quat'Saisons, Great Milton (see entry), instilled in him the love of food from the wild that is now his signature. His menus (including one for vegetarians) feature 'absolutely delicious' dishes such as squab pigeon, cauliflower, forced rhubarb, charred kale, wild chervil, and Cornish brill, mussel cream, purple sprouting brassica, three-cornered garlic. 'We had the wine flight, which was a good choice.' Four bedrooms have been refurbished, with a large double-ended bath and walk-in shower. Two have a sleigh bed and a seating area, one has a stone wet room. They are smart, but the food is the star. (DH)

Whitebrook NP25 4TX

T: 01600 860254
E: info@thewhitebrook.co.uk
W: thewhitebrook.co.uk

BEDROOMS: 8.
OPEN: all year, except 24 Dec (rooms), 25/26 Dec, 1 Jan, 2 weeks in Jan, restaurant closed Mon, Tues, Wed, and for lunch on Thurs.
FACILITIES: lounge/bar, restaurant (vegetarian menu), in-room TV (Freeview), terrace, 1-acre garden, restaurant and women's toilet wheelchair accessible.
BACKGROUND MUSIC: 'chill-out' in restaurant and lounge.
LOCATION: 6 miles S of Monmouth.
CHILDREN: all ages welcomed, over-8s only in restaurant on weekdays, over-16s only at weekends.
DOGS: only guide dogs allowed.
CREDIT CARDS: Amex, MC, Visa.
PRICES: D,B&B doubles from £330. Fixed-price 3-course menu £42, tasting menus lunch, 5 courses, £55, dinner, 7 courses £85.

CHANNEL ISLANDS

La Coupée, Sark

HERM

THE WHITE HOUSE

Time stands still at this country house – a family-friendly hotel since 1949, with fine-dining restaurant – on a tiny, car-free island of white-sand beaches. In the garden, Herm's own flag, with its silver embowed dolphins and cowled monks, flutters in the breeze in the gentle oceanic climate. Bedrooms have a sea or garden view, some with a furnished balcony, some with access to the swimming pool through French doors. All have the same palette – dark wood furniture, crisp white linen, turquoise throw, blue-striped curtains, taupe carpet, no telephone, no TV, no clock. (Why come here if not to take a break from the frenetic modern world?) You are expected to dress up (smart casual) for dinner in the Conservatory restaurant, where executive head chef Krzysztof Janiak's menus are sophisticated and modern. A typical dish: turbot, steamed mussels, fregola, gremolata, lemon beurre blanc, foraged rock samphire. There is more casual dining and pub fare in The Ship Inn. A designated Ramsar site, Herm is a wildlife-spotters' paradise, with a seal colony resident on the sandbanks known as the 'Humps'.

Herm GY1 3HR

T: 01481 750075
E: reservations@herm.com
W: herm.com

BEDROOMS: 40. 23 in cottages, some on ground floor.
OPEN: early Apr–31 Oct.
FACILITIES: 3 lounges, 2 bars, 2 restaurants, conference room, 1-acre gardens (tennis), 7-metre outdoor swimming pool, wheelchair access to island difficult.
BACKGROUND MUSIC: in The Ship Inn.
LOCATION: by harbour, ferry from Guernsey (20 mins).
CHILDREN: all ages welcomed, no charge for under-6s, under-14s on extra bed £50.
DOGS: allowed in 8 bedrooms by prior arrangement (£25 per night), reception lounge, garden, bars, with restrictions.
CREDIT CARDS: MC, Visa.
PRICES: B&B doubles from £145, singles from £70. Set dinner £38, à la carte £29.

LITTLE SARK Sark

MAP 1: inset E6

LA SABLONNERIE

♔ Previous César winner

Arriving at this pretty 17th-century farmhouse with roses round the door 'is part of its enormous charm': guests are met at the ferry from Guernsey in horse-drawn carriage and clip-clop over La Coupée, a dramatic, narrow isthmus 80 metres above the sea. In a beautiful corner of the car-free dark-sky island, 'effervescent and charismatic' owner Elizabeth Perrée devotes heart and soul to the enterprise begun by her family in 1948. Early visitors included Vivien Leigh and Laurence Olivier. 'Quaint and pleasingly simple' bedrooms are in the main house and surrounding cottages. On cold days a fire burns in the inglenook in a beamed lounge. Colin Day's locally sourced menus, served in the rustic dining room or among the brimming flower borders of the tea garden, include dishes such as roasted scallops, duckling with green peppercorn sauce. 'We feasted on lobster in the pretty garden.' You can bathe in the tidal Venus rock pool, go cycling or take boat trips. Time and tide were against one reader who had hoped both 'to visit the caves in Derrible Bay' and to return for a 25th stay on Sark when lockdown hit. Paradise postponed.

Little Sark GY10 1SD

T: 01481 832061
E: reservations@sablonneriesark.com
W: sablonneriesark.com

BEDROOMS: 22. Some in nearby cottages.
OPEN: mid-Apr–Oct.
FACILITIES: 3 lounges, 2 bars, restaurant, Wi-Fi by arrangement, civil wedding licence, 1-acre garden (tea garden/bar, croquet), unsuitable for disabled.
BACKGROUND MUSIC: classical/piano in bar.
LOCATION: Little Sark, via boat from Guernsey (guests will be met at the harbour on arrival).
CHILDREN: all ages welcomed, terms on application.
DOGS: allowed in some cottages and bedrooms at hotel's discretion (no charge), not in public rooms.
CREDIT CARDS: MC, Visa.
PRICES: B&B doubles from £97.50. Set menus £35, à la carte £55.

ST BRELADE Jersey

MAP 1: inset E6

THE ATLANTIC HOTEL

Overlooking St Ouen's Bay on Jersey's west coast,
The Atlantic has a hint of ocean-cruising glamour
with its retro, streamlined looks, fine dining and
emphasis on relaxation. Big windows, balconies,
pale or nautical colours, and light oak furniture
give bedrooms a breezy feel, relaxing rather
than flashy. Grander rooms have more stately
furnishings. All have marble bathrooms, robes,
fruit and water, sea or golf-course views, and
'generous extras' – readers appreciated the half
bottle of complimentary champagne. As much
as the views – the sunsets are spectacular – it's
the good food that's the draw, with sophisticated
dishes making full use of Jersey's produce:
perhaps pickled Jersey crab and mango salsa
followed by glazed duck breast with stem ginger
and blackcurrant, or sea bass with Jersey Royals.
Tasting menus and market menus add to the
choice. Breakfast brings freshly squeezed juice
and made-to-order dishes, including choices such
as chorizo and eggs, and avocado, tomato and
chilli. With gardens, a palm-fringed outdoor pool,
tennis court, indoor pool and small spa, the hotel
provides a 'wonderfully' relaxing stay. (K and VS)

Le Mont de la Pulente
St Brelade JE3 8HE

T: 01534 744101
E: info@theatlantichotel.com
W: theatlantichotel.com

BEDROOMS: 50. Some on ground floor,
unsuitable for disabled.
OPEN: all year except 3–25 Jan.
FACILITIES: lift, lounge, library, cocktail
bar, restaurant, private dining room,
fitness centre, in-room TV (Sky),
civil wedding licence, 10-acre garden
(tennis, indoor and outdoor heated
swimming pools), public rooms
wheelchair accessible, no adapted
toilet.
BACKGROUND MUSIC: in restaurant,
lounge and cocktail bar in evenings.
LOCATION: 5 miles W of St Helier.
CHILDREN: all ages welcomed, extra
bed free.
DOGS: guide dogs only.
CREDIT CARDS: Amex, MC, Visa.
PRICES: B&B doubles from £150,
singles from £130. Market menu £55,
à la carte £65.

ST PETER Jersey

MAP 1: inset E6

GREENHILLS COUNTRY HOUSE HOTEL

The pace of life slows amid Jersey's tranquil Green Lanes, where the Seymour family's hotel – a 17th-century granite house flanked by sympathetically designed modern wings – sits in flower-filled gardens. Guide readers were 'very impressed' by the service under the stewardship of highly praised manager Carmelita Fernandes. 'Any questions were answered with a smile.' The cheerful, long-serving staff are also a great asset. A garden-view room had a king-size bed ('I needed a telescope to see my wife'), a sofa and armchair, and ample storage. The bathroom, though smallish, had a good walk-in shower. There was only instant coffee and UHT milk, as only top-price rooms have a coffee machine, but all have White Company toiletries. In the restaurant, Lukasz Pietrasz's regularly changing menus include locally sourced dishes such as lamb rump with romesco sauce and pickled cherry tomatoes, or you might opt for a crab sandwich on the terrace from the all-day bar/lounge menu. Loungers surround a small pool, which is open late for a dip on warm summer nights, while sandy beaches are ten minutes' drive away. (AK)

Mont de l'École
St Peter JE3 7EL

T: 01534 481042
E: reservations@greenhillshotel.com
W: greenhillshotel.com

BEDROOMS: 33. 10 on ground floor, 1 suitable for disabled.
OPEN: all year except 2 Dec–mid-Feb.
FACILITIES: 2 lounges, bar, restaurant (vegetarian/vegan menu), garden, terrace, in-room TV, civil wedding licence, outdoor heated swimming pool, access to leisure club at sister hotel, public rooms wheelchair accessible, adapted toilet.
BACKGROUND MUSIC: in public areas.
LOCATION: 8 miles NW of St Helier.
CHILDREN: all ages welcomed.
DOGS: allowed in 4 ground-floor bedrooms on request (£10 per dog per night), not in public areas, but assistance dogs 'always welcome'.
CREDIT CARDS: Amex, MC, Visa.
PRICES: B&B doubles from £109. Set dinner £31.50–£39.50, à la carte £50.

ST PETER PORT Guernsey

MAP 1: inset E5

LA FREGATE

High above St Peter Port, this extended 18th-century manor house made over in contemporary hotel style has views down to the busy harbour and the islands of Sark, Herm and Brecqhou beyond. Even the smallest room looks out to sea, but if you want to watch the boats plying the harbour, it's best to book one with a balcony or terrace. All are bright, light and spacious with subtle paint finishes, bleached-wood furniture and leather armchairs, though with a slightly corporate feel. A top-floor suite with the most commanding outlook has a separate lounge and a dining table. You can take a light lunch in the sun on the terrace, while in the modern restaurant, with its wall of picture windows, Tony Leck's monthly-changing menu is big on local shellfish – Guernsey lobster, hand-dived scallops, Herm oysters – while reprising greatest hits of the 1970s with beef stroganoff, steak tartare and crêpe Suzette. If you have particular dietary needs, just give them notice. Before dinner, take the steep path down to the town and harbour – the walk back will surely sharpen your appetite. Reports, please.

Beauregard Lane
Les Cotils
St Peter Port GY1 1UT

T: 01481 724624
E: enquiries@lafregatehotel.com
W: lafregatehotel.com

BEDROOMS: 22.
OPEN: all year, closed Sun pm, Mon, Tues.
FACILITIES: lounge/bar, restaurant, lift, private dining/function rooms, in-room TV (Freeview), civil wedding licence, terrace (alfresco dining), ½-acre terraced garden, parking, unsuitable for disabled.
BACKGROUND MUSIC: in lounge/bar and restaurant.
LOCATION: hilltop, 5 mins' walk from centre.
CHILDREN: all ages welcomed, extra bed for under-8s £20.
DOGS: guide dogs only.
CREDIT CARDS: Amex, MC, Visa.
PRICES: B&B doubles from £210, suite £475, singles from £105. À la carte £50.

SEE ALSO SHORTLIST

ST SAVIOUR Jersey

MAP 1: inset E6

LONGUEVILLE MANOR

A fountain plays before the magnificent arched entrance to Malcolm and Patricia Lewis's luxury spa hotel (Relais & Châteaux), occupying an ancient, much-altered manor house in landscaped grounds. There's plenty of history here, with medieval fireplaces, beams from the Spanish Armada in one bedroom, and a Victorian garden, but service is bang up to date. 'The general manager is very much in evidence, very hands-on, and boy does it show!' Rooms range from 'standard' to a suite in the turret, with stone bath, oversized shower and access to garden and pool. 'We had a suite. Lovely comfortable bed, well lit, spacious, lots of seating, fabulous bathroom.' A room-service meal was delivered by 'a whole gang of liveried foot soldiers', including the sommelier (the cellar holds 4,000 bottles). But don't miss the restaurant with its oak panelling, and dress up to sample Andrew Baird's creative dishes – maybe deep-water cod, oxtail ravioli, garden kale and white bean velouté. Breakfast is 'a treat'. 'It was all there, Prosecco, loads of fresh fruit, meats, smoked salmon … Coffee was a bit weak. There we are! A criticism – the only one!' (RM-P)

Longueville Road
St Saviour JE2 7WF

T: 01534 725501
E: info@longuevillemanor.com
W: longuevillemanor.com

BEDROOMS: 30. 8 on ground floor, suite in cottage.
OPEN: all year except 22 Dec–13 Jan.
FACILITIES: lift, 2 lounges, cocktail bar, 2 dining rooms, in-room smart TV, conference facilities, civil wedding licence, spa, 18-acre grounds (croquet, tennis, outdoor heated pool), public areas wheelchair accessible, no adapted toilet.
BACKGROUND MUSIC: in bar and restaurant.
LOCATION: 1½ miles E of St Helier.
CHILDREN: all ages welcomed, extra bed for ages 2–12 £75.
DOGS: allowed in bedrooms (£25) and public rooms but not in restaurant.
CREDIT CARDS: MC, Visa.
PRICES: B&B doubles from £200. À la carte £75. 1-night bookings refused at weekends, bank holidays.

IRELAND

Carrauntoohil, in Maegillycuddy's Reeks, Co. Kerry

BAGENALSTOWN Co. Carlow

LORUM OLD RECTORY

♻ Previous César winner

A stay at Lorum is like being invited as a family friend to enjoy the antique-filled country house, candlelit dinners and mountain views. Bobbie Smith and daughter Rebecca welcome guests into their large, granite-stone Victorian rectory – Bobbie's childhood home – filled with fine furniture, curios, fresh flowers and family photographs. Relax over afternoon tea on a plump sofa in front of the drawing-room fire while browsing through one of the many books or gazing at views of Mount Leinster. Drinks are taken here before dinner around the mahogany table in the fire-warmed and red-walled dining room – guests are charmed by the entertaining, communal style – where imaginative home-cooked dinners (mother and daughter are members of chefs' group Euro-Toques) use home-grown and local produce. Quirky diets can be catered for with little fuss. Spacious bedrooms are comfortable country house in style, with solid furniture, family heirlooms, well-padded armchairs and stacks of books. Large bathrooms have a power shower. Guests regularly mention the attention to detail, and the restorative peace of the setting.

Kilgraney
Bagenalstown R21 RD45

T: 00 353 59 977 5282
E: bobbie@lorum.com
W: lorum.com

BEDROOMS: 3.
OPEN: Feb–end Nov.
FACILITIES: drawing room, study (with TV), dining room, snug, 1-acre garden (croquet) in 18-acre grounds, wedding facilities, unsuitable for disabled.
BACKGROUND MUSIC: none.
LOCATION: 4 miles S of Bagenalstown on R705 to Borris.
CHILDREN: aged 16 and over welcomed.
DOGS: by arrangement, not on furniture or in dining room (no charge).
CREDIT CARDS: MC, Visa.
PRICES: B&B doubles from €180, singles from €130. Set 5-course dinner €50.

BALLINGARRY Co. Limerick

MAP 6:D5

THE MUSTARD SEED
AT ECHO LODGE

Everything is peachy at this apricot-washed Victorian mansion, now a lavishly furnished hotel and fine-dining restaurant, in landscaped grounds with orchard and working kitchen garden. John Edward Joyce, who bought the place in 2016 after 25 years as manager, is still keen as mustard. 'We were welcomed personally by him on arrival, and he was on hand to wish us a safe journey on departure.' There's a feel of a private home to the heritage hideaway, its 'spacious public rooms bedecked with flowers'. Bedrooms, either in the main house with its hand-carved oak staircase or in a separate wing, are traditionally styled, with antique furniture, designer fabrics and perhaps a four-poster or original fireplace. Some have dual-aspect valley views, others have doors opening on to the gardens. In the twin Georgian dining rooms, where 'paintings and gilt mirrors delight the eye', service is 'efficient and seemingly effortless'. Chef Angel Pirev's highly creative menus include dishes such as venison loin, kofta, rainbow carrot, gooseberries and hazelnuts. 'Definitely a place to put on our "revisit" list.' (PH, and others)

Ballingarry V94 EHN8

T: 00 353 69 68508
E: info@mustardseed.ie
W: mustardseed.ie

BEDROOMS: 16. 1, on ground floor, suitable for disabled.
OPEN: all year except 24–26 Dec.
FACILITIES: entrance hall, library, restaurant, sunroom, in-room TV (terrestrial), wedding facilities, 12-acre grounds, restaurant and public rooms wheelchair accessible, adapted toilet.
BACKGROUND MUSIC: in restaurant.
LOCATION: in village, 18 miles SW of Limerick.
CHILDREN: all ages welcomed, extra bed no charge.
DOGS: 'well-behaved' pets welcome, in designated bedrooms (not unattended, no charge), not in public rooms.
CREDIT CARDS: Amex, MC, Visa.
PRICES: B&B doubles from €140. Twilight Dinner (4 courses) €49, Classic Dinner (4 courses) €68.

BALLYCASTLE Co. Mayo

MAP 6:B4

STELLA MARIS

You can drift off to sleep to the sound of the waves and wake to the view over Bunatrahir Bay at this Victorian coastguard's fortress turned one-of-a-kind hotel. Almost all the bedrooms are sea facing. This is a summer place, open from May through September, when warmth and light flood a sun lounge that runs the length of the building, filled with mix-and-match furniture. Cosy public rooms open one into another, warmed by blazing fires on chilly days, and adorned with antiques, clocks, photos and whatnots. There is so much character here, in the fabric of the extraordinary building, with Gothic windows, walls that in places are three feet thick, and gun turrets. Today, binoculars rather than guns are trained on the ocean, in the hope of spotting playful dolphins. At night, tables are set with crisp linen for a dinner of local ingredients – perhaps roast rack of Mayo lamb, fish from the day boats and home-grown vegetables – from a short menu devised by chef/proprietor Frances Kelly-McSweeney. After a full Irish breakfast, you might set out to explore the Wild Atlantic Way or head to the links at Enniscrone.

Killerduff
Ballycastle

T: 00 353 96 43322
E: info@stellamarisireland.com
W: stellamarisireland.com

BEDROOMS: 11. 1, on ground floor, suitable for disabled.
OPEN: 1 May–30 Sept, restaurant closed Mon evening.
FACILITIES: lounge, bar, restaurant, conservatory, in-room TV (terrestrial), Wi-Fi in public areas, 2-acre grounds, public rooms wheelchair accessible, adapted toilet.
BACKGROUND MUSIC: none.
LOCATION: 1½ miles W of Ballycastle.
CHILDREN: not under 5.
DOGS: not allowed.
CREDIT CARDS: MC, Visa.
PRICES: B&B doubles from €150, singles from €95. À la carte €40.

BALLYMOTE Co. Sligo

MAP 6:B5

TEMPLE HOUSE

A ruined Knights Templar castle sits beside a mile-long lake in the grounds belonging to Roderick and Helena Perceval's impressive classical mansion. The Perceval family home since 1665, the present house dates from 1825 and was remodelled in the 1860s. It's all very grand, with a half-mile driveway to the door, through which an imperial staircase leads up from a double-height vestibule. But it's also very much a family home, filled with antiques and ancestral portraits. Your bedroom might have a sleigh bed, a half-tester – two identical half-testers in the case of Twins room. If you need a lot of hanging space choose Porch; it has a 14-foot wardrobe. Maple has original furniture from 1864 and views across parkland and downriver. At night, guests gather for drinks by the fire, house-party style, before eating communally in the dining room. Here, dishes of perhaps braised Temple House lamb or cod with tempura wild Atlantic oyster are complemented by the historic setting, with a portrait of Roderick's great-great-great-grandfather above the fireplace, and the family silver laid out on the mahogany dining table.

Temple House Demesne
Ballymote F56 NN50

T: 00 353 71 918 3329
E: stay@templehouse.ie
W: templehouse.ie

BEDROOMS: 7. Plus 3 non-B&B reserved for house parties.
OPEN: Apr–mid-Nov.
FACILITIES: morning room, dining room, vestibule, table-tennis room, wedding facilities, 1½-acre garden on 1,000-acre estate, water sports on site.
BACKGROUND MUSIC: none.
LOCATION: 12 miles S of Sligo.
CHILDREN: all ages welcomed, extra bed €30, kitchen supper for 3–12s.
DOGS: not allowed.
CREDIT CARDS: Amex, MC, Visa.
PRICES: B&B doubles from €179, singles from €125. Set dinner €59.

BALLYVAUGHAN Co. Clare   MAP 6:C4

GREGANS CASTLE HOTEL

♔ Previous César winner

There isn't a castle, but there is a 15th-century tower house, built for the 'Prince of the Burren', the unearthly glaciokarst landscape said to have inspired J R R Tolkien. The author stayed in the 18th-century manor house opposite the tower, which is now run as a hotel in an 'idyllic setting', with a 'warm welcome' from owners Simon Haden and Frederieke McMurray. Everything is beautifully styled, with antiques, modern artwork and quirky ornaments; the hotel retains its historic charm yet feels completely of the moment. Rooms are 'ample and comfortable'; some have a sea view where you can watch the sun go down on Galway Bay, others have a private garden. Robbie McCauley's menus combine modern cooking with artisan and foraged ingredients in dishes such as East Clare rabbit, celeriac, cèpe, pear, tarragon. 'The five-course dinner was outstanding.' At breakfast there are pancakes with organic apple syrup, smoked haddock with hollandaise. You can wander lovely grounds, have a drink by the drawing-room fire, and lunch on Flaggy Shore oysters in the Corkscrew bar, named after the scenic winding road from Lisdoonvarna. (RP)

Gragan East
Ballyvaughan H91 CF60

T: 00 353 65 707 7005
E: stay@gregans.ie
W: gregans.ie

BEDROOMS: 21. 7 on ground floor, 1 suitable for disabled.
OPEN: mid-Feb–early Dec, restaurant closed Mon, Thurs.
FACILITIES: drawing room, bar, dining room, 15-acre grounds, wedding facilities, EV charging, public areas wheelchair accessible, no adapted toilet.
BACKGROUND MUSIC: in bar and dining room.
LOCATION: 3½ miles SW of Ballyvaughan.
CHILDREN: all ages welcomed, extra bed €25–€50.
DOGS: allowed in some ground-floor bedrooms (€25 per stay), not in public rooms.
CREDIT CARDS: Amex, MC, Visa.
PRICES: B&B doubles from €279. Set menu and à la carte €80, tasting menu €100. 1-night bookings sometimes refused Sat, bank holidays.

CASTLEHILL Co. Mayo

MAP 6:B4

ENNISCOE HOUSE

A single-track road meanders through woodlands to this Georgian mansion at the foot of lonely Nephin mountain, overlooking Lough Conn, where Susan Kellett and son DJ are 'welcoming hosts'. Built on to an older house in 1790 (you can still see the 'join') Enniscoe is a trove of antiques, ancestral portraits and hunting trophies. The drawing room has the original – if faded – silk Adamesque wallpaper. The front bedrooms, up an elliptical grand staircase, have a four-poster or canopy bed and lake view. There has been some updating since last year – a 'new' heritage carpet from an aunt's house in one bedroom, a remodelled bathroom for another – but the timeless ethos remains. A peat fire was burning merrily and 'an excellent tea' awaited when readers returned from exploring the grounds, with Victorian walled garden and woodland trail. Dinner, cooked by Susan with produce from the garden, is served in the wood-panelled dining room. Maybe savoury tart, salmon in creamy sauce, a super-fresh salad. After a breakfast of home-baked bread, a 'generous buffet' and the full Irish, you might visit the North Mayo Heritage Centre on the property.

Castlehill
Ballina F26 EA34

T: 00 353 96 31112
E: mail@enniscoe.com
W: enniscoe.com

BEDROOMS: 6. Plus self-catering units behind house.
OPEN: Apr–Oct, New Year.
FACILITIES: 2 sitting rooms, dining room, no in-room TV, wedding facilities, 3-acre garden in 30-acre grounds.
BACKGROUND MUSIC: occasionally in public areas.
LOCATION: 2 miles S of Crossmolina, 12 miles SW of Ballina.
CHILDREN: all ages welcomed, 12s and under stay free, over-12s €20.
DOGS: allowed in certain bedrooms (no charge), public rooms, not dining room.
CREDIT CARDS: MC, Visa.
PRICES: B&B doubles from €190, singles from €125. Set menu €50. Sat min. 2-night stay.

CASTLELYONS Co. Cork

MAP 6:D5

BALLYVOLANE HOUSE

Amid gardens and parkland, with bluebell woods and trout lakes, this Georgian country house, remodelled in the 19th century, is not a hotel but a family home, say third-generation owners Justin and Jenny Green. It is filled with possessions accumulated over nearly 70 years – antiques, portraits, landscapes, stuffed pheasants, lamps, figurines, vintage sofas. Log fires blaze; spaniels fawn. Bedrooms are full of character. Some have views to the Galtee mountains, or a huge bathroom with a trophy stag's head over a freestanding bath. All have a coffee machine, home-made cordials, cookies and chocolate. A convivial dinner might include home-reared meat, salmon from their beats on the River Blackwater, fruit and vegetables from the walled garden, and foraged ingredients. Or perhaps nettle soup; gravadlax; roast saddleback pork, baked apple, Longueville House cider sauce; lemon posset; artisan cheeses. Children love to pet the donkeys, feed the hens and collect eggs for breakfast, or hop aboard for a trailer ride around the estate. A laburnum walk leads to bell tents and a 'pig ark' if you want to 'glamp' under the stars.

Castlelyons
Fermoy P61 FP70

T: 00 353 25 36349
E: info@ballyvolanehouse.ie
W: ballyvolanehouse.ie

BEDROOMS: 6. Plus 'glamping' tents May–Sept.
OPEN: all year, but closed Mon, Tues, Wed in winter except for group bookings, Christmas/New Year (self-catering only).
FACILITIES: hall, drawing room, garden hall (honesty bar), dining room, wedding facilities, barn (table tennis), 80-acre grounds (15-acre garden, croquet, tennis, trout lakes).
BACKGROUND MUSIC: none.
LOCATION: 22 miles NE of Cork.
CHILDREN: all ages welcomed, free cots, extra bed €30, high tea for under-13s €15.
DOGS: allowed (no charge) but kept on lead during shooting season July–Jan.
CREDIT CARDS: MC, Visa.
PRICES: B&B doubles from €250. Set dinner €67.50.

CLIFDEN Co. Galway

MAP 6:C4

THE QUAY HOUSE

♔ Previous César winner

With its harbour views, eclectic furnishings, bedrooms full of home comforts and hosts who exude warmth and joviality, Quay House is a Connemara institution. The former Georgian harbourmaster's house and neighbouring buildings, run by 'extremely welcoming' Paddy and Julia Foyle as a B&B for 28 years, is delightfully unique. Antiques, curios, paintings and mirrors dot the fire-warmed ground-floor rooms: a zebra rug here, vintage binoculars there, and antlers and bison horns clustered on walls. With 'good-quality' Georgian and Victorian furniture, the overall feel is comfortable rather than cluttered. 'Spacious, country house' bedrooms follow the same style, most with harbour views and many with balcony or terrace. Bathrooms are large, with bathtub and shower. Breakfasts, in the plant-filled conservatory, are 'delicious and filling' with freshly squeezed juice, home-baked bread, and cooked dishes including devilled kidneys, the 'full Irish', locally smoked salmon and scrambled eggs. 'As good as anything we have eaten anywhere.' Service is 'warm and prompt' and the Foyles love sharing local knowledge. (RH, and others)

Beach Road
Clifden H71 XF76

T: 00 353 95 21369
E: res@thequayhouse.com
W: thequayhouse.com

BEDROOMS: 14. 2 on ground floor, 1 suitable for disabled, 8 in annexe.
OPEN: end Mar–end Oct.
FACILITIES: 2 sitting rooms, breakfast conservatory, in-room TV, small garden, fishing, sailing, golf, riding nearby, free road parking, breakfast room and public areas wheelchair accessible.
BACKGROUND MUSIC: none.
LOCATION: on harbour, 8 mins' walk from centre.
CHILDREN: all ages welcomed, free cots, no charge for under-12s sharing room with parents.
DOGS: not allowed.
CREDIT CARDS: MC, Visa.
PRICES: B&B doubles from €160, singles from €90. 1-night bookings may be refused bank holiday weekends.

SEE ALSO SHORTLIST

CLIFDEN Co. Galway

MAP 6:C4

SEA MIST HOUSE

The colourful cottage-style flowers surrounding the red door of this pretty, stone-built Georgian house are a clue to the warm welcome and cosy atmosphere inside. Sheila Griffin grew up in Sea Mist House, just a couple of minutes from Clifden centre, and that sense of a well lived-in house – photographs, memorabilia, a huge collection of art – is palpable. Guests comment on Sheila's genial hospitality and the B&B's relaxed atmosphere. Downstairs, there are two welcoming sitting rooms, a peat fire in one and wood-burning stove in the other, with tables of books, walls of paintings, deep sofas and well-loved antiques. More books are found in a mini-library on the landing. Neat bedrooms have bright rugs and curtains, more paintings, an inviting mix of furniture and often a window seat, but no TVs. Shower-only bathrooms can be a squeeze. Breakfast in the conservatory overlooking the cottage garden is a proper affair with decorative china, fresh flowers and linen napkins. The menu includes home-made compote, bread and scones, as well as pancakes and the full Irish, with eggs courtesy of Sheila's hens.

Seaview
Clifden H71 NV63

T: 00 353 95 21441
E: sheila@seamisthouse.com
W: seamisthouse.com

BEDROOMS: 4.
OPEN: mid-Mar–end Oct.
FACILITIES: 2 sitting rooms, conservatory dining room, mini-library, ¾-acre garden, parking, unsuitable for disabled.
BACKGROUND MUSIC: none.
LOCATION: just down from the main square, on the edge of town.
CHILDREN: by arrangement.
DOGS: not allowed.
CREDIT CARDS: MC, Visa.
PRICES: B&B doubles from €90.

SEE ALSO SHORTLIST

CLONES Co. Monaghan

MAP 6:B6

HILTON PARK

Built in 1734, burnt down in 1803, rebuilt over 15 years and remodelled in the 1870s in the style of an Italian palazzo, the ancestral home of the Maddens is the perfect place for an escapist Irish country house weekend. Fred and Joanna Madden have been the delightful hosts for more than 30 years since opening Hilton Park to paying guests. Interiors are filled with antiques, portraits and family heirlooms accumulated over nine generations. The principal bedrooms have views across parkland to a lake, through eight-foot windows, a four-poster, an antique bath. There is a billiard room and drawing rooms, while outdoor diversions include golf, fishing, wild swimming, or simply exploring the accredited wildlife estate. Breakfast, in the vaulted servants' hall, brings poached fruit, fresh-baked bread, home-made granola, superior sausages, sorrel and haddock fishcakes. At night guests sit down to a dinner cooked by Fred, who trained under Rowley Leigh at London's Kensington Place, and uses produce from the walled kitchen garden, pork from the free range pigs that forage in the woodland, venison and trout from the estate.

Clones H23 C582

T: 00 353 47 56007
E: mail@hiltonpark.ie
W: hiltonpark.ie

BEDROOMS: 6.
OPEN: Mar–mid-Dec, groups only at Christmas/New Year.
FACILITIES: 3 drawing rooms, study, breakfast room, dining room, games room, billiard room, Wi-Fi in public areas, wedding facilities, 600-acre grounds (3 lakes for fishing and wild swimming, golf course, croquet).
BACKGROUND MUSIC: occasionally in dining room.
LOCATION: 4 miles S of Clones.
CHILDREN: all ages welcomed, extra bed €40–€50 (under-3s stay free), children's high tea.
DOGS: not allowed in house, only in garden.
CREDIT CARDS: MC, Visa.
PRICES: B&B doubles from €210. Set dinner €65.

DRINAGH Co. Wexford

MAP 6:D6

KILLIANE CASTLE
COUNTRY HOUSE AND FARM

A 15th-century fortified tower complete with massive walls and murder holes abuts this handsome B&B in the heart of a working farm. The past may have been turbulent, but today you can be assured of a warm welcome from the Mernagh family, who have owned the estate since 1920, giving the farmhouse the feel of a cherished home. Guests are welcomed by Patrycja with tea and home-baked biscuits, while husband Paul is manager. Up an elegant staircase, past the grandfather clock, lie eight comfortable bedrooms, supplied with water from an artesian well. Two more rooms are in the courtyard and stable block. In the summer, Patrycja cooks dinner with meat from the farm and salads from the garden. Her substantial farmhouse breakfast includes porridge with whiskey and cream, the full Irish, Duncannon smoked salmon, new-laid eggs from hens in the garden, honey from the hives, home-made soda bread and toast. To work it all off, you can play tennis or pitch and putt, get swinging on the driving range, or climb to the top of the tower where Paul's grandfather once stored potatoes, and admire the views of Wexford.

Drinagh Y35 E1NC

T: 00 353 53 915 8885
E: info@killianecastle.com
W: killianecastle.com

BEDROOMS: 10. 2 in former stable block.
OPEN: mid-Feb–mid-Dec.
FACILITIES: lounge (honesty bar), snug, dining room, in-room TV (Freeview), garden, grounds (nature trail, tennis, croquet, pitch and putt, 300-metre driving range), 230-acre dairy farm, unsuitable for disabled.
BACKGROUND MUSIC: in dining room and reception.
LOCATION: 1½ miles S of Drinagh.
CHILDREN: all ages welcomed, family rooms sleep 1 or 2 children under 12.
DOGS: allowed in grounds, not indoors.
CREDIT CARDS: MC, Visa.
PRICES: B&B doubles from €125, singles from €85. Set 3-course dinner (June–Aug) €45.

DUBLIN

THE WILDER TOWNHOUSE

Once a home for retired governesses and for
'bewildered women', this Victorian red brick
property a stroll from St Stephen's Green also
draws its name from Oscar Wilde's association
with Dublin. Today, it has been transformed
for hoteliers Frankie and Josephine Whelehan
into a luxurious boutique hotel with a 'stunning
combination of white paint, mirrors, modern
paintings and eccentric antiques'. Bedrooms,
ranging from 'shoebox' to suites, have amusing
artwork and quirky features, perhaps a
dressmaker's form, gilded butterflies in a bell jar,
a log-effect fire, velvet Art Deco chairs. All have
Parisian toiletries, books by Irish authors, here
and there a bon mot ('Life is too short to be taken
seriously' – Oscar Wilde). Bathrooms have a walk-
in rainforest shower. Craft gins and 'excellent
light bites' such as a charcuterie or cheese plate are
served in a 'charming tea room' which opens on
to a 'flowery terrace'. 'Delicious breakfasts' might
include eggs Benedict or, should you prefer it, you
can sit serenely over a muffin ('One should always
eat muffins quite calmly,' as Wilde also wrote).
(Anne Chisholm)

22 Adelaide Road
Dublin 2

T: 00 353 1 969 65 98
E: stay@thewilder.ie
W: thewilder.ie

BEDROOMS: 42. Some suitable for
disabled.
OPEN: all year except 23–27 Dec.
FACILITIES: Gin and Tea Rooms,
Garden Room, terrace, in-room TV
(terrestrial), 8 parking spaces, public
rooms wheelchair accessible.
BACKGROUND MUSIC: in lobby and bar.
LOCATION: near St Stephen's Green.
CHILDREN: all ages welcomed, but not
an ideal place for children, under-3s
stay free.
DOGS: not allowed.
CREDIT CARDS: Amex, MC, Visa.
PRICES: B&B doubles from €169.

SEE ALSO SHORTLIST

GLASLOUGH Co. Monaghan

MAP 6:B6

CASTLE LESLIE ESTATE

'This is such a unique and interesting place,'
writes a reader, of the Leslie clan's 19th-century
mansion on a vast estate with gardens, lakes
and woodland. 'I felt like I was in a fairy tale.'
Inside a slightly dour building, the feel is more
Italian Renaissance, with paintings, Grand Tour
souvenirs and heirlooms. 'Every corner is filled
with stories and charm. The staff are warm,
friendly and helpful.' Heritage bedrooms come
with their own gem of Leslie lore. Aggie's room,
with a slipper bath and four-poster, recalls Agnes
Bernelle, 'wartime secret agent, actress and
Ireland's oldest punk'. New this year, the West
Wing suite has a four-poster, a bathroom with
roll-top bath, walk-in shower and Juliet balcony,
a double bedroom and bathroom above. Further
great bedrooms are found at The Lodge by the
equestrian centre, or stay with your dog in the Old
Stable Mews apartments. You can eat casually in
Conor's Lounge at The Lodge, take out a picnic,
or dine in Snaffles restaurant, where head chef
Aaron Duffy will prepare dishes such as Irish beef
fillet with slow-cooked short rib, salt-baked carrot
and bone-marrow crust.

Glaslough H18 FY04

T: 00 353 47 88100
E: info@castleleslie.com
W: castleleslie.com

BEDROOMS: 95 bedrooms. 50 in Lodge
(2 suitable for disabled), self-catering
cottages.
OPEN: all year except 16–27 Dec.
FACILITIES: drawing rooms, bar,
breakfast room, restaurant,
conservatory, billiard room, library,
private dining rooms, cinema, some
in-room TV, wedding facilities, spa
(outdoor hot tub), equestrian centre,
14-acre gardens on 1,000-acre estate,
public areas wheelchair accessible,
adapted toilet.
BACKGROUND MUSIC: in public areas
of Lodge.
LOCATION: 7 miles NE of Monaghan.
CHILDREN: all ages welcomed.
DOGS: allowed in Old Stable mews
rooms only (no charge).
CREDIT CARDS: Amex, MC, Visa.
PRICES: B&B doubles from €195.
6-course dinner €68. 1-night bookings
sometimes refused.

GOREY Co. Wexford

MAP 6:D6

MARLFIELD HOUSE

George the peacock struts some of the 40-acre grounds of this rural Regency-style country house, run as a hotel (Relais & Châteaux) for more than four decades by the Bowe family. The interiors are a blend of elegance and comfort, with antiques, oil portraits, blazing fires, fresh flowers and the odd snoozing cat. Bedrooms have a marble bathroom, some a four-poster, a working fireplace, and a view of the lake. New this year are the Pond Suites, in a woodland setting, with a freestanding bath under a circular picture window, a walk-in shower, and patio doors to a private terrace. In the fine-dining Conservatory restaurant, the menu might include fillet of turbot with brown shrimp, with vegetables from the kitchen garden. Vegans have good choices here and at the more informal Duck Terrace, in converted courtyard buildings, with a log fire, café bar and glasshouse, and tables on a terrace overlooking the kitchen garden. After a breakfast featuring Duncannon smoked salmon, free-range eggs, or pancakes with bacon and maple syrup, you can set off and explore on one of the woodland walks.

Courtown Road
Gorey Y25 DK23

T: 00 353 53 942 1124
E: margaret@marlfieldhouse.ie
W: marlfieldhouse.com

BEDROOMS: 22. 8 on ground floor, 6 annexe suites, 6 suitable for disabled.
OPEN: 1 Feb–9 Jan, Wed–Sun, all week Easter to Sept (check website for restaurants as opening times may change).
FACILITIES: reception hall, drawing room, library/bar, 2 restaurants, in-room TV (terrestrial, Virgin), wedding facilities, 36-acre grounds, reception area and restaurant wheelchair accessible.
BACKGROUND MUSIC: in library/bar, restaurant.
LOCATION: 1 mile E of Gorey.
CHILDREN: all ages welcomed, extra bed €25.
DOGS: allowed in bedroom and grounds by arrangement (€25 a night), not in public rooms.
CREDIT CARDS: Amex, MC, Visa.
PRICES: D,B&B from €154 per person. Set-price dinner (5-course) €67, à la carte €45. 1-night bookings sometimes refused weekends.

HOLYWOOD Co. Down

MAP 6:B6

♔RAYANNE HOUSE

César award: eccentric hotel of the year

'Rayanne House isn't your typical bed and breakfast accommodation,' say Conor and Bernie McClelland of their Victorian merchant's house overlooking Belfast lough. No, indeed! Described by our inspectors as 'lavish, eccentric, endearing', it combines striking original features with bold fabrics, wallpaper and murals. Most novel is the golf-themed Rory McIlroy bedroom with wet-room shower. Some rooms have a balcony with a lough view. Conor's seasonal menus include dishes such as seared duck breast, blackberry and sloe gin reduction; halibut fillet, oyster mushroom and morel beurre blanc, crab and apple salad. There are themed Titanic nights, when he replicates, from soup to nuts, canapés to petits fours, the extravagant nine-course last meal served on the doomed ship, which sailed out of the Harland and Wolff shipyard beneath these windows. The award-winning breakfast, too, can be a Titanic affair, bringing goodies such as chilled cream porridge with raspberry purée; oven-baked ham and organic eggs; grilled kipper or oak-smoked salmon; and potato waffles drizzled with Dijon mustard, cider and honey sauce.

60 Demesne Road
Holywood BT18 9EX

T: 28 9042 5859
E: info@rayannehouse.com
W: rayannehouse.com

BEDROOMS: 10. 1, on ground floor, suitable for disabled.
OPEN: all year, 'limited service' Christmas/New Year.
FACILITIES: 2 lounges, dining room, conference facilities, wedding facilities, 1-acre grounds, parking, public rooms wheelchair accessible, adapted toilet.
BACKGROUND MUSIC: in dining room.
LOCATION: ½ mile from Holywood town centre, 6 miles NE of Belfast.
CHILDREN: all ages welcomed, under-2s stay free, cots, baby-listening.
DOGS: may be allowed by prior arrangement.
CREDIT CARDS: MC, Visa.
PRICES: B&B doubles from £150, singles from £90, triple from £150. Set-price à la carte, £52 (10% service added), Titanic package, D,B&B £250 for 2 sharing.

LETTERFRACK Co. Galway
MAP 6:C4

ROSLEAGUE MANOR

Overlooking Ballinakill Bay, and tucked among private woodland, this fine-looking, family-run hotel offers rooms and service as serene as its surroundings. 'Lovely staff', together with the hotel's peaceful setting, ensured 'our shoulders began to relax', report guests. With its creeper-covered blush-pink facade, the Regency building is as handsome inside as out. The two drawing rooms and dining room, with original cornicing, high ceilings and log fires, are elegantly furnished, and the walls hung with paintings and mirrors. Bedrooms are large – some 'enormous' – with a traditional country house style including antiques, comfortable reading chairs, books and fresh flowers. All have views of either the sea or woodland. Dinner is a leisurely affair in the rich red-walled dining room that might start with local scallops followed by roast rack of Connemara lamb or turbot with saffron beurre blanc. After a feast-like breakfast, spend the day exploring unspoilt Connemara – part of the Wild Atlantic Way scenic route passes through the district – and return to afternoon tea in the plant-filled Victorian conservatory. (BT)

Letterfrack

T: 00 353 95 41101
E: info@rosleague.com
W: rosleague.com

BEDROOMS: 21. 2 on ground floor.
OPEN: mid-Mar–end Oct.
FACILITIES: 2 drawing rooms, conservatory/bar, dining room, in-room TV (terrestrial), wedding facilities, 25-acre grounds (tennis).
BACKGROUND MUSIC: none.
LOCATION: 7 miles NE of Clifden.
CHILDREN: all ages welcomed, extra bed €30, also family rooms.
DOGS: 'well-behaved' dogs allowed (no charge).
CREDIT CARDS: MC, Visa.
PRICES: B&B doubles from €146, singles from €107. Set dinner €38–€55, à la carte €42. Min. 2-night stay at bank holiday weekends.

LIMERICK Co. Limerick   MAP 6:D5

NO. 1 PERY SQUARE

This town-house hotel, overlooking Limerick's
People's Park, packs a lot into its Georgian rooms,
from a spa and swish restaurant to a choice of
period and chic bedrooms. There's even space for
a terrace and garden. Sweeping sash windows
form the backdrop to a low-key glamour of
deep-hued walls, velvet-covered chairs, mirrors
and candlesticks. 'Smartly dressed' porters whisk
bags to bedrooms, either smaller Club rooms in
an adjoining building with a classic contemporary
style, or larger sash-windowed Period rooms.
Overlooking the park or garden, these are elegant
with brass bedsteads, Sanderson wallpapers and
roll-top baths. All offer bathrobes and organic
Voya bathroom products. The latter are used in
the basement spa, a serene space with a thermal
suite and treatment rooms. 'Excellent' dinners
are served in the club-style Long Room bar,
recently extended with a garden room, from a
menu of confident, sophisticated dishes such as
smoked salmon with preserved rhubarb, and
duck breast with lentil and beet dhal. The
Drawing Room's afternoon tea is a classy
event, too. Walk it off with a stroll around the
surrounding Georgian Quarter.

Georgian Quarter
1 Pery Square
Limerick V94 EKP9

T: 00 353 61 402402
E: info@oneperysquare.com
W: oneperysquare.com

BEDROOMS: 21, 2 suitable for disabled.
OPEN: all year except 24–26 Dec.
FACILITIES: lift, lounge/bar, drawing
room, restaurant (vegetarian & vegan
menus), private dining room, in-room
TV (RTÉ, Virgin), wedding facilities,
small kitchen garden, terrace,
basement spa, car park (free), public
rooms wheelchair accessible.
BACKGROUND MUSIC: in restaurant and
lounge.
LOCATION: central.
CHILDREN: all ages welcomed, extra
bed €35.
DOGS: 1 dog-friendly bedroom
(€25 per night).
CREDIT CARDS: Amex, MC, Visa.
PRICES: B&B doubles from €165, singles
from €135. À la carte €49.

LISDOONVARNA Co. Clare

MAP 6:C4

SHEEDY'S

The Sheedy family's old farmhouse on the edge of the Burren's dramatic karst landscape is today a smart hotel and restaurant. Sheedy hospitality stretches back to the 1930s, when Alice Sheedy first welcomed paying guests. Today grandson John, with his wife, Martina, are natural hosts. When our inspectors visited, Martina showed them to a 'spacious, squeaky-clean' bedroom with 'a mix of antiques and contemporary pieces', comfy armchairs and 'well-stocked' tray. The bathroom had a bath and power shower, Gilchrist & Soames toiletries. A pot of tea awaited in a downstairs lounge with 'squashy sofas round a crackling fire'. At night in the dual-aspect dining room, John uses 'locally sourced ingredients in generous portions', with herbs and vegetables from the garden, in dishes such as St Tola goat's curd salad, beetroot, asparagus and hazelnut dressing, or slow-cooked Burren lamb with herb gravy. Breakfast on porridge or apricots cooked in Cointreau and cinnamon, with perhaps a toasted bagel with salmon from the local smokery before heading out for a walk on the Burren Way or to marvel at the Cliffs of Moher.

Lisdoonvarna V95 NH22

T: 00 353 65 707 4026
E: info@sheedys.com
W: sheedys.com

BEDROOMS: 11. 5 on ground floor.
OPEN: Apr hotel and restaurant Thurs–Sun, May–Sept daily (restaurant closed Sun).
FACILITIES: sitting room/library, sun lounge, bar, restaurant, in-room TV (terrestrial), ½-acre garden, restaurant wheelchair accessible, adapted toilet, parking.
BACKGROUND MUSIC: in restaurant and bar, Lyric FM at breakfast, 'easy listening' jazz at dinner.
LOCATION: 20 miles SW of Galway.
CHILDREN: over-12s welcomed.
DOGS: not allowed.
CREDIT CARDS: MC, Visa.
PRICES: B&B doubles from €185. Set-price menu, dinner, €60. 1-night bookings refused weekends in Sept.

SEE ALSO SHORTLIST

LONGFORD Co. Longford   MAP 6:C5

VIEWMOUNT HOUSE

♛ Previous César winner

It is the attention to detail that so impresses at
Beryl and James Kearney's classical Georgian
rebuild of a 17th-century house, set in themed
gardens with a pond and orchard. From fresh-
cut flowers to handmade Irish toiletries and
manuka honey with your morning porridge,
everything speaks of pride in their enterprise. It
is 'such a wonderful hotel', writes a reader, who
was welcomed by Beryl and shown to a ground-
floor suite with 'wooden floors, large rugs, period
furniture (all dark wood) and antique mirrors',
a bathroom with 'a shower as powerful as any
I've come across'. Service bells still hang in the
original vaulted kitchens, now the guest lounge.
In VM restaurant, in the beamed, stone-walled
old stables, tables are set with 'starched napery, a
candle and elegant china', for a dinner cooked by
Marcio Laan. Short menus include dishes such
as salt-fried sirloin steak, saffron potato, shallot,
porcini; monkfish, Jerusalem artichoke, kale,
pickle, fish sauce. The next day, there is freshly
squeezed orange juice, free-range local eggs, Irish
sausages and bacon. 'As delicious a breakfast as
I could ever desire.'

Dublin Road
Longford N39 N2X6

T: 00 353 43 334 1919
E: info@viewmounthouse.com
W: viewmounthouse.com

BEDROOMS: 12. 7 in modern extension,
some on ground floor, 1 suitable for
disabled.
OPEN: all year except 25 Oct–4 Nov,
restaurant open Wed–Sat for dinner,
Sun lunch, closed 24–27 Dec.
FACILITIES: reception room, library,
sitting room, breakfast room,
restaurant, in-room TV (terrestrial),
wedding facilities, 4-acre grounds,
breakfast room and restaurant
wheelchair accessible, adapted toilet.
BACKGROUND MUSIC: in restaurant.
LOCATION: 1 mile E of town centre.
CHILDREN: all ages welcomed, family
room.
DOGS: not allowed.
CREDIT CARDS: Amex, MC, Visa.
PRICES: B&B doubles from €160, family
room from €200. Set-price dinner €60,
early bird dinner €35.

MAGHERALIN Co. Armagh

MAP 6:B6

NEWFORGE HOUSE

Previous César winner

Set on the edge of a small village, in mature gardens and pastureland, this creeper-clad Georgian mansion offers a taste of country house living only 40 minutes from Belfast. John and Louise Mathers are sixth-generation owners, and the house is filled with antiques and family possessions. Readers praise the 'very good' hospitality at this 'lovely place'; John was awarded a British Empire Medal for hospitality in 2018. Bedrooms are furnished in period style, with fresh flowers, a cafetière and china teapot. Hanna has a four-poster, floor-to-ceiling windows; a bathroom with a fireplace, bath and walk-in shower. Small but pretty Waddell has a canopy bed draped with toile de Jouy fabric. At 8 pm, after maybe a Newforge plum fizz or an Armagh Appletini by the drawing-room fire, guests sit down to a three-course dinner with either/or choices – perhaps roast cod loin with lemon dulse butter or dry-aged lamb with rosemary and garlic pan juices. Breakfast is just as tasty, with an Ulster fry and eggs from hens in the orchard. 'One of our main holiday requirements is good food, and we certainly were not disappointed.' (PH, SM)

58 Newforge Road
Magheralin BT67 0QL

T: 028 9261 1255
E: enquiries@newforgehouse.com
W: newforgehouse.com

BEDROOMS: 6.
OPEN: Feb–mid-Dec, restaurant closed Sun/Mon evenings.
FACILITIES: drawing room, dining room, in-room TV (Freeview), wedding facilities, 2-acre gardens (vegetable garden, wild-flower meadow, orchard, woodland) in 50 acres of pastureland, unsuitable for disabled.
BACKGROUND MUSIC: in dining room.
LOCATION: on edge of village, 20 miles SW of Belfast.
CHILDREN: aged 10 and over welcomed.
DOGS: not allowed.
CREDIT CARDS: MC, Visa.
PRICES: B&B doubles from £145, singles from £115. À la carte £50.

MOUNTRATH Co. Laois

MAP 6:C5

ROUNDWOOD HOUSE

Ω Previous César winner

Combine a Georgian mansion, rambling grounds, creative cooking served by serenading chefs, and big-hearted hosts, and you understand Roundwood's allure. Guests enthuse about convivial evenings spent drinking wine and talking with owners Hannah and Paddy Flynn, who took over from Hannah's parents' 25-year reign, continuing the tradition of warm hospitality. High-ceilinged rooms of sash windows, rococo plasterwork and marble fireplaces are rich with heritage-coloured walls, family heirlooms and artwork. Bedrooms have a comfortable country house air in the main building, with shuttered windows and fine antiques, and are cosy cottage style in the separate Yellow House. All have books, flowers, views, and a bathroom with both bath and shower. Browse the double-height library in the former stables or explore the native woodland and meadow. Pop into the kitchen to see what Paddy's cooking; perhaps roast lamb with blueberry sauce and sweet potato purée, or wild venison with caramelised parsnips. Almost all is made from scratch (the bread, too), while breakfast, including a full Irish, tempts until a blissful 11 am.

Mountrath R32 TK79

T: 00 353 57 873 2120
E: info@roundwoodhouse.com
W: roundwoodhouse.com

BEDROOMS: 10. 4 in separate house.
OPEN: all year except 24–26 Dec.
FACILITIES: drawing room, dining room, study, library, wedding facilities, 18-acre grounds, unsuitable for disabled.
BACKGROUND MUSIC: none.
LOCATION: 3 miles N of village.
CHILDREN: all ages welcomed, under-5s free, extra bed €30, children's supper €12.50.
DOGS: not allowed.
CREDIT CARDS: Amex, MC, Visa.
PRICES: B&B doubles from €180, singles from €120. Set 4-course dinner €60, supper of soup, cheese and dessert €25.

NEWPORT Co. Mayo
MAP 6:B4

NEWPORT HOUSE

You don't have to be a fly-fisher to check in at Kieran Thompson's creeper-swathed, late-Georgian mansion with views over the Newport river and Clew Bay, but if you are into the sport, this is indeed the place to stay. The ambience is old-fashioned: 'The description "traditional country house" is entirely accurate.' Interiors are filled with time-darkened portraits, antiques, fish in glass cases. 'The website doesn't seem to have changed at all over the years' and 'if you're looking for a rainfall shower and huge, flat-screen TV', look elsewhere. What you will find is traditional hospitality, a feeling of staying with friends, a welcome on arrival with tea by the drawing-room fire. And while dinner is not haute cuisine, we're assured it is consistently good, with a varied menu of dishes such as chicken liver pâté, Connemara scallops or duck breast with ginger and plum sauce. You can take along a picnic basket for a day's fishing on eight miles of the river, or join a ghillie with a boat trip on Lough Beltra. Catch a salmon and they can arrange to have it smoked. Note that Newport House will remain closed until April 2022. (FT)

Newport F28 F243

T: 00 353 98 41222
E: info@newporthouse.ie
W: newporthouse.ie

BEDROOMS: 14. 4 in courtyard, 2 on ground floor.
OPEN: Apr 2022–Oct 2022.
FACILITIES: bar, drawing room, sitting room, dining room, Wi-Fi only in reception and some bedrooms, in-room TV, 15-acre grounds, walled garden, private fishery, bicycle hire.
BACKGROUND MUSIC: none.
LOCATION: in village, 7 miles N of Westport.
CHILDREN: all ages welcomed, under-2s free, cots, high chairs, baby monitors provided.
DOGS: allowed in courtyard bedrooms (no charge), not in public rooms.
CREDIT CARDS: Amex, MC, Visa.
PRICES: B&B doubles from €250, singles from €125. Fixed-price 5-course dinner €68.

OUGHTERARD Co. Galway

MAP 6:C4

CURRAREVAGH HOUSE

With cakes on the sideboard, drinks by the fire, and a gong to summon guests to dinner, Henry and Lucy Hodgson's Victorian mansion in parkland on Lough Corrib has the atmosphere of a much-loved home. Interiors tell a tale of 180 years of family ownership, with clocks, books and bibelots, a tiger skin (sorry, tiger!), fish in glass cases, framed maps and paintings, a vintage bagatelle machine. Spacious, refurbished bedrooms have vintage furniture, cut flowers, Irish toiletries, hand-woven rugs, water from the spring, views of the lough or the Maam mountains, no door key (you're among friends). At night Lucy, who was trained by Prue Leith, cooks a no-choice, locally sourced, four-course dinner of such dishes as spring lamb with wild garlic gremolata and redcurrant jus. At breakfast there is granola, kombucha, local cheeses, home-baked ham, the full Irish, while picnics come packed in a colourful 1940s tin. The wooded grounds are a wildlife reserve: keep your eyes trained for otters, hen harriers, tufted ducks and pochards – not to mention brook lampreys, freshwater pearl mussels and sickle moss.

Oughterard H91 X3C2

T: 00 353 91 552312
E: rooms@currarevagh.com
W: currarevagh.com

BEDROOMS: 10.
OPEN: 1 Mar–30 Nov.
FACILITIES: sitting room/library, drawing room, dining room, 180-acre grounds (lakeshore, fishing, ghillies available, boating, tennis, croquet), golf, riding nearby, unsuitable for disabled.
BACKGROUND MUSIC: none.
LOCATION: 4 miles NW of Oughterard.
CHILDREN: aged 10 and upwards welcomed.
DOGS: allowed in 1 bedroom, not in public rooms.
CREDIT CARDS: MC, Visa.
PRICES: B&B doubles from €160, single occupancy from €110. Set dinner €50.

RATHMULLAN Co. Donegal

MAP 6:B5

RATHMULLAN HOUSE

Second-generation owners Mark and Mary Wheeler continue a 60-year tradition of welcoming guests to their Georgian-cum-Victorian house in landscaped grounds and gardens, with a sandy beach on Lough Swilly. Stay at New Year and you can join the villagers for their annual dip – at other times, snuggle in by a turf fire in Batt's bar or one of the lounges, or take a stroll to discover champion trees, a tranquillity garden with plashing fountain, and a Victorian walled vegetable garden. Bedrooms are highly individual with carefully chosen antiques, perhaps a wall of vintage plates. Rooms in a contemporary wing have French doors to a balcony or patio. Most sought-after are bay-window rooms in the main house with views across the lough to the hills of Inishowen. You can dine in the Cook & Gardener restaurant under a blue tented ceiling, on dishes such as locally landed fish and Donegal farmed meats, with home-grown vegetables and foraged wild garlic – maybe roast black sole, wild mushroom linguine, or roast rump of Lisdergan lamb. Alfresco Pavilion also offers stone-baked pizza. Sailing, horse riding and golf are all available nearby.

Rathmullan F92 YA0F

T: 00 353 74 915 8188
E: reception@rathmullanhouse.com
W: rathmullanhouse.com

BEDROOMS: 32. Some on ground floor.
OPEN: open all year except 24–27 Dec, 6 Jan–6 Feb.
FACILITIES: bar, 2 lounges, library, TV room, playroom, cellar bar/ pizza parlour, restaurant, in-room TV, wedding facilities, 15-metre heated indoor swimming pool, 7-acre grounds, EV charging, lounges wheelchair accessible.
BACKGROUND MUSIC: none.
LOCATION: ½ mile N of village.
CHILDREN: all ages welcomed, 6 interconnecting family rooms, cots available.
DOGS: some pet-friendly bedrooms (€20 per night), not allowed in public rooms.
CREDIT CARDS: Amex, MC, Visa.
PRICES: B&B doubles from €160, singles from €90. Set-price menu €42–€50 (2/3 courses). 1-night bookings refused Sat and bank holidays.

RIVERSTOWN Co. Sligo

MAP 6:B5

COOPERSHILL

A mile-long avenue leads across the River Unshin to Simon and Christina O'Hara's Georgian ancestral home in 500 acres, with a deer park, venerable oaks and exhibitionist peacocks. Beyond the front door – said to be the tallest in Sligo, allowing the first owner, Arthur Cooper, to enter on horseback – the house is replete with antiques, paintings, busts in niches, hunting trophies, testifying to seven generations of Cooper-O'Hara occupation. Among the bedrooms, the Venetian Room has twin queen-size four-posters. The Georgian Room has a king-size canopy bed and views to Keshcorran mountain. There is no TV or radio, but spring water on tap, and Penhaligon toiletries. Christina uses local, home-reared and home-grown ingredients for a dinner served at 8 pm. Maybe spinach soup, venison in juniper cream sauce or wild turbot, and gooseberry tart with elderflower ice cream. Breakfast brings home-baked sourdough, farm-pressed apple juice, honey from the hives, free-range eggs, kippers, a full Irish. Special deals include a two-night stay with a picnic to take to Benbulben, Sligo's 'Table Mountain', for views over Yeats country.

Riverstown F52 EC52

T: 00 353 71 916 5108
E: reservations@coopershill.com
W: coopershill.com

BEDROOMS: 7.
OPEN: Apr–Oct, off-season house parties by arrangement.
FACILITIES: front hall, drawing room, dining room, snooker room, wedding facilities, 500-acre estate (garden, tennis, croquet, woods, farmland, river with trout fishing), EV charging, unsuitable for disabled.
BACKGROUND MUSIC: none.
LOCATION: 11 miles SE of Sligo.
CHILDREN: all ages welcomed, extra bed €50.
DOGS: not allowed.
CREDIT CARDS: MC, Visa.
PRICES: B&B doubles from €234, single occupancy from €151. Set dinner €60. 1-night bookings refused weekends.

SHANAGARRY Co. Cork

MAP 6:D5

BALLYMALOE HOUSE

When farmer's wife Myrtle Allen opened a restaurant in her Georgian farmhouse back in 1964, she did not dream that she was starting a quiet revolution in Irish food, or that her home would become the epitome of country house hotel style. Mrs Allen died in 2018, but Ballymaloe remains a family concern. Daughter Fern runs the hotel with general manager Peter Loughnane. Fern's sister-in-law Darina runs the cookery school, while in the kitchen, Ballymaloe head chef Dervilla O'Flynn remains true to Myrtle's values. Menus are determined by what is best on the day of organic home-grown, locally produced and fished ingredients, and might include dishes such as seared Ballycotton brill with salsa verde, braised Ballymaloe pork or ruby beetroot risotto, with scallion champ and garden vegetables. A wide choice of bedrooms, which have undergone 'continuous refurbishment' during lockdown, includes some with French doors to a private terrace. The most novel is a split-level twin room in the 16th-century estate gatehouse. Breakfast brings fresh-baked breads, local honey, and free-range eggs from the farm.

Shanagarry P25 Y070

T: 00 353 21 465 2531
E: res@ballymaloe.ie
W: ballymaloe.ie

BEDROOMS: 32. 12 in annexe, 4 on ground floor with wheelchair access.
OPEN: all year except 25/26 Dec, closed Mon and Tues in Jan–Mar, Oct–Dec.
FACILITIES: drawing room, bar, 2 TV rooms, conservatory, restaurant, private dining, wedding facilities, 6-acre gardens, tennis, 5-hole golf course, swimming pool, cookery school, café/kitchen shop, EV charging, restaurant wheelchair accessible.
BACKGROUND MUSIC: none.
LOCATION: 20 miles E of Cork.
CHILDREN: all ages welcomed, extra bed €75.
DOGS: small dogs in 3 bedrooms (no charge), not in public areas.
CREDIT CARDS: Amex, MC, Visa.
PRICES: B&B doubles from €280, singles from €150. Set dinner 5 courses (Mon–Sat) €85, Sun night buffet €70.

SHORTLIST

The Old Hall, Ely

LONDON
BATTY LANGLEY'S

Georgian 'Grand Taste' fuses with sybaritic
comforts at this eccentric Spitalfields hotel, a
tribute to the area's novelists, silk weavers and
colourful characters over the years. The two
artfully restored 18th-century buildings are
decorated with tapestries, gilt-framed paintings
and sumptuous seating; there's calm and
sanctuary in its wood panelling, cosy nooks and
honesty gin and tonics. In the bedrooms, crushed
velvet bedspreads and goose down-filled pillows
sit comfortably with vintage fittings; bathrooms
might have a throne loo or a 'bathing machine'.
Breakfast, delivered to the room, has yogurt, fruit,
granola, pastries and bagels. A sister to London's
Hazlitt's and The Rookery (see main entries).
(Underground: Liverpool Street)

MAP 2:D4
12 Folgate Street
Spitalfields
London E1 6BX
T: 020 7377 4390
W: battylangleys.com

BEDROOMS: 29. 1 suitable for disabled.
OPEN: all year.
FACILITIES: lift, library, parlour,
lounge, meeting rooms, in-room TV
(Freeview), small courtyard.
BACKGROUND MUSIC: none.
LOCATION: 5 mins' walk from
Liverpool Street Underground and
rail stations.
CHILDREN: all ages welcomed.
DOGS: assistance dogs only.
CREDIT CARDS: Amex, MC, Visa.
PRICES: per room £235–£1,200.
Breakfast £11.95.

LONDON
THE BUXTON

A hip, youthful air fills this modish Spitalfields
gastropub-with-rooms, a stroll up the colourful
street from the Whitechapel Gallery. Named after
Victorian social reformer, abolitionist and brewer
Sir Thomas Fowell Buxton, it runs on sustainable
values and a selection of local beers. Each of the
compact, neatly designed bedrooms has coffee,
teas and a micro-library of East London-themed
books; handwoven artworks, rugs and blankets
made by local weavers add zest. Guests can ascend
to the roof terrace for 360-degree views across
the East End and the City, or head down to the
brick-painted bar and bistro, for friendly service
and seasonally changing British-European menus.
(Underground: Aldgate East, Whitechapel)

MAP 2:D4
42 Osborn Street
Spitalfields
London E1 6TD
T: 020 7392 2219
W: thebuxton.co.uk

BEDROOMS: 15.
OPEN: all year except 22 Dec–1 Jan.
FACILITIES: pub/bistro, in-room TV,
rooftop garden terrace, eating and
drinking areas wheelchair accessible.
BACKGROUND MUSIC: all day in public
areas.
LOCATION: 2 mins' walk from Aldgate
East Underground station.
CHILDREN: all ages welcomed.
DOGS: allowed in pub.
CREDIT CARDS: Amex, MC, Visa.
PRICES: per room B&B (continental)
£100–£125. À la carte £25.

LONDON
CHARLOTTE STREET HOTEL

Close to Soho and the West End theatres, this Firmdale hotel raises the curtain on a burst of colour and contemporary British art. Wide, striped awnings jauntily shelter the café tables lined up out front; inside, a lounge and library are inviting, with open fires, an honesty bar and plenty of space to sit. Thoughtfully equipped bedrooms and suites (some interconnecting) are bold, bright and beckoning – particularly for the youngest guests, who receive a welcome gift, and milk and cookies in the evening. In the lively restaurant and on the heated terrace, modern British dishes might include baked cod, saffron, mussels and leek broth, plus pastas, salads and grills. (Underground: Goodge Street)

MAP 2:D4
15–17 Charlotte Street
Fitzrovia
London W1T 1RJ
T: 020 7806 2000
W: charlottestreethotel.com

BEDROOMS: 52. 1 suitable for disabled.
OPEN: all year.
FACILITIES: bar/restaurant, drawing room, library, in-room TV (Freeview), civil wedding licence, cinema, gym.
BACKGROUND MUSIC: in restaurant and bar.
LOCATION: 5 mins' walk from Goodge Street Underground station.
CHILDREN: all ages welcomed.
DOGS: allowed 'on a case-by-case basis'.
CREDIT CARDS: Amex, MC, Visa.
PRICES: per room from £389. Breakfast £8.50–£19, à la carte £50.

LONDON
ECCLESTON SQUARE HOTEL

At the touch of a button, guests take control in this intimate Pimlico hotel on a tranquil garden square. 'Comfortable' bedrooms in the Georgian building, some with a patio or a balcony, have a sober palette and high-tech features: a 'digital concierge' on a tablet, smart-glass shower walls, electronically operated blinds or curtains, an adjustable bed with massage settings. Rooms are equipped with a coffee machine; pots of tea are freshly brewed and delivered on request. Guests also receive a smartphone loaded with local information and free mobile Internet. Throughout, friendly staff maintain an 'impeccable' standard. Close to a major transport hub; neighbourhood eateries abound. (Underground: Victoria)

MAP 2:D4
37 Eccleston Square
Pimlico
London SW1V 1PB
T: 020 3503 0692
W: ecclestonsquarehotel.com

BEDROOMS: 39. Plus 2-bed town house with patio garden.
OPEN: all year.
FACILITIES: drawing room, cocktail lounge, in-room TV (Sky), parking discounts.
BACKGROUND MUSIC: in public areas.
LOCATION: 5 mins' walk from Victoria Underground and rail stations.
CHILDREN: not under 13.
DOGS: not allowed.
CREDIT CARDS: Amex, MC, Visa.
PRICES: per room from £160.

LONDON

THE FIELDING

A hop, a skip and a grand jeté from the Royal
Opera House, this small hotel, named after
the 18th-century novelist Henry Fielding, is a
'good-value' option in a central location. It is
'remarkably quiet' considering its prime position
in bustling Covent Garden. Past the pretty,
plant-decked Georgian exterior, individually
decorated bedrooms, set over four floors, are air
conditioned and 'excellently lit'. Each room has a
well-equipped shower room (two rooms also have
a bath), plus tea- and coffee-making facilities.
Families might ask for a room with an extra sofa
bed. No breakfast is provided, but there's plenty
of choice in the surrounding streets – just ask
the 'helpful staff' at reception to point the way.
(Underground: Covent Garden)

MAP 2:D4
4 Broad Court
Covent Garden
London WC2B 5QZ
T: 020 7836 8305
w: thefieldinghotel.co.uk

BEDROOMS: 25. Some, on ground
floor, wheelchair accessible, plus
1- and 4-bed apartments in adjoining
building.
OPEN: all year.
FACILITIES: in-room TV (Freeview),
free access to nearby spa and fitness
centre.
BACKGROUND MUSIC: none.
LOCATION: 3 mins' walk from Covent
Garden Underground station.
CHILDREN: all ages welcomed.
DOGS: not allowed.
CREDIT CARDS: Amex, MC, Visa.
PRICES: per room £175–£195.

LONDON

54 QUEEN'S GATE HOTEL

One in an elegant row of white stucco Edwardian
town houses, this small hotel is a short walk
from Hyde Park, the Royal Albert Hall and the
museums. Within the smartly refurbished Grade
II listed building, serene modern bedrooms
are each dedicated to a renowned Londoner
(Pankhurst, Eliot, Elgar, etc), and made
comfortable with air conditioning, dressing gowns
and slippers, a coffee machine and a minibar
of soft drinks. (Front-facing rooms may have
some traffic noise.) A small buffet accompanies
a freshly cooked full English at breakfast. After
a day out exploring, the lounge, bar and rear
terrace are inviting retreats. Plentiful restaurant
choice nearby. Part of the Bespoke Hotels group.
(Underground: South Kensington)

MAP 2:D4
54 Queen's Gate
South Kensington
London SW7 5JW
T: 020 7761 4000
w: 54queensgate.com

BEDROOMS: 24.
OPEN: all year.
FACILITIES: lounge, bar, breakfast
room, in-room smart TV, terrace.
BACKGROUND MUSIC: none.
LOCATION: 10 mins' walk from South
Kensington Underground station.
CHILDREN: not under 16.
DOGS: not allowed.
CREDIT CARDS: Amex, MC, Visa.
PRICES: per room B&B £199–£499.

LONDON

GEORGIAN HOUSE HOTEL

By turns style-conscious and spellbinding, this modern Pimlico hotel holds surprises for wizards and Muggles alike. Spread between the main, Grade II listed building and two town houses nearby, bright, contemporary accommodation ranges from small single rooms to spacious family apartments. Harry Potter fans of all ages might choose wizard-themed basement 'chambers' in the main house: accessed via a hidden door in a bookcase, they reveal (faux) stained-glass windows, velvet drapes, trunks and tapestries. A café/bar serves breakfast, drinks, snacks and an enchanting afternoon tea. Potion-mixing is an option. Stairs are steep; cheerful staff help with luggage. (Underground: Victoria, Pimlico)

MAP 2:D4
35–39 St George's Drive
Pimlico
London SW1V 4DG
T: 020 7834 1438
W: georgianhousehotel.co.uk

BEDROOMS: 63. Some on ground floor, 18 in nearby town houses.
OPEN: all year.
FACILITIES: reception, café/bar (closed Sun eve), breakfast room, private meeting/function room, 2-person 'cinema', in-room TV.
BACKGROUND MUSIC: in café/bar.
LOCATION: 10 mins' walk from Victoria Underground and rail stations.
CHILDREN: all ages welcomed.
DOGS: not allowed.
CREDIT CARDS: MC, Visa.
PRICES: per room B&B £120–£450.

LONDON

THE GYLE

Conveniently located a short pace from the Eurostar terminal, three 19th-century town houses on a leafy public square have been converted into one contemporary hotel. Decorated in a modern palette of greens and greys, bedrooms in various sizes are spruced up with Scottie dog cushions and tartan textiles. Some basement rooms have a decadent sunken bath; other rooms, on upper floors, have a balcony overlooking the inner courtyard. Complimentary hot drinks are available all day in the moss-walled lounge. Breakfast has a continental buffet of meats and cheeses, home-baked breads and pastries; at gloaming, choose among fine single malts, regional wines and craft beers. (Underground: King's Cross, St Pancras)

MAP 2:D4
16–18 Argyle Square
Kings Cross
London WC1H 8AS
T: 020 3301 0333
W: thegyle.co.uk

BEDROOMS: 33. Some on ground floor.
OPEN: all year.
FACILITIES: bar/lounge, in-room smart TV, interior courtyard.
BACKGROUND MUSIC: in bar/lounge.
LOCATION: 5 mins' walk from King's Cross St Pancras Underground and rail stations.
CHILDREN: all ages welcomed.
DOGS: allowed.
CREDIT CARDS: Amex, MC, Visa.
PRICES: per room B&B £155–£270.

LONDON

HAM YARD HOTEL

An apt choice for the animated neighbourhood, a Tony Cragg bronze sculpture seemingly in motion greets visitors in the tree-lined courtyard of this design-conscious Soho hotel. Inside the modern building, vibrant fabrics, quirky furniture and the latest works from an international roster of artists serve up Kit Kemp's signature Firmdale Hotels look. There's top-to-bottom allure, from a residents-only roof terrace to a buzzy basement bar; in between, the well-stocked library and vast restaurant have afternoon teas and leisurely meals. Bedrooms decorated with a sense of upmarket fun take in city or courtyard views through huge windows. A spa and a 1950s bowling alley round out the offer. (Underground: Piccadilly Circus)

MAP 2:D4
1 Ham Yard
Soho
London W1D 7DT
T: 020 3642 2000
W: hamyardhotel.com

BEDROOMS: 91. 6 suitable for disabled.
OPEN: all year.
FACILITIES: lift, bar, restaurant, drawing room, library, meeting rooms, in-room TV (Freeview), civil wedding licence, spa, gym, bowling alley, heated courtyard, rooftop terrace and garden, valet parking (charge).
BACKGROUND MUSIC: in bar.
LOCATION: 3 mins' walk from Piccadilly Circus Underground station.
CHILDREN: all ages welcomed.
DOGS: allowed 'on a case-by-case basis'.
CREDIT CARDS: Amex, MC, Visa.
PRICES: per room from £520. Breakfast from £15, à la carte £45.

LONDON

HAYMARKET HOTEL

Vintage furnishings and modern artwork make a lively mix at this 'elegant, sophisticated' Firmdale hotel in the heart of Theatreland. The library and conservatory are made for relaxation; in the basement, the glamorous swimming pool area is 'more bar than spa'. 'Lovely' bedrooms, each with their own style, have 'a very comfortable bed'; larger rooms and suites can accommodate extra beds or cots to suit a family. Guests in the Townhouse have their own front door and direct access to the main hotel. Pre- and post-theatre, order bistro dishes in the restaurant, or on the terrace when the weather's fine; 'breakfast is top quality'. The National Gallery is a stroll away; the South Bank is within 'easy walking distance'. (Underground: Piccadilly Circus)

MAP 2:D4
1 Suffolk Place
Piccadilly
London SW1Y 4HX
T: 020 7470 4000
W: haymarkethotel.com

BEDROOMS: 50. Some suitable for disabled, plus 5-bed town house.
OPEN: all year.
FACILITIES: lift, lobby, library, conservatory, bar, restaurant, in-room TV, civil wedding licence, indoor swimming pool, gym.
BACKGROUND MUSIC: in bar and restaurant.
LOCATION: 5 mins' walk from Piccadilly Circus Underground station.
CHILDREN: all ages welcomed.
DOGS: allowed 'on a case-by-case basis'.
CREDIT CARDS: Amex, MC, Visa.
PRICES: per room B&B from £396. 3-course set menu £19.95, à la carte £40.

LONDON
HOTEL 41

Guests receive the royal treatment at this chic, discreet hotel on the fifth floor of a historic building close to Buckingham Palace. A pre-arrival questionnaire ensures residents' preferences are met (pillow firmness, a humidifier, etc) in the smart bedrooms and suites; other perks include home-made treats and season-specific bathrobes. 'Plunder the pantry' of pastries, cold meats, cheeses and desserts in the clubby lounge, then pair up with a 'sports buddy' for a game of tennis or a brisk walk around St James's Park nearby. Lunch and dinner may be had at sister hotel The Rubens, within the same building. A pet concierge guarantees dogs are nobly treated, too. Part of the Red Carnation group. (Underground: Victoria)

MAP 2:D4
41 Buckingham Palace Road
Victoria
London SW1W 0PS
T: 020 7300 0041
W: 41hotel.com

BEDROOMS: 30. Some suitable for disabled, if requested.
OPEN: all year.
FACILITIES: lounge, in-room TV (Sky), room service, butler and chauffeur service, valet parking, free access to nearby spa and gym.
BACKGROUND MUSIC: in public areas.
LOCATION: 5 mins' walk from Victoria Underground and rail stations.
CHILDREN: all ages welcomed.
DOGS: allowed in bedrooms, public rooms.
CREDIT CARDS: Amex, MC, Visa.
PRICES: per room B&B from £387.

LONDON
LIME TREE HOTEL

Occupying a pair of Grade II listed Georgian town houses, Charlotte and Matt Goodsall's peaceful, personally run Belgravia hotel is within walking distance of some of the city's most popular tourist spots. The smartly refurbished bedrooms may vary in size, shape and layout, but all retain their original high ceiling, cornices and sash windows. In every room: comfy beds, crisp linens and natural toiletries. Upper-floor rooms are up several flights of stairs (staff are on hand to help with luggage). The lounge has guidebooks and magazines; the laid-back Buttery café serves breakfast, light lunches, savoury treats and home-made cakes until teatime, to be enjoyed in the compact walled garden if preferred. (Underground: Victoria)

MAP 2:D4
135–137 Ebury Street
Belgravia
London SW1W 9QU
T: 020 7730 8191
W: limetreehotel.co.uk

BEDROOMS: 27.
OPEN: all year.
FACILITIES: lounge, restaurant, in-room TV (Freeview), meeting facilities, small garden.
BACKGROUND MUSIC: 'quiet' in lounge, restaurant.
LOCATION: 5 mins' walk from Victoria Underground and rail stations.
CHILDREN: not under 5.
DOGS: only assistance dogs allowed.
CREDIT CARDS: Amex, MC, Visa.
PRICES: per room B&B single £125–£175, double £170–£340. 1-night bookings sometimes refused Sat and peak periods.

NEW

LONDON

THE MAYFAIR TOWNHOUSE

In a well-heeled neighbourhood, this flamboyant hotel occupies a spread of converted Georgian houses filled with deep colours, original artwork, plush furnishings and a sense of fun. A Mayfair town mouse to country cousins Cliveden House, Taplow, and Chewton Glen, New Milton (see main entries), it shares their smart, sophisticated feel. Decorated in seductive shades, bedrooms and suites (some interconnecting) have plenty of treats, including a minibar stocked with complimentary tipples. Some superior rooms have a private garden terrace. Available all day, small and large plates served in the glamorous cocktail bar and underground dining room have good vegan and vegetarian options. (Underground: Green Park)

MAP 2:D4
27–41 Half Moon Street
Mayfair
London W1J 7BG
T: 020 8138 3400
W: themayfairtownhouse.com

BEDROOMS: 172. Some suitable for disabled.
OPEN: all year.
FACILITIES: lifts, cocktail bar, dining room, private dining room, in-room TV, room service, meeting/function facilities, gym.
BACKGROUND MUSIC: in public areas.
LOCATION: 3 mins' walk from Green Park Underground station.
CHILDREN: all ages welcomed.
DOGS: allowed in some bedrooms, bar.
CREDIT CARDS: Amex, MC, Visa.
PRICES: per room from £252. Breakfast £14, à la carte £32.

LONDON

ROSEATE HOUSE

A saunter from Hyde Park, this elegant hotel is spread over three Victorian town houses on a tree-lined avenue. Public spaces decorated with period furnishings and oil paintings lead to traditionally styled bedrooms equipped with modern comforts (including thoughtful treats for accompanying dogs). Rooms vary in size – the four-poster suite has its own sitting room – but all have a well-supplied limestone bathroom with robes, slippers and high-end toiletries. Cocktails and a short menu of modern European dishes may be taken in the bar and restaurant or on the leafy terrace; breakfast in bed is an option. Sister hotel The Roseate Villa is in Bath (see Shortlist entry). (Underground: Paddington, Lancaster Gate)

MAP 2:D4
3 Westbourne Terrace
Paddington
London W2 3UL
T: 020 7479 6600
W: roseatehotels.com/london/
    roseatehouse

BEDROOMS: 48.
OPEN: all year.
FACILITIES: lift, bar, restaurant, in-room TV, business/function facilities, beauty treatment rooms, terrace, garden, limited parking.
BACKGROUND MUSIC: in reception, bar and restaurant during the day.
LOCATION: 5 mins' walk from Paddington and Lancaster Gate Underground stations.
CHILDREN: all ages welcomed.
DOGS: allowed in bedrooms only.
CREDIT CARDS: Amex, MC, Visa.
PRICES: per room B&B from £180.

LONDON
ST JAMES'S HOTEL AND CLUB

In a quiet corner of tony Mayfair, this sophisticated hotel (Althoff Collection) houses silkily decorated bedrooms, a Michelin-starred restaurant, and a plush, velvet-seated bistro and bar. Down panelled corridors, fine artworks are hung throughout the former diplomats' club; a shortcut leads directly to Green Park. Bedrooms are kitted out with state-of-the-art technology, though the luckiest guests might simply turn their gaze outward: many of the rooms have their own balcony, and views over neighbourhood rooftops. Meals may be taken in the bistro or refined Seven Park Place restaurant; in the morning, 'wellness breakfasts' include green smoothies, almond-milk porridge and quinoa crumpets. (Underground: Green Park)

MAP 2:D4
7–8 Park Place
Mayfair
London SW1A 1LS
T: 020 7316 1600
W: stjameshotelandclub.com

BEDROOMS: 60. 2 on ground floor, some suitable for disabled.
OPEN: all year.
FACILITIES: lounge, bar/bistro, restaurant (closed Sun, Mon), 4 private dining rooms, in-room TV, civil wedding licence, function rooms.
BACKGROUND MUSIC: in public areas.
LOCATION: 5 mins' walk from Green Park Underground station.
CHILDREN: all ages welcomed.
DOGS: not allowed.
CREDIT CARDS: Amex, MC, Visa.
PRICES: per room B&B from £320. À la carte (bistro) £45, 2- or 3-course menus (restaurant) £65–£75, tasting menu (restaurant) £95.

LONDON
SOUTH PLACE HOTEL

'Distinctly cool', this City hotel, designed with playful flair by Terence Conran, is filled with eye-catching works of contemporary art. It is a buzzy, after-work haunt of business types, who come for the pick of eating places: sophisticated seafood in the Michelin-starred Angler restaurant; updated British classics in the Chop House; cocktails and snacks in the glamorous bars. Overnight guests stay in one of the 'quiet, truly relaxing' bedrooms, each decorated with original artwork and bespoke furniture; their well-equipped bathrooms have a deep bathtub or walk-in shower. At breakfast, the extensive menu may include coconut granola, buttermilk pancakes, eggs many ways. (Underground: Liverpool Street, Moorgate)

MAP 2:D4
3 South Place
City of London
London EC2M 2AF
T: 020 3503 0000
W: southplacehotel.com

BEDROOMS: 80. 4 suitable for disabled.
OPEN: all year, restaurant closed Sun, Mon.
FACILITIES: lift, 3 bars, 2 restaurants, residents' lounge, in-room TV (Sky, Freeview), civil wedding licence, meeting/function facilities, gym, spa, art gallery, rooftop terraces.
BACKGROUND MUSIC: in public areas, live DJ weekends in bars.
LOCATION: 5 mins' walk from Liverpool Street Underground and rail stations.
CHILDREN: all ages welcomed.
DOGS: small- and medium-size dogs allowed in rooms, bars, assistance dogs in restaurant.
CREDIT CARDS: Amex, MC, Visa.
PRICES: per room £250–£900. À la carte (Chop House) £37, à la carte (Angler) £75, tasting menu (Angler) £100.

ALFRISTON Sussex

DEANS PLACE

Country walks and cream teas are the order of the day at this family-run hotel, which stands in large grounds on the banks of the Cuckmere river. In good weather, take afternoon tea on the terrace; when the temperature dips, retreat to a spot by the log fire in the bar with a local ale or a glass of Sussex sparkling wine. Modern British dishes are served in the refined restaurant (Thurs–Sat) and the cosy bar (Sun–Wed) at lunch and dinner. Bedrooms in the extensively enlarged old farmhouse vary in size. Every room is individually styled; the best, recently revamped, overlook the 'beautifully cared-for' gardens. After a hearty breakfast, tackle the South Downs Way, which runs through the historic village.

MAP 2:E4
Seaford Road
Alfriston BN26 5TW
T: 01323 870248
W: deansplace.co.uk

BEDROOMS: 36. 1 suitable for disabled.
OPEN: all year.
FACILITIES: bar, restaurant, function rooms, in-room TV (Freeview), civil wedding licence, terrace, 4-acre garden, heated outdoor swimming pool (May–Sept), paddock for visiting horses.
BACKGROUND MUSIC: in bar and dining room, occasional live jazz at Sun lunch.
LOCATION: in village, 3 miles from the coast and walking distance of South Downs.
CHILDREN: all ages welcomed.
DOGS: allowed in some bedrooms, public rooms, not in restaurant.
CREDIT CARDS: MC, Visa.
PRICES: per room B&B £99–£235.
À la carte £35.

ALFRISTON Sussex

WINGROVE HOUSE

Charming inside and out, this restaurant-with-rooms occupies a 19th-century colonial-style house in a pretty village within the South Downs national park. An elegant veranda wraps around the house; inside, an open fire burns in the cosy lounge in winter. Bedrooms, some in an ancient malthouse, have an appealingly understated style; several have a terrace or balcony; most have verdant views. Footfall from above may be noticeable. Modern British dishes are served in the bright, 'well-decorated' restaurant (candlelit at night) or on the terrace in good weather. Inspired by seasonal, locally grown produce, menus include interesting vegetarian options, perhaps roasted cauliflower, baba ghanoush, harissa chickpeas.

MAP 2:E4
High Street
Alfriston BN26 5TD
T: 01323 870276
W: wingrovehousealfriston.com

BEDROOMS: 16. 5 on ground floor, plus 3-bed pet-friendly cottage.
OPEN: all year.
FACILITIES: lounge/bar, restaurant, private dining room, in-room TV (Freeview), terrace, walled garden, restaurant wheelchair accessible.
BACKGROUND MUSIC: in restaurant.
LOCATION: at the end of the village High Street, 20 mins' drive from Glyndebourne.
CHILDREN: welcomed in restaurant, not overnight.
DOGS: not in bedrooms, 'although well-behaved dogs are welcome on the terrace'.
CREDIT CARDS: Amex, MC, Visa.
PRICES: per room B&B £100–£250.
À la carte £36.

ALNMOUTH Northumberland
THE RED LION INN

Watch the sun go down over the Aln estuary from the sheltered garden of this traditional 18th-century coaching inn, which stands opposite the parish church in a pretty village. 'A popular local watering hole', the place is run with 'friendly' staff. The wood-panelled bar entices with real ales and beers from artisan brewers; daytime pizzas come straight from a wood-fired oven. 'Tasteful, well-appointed' bedrooms on the first floor have modern oak furniture, a 'comfortable' bed and a smart bathroom, plus local teas and biscuits. Breakfast, ordered the night before, has 'trencher portions', including vegetarian options. Dinner suggestions at village eateries and places nearby are supplied.

MAP 4:A4
22 Northumberland Street
Alnmouth NE66 2RJ
T: 01665 830584
W: redlionalnmouth.com

BEDROOMS: 7. 4 in annexe.
OPEN: all year.
FACILITIES: bar, restaurant, in-room TV (Freeview), beer garden.
BACKGROUND MUSIC: in bar, restaurant, live music events throughout the year.
LOCATION: in village centre.
CHILDREN: all ages welcomed.
DOGS: allowed in bar area, not in restaurant, bedrooms.
CREDIT CARDS: MC, Visa.
PRICES: per room B&B £110–£170. 2-night min. stay at weekends.

AMBLESIDE Cumbria
RIVERSIDE BED & BREAKFAST

An easy walk from Ambleside, Richard and Diney Standen's B&B is on a quiet lane, opposite a 'delightful, babbling' river. The large Victorian house has sofas in a light-filled lounge, a blazing fire in the wood-burner, wines and spirits in the honesty bar, and 'every imaginable' area map and guidebook. Bedrooms with views of the garden, river or Loughrigg Fell have 'quality linens', coffee, tea and biscuits; the immaculate bathrooms are supplied with fluffy towels and local toiletries. 'Breakfast is a highlight': the orange juice is freshly squeezed; the bread, freshly baked. Let Diney press upon you a slice of home-made cake before you head off on a walk. Return for a cup of tea or a drink in the peaceful garden.

MAP 4: inset C2
Under Loughrigg
Ambleside LA22 9LJ
T: 015394 32395
W: riverside-at-ambleside.co.uk

BEDROOMS: 6.
OPEN: all year except 15 Dec–1 Feb.
FACILITIES: lounge, breakfast room, in-room smart TV, 2 terrace areas, garden.
BACKGROUND MUSIC: none.
LOCATION: ¾ mile W of Ambleside.
CHILDREN: not under 10.
DOGS: not allowed.
CREDIT CARDS: MC, Visa.
PRICES: per room B&B £120–£150. 2-night min. stay.

AMBLESIDE Cumbria

ROTHAY MANOR

With newly landscaped grounds, tastefully refreshed decor and ambitious cooking that's 'a class act', Jamie and Jenna Shail's Grade II listed manor house pleases, inside and out. (Canine companions give it two paws up, too.) Individually decorated bedrooms are supplied with bathrobes, a coffee machine and Fairtrade tea; some have a balcony with views to the fells beyond. Work was underway on eight new suites in a stylish garden annexe as the Guide went to press. Chef Daniel McGeorge's menus in the fine-dining restaurant have excellent vegetarian options; the laid-back lounge has classic fare. Lakeside strolls and hilly hikes are within reach; guests also have complimentary use of a local health club.

MAP 4: inset C2
Rothay Bridge
Ambleside LA22 0EH
T: 015394 33605
W: rothaymanor.co.uk

BEDROOMS: 23. 8 in Pavillion, 2 suitable for disabled.
OPEN: all year except 2–21 Jan.
FACILITIES: bar, lounge, drawing room, restaurant (3 dining areas), in-room TV (Sky), civil wedding licence, boot room, dog wash, 2-acre landscaped gardens (croquet), public rooms wheelchair accessible.
BACKGROUND MUSIC: all day in bar, lounge and restaurant.
LOCATION: ¼ mile SW of Ambleside.
CHILDREN: all ages welcomed.
DOGS: allowed in some bedrooms, public rooms, separate area of restaurant.
CREDIT CARDS: Amex, MC, Visa.
PRICES: per room B&B £180–£450. À la carte £60, tasting menu £70 (5 courses), £90 (7 courses). 1-night bookings normally refused Sat, bank holidays.

ANGMERING Sussex

THE LAMB AT ANGMERING

On the edge of the South Downs national park, the Newbon family's revived village pub enfolds locals and visitors alike in its warmly welcoming atmosphere. Sussex brews, local gins, Sunday roasts and 'delicious' gastropub dishes are served by 'consistently friendly and helpful' staff in the oak-floored bar and smart, informal restaurant; in clement weather, the terrace overlooking St Nicholas Gardens is just the spot for an alfresco meal. Come winter, a log fire burns in the inglenook fireplace. 'Comfortably furnished' bedrooms with vintage touches and modern amenities have country charm in their florals and plaids; some rooms can accommodate an extra bed for a child. Breakfast is cooked to order.

MAP 2:E3
The Square
Angmering
nr Littlehampton BN16 4EQ
T: 01903 774300
W: thelamb-angmering.com

BEDROOMS: 8. 1 on ground floor with private entrance.
OPEN: all year, restaurant closed 25 Dec.
FACILITIES: bar, restaurant, in-room TV (Freeview), terrace, garden.
BACKGROUND MUSIC: 'quiet music' in public spaces.
LOCATION: in village, 15 miles E of Chichester.
CHILDREN: all ages welcomed, not in bar area after 9 pm.
DOGS: allowed in pub, on terrace.
CREDIT CARDS: MC, Visa.
PRICES: per room B&B £115–£215. À la carte £40.

NEW

ASKHAM Cumbria

THE QUEEN'S HEAD

Low-ceilinged and wood fire-warmed, this smartly refurbished 17th-century pub in the centre of a Lake District village is 'friendly, fun and very convivial'. It is owned by the Lowther family, whose Askham Hall (see main entry in Penrith) and Michelin-starred restaurant are a stroll away. Mismatched cushions nudge up along the wooden banquettes, and there are posy-topped tables; five evenings a week, sit down to a five-course menu of refined pub dishes (perhaps wild mushroom and roast onion broth, rosemary dumplings; malt-cured Shorthorn bavette). Spacious, country-style bedrooms are made modern with colour; three rooms can accommodate a family. Guests receive free entry to Askham Hall's Grade II listed gardens.

MAP 4: inset C2
Askham
nr Penrith CA10 2PF
T: 01931 712225
W: queenshead-askham.co.uk

BEDROOMS: 6. 3 on ground floor, 1 suitable for disabled.
OPEN: all year except Christmas, restaurant closed Sun evening–Tues evening.
FACILITIES: bar, restaurant, in-room TV, small beer garden, parking.
BACKGROUND MUSIC: none.
LOCATION: in village, 5½ miles S of Penrith.
CHILDREN: all ages welcomed.
DOGS: allowed.
CREDIT CARDS: Amex, MC, Visa.
PRICES: per room B&B single £117.50–£177, double £130–£190. 5-course prix-fixe menu £45.

ASTHALL Oxfordshire

THE MAYTIME INN

Creepers climb up the front of this mellow stone 17th-century coaching inn, a short stroll from the River Windrush. A 'delightful, friendly' place, it retains an authentic country air. Against centuries-old stonework and timbers in the popular bar, choose from a 'good selection' of gins, ales and ciders; the kitchen sends out seasonal rustic dishes and pub classics, perhaps beetroot tarte Tatin, broad bean crème fraîche; fish pie. A large rear garden has an outdoor gin bar, a boules pitch and fine views over rolling countryside. Sleep in one of the 'comfortable, beautifully converted' bedrooms in the main building or around the courtyard; in the morning, breakfast – Bloody Mary optional – is 'top-notch'.

MAP 2:C2
Asthall OX18 4HW
T: 01993 822068
W: themaytime.com

BEDROOMS: 6. All on ground floor.
OPEN: all year except 25 Dec.
FACILITIES: bar, restaurant, in-room TV (Freeview), large terrace, garden with outdoor bar, boules pitch.
BACKGROUND MUSIC: in bar and restaurant.
LOCATION: 2 miles from Burford.
CHILDREN: all ages welcomed (not under 18 in own room).
DOGS: allowed in public areas, not in bedrooms.
CREDIT CARDS: MC, Visa.
PRICES: per room B&B single £85–£160, double £95–£160. À la carte £30.

AYSGARTH Yorkshire
STOW HOUSE

The vista sweeps over the Yorkshire Dales from Phil and Sarah Bucknall's stone-built Victorian rectory, on the edge of a small Wensleydale village near the Aysgarth Falls. A welcoming place run by personable hosts, the B&B is filled with contemporary art, books and the crackling fire of several wood-burners. Bedrooms are an eclectic mix of period furniture and modern pieces, exposed timbers and countryside views. They're all different: an antique dresser here, a red-painted cast-iron bath there. Bolton Castle is a four-mile yomp from the door – and the hostess's made-to-order cocktails are the perfect pick-me-up after a hike. Breakfast features freshly squeezed juice, home-made bread and granola and local produce.

MAP 4:C3
Aysgarth
nr Leyburn DL8 3SR
T: 01969 663635
W: stowhouse.co.uk

BEDROOMS: 7. 1 on ground floor.
OPEN: all year except 23–28 Dec.
FACILITIES: sitting room (honesty bar), snug, dining room, in-room TV (Freeview), 2-acre grounds.
BACKGROUND MUSIC: none.
LOCATION: 7 miles from Leyburn, 9 miles from Hawes.
CHILDREN: all ages welcomed.
DOGS: well-behaved dogs allowed in 5 bedrooms, public rooms.
CREDIT CARDS: MC, Visa.
PRICES: per room B&B £115–£185. 2-night min. stay at weekends May–Sept.

BAINBRIDGE Yorkshire
YOREBRIDGE HOUSE

The atmosphere is one of 'laid-back luxury without pretensions' at this contemporary restaurant-with-rooms in a 'beautiful Yorkshire Dales setting'. The restored Victorian schoolhouse and headmaster's house stand on the outskirts of a village by the River Ure; inside, owners Charlotte and David Reilly have decorated the spacious bedrooms with items inspired by far-flung places. Several rooms have a private terrace or riverside garden, plus an outdoor hot tub for a soak while star-gazing. Light bites and afternoon tea are available by day (perhaps with a Yorkshire gin and tonic); evenings, 'well-presented' modern dishes such as wild halibut, langoustine bisque are served in the candlelit dining room.

MAP 4:C3
Bainbridge DL8 3EE
T: 01969 652060
W: yorebridgehouse.co.uk

BEDROOMS: 12. 4 in schoolhouse; 1 suite in village, 5 mins' walk; 6 on ground floor.
OPEN: all year.
FACILITIES: lounge, bar, restaurant, tasting room, in-room TV (Sky), civil wedding licence, function facilities, 5-acre grounds.
BACKGROUND MUSIC: all day in public areas.
LOCATION: village outskirts.
CHILDREN: all ages welcomed.
DOGS: allowed in 2 rooms, by arrangement.
CREDIT CARDS: MC, Visa.
PRICES: per room B&B £220–£380. 3-course menu £60, tasting menu £80.

BARNSLEY Gloucestershire

THE VILLAGE PUB

With a refined pub menu and a relaxed, dog-friendly atmosphere, this mellow-stone pub-with-rooms (Calcot Collection) is the hub of a pretty Cotswolds village. Seasonal produce, much grown just down the road, is the highlight of meals served in the dining room and alfresco in the courtyard; a sausage roll might accompany a craft ale or West Country cider. Accessed via a separate entrance from the pub, the bedrooms, country chic and very smart, are supplied with a pantry and a capsule coffee machine; perhaps a roll-top bath. Light sleepers should request a room away from the road. A bonus: residents may visit the Rosemary Verey-designed gardens at sister hotel Barnsley House, nearby (see main entry).

MAP 3:E6
Barnsley GL7 5EF
T: 01285 740421
W: thevillagepub.co.uk

BEDROOMS: 6.
OPEN: all year.
FACILITIES: bar, restaurant, in-room TV (Freeview), courtyard, bicycles to borrow.
BACKGROUND MUSIC: in bar, restaurant.
LOCATION: on the B4425 Cirencester to Bibury road, 4 miles NE of Cirencester town.
CHILDREN: all ages welcomed.
DOGS: allowed in bedrooms, public areas.
CREDIT CARDS: Amex, MC, Visa.
PRICES: per room B&B £114–£219. À la carte £40.

NEW

BARNSTAPLE Devon

THE IMPERIAL HOTEL

A country house atmosphere prevails at this town-centre hotel, which occupies a grand, Grade II listed Edwardian building by the River Taw. 'Without exception, all the staff are well trained, charming and helpful,' report regular Guide readers this year, who had a 'faultless' stay. Recent refurbishment has resulted in 'outstanding' bedrooms and 'immaculate' public spaces, including options for casual and formal dining. Each of the classically decorated bedrooms is different: some overlook the river; some can accommodate a family. 'The excellent lighting and quality of the fittings made our room a real joy.' Guests may use the indoor and outdoor swimming pools at sister Brend hotel The Barnstaple, a short drive away.

MAP 1:B4
Taw Vale Parade
Barnstaple EX32 8NB
T: 01271 345861
W: brend-imperial.co.uk

BEDROOMS: 63. 8 in annexe across the car park, 1 suitable for disabled.
OPEN: all year.
FACILITIES: lift, lounge, bar, restaurant, bistro, function rooms, in-room TV, room service, civil wedding licence, terrace.
BACKGROUND MUSIC: classical in restaurant.
LOCATION: in town centre.
CHILDREN: all ages welcomed.
DOGS: allowed in annexe bedrooms.
CREDIT CARDS: MC, Visa.
PRICES: per room B&B £190–£320. À la carte £35.

BATH Somerset

THE BIRD

Jollity swoops through this chirpy, contemporary
hotel close to the centre. Birds of all feathers
are judiciously displayed on walls, cushions and
crockery throughout the remodelled Victorian
mansion; vivid artwork and glittering chandeliers
add to the eclectic style. Snug or more spacious,
the modish bedrooms are supplied with a capsule
coffee machine, teas and fancy toiletries to
make guests happy as larks; several have views
stretching across recreation grounds to Bath
Abbey. An all-day menu of modern British dishes
is served in the lower-ground Plate restaurant
or on the terrace, amid dining pavilions, domes
and fire pits. Not far, sister hotel Homewood (see
main entry) has country house flair.

MAP 2:D1
18–19 Pulteney Road
Bath BA2 4EZ
T: 01225 580438
W: thebirdbath.co.uk

BEDROOMS: 31.
OPEN: all year, restaurant closed Mon
lunch and Sun dinner.
FACILITIES: lounge, bar, restaurant,
conservatory, in-room TV, terrace,
garden, parking.
BACKGROUND MUSIC: all day in public
areas.
LOCATION: 10 mins' walk from the
centre.
CHILDREN: all ages welcomed.
DOGS: 'very warmly welcomed'.
CREDIT CARDS: Amex, MC, Visa.
PRICES: per room B&B £144–£315.
À la carte £35. 1-night bookings
sometimes refused at peak weekends.

BATH Somerset

HARINGTON'S HOTEL

In the heart of the city, this genial small hotel
spreads over three Georgian houses on a quiet
cobbled street. Up the stairs, bright bedrooms
(some compact) decorated with statement
wallpapers are equipped with tea- and coffee-
making facilities, plus oversized towels and a
power shower. A blanket, towel and treats are
provided for accompanying dogs. Light bites,
salads and afternoon teas are served in the lounge;
cocktails and Bath ales are available in the bar.
At breakfast, find fruit, freshly squeezed orange
juice, leaf teas, and a comprehensive menu of hot
dishes, including vegetarian options. A hot tub in
a secluded courtyard (extra charge) is a modern
take on the thermal baths. Off-site parking can
be arranged.

MAP 2:D1
8–10 Queen Street
Bath BA1 1HE
T: 01225 461728
W: haringtonshotel.co.uk

BEDROOMS: 13. Plus self-catering town
house and apartments.
OPEN: all year except 25–26 Dec.
FACILITIES: lounge, breakfast room,
café/bar, in-room TV (Freeview),
room service, conference room,
small courtyard with hot tub, secure
pre-bookable parking nearby (extra
charge).
BACKGROUND MUSIC: in public areas.
LOCATION: in city centre.
CHILDREN: all ages welcomed.
DOGS: allowed.
CREDIT CARDS: Amex, MC, Visa.
PRICES: per room B&B £84–£208.
2-night min. stay some weekends.

BATH Somerset

THE ROSEATE VILLA

'Within walking distance of everything', this
villa formed from two Victorian houses stands
in 'pretty gardens' overlooking Henrietta Park.
Managers Jean-Luc Bouchereau and Caroline
Browning extend a 'delightful welcome'. Public
rooms are decorated with antiques and prints; in
the crisply styled bedrooms – some snug, others
generously sized – a guest's gaze may well fall on
the supply of home-baked shortbread. This is a
place that encourages delicious lounging: in the
chic new bar, morning coffee, light meals, Sunday
brunch and afternoon teas give way to creative
cocktails in the evening; breakfast brings Buck's
Fizz paired with interesting choices. Sister hotel
Roseate House is in London (see Shortlist entry).

MAP 2:D1
Henrietta Road
Bath BA2 6LX
T: 01225 466329
W: roseatehotels.com/bath/
theroseatevilla

BEDROOMS: 21. One 2-bed suite on
lower ground floor.
OPEN: all year.
FACILITIES: bar, breakfast/dining room,
in-room TV (Freeview), small front
garden, rear garden with seating,
terrace, parking.
BACKGROUND MUSIC: in bar.
LOCATION: by Henrietta Park, 5 mins'
walk from the city centre.
CHILDREN: all ages welcomed.
DOGS: allowed, if more than 10 months
old.
CREDIT CARDS: Amex, MC, Visa.
PRICES: per room B&B single £45,
double £150–£495.

BEXHILL-ON-SEA Sussex

THE DRIFTWOOD

Steps from the seafront and the De La Warr
Pavilion, this smart restaurant-with-rooms in
a refurbished Victorian town house brings a
coolly contemporary touch to the High Street.
In the ground-floor restaurant, well-regarded
Asian-influenced dishes (tiger prawn tempura;
Sri Lankan black curry, turmeric currant rice)
are served against a brasserie-style backdrop of
deep leather banquettes and exposed brick walls.
Handsome bedrooms decorated in moody tones
are on the first and second floors. Rooms vary in
size, but all are supplied with pleasing extras such
as bathrobes and slippers, a coffee machine and a
mini-fridge. Breakfast, perhaps brioche French
toast with a berry compote, is cooked to order.

MAP 2:E4
40 Sackville Road
Bexhill-on-Sea TN39 3JE
T: 01424 732584
W: thedriftwoodbexhill.co.uk

BEDROOMS: 6.
OPEN: all year.
FACILITIES: restaurant, in-room TV.
BACKGROUND MUSIC: none.
LOCATION: in town centre.
CHILDREN: all ages welcomed.
DOGS: not allowed.
CREDIT CARDS: Amex, MC, Visa.
PRICES: per room B&B £95–£145.
1-night bookings refused at weekends
in high season.

BIBURY Gloucestershire

THE SWAN

Here is a setting that elicits admiring exclamation: green creepers climbing up old stone, this stylishly updated 17th-century coaching inn stands on the banks of the River Coln, in a village William Morris described as the most beautiful in England. Country-style bedrooms have views of river, village or courtyard; cottage suites in the pretty garden are ideal for larger groups. There's a choice of dining areas: gastropub fare is served in the dog-friendly bar and courtyard; the brasserie has modern European cooking, perhaps Bibury trout. In clement weather, find a spot for sunning in the riverside garden across the lane. Part of the Fuller's portfolio; see also Bay Tree Hotel, Burford (Shortlist entry).

MAP 3:E6
Bibury GL7 5NW
T: 01285 740695
W: cotswold-inns-hotels.co.uk/
the-swan-hotel

BEDROOMS: 22. Some on ground floor, 4 in adjacent garden cottages.
OPEN: all year.
FACILITIES: lift, lounge, bar, brasserie, in-room TV (Freeview), civil wedding licence, function facilities, courtyard, ½-acre garden, electric car charging point.
BACKGROUND MUSIC: 'subtle' in public spaces.
LOCATION: village centre.
CHILDREN: all ages welcomed.
DOGS: allowed in bar, lounge, garden, some bedrooms.
CREDIT CARDS: Amex, MC, Visa.
PRICES: per room B&B £170–£405. À la carte (brasserie) £36.

BIRMINGHAM Warwickshire

THE HIGH FIELD TOWN HOUSE

In upmarket Edgbaston, this white-fronted Victorian villa has the feel of a 'boutique country house'. It is run in conjunction with the popular High Field gastropub next door. The bright sitting room has complimentary newspapers, vases of flowers and a capsule coffee machine; something a little stronger may be found in the honesty bar. Modern and lively, bedrooms (some large enough to accommodate a family) are decorated with well-chosen antiques and retro furnishings. Pop across the driveway when hunger strikes: along with cocktails and bubbly, imaginative sharing platters and elevated pub grub include the likes of maple-roasted butternut squash, puy lentils; 14-hour-braised beef and ale pie. Plenty of choice at breakfast.

MAP 3:C6
23 Highfield Road
Birmingham B15 3DP
T: 0121 647 6466
W: highfieldtownhouse.co.uk

BEDROOMS: 12. 1 suitable for disabled.
OPEN: all year, except 24/25 Dec.
FACILITIES: sitting room (honesty bar), restaurant in adjacent building, private dining room, in-room TV (Freeview), terrace, garden, parking.
BACKGROUND MUSIC: in sitting room.
LOCATION: 10 mins' drive from city centre.
CHILDREN: all ages welcomed.
DOGS: allowed in pub, not in bedrooms.
CREDIT CARDS: Amex, MC, Visa.
PRICES: per room B&B £115–£210. À la carte £35.

BLACKPOOL Lancashire

NUMBER ONE ST LUKE'S

Experienced hosts Mark and Claire Smith have
run their well-liked South Shore B&B for close
to two decades. Spacious, individually decorated
bedrooms in the red-brick detached house
each have a king-size bed and plenty of perks:
snacks and drinks; a music system and wide
TV; bathrobes, a power shower and spa bath in
the bathroom. A large conservatory overlooks
the garden; outside, there are sun loungers,
a greenhouse and a hot tub. Fill up on a 'full
Blackpool' at breakfast or choose something
lighter from the menu (special diets are willingly
catered for), then head out to explore: the famous
promenade and Pleasure Beach are minutes
away on foot, and the hosts have many local
recommendations to share.

MAP 4:D2
1 St Luke's Road
Blackpool FY4 2EL
T: 01253 343901
W: numberoneblackpool.com

BEDROOMS: 3.
OPEN: all year.
FACILITIES: dining room, conservatory,
in-room TV (Freeview), garden
(putting green, hot tub), electric car
charging point, parking.
BACKGROUND MUSIC: none.
LOCATION: 2 miles S of town centre.
CHILDREN: not under 4.
DOGS: 'possibly a small dog', by prior
arrangement; allowed in bedroom, not
in dining room.
CREDIT CARDS: Amex, MC, Visa.
PRICES: per room B&B £120–£150.
1-night bookings occasionally refused
weekends.

BOURNEMOUTH Dorset

THE GREEN HOUSE

A green ethos prevails at this 'friendly' hotel,
in a handsome Victorian villa within strolling
distance of the beach. Ethically run, the hotel has
implemented many sustainable initiatives, from
its community vegetable garden and responsibly
sourced furnishings to the solar panels and
beehives on the roof. Bedrooms (some snug)
are smartly decorated in pleasing, earthy tones;
they have 'crisp' organic bed linens, 'soft pillows'
and a bathroom with 'proper fluffy towels',
perhaps even a reclaimed Victorian roll-top bath.
Rear rooms are quietest. In Arbor restaurant,
uncomplicated but imaginative dishes use organic,
Fairtrade and locally sourced ingredients, and
may be served on the terrace in good weather.

MAP 2:E2
4 Grove Road
Bournemouth BH1 3AX
T: 01202 498900
W: thegreenhousehotel.co.uk

BEDROOMS: 32. 1 suitable for disabled.
OPEN: all year.
FACILITIES: lift, bar, restaurant, in-
room TV (Freeview), civil wedding
licence, private event facilities, 1-acre
garden, terrace, parking.
BACKGROUND MUSIC: in public areas.
LOCATION: 5 mins' walk from beach,
10 mins' walk from town centre.
CHILDREN: all ages welcomed, not in
restaurant after 7 pm.
DOGS: not allowed.
CREDIT CARDS: Amex, MC, Visa.
PRICES: per room B&B £157–£247.
À la carte £35. 1-night bookings
refused Sat in peak season.

BRADFORD-ON-AVON Wiltshire
TIMBRELL'S YARD

'Friendly, enthusiastic staff' animate this popular
bar/restaurant-with-rooms, which occupies an
18th-century merchant's house by a footpath
skirting the River Avon. Snacks, small plates and
refined pub food are plied in the industrial-style
dining areas throughout the day; the bar has craft
spirits, local ales and ciders. Alfresco meals may
be taken on the river-facing terrace. Along a maze
of stairs and corridors, style-conscious bedrooms
(most with views of the water) are stocked with
freshly ground coffee, tea and sweet treats; split-
level suites (with 'steep, polished steps') have
window seats. Part of the Stay Original Co.; see
also The Swan, Wedmore, and The White Hart,
Somerton (Shortlist entries).

MAP 2:D1
49 Saint Margaret's Street
Bradford-on-Avon BA15 1DE
T: 01225 869492
W: timbrellsyard.com

BEDROOMS: 17.
OPEN: all year.
FACILITIES: bar, restaurant, private
dining room, in-room TV (Freeview),
river-facing terrace.
BACKGROUND MUSIC: in public spaces
'to suit time and ambience'.
LOCATION: in town centre, 3 mins'
walk from railway station.
CHILDREN: all ages welcomed.
DOGS: allowed in bedrooms, bar.
CREDIT CARDS: MC, Visa.
PRICES: per room B&B from £115.
À la carte £34.

BREEDON ON THE HILL Leicestershire
BREEDON HALL

In a village within the National Forest, this listed
Georgian manor house in the shade of ancient
yew trees has an inviting country feel. Warm and
welcoming, it is run as a B&B by Charles and
Charlotte Meynell. The elegantly restored home
has a fire-warmed drawing room, and bedrooms
decorated with character. Some rooms have
handsome beams; all have views over gardens
front and rear. No keys are provided (though
bedrooms can be bolted from the inside): 'It's a
family home, and feels like one,' the hosts say.
Breakfast on fresh fruit, home-made granola and
jams, and eggs from the house's hens; pub grub
is as near as the end of the drive. Market towns
Melbourne and Ashby-de-la-Zouch are close.

MAP 2:A2
Breedon on the Hill DE73 8AN
T: 01332 864935
W: breedonhall.co.uk

BEDROOMS: 5. Plus 3 self-catering
cottages.
OPEN: all year except Sun, 'sometimes'
in Feb and Mar, first 2 weeks July,
Christmas and New Year.
FACILITIES: drawing room (honesty
bar), main kitchen, dining room,
in-room TV (Freeview), civil wedding
licence, 1-acre grounds, electric car
charging point, parking.
BACKGROUND MUSIC: none.
LOCATION: in village centre.
CHILDREN: preferably not under 12,
'but we may make exceptions upon
request'.
DOGS: well-behaved dogs allowed in
bedrooms, public rooms (resident
dog).
CREDIT CARDS: Amex, MC, Visa.
PRICES: per room B&B £95–£165.
2-night min. stay.

BRIGHTON Sussex

BRIGHTONWAVE

In a row of Victorian town houses, a five-minute stroll from the pier, this Kemptown B&B has some 'lovely little touches'. Richard Adams and Simon Throp are the helpful, informative owners. Painted in subtle colours, the crisp, contemporary bedrooms (some compact) have 'everything you need': a DVD/CD player, bottles of water, tea- and coffee-making facilities, a little tub of chocolates. One room has a private patio garden with seating; another, a Juliet balcony. Works by local artists decorate the lounge, where there are books to borrow, and a laptop and printer for guests' use. Cooked-to-order breakfasts are served till 10.30 am at the weekend; a continental breakfast may be taken in the room.

MAP 2:E4
10 Madeira Place
Brighton BN2 1TN
T: 01273 676794
W: brightonwave.com

BEDROOMS: 8.
OPEN: all year except Christmas.
FACILITIES: lounge, in-room TV (Freeview).
BACKGROUND MUSIC: none.
LOCATION: in Kemptown, just off the seafront.
CHILDREN: not under 14.
DOGS: not allowed.
CREDIT CARDS: Amex, MC, Visa.
PRICES: per room B&B £96–£180.
2-night min. stay preferred.

BRISLEY Norfolk

THE BRISLEY BELL

A buzzy local landmark, this 17th-century inn facing the village common is just the place for lively quiz nights and Friday-evening cricket matches; for more peaceful diversion, there's also afternoon tea and board games by the original inglenook fireplaces. It is owned and run by Norfolk-bred Amelia Nicholson and Marcus Seaman, who restored the old pub and extended it to include stylish modern bedrooms in converted barns, set in a spread of lawns and landscaped gardens. Served across dining areas inside and out, well-regarded pub lunches and dinners feature English favourites tweaked with French techniques. Nature trails, country estates and the north Norfolk coastline are within easy reach.

MAP 2:A5
The Green
Brisley
nr Dereham NR20 5DW
T: 01362 705024
W: thebrisleybell.co.uk

BEDROOMS: 6. All on ground floor in converted barns, 1 suitable for disabled.
OPEN: all year, contact inn directly for Christmas and New Year details.
FACILITIES: bar, snug, restaurant, garden room, in-room TV (Freeview), pre-bookable in-room massages, covered patio, 2-acre garden (croquet lawn, herb garden, meadow) extending to village common, electric car charging point.
BACKGROUND MUSIC: none, except for occasional live music events.
LOCATION: just outside village.
CHILDREN: all ages welcomed.
DOGS: allowed in 2 bedrooms, bar, snug, garden.
CREDIT CARDS: MC, Visa.
PRICES: per room B&B £112–£199.
À la carte £35.

BROADWAY Worcestershire

THE OLIVE BRANCH

In a honey-hued village within easy reach of
National Trust properties and gardens, this
'beautifully appointed' B&B occupies a 16th-
century Cotswold stone building liked for its
traditional country cottage charm. Pam Talboys,
the welcoming hostess, has plenty of local
knowledge to share. The cosy sitting room has
books to borrow, and a wood burner for cool days;
in fine weather, the rear garden is a pleasant place
to be – perhaps with a drink from the honesty bar.
Bedrooms are well equipped, and have a 'lavishly
provisioned' bathroom. 'First-rate breakfasts',
taken in the front parlour with its original stone
flags, are a feast of home-baked breads and muesli
bars, plus local jam, marmalade and honey.

MAP 3:D6
78 High Street
Broadway WR12 7AJ
T: 01386 853440
W: theolivebranch-broadway.com

BEDROOMS: 7. Some on ground floor,
1 suitable for disabled.
OPEN: all year except 25–27 Dec.
FACILITIES: lounge, breakfast room,
in-room TV, ¼-acre garden, gazebo,
'easy parking', dining room and
lounge wheelchair accessible.
BACKGROUND MUSIC: in lounge,
breakfast room.
LOCATION: in village centre.
CHILDREN: all ages welcomed.
DOGS: not allowed.
CREDIT CARDS: MC, Visa.
PRICES: per room B&B single
£110–£125, double £130–£150. 1-night
bookings generally refused weekends
in high season.

BUCKFASTLEIGH Devon

KILBURY MANOR

Thick hedgerows border the approach to Julia
and Martin Blundell's peaceful rural B&B, in
meadowland that leads down to the River Dart.
Pretty, country-style bedrooms are in the 17th-
century Devonshire longhouse or a converted
barn across the courtyard; each room is supplied
with coffee, tea, hot chocolate, locally bottled
water and all-natural toiletries. Breakfast, served
by a wood-burning stove on chilly mornings,
has fruit, juice and yogurts, plus home-made
preserves and compotes; specials such as devilled
tomatoes on granary toast are cooked to order.
Stretch your legs around the flower borders, pond
and fruit trees in the grounds or head further
afield – Dartmoor national park is within reach.

MAP 1:D4
Colston Road
Buckfastleigh TQ11 0LN
T: 01364 644079
W: kilburymanor.co.uk

BEDROOMS: 3. 2 in converted stone barn
across the courtyard.
OPEN: Apr–Oct.
FACILITIES: breakfast room, in-room
TV (Freeview), 4-acre grounds,
courtyard, bicycle and canoe storage.
BACKGROUND MUSIC: 'gentle classical
music played at low level' in breakfast
room.
LOCATION: 1 mile from Buckfastleigh
centre.
CHILDREN: not under 8.
DOGS: not allowed.
CREDIT CARDS: MC, Visa.
PRICES: per room B&B £85–£105.
2-night min. stay Apr–Sept.

BURFORD Oxfordshire

BAY TREE HOTEL

Forged from a row of 17th-century houses, this prettily refurbished hotel is a charming mix of flagstone floors, ancient beams and 'immaculate' modern bedrooms. Past the wisteria-festooned arch, there are huge open fireplaces and a grand galleried staircase; everywhere, the 'endlessly pleasant, helpful and efficient' staff make visitors feel very welcome. In a flourish of florals, checks and tweeds, bedrooms have 'good lighting' and a 'large, comfortable bed'. Guests with a dog should ask for a garden room with outdoor access. There are local ales, light meals and board games in the bar; in the restaurant, 'delicious' modern British cuisine. Part of the Fuller's portfolio; see also The Swan, Bibury (Shortlist entry).

MAP 3:D6
Sheep Street
Burford OX18 4LW
T: 01993 822791
W: cotswold-inns-hotels.co.uk/
the-bay-tree-hotel

BEDROOMS: 21. 2 adjoining garden rooms on ground floor.
OPEN: all year.
FACILITIES: library, bar, restaurant, in-room TV (Freeview), civil wedding licence, function facilities, patio, walled garden, parking.
BACKGROUND MUSIC: 'subtle' in public areas.
LOCATION: 5 mins' walk from Burford High Street.
CHILDREN: all ages welcomed.
DOGS: well-behaved dogs allowed in some bedrooms, public rooms except restaurant.
CREDIT CARDS: Amex, MC, Visa.
PRICES: per room B&B £139–£310. À la carte £43.

BURLEY Hampshire

BURLEY MANOR

In rolling New Forest countryside, this Victorian verderer's manor house overlooking grazing deer is today a stylishly updated hotel with a well-regarded restaurant and a cosy duo of spa treatment rooms. Country-chic bedrooms (most dog friendly) range from snug to capacious; 'spacious' garden suites have a private terrace with seating. At lunch and dinner, 'unusual, eclectic' menus list Mediterranean-inspired and locally sourced small and large plates – seared Jerusalem artichoke, Tunworth custard, perhaps, or tea-smoked lamb shoulder, Turkish ezme, figs. There's 'plenty of choice' at breakfast in the conservatory: fruit and yogurts, 'good-quality breads', eggs any way. The village is within a short stroll.

MAP 2:E2
Ringwood Road
Burley BH24 4BS
T: 01425 403522
W: burleymanor.com

BEDROOMS: 40. Some in garden wing, 2 suitable for disabled.
OPEN: all year, 'house party retreats' over Christmas, New Year.
FACILITIES: drawing room, lounge/bar, 3 dining areas (1 conservatory), in-room TV, civil wedding licence, meeting/function facilities, treatment rooms, 8-acre grounds, heated outdoor pool (Jun–Sept).
BACKGROUND MUSIC: in public rooms.
LOCATION: 7 mins' walk from Burley village.
CHILDREN: all ages welcomed at lunch, no under-13s overnight.
DOGS: allowed in most bedrooms, public rooms, not in restaurant.
CREDIT CARDS: MC, Visa.
PRICES: per room B&B £139–£345. À la carte £35. 2-night min. stay at weekends.

BURRINGTON Devon

NORTHCOTE MANOR HOTEL & SPA

Surrounded by orchards and woodland deep in the Taw valley, this wisteria-hung 18th-century manor house is a 'very comfortable' hideaway. There are books to borrow and 'great log stoves' by deep sofas; a modern spa has treatments for lazy days. Snug or spacious, traditional or modern, with terrace or garden views, bedrooms have 'all the necessities', including freshly baked biscuits. Stay in for dinner: the modern British menus are much commended and include good choice for vegetarians. Next day, keep an eye out for the resident roe deer in the extensive grounds. Fly fishing can be arranged. Sister hotel The Lake Country House Hotel & Spa is in Llangammarch Wells, Wales (see main entry).

MAP 1:C4
Burrington
nr Umberleigh EX37 9LZ
T: 01769 560501
W: northcotemanor.co.uk

BEDROOMS: 16. 5 in extension, 1 suitable for disabled.
OPEN: all year.
FACILITIES: lounge/bar, snug, restaurant, in-room TV (Freeview), civil wedding licence, spa (steam room, sauna, hot tub, 12.5-metre swimming pool, gym, treatment rooms, lounge/café area), 20-acre grounds.
BACKGROUND MUSIC: classical in public areas after midday.
LOCATION: 3 miles S of Umberleigh.
CHILDREN: all ages welcomed, not under 9 in restaurant at dinner.
DOGS: allowed in some bedrooms, not in 1 lounge, restaurant.
CREDIT CARDS: Amex, MC, Visa.
PRICES: per room B&B £190–£295. À la carte £49.50, 6-course tasting menu £65.

BURY ST EDMUNDS Suffolk

THE NORTHGATE

Two Victorian town houses have been transformed into this glamorous hotel, minutes from Bury's ancient abbey. Spacious, creamy-hued bedrooms, including a two-bedroom suite to accommodate a family, are 'nicely furnished' with French-inspired pieces; garden-facing rooms are quietest. Order a cocktail from the slick, 'well-stocked' bar before tucking in to the 'ambitious' menu in the modish restaurant or on the large terrace. Here, sustainably sourced regional produce informs the modern dishes and seasonal small plates – perhaps grilled mackerel, local wild garlic and anchovy salsa. Part of the Chestnut group; see also The Westleton Crown, Westleton, and The Ship at Dunwich (Shortlist entries).

MAP 2:B5
Northgate Street
Bury St Edmunds IP33 1HP
T: 01284 339604
W: thenorthgate.com

BEDROOMS: 9.
OPEN: all year.
FACILITIES: bar/lounge, restaurant, private function room, in-room TV (Freeview), garden, terrace, parking.
BACKGROUND MUSIC: in public areas.
LOCATION: 6 mins' walk from town.
CHILDREN: all ages welcomed.
DOGS: allowed in 1 bedroom, in public rooms except chef's table.
CREDIT CARDS: Amex, MC, Visa.
PRICES: per room B&B £140–£280. À la carte £40.

CAMBRIDGE Cambridgeshire

GONVILLE HOTEL

An easy walk to colleges, shops and cafés, this
large, family-owned hotel overlooking Parker's
Piece has a 'friendly, personable feel'. Smartly
updated, it is a 'comfortable' place, with jazz
evenings, spa treatments, drinks and meals on
the lawn, and bicycles to borrow. Air-conditioned
bedrooms in the main building and a renovated
Victorian villa range from classically designed
rooms to sumptuous floral-themed rooms with a
seating area. Some have French doors that open
on to the garden; others, interconnecting, suit a
family. (The hotel is set back from a busy road;
rooms at the rear are quietest.) On-site parking
(extra charge) is a bonus. Complimentary pick-
ups and drop-offs in the hotel's Bentley can be
pre-arranged.

MAP 2:B4
Gonville Place
Cambridge CB1 1LY
T: 01223 366611
W: gonvillehotel.co.uk

BEDROOMS: 84. Some on ground
floor, some suitable for disabled, 8 in
Gresham House within the grounds.
OPEN: all year.
FACILITIES: lift, bar, lounge, restaurant,
in-room TV (Freeview), spa beauty
treatments, parking (£15 council
charge), bicycles to borrow.
BACKGROUND MUSIC: in public areas,
live jazz in bar, garden on Fri, Sat
evenings.
LOCATION: in city centre.
CHILDREN: all ages welcomed.
DOGS: allowed in some bedrooms,
reception area.
CREDIT CARDS: Amex, MC, Visa.
PRICES: per room B&B £220–£400.
À la carte £50.

CARBIS BAY Cornwall

THE GANNET INN

In a pretty village that slopes down to the bay,
this 'friendly' place with a view over the water
has 'the feel of a boutique hotel'. Thick armchairs
cluster in comfortable groups, some by the
wood-burner, in the spacious bar; in the smart
dining areas, guests sit down to hearty grills,
classic Cornish fare and Sunday lunches. The
bedrooms are 'lovely': styled in hues inspired by
sand, sea and sky, they range in size from cosy to
family friendly. Some have views of spectacular
seascapes. A short walk down the hill, guests
may use the spa, pool and salon at sister property
Carbis Bay Hotel before stepping on to the Blue
Flag beach; here, too, is the St Ives branch line for
the short train ride into town.

MAP 1:D1
St Ives Road
Carbis Bay TR26 2SB
T: 01736 795651
W: gannetstives.co.uk

BEDROOMS: 16.
OPEN: all year.
FACILITIES: lounge/bar (darts, pool
table), restaurant, in-room TV, civil
wedding licence, terrace, beauty salon,
yacht charter.
BACKGROUND MUSIC: in public areas.
LOCATION: 1 mile from St Ives.
CHILDREN: all ages welcomed.
DOGS: only assistance dogs allowed.
CREDIT CARDS: Amex, MC, Visa.
PRICES: per room B&B £200–£405.

CHATTON Northumberland

CHATTON PARK HOUSE

A 'most welcoming' place, this peaceful Georgian house stands in neat gardens that stretch towards Northumberland countryside. The spacious sitting room has deep leather armchairs, books to browse, and an open fire in cool weather; adults-only B&B accommodation is in large, garden-facing bedrooms on the first floor. Each room has thoughtful extras, such as tea- and coffee-making facilities, a mini-fridge and fluffy bathrobes; two rooms have a separate lounge. Ordered in advance, generous breakfasts include oak-smoked local kippers, a vegetarian platter, toasted crumpets and locally made jams. Special diets can be catered for. Well located for castle visiting, garden admiring and tootling along the coast.

MAP 4:A3
New Road
Chatton
nr Alnwick NE66 5RA
T: 01668 215507
W: chattonpark.com

BEDROOMS: 4. Plus 2-bed self-catering lodge with private garden.
OPEN: Easter–31 Oct.
FACILITIES: sitting room, breakfast room, in-room TV (Sky, Freeview), 4-acre grounds, electric car charging points.
BACKGROUND MUSIC: none.
LOCATION: ½ mile from Chatton.
CHILDREN: not allowed.
DOGS: not allowed.
CREDIT CARDS: MC, Visa.
PRICES: per room B&B single £124–£380, double £139–£395. 2-night min. stay at weekends June–Sept, bank holidays.

CHELTENHAM Gloucestershire

BUTLERS

An 'easy stroll' to the promenade and the Montpellier district, Paul Smyth and Shaun Bailey's butler-themed B&B occupies a 19th-century gentleman's residence. 'Spacious', traditionally decorated bedrooms bearing the name of a famous butler (Brabinger, Jeeves, Hudson, etc) are gracefully turned out: each has a hospitality tray, a candlestick telephone and an 'immaculate' bathroom with a powerful shower. The lounge is 'well stocked' with books and magazines; in warm weather, the small garden is a pleasing place to sit. Breakfast has a short menu of 'nicely presented' favourites: home-made oat porridge, pancakes with bacon and maple syrup, eggs any way. Close by: 'an abundance of good places to eat in the evening'.

MAP 3:D5
Western Road
Cheltenham GL50 3RN
T: 01242 570771
W: butlers-hotel.co.uk

BEDROOMS: 8.
OPEN: all year except Christmas.
FACILITIES: drawing room, breakfast room, in-room TV (Freeview), roof terrace, ¼-acre garden, parking.
BACKGROUND MUSIC: quiet radio in the morning.
LOCATION: 15 mins' stroll to the promenade or Montpellier.
CHILDREN: not under 9.
DOGS: not allowed.
CREDIT CARDS: MC, Visa.
PRICES: per room B&B single £60–£75, double £85–£120. 2-night min. stay at weekends and during festivals.

CHELTENHAM Gloucestershire

COTSWOLD GRANGE

Set in gardens front and back, its terrace bordered by pleached ornamental pear trees, Nirav and Dhruti Sheth's friendly hotel is in a fine stone mansion in leafy Pittville. The 1830s building retains its original high ceilings, cantilevered staircase and decorative mouldings; its bijou bar and garden-facing breakfast room are stylish spaces in which to eat and drink. Individually decorated, pleasing bedrooms vary in size from cosy doubles to spacious rooms that can accommodate an extra bed for a child. Each room has tea- and coffee-making facilities, plus British-made toiletries in a modern bathroom. Between town and racecourse; the shops and eating places in the centre are a 15-minute walk away.

MAP 3:D5
Pittville Circus Road
Cheltenham GL52 2QH
T: 01242 515119
W: cotswoldgrangehotel.co.uk

BEDROOMS: 20.
OPEN: all year except Christmas.
FACILITIES: bar, breakfast room, in-room TV (Freeview), terrace, front and rear gardens.
BACKGROUND MUSIC: in bar, breakfast room.
LOCATION: in Pittville.
CHILDREN: all ages welcomed.
DOGS: in some bedrooms, bar.
CREDIT CARDS: Amex, MC, Visa.
PRICES: per room B&B single £70–£125, double £80–£250. 2-night min. stay May–Oct.

CHESTER Cheshire

THE CHESTER GROSVENOR

'The service is second to none' at this 'very smart' Grade II listed hotel, which has stood in the heart of the city since 1865. While 'its central location can hardly be bettered if you're keen to be in the thick of things', its 'exceptionally comfortable' bedrooms are 'very quiet'. Whether traditional or more modern, rooms have 'a comfy bed, proper seating and excellent lighting'; 'every amenity' is provided. Informal brunches, lunches and dinners are served in the 'likeable' brasserie; in chef Simon Radley's Michelin-starred restaurant, à la carte and tasting menus include imaginative vegetarian options. And when you've had enough of the 'charms of the historic centre', head inward to the restorative spa.

MAP 3:A4
Eastgate
Chester CH1 1LT
T: 01244 324024
W: chestergrosvenor.com

BEDROOMS: 79. 1 suitable for disabled.
OPEN: all year except 24–25 Dec.
FACILITIES: lift, drawing room, lounge, bar, brasserie, restaurant, meeting/private dining rooms, in-room TV (Sky, Freeview), civil wedding licence, function facilities, spa, electric car charging points, 'convenient' parking.
BACKGROUND MUSIC: in public areas.
LOCATION: in city centre.
CHILDREN: all ages welcomed, not under 12 in bar and restaurant, not under 16 in spa.
DOGS: not allowed.
CREDIT CARDS: Amex, MC, Visa.
PRICES: per room B&B from £155. Tasting menu (restaurant) £89 or £110, à la carte (brasserie) £45.

CHIDDINGFOLD Surrey
THE CROWN INN

'Traditional character' defines this 'lovely' country inn on the corner of the village green, where weary pilgrims and travellers have stopped in for centuries. Constructed in 1441, the timber-framed building has a popular bar, where local tipples are served amid medieval carvings, 'massive beams', stained-glass windows and inglenook fireplaces. Classic fare may be eaten here and in the oak-panelled restaurant. Well-appointed bedrooms, all sloping floors, ancient beams and antique furnishings, have chic toiletries and a digital radio; across the courtyard, two rooms open on to a private garden. Breakfast, served till 11 am at the weekend, has good cooked choices and a buffet of morning-baked pastries.

MAP 2:D3
The Green
Petworth Road
Chiddingfold GU8 4TX
T: 01428 682255
W: thecrownchiddingfold.com

BEDROOMS: 8.
OPEN: all year.
FACILITIES: lounge, bar, lower bar, restaurant, in-room TV (Sky, Freeview), private dining room, 2 small courtyard gardens, large terrace, parking, public rooms wheelchair accessible.
BACKGROUND MUSIC: 'gentle' in public spaces.
LOCATION: 20 mins from Guildford.
CHILDREN: all ages welcomed.
DOGS: allowed on lead in bar and lounge, not in bedrooms.
CREDIT CARDS: Amex, MC, Visa.
PRICES: per room B&B £130–£220. À la carte £32.

NEW

CHURCH ENSTONE Oxfordshire
THE CROWN INN

On stone walls unchanged for centuries, a regularly renewed collection of art enlivens this 'friendly' 400-year-old Cotswold inn. Artist George Irvine and his wife, Victoria, are the owners; the artworks are his, alongside those of other local artists. Wines, gins and seasonal ales are served against a backdrop of sloping floors, low beams and wide hearths in the bar; cream teas and updated pub fare are presented on stoneware crockery in the restaurant and airy conservatory. Upstairs, handsome, country-style bedrooms have village or valley views, and a modern bathroom stocked with Cotswolds-made toiletries. Out back, the small garden is festive with oversized parasols, beer-barrel tables and pots billowing with flowers.

MAP 2:C2
Mill Lane
Church Enstone
nr Chipping Norton OX7 4NN
T: 01608 677262
W: crowninnenstone.co.uk

BEDROOMS: 5. Plus 2-bed cottage.
OPEN: all year.
FACILITIES: bar, restaurant, in-room TV (Freeview), conservatory, ⅓-acre garden.
BACKGROUND MUSIC: occasionally in public areas.
LOCATION: in village.
CHILDREN: all ages welcomed.
DOGS: allowed in 1 bedroom, bar, garden, cottage.
CREDIT CARDS: MC, Visa.
PRICES: per room B&B £120–£170. À la carte £25. 2-night min. stay at weekends.

CHURCH STRETTON Shropshire
VICTORIA HOUSE

In the centre of a lively market town within walking distance of the Shropshire hills, this 'splendid' B&B is run by Diane Chadwick, a 'wonderfully energetic, helpful' hostess. The Victorian town house has 'well-priced, convenient' accommodation in 'comfortable' bedrooms, each 'tastefully decorated' with artworks and antiques that lend much character. Guests appreciate the hostess's generous touch and eye for detail: each bedroom is supplied with bathrobes and toiletries, teas, coffee, hot chocolate, sherry and biscuits. Served in a garden-facing room, breakfast has freshly baked pastries, and sausages from locally reared pigs. Light lunches and sweet treats may be taken in the cosy, on-site café, Jemima's Kitchen.

MAP 3:C4
48 High Street
Church Stretton SY6 6BX
T: 01694 723823
W: victoriahouse-shropshire.co.uk

BEDROOMS: 6.
OPEN: all year, café closed Mon, Tues.
FACILITIES: seating area, breakfast room, café/tea room, in-room TV (Freeview), walled garden, pay-and-display parking (deducted from hotel bill or permits supplied, electric car charging points available).
BACKGROUND MUSIC: in breakfast room and café.
LOCATION: in town centre.
CHILDREN: all ages welcomed.
DOGS: allowed in some bedrooms, café.
CREDIT CARDS: Amex, MC, Visa.
PRICES: per room B&B single £71–£90, double £91–£110. 2-night min. stay at bank holiday weekends.

NEW

CLIFTON Cumbria
GEORGE AND DRAGON

A 'convivial' country pub with cosy rooms and 'very good' food, the Lowther family's restored 18th-century coaching inn near Ullswater retains its rural roots. Roaring fires supply a cheering welcome in the hop-hung bar and dining areas in cool weather; in sunshine, eat alfresco in the courtyard or beer garden. Farm and garden produce from the family estate and sister hotel Askham Hall (see main entry in Penrith) supply the blackboard specials and monthly menu. Upstairs, uncluttered bedrooms – some snug, others able to accommodate a family – are decorated with an antique piece or two. Light sleepers should ask for a room away from the road. The family also owns The Queen's Head, Askham (see Shortlist entry), nearby.

MAP 4: inset C2
Clifton
nr Penrith CA10 2ER
T: 01768 865381
W: georgeanddragonclifton.co.uk

BEDROOMS: 11.
OPEN: all year, except 26 Dec.
FACILITIES: bar, restaurant, in-room TV (Freeview), beer garden, secure bicycle storage, electric car charging point.
BACKGROUND MUSIC: contemporary in public areas.
LOCATION: on A6, on the edge of the Lake District, 10 mins' drive from Ullswater.
CHILDREN: all ages welcomed.
DOGS: allowed in bedrooms, bar, not in restaurant.
CREDIT CARDS: MC, Visa.
PRICES: per room B&B single £90–£130, double £100–£160. À la carte £40. 2-night min. stay at weekends in high season.

COLERNE Wiltshire
LUCKNAM PARK

Down a mile-long avenue of lime and beech trees, this 'very grand and lovely' 18th-century mansion exults in 500 acres of parkland and gardens. There are an arboretum and a rose garden to wander through; trails to explore, on horseback if desired; cookery classes for all tastes. In a walled garden, the award-winning spa has swimming pools and treatments galore. Young visitors aren't neglected: they have sports and pony rides, plus indoor and outdoor play areas. At mealtimes, choose between chef Hywel Jones's Michelin-starred fine dining restaurant and the informal modern brasserie. Wind down, afterward, in one of the elegant, classically decorated bedrooms – each is supplied with fluffy robes and slippers.

MAP 2:D1
Colerne
nr Chippenham SN14 8AZ
T: 01225 742777
W: lucknampark.co.uk

BEDROOMS: 43. 18 in courtyard, 1 suitable for disabled, plus five 3- and 4-bed cottages.
OPEN: all year, restaurant closed Mon–Wed.
FACILITIES: drawing room, library, restaurant, brasserie, in-room TV, civil wedding licence, spa, indoor pools, outdoor hydrotherapy and saltwater plunge pools, terrace, tennis, croquet, football pitch, equestrian centre, 5-acre grounds within 500 acres, electric car charging point.
BACKGROUND MUSIC: in public areas.
LOCATION: 7 miles W of Chippenham.
CHILDREN: all ages welcomed.
DOGS: allowed in 4 bedrooms, part of brasserie.
CREDIT CARDS: Amex, MC, Visa.
PRICES: per room B&B £439–£1,714. 2-night min. stay at weekends.
À la carte (brasserie) £50.

CORNWORTHY Devon
KERSWELL FARMHOUSE

Woodland and riverside walks unfurl from the door of Nichola and Graham Hawkins's rural B&B, which stands in peaceful seclusion amid rolling South Hams countryside. Antiques, farmhouse furnishings and freshly cut flowers decorate the renovated 400-year-old longhouse; works by contemporary ceramicists, glassmakers, painters and photographers are on display in the old milking parlour. Spacious bedrooms have a wide bed and all the essentials, plus thoughtful extras (bathrobes, novels, magazines); two suites, in a converted barn, each have a private sitting room and a fully stocked minibar. Award-winning farm-fresh breakfasts include a full Devon with bacon and sausages from home-reared pigs.

MAP 1:D4
Cornworthy TQ9 7HH
T: 01803 732013
W: kerswellfarmhouse.co.uk

BEDROOMS: 5. 2 in adjacent barns, 1 on ground floor.
OPEN: Mar–mid-Dec.
FACILITIES: sitting room, 2 dining rooms, art gallery, in-room TV (Freeview), 14-acre grounds.
BACKGROUND MUSIC: none.
LOCATION: 4 miles S of Totnes, 4 miles N of Dartmouth.
CHILDREN: not under 12.
DOGS: not allowed.
CREDIT CARDS: none accepted.
PRICES: per room B&B £145–£155. 2-night min. stay Apr–end Sept, unless a single night becomes available.

COVENTRY Warwickshire

BARNACLE HALL

Rose Grindal's 'charming old house' stands in lush gardens swaddled by sheep-grazed fields, with a 'warm welcome' awaiting B&B guests beyond the great oak door. Three miles from the M6, a 20-minute drive from Coventry, it feels a world away from both. The 16th-century farmhouse has low doorways, characterful beams, nooks and crannies; a log fire is lit in the inglenook fireplace on cold evenings. Steps of varying heights betray the age of the house, but the large, traditionally decorated bedrooms on the first floor have all the modern essentials, plus fresh flowers and a generous hospitality tray. A 'good breakfast' caters for all, with fresh fruit and cereal, as well as hot dishes cooked to order.

MAP 3:C6
Shilton Lane
Shilton
Coventry CV7 9LH
T: 02476 612629
W: barnaclehall.co.uk

BEDROOMS: 3.
OPEN: all year except 24 Dec–2 Jan.
FACILITIES: sitting room, dining room, in-room TV (Freeview), patio, garden.
BACKGROUND MUSIC: none.
LOCATION: 7 miles NE of Coventry, SE of Nuneaton.
CHILDREN: all ages welcomed.
DOGS: assistance dogs allowed.
CREDIT CARDS: none accepted.
PRICES: per room B&B single £50–£60, double £75–£85.

CRAYKE Yorkshire

THE DURHAM OX

In a hilltop village along an ancient Celtic trail to York, this 'friendly', personally run pub-with-rooms has hosted visitors for centuries. Today, owners Michael and Sasha Ibbotson ensure guests, and their dogs, continue to feel taken care of. The busy dining areas indoors have stone flags, wood panelling and inglenook fireplaces – a 'delightfully decorated' backdrop to the 'excellent' menu of regional pub classics. Alfresco meals may be taken on the heated patio. Most of the 'comfy, well-lit' bedrooms are in stone-built farm cottages behind the pub; some have a terrace with outdoor seating. On clear days, soak in 'superb' views over the Vale of York. Maps are available to borrow, for gentle strolls and serious hikes alike.

MAP 4:D4
Westway
Crayke YO61 4TE
T: 01347 821506
W: thedurhamox.com

BEDROOMS: 6. 5 in converted farm buildings, 3 on ground floor, 1 suite accessed via external stairs. Plus 3-bed self-catering cottage in village.
OPEN: all year.
FACILITIES: 3 bars, restaurant, private dining room, in-room TV (Freeview), function facilities, patio, 2-acre grounds.
BACKGROUND MUSIC: in pub and restaurant.
LOCATION: 2 miles E of Easingwold.
CHILDREN: all ages welcomed.
DOGS: allowed in public areas, most bedrooms.
CREDIT CARDS: Amex, MC, Visa.
PRICES: per room B&B single £100–£150, double £120–£170. À la carte £35.

DARTMOUTH Devon
STRETE BARTON HOUSE
Stuart Litster and Kevin Hooper's 'superbly decorated' B&B is in a seaside village, steps from the South West Coast Path. Guests come for 'the warmth of the welcome' as much as they do for the tea and home-baked cake that are served on arrival. Large sofas in the lounge of the Jacobean manor house take in the views across Start Bay; a log fire is lit here in cool weather. In the main house and a duplex cottage suite, contemporary bedrooms have 'pristine bedding', fresh flowers, biscuits and a beverage tray; 'windows open to let in sea air and birdsong'. After a 'comprehensive' breakfast with 'beautifully cooked' hot dishes, head for the pine-fringed bay around Blackpool Sands, a 20-minute walk away.

MAP 1:D4
Totnes Road
Strete
Dartmouth TQ6 0RU
T: 01803 770364
W: stretebarton.co.uk

BEDROOMS: 6. 1 in cottage annexe.
OPEN: Mar–Oct.
FACILITIES: sitting room, breakfast room, library, in-room TV (Freeview), ⅓-acre garden.
BACKGROUND MUSIC: none.
LOCATION: 5 miles W of Dartmouth.
CHILDREN: not under 8.
DOGS: allowed in cottage suite.
CREDIT CARDS: Amex, MC, Visa.
PRICES: per room B&B £105–£180. 1-night bookings sometimes refused in high season.

DELPH Lancashire
THE OLD BELL INN
In a scenic, stone-built Saddleworth village not far from Manchester, Philip Whiteman's 'well-kept, traditional' inn is home to the Guinness World Record-breaking Gin Emporium, its 1,100 bottles available for the tasting. The 18th-century coaching house shelters a busy bar ('all polished brass, shiny bottles and hard-working staff'), an informal brasserie and a cosy restaurant whose regularly changing menus include 'flavoursome' daily specials. 'Clean, workaday bedrooms' have all the essentials. There are rooms for solo travellers and ones to accommodate a family; quieter rooms are at the rear. Overnight guests have access to a conservatory lounge on the first floor. Breakfast has hearty cooked options.

MAP 4:E3
Huddersfield Road
Delph OL3 5EG
T: 01457 870130
W: theoldbellinn.co.uk

BEDROOMS: 18. 4 in extension.
OPEN: all year.
FACILITIES: bar, lounge, brasserie, restaurant, in-room TV (Freeview), function facilities, terrace, parking, restaurant wheelchair accessible.
BACKGROUND MUSIC: in public areas.
LOCATION: 5 miles from Oldham.
CHILDREN: all ages welcomed.
DOGS: not allowed.
CREDIT CARDS: Amex, MC, Visa.
PRICES: per room B&B single £79–£89, double £130–£150. À la carte £32.

DIDMARTON Gloucestershire
THE KING'S ARMS

Deep in Cotswold countryside, this traditional inn looks just the part: there are old photos on heritage-hued walls and candlesticks on tables; a log fire is lit when the temperature dips. In the main building and renovated stables, dog-friendly, cottage-style bedrooms are decorated with equestrian paintings and sheepskin rugs. Canine guests receive a bed and a bottle of dog beer; their human companions have tea, coffee, biscuits and eco-friendly toiletries. Seasonal British dishes in the restaurant feature game sourced from neighbouring estates, plus daily blackboard specials – perhaps roasted river trout fillet, mussels, white wine and cream chowder. Summertime pizzas are cooked in a wood-fired oven in the garden.

MAP 3:E5
The Street
Didmarton
nr Badminton GL9 1DT
T: 01454 238245
W: kingsarmsdidmarton.co.uk

BEDROOMS: 6. Plus 2 self-catering cottages.
OPEN: all year.
FACILITIES: 2 bars, restaurant, private dining room, garden (boules), main pub and restaurant wheelchair accessible.
BACKGROUND MUSIC: in pub.
LOCATION: in village.
CHILDREN: all ages welcomed.
DOGS: allowed in bedrooms, public areas.
CREDIT CARDS: MC, Visa.
PRICES: per room B&B single from £110, double from £120. À la carte £33.

NEW

DOUGLAS Isle of Man
THE REGENCY HOTEL

Flags fly in the sea breeze over the entrance of this traditional hotel, which has stood for nearly three decades in a 'very convenient location' on the promenade of the island's main town. (Listen out for the clip-clop of horse-drawn trams along the prom throughout spring and summer.) It is liked for its amiable staff, who are 'very helpful with local recommendations'. Manx artwork hangs in the lounge and 'gorgeously panelled' bar; 'certainly the narrowest lift we've ever been in' takes guests to upper-floor bedrooms (some with sea views). In L'Experience restaurant, the menu of brasserie classics might include French onion soup and steak au poivre. A free shuttle takes guests to the town centre.

MAP 4: inset E1
Queens Promenade
Douglas IM2 4NN
T: 01624 680680
W: regency.im

BEDROOMS: 38.
OPEN: all year, restaurant closed Sun.
FACILITIES: lift, lounge, bar, restaurant, in-room TV, civil wedding licence, meeting/function facilities.
BACKGROUND MUSIC: none.
LOCATION: on the promenade.
CHILDREN: all ages welcomed.
DOGS: not allowed.
CREDIT CARDS: Amex, MC, Visa.
PRICES: per room B&B £100–£210. À la carte £40.

NEW

DUNSFORD Devon

WEEKE BARTON

Play pétanque on the wide lawn here, or stroll down to the pond; on clear nights, settle in to stargaze: surrounded by the rolling hills and pastures of the Teign valley, Jo Gossett and Sam Perry's rustic chic country guest house is just as inviting outside as in. The Grade II listed longhouse is pleasing with its wood-burning stoves, deep sofas, and Dartmoor- and Devon-focused honesty bar; dogs and children are welcome in equal measure. Uncluttered bedrooms have cotton robes, bags of style, rural views from a sheep-skinned window seat. Four nights a week, stay in for a home-cooked dinner of locally sourced produce (special diets are catered for); at breakfast, the home-made granola wins praise.

MAP 1:C4
Dunsford EX6 7HH
T: 01647 253505
W: weekebarton.com

BEDROOMS: 6. 1 in converted cob barn.
OPEN: all year, dinner available Mon, Thurs, Fri and Sun.
FACILITIES: lounge, bar, dining room, in-room flat screens for movies (no TV signal), patio, 4-acre grounds (lawns, paddock, pond, play den for children).
BACKGROUND MUSIC: 'chilled tunes' all day (adjustable volume).
LOCATION: 8 miles SW of Exeter.
CHILDREN: all ages welcomed.
DOGS: allowed (resident dogs).
CREDIT CARDS: MC, Visa.
PRICES: per room B&B single £120–£165, double £130–£175. 2-night min. stay at weekends.

DUNWICH Suffolk

THE SHIP AT DUNWICH

Once a smugglers' haunt, this 'friendly', creeper-covered inn is close to the unspoiled salt marshes of Dunwich Heath and the RSPB reserves at Dingle Marshes and Minsmere. The red-brick building has a nautical-themed bar and three handsomely updated dining areas where pub favourites and daily specials (perhaps wild garlic arancini; pan-fried sea trout) are served. An ancient fig tree and an old fishing boat watch over the beer garden and heated courtyard. Bedrooms, some snug, have simple country charm. The best have marsh views; some, in converted outbuildings, are 'perfect for dogs'. Part of the Chestnut group; see also The Northgate, Bury St Edmunds, and The Westleton Crown, Westleton (Shortlist entries).

MAP 2:B6
St James Street
Dunwich IP17 3DT
T: 01728 648219
W: shipatdunwich.co.uk

BEDROOMS: 16. 4 on ground floor in converted stables, 1 suitable for disabled.
OPEN: all year.
FACILITIES: bar, restaurant (3 dining areas), in-room TV (Freeview, smart TV in family rooms), courtyard, large beer garden.
BACKGROUND MUSIC: in bar and dining areas.
LOCATION: a few hundred yards from Dunwich beach.
CHILDREN: all ages welcomed.
DOGS: warmly welcomed inside and out.
CREDIT CARDS: MC, Visa.
PRICES: per room B&B £95–£165. À la carte £25–£30. 2-night min. stay at weekends in peak season.

MAP 4:C4
Main Road
East Witton DL8 4SN
T: 01969 624273
W: thebluelion.co.uk

EAST WITTON Yorkshire
THE BLUE LION

Log fires and settles downstairs, country-style bedrooms up: in this 'sophisticated' 18th-century inn, Paul and Helen Klein offer an 'utterly authentic' slice of rural Wensleydale hospitality. The former coaching house is liked for its 'pleasant, knowledgeable staff' and 'good atmosphere': there are real ales from nearby Masham, and a warm welcome for visiting dogs. In the bar and candlelit restaurant, 'well-executed comfort food' might include a twice-baked Wensleydale cheese soufflé. Bedrooms have a more rustic style in the main building, and some have views across the village to the dales; more contemporary rooms in the converted outbuildings lead to the courtyard. Country pursuits are all around.

BEDROOMS: 15. 9 in courtyard annexe.
OPEN: all year.
FACILITIES: 2 bars, 2 dining areas, private dining room, in-room TV (Freeview), 1-acre garden, parking, restaurant, bar wheelchair accessible.
BACKGROUND MUSIC: none.
LOCATION: in village, 4½ miles from Leyburn.
CHILDREN: all ages welcomed.
DOGS: allowed in bar, garden, some bedrooms.
CREDIT CARDS: MC, Visa.
PRICES: per room B&B £105–£155. À la carte £43. 1-night bookings occasionally refused Sat nights.

MAP 2:E4
King Edwards Parade
Eastbourne BN21 4EQ
T: 01323 412345
W: grandeastbourne.com

EASTBOURNE Sussex
THE GRAND HOTEL

On the seafront, this great, white Victorian hotel gazes majestically over the water, the views stretching along the coast. 'All is glamorous' inside: there are spacious public rooms, long corridors with patterned carpets, lofty ceilings and arched windows. Throughout, guests commend the 'slick service' from 'such kind, pleasant staff'. 'Beautiful and well-equipped', the classically decorated bedrooms and suites have towelling robes, an espresso machine and high-end toiletries; room service is available around the clock. Afternoon tea is served on the terrace, or in the great hall with musical accompaniment; there are two restaurants to choose from at lunch and dinner (plus a 'nice selection of wines by the glass'). Breakfast is 'excellent'.

BEDROOMS: 152. 1 suitable for disabled.
OPEN: all year, Mirabelle closed Sun, Mon, first 2 weeks Jan.
FACILITIES: lifts, 5 lounges, bar, 2 restaurants, function facilities, in-room TV (BT, Freeview), civil wedding licence, large terrace, spa/ health club (indoor and outdoor swimming pools), 2-acre garden, public areas wheelchair accessible.
BACKGROUND MUSIC: in lounges, live music at weekends.
LOCATION: on the seafront, outside the centre.
CHILDREN: all ages welcomed.
DOGS: allowed in bedrooms.
CREDIT CARDS: Amex, MC, Visa.
PRICES: per room B&B single from £165, double £240–£545. À la carte £55 (Mirabelle).

EDENBRIDGE Kent

HEVER CASTLE B&B

Fit for a queen, this sumptuous B&B occupies the Tudor-style Edwardian wings of Hever Castle, the childhood home of ill-fated Anne Boleyn. The double-moated 13th-century castle stands in a spread of award-winning gardens; bedrooms are in the richly decorated Aster and Anne Boleyn wings, where moulded ceilings, grand chimney pieces and rich tapestries heighten the grandeur. Every room is different: choose one with a gold chaise longue, or one with a four-poster bed; all are supplied with tea- and coffee-making facilities, and spoiling toiletries in a bathroom of limestone or marble. Breakfast, a lavish affair, is served in each wing's own dining room. Residents have free access to the castle and grounds.

MAP 2:D4
Hever
Edenbridge TN8 7NG
T: 01732 861800
W: hevercastle.co.uk

BEDROOMS: 28. Some on ground floor, some suitable for disabled, plus self-catering Medley Court cottage.
OPEN: all year except 25 and 31 Dec.
FACILITIES: lounge, billiard room, in-room TV (Sky, Freeview), civil wedding licence, courtyard garden, tennis court, 625-acre grounds.
BACKGROUND MUSIC: none.
LOCATION: 1½ miles from Hever station.
CHILDREN: all ages welcomed.
DOGS: not allowed.
CREDIT CARDS: Amex, MC, Visa.
PRICES: per room B&B single from £110, double £180–£345.

EDINGTON Wiltshire

THE THREE DAGGERS

With a dash of country cool, this spruced-up pub-with-rooms serves as a village hub, and then some. The enterprise consists of an award-winning microbrewery, a well-stocked deli/farm shop, a hillside spa barn, a lively restaurant serving modern comfort food, and a trio of rustic-chic bedrooms to fall into at the end of the day. Each room is different – a spacious suite has a claw-footed bath in the bathroom – but all are supplied with fresh flowers, natural toiletries, and fluffy towels warmed on towel rails. A continental breakfast is served in the room. A bonus: the residents' lounge has a generous stash of drinks and snacks. Just beyond the village, scenic trails wind through this stretch of the Salisbury Plain.

MAP 2:D1
47 Westbury Road
Edington BA13 4PG
T: 01380 830940
W: threedaggers.co.uk

BEDROOMS: 3. Plus 6-bed self-catering cottage.
OPEN: all year.
FACILITIES: residents' living room/kitchen, bar, restaurant, private dining room, in-room TV (Freeview), civil wedding licence, garden (direct access to village park), pizza shack (summer months), spa barn, microbrewery, farm shop.
BACKGROUND MUSIC: in the pub.
LOCATION: 10 mins' drive from Westbury.
CHILDREN: all ages welcomed.
DOGS: allowed in bedrooms, public rooms.
CREDIT CARDS: Amex, MC, Visa.
PRICES: per room B&B £120–£160. À la carte £40.

EGHAM Surrey

THE RUNNYMEDE ON THAMES HOTEL AND SPA

In glints and gleams, the river provides plenty of diversion at this 'very relaxing' Thames-side hotel and spa: there are swans for feeding, fish for enticing, riverboats for messing about in. Clean-cut bedrooms in the 1970s building have 'every amenity'; those facing the river take in 'spectacular' views. Quieter rooms are away from the road. Two restaurants (both with a terrace for alfresco meals) provide plenty of options at lunch and dinner; the bright, spacious lounge/café has sandwiches, salads and sharing platters. Breakfast brings 'extensive choice'. This is a place for all the family: there are interconnecting bedrooms, gardens to stroll or skip through, space for picnics and outdoor play.

MAP 2:D3
Windsor Road
Egham TW20 0AG
T: 01784 220600
W: runnymedehotel.com

BEDROOMS: 180. 2 suitable for disabled.
OPEN: all year.
FACILITIES: lounge, 2 restaurants, in-room TV (Freeview), civil wedding licence, function facilities, indoor and outdoor swimming pools, 12-acre grounds, electric car charging point, parking.
BACKGROUND MUSIC: in public areas.
LOCATION: on the riverbank, in town 5 miles SE of Windsor.
CHILDREN: all ages welcomed.
DOGS: allowed in some bedrooms, by prior arrangement, not in public areas.
CREDIT CARDS: Amex, MC, Visa.
PRICES: per room B&B single from £145, double from £170.

NEW

ELY Cambridgeshire

THE OLD HALL

Take in 'an incomparable view' of Ely cathedral from this family-run B&B on the Morbey family's historic estate of lakes, arable farmland and green countryside, a few minutes' drive from the city. Rebuilt from the ruins of a Jacobean brick manor house, this 'most extraordinary building' stands in manicured grounds, making it a popular exclusive-use wedding venue. Spacious sitting areas have deep sofas and armchairs by an open fireplace; several nights a week, the restaurant serves a short, straightforward menu (perhaps butternut squash and feta tart; pan-fried salmon, salsa verde). Individually decorated with antiques and handmade furniture, elegant bedrooms overlook the garden or surrounding farmland.

MAP 2:B4
Stuntney
Ely CB7 5TR
T: 01353 663275
W: theoldhallely.co.uk

BEDROOMS: 15. 2 on ground floor, suitable for disabled.
OPEN: all year except Christmas and New Year, restaurant closed Mon, Tues.
FACILITIES: drawing room, main hall, bar, 2 dining rooms, in-room TV, civil wedding licence, terrace, 3,000-acre grounds (garden, lakes, farmland).
BACKGROUND MUSIC: 'low-key' in public rooms.
LOCATION: 2 miles S of Ely.
CHILDREN: not allowed.
DOGS: not allowed.
CREDIT CARDS: MC, Visa.
PRICES: per room B&B £120–180. Set dinner £32.95 (2 courses), £38.95 (3 courses).

FAIRFORD Gloucestershire

THE BULL HOTEL

In a Cotswold town known for its fine 'wool church', this stone-built 15th-century building has variously hosted a monks' chanting-house, a post office and a coaching inn. Today a stylishly updated pub and hotel (part of the Barkby group), it has a stone-walled bar with exposed timbers, local cask ales and plush seating by a crackling fire. A bull's head above an open fireplace oversees proceedings. Rustic pub staples and pizzas are served in the moodily lit dining areas: eat in, then stay over in one of the contemporary, country-style bedrooms decorated with vintage finds and wool throws. Fishing enthusiasts appreciate the hotel's stretch of the River Coln; riverside walks please everyone else.

MAP 3:E6
Market Place
Fairford GL7 4AA
T: 01285 712535
W: thebullhotelfairford.co.uk

BEDROOMS: 21.
OPEN: all year.
FACILITIES: bar, lounge, morning room, 3 dining rooms, function facilities, in-room TV (Freeview), terraces, private fishing rights.
BACKGROUND MUSIC: in bar, dining rooms.
LOCATION: in town centre.
CHILDREN: all ages welcomed.
DOGS: allowed in bar only.
CREDIT CARDS: Amex, MC, Visa.
PRICES: per room B&B £75–£220. À la carte £35. 2-night min. stay preferred at weekends.

FALMOUTH Cornwall

THE GREENBANK

With boats bobbing on the water and 'magnificent' vistas across the harbour, life on the water's edge doesn't come much closer than at this large hotel, the oldest in the maritime town. The building is an amalgam of modern additions to a 17th-century sailors' pub; today, coastal light floods in to its public spaces, and its bedrooms and suites, some harbour facing, are bright and contemporary. Food is served all day in the restaurant (perhaps shellfish lasagne, pan-fried brill); in the dog-friendly Working Boat pub, find hearty portions, Sunday roasts and a home brew. Step straight on to a boat from the hotel's pontoons; a ten-minute stroll away, board the Flushing Ferry to the historic fishing village.

MAP 1:E2
Harbourside
Falmouth TR11 2SR
T: 01326 312440
W: greenbank-hotel.co.uk

BEDROOMS: 61.
OPEN: all year.
FACILITIES: lift, bar, pub, restaurant, lounge, in-room TV, civil wedding licence, spa treatments, electric car charging point.
BACKGROUND MUSIC: in bar, restaurant.
LOCATION: on Falmouth harbour.
CHILDREN: all ages welcomed.
DOGS: allowed in 9 bedrooms, pub, not in restaurant, bar.
CREDIT CARDS: Amex, MC, Visa.
PRICES: per room B&B £99–£319. À la carte £35. 1-night bookings sometimes refused.

FAR SAWREY Cumbria
CUCKOO BROW INN

In a pretty village between Lake Windermere and Hawkshead, this unpretentious 18th-century inn stands atop a hill, the views over lakeland countryside stretching out before it. Past the gabled entrance, a wide, double-sided wood-burning stove takes pride of place in the dog-friendly bar and dining room. Local ales and modern pub fare (wild mushrooms, fried hen's egg, charred beetroot sourdough, say, or steak and Flakebridge cheese pie) are served here; in former stables, sofas, games and a log-burning stove create a cosy retreat. Most of the contemporary bedrooms are in an annexe attached to the main building; family rooms have a screened-off area for children. Hiking and cycling trails abound.

MAP 4: inset C2
Far Sawrey LA22 0LQ
T: 015394 43425
W: cuckoobrow.co.uk

BEDROOMS: 14. Some on ground floor.
OPEN: all year.
FACILITIES: lobby lounge, bar, dining room, games room, in-room TV (Freeview), terrace, small garden.
BACKGROUND MUSIC: in bar, games room.
LOCATION: village centre.
CHILDREN: all ages welcomed.
DOGS: 'very welcome' in bedrooms, public rooms.
CREDIT CARDS: MC, Visa.
PRICES: per room B&B single from £77, double £110–£165. 2-night min. stay over Easter, Christmas and New Year.

FERRENSBY Yorkshire
THE GENERAL TARLETON

A welcome staging post for travellers between Scotland and England, this revamped 18th-century coaching inn is now under new ownership. Extensive refurbishment in 2021 resulted in spruced-up eating and drinking areas, and a collection of stylishly updated bedrooms. In the bar or on the terrace, small and large plates of 'world-inspired' cooking might include cod ceviche or sticky apple-glazed pork belly bites, kimchi; the fine-dining restaurant, Ralph's, serves a multi-course tasting menu. Overnight guests stay in one of the contemporary bedrooms, each supplied with tea, coffee and organic toiletries. Residents also have access to a lounge with an honesty bar. Harrogate, York and the Dales are an easy drive away.

MAP 4:D4
Boroughbridge Road
Ferrensby HG5 0PZ
T: 01423 340284
W: the-gt.co.uk

BEDROOMS: 15. Some, on ground floor, suitable for disabled.
OPEN: all year, closed Mon, Tues during school term; restaurant open for dinner Wed–Sat evenings.
FACILITIES: residents' lounge, bar, restaurant, conservatory, in-room TV (Freeview), 2 terraces, small herb garden, parking.
BACKGROUND MUSIC: all day in public areas.
LOCATION: 4 miles from Knaresborough.
CHILDREN: all ages welcomed.
DOGS: not allowed, except on terraces.
CREDIT CARDS: Amex, MC, Visa.
PRICES: per room B&B single from £115, double £115–£165. À la carte £50, tasting menu (Ralph's) £55.

GILSLAND Cumbria

THE HILL ON THE WALL

Elaine Packer's farmhouse B&B overlooks
Hadrian's Wall near Birdoswald, one of the
Roman monument's best-preserved forts. Visitors
praise the welcome they receive at this Georgian
building filled with 'every comfort'. The
traditionally decorated bedrooms are supplied
with bathrobes, freshly ground coffee and a jar
of biscuits; at teatime, there are hot drinks and
home-made cake to be had. On cool days, browse
the library by the wood-burning stove; when
the weather's fine, sit in the 'beautiful' walled
garden and watch the light change over the
North Pennines and the Lakeland fells beyond.
'So peaceful.' Breakfast on 'gigantic portions' of
home-cooked Northumbrian fare, ordered the
night before.

MAP 4:B3
The Hill
Gilsland CA8 7DA
T: 016977 47214
W: hillonthewall.co.uk

BEDROOMS: 3. 1 on ground floor.
OPEN: Mar–Oct.
FACILITIES: lounge, breakfast room, in-
room TV (Freeview), 1-acre garden,
terrace, secure bicycle storage.
BACKGROUND MUSIC: none.
LOCATION: 1 mile W of Gilsland on
the B6318.
CHILDREN: not under 10.
DOGS: not allowed.
CREDIT CARDS: MC, Visa for online
bookings only.
PRICES: per room B&B single £75–£85,
double £95.

GOATHLAND Yorkshire

FAIRHAVEN COUNTRY
GUEST HOUSE

Peter and Sarah Garnett's 'very comfortable'
Edwardian guest house is in a scenic village
surrounded by wooded valleys and thick heather
moorland. The 'friendly, helpful' hosts provide
a welcoming pot of tea and home-baked cake in
the large lounge; there are games and books, and
an open fire when the temperature dips. Homely
bedrooms with 'beautiful moorland views' are
'well stocked' with hot drinks and biscuits; fresh
milk and filtered water are in the dining-room
fridge. 'Superb' breakfasts with home-made
granola, marmalade and jams include daily
specials – a Whitby kipper and a poached egg,
say. Countryside and coast are easily explored; the
North York Moors Railway is close.

MAP 4:C5
The Common
Goathland YO22 5AN
T: 01947 896361
W: fairhavencountryguesthouse.co.uk

BEDROOMS: 9. 1 with separate private
bathroom.
OPEN: all year except 1 week over
Christmas.
FACILITIES: lounge, dining room,
in-room TV (Freeview), front terrace,
large garden, secure bicycle storage,
dinner available on certain evenings
in winter, all year for parties of 6 or
more.
BACKGROUND MUSIC: during breakfast.
LOCATION: 8 miles from Whitby.
CHILDREN: all ages welcomed.
DOGS: not allowed.
CREDIT CARDS: MC, Visa.
PRICES: per room B&B single £47–£80,
double £90–£112.

NEW

GOSFORTH Cumbria

1692 WASDALE

Sleekly designed and with many modern comforts, Faith and Stephen Newell's fantastically secluded B&B in the rugged western Lake District is 'one of the best we've stayed at', a Guide reader reports. Bursts of vibrant colour complement the high beamed ceilings and timber and flagstone floors in the stone-built house, but guests may find their attention drawn outside instead: the Wasdale valley views stretch from Scafell Pike in the east to the Isle of Man, over the Irish Sea, to the west. The lounge has an honesty bar, a piano, an open fire for cool evenings; each spacious suite has a private patio. Picnics and home-cooked dinners may be pre-ordered; breakfast, served in the courtyard on sunny days, is 'excellent'.

MAP 4: inset C2
Bolton Head Farm
Gosforth CA20 1EW
T: 019467 25777
W: 1692wasdale.co.uk

BEDROOMS: 6.
OPEN: all year except 23–26 Dec.
FACILITIES: lounge, dining room, in-room smart TV, courtyard, 3-acre garden, boot room, sheltered outdoor hot tub, electric car charging point.
BACKGROUND MUSIC: in public rooms.
LOCATION: 1½ miles E of Gosforth.
CHILDREN: not under 12.
DOGS: allowed in 3 suites, not in lounge, dining room.
CREDIT CARDS: MC, Visa.
PRICES: per room B&B single £155–£175, double £170–£190. À la carte £40.

GRANGE-IN-BORROWDALE Cumbria

BORROWDALE GATES

Broad views and the promise of walks from the door draw returning guests to this 'very friendly' traditional Lakeland hotel with up-to-date facilities. 'Tranquil, well-appointed' bedrooms look over the Borrowdale valley and surrounding fells. Many rooms have a balcony, or patio access to the garden; all have a refreshment tray, bathrobes, a digital library of magazines and newspapers via a smart phone or tablet. On inclement days, the lounge's picture windows provide immersive views with no need to move a muscle. A showcase for Cumbrian produce (Borrowdale trout, fell-bred lamb), the restaurant has 'superb food for all, including vegetarians'. 'Breakfast sustains walkers through a long day.'

MAP 4: inset C2
Grange-in-Borrowdale
nr Keswick CA12 5UQ
T: 01768 777204
W: borrowdale-gates.com

BEDROOMS: 32. Some on ground floor.
OPEN: all year.
FACILITIES: lift, open-plan bar, dining room and lounge (log fire), reading room, in-room TV (Freeview), wedding facilities (exclusive use only), 2-acre grounds, terrace.
BACKGROUND MUSIC: none.
LOCATION: 5 miles from Keswick, in the heart of the Borrowdale valley.
CHILDREN: all ages welcomed.
DOGS: allowed in 3 bedrooms, not in dining room, bar, lounge.
CREDIT CARDS: MC, Visa.
PRICES: per room B&B £224–£300. À la carte £49.

GRANGE-OVER-SANDS Cumbria
CLARE HOUSE

In green grounds with sweeping views over Morecambe Bay, two generations of the Read family have run this comfortable hotel for more than half a century; in that time, it has retained the affection of its many returning guests, who speak of 'marvellous' stays. 'Wonderfully old-fashioned', the Victorian house has well-appointed bedrooms, most overlooking the water. Morning coffee, light lunches and afternoon tea can be taken in bay-view lounges or under parasols in the 'well-tended' garden. At dinner, 'beautifully presented' dishes might include twice-baked gruyère soufflé; roast lamb, celeriac cream, rösti potato. Breakfast is served on linen-dressed tables. 'Friendly staff' readily advise on Lake District day trips.

MAP 4: inset C2
Park Road
Grange-over-Sands LA11 7HQ
T: 015395 33026
W: clarehousehotel.co.uk

BEDROOMS: 16. 1 on ground floor suitable for disabled.
OPEN: mid-Mar–mid-Dec.
FACILITIES: 2 lounges, dining room, in-room TV (Freeview), 1-acre grounds, parking.
BACKGROUND MUSIC: none.
LOCATION: in village.
CHILDREN: all ages welcomed, but no special facilities.
DOGS: only assistance dogs allowed.
CREDIT CARDS: MC, Visa.
PRICES: per person D,B&B £120–£135.

GRASMERE Cumbria
THE YAN AT BROADRAYNE

On a hillside flanked by grazing Herdwick sheep – 'a beautiful setting' – this 17th-century barn and cluster of old outbuildings have been reinvented as a 'refreshingly different' contemporary hotel and bistro. It's a hands-on family affair, run by Jess Manley with her husband, Will (the chef), and her parents, Dave and Sally Keighley. Uncluttered modern bedrooms all have views of the fells; 'useful charging sockets and good reading lights' are thoughtful touches. Cumbrian classics and lamb from the family farm appear on 'adventurous, very good' seasonal menus in the 'informal' bistro. Walking sticks, maps and guides are available to borrow; the 555 Kendal–Grasmere bus nearby makes a car 'almost unnecessary'.

MAP 4: inset C2
Broadrayne Farm
Grasmere LA22 9RU
T: 015394 35055
W: theyan.co.uk

BEDROOMS: 7. Plus self-catering cottages.
OPEN: all year except 3–21 Jan.
FACILITIES: lounge, bar/bistro, in-room TV (Freeview), tiered terrace, drying room, bicycle storage, 10-acre farmland.
BACKGROUND MUSIC: 'chilled' in bistro.
LOCATION: close to A591, 1 mile N of Grasmere.
CHILDREN: all ages welcomed.
DOGS: allowed in 2 rooms (1 dog per room), on lead in public areas.
CREDIT CARDS: MC, Visa.
PRICES: per room £100–£220. Breakfast £10, à la carte £30. 2-night min. stay.

HALIFAX Yorkshire

SHIBDEN MILL INN

In the wooded Shibden valley, this wisteria-covered 17th-century inn stands near Red Beck, the stream that powered the corn and spinning mill that once stood here. Today's oak-beamed bar, with a vast open fireplace, has a wide range of gins and whiskies, plus Shibden Mill's own brew; ambitious, Yorkshire-inspired dishes are served here, in the dining room or on the patio. Characteristic dishes: basil gnocchi; lamb shoulder, barbecue leek, Mrs Kirkham's Lancashire. Individually styled bedrooms (some compact) are supplied with bathrobes, teas and coffee. There are checks and floral prints in one; in another, a deep velvet sofa at the foot of a half-tester bed. Rest well: circular walks (ask for a map) start from the garden.

MAP 4:D3
Shibden Mill Fold
Shibden
Halifax HX3 7UL
T: 01422 365840
W: shibdenmillinn.com

BEDROOMS: 11.
OPEN: all year except 25–26 Dec, 1 Jan.
FACILITIES: bar, lounge, restaurant, private dining room, in-room TV (Freeview), small conference facilities, patio, 2-acre garden, complimentary access to local health club.
BACKGROUND MUSIC: in main bar, restaurant.
LOCATION: 2 miles from Halifax town centre.
CHILDREN: all ages welcomed.
DOGS: allowed in bar.
CREDIT CARDS: Amex, MC, Visa.
PRICES: per room B&B single £90–£180, double £95–£245. À la carte £35.

HARROGATE Yorkshire

THE WEST PARK HOTEL

Facing the Stray's 200 acres of open parkland, a Victorian coach house is today this jazzily refurbished town-centre hotel. It has a zinc-topped bar serving cocktails and Yorkshire ales; breakfast, light lunches and a seasonal dinner menu are taken in the buzzy brasserie or under fairy lights on the covered, heated terrace. The well-appointed bedrooms, some with a private terrace, are bright and contemporary. Each room is supplied with teas and a capsule coffee machine, plus bathrobes and good toiletries in a bathroom with under-floor heating. Two spacious duplex suites also have a lounge and dining area, and access to the roof terrace. Part of the Provenance Inns & Hotels group.

MAP 4:D4
19 West Park
Harrogate HG1 1BJ
T: 01423 524471
W: thewestparkhotel.com

BEDROOMS: 25. Some suitable for disabled.
OPEN: all year.
FACILITIES: bar, brasserie, meeting/private dining rooms, in-room TV (Freeview), large walled terrace, adjacent NCP car park, pay and display street parking.
BACKGROUND MUSIC: all day in public areas.
LOCATION: in town centre.
CHILDREN: all ages welcomed.
DOGS: well-behaved dogs allowed in some bedrooms, bar.
CREDIT CARDS: Amex, MC, Visa.
PRICES: per room B&B £162–£500. À la carte £35.

HASTINGS Sussex
THE LAINDONS

A stroll from the beach, Karen and Malcolm Twist's B&B in a handsome Grade II listed Georgian coaching house has a modern, seasidey feel. Bright and cheery, well-proportioned, high-ceilinged bedrooms have quality linens on a bed handcrafted from reclaimed timber; perhaps also a period fireplace, window seat or chaise longue. Home-made biscuits, ground coffee, organic teas – even earplugs to combat seagull squawks – are welcome extras. The hosts whip up fresh smoothies, bake their own bread and roast their own coffee for breakfast in the conservatory overlooking the Old Town. There's good choice on the morning menu: a full English, blueberry pancakes, granola with yogurt and home-made compote, and more.

MAP 2:E5
23 High Street
Hastings TN34 3EY
T: 01424 437710
W: thelaindons.com

BEDROOMS: 5. Plus 2 with shared bathroom, suitable for a family or group travelling together.
OPEN: all year except 24–26 Dec, first 2 weeks Jan.
FACILITIES: drawing room (honesty bar), breakfast room, in-room TV (Freeview), parking permits provided.
BACKGROUND MUSIC: 'gentle' in public areas at breakfast.
LOCATION: in the heart of the Old Town.
CHILDREN: not under 10.
DOGS: not allowed.
CREDIT CARDS: MC, Visa.
PRICES: per room B&B £145–£175. 2-night min. stay at weekends Apr–Sept.

HAWKHURST Kent
THE QUEEN'S INN

All hail this revived 16th-century coaching inn, in a historic Wealden village close to National Trust attractions Scotney Castle and Sissinghurst Castle Garden. Against an old-meets-new backdrop of beams, brick walls, velvet wingback chairs and plush banquettes, Kentish wines, ales and ciders headline the drinks list in the timbered bar. Hungry visitors have a choice of dining areas. The smart, rustic restaurant serves Kentish cider mussels and grilled steaks alongside vegan and vegetarian options; pizzas are available in the industrial-chic Charcoal Kitchen. Upstairs, creatively decorated bedrooms (some of which will accommodate a family) have coffee and tea, fresh milk, home-made brownies and botanical toiletries.

MAP 2:E4
Rye Road
Hawkhurst TN18 4EY
T: 01580 754233
W: thequeensinnhawkhurst.co.uk

BEDROOMS: 8.
OPEN: all year.
FACILITIES: bar, snug, 3 dining areas, in-room TV (Freeview), function facilities, front patio.
BACKGROUND MUSIC: in bar, restaurant.
LOCATION: in village, within the High Weald Area of Outstanding Natural Beauty.
CHILDREN: all ages welcomed.
DOGS: allowed in bar, one area of restaurant.
CREDIT CARDS: Amex, MC, Visa.
PRICES: per room B&B £115–£195. À la carte £35. 2-night min. stay at weekends.

NEW

HEALING Lincolnshire

HEALING MANOR HOTEL

Spot Sidney the swan on the willow-draped pond: this centuries-old manor house on the village outskirts stands in extensive grounds stretching from landscaped gardens to parkland. Individually styled bedrooms are spread among the main house and converted outbuildings. They range in size and aspect – some overlook the pond while others have direct access to a shared courtyard – though all have a neat, contemporary country air. Guests have a choice of places to eat: the dog-friendly Pig & Whistle pub, where accompanying pooches have their own menu, and the Portman restaurant, whose à la carte and tasting menus make the most of locally grown and foraged ingredients. A popular wedding venue.

MAP 4:E5
Stallingborough Road
Healing DN41 7QF
T: 01472 884544
W: healingmanorhotel.co.uk

BEDROOMS: 37. 24 in converted outbuildings, 2 suitable for disabled.
OPEN: all year.
FACILITIES: pub, restaurant, function rooms, in-room TV (Freeview), civil wedding licence, terrace, 36-acre grounds (gardens, fields, woodland, moated island), electric car charging points.
BACKGROUND MUSIC: all day in dining areas.
LOCATION: 5 miles W of Grimsby.
CHILDREN: all ages welcomed.
DOGS: allowed in pub, some bedrooms.
CREDIT CARDS: Amex, MC, Visa.
PRICES: per room B&B £95–£200.
À la carte £40.

HERTFORD Hertfordshire

NUMBER ONE PORT HILL

'Every corner contains a curiosity' at Annie Rowley's 'artful' B&B in a historic market town. The Georgian house, featured in Pevsner's guide to Hertfordshire, is filled with vintage glassware, chandeliers and sculptures. Immaculate bedrooms are on the top floor: one is large, with a French gilt bed and a raised boat bath in the bathroom; two are cosy. Plentiful extras include Belgian hot chocolate, sweet and savoury snacks, bathrobes and 'eclectic' reading material. Traffic noise is muted by 'very good' double glazing. Breakfast, with freshly ground coffee and home-made preserves, is taken communally, or under ancient wisteria in the walled garden. A fine dinner is available some nights; eating places are close by.

MAP 2:C4
1 Port Hill
Hertford SG14 1PJ
T: 01992 587350
W: numberoneporthill.co.uk

BEDROOMS: 3.
OPEN: all year except Christmas.
FACILITIES: drawing room, in-room TV (Sky, Freeview), front and back gardens, limited street parking.
BACKGROUND MUSIC: none.
LOCATION: 5 mins' walk from town centre.
CHILDREN: not under 12 ('though exemptions may be made, if discussed, for younger children').
DOGS: not allowed.
CREDIT CARDS: MC, Visa.
PRICES: per room B&B £130–£160.
Dinner £45 (dependent on number of guests).

HEXHAM Northumberland

BATTLESTEADS

A stroll from 'the majestic flow' of the North Tyne river, Dee and Richard Slade's 'well-run' hotel, restaurant and village pub stand out for their 'laudable' approach to sustainable tourism. Modern menus at mealtimes use locally sourced produce and the bounty from the kitchen garden and mushroom farm; the walled garden is a popular stop for birds and red squirrels; the dark sky observatory is simply 'amazing'. Bedrooms are in the main building (part of an 18th-century farmstead) and in wood-built lodges to the rear. Some may be 'on the small side, though adequate', while others, in the lodges, are 'vast'. Rooms away from the road are quietest. The hosts readily advise on the best walks for spotting local wildlife.

MAP 4:B3
Wark-on-Tyne
Hexham NE48 3LS
T: 01434 230209
W: battlesteads.com

BEDROOMS: 22. 4 on ground floor, 5 in lodges, 2 suitable for disabled.
OPEN: all year except 25 Dec.
FACILITIES: bar, dining room, in-room TV (Freeview), civil wedding licence, function facilities, drying room, 2-acre grounds (walled garden, kitchen garden, dark sky observatory), electric car charging points.
BACKGROUND MUSIC: in bar, restaurant.
LOCATION: 12 miles N of Hexham.
CHILDREN: all ages welcomed.
DOGS: allowed in public rooms, some bedrooms (resident dog).
CREDIT CARDS: Amex, MC, Visa.
PRICES: per room B&B from £135.
À la carte £33.

HEXHAM Northumberland

THE BEAUMONT

Facing the park in the historic market town, this 'bustling' town house hotel is liked for its 'unfailingly welcoming, helpful and friendly' staff. 'It clearly has a good local reputation.' It is owned by Roger Davy, a Hexham native, and his wife, Magda, who run it with 'energy and commitment to high standards'. The Victorian building is lively with pleasingly mismatched fabrics and colourful local artwork; 'well-appointed' bedrooms, freshly refurbished, are supplied with essential-oil toiletries. In the smart, open-plan bar/lounge/restaurant on the ground floor, 'the food and service represent excellent value for money'. Here, 'interesting and varied' dishes might include an 'impressive' courgette and goat's curd risotto. 'Good coffee at breakfast, too.'

MAP 4:B3
Beaumont Street
Hexham NE46 3LT
T: 01434 602331
W: thebeaumonthexham.co.uk

BEDROOMS: 33. 1 suitable for disabled.
OPEN: all year.
FACILITIES: open-plan bar/lounge/restaurant, in-room TV (Freeview), function facilities, electric car charging point, parking, restaurant and bar wheelchair accessible.
BACKGROUND MUSIC: in bar, restaurant.
LOCATION: in town centre.
CHILDREN: all ages welcomed.
DOGS: allowed in designated public areas only, not in bedrooms.
CREDIT CARDS: Amex, MC, Visa.
PRICES: per room B&B £140–£160.
À la carte £30.

HITCHIN Hertfordshire

THE FARMHOUSE AT REDCOATS

In serene countryside, this well-restored old farmhouse, its many characterful features dating from the 15th century, stands in large landscaped gardens. The hotel and restaurant, part of the Nye family's Anglian Country Inns, have intimate sitting areas, and warming fires in inglenook fireplaces. Modern British dishes in the conservatory restaurant use much locally sourced produce and home-grown fruit and vegetables; cocktails, wines and real ales accompany. Creatively decorated bedrooms (some family-friendly) are spread across the main house, converted stables and Grade II listed barns across the courtyard, where events may be held. In the morning, choose an in-room breakfast box or a hearty dish from the farmhouse menu.

MAP 2:C4
Redcoats Green
Hitchin SG4 7JR
T: 01438 729500
W: farmhouseatredcoats.co.uk

BEDROOMS: 27. 8 in converted stables and coach house, 15 in Grade II listed barn conversion across the yard, some on ground floor.
OPEN: all year.
FACILITIES: bar, lounge, conservatory restaurant, 3 private dining rooms, in-room TV (Freeview), civil wedding licence, events barn, 4-acre grounds.
BACKGROUND MUSIC: 'subtle' in public areas.
LOCATION: 9 mins' drive from Stevenage.
CHILDREN: all ages welcomed.
DOGS: well-behaved dogs allowed in some bedrooms, bar, lounge.
CREDIT CARDS: Amex, MC, Visa.
PRICES: per room B&B £120–£165.
À la carte £45.

HOLKHAM Norfolk

THE VICTORIA INN

In beach flint and brick, this genteelly refurbished 18th-century inn on the Earl of Leicester's Holkham estate is 'perfect for exploring the north Norfolk coast'. Enthusiastic staff welcome locals, tourists and their dogs to the popular bar, where hunting trophies and taxidermied wildfowl are displayed; in the dining rooms, local produce (including beef from the estate) dictates the daily specials on the unfussy, brasserie-style menu. Bedrooms and family-friendly suites in country-cottage hues have a few antiques and plenty of perks, including a mini-fridge with complimentary drinks. Ancient House residents have a walled rose garden to enjoy, too. A few minutes' walk away: 'one of the most beautiful, isolated beaches'.

MAP 2:A5
Park Road
Holkham NR23 1RG
T: 01328 711008
W: holkham.co.uk/stay-eat/
the-victoria-inn/welcome

BEDROOMS: 20. 10 in Ancient House, opposite, 1 on ground floor suitable for disabled.
OPEN: all year.
FACILITIES: bar, lounge, restaurant with conservatory extension, in-room TV, courtyard, garden, children's play area.
BACKGROUND MUSIC: in public areas.
LOCATION: on the Holkham estate, 1¾ miles W of Wells-next-the-Sea.
CHILDREN: all ages welcomed.
DOGS: allowed in inn bedrooms, bar, restaurant, not in Ancient House.
CREDIT CARDS: MC, Visa.
PRICES: per room B&B from £125.
À la carte £35.

HOLT Norfolk
BYFORDS

A lively spot, this higgledy-piggledy place, said to be Holt's oldest building, stands at the heart of the 'bustling' market town. It is popular with locals, who drop in at the all-day café and food shop; overnight guests stay in 'very comfortable' accommodation. Bedrooms revamped with character are accessed via a winding staircase at the back of the deli. Each room has its own style (and some suit a family), but all have vintage furnishings on stripped-wood floors; an entertainment system; home-made biscuits, fresh milk and water. In the conservatory eating area, the comprehensive menu includes something-for-everyone dishes alongside sharing platters, salads and pizzas. Picnic items and takeaway treats are in the deli.

MAP 2:A5
1–3 Shirehall Plain
Holt NR25 6BG
T: 01263 711400
W: byfords.org.uk

BEDROOMS: 16. Plus self-catering apartment.
OPEN: all year.
FACILITIES: café/bar, deli, in-room TV (Sky), terrace, private secure parking.
BACKGROUND MUSIC: in café.
LOCATION: in town centre.
CHILDREN: all ages welcomed.
DOGS: not allowed.
CREDIT CARDS: Amex, MC, Visa.
PRICES: per room B&B £170–£240.

NEW

HUDDERSFIELD Yorkshire
MANOR HOUSE LINDLEY

An alluring update has brought zesty eating and drinking spaces, refined bedrooms, a rooftop terrace and a modern fitness studio to this stately Georgian manor. Set back from the High Street in a smart Huddersfield suburb, the hotel has a conservatory-like bistro for daytime comfort food, and a stylish restaurant serving sophisticated dinners (perhaps native lobster and pickled strawberry tart; wild garlic gnocchi, baked Tunworth). Cocktails may be shaken and stirred in the lounge or on the roof terrace overlooking St Stephen's church. The bedrooms and suites are all different, though every one is supplied with a capsule coffee machine, a designer scented candle and a dose of contemporary glamour.

MAP 4:E3
1 Lidget Street
Huddersfield HD3 3JB
T: 01484 504000
W: manorhouselindley.co.uk

BEDROOMS: 10. 1 suitable for disabled, plus duplex apartment.
OPEN: all year, restaurant closed Mon, Tues.
FACILITIES: 3 bars, restaurant, bistro, in-room TV (Freeview), civil wedding licence, meeting/function facilities, gym (open to non-residents), courtyard, electric car charging point.
BACKGROUND MUSIC: 'relaxing' music all day in public areas.
LOCATION: 2 miles NW of Huddersfield town centre.
CHILDREN: all ages welcomed, not under 12 in lounge and restaurant (except at Sunday lunch), adults only on rooftop terrace.
DOGS: allowed in apartment, grounds, not in main building.
CREDIT CARDS: Amex, MC, Visa.
PRICES: per room B&B £139–£299. À la carte £50.

HUDDERSFIELD Yorkshire

THE THREE ACRES INN & RESTAURANT

There are 'tremendous views to all sides' from this 'friendly' roadside drovers' inn in Pennine countryside, but diners may find their attention drawn, instead, to the 'detour-worthy food' served within. A family enterprise for more than 50 years, it is owned by Neil Truelove and his son, Tom. The 'high-quality' cooking follows the seasons: perhaps fresh native lobster, beef-drip chips in the summer; forest mushrooms, crispy egg, truffle in the autumn. Vegetarians have their own menu. Spread across the main building and garden cottages, bedrooms are 'comfortable and clean, with an agreeable bed'. In the morning: home-made muesli, home-baked sourdough, local bacon and sausage.

MAP 4:E3
Roydhouse
Shelley
Huddersfield HD8 8LR
T: 01484 602606
W: 3acres.com

BEDROOMS: 17. 1 suitable for disabled, 8 in annexe.
OPEN: all year except evenings 25 and 26 Dec, midday 31 Dec, evening 1 Jan.
FACILITIES: bar, restaurant, in-room TV (Freeview), civil wedding licence, small function/private dining facilities, terraced garden, electric car charging points.
BACKGROUND MUSIC: in bar, restaurant.
LOCATION: in hamlet, 6 miles from Huddersfield town centre.
CHILDREN: well-behaved children welcomed.
DOGS: only guide dogs allowed.
CREDIT CARDS: Amex, MC, Visa.
PRICES: per room B&B single £60–£195, double £150–£225. À la carte £50.

HURLEY Berkshire

HURLEY HOUSE

Within reach of historic houses, vineyards and Thames river cruises, this upmarket Berkshire hotel makes a fine base for exploring the Chilterns. Styled in creams and greys, urbane bedrooms, some with a private patio, have up-to-date comforts such as air conditioning and under-floor heating; efficient insulation subdues noise from the adjacent busy road. There's a choice of eating areas: the well-regarded restaurant, a sophisticated space (sleek wood panelling, leather banquettes, oversized artwork) where guests have their pick from Japanese and British menus; the smartly rustic bar; and large, heated terraces, ideal for alfresco meals in fine weather. At breakfast, find a 'good choice' of cooked dishes.

MAP 2:D3
Henley Road
Hurley SL6 5LH
T: 01628 568500
W: hurleyhouse.co.uk

BEDROOMS: 10. Some suitable for disabled.
OPEN: all year, restaurant closed Sun evenings.
FACILITIES: bar, snug, restaurant, private dining room, in-room TV (Freeview), function facilities, civil wedding licence, spa treatment room, large terrace, electric car charging points.
BACKGROUND MUSIC: in public areas until 11 pm, plus live music at Sun lunch and on selected evenings.
LOCATION: 5 miles E of Henley-on-Thames, 10 miles NW of Windsor.
CHILDREN: all ages welcomed.
DOGS: allowed in bar, on terrace.
CREDIT CARDS: Amex, MC, Visa.
PRICES: per room B&B £190–£270. À la carte £55.

IRONBRIDGE Shropshire

THE LIBRARY HOUSE

In the heart of a historic town, the once-upon-a-time village library is today this 'beautifully decorated' B&B run by Sarah and Tim Davis. Neat, pretty bedrooms in the Grade II listed Georgian town house are named after writers: Chaucer opens on to a garden terrace; high-ceilinged Eliot overlooks the River Severn; spacious Milton has a large bed and a reading corner. Each room is supplied with waffle robes, fresh milk and a hot-water bottle. A log-burner blazes in the book-lined sitting room when the temperature dips; in good weather, take tea in the terraced garden. Breakfast, with home-made marmalade, is served at linen-topped tables; special diets are catered for. Ironbridge Gorge, a UNESCO World Heritage site, is close.

MAP 3:C5
11 Severn Bank
Ironbridge TF8 7AN
T: 01952 432299
W: libraryhouse.com

BEDROOMS: 3.
OPEN: all year.
FACILITIES: sitting room, breakfast room, in-room TV (Freeview), courtyard, mature garden, permits for on-street parking.
BACKGROUND MUSIC: none.
LOCATION: in town centre.
CHILDREN: not under 13.
DOGS: not allowed.
CREDIT CARDS: MC, Visa.
PRICES: per room B&B single £75–£95, double £100–£140.

KELLING Norfolk

THE PHEASANT

Part of a sprawling estate of woods and parkland, this country house hotel is a tranquil retreat. Take tea on the lawn on a fine day; at lunch and dinner, sample local and estate-grown produce in the restaurant or orangery. The daily changing menu might include smoked duck salad, celeriac remoulade; Cromer crab thermidor, buttered new potatoes, chargrilled asparagus. Among the classically styled bedrooms (some dog friendly), some interconnect to suit a family or a group. A coffee machine and good toiletries are provided; bathrobes and slippers, too, in superior rooms. Varied breakfasts (omelettes, Cley smoked kipper, etc) provide ample fuel for exploring north Norfolk's coastal walks and nature reserves.

MAP 2:A5
Coast Road
Kelling NR25 7EG
T: 01263 588382
W: pheasanthotelnorfolk.co.uk

BEDROOMS: 32. 24 on ground floor, 1 suitable for disabled.
OPEN: all year.
FACILITIES: bar/lounge, restaurant, orangery, private dining room, in-room TV, civil wedding licence, terrace, 2½-acre garden in 2,000-acre estate.
BACKGROUND MUSIC: in public areas.
LOCATION: 3½ miles NE of Holt.
CHILDREN: all ages welcomed.
DOGS: allowed in 4 bedrooms, bar, orangery, not in restaurant.
CREDIT CARDS: Amex, MC, Visa.
PRICES: per room B&B £200–£260. À la carte £35. 2-night min. stay at weekends July–Aug, bank holidays.

KING'S LYNN Norfolk

BANK HOUSE

Well placed for visiting the market town, this 'distinguished' Georgian bank-turned-town hotel is in a 'fine waterfront setting' within strolling distance, along cobbled streets, of historical buildings and handsome squares. Owned by the Goodrich family (see The Rose & Crown, Snettisham, main entry), it is popular with locals, who gather in its bar and newly redecorated brasserie. The individually styled bedrooms vary in size and layout: call ahead to discuss best options. Most rooms have a river view; all have pampering toiletries, 'good-quality magazines', a 'well-researched guide' of local hotspots. 'Great British classics' are served indoors and out, across several dining areas. Pay-and-display parking is close by.

MAP 2:A4
King's Staithe Square
King's Lynn PE30 1RD
T: 01553 660492
W: thebankhouse.co.uk

BEDROOMS: 12.
OPEN: all year.
FACILITIES: bar, 3 dining rooms, meeting/function rooms, vaulted cellars for private functions, in-room smart TV, riverside terrace, courtyard, all public rooms wheelchair accessible, adapted toilet.
BACKGROUND MUSIC: from mid-morning onwards, in public areas (but 'turned off on demand').
LOCATION: on the quayside.
CHILDREN: all ages welcomed.
DOGS: allowed in restaurant, bar, terrace, 2 bedrooms.
CREDIT CARDS: Amex, MC, Visa.
PRICES: per room B&B single £105–£170, double £125–£185.
À la carte £36.

KINGSBRIDGE Devon

THURLESTONE HOTEL

Approached by lanes 'resplendent with wildflowers', this 'thoroughly dependable' hotel is set in 19 acres of sub-tropical gardens along the South Devon National Trust coastline. It has been owned and run by generations of the Grose family since 1896. 'Stunning' views over the grounds reach to the sea beyond; inside the hotel are well-equipped bedrooms (several to accommodate a family) and many 'stylish' areas for lunches, dinners and cream teas. The menu in the smart Trevilder restaurant lists 'good classic stuff'; real ales and pub fare are served beneath shipwreck timbers in the 16th-century village inn. Play croquet, tennis or golf in the grounds, or head out: coastal walks and rock pools are minutes away.

MAP 1:D4
Thurlestone
Kingsbridge TQ7 3NN
T: 01548 560382
W: thurlestone.co.uk

BEDROOMS: 65. 2 suitable for disabled.
OPEN: all year.
FACILITIES: lift, lounge, bar, restaurant, poolside café, village pub, in-room TV (Sky), civil wedding licence, function facilities, terrace, spa, outdoor heated swimming pool, tennis, 9-hole golf course, children's club during school holidays, electric car charging point.
BACKGROUND MUSIC: none.
LOCATION: 4 miles SW of Kingsbridge.
CHILDREN: all ages welcomed.
DOGS: allowed in some bedrooms, not in public rooms.
CREDIT CARDS: Amex, MC, Visa.
PRICES: per room B&B from £235.
À la carte £40, tasting menu £70.
2-night min. stay.

KINGSWEAR Devon

KAYWANA HALL

Tony Pithers and Gordon Craig's ultra-modern B&B stands in hillside woodland across the estuary from Dartmouth. One of just four in Devon, the 1960s Le Corbusier-inspired 'butterfly house' is a tranquil, adults-only space. Sleek, light-filled bedrooms decorated with abstract art each have their own entrance and private terrace with outdoor seating (some reached via steep steps). Well equipped, they have robes and slippers, a mini-fridge, an espresso machine and home-made sweet treats. Breakfast is in an airy room overlooking the swimming pool. Start with freshly squeezed juices, locally baked bread and fruit compote; eggs Benedict, home-made vegetarian sausages or other cooked dishes follow.

MAP 1:D4
Higher Contour Road
Kingswear TQ6 0AY
T: 01803 752200
W: kaywanahall.co.uk

BEDROOMS: 4.
OPEN: mid-May–end Oct.
FACILITIES: pool room lounge, kitchen/breakfast room, free Wi-Fi in bedrooms, in-room TV (Freeview), 12-acre grounds, 9-metre heated outdoor swimming pool (in summer months), electric car charging point, parking.
BACKGROUND MUSIC: none.
LOCATION: 5 mins from Dartmouth via ferry.
CHILDREN: not allowed.
DOGS: only assistance dogs allowed.
CREDIT CARDS: Amex, MC, Visa.
PRICES: per room B&B £210–£245. 2-night min. stay.

KNARESBOROUGH Yorkshire

NEWTON HOUSE

In the centre of a 'fascinating' town, Denise Carter's B&B 'offers good value and plenty of Yorkshire friendliness'. 'Well-appointed' bedrooms in the 300-year-old town house and converted stables are supplied with a hot drinks tray and glass bottles of filtered water; 'the collection of books is a nice touch'. Guests may help themselves to local beers, spirits or soft drinks from the well-stocked honesty bar in the sitting room. In the evening, light bites (soup or an omelette) might be 'rustled up'; the hostess can recommend nearby eateries for more substantial fare. Home-made sourdough bread, jams and compotes are part of the 'excellent' 'slow-food' breakfasts that 'set you up for the day'. On-site parking is a bonus.

MAP 4:D4
5–7 York Place
Knaresborough HG5 0AD
T: 01423 863539
W: newtonhouseyorkshire.com

BEDROOMS: 12. 1 in adjacent building, 2 in converted stables, 2 on ground floor suitable for disabled.
OPEN: all year.
FACILITIES: sitting room (honesty bar), dining room, in-room TV (Freeview), small courtyard garden (wildlife area), parking.
BACKGROUND MUSIC: Classic FM at breakfast.
LOCATION: in town centre, 4 miles from Harrogate.
CHILDREN: all ages welcomed.
DOGS: allowed in 2 rooms with outside access, not in public rooms.
CREDIT CARDS: Amex, MC, Visa.
PRICES: per room B&B single £70–£110, double £95–£145. 1-night bookings generally refused weekends.

LANCHESTER Co. Durham
BURNHOPESIDE HALL

There are log fires, country views and a warm welcome to be had at this Grade II* listed house, in a spread of gardens surrounded by acres of farmland and forest. Engineer William Hedley, inventor of Puffing Billy, once lived here. Today, Christine Hewitt, the 'attentive' hostess, offers 'good-value' B&B accommodation in 'clean, quiet and comfortable' traditionally decorated bedrooms in the main house, adjoining farmhouse and cottage. Home-made, home-reared and home-grown fare features at breakfast; dinner may be requested in advance. The grounds provide generous scope for gentle strolls or for exercising dogs and exuberant children; trails lead to the river and the Lanchester Valley Railway Path. Well placed for Durham.

MAP 4:B4
Durham Road
Lanchester DH7 0TL
T: 01207 520222
W: burnhopeside-hall.co.uk

BEDROOMS: 13. 5 in adjoining farmhouse, 3 in cottage, 2-bed apartment on top floor in main house.
OPEN: all year, except when booked for exclusive use.
FACILITIES: sitting room, dining room, library, billiard room, in-room TV (Freeview), 18-acre gardens in 475-acre grounds; farmhouse rooms have a sitting room, dining room; cottages have a sitting room where breakfast can be served; all with log fires.
BACKGROUND MUSIC: none.
LOCATION: 5 miles NW of Durham.
CHILDREN: all ages welcomed.
DOGS: welcomed (resident dogs).
CREDIT CARDS: Amex, MC, Visa.
PRICES: per room B&B single from £85, double £120–£145. Dinner, by arrangement, £40.

LAVENHAM Suffolk
THE SWAN HOTEL & SPA

In the heart of a historic wool village whose crooked houses splendidly lean, a trio of timber-framed 15th-century buildings hosts this updated hotel and spa. Modern, country-style bedrooms in a variety of sizes (some accessed via 'picturesque corridors with ups and downs and twists and turns') retain characterful features such as old beams, mullioned windows or an inglenook fireplace; they have all the essentials, including bathrobes and upmarket toiletries. Guests have a choice of dining areas: light bites in the Airmen's bar; British favourites in the garden-facing brasserie; refined dishes in the Gallery restaurant. Part of The Hotel Folk; see also The Crown, Woodbridge (Shortlist entry).

MAP 2:C5
High Street
Lavenham CO10 9QA
T: 01787 247477
W: theswanatlavenham.co.uk

BEDROOMS: 45. 1 suitable for disabled.
OPEN: all year.
FACILITIES: 3 lounges, bar, brasserie, restaurant, in-room TV (Freeview), civil wedding licence, private dining/function facilities, spa (treatment rooms, sauna, steam room, outdoor hydrotherapy pool), terrace, garden.
BACKGROUND MUSIC: occasionally in public areas.
LOCATION: in village.
CHILDREN: all ages welcomed.
DOGS: in some bedrooms, bar, lounge, garden, not in restaurants.
CREDIT CARDS: Amex, MC, Visa.
PRICES: per room B&B £130–£280. À la carte £40.

LEATHERHEAD Surrey
BEAVERBROOK

In a sweep of Surrey parkland, this opulent, art-
and memorabilia-filled hotel is in a late Victorian
mansion, once the rural retreat of press baron
Lord Beaverbrook. The politicians and luminaries
he entertained here are remembered in elegant
bedrooms in the main building; in the Garden
House and dog-friendly Coach House, botanical
prints and smart rustic features give bedrooms
a Victorian cottage feel. Find a spot to call your
own in the well-stocked library or fashionably
old-world bar; take afternoon tea on the terrace;
soak in countryside views from the swimming
pool. A trio of restaurants caters for varying tastes,
from Japanese fine dining to Anglo-Italian fare to
superfood specials in the holistic spa.

MAP 2:D4
Reigate Road
Leatherhead KT22 8QX
T: 01372 227670
W: beaverbrook.co.uk

BEDROOMS: 35. 11 in Garden House,
6 in Coach House, 1 suitable for
disabled.
OPEN: all year.
FACILITIES: bar, snug, lounge, 3
restaurants, library, cinema, in-room
TV (Sky), civil wedding licence,
indoor and outdoor swimming pools,
470-acre grounds, walled garden,
woodlands, lake, cookery school,
kids' club.
BACKGROUND MUSIC: in restaurant, bar.
LOCATION: on estate, 2 miles from
town centre.
CHILDREN: all ages welcomed.
DOGS: allowed in some bedrooms,
public areas.
CREDIT CARDS: Amex, MC, Visa.
PRICES: per room B&B £490–£1,550.
À la carte (Garden House restaurant)
£55. 2-night min. stay on Sat, bank
holidays, Christmas, New Year's Eve.

LEDBURY Herefordshire
THE FEATHERS

'An attractive building in a lovely town', this
former coaching inn is today a modern hotel
whose many original features – exposed ancient
beams, leaded windows, a centuries-old staircase
– lend much character. Behind the striking
Tudor facade (a local landmark), 'very clean and
pleasant', recently refurbished bedrooms vary in
size; the best have a sitting area, perhaps a four-
poster bed. Light sleepers should ask for a room
away from the street. Small plates, sharing platters
and brasserie dishes can be eaten in the restaurant,
dog-friendly bar or lounge; when the weather
allows, have an alfresco meal in the courtyard. In
every area, 'the staff are all charming'. Part of the
Coaching Inn group.

MAP 3:D5
25 High Street
Ledbury HR8 1DS
T: 01531 635266
W: feathersledbury.co.uk

BEDROOMS: 20. 1 suite in cottage, plus
self-catering apartments.
OPEN: all year.
FACILITIES: bar, lounge, restaurant,
coffee house, in-room TV (Freeview),
civil wedding licence, function
facilities, courtyard garden, parking.
BACKGROUND MUSIC: none.
LOCATION: in town centre.
CHILDREN: all ages welcomed.
DOGS: allowed in bedrooms, most
public areas, not in restaurant.
CREDIT CARDS: Amex, MC, Visa.
PRICES: per room B&B £85–£255. À la
carte £30. 1-night bookings sometimes
refused weekends.

LEVENS Cumbria

HARE AND HOUNDS

In a Lyth valley village on the edge of the Lake District, Becky and Ash Dewar transformed a 16th-century hostelry into this family-friendly village pub nearly a decade ago. The beamed bar has cask ales, craft beers and cocktails made with locally produced spirits; pub classics (burgers, pizzas, grills) are served here, in the bright restaurant and on the terrace. Upstairs, and in a spacious barn annexe, contemporary, country-style bedrooms have welcome extras, such as freshly baked brownies, ground coffee and Cumbrian-made toiletries. At breakfast: fresh fruit, local bread, a choice of hot dishes cooked to order. There are knolls and fells to walk in the area, and the celebrated topiary of Levens Hall close by.

MAP 4: inset C2
Church Road
Levens
nr Kendal LA8 8PN
T: 015395 60004
w: hareandhoundslevens.co.uk

BEDROOMS: 5. 1 in barn annexe.
OPEN: all year, no accommodation 24–25 Dec.
FACILITIES: pub, residents' lounge, restaurant, in-room TV (Freeview), ½-acre beer garden, parking.
BACKGROUND MUSIC: in pub and restaurant.
LOCATION: in village.
CHILDREN: all ages welcomed.
DOGS: allowed in barn annexe, pub, garden, not in restaurant.
CREDIT CARDS: Amex, MC, Visa.
PRICES: per room B&B single £85–£185, double £95–£195. À la carte £30. 2-night min. stay at weekends, unless there is last-minute single-night availability.

LEWANNICK Cornwall

COOMBESHEAD FARM

In meadows and woodland between Bodmin Moor and Dartmoor, this rustic-chic guest house and restaurant make an ideal base for countryside exploration – or simply for eating 'stupendously' well. Occupying a centuries-old farmhouse and its surrounding barns, it is owned by chefs Tom Adams and April Bloomfield, who have won a Michelin green star for the farm-to-fork cooking in their 'feasting barn'. Home-grown, -reared, -smoked, -cured and -pickled ingredients are paired with organic Cornish produce and locally foraged food at dinner and weekend lunch. Accommodation is in handsomely countrified bedrooms in the farmhouse and a newly converted grain store. On-site sourdough bakery; monthly bread workshops.

MAP 1:D3
Lewannick PL15 7QQ
T: 01566 782009
w: coombesheadfarm.co.uk

BEDROOMS: 10. 1 bunk-bedroom, 4 in converted barn, 2 suitable for disabled. Plus 2-bed self-catering cottage.
OPEN: all year except Jan, restaurant closed Mon–Wed.
FACILITIES: living room, lounge, library, dining room, kitchen, bakery, civil wedding licence, 66-acre grounds.
BACKGROUND MUSIC: in evening in living room, dining room and kitchen.
LOCATION: in village, 3 miles from A30, 6 miles from Launceston.
CHILDREN: not under 12, except at weekend lunch.
DOGS: allowed in 2 bedrooms, on lead in grounds, not in restaurant.
CREDIT CARDS: Amex, MC, Visa.
PRICES: per room B&B £195–£255. Set dinner £80.

LICHFIELD Staffordshire

SWINFEN HALL

The setting is 'superb': in formal walled gardens that lead to wild hay meadows, woodland, and parkland where Sika deer roam, the Wiser family's ethically run hotel occupies a grand Georgian manor. Guests enter a magnificent hall with a hand-carved ceiling and balustraded minstrels' gallery; beyond are spacious, well-equipped bedrooms, a fine, oak-panelled restaurant, and pleasing places to take afternoon tea. A fire burns in the cocktail lounge when the weather calls for it; in sunshine, sit on the terrace overlooking the wide grounds. At dinner, choose between à la carte and tasting menus in the restaurant – the cooking focuses on home-grown and -reared produce – or have a more casual meal in the bar.

MAP 2:A2
Swinfen
Lichfield WS14 9RE
T: 01543 481494
W: swinfenhallhotel.co.uk

BEDROOMS: 17.
OPEN: all year except 25 Dec evening, 26 Dec, restaurant closed Sun, Mon evenings (bar menu available).
FACILITIES: bar, lounge, cocktail lounge, restaurant, private dining rooms, in-room TV (Sky), civil wedding licence, 100-acre grounds (formal gardens, walled kitchen garden, courtyard garden, deer park, meadows, woodland), electric car charging points.
BACKGROUND MUSIC: in public areas.
LOCATION: 2 miles S of Lichfield, just off the A38.
CHILDREN: all ages welcomed.
DOGS: not allowed.
CREDIT CARDS: Amex, MC, Visa.
PRICES: per room B&B single £125–£335, double £150–£375.
À la carte £50.

LINCOLN Lincolnshire

BRIDLEWAY BED & BREAKFAST

A 'lovely welcome' of home-made cream scones awaits arriving guests at this 'excellent' B&B, a relaxed, rural spot next to a thick oak wood. It is run by Jane Haigh, an artist. Country-cosy rooms in the converted stables and cart shed have their own entrance; inside are calming hues, mellow wood, bathrobes and daily baked treats. 'Magnificent' breakfasts in the conservatory include fresh fruit salad, local honey, Aga-cooked Scotch pancakes, and eggs from the house's hens; a continental hamper, with warm pastries, can be delivered to the room. Borrow wellies and the family dogs for walks; the hostess readily provides advice on local restaurants and even a lift into Lincoln, nearby. Stabling is provided.

MAP 4:E5
Riseholme Gorse
Hall Lane
Lincoln LN2 2LY
T: 01522 545693
W: bridlewaybandb.co.uk

BEDROOMS: 4. All on ground floor in converted outbuildings.
OPEN: Jan–mid-Dec.
FACILITIES: conservatory, in-room TV (Freeview), ½-acre grounds, 2 stables, manège, paddock for guests' horses.
BACKGROUND MUSIC: none.
LOCATION: 3½ miles from Lincoln.
CHILDREN: not under 16.
DOGS: only assistance dogs allowed.
CREDIT CARDS: Amex, MC, Visa.
PRICES: per room B&B single £79–£110, double £90–£160. 1-night bookings refused weekends, high season.

LITTLE ECCLESTON Lancashire

THE CARTFORD INN

By the bridge over the River Wyre, this quirky coaching inn has looked across the rural panorama to the Bowland fells for centuries. Today owned by Julie and Patrick Beaumé, it is 'excellent in every way'. A much-loved local hub, it has a lively pub and well-regarded restaurant, a collection of 'rustic chic' bedrooms, and a deli and community art gallery to boot. Most of the modern bedrooms overlook the winding river; four attic rooms have a skylight for stargazing. Two imaginatively decorated cabins, each with a split-level bedroom, spacious lounge and river-view balcony, stand in landscaped grounds. Lancastrian produce is cooked with a Gallic tweak at lunch and dinner; the farm shop has snacks for the journey home.

MAP 4:D2
Cartford Lane
Little Eccleston PR3 0YP
T: 01995 670166
W: thecartfordinn.co.uk

BEDROOMS: 16. Some in riverside annexe, 1 suitable for disabled, 2 cabins in grounds.
OPEN: all year except 24–28 Dec, restaurant closed Mon lunch except on bank holidays.
FACILITIES: bar, restaurant, in-room TV (Freeview), function facilities, deli/coffee shop, riverside terrace, garden.
BACKGROUND MUSIC: in public areas.
LOCATION: 8 miles E of Blackpool, easily reached from M6 and M55.
CHILDREN: all ages welcomed (some time restrictions in bar, restaurant).
DOGS: not allowed.
CREDIT CARDS: Amex, MC, Visa.
PRICES: per room B&B single £80–£150, double £130–£250. À la carte £33.

LIVERPOOL Merseyside

HOPE STREET HOTEL

In the buzzy Georgian quarter, this contemporary hotel with a sleek spa and a private cinema is well placed for exploring the wealth of the city's cultural and educational venues. Transformed from a former Victorian carriage works, it is 'airy and modern', its stripped-back style defined by exposed brick walls, pitch pine beams and iron pillars. Minimalist bedrooms – white-painted, with wood floors and cherry and walnut furniture – range from snug double rooms to rooftop suites with a hot tub terrace and 'wonderful views' of city landmarks. From breakfast till late, modern British dishes (including vegan options) are served in the restaurant; in the bar, sharing platters and easy eats pair with made-to-order cocktails.

MAP 4:E2
40 Hope Street
Liverpool L1 9DA
T: 0151 709 3000
W: hopestreethotel.co.uk

BEDROOMS: 150. 2 suitable for disabled.
OPEN: all year.
FACILITIES: lift, bar, 2 lounges, restaurant, private dining rooms, in-room TV (Sky, Freeview), civil wedding licence, spa (treatment rooms, indoor swimming pool, indoor/outdoor vitality pool), gym, cinema, limited parking nearby (charge).
BACKGROUND MUSIC: in public rooms.
LOCATION: in city centre.
CHILDREN: all ages welcomed.
DOGS: allowed in some bedrooms, public areas, bar side of restaurant.
CREDIT CARDS: Amex, MC, Visa.
PRICES: per room B&B £130–£520. À la carte £40.

LOOE Cornwall

THE BEACH HOUSE

Overlooking Whitsand Bay, Rosie and David Reeve's laid-back B&B is steps away from a sandy beach with rock pools to explore. Guests arrive to tea and a home-baked treat, then head to one of the simply decorated, 'spotlessly clean' bedrooms, each supplied with bathrobes, slippers, bottles of Cornish water, and a hospitality tray with fresh milk. Three rooms have a panoramic view of the sea; two access the garden. The breakfast buffet is a spread of cereals, fresh fruit, muffins and yogurt; hot cooked dishes, ordered the night before, include French toast, pancakes and Cornish sausages. The South West Coast Path in front of the house leads, past smugglers' caves, to Polperro. The hosts readily share local tips.

MAP 1:D3
Marine Drive
Hannafore
Looe PL13 2DH
T: 01503 262598
W: thebeachhouselooe.co.uk

BEDROOMS: 5.
OPEN: all year except Christmas.
FACILITIES: garden room, breakfast room, in-room TV (Freeview), terrace, ½-acre garden, beach opposite, spa treatments, parking.
BACKGROUND MUSIC: classical radio in breakfast room.
LOCATION: ½ mile from centre.
CHILDREN: not under 16.
DOGS: only assistance dogs allowed.
CREDIT CARDS: MC, Visa.
PRICES: per room B&B £80–£135. 2-night min. stay.

LUDLOW Shropshire

THE CLIVE ARMS

A ten-minute drive from Ludlow, this updated 18th-century building on the Earl of Plymouth's Oakly Park estate has a string of smart bedrooms and a modern, open-plan bar and restaurant. Most of the bedrooms, including a family suite, are in the rear courtyard. Individually styled, each is supplied with pleasing extras: ground coffee, loose-leaf teas, locally baked biscuits; a choice of pillows. Guests sensitive to traffic noise (an A road runs close by) should call to discuss their best options. In the 'field-to-fork' restaurant, seasonal menus reflect the freshest produce from the hotel's walled garden and surrounding farms. The Ludlow Farmshop is steps away; walking maps are available for exploration further afield.

MAP 3:C4
Bromfield
Ludlow SY8 2JR
T: 01584 856565
W: theclive.co.uk

BEDROOMS: 17. 14 in courtyard annexe, some on ground floor, 1 suitable for disabled.
OPEN: all year, restaurant and bar closed Mon, Tues.
FACILITIES: bar, lower bar, restaurant, snug, private dining room, conference room, in-room TV (Freeview), courtyard, beer garden.
BACKGROUND MUSIC: in public areas.
LOCATION: 4 miles NW of Ludlow.
CHILDREN: all ages welcomed.
DOGS: allowed in public rooms, some bedrooms.
CREDIT CARDS: Amex, MC, Visa.
PRICES: per room B&B £107–£207. À la carte £28–£40.

LUDLOW Shropshire

THE FEATHERS

A local landmark, this Grade I listed Jacobean
building with an ornate, timber-framed facade
stands in a 'wonderful position' in the heart
of town, a few minutes' walk from the main
square and castle. 'The hotel has been completely
revamped internally without losing its renowned
historical features,' a regular Guide reader, and
return visitor, reports. Inside are 'huge fireplaces',
'fine timberwork' and restored oak panelling; it is
'immaculately clean' throughout. The bedrooms
are pleasingly modern: while some may be snug,
all have a 'very comfortable' bed and a choice of
pillows, plus a mini-fridge, coffee and loose-leaf
teas. Service at mealtimes is 'fast and cheerful';
there is 'decent variety' at breakfast.

MAP 3:C4
24–25 Bull Ring
Ludlow SY8 1AA
T: 01584 875261
w: feathersatludlow.co.uk

BEDROOMS: 42. Some suitable for
disabled.
OPEN: all year.
FACILITIES: lift, lounge, bar, tea room,
restaurant, function rooms, in-room
smart TV, civil wedding licence,
courtyard, limited parking (charge).
BACKGROUND MUSIC: jazz in public
areas.
LOCATION: in town centre.
CHILDREN: all ages welcomed.
DOGS: allowed, not in restaurant.
CREDIT CARDS: MC, Visa.
PRICES: per room £95–£219. Breakfast
£10, à la carte £30.

LYME REGIS Dorset

GREENHILL HOUSE

'If Lyme Regis is the pearl of the Dorset coast,
then this beautiful B&B is surely one of its
diamonds.' Sara and Ed Hollway's 'restful,
relaxing' 1930s home overlooking Lyme Bay
offers guests 'a blissful experience'. 'Everything
has been carefully thought out to provide the
utmost comfort and convenience': there are maps,
books, jigsaw puzzles and board games in the
sitting room; in the well-equipped bedrooms,
'top-quality design, with a hint of the '30s, is
executed with panache and a touch of humour'.
A generous breakfast is served in the dining room
or the 'delightful' garden, where the views to
Golden Cap and the Jurassic Coast are 'sublime'.
The walk back from town is steep – let the bus or
a taxi take the strain.

MAP 1:C6
Somers Road
Lyme Regis DT7 3EX
T: 01297 445497
w: greenhillhousebandb.co.uk

BEDROOMS: 3.
OPEN: all year except 20–29 Dec.
FACILITIES: sitting room, dining room,
in-room TV (Freeview), ½-acre
garden.
BACKGROUND MUSIC: none.
LOCATION: on a hillside, above the
town.
CHILDREN: all ages welcomed (but no
special facilities).
DOGS: not allowed.
CREDIT CARDS: not accepted.
PRICES: per room B&B £155–£180.

MALVERN WELLS Worcestershire

THE COTTAGE IN THE WOOD

'The location can hardly be bettered': high in
the Malvern hills, this refurbished Georgian
dower house has 'fabulous, far-reaching' views
over the Severn valley. Extensive refurbishment
has resulted in contemporary public spaces and
a collection of smart, 'very pleasant' bedrooms,
some with a patio or small balcony. Floor-to-
ceiling windows in the restaurant frame a rural
panorama that stretches to the Cotswolds, a fine
backdrop for the modern cooking at lunch and
dinner. Typical dishes: Cotswold chicken terrine;
truffle gnocchi, hazelnut, shallot. Casual meals
and drinks may also be taken alfresco on the
covered terrace – all the better to soak in the fresh
air. The Elgar route is close by.

MAP 3:D5
Holywell Road
Malvern Wells WR14 4LG
T: 01684 588860
W: cottageinthewood.co.uk

BEDROOMS: 32. 4 in Beech Cottage,
19 in Coach House, 10 on ground
floor, 1 suitable for disabled.
OPEN: all year.
FACILITIES: bar, restaurant, meeting
room, in-room TV (Freeview),
covered terrace, 8-acre grounds.
BACKGROUND MUSIC: 'ambient' in bar,
restaurant.
LOCATION: 4 miles from Malvern
Wells.
CHILDREN: all ages welcomed.
DOGS: allowed in some bedrooms, not
in public rooms.
CREDIT CARDS: Amex, MC, Visa.
PRICES: per room B&B £119–£229.
À la carte £40.

MANCHESTER

DIDSBURY HOUSE

Between two parks, this voguish hotel occupies
a refurbished Victorian villa within easy reach
of the city. Vintage prints, statement wallpapers
and an impressive stained-glass window form a
sophisticated setting for fresh flowers, books, open
fires and deep sofas; tasteful bedrooms and suites,
some set over two levels, retain original high
windows and delicate cornices. Among up-to-date
amenities in the rooms are a butler tray with fresh
milk, perhaps a roll-top bath or two. Afternoon
tea may be taken in one of two lounges. A deli
menu accompanies an aperitif or nightcap in the
bar or on the atmospherically lit walled terrace;
on the weekend, breakfast is served until late. A
sister hotel is just up the street.

MAP 4:E3
Didsbury Park
Manchester M20 5LJ
T: 0161 448 2200
W: didsburyhouse.co.uk

BEDROOMS: 27. Some on ground floor,
1 suitable for disabled.
OPEN: all year.
FACILITIES: bar, 2 lounges, breakfast
room, in-room TV (Sky), civil
wedding licence, meeting/function
facilities, heated walled terrace.
BACKGROUND MUSIC: in public
areas, volume adjusted to suit the
atmosphere and time of day.
LOCATION: 6 miles from Manchester
city centre and airport, easy access
to M60.
CHILDREN: all ages welcomed.
DOGS: not allowed.
CREDIT CARDS: Amex, MC, Visa.
PRICES: per room £150–£300.
Breakfast £16.

MARAZION Cornwall

THE GODOLPHIN

Across the causeway from St Michael's Mount, this beachfront restaurant-with-rooms, 'tactfully modernised and enlarged', is decorated with uplifting coastal colours and local artwork. Smart bedrooms face the village or the sea – the view over Mount's Bay is worth the upgrade. 'Our sea-view balcony was sunny from lunchtime on.' In the breezy restaurant or on the glass-fronted terrace, a short, seasonal menu favours fish and seafood, maybe St Austell Bay mussels, whole fried crispy sea bass or local lobster. Breakfast has good choice: a full Cornish, a vegetarian platter, buttermilk pancakes and more. Children have their own menu; doggy companions receive a welcome pack with treats, a bowl and a blanket.

MAP 1:E1
West End
Marazion TR17 0EN
T: 01736 888510
W: thegodolphin.com

BEDROOMS: 10. Some suitable for disabled.
OPEN: all year.
FACILITIES: 2 bars, split-level dining area, in-room TV (Freeview), civil wedding licence, function facilities, 2 terraces, parking, dining room wheelchair accessible.
BACKGROUND MUSIC: in public areas, occasional live acoustic music.
LOCATION: 4 miles E of Penzance.
CHILDREN: all ages welcomed.
DOGS: allowed in 2 bedrooms, designated dining area, on terrace.
CREDIT CARDS: MC, Visa.
PRICES: per room B&B £120–£370. À la carte £30. 2-night min. stay at weekends in high season.

MARCHAM Oxfordshire

B&B RAFTERS

Sigrid Grawert's inviting B&B, complete with suntrap garden, is on the outskirts of an Oxfordshire village, within reach of historic houses, Cotswold communities and the city of dreaming spires. Modern bedrooms (one with a private balcony) are equipped with fluffy robes and a power shower in the bathroom; on the landing are honesty-box soft drinks and snacks, and a capsule coffee machine. In the morning, an award-winning breakfast is taken communally: freshly squeezed orange juice, home-baked sourdough bread, home-made marmalade and jams, a superb porridge menu. Special diets are willingly catered for. Visitors keen on local tips only have to ask – the hostess has much helpful information to share.

MAP 2:C2
Abingdon Road
Marcham OX13 6NU
T: 01865 391298
W: bnb-rafters.co.uk

BEDROOMS: 4.
OPEN: all year except Christmas, New Year.
FACILITIES: breakfast room, in-room smart TV (Freeview), garden, parking.
BACKGROUND MUSIC: none.
LOCATION: 3 miles W of Abingdon, 10 miles S of Oxford.
CHILDREN: not under 12.
DOGS: not allowed.
CREDIT CARDS: MC, Visa.
PRICES: per room B&B single from £64, double from £99. 2-night min. stay at bank holiday weekends.

MATLOCK BATH Derbyshire

HODGKINSON'S HOTEL

Well located for exploring the Peak District, Zoe and Chris Hipwell's personable small hotel overlooks a bend of the River Derwent in the centre of a historic spa resort. Most of the restored features in the Georgian town house (ornate glasswork, a tiled entrance hall, the wood-and-glass bar) date to the ownership of Victorian wine merchant Job Hodgkinson, who stored his wares in the Roman-era cave. Bedrooms are traditionally furnished in period style; one has a four-poster bed and a roll-top bath; several have river views. There is a terraced garden with space to sit, and an intimate restaurant serving modern European dishes. 'Excellent walks' from the door; stately homes are within an easy drive.

MAP 3:B6
150 South Parade
Matlock Bath DE4 3NR
T: 01629 582170
W: hodgkinsons-hotel.co.uk

BEDROOMS: 8.
OPEN: all year except Christmas week, restaurant closed Sun, Mon eve, except on bank holiday Sun and for guests who have pre-booked.
FACILITIES: sitting room, restaurant with bar, in-room TV (Freeview), terraced garden, drying room, limited parking (parking nearby, permits supplied).
BACKGROUND MUSIC: in public areas.
LOCATION: centre of village, 1 mile from Matlock and Cromford.
CHILDREN: all ages welcomed.
DOGS: allowed in some bedrooms, lounge, not in restaurant.
CREDIT CARDS: MC, Visa.
PRICES: per room B&B £95–£165. Set dinner £28 (2 courses), £32 (3 courses). 2-night min. stay at weekends Easter–Oct.

MAWNAN SMITH Cornwall

BUDOCK VEAN

Walk through the 'pretty' garden to reach the Helford river from this spa hotel and golf resort: 'The peacefulness and sheer enchantment at the water's edge, where all you hear is the clop of water against the boats riding at anchor and the sounds of wading birds diving, really is stunning.' The hotel, in an 18th-century manor house, has been owned by the Barlow family since 1987; Guide readers praise the 'really super, long-serving staff'. Refurbishment continues in the bedrooms, which are 'pleasant', 'comfortable' and supplied with Cornish biscuits. In the evening, dinner – from the 'wonderful canapés' to the 'reassuringly homely desserts' on the 'well-balanced menus' – is 'truly outstanding'.

MAP 1:E2
nr Helford Passage
Mawnan Smith
Falmouth TR11 5LG
T: 01326 252100
W: budockvean.co.uk

BEDROOMS: 55. Plus 4 self-catering cottages, 1 suitable for disabled.
OPEN: all year.
FACILITIES: lift, 2 lounges, cocktail bar, conservatory, golf bar, restaurant, in-room TV (Freeview), civil wedding licence, 65-acre grounds (golf, tennis, woodlands, private quay), spa, sauna, indoor swimming pool, outdoor hot tub, electric car charging points.
BACKGROUND MUSIC: 'gentle' live piano or guitar at dinner.
LOCATION: 6 miles SW of Falmouth.
CHILDREN: all ages welcomed.
DOGS: allowed in some bedrooms, lobby, conservatory, terrace, not in other public rooms.
CREDIT CARDS: MC, Visa.
PRICES: per person B&B £75–£152. Prix fixe dinner £29 (£48 for non-residents).

MEVAGISSEY Cornwall

PEBBLE HOUSE

Panoramic sea views reach across Mevagissey Bay to historic Chapel Point and beyond, from Andrea and Simon Copper's sleekly designed B&B set high above the 14th-century fishing village. Clean-cut bedrooms in the child-free retreat have floor-to-ceiling windows to bring the outside in; one also has wide roof windows for bedtime stargazing. Light lunches, cream teas and award-winning breakfasts (home-made granola and soda bread; special diets catered for with advance notice) are served in the breakfast room/lounge, against the stunning seascape; in fine weather, the front terrace is the place to be. Picnics may be arranged, perhaps for a walk along the South West Coast Path, steps away.

MAP 1:D2
Polkirt Hill
Mevagissey PL26 6UX
T: 01726 844466
W: pebblehousecornwall.co.uk

BEDROOMS: 5. 1 on ground floor with private terrace.
OPEN: Feb–early Nov, exclusive-use self-catering over Christmas, New Year.
FACILITIES: open-plan lounge/breakfast room, in-room TV (Freeview, Sky in some rooms), terrace, small functions, parking.
BACKGROUND MUSIC: in breakfast room.
LOCATION: on South West Coast Path, 10 mins' walk to Mevagissey, 16 miles E of Truro.
CHILDREN: not allowed, except for self-catering bookings.
DOGS: not allowed.
CREDIT CARDS: MC, Visa.
PRICES: per room B&B £175–£225. 2-night min. stay.

MINSTER LOVELL Oxfordshire

OLD SWAN

One of the oldest buildings in a village of thatched houses, this 600-year-old inn stands steps away from the willows leaning over the River Windrush. Outside are gardens, wildflower meadows and woodland; inside, cosy nooks, log fires, flagstone floors and sturdy beams form a characterful setting for pie-and-brew evenings or celebratory drinks. Well-ordered bedrooms (three with a four-poster bed; some to suit a family) have rustic charm in their plaid throws and cushions, plus bathrobes, slippers and upmarket toiletries. Tackle a rural walk or fish from a mile of river bank; return to take afternoon tea on the terrace. Guests may use the tennis and spa facilities at sister hotel Minster Mill, across the road.

MAP 3:D6
Minster Lovell OX29 0RN
T: 01993 862512
W: oldswan.co.uk

BEDROOMS: 15. 6 on ground floor, plus 3-bed cottage.
OPEN: all year.
FACILITIES: bar, restaurant, in-room TV (Freeview), terrace, 65-acre grounds (croquet, fishing), bicycle hire.
BACKGROUND MUSIC: none.
LOCATION: in village 3 miles W of Witney, 15 miles from Oxford.
CHILDREN: all ages welcomed.
DOGS: in some bedrooms, bar.
CREDIT CARDS: Amex, MC, Visa.
PRICES: per room B&B £165–£365. 2-night min. stay some weekends.

MORECAMBE Lancashire

THE MIDLAND

Overlooking the sand flats of Morecambe Bay, this 'superbly positioned Art Deco wonder' was restored to its former glory by the English Lakes group. Its long dining room – 'a joy' – follows the curve of the building; every diner has a 'spectacular' sea view through huge windows. Modern British dishes are served here; sandwiches, salads and sharing platters may be taken on the terrace of the Rotunda bar. Up a spiral staircase or via a compact lift, red-carpeted corridors lead to urbane, 'surprisingly spacious' bedrooms, many with a view over the sea. (The landward view is rather more prosaic.) Breakfast is 'plentiful'. A sister hotel's health club is available to guests. Ideal for the Isle of Man ferry.

MAP 4:D2
Marine Road West
Morecambe LA4 4BU
T: 01524 424000
W: englishlakes.co.uk/the-midland

BEDROOMS: 44. 2 suitable for disabled.
OPEN: all year.
FACILITIES: lift, lounge, bar, restaurant, in-room TV, function rooms, civil wedding licence, lawns, parking.
BACKGROUND MUSIC: all day in lounge.
LOCATION: overlooking Morecambe Bay, steps from the stone jetty.
CHILDREN: all ages welcomed.
DOGS: well-behaved dogs allowed, not in restaurant.
CREDIT CARDS: Amex, MC, Visa.
PRICES: per room B&B £125–£560. À la carte £31. 1-night bookings refused Sat.

MULLION Cornwall

POLURRIAN ON THE LIZARD

In a 'wonderful clifftop position' on the Lizard peninsula, this relaxed hotel exults in stunning coastal views over Mount's Bay. Praised for its friendly staff – 'an asset to the hotel' – it is an airy retreat that appeals to guests of all ages. Tennis, kayaking, spa treatments and yoga sessions are available all year round; child-friendly activities are organised during the holidays. In the restaurant and on the sea-view terrace, informal, Mediterranean-inspired dishes make the best of Cornish ingredients, much sourced from within a 20-mile radius. Bedrooms are neat and modern; many face the water. Order a picnic, then borrow fishing nets, buckets and spades: a path leads to a private beach, a 10-minute stroll away.

MAP 1:E2
Polurrian Road
Mullion TR12 7EN
T: 01326 240421
W: polurrianhotel.com

BEDROOMS: 41. Some on ground floor, 1 suitable for disabled. Plus four 3-bed self-catering villas.
OPEN: all year.
FACILITIES: lift, bar, lounge, snug, restaurant, in-room TV, civil wedding licence, function facilities, cinema, games room (table football, table tennis), spa, indoor pool, 9-metre outdoor pool (Apr–Sept), 12-acre grounds, terrace, tennis court, climbing frame.
BACKGROUND MUSIC: in public areas.
LOCATION: in village.
CHILDREN: all ages welcomed.
DOGS: allowed in some bedrooms, not in restaurant.
CREDIT CARDS: Amex, MC, Visa.
PRICES: per room B&B £119–£339.

NEWQUAY Cornwall
THE HEADLAND HOTEL

From sunrise to sunset, bask in 'spectacular views' of the Atlantic ocean from the Armstrong family's child- and dog-friendly hotel above Fistral beach. The impressive Victorian building and its strikingly contemporary Aqua Club are packed with diversions: six swimming pools, indoors and out; a host of treatments in the adults-only spa; buckets and spades for the beach; games, books and DVDs for duvet days. A golf course and surf school round out the offer. Most of the bedrooms have coastal hues and views; some rooms have a balcony, too. Day or night, varied menus and venues – on the waterfront terrace, in the sophisticated Samphire restaurant, or poolside – highlight Cornish produce in season.

MAP 1:D2
Headland Road
Newquay TR7 1EW
T: 01637 872211
W: headlandhotel.co.uk

BEDROOMS: 139. 1 suitable for disabled, plus self-catering cottages in the grounds.
OPEN: all year.
FACILITIES: 5 lounges, bar, 4 restaurants, in-room TV (Freeview), civil wedding licence, conference/event facilities, 10-acre grounds, spa, gym, indoor and outdoor heated swimming pools, sun terrace, electric car charging point.
BACKGROUND MUSIC: 'easy listening' in restaurants.
LOCATION: on a headland overlooking Fistral beach.
CHILDREN: all ages welcomed.
DOGS: allowed in bedrooms, public rooms, not in restaurants.
CREDIT CARDS: Amex, MC, Visa.
PRICES: per room B&B £185–£655. À la carte £39.

NEWQUAY Cornwall
LEWINNICK LODGE

Atop the craggy Pentire headland, this cliff-edge hotel looking north along the Cornish coast dispenses 'fabulous' views and the soothing sounds of the Atlantic. Sleek and stylish inside, it has 'friendly, helpful and efficient' staff and a laid-back atmosphere. Most bedrooms take in a vista that stretches towards Towan Head and Fistral beach. Each room has home-made biscuits and binoculars; in the bathroom are robes, organic toiletries, perhaps a slipper bath. The restaurant and bar are popular with locals. In the dining room and on the terrace above the waves, 'all the meals are good (though the menu was unchanged over our multi-night stay)'. Good walks from the door. 'We, and our dog, will return.'

MAP 1:D2
Pentire Headland
Newquay TR7 1QD
T: 01637 878117
W: lewinnicklodge.co.uk

BEDROOMS: 17. Some suitable for disabled.
OPEN: all year.
FACILITIES: lift, bar, lounge, snug, restaurant, in-room smart TV (Sky, Freeview), in-room spa treatments, terraced beer garden, electric car charging points.
BACKGROUND MUSIC: all day in public spaces.
LOCATION: 3 miles W of Newquay centre.
CHILDREN: all ages welcomed.
DOGS: allowed in some bedrooms, bar, terrace, not in restaurant.
CREDIT CARDS: MC, Visa.
PRICES: per room B&B £120–£300. À la carte £32. 1-night bookings sometimes refused high season.

NORTHALLERTON Yorkshire

THE CLEVELAND TONTINE

'Good food' and 'a friendly welcome' await visitors at this Georgian roadside hostelry, on the western edge of the North York Moors. A fire burns in the lounge of the former coaching inn in cool weather; all year round, seasonal menus of modern British dishes in the 'busy' bistro focus on produce from regional farmers. Afternoon tea may be taken on the garden terrace or in the morning room overlooking the Cleveland hills. Recently refurbished, colourful bedrooms are supplied with tea- and coffee-making facilities, plus bathrobes in a bathroom with under-floor heating. Continental or cooked breakfasts include vegetarian options. Part of the Provenance Inns & Hotels group; see The Carpenters Arms, Felixkirk (main entry).

MAP 4:C4
Staddlebridge
Northallerton DL6 3JB
T: 01609 882671
W: theclevelandtontine.com

BEDROOMS: 7.
OPEN: all year.
FACILITIES: bar, 2 lounges, morning room, bistro, in-room TV (Freeview), room service, function facilities, small garden, parking.
BACKGROUND MUSIC: in public rooms.
LOCATION: 8 miles NE of Northallerton.
CHILDREN: all ages welcomed.
DOGS: allowed in bar, 1 lounge.
CREDIT CARDS: Amex, MC, Visa.
PRICES: per room B&B £149–£310. À la carte £35.

NEW

NUN MONKTON Yorkshire

THE ALICE HAWTHORN

On the green of a peaceful village where the rivers Nidd and Ouse meet, this smartly revamped Grade II listed country pub is one visitors make detours for. Chef/patron John Topham, previously widely praised for his cooking at the General Tarleton, Ferrensby (see Shortlist entry), brings his culinary flair to seasonal menus of elevated, Yorkshire-influenced pub food, perhaps Dales lamb or local asparagus, ricotta and hazelnut tortellini. A pizza oven is fired up in the summer. Decorated in a calm, contemplative style, well-equipped bedrooms are above the pub and in newly built Douglas-fir outbuildings set around the landscaped beer garden. Close by, a ferry boat heads upriver to the National Trust's Beningbrough Hall.

MAP 4:D4
The Green
Nun Monkton YO26 8EW
T: 01423 330303
W: thealicehawthorn.com

BEDROOMS: 12. 8 in garden, 1 suitable for disabled.
OPEN: Wed–Sun all year.
FACILITIES: bar, 3 dining areas, in-room TV, beer garden.
BACKGROUND MUSIC: all day in public areas.
LOCATION: in village, 11 miles NW of York.
CHILDREN: all ages welcomed.
DOGS: allowed in 2 bedrooms, bar.
CREDIT CARDS: MC, Visa.
PRICES: per room B&B single £100–£225, double £120–£245. À la carte £45.

OUNDLE Northamptonshire
LOWER FARM

Where the village gives way to green fields, the
Marriott family has converted a series of farm
buildings into comfortable B&B accommodation.
Robert Marriott and his brother, John, run the
adjoining arable farm; Caroline Marriott is the
'friendly, accommodating' hostess. Arranged
around a neatly landscaped courtyard with
seating, up-to-date bedrooms occupy the former
milking parlour and stables; connecting rooms
suit a family. Hearty farmhouse breakfasts might
include porridge with fresh cream, or avocado
with locally sourced sausages and eggs – fuel for
tackling the walking and cycling tracks from the
door. The Nene Way footpath runs through the
farm; the village pub is a short stroll away.

MAP 2:B3
Main Street
Barnwell
Oundle PE8 5PU
T: 01832 273220
W: lower-farm.co.uk

BEDROOMS: 10. All on ground floor,
1 suitable for disabled.
OPEN: all year.
FACILITIES: breakfast room, in-room
TV (Freeview), courtyard garden,
parking.
BACKGROUND MUSIC: radio 'if guests
wish' in breakfast room.
LOCATION: at one end of the village,
3 miles from Oundle.
CHILDREN: all ages welcomed.
DOGS: allowed in 2 bedrooms, not in
public rooms.
CREDIT CARDS: Amex, MC, Visa.
PRICES: per person B&B £55–£90.

PAKEFIELD Suffolk
THE HOG HOTEL

'Excellent meals, comfortable accommodation
and responsive owners' make this family-owned
hotel, in an old maritime village on the Suffolk
coast, a welcome addition to the area. 'Cathy
Jones, the manager, was very helpful with ideas
of restaurants and activities, before we'd even
arrived,' write Guide readers this year. 'Clean-
lined and modern but grey' bedrooms (some
with their own entrance) vary in size; some can
accommodate a family. 'Our suite overlooking
the well-kept garden had an extremely comfy
bed. In the bathroom: fluffy towels, super-soft
robes, a wonderful drench shower.' A continental
breakfast is served Sun–Wed; hot breakfasts
Thurs–Sat might include 'a very fine kipper'.
Dinner has good choice.

MAP 2:B6
41 London Road
Pakefield NR33 7AA
T: 01502 569805
W: thehoghotel.co.uk

BEDROOMS: 16. 1 suite suitable for
disabled.
OPEN: all year, restaurant open for
dinner Wed and Thurs, lunch and
dinner Fri and Sat, Sun lunch.
FACILITIES: bar, restaurant, in-room
smart TV, function facilities,
conservatory, terrace, garden.
BACKGROUND MUSIC: in public areas.
LOCATION: in village, 2 miles S of
Lowestoft.
CHILDREN: all ages welcomed.
DOGS: welcomed in some bedrooms,
not in main hotel, bar, restaurant.
CREDIT CARDS: Amex, MC, Visa.
PRICES: per room B&B £120–£230.
À la carte £32.

PENZANCE Cornwall

ARTIST RESIDENCE CORNWALL

Up a sloping lane from the harbour, this revitalised Georgian coach house brims with a sense of fun. Typical of Justin and Charlotte Salisbury's eclectic hotel collection (see main entries for Artist Residence in London, Brighton and South Leigh, Oxfordshire), the peppy, thoughtfully supplied bedrooms are individually decorated with bright artworks and vintage furniture. Set across three floors, they range in size from snug to capacious, with space for an accompanying dog or entire family. Downstairs, eating, drinking and merry-making take place in the informal bar, restaurant and garden, where menus feature Cornish produce, and meat and fish from the on-site smokehouse.

MAP 1:E1
20 Chapel Street
Penzance TR18 4AW
T: 01736 365664
W: artistresidence.co.uk

BEDROOMS: 19. Plus 3-bed cottage in grounds.
OPEN: all year.
FACILITIES: bar, restaurant, in-room TV (Freeview), terrace, beer garden (outdoor seafood shack and bar in summer).
BACKGROUND MUSIC: in public areas.
LOCATION: in town centre.
CHILDREN: all ages welcomed.
DOGS: allowed in some bedrooms, restaurant.
CREDIT CARDS: Amex, MC, Visa.
PRICES: per room £125–£345, suite £345–£435, cottage £465–£565. Breakfast £4–£10.50, à la carte £35. 1-night stay sometimes refused weekends.

PENZANCE Cornwall

VENTON VEAN

By Penlee Park, this modern B&B has a pleasing mix of contemporary art and vintage furnishings, the stylish whole set against the period features of the immaculately restored Victorian house. It is owned by Philippa McKnight and David Hoyes. Spacious bedrooms have a king-size bed and welcome extras (refreshments, bathrobes, eco-friendly toiletries); books are available to borrow in the airy sitting room. When it comes to food, 'our emphasis is on special and unusual dishes,' the hosts say: home-made corn tortillas and refried beans at breakfast, perhaps, or a Sri Lankan hodi broth with fresh Newlyn mussels at dinner (served Sat–Mon). Vegan and vegetarian diets are willingly catered for.

MAP 1:E1
Trewithen Road
Penzance TR18 4LS
T: 01736 351294
W: ventonvean.co.uk

BEDROOMS: 5. 1 with adjoining single room, suitable for a family.
OPEN: all year except 25–26 Dec.
FACILITIES: sitting room, dining room, in-room smart TV, garden.
BACKGROUND MUSIC: at breakfast in dining room.
LOCATION: 7 mins' walk from the centre of Penzance and Penzance seafront.
CHILDREN: not under 5.
DOGS: not allowed.
CREDIT CARDS: MC, Visa.
PRICES: per room B&B single £77–£97, double £87–£107. À la carte £30. 2-night min. stay May–Sept.

RAMSGATE Kent

ALBION HOUSE

Ben and Emma Irvine's stylish small hotel occupies a restored Regency building in a clifftop position overlooking the beach and Royal Harbour. It has been visited, in the past, by politicians, actors, even Princess Victoria, who stayed while recuperating from an illness. A sense of grandeur remains today, in its high ceilings, ornate cornices and carved fireplaces. Elegant public spaces have mirrors, plants, walls painted deep heritage shades; a lounge is a 'welcoming' spot. Most of the well-equipped bedrooms, some high up in the eaves, have views towards the water. (A busy road at the front may affect light sleepers.) In Townley's restaurant, seasonal produce, including locally caught seafood, dictates the menu.

MAP 2:D6
Albion Place
Ramsgate CT11 8HQ
T: 01843 606630
W: albionhouseramsgate.co.uk

BEDROOMS: 14. 1 suitable for disabled.
OPEN: all year.
FACILITIES: 2 lounges, bar/restaurant, snug, in-room TV (Freeview), private dining room, electric bicycle hire.
BACKGROUND MUSIC: all day in public areas.
LOCATION: above Ramsgate Main Sands beach.
CHILDREN: all ages welcomed.
DOGS: allowed in bedrooms, public rooms.
CREDIT CARDS: MC, Visa.
PRICES: per room B&B £125–£390. À la carte £60. 1-night bookings refused weekends in July, Aug.

REETH Yorkshire

CAMBRIDGE HOUSE

On the outskirts of a rural village, in an area popular with walkers and cyclists for its vast open moors, this Swaledale B&B is run by 'marvellous hosts' Sheila and Robert Mitchell. Bedrooms with 'superb' countryside views are supplied with hot drinks and dressing gowns; all but a single room have a bath and shower. Tea and home-made cake are served in the conservatory; the lounge has an honesty bar, and a log fire in winter. 'A great start to the day', the 'varied' breakfast includes kippers and Yorkshire rarebit alongside home-baked bread and award-winning marmalades. Special diets can be catered for. The 'thoughtful' owners provide bicycle storage and a drying room; the packed lunches are 'very good', too.

MAP 4:C3
Arkengarthdale Road
Reeth DL11 6QX
T: 01748 884633
W: cambridgehousereeth.co.uk

BEDROOMS: 5.
OPEN: Feb–mid-Dec.
FACILITIES: lounge, dining room, conservatory, in-room TV (Freeview), small garden, terrace, bicycle storage, parking.
BACKGROUND MUSIC: none.
LOCATION: 500 yards from centre of Reeth.
CHILDREN: not allowed.
DOGS: 1 well-behaved dog allowed, by arrangement, in bedroom (not unattended), conservatory.
CREDIT CARDS: MC, Visa.
PRICES: per room B&B single £90–£100, double £80–£115. Limited availability of 1-night bookings Apr–Sept.

RIPLEY Surrey

BROADWAY BARN

The eggs Benedict are 'made right' at Mindi
McLean's B&B, in this 'beautifully and tastefully
restored' 200-year-old barn at the heart of a
historic village. 'Exquisitely furnished' bedrooms
(one with a roll-top bath) are equipped with little
luxuries: dressing gowns, slippers, flowers and
home-made shortbread. In the morning, guests
find a feast in the conservatory overlooking the
small walled garden. With a spread of home-
baked breads, home-made jams and granola, and
house-recipe chipolatas, 'the breakfast is a fitting
end to an amazing stay'. 'Engaging, thoughtful
and attentive', the hostess has eating places to
recommend in this foodie area. 'Very easy access'
to Guildford, Woking and other Surrey towns.

MAP 2:D3
High Street
Ripley
nr Woking GU23 6AQ
T: 01483 223200
W: broadwaybarn.com

BEDROOMS: 3. Plus self-catering flat
and cottages.
OPEN: all year.
FACILITIES: conservatory sitting
room/breakfast room, in-room TV
(Freeview), small garden, parking.
BACKGROUND MUSIC: 'subtle' at
breakfast.
LOCATION: village centre.
CHILDREN: not under 12.
DOGS: not allowed.
CREDIT CARDS: Amex, MC, Visa.
PRICES: per room B&B £130.

ST ALBANS Hertfordshire

SOPWELL HOUSE HOTEL

In extensive grounds, the former home of Lord
Louis Mountbatten is today a 'well-run' hotel
with contemporary bedrooms, cosseting suites,
a choice of eating and drinking spaces, and a
sleek spa. Bedrooms in the extended 300-year-old
manor house are 'practical and well furnished,
with all the amenities'; upmarket mews suites, in
landscaped gardens in a gated compound, offer
extra privacy. The 'bustling', light-drenched
brasserie has classic bistro dishes ('seemingly
something for everyone'); more formal, modern
British dinners are taken in the restaurant (Fri
and Sat). Besides the state-of-the-art spa, several
walled gardens provide space for relaxation and
reflection. 'Plentiful' breakfasts are 'nicely served'.

MAP 2:C3
Cottonmill Lane
St Albans AL1 2HQ
T: 01727 864477
W: sopwellhouse.co.uk

BEDROOMS: 128. 16 mews suites.
OPEN: all year, restaurant open Fri, Sat
for dinner.
FACILITIES: cocktail lounge, bar,
2 restaurants, sitting room, in-room
TV (Sky, BT), civil wedding licence,
meeting and conference facilities, spa,
indoor pool, gym, 12-acre grounds,
electric car charging points.
BACKGROUND MUSIC: in lobby and
restaurants.
LOCATION: 1½ miles from the city
centre and rail station.
CHILDREN: not under 12 to stay, not
under 16 in spa or swimming pool.
DOGS: not allowed.
CREDIT CARDS: Amex, MC, Visa.
PRICES: per room B&B £209–£439.
À la carte £45.

ST IVES Cornwall

HEADLAND HOUSE

On a steep hill above Carbis Bay, Mark and
Fenella Thomas's chic Edwardian house is a
tranquil retreat from lively St Ives nearby. The
snug lounge has an honesty bar, plus books and
magazines to browse; in good weather, loll about
in a garden hammock – complimentary aperitif
optional. Each of the well-equipped bedrooms
(dressing gowns, a coffee machine, fresh milk,
etc) is individually decorated in a smart, airy
style. Choose a room with beachy views from a
broad window seat, perhaps, or one, off the rear
courtyard garden, with sun loungers on a private
deck; in every room, home-baked cake turns up
at teatime. Hearty Cornish breakfasts (including
a weekly special) kick-start the day with a view
across the water.

MAP 1:D1
Headland Road
Carbis Bay
St Ives TR26 2NS
T: 01736 796647
W: headlandhousehotel.co.uk

BEDROOMS: 9. 3 off the courtyard
garden.
OPEN: end Mar/early Apr–Oct.
FACILITIES: lounge, conservatory
breakfast room, in-room TV
(Freeview), large front garden, sun
deck, parking.
BACKGROUND MUSIC: none.
LOCATION: 1½ miles from St Ives
centre, 5 mins from Carbis Bay beach.
CHILDREN: not under 16.
DOGS: not allowed.
CREDIT CARDS: MC, Visa.
PRICES: per room B&B single
£120–£175, double £130–£185. 2-night
min. stay preferred.

ST IVES Cornwall

TREVOSE HARBOUR HOUSE

With views over the harbour, and a crisp blue-
and-white interior, Angela and Olivier Noverraz's
1850s mid-terrace house is 'a delight'. The creative
owners have mixed vintage finds and upcycled
furniture with original art by St Ives artists; a
terrace has seating for a sunny day. Beyond the
snug, with its books to borrow and honesty-bar
cocktails to mix, B&B accommodation is in serene
bedrooms supplied with coffee, tea and organic
toiletries. Most rooms have views of the harbour
and the bay; a spacious split-level annexe room has
a separate seating area. There's plenty of choice
at breakfast, where local produce is highlighted:
Cornish cheeses, smoked salmon from St Mawes,
home-made granola and preserves.

MAP 1:D1
22 The Warren
St Ives TR26 2EA
T: 01736 793267
W: trevosehouse.co.uk

BEDROOMS: 6. 1 in rear annexe.
OPEN: late Mar–Nov.
FACILITIES: snug, breakfast room,
in-room TV, in-room treatments,
terrace, limited parking close by.
BACKGROUND MUSIC: in snug.
LOCATION: in town centre.
CHILDREN: not under 12.
DOGS: not allowed.
CREDIT CARDS: Amex, MC, Visa.
PRICES: per room B&B £180–£315.
2-night min. stay.

ST LEONARDS-ON-SEA Sussex
THE CLOUDESLEY

A short walk from the seafront, this eclectic, modern B&B is owned and run by Shahriar Mazandi, a holistic therapist, photographer and award-winning gardener. His home is a reflection of his interests: the drawing room is stocked with art, gardening and photography books; the walls are hung with his photographs. Decorated with original works of art, the serene bedrooms have a large bed and a compact shower room; no TV, but plenty to read. In the bright dining room or on the sunny bamboo terrace, there's good choice at breakfast, including vegan options and an impressive omelette menu (sausage, sage and courgette; fruit and Armagnac; etc). In-room massages and reflexology treatments are available.

MAP 2:E4
7 Cloudesley Road
St Leonards-on-Sea TN37 6JN
T: 07507 000148
w: thecloudesley.co.uk

BEDROOMS: 4.
OPEN: all year.
FACILITIES: drawing room (honesty bar), dining room, in-room spa treatments, ¼-acre garden, patio.
BACKGROUND MUSIC: none.
LOCATION: 10 mins from St Leonards-on-Sea town centre.
CHILDREN: well-behaved children accepted.
DOGS: not allowed.
CREDIT CARDS: MC, Visa.
PRICES: per room B&B £75–£135. 2-night min. stay preferred at weekends.

ST MARTIN'S Isles of Scilly
KARMA ST MARTIN'S

The ferry from St Mary's docks at the private jetty of this waterfront hotel, which basks in the full azure panorama of Teän Sound. A laid-back, dog-friendly place, it is the only hotel on the island. Light, modern bedrooms in the low-built building have books, freshly ground Cornish coffee and vintage-style furnishings; large bay windows gaze over the stretch of white sand and the sea. In the restaurant, or alfresco in the sub-tropical garden, lobster rolls and platters of freshly caught seafood are menu mainstays. Accompanying dogs can relish a dish from the Kanine Kitchen, then toast their good fortune with some 'Pawsecco'. Active sorts might hire a day boat or snorkel with seals; soothing spa treatments are also available.

MAP 1: inset C1
Lower Town
St Martin's TR25 0QW
T: 01720 422368
w: karmastmartins.com

BEDROOMS: 30. 12 on ground floor, 5 suitable for disabled.
OPEN: Easter–end Oct.
FACILITIES: bar, restaurant, 2 lounges, in-room TV (Freeview), civil wedding licence, treatment room, children's games room, 7-acre grounds.
BACKGROUND MUSIC: jazz in bar, restaurant, muted on request.
LOCATION: 2 mins' walk from Lower Town Quay.
CHILDREN: all ages welcomed.
DOGS: allowed in upper dining room, some bedrooms.
CREDIT CARDS: Amex, MC, Visa.
PRICES: per room B&B £250–£600. À la carte £50.

ST MARY'S Isles of Scilly
ST MARY'S HALL HOTEL

A few sandy footsteps from two of Hugh Town's beaches, this privately owned hotel on the largest of the Isles of Scilly occupies an extended town house standing in sub-tropical gardens. Roger Page, a familiar face to returning guests, is the 'helpful, knowledgeable' manager. Airy bedrooms decorated in soothing shades vary in size, though all have a large bed, high-end toiletries and home-made biscuits on a well-stocked tray. Family-friendly suites, most with a galley kitchenette, accommodate up to four guests. At mealtimes, choose from local seafood, and meat from the owners' rare-breeds farm; at breakfast, there are eggs from St Mary's hens. Ask for a picnic before setting off to explore the neighbouring islands.

MAP 1: inset C1
Church Street
St Mary's TR21 0JR
T: 01720 422316
w: stmaryshallhotel.co.uk

BEDROOMS: 27.
OPEN: mid-Mar–mid-Oct.
FACILITIES: 2 lounges, bar, 2 restaurants, in-room TV (Freeview), garden.
BACKGROUND MUSIC: in bar, restaurants.
LOCATION: 5 mins' walk from town centre, 10 mins' walk from quay.
CHILDREN: all ages welcomed.
DOGS: allowed in ground-floor suites, public rooms.
CREDIT CARDS: MC, Visa.
PRICES: per room single £109–£256, double £189–£342. À la carte £45.

SALCOMBE Devon
SOUTH SANDS

In a sheltered cove along the coast from the popular sailing resort town, this dog- and family-friendly hotel has a breezy, informal feel. Ranging in size and outlook, up-to-date bedrooms have some seaside touches; large two-bedroom suites have a kitchen and a balcony or patio. Preprandials on the wide, beach-facing terrace might be followed by fresh-as-can-be fish and shellfish, plus seasonal West Country dishes off an all-day menu. (Good veggie options, too.) Coastal paths start from the back door; the National Trust garden Overbeck's is up the hill. Leave the car where you've parked it: the most delightful way to reach the town centre is via sea tractor down South Sands beach to meet the passenger ferry.

MAP 1:E4
Bolt Head
Salcombe TQ8 8LL
T: 01548 845900
w: southsands.com

BEDROOMS: 27. Some on ground floor, 1 suitable for disabled, 5 suites with separate entrance.
OPEN: all year.
FACILITIES: bar, restaurant, in-room TV (Freeview), civil wedding licence, electric car charging point, terrace, bar and restaurant wheelchair accessible.
BACKGROUND MUSIC: in public areas.
LOCATION: on South Sands beach, 1½ miles from Salcombe town centre.
CHILDREN: all ages welcomed.
DOGS: allowed in some bedrooms, bar, half the restaurant.
CREDIT CARDS: MC, Visa.
PRICES: per room B&B £250–£750. À la carte £45. 2-night min. stay at weekends.

SCARBOROUGH Yorkshire
PHOENIX COURT

Atop the cliffs overlooking the surf-licked sands of North Bay, Donna and Mike Buttery's personably run guest house is in a 'great central location' within walking distance of the town. Many of the spacious bedrooms in the twin Victorian town houses have sweeping sea views through large windows; two rooms can accommodate a family. Refurbishments continued in 2021, and most rooms now have a new orthopaedic bed. Returning guests praise the host's cooked-to-order breakfasts; lighter options include locally smoked kippers or fruit and nut toast with Wensleydale cheese. Special diets are catered for, with advance notice. Leave the car in the private car park and easily access the path down to the seafront.

MAP 4:C5
8–9 Rutland Terrace
Scarborough YO12 7JB
T: 01723 501150
W: phoenixcourt.co.uk

BEDROOMS: 12. 1 on ground floor.
OPEN: Mar–Oct.
FACILITIES: lounge (honesty bar), breakfast room, in-room TV (Freeview), drying facilities, parking.
BACKGROUND MUSIC: local radio in breakfast room.
LOCATION: 10 mins' walk from the town centre and South Bay.
CHILDREN: all ages welcomed.
DOGS: not allowed.
CREDIT CARDS: MC, Visa.
PRICES: per room B&B single £50–£75, double £60–£80, family £80–£95. 2-night min. stay at weekends.

SEDBERGH Cumbria
THE BLACK BULL

On the High Street of a small, book-loving town at the foot of the Howgill fells, this 17th-century inn has been sympathetically updated by chef/patron Nina Matsunaga and her husband, James Ratcliffe, a Dales native. Pots of moss and fern bring the outdoors in to the modern bar and restaurant; at mealtimes, local produce is transformed by Nina's innovative Japanese-inspired cooking: wild halibut, haddock, shiso, apple, perhaps, or Lune valley pork belly, fermented rhubarb. A list of biodynamic wines and local craft beers accompanies. Upstairs, serene, clean-lined bedrooms have locally made wool blankets and photographs of the surrounding landscape; sleek bathrooms are stocked with essential-oil toiletries.

MAP 4:C3
44 Main Street
Sedbergh LA10 5BL
T: 015396 20264
W: theblackbullsedbergh.co.uk

BEDROOMS: 18.
OPEN: all week May–Oct, 5 days a week Nov–Apr, restaurant open Wed–Sun all year round.
FACILITIES: bar, restaurant, in-room TV, 1-acre garden, bar and restaurant wheelchair accessible.
BACKGROUND MUSIC: in public rooms.
LOCATION: in town centre, close to M6 (Junction 37).
CHILDREN: all ages welcomed.
DOGS: allowed in 3 bedrooms, bar, not in restaurant.
CREDIT CARDS: Amex, MC, Visa.
PRICES: per room B&B single £112.50–£172, double £125–£205. À la carte £34. 2-night min. stay at weekends in high season.

SEDGEFORD Norfolk
MAGAZINE WOOD

In a secluded swath of green countryside, Pip and Jonathan Barber's chic B&B looks over the village towards the Norfolk coast. Just right for cocooning, each spacious, newly refurbished suite has a private entrance and terrace; inside are a large bed and mood lighting, plus a deep bath and separate shower in the bathroom. Books, DVDs and binoculars are provided; a tablet computer serves as an online concierge, to download a newspaper or create a travel itinerary. The day begins 'anytime': a well-stocked cupboard contains muesli, cereals, fruit and croissants; milk and organic yogurts are in the fridge. Cooked breakfasts (charged extra) are ordered the night before. A dining pub is within walking distance.

MAP 2:A5
Peddars Way
Sedgeford PE36 5LW
T: 01485 750740
W: magazinewood.co.uk

BEDROOMS: 3. All on ground floor, 2 in converted barn.
OPEN: all year except Christmas.
FACILITIES: in-room TV (on-demand movies), in-room spa treatments, 3-acre grounds.
BACKGROUND MUSIC: none.
LOCATION: 5 miles from Hunstanton.
CHILDREN: infants welcomed.
DOGS: allowed (not unattended) in 1 bedroom.
CREDIT CARDS: MC, Visa.
PRICES: per room B&B (continental) £115–£149. Cooked breakfast £7.50. 2-night min. stay most weekends.

SHAFTESBURY Dorset
THE GROSVENOR ARMS

'A lovely, intimate hotel in a beautiful town', this former coaching inn with 'friendly, helpful' staff has been updated with a pared-back, modern rustic feel. The wood-floored bar has a wood burner and well-worn leather armchairs; in the buzzy restaurant and conservatory, or around a central courtyard, 'excellent' food on the locally sourced menus might include flat-iron chicken, Somerset Camembert, squash and chestnut pie, or a pizza from the wood-fired oven. 'Attractive' bedrooms and suites are well equipped with teas and a capsule coffee machine; some rooms can accommodate a cot or an extra bed for a child. At breakfast, stoke up on Old Spot sausage and bacon, smoky beans and hash browns for the climb up Gold Hill.

MAP 2:D1
The Commons
Shaftesbury SP7 8JA
T: 01747 850580
W: grosvenorarms.co.uk

BEDROOMS: 16. 2 on first floor accessible by lift.
OPEN: all year.
FACILITIES: lift to first-floor rooms, bar, lounge, restaurant, conservatory, private dining room, ballroom, in-room smart TV (Freeview), courtyard garden, parking permits supplied for local car park, bar and restaurant wheelchair accessible, adapted toilet.
BACKGROUND MUSIC: in bar.
LOCATION: in town centre, 1-min. walk from Gold Hill.
CHILDREN: all ages welcomed.
DOGS: allowed in bedrooms, bar, conservatory, not in restaurant.
CREDIT CARDS: Amex, MC, Visa.
PRICES: per room B&B £115–£240. À la carte £35.

SHANKLIN Isle of Wight

HAVEN HALL HOTEL

Looking out to sea, Arielle and David Barratt's cliff-top Edwardian house on the Isle of Wight is just a stroll, along the coastal path, from the beach on Sandown Bay. The engaging owners, who live in a separate wing, have furnished their guest house with carefully chosen period pieces that give the bedrooms and suites an Arts and Crafts appeal. Nearly all the rooms have views over the water. The day begins with a spread of fruit, cereals, breads, jams and home-made compotes in the breakfast room, whose doors open to the patio and the flowerbeds in the award-winning landscaped gardens. A swimming pool and grass tennis court are ideal for active sorts. Guests may ask to dine in, or try a recommended restaurant.

MAP 2:E2
5 Howard Road
Shanklin PO37 6HD
T: 07914 796494
W: havenhallhotel.com

BEDROOMS: 14. 3 on ground floor, 7 available for self-catering.
OPEN: all year except Christmas, New Year.
FACILITIES: bar, lounge, dining room, in-room TV (Freeview), outdoor pool (heated May–Sept), grass tennis court, croquet, 2-acre grounds, electric car charging point.
BACKGROUND MUSIC: none.
LOCATION: on E side of island, overlooking the English Channel.
CHILDREN: not under 7.
DOGS: welcomed in 3 bedrooms.
CREDIT CARDS: Amex, MC, Visa.
PRICES: per room B&B £420–£1,250. À la carte £40. 2-night min. stay.

SHANKLIN Isle of Wight

RYLSTONE MANOR

'Delightfully relaxing', Carole and Mike Hailston's Isle of Wight B&B stands within serene public gardens above Sandown Bay. There's plenty of space inside the 19th-century gentleman's residence, where the bar and homely sitting rooms sport rich hues, period furnishings and leaded windows. Some of the traditionally styled bedrooms offer glimpses of the sea through leafy trees; one has a four-poster bed; another, a window seat perfect for looking over the Chine. A secluded private garden surrounds the house; not far, steps lead down to the sandy beach. Founts of island information, the genial hosts can arrange ferry crossings and point out the easy walk to the shops and restaurants in Old Shanklin.

MAP 2:E2
Rylstone Gardens
Shanklin PO37 6RG
T: 01983 862806
W: rylstone-manor.co.uk

BEDROOMS: 8.
OPEN: Mar–early Nov.
FACILITIES: drawing room, bar/lounge, breakfast room, in-room TV (Freeview), terrace, ¼-acre garden in 4-acre public gardens.
BACKGROUND MUSIC: none.
LOCATION: in Shanklin Old Village.
CHILDREN: not under 16.
DOGS: only assistance dogs allowed.
CREDIT CARDS: MC, Visa.
PRICES: per room B&B single £110–£130, double £135–£165. 3-night min. stay June–Aug 'unless space allows'.

SHEFFORD WOODLANDS Berkshire
THE PHEASANT INN
Old photographs and the odd stuffed pheasant add to the appealing character of this revamped sheep drover's inn, which overlooks a wide spread of the Berkshire Downs. Amid quirky prints and shelves of books, locals and visitors easily find places to perch on red leather settles and vintage bar stools. Overnighters roost in one of the smart bedrooms, each supplied with cafetière coffee, quality teas and fresh milk, plus natural toiletries and towelling robes in the shower- or bathroom. Served on bare-wood tables, elevated pub food (cured and torched mackerel, miso; Wiltshire lamb rump) includes vegan options; breakfast has plenty of choice. Hampers can be made up for a day out walking on the North Wessex Downs.

MAP 3:E6
Ermin Street
Shefford Woodlands RG17 7AA
T: 01488 648284
W: thepheasant-inn.co.uk

BEDROOMS: 11.
OPEN: all year.
FACILITIES: bar, restaurant, private dining room, in-room TV (Sky), courtyard, garden, parking.
BACKGROUND MUSIC: in public areas.
LOCATION: 9½ miles NW of Newbury.
CHILDREN: all ages welcomed.
DOGS: allowed in bedrooms, public rooms, by arrangement.
CREDIT CARDS: Amex, MC, Visa.
PRICES: per room B&B £125–£150.
À la carte £35.

SHERBORNE Dorset
THE EASTBURY HOTEL & SPA
Close to Sherborne Abbey, this handsome Georgian town house in 'lovely' walled gardens makes a 'pleasant retreat' in the heart of the historic market town. The hotel, restored by Peter and Lana de Savary, has 'comfortable, well-furnished' bedrooms (classic, or with a chic, modern edge), all supplied with bathrobes and slippers, teas, coffees and home-made biscuits. In the garden, five green-roofed suites, all dog friendly, each have a private terrace. Afternoon teas and brasserie dishes are served in the bar and lounge, or on the terrace in good weather; in the evening, chef Matthew Street's creative fine-dining and tasting menus are a high point. A snug spa is tucked away at the bottom of the garden.

MAP 2:E1
Long Street
Sherborne DT9 3BY
T: 01935 813131
W: theeastburyhotel.co.uk

BEDROOMS: 26. 5 in walled gardens, 2 suitable for disabled. Plus 3-bed self-catering cottage.
OPEN: all year.
FACILITIES: bar/dining room, morning room, drawing room, library, private dining room, in-room TV (Freeview), wedding/function facilities, spa (hydrotherapy pool, outdoor hot tub), terrace, 1-acre walled garden, electric car charging point.
BACKGROUND MUSIC: in bar, restaurant.
LOCATION: in town centre.
CHILDREN: all ages welcomed.
DOGS: allowed in 9 bedrooms, morning room, part of restaurant.
CREDIT CARDS: Amex, MC, Visa.
PRICES: per room B&B £145–£350.
À la carte £40. 1-night bookings sometimes refused.

SHERBORNE Dorset

THE KINGS ARMS

Just up the street from the village church, this
19th-century inn is today a 'friendly' country pub
run by chef/patron Sarah Lethbridge and her
husband, Anthony. Local artwork (all for sale)
hangs in the public spaces; in the snug, where a
wood-burning stove is lit in cool weather, a stack
of the day's newspapers is ready for flipping
through. Local ales and 'great' ciders in the bar
pair nicely with the updated pub grub served in
the smart dining room and on the large terrace;
in barbecue season, the grill on the lawn is fired
up. Staying guests have a choice of colourful
bedrooms, each with a marble wet room; a family
might ask for interconnecting rooms. The historic
town of Sherborne is four miles away.

MAP 2:E1
North Street
Charlton Horethorne
Sherborne DT9 4NL
T: 01963 220281
w: thekingsarms.co.uk

BEDROOMS: 10. 1 suitable for disabled.
OPEN: all year, restaurant closed
25–26 Dec.
FACILITIES: lift, snug, bar, restaurant,
in-room TV (Freeview), meeting/
function facilities, terrace, garden
(outdoor barbecue kitchen), free use
of local sports centre, discounts at
Sherborne Golf Club.
BACKGROUND MUSIC: none.
LOCATION: in village 4 miles NE of
Sherborne.
CHILDREN: all ages welcomed.
DOGS: allowed in bar.
CREDIT CARDS: MC, Visa.
PRICES: per room B&B £95–£145.
À la carte £32.

SHIPSTON-ON-STOUR Warwickshire

THE BOWER HOUSE

Decorated with 'immense panache', this
restaurant-with-rooms is on the pretty square
of a historic market town on the edge of the
Cotswolds. 'An impressive assortment of pictures
and eclectic furniture' fills the public areas, but
its biggest attraction is arguably its bistro menu:
'locals flock to the place' for dishes such as
chicken Milanese, wild garlic butter; miso-glazed
aubergine, tahini, pomegranate. Overnight guests
have 'first-class' accommodation. Through a
separate entrance, 'elegant' bedrooms are reached
via a steep staircase. They're worth the climb, for
within them 'every possible need has been thought
of' – tea and coffee, Scrabble, books and playing
cards among them. Breakfast is served until late.

MAP 3:D6
Market Place
Shipston-on-Stour CV36 4AG
T: 01608 663333
w: bower.house

BEDROOMS: 5.
OPEN: all year except 25–26 Dec,
restaurant closed Sun eve, Mon.
FACILITIES: bar, dining rooms, in-
room TV (Freeview), dining areas
wheelchair accessible.
BACKGROUND MUSIC: in restaurant.
LOCATION: in town centre.
CHILDREN: all ages 'warmly
welcomed'.
DOGS: allowed in bar area of
restaurant.
CREDIT CARDS: Amex, MC, Visa.
PRICES: per room B&B £115–£205.
À la carte £42. 2-night min. stay bank
holidays, summer weekends.

SHREWSBURY Shropshire

DARWIN'S TOWNHOUSE

Steps from the footpath along the River Severn, this listed town house with 18th-century origins has evolved into a contemporary B&B that pays homage to Shrewsbury's most revered son, Charles Darwin. The sitting room and snug have ample space for repose; there are board games, books and an honesty bar. Individually decorated bedrooms, some overlooking the garden, have appropriate curiosities and 'a number of thoughtful touches': dressing gowns, a digital alarm radio, tea- and coffee-making facilities. A 'delicious' breakfast is served in the conservatory – 'and the options appear endless'. Discount cards are offered to residents for two sister restaurants, both within a ten-minute walk of the B&B.

MAP 3:B4
37 St Julian's Friars
Shrewsbury SY1 1XL
T: 01743 343829
W: darwinstownhouse.com

BEDROOMS: 19. 5 on ground floor, 8 in garden annexe, 1 suitable for disabled.
OPEN: all year, continental breakfast only on 25 Dec.
FACILITIES: lounge, snug (honesty bar), conservatory breakfast room, in-room TV, garden, bicycle storage.
BACKGROUND MUSIC: in lounge, snug.
LOCATION: in town centre.
CHILDREN: all ages welcomed.
DOGS: allowed in garden bedrooms, not in breakfast room.
CREDIT CARDS: Amex, MC, Visa.
PRICES: per room B&B £100–£200. À la carte (at sister restaurants) £25, residents' discount cards supplied.

SHREWSBURY Shropshire

LION AND PHEASANT

There's a fresh, modern feel at this updated 16th-century coaching inn, in a convenient central position near the English Bridge. 'Friendly staff' dish out regional real ales against a backdrop of characterful original features in the buzzy bar; a fire burns in the inglenook fireplace in cooler months. Served in the split-level restaurant and the courtyard garden, chef Callum Smith's well-regarded cooking focuses on Shropshire produce. Small plates and sustainable wines are in the brick-walled wine bar next door. Staying guests choose among bedrooms with a contemporary country air; some rooms also have river views. (Rooms at the front may have some street noise.) Close by: riverside walks; medieval streetscapes.

MAP 3:B4
49–50 Wyle Cop
Shrewsbury SY1 1XJ
T: 01743 770345
W: lionandpheasant.co.uk

BEDROOMS: 22.
OPEN: all year except 25–26 Dec.
FACILITIES: bar, wine bar, restaurant, function room, in-room TV (Freeview), garden terrace, parking (narrow entrance).
BACKGROUND MUSIC: in public areas, occasional live music in bar.
LOCATION: in town centre.
CHILDREN: all ages welcomed.
DOGS: allowed on garden terrace only.
CREDIT CARDS: MC, Visa.
PRICES: per room B&B £150–£240. À la carte £38.

SOMERTON Somerset

THE WHITE HART

A foodie spot in a friendly town skirting the
Somerset Levels, this updated pub-with-rooms
on the market square draws tourists and locals
with its 'good atmosphere' and 'delicious' West
Country menus. The wood-floored restaurant
is bright and spacious; here, diners tuck in to
modern gastropub dishes – Somerset Camembert,
squash and chestnut pie, say. Cocktails, local
ciders and organic wines are quaffed in the wood
burner-warmed bar. 'Well-presented' bedrooms
upstairs have a large bed, fresh coffee and tea,
and natural toiletries. At breakfast: wood-roasted
kippers, Old Spot sausages and more. Part of
the Stay Original Co.; see also Timbrell's Yard,
Bradford-on-Avon, and The Swan, Wedmore
(Shortlist entries).

MAP 1:C6
Market Place
Somerton TA11 7LX
T: 01458 272273
W: whitehartsomerton.com

BEDROOMS: 8.
OPEN: all year.
FACILITIES: bar, restaurant, in-room
smart TV, large courtyard garden,
bicycle storage.
BACKGROUND MUSIC: in bar.
LOCATION: in town centre.
CHILDREN: all ages welcomed.
DOGS: 'very welcome' in bedrooms,
bar, terrace and garden.
CREDIT CARDS: MC, Visa.
PRICES: per room B&B £85–£160.
À la carte £27.

SOUTH ALKHAM Kent

ALKHAM COURT

'Wonderful, engaging hosts' Wendy and Neil
Burrows welcome B&B guests to their Alkham
valley farmhouse with home-baked cake; their
warm thoughtfulness lasts the stay. Country-
style bedrooms each have a private entrance, and
treats within: flowers, robes and slippers, a coffee
machine, biscuits and sherry. Guests also have
use of a spa barn with a hot tub and sauna. The
hosts 'have a love for the area', and can advise
on diversions in countryside and along the coast.
Packed lunches and, in the evening, bowls of
soup with warm, crusty rolls can also be provided.
Breakfast wins fans with a spread of Kentish
produce, plus home-made preserves, freshly
baked muffins and a large choice of hot dishes.

MAP 2:D5
Meggett Lane
South Alkham CT15 7DG
T: 01303 892056
W: alkhamcourt.co.uk

BEDROOMS: 4. 3 on ground floor,
1 suitable for disabled. Plus 2 restored
vintage shepherd's huts for self-
catering.
OPEN: all year except 23–27 Dec.
FACILITIES: sitting/breakfast room,
in-room TV (Freeview), spa barn
(hot tub, sauna), large garden, 60-acre
farm.
BACKGROUND MUSIC: none.
LOCATION: in a rural location near
Dover; 5 mins from M20, 10 mins
from Eurotunnel.
CHILDREN: all ages welcomed.
DOGS: allowed (not unattended) in
1 bedroom, on lead at all times outside
because of livestock.
CREDIT CARDS: Amex, MC, Visa.
PRICES: per room B&B single £85–£100,
double £140–£170. 2-night min. stay in
summer, 3-night min. stay over bank
holidays.

SOUTH HARTING Sussex
THE WHITE HART

Locals, ramblers and overnighters gather at this dog- and family-friendly 16th-century inn, in walking country near the South Downs Way. It is in a peaceful village close to the National Trust's Uppark House. There's character in the beams and log fires of the wood- and flagstone-floored bar, a setting that's just right for the ales, wines and spirits on offer; in the walled garden, picnic tables and parasols await clement weather. Hearty meals, listed on frequently changing menus, might include classic fish pie or lemon and parmesan chicken schnitzel. In the main building and a converted barn in the rear, well-refurbished bedrooms and family suites have rustic charm in their exposed timbers, plaids and patterns.

MAP 2:E3
The Street
South Harting GU31 5QB
T: 01730 825124
W: the-whitehart.co.uk

BEDROOMS: 7. 4 in annexe.
OPEN: all year except evenings of 25 and 26 Dec, 1 Jan.
FACILITIES: bar, restaurant, snug, in-room TV, terrace, garden.
BACKGROUND MUSIC: in public areas.
LOCATION: in village, 4½ miles SE of Petersfield.
CHILDREN: all ages welcomed.
DOGS: allowed in some bedrooms, bar, snug.
CREDIT CARDS: Amex, MC, Visa.
PRICES: per room B&B £89–£169.
À la carte £30.

NEW

SOUTHLEIGH Devon
GLEBE HOUSE

'Divine countryside views' sweep away from Olivia and Hugo Guest's Georgian house, on the hilltop of their 15-acre smallholding. Outside are 'very pretty gardens', a swimming pool and a tennis court; inside, uplifting colours, mismatched fabrics and original artworks 'all make for a gracious impression'. Creatively decorated bedrooms share rural or garden views. A simple supper is available all week; Thursdays through Sundays, a fixed four-course Italian-inspired dinner might include wild garlic tortellini or roast cod, borlotti beans. 'We enjoyed the food, but would have preferred some choice.' To accompany the home-made farmhouse breakfast, guests may ask for Aga-cooked 'eggs one way'.

MAP 1:C5
Southleigh
nr Colyton EX24 6SD
T: 01404 871276
W: glebehousedevon.co.uk

BEDROOMS: 6. 1 in annexe.
OPEN: all year except Christmas, exclusive use over New Year.
FACILITIES: 2 sitting rooms, 4 dining areas, 15-acre grounds, heated outdoor swimming pool, tennis court.
BACKGROUND MUSIC: in public areas.
LOCATION: 3 miles W of Colyton.
CHILDREN: all ages welcomed.
DOGS: allowed in 2 bedrooms, not in restaurant.
CREDIT CARDS: Amex, MC, Visa.
PRICES: per room B&B single £109–£187, double £129–£220. Supper £20, 4-course fixed menu £48. 2-night min. stay at weekends unless single night becomes available.

SOUTHWOLD Suffolk
THE SWAN

A stroll from the pier, this Southwold stalwart has stood on the market square for centuries. Bright and jazzy following a fashionable facelift – with stripped oak floorboards, a gleaming copper-topped bar and a green velvet sofa or two – it has a hip, modern feel. It is owned by Adnams, the brewers; guests may tour the on-site brewery and distillery, and make their own gin. 'Light, airy and well fitted-out', bedrooms are supplied with 'very nice touches', such as good biscuits and an espresso machine. Pub classics mix with imaginative options in the banquette-lined Tap Room and bar; in the Still Room restaurant, 'the food is particularly good'. Borrow picnic rugs and deckchairs: the beach is at the end of the street.

MAP 2:B6
Market Place
Southwold IP18 6EG
T: 01502 722186
W: theswansouthwold.co.uk

BEDROOMS: 35. 12 in garden extension, 1 suitable for disabled.
OPEN: all year.
FACILITIES: 2 restaurants, lounge, private dining rooms, in-room TV, civil wedding licence, large garden, bicycle hire, electric car charging point, parking.
BACKGROUND MUSIC: in restaurant.
LOCATION: on market square.
CHILDREN: all ages welcomed.
DOGS: allowed in garden rooms, not in main hotel building.
CREDIT CARDS: MC, Visa.
PRICES: per room B&B £189–£430. À la carte £35. 1-night bookings generally refused in summer.

STOW-ON-THE-WOLD Gloucestershire
THE OLD STOCKS INN

In a historic wool town, the classic Cotswold-stone exterior of this 17th-century inn gives way to a cool, contemporary interior that mixes wooden beams and ancient floorboards with cocktails, Scandi-chic furnishings and a family-friendly feel. Past the board games in the bar, colourful bedrooms (ranging from cosy doubles to spacious garden rooms that open on to a terrace) have a coffee machine, fresh milk and local snacks. 'We like the location, the ambience, the staff and the quirky features': exposed stone walls in one room; a private, slanted staircase in another; 'some creaks and footfalls from neighbouring rooms'. Hearty British cuisine in the restaurant includes interesting vegetarian and vegan options.

MAP 3:D6
The Square
Stow-on-the-Wold GL54 1AF
T: 01451 830666
W: oldstocksinn.com

BEDROOMS: 16. 3 in garden annexe.
OPEN: all year except 24–25 Dec, restaurant closed for lunch Mon–Thurs.
FACILITIES: restaurant, bar, library, coffee shop, private dining room, in-room TV (Freeview), terrace.
BACKGROUND MUSIC: in public areas.
LOCATION: in town centre.
CHILDREN: all ages welcomed.
DOGS: allowed in 3 bedrooms, bar, library, coffee shop.
CREDIT CARDS: Amex, MC, Visa.
PRICES: per room B&B £129–£289. À la carte £38. 1-night bookings sometimes refused Sat night.

STRATFORD-UPON-AVON Warwickshire

WHITE SAILS

Within a 20-minute stroll of the medieval market town, Tim and Denise Perkin's well-regarded B&B is in a suburban house well placed for visiting castles and historic cottages alike. The hosts maintain a home-away-from-home atmosphere, with help-yourself extras (sherry, espresso coffee, home-made treats) in the compact lounge, and a neat garden to sit in on warm days. 'Clean and comfy' bedrooms, including one with a four-poster bed, are supplied with bathrobes, a digital radio and home-baked cake; chilled water and fresh milk are in a silent fridge. Breakfast has yogurt, fruit and compotes, plus home-made granola, bread and cakes; cooked-to-order dishes include smoked haddock with poached eggs.

MAP 3:D6
85 Evesham Road
Stratford-upon-Avon CV37 9BE
T: 01789 550469
w: white-sails.co.uk

BEDROOMS: 4.
OPEN: all year except 25 Dec, 1 Jan.
FACILITIES: lounge, dining room, in-room TV (Freeview), garden, bicycle storage, parking.
BACKGROUND MUSIC: in breakfast room.
LOCATION: 1 mile W of centre.
CHILDREN: not under 12.
DOGS: not allowed.
CREDIT CARDS: Amex, MC, Visa.
PRICES: per room B&B single £95–£120, double £110–£135. 2-night min. stay May–Sept.

SUMMERHOUSE Co. Durham

THE RABY HUNT RESTAURANT AND ROOMS

Drive past fields of grazing cows to come to this Grade II listed 19th-century drover's inn, its strikingly modern zinc extension glinting, on a sunny day, in the light. In a rural hamlet, the tiny restaurant-with-rooms is as surprising inside as out. It is owned by James Close, a self-taught chef, who has two Michelin stars for his innovative cooking. An open-view kitchen in the restaurant lets diners watch the drama as a busy team prepares the tasting menu of some 15 succinctly described courses: suckling pig, perhaps, or sea bass, or squab. A chocolate skull provides a theatrical finish. Up close, the Kitchen Table has front-row seats for six. Stay for breakfast: there are three spacious, contemporary bedrooms.

MAP 4:C4
Summerhouse
nr Darlington DL2 3UD
T: 01325 374237
w: rabyhuntrestaurant.co.uk

BEDROOMS: 3.
OPEN: all year except Christmas, New Year, restaurant closed Sun–Tues.
FACILITIES: restaurant, in-room TV.
BACKGROUND MUSIC: in restaurant.
LOCATION: 6 miles NW of Darlington.
CHILDREN: not under 12.
DOGS: not allowed.
CREDIT CARDS: Amex, MC, Visa.
PRICES: per room B&B £275. Tasting menu (14–18 courses) £210, Kitchen Table menu £285.

TAUNTON Somerset

THE CASTLE AT TAUNTON

History is in the walls – in the 150-year-old
wisteria, even – of this 'very comfortable' hotel in
the heart of the county town. The medieval castle
has been extended and rebuilt over centuries;
today, it is run by the third generation of the
Chapman family, who have owned it since 1950.
'Cheerful' bedrooms and suites, some newly
refurbished in a 'retro chic' style, vary in size
and shape; larger or interconnecting rooms suit
a family. In the buzzy brasserie, the set menus,
blackboard specials and sharing platters might
include ham hock terrine, pickled summer
vegetables; linguini, chili and basil butter, truffle.
Breakfast includes a buffet with home-made
bread and jams; 'excellent' cooked dishes are
served 'piping hot'.

MAP 1:C5
Castle Green
Taunton TA1 1NF
T: 01823 272671
W: the-castle-hotel.com

BEDROOMS: 44.
OPEN: all year.
FACILITIES: lift, lounge/bar, snug,
restaurant, private dining/meeting
rooms, in-room TV (Freeview), civil
wedding licence, ¼-acre garden,
electric car charging points, public
rooms wheelchair accessible, adapted
toilet.
BACKGROUND MUSIC: 'easy listening'
in bar, restaurant.
LOCATION: in town centre.
CHILDREN: all ages welcomed.
DOGS: allowed in bedrooms, bar.
CREDIT CARDS: Amex, MC, Visa.
PRICES: per room B&B single
£125–£235, double £145–£255.
À la carte £30.

THORNHAM Norfolk

THE LIFEBOAT INN

Look out toward the sea and the salt marshes
from this 16th-century beer house, which takes
in the changing landscape from its 'spectacular'
location facing the north Norfolk coast. Today
a family-friendly, dog-welcoming inn (Agellus
Hotels), the white-painted building has an oak-
beamed bar with settles and open fires; a relaxed
restaurant serving seasonal dishes and daily
specials; a conservatory crowned by a 200-year-
old vine; and up-to-date bedrooms with views
of countryside or coast. (A pitch-penny slot in a
bar bench adds extra character.) Sit down to a
hearty meal, or head out to Holme Dunes – the
company of migrating birds, natterjack toads and
dragonflies can be just as delicious.

MAP 2:A5
Ship Lane
Thornham PE36 6LT
T: 01485 512236
W: lifeboatinnthornham.com

BEDROOMS: 16. 1 on ground floor, in
cottage.
OPEN: all year.
FACILITIES: bar, 2 lounge areas,
conservatory, restaurant, meeting
room, private dining room, in-room
smart TV, terrace, garden, parking.
BACKGROUND MUSIC: all day in
restaurant, bar.
LOCATION: in a small coastal village,
14 miles NE of Hunstanton.
CHILDREN: all ages welcomed.
DOGS: allowed in bedrooms, public
rooms.
CREDIT CARDS: MC, Visa.
PRICES: per room B&B £160–£240. À la
carte £28. 2-night min. stay preferred.

THORNTON HOUGH Merseyside
MERE BROOK HOUSE

A 'peaceful haven' set within a dell of mature trees, this Edwardian country house is considered a 'home away from home' by its many returning guests. The B&B is run with 'thoughtful hospitality' by Lorna Tyson and her husband, Donald, a farmer, who are keen to treat visitors to the bounty of their land. Supplied with home-baked cake, pretty bedrooms overlooking garden or countryside are in the main building and a converted coach house 20 yards away. Both buildings have their own lounge and kitchen stocked with cheese, home-made chutneys, juice and hot drinks. Breakfast in the conservatory brings more super-local treats: honey from garden beehives, apple juice or cider from orchard fruit, and more.

MAP 4:E2
Thornton Common Road
Thornton Hough CH63 0LU
T: 07713 189949
W: merebrookhouse.co.uk

BEDROOMS: 8. 4 in coach house, 3 on ground floor, 2 wheelchair accessible.
OPEN: all year, limited availability over Christmas, New Year.
FACILITIES: 3 lounges, conservatory, dining room, guest kitchens, in-room TV (Freeview), wedding/function facilities, 1-acre garden in 4-acre grounds (paddocks).
BACKGROUND MUSIC: none.
LOCATION: centre of Wirral peninsula, 20 mins' drive from Chester and Liverpool.
CHILDREN: all ages welcomed.
DOGS: only assistance dogs allowed.
CREDIT CARDS: MC, Visa.
PRICES: per room B&B single from £79, double £99–£139.

THURNHAM Kent
THURNHAM KEEP

Built from the ruins of Thurnham Castle, Amanda Lane's 'magnificent place' stands in a 'perfect setting' on the crest of the North Downs. Guests reach this 'simply wonderful' B&B, the hostess's childhood home, down a long drive through landscaped gardens; upon arrival, they may be rewarded with 'the best shortbread ever'. Up an oak staircase, spacious bedrooms are traditionally decorated with period furniture; each room looks across the lawns to spreading countryside. Breakfast, served communally, is 'lavish and tasty': home-made jams, garden honey, eggs fresh from the coop. Supper can be arranged in advance. Play croquet or tennis in fine weather; in summer, there's a heated swimming pool, too.

MAP 2:D4
Castle Hill
Thurnham ME14 3LE
T: 01622 734149
W: thurnhamkeep.co.uk

BEDROOMS: 3. Plus self-catering suite in grounds.
OPEN: Mar–Oct.
FACILITIES: sitting room, dining room, conservatory, billiard room, in-room TV (Freeview), 7-acre terraced garden, terrace, heated outdoor swimming pool (May–Sept), tennis.
BACKGROUND MUSIC: none.
LOCATION: 3 miles from Maidstone.
CHILDREN: not under 10.
DOGS: not allowed.
CREDIT CARDS: Amex, MC, Visa.
PRICES: per room B&B single £140–£160, double £160–£180. 2-night min. stay at weekends.

TISBURY Wiltshire
THE COMPASSES INN

Hidden down rural lanes bordered by hedgerows, Ben Maschler's contemporary country pub-with-rooms occupies a thatch-roofed 14th-century inn whose flagstone floors and ancient beams lend it much character. There are nooks and crannies, and candles lit on wooden tables; a fire burns in the inglenook fireplace when the mercury dips. Come hungry, as the locals do, for the 'exceptional' cooking: sophisticated pub standbys are ably accompanied by cocktails and local ales. Above the pub, 'simple but more than adequate' bedrooms are pleasingly pared-back; modern bath- and shower rooms are supplied with British-made toiletries. The Nadder valley's footpaths and sheep trails start from the door.

MAP 2:D1
Lower Chicksgrove
Tisbury SP3 6NB
T: 01722 714318
W: thecompassesinn.com

BEDROOMS: 4. Plus 3-bed self-catering cottage.
OPEN: all year except 25 Dec.
FACILITIES: bar, restaurant, in-room TV (Freeview), terrace, ¼-acre garden.
BACKGROUND MUSIC: none, occasional live music events.
LOCATION: 2 miles E of Tisbury.
CHILDREN: all ages welcomed.
DOGS: allowed in bedrooms, public areas.
CREDIT CARDS: MC, Visa.
PRICES: per room B&B single £110, double £120. À la carte £38. 2-night min. stay bank holidays and summer weekends.

TOPSHAM Devon
THE SALUTATION INN

In an old ship-building town on the Exe estuary, this updated 18th-century coaching inn is today a contemporary restaurant-with-rooms with clean-cut, modern accommodation and a reputation for fine food. The enterprise, including a new wet fish deli, is run by chef/patron Tom Williams-Hawkes and his wife, Amelia. Well-regarded menus, including ones for vegetarians, are served in the glass-covered atrium café or in the intimate restaurant. Typical dishes: wild garlic arancini, braised fennel; East Devon turbot, creel-caught langoustines, asparagus. Bedrooms (some snug, with a 'bijou' shower room) are airy and restrained; guests may help themselves to drinks, snacks and continental breakfast items in a shared kitchen.

MAP 1:C5
68 Fore Street
Topsham EX3 0HL
T: 01392 873060
W: salutationtopsham.co.uk

BEDROOMS: 6.
OPEN: all year except 25 Dec evening, 26 Dec, 1 Jan, restaurant and café closed Sun eve.
FACILITIES: 2 lounges, restaurant, café, meeting/function room, in-room TV (Freeview), walled yard with seating, wet fish deli, parking.
BACKGROUND MUSIC: in public areas.
LOCATION: in town centre.
CHILDREN: all ages welcomed.
DOGS: allowed in bedrooms, public rooms.
CREDIT CARDS: MC, Visa.
PRICES: per room £145–£230. Breakfast £14, à la carte £45. 2-night min. stay at weekends May–Sept.

TORQUAY Devon

THE MEADFOOT BAY

On the English Riviera, Phil Hartnett and Vicki Osborne encourage 'home-away-from-home' relaxation at their adults-only hotel, in a Victorian villa close to the beach and coastal path. Past the light-filled sitting room, graceful with its chandelier and deep sofas, newly refurbished bedrooms and suites have all the amenities: teas and coffee; fresh milk and chilled water in a mini-fridge; bathrobes and slippers, too, in superior rooms. Three rooms have a private terrace. At dinner and Sunday lunch, modern British menus in the brasserie might include seared Brixham scallops or Devon new-season lamb. Cooked-to-order breakfasts accompany home-made muesli and granola. It's a 15-minute walk to town.

MAP 1:D5
Meadfoot Sea Road
Torquay TQ1 2LQ
T: 01803 294722
W: meadfoot.com

BEDROOMS: 15. 1 on ground floor.
OPEN: all year, restaurant closed Sun eve and Mon eve Oct–Mar (supper menu available).
FACILITIES: lounge, bar, dining room, library, in-room TV (Freeview), terrace, parking.
BACKGROUND MUSIC: in public areas.
LOCATION: 3 mins' walk behind Meadfoot beach, 15 mins' walk from Torquay harbour.
CHILDREN: not under 15.
DOGS: allowed in 1 bedroom with own entrance, not inside main hotel.
CREDIT CARDS: Amex, MC, Visa.
PRICES: per room B&B single from £82.50, double £110–£250. À la carte £46, tasting menu £65. 2-night min. stay in high season and on bank holidays.

TRESCO Isles of Scilly

THE NEW INN

In a 'fantastic location' close to the harbour, the only pub on Robert Dorrien-Smith's private, car-free island is a 'relaxed' gathering place where the 'lovely staff' warmly welcome locals and holidaymakers alike. There's a canopied garden for hanging about in good weather; in the 'well-stocked' bar, a wood-burning stove is fired up on chilly days. Unfussy menus showcase 'very good' Scillonian produce, perhaps a 'catch of the day' with crushed Cornish new potatoes. Substantial renovation is planned in the bedrooms over winter 2021/22; in-room treats including ground coffee and home-made biscuits will remain. Guests may access the tennis and spa facilities at Tresco Island Spa (extra charge).

MAP 1: inset C1
New Grimsby
Tresco TR24 0QQ
T: 01720 422849
W: tresco.co.uk/staying/the-new-inn

BEDROOMS: 16. Some on ground floor.
OPEN: all year, limited opening in winter months.
FACILITIES: bar, residents' lounge, restaurant, in-room TV (Freeview), pavilion, beer garden, heated outdoor swimming pool (seasonal), use of Tresco Island Spa facilities (extra fee).
BACKGROUND MUSIC: in pub and restaurant, occasional live music events.
LOCATION: near New Grimsby harbour.
CHILDREN: all ages welcomed.
DOGS: allowed in public bar, beer garden, assistance dogs allowed in bedrooms.
CREDIT CARDS: MC, Visa.
PRICES: per room B&B £175–£245. À la carte £35.

TRUSHAM Devon

THE CRIDFORD INN

Come down a single-track road to reach this Teign valley pub, its thatched roof, cob walls and wide stone fireplaces. Quite likely as old as Trusham itself, the Devon longhouse was a nunnery, property of Buckfast Abbey, when it was listed in the Domesday Book. Today, under the hands-on ownership of Paul and Ness Moir, it is a dog-friendly inn and a convivial gathering spot for locals. The slate-floored pub and restaurant host Sunday roasts and everyday lunches and dinners (with interesting choices for vegetarians); alfresco meals and drinks may be taken on the suntrap terrace. Up the stairs, recently revamped bedrooms retain their sloping ceilings and exposed beams. Restorative country walks start from the door.

MAP 1:D4
Trusham TQ13 0NR
T: 01626 853694
W: thecridfordinn.co.uk

BEDROOMS: 4. Plus 2-bed cottage.
OPEN: all year.
FACILITIES: pub, restaurant, function room, in-room TV (Freeview), terrace, drying shed, pub and restaurant wheelchair accessible.
BACKGROUND MUSIC: 'appropriate' in pub and restaurant, occasional live music.
LOCATION: 12 miles SW of Exeter.
CHILDREN: all ages welcomed.
DOGS: allowed in 1 bedroom and cottage, pub, dog-friendly eating area.
CREDIT CARDS: MC, Visa.
PRICES: per room B&B £59–£169. À la carte £25. 1-night bookings refused weekends in high season.

TUNBRIDGE WELLS Kent

THE MOUNT EDGCUMBE

Surrounded by greenery, this family-run hotel and restaurant by the Common has been brought up to date with contemporary style and a sense of fun. Downstairs, wood floors, exposed brick walls and eye-catching pieces surround the real-ale connoisseurs and gastropub diners in the informal, split-level restaurant; a 6th-century sandstone cave shelters a snug bar. In warm weather, parasols spring up over picnic tables on the large patio. Perky bedrooms decorated in harmonious hues are up the stairs in the Grade II listed building. Each room is supplied with biscuits, a capsule coffee machine and all-natural toiletries; views are over leafy trees or the Edgcumbe Rocks. The town centre is a short walk away.

MAP 2:D4
The Common
Tunbridge Wells TN4 8BX
T: 01892 618854
W: themountedgcumbe.com

BEDROOMS: 6.
OPEN: all year, restaurant closed 25 Dec.
FACILITIES: bar, restaurant, cave, in-room TV (Freeview), garden.
BACKGROUND MUSIC: in bar, restaurant.
LOCATION: ½ mile from Tunbridge Wells train station.
CHILDREN: all ages welcomed.
DOGS: in bar, restaurant, garden, not in bedrooms.
CREDIT CARDS: Amex, MC, Visa.
PRICES: per room B&B £120–£180. À la carte £35.

ULVERSTON Cumbria

THE BAY HORSE

Watch the tide race in from Robert Lyons and Lesley Wheeler's traditional pub-with-rooms overlooking the Levens estuary – it's a thrilling sight that harks centuries back to the days when the inn was a stopover for coaches and horses before they crossed the sands to Lancaster. An 'amiable' place, this is a community hub that draws back birdwatchers, cyclists, walkers, dog owners and fishermen year after year. Homely bedrooms are supplied with board games, books and magazines; six rooms have an estuary-view balcony – all the better to watch the sunrise from. There are casual bar meals to be had, or candlelit dinners in the newly redecorated conservatory restaurant by the water's edge; mornings, breakfast is praised.

MAP 4: inset C2
Canal Foot
Ulverston LA12 9EL
T: 01229 583972
W: thebayhorsehotel.co.uk

BEDROOMS: 9.
OPEN: all year, restaurant closed Mon lunchtime (light bites available).
FACILITIES: bar/lounge, conservatory restaurant, in-room TV (Freeview), picnic area, parking, bar and restaurant wheelchair accessible.
BACKGROUND MUSIC: in bar, restaurant.
LOCATION: 1½ miles from town centre.
CHILDREN: not under 10.
DOGS: well-behaved dogs allowed in bedrooms, bar area, not in restaurant.
CREDIT CARDS: Amex, MC, Visa.
PRICES: per room B&B £110–£117.50. À la carte £40. 2-night min. stay at weekends May–Sept, bank holidays.

WARTLING Sussex

WARTLING PLACE

In a quiet hamlet close to the Pevensey Levels nature reserve, this Grade II listed former Georgian rectory stands in 'beautiful' gardens; 'delightful' bedrooms and 'delicious' breakfasts are within. Returning guests praise the 'attentive, responsive' hosts, Rowena and Barry Gittoes. There are prints, pictures and comfortable seating in the drawing room; bedrooms, supplied with coffee and Fairtrade teas, may have an antique four-poster bed and rural views towards the South Downs. In the garden-facing dining room, breakfast includes smoked salmon from Hastings, local sausages and eggs, and herbs from the garden. 'Convenient for Glyndebourne and the coast'; historic villages and National Trust houses are within reach.

MAP 2:E4
Wartling BN27 1RY
T: 01323 832590
W: wartlingplace.co.uk

BEDROOMS: 4. Plus 2-bed self-catering cottage, suitable for disabled.
OPEN: all year.
FACILITIES: drawing room, dining room, in-room smart TV, 3-acre garden, parking.
BACKGROUND MUSIC: none.
LOCATION: 5 miles E of Hailsham.
CHILDREN: not under 12.
DOGS: not allowed.
CREDIT CARDS: Amex, MC, Visa.
PRICES: per room B&B single £105–£120, double £140–£165. 2-night min. stay.

WARWICK Warwickshire

PARK COTTAGE

Bestrewn with hanging baskets of colourful blooms, Janet and Stuart Baldry's wonderfully wonky Grade II listed 15th-century house is by the entrance to Warwick Castle. 'Warm and welcoming', the owners exhibit 'truly attentive care and concern' for their B&B guests. Most of the 'comfortable' bedrooms, all different, are accessed across sloping floors and up a steep, narrow staircase. One has an antique four-poster bed under original beams; two can accommodate a family. A room on the ground floor has access to the pretty patio garden, home to a 300-year-old listed yew tree. 'Splendid' breakfasts, 'expertly cooked' by the host, are served at tables set on the original sandstone floor of the former castle dairy.

MAP 3:C6
113 West Street
Warwick CV34 6AH
T: 01926 410319
W: parkcottagewarwick.co.uk

BEDROOMS: 4. 1 on ground floor. Plus 2 self-catering cottages.
OPEN: all year except Christmas, New Year.
FACILITIES: reception/sitting area, breakfast room, in-room TV (Freeview), small garden, parking.
BACKGROUND MUSIC: none.
LOCATION: in town centre.
CHILDREN: all ages welcomed.
DOGS: allowed by prior arrangement in bedrooms (not unattended, own bed required), on lead in public areas.
CREDIT CARDS: Amex, MC, Visa.
PRICES: per room B&B from £96.
1-night bookings sometimes refused.

WATCHET Somerset

SWAIN HOUSE

In the heart of the historic harbour town that inspired Samuel Taylor Coleridge, Jason Robinson's chic, cocooning B&B is an ideal place in which to be idle as a painted ship upon a painted ocean. Ramble along the Coleridge Way if you must, or easily access the heritage West Somerset Railway. Alternatively, simply make yourself comfortable in one of the large bedrooms in this refurbished 18th-century house: each has been thoughtfully supplied with teas, coffee and fresh milk; waffle bathrobes and high-end toiletries; a slipper bath and walk-in shower in the bathroom. 'Beautifully laid out' breakfasts include a full veggie option; in the evening, a light cheese or charcuterie supper is available.

MAP 1:B5
48 Swain Street
Watchet TA23 0AG
T: 01984 631038
W: swain-house.com

BEDROOMS: 4.
OPEN: all year except Christmas, New Year.
FACILITIES: lounge/dining room, in-room TV (Freeview), public car park 20 yards away.
BACKGROUND MUSIC: none.
LOCATION: 100 yards from harbour marina.
CHILDREN: not under 12.
DOGS: not allowed.
CREDIT CARDS: Amex, MC, Visa.
PRICES: per room B&B single from £125, double from £140.

WEDMORE Somerset

THE SWAN

Go where the locals go, in this lively village in the Somerset Levels: this bring-the-dog, kids-in-tow pub-with-rooms humming with a 'lovely, informal atmosphere'. There are real ales and ciders, plus an all-day snack menu, in the bar; at lunch and dinner, perhaps eaten alfresco on the garden terrace, the menu of unfussy gastropub dishes might include such vegetarian options as spiced beetroot Wellington, nettle pesto. Staying guests spend the night in one of the 'smart', rustic-chic bedrooms upstairs. 'Breakfast is a real treat.' Beyond the village, walking and cycling paths reach out and far about. Part of the Stay Original Co.; see also Timbrell's Yard, Bradford-on-Avon, and The White Hart, Somerton (Shortlist entries).

MAP 1:B6
Cheddar Road
Wedmore BS28 4EQ
T: 01934 710337
W: theswanwedmore.com

BEDROOMS: 7.
OPEN: all year.
FACILITIES: bar, restaurant, in-room TV, civil wedding licence, function facilities, terrace, large garden, parking.
BACKGROUND MUSIC: in bar.
LOCATION: in village centre.
CHILDREN: all ages welcomed.
DOGS: allowed in bedrooms, public rooms.
CREDIT CARDS: MC, Visa.
PRICES: per room B&B £85–£195.
À la carte £27.

WESTGATE Co. Durham

WESTGATE MANOR

A stroll from ancient woodland, in a Weardale village in the heart of the North Pennines, this personably run guest house is owned by 'welcoming, friendly and helpful' hosts Kathryn and Stuart Dobson. The Victorian manor house has chandeliers, antique furnishings and displays of fresh flowers; huge windows in the wood burner-warmed lounge look toward the rolling slopes – look out for grazing sheep, strolling pheasants and deer. High-ceilinged and traditionally decorated, characterful bedrooms take in countryside views. Two rooms have a grand four-poster bed; all have a walk-in shower and a roll-top bath in the bathroom. Breakfast is taken in the orangery; evening meals may be ordered in advance.

MAP 4:B3
Westgate DL13 1JT
T: 01388 517371
W: westgatemanor.co.uk

BEDROOMS: 5.
OPEN: all year except Christmas, New Year.
FACILITIES: lounge, dining room, orangery, garden room, in-room TV (Freeview), patio, secure bicycle storage.
BACKGROUND MUSIC: in reception, dining room.
LOCATION: 25 miles W of Durham.
CHILDREN: all ages welcomed.
DOGS: not allowed.
CREDIT CARDS: Amex, MC, Visa.
PRICES: per room B&B £129–£145.
À la carte £27.

WESTLETON Suffolk

THE WESTLETON CROWN

Ramblers, birders and seaside-seekers make their
way to this refreshed 12th-century coaching inn,
in a quiet village close to the Suffolk coast. Wood
fires, deep armchairs, snug corners and a dog-
friendly approach create an informal atmosphere
in the bar and lounge; at mealtimes, diners sit
in the cosy pub parlour, bright conservatory or
terraced courtyard for unfussy modern dishes –
pan-fried bream, saffron and chorizo risotto, say.
Recently refurbished bedrooms are decorated in
an updated rustic style; duplex rooms have bunk
beds for young guests. The RSPB nature reserve
at Minsmere is a ten-minute drive away; a circular
walk calls for a pit stop at sister inn The Ship at
Dunwich (see Shortlist entry).

MAP 2:B6
The Street
Westleton IP17 3AD
T: 01728 648777
W: westletoncrown.co.uk

BEDROOMS: 34. Most in cottages,
converted stables and purpose-built
blocks in grounds, 1 suitable for
disabled.
OPEN: all year.
FACILITIES: bar, lounge, snug, 2 dining
areas, in-room TV (Freeview), civil
wedding licence, terraced garden.
BACKGROUND MUSIC: all day in dining
areas.
LOCATION: in countryside, 3 miles from
Dunwich beach.
CHILDREN: all ages welcomed.
DOGS: allowed in bar/lounge,
bedrooms.
CREDIT CARDS: Amex, MC, Visa.
PRICES: per room B&B £99–£230.
À la carte £30. 2-night min. stay at
weekends.

WHEATHILL Shropshire

THE OLD RECTORY

Izzy Barnard's flower-filled Georgian house is
a rural retreat in prime Shropshire hacking and
walking country – horses, hikers and hounds
are cheerfully welcomed. Piles of books and, in
cool weather, a blazing fire in the drawing room
help guests wind down; a small but soothing
sauna completes the job. Country-style bedrooms
have homely comforts, with a large bed, antique
furnishings and biscuits. Horses and dogs have
their own quarters. Ask for a four-course dinner,
served communally and by candlelight, or sup,
simply, on soup and a sandwich. Mornings, find
home-made granola and compotes, local sausages,
and eggs from resident hens and ducks. Guides
and route cards detail nearby bridleways.

MAP 3:C5
Wheathill WV16 6QT
T: 01746 787209
W: theoldrectorywheathill.com

BEDROOMS: 3.
OPEN: all year except Christmas, Jan.
FACILITIES: drawing room, dining
room, in-room TV (Freeview), sauna,
7-acre gardens, boot room, tack room,
loose boxes for horses.
BACKGROUND MUSIC: none.
LOCATION: 7 miles from Ludlow.
CHILDREN: all ages welcomed, by
arrangement.
DOGS: allowed in boot room.
CREDIT CARDS: MC, Visa.
PRICES: per room B&B single £80–£120,
double £95–£139. Set dinner £35,
supper tray £10. 2-night min. stay
preferred.

WILLIAN Hertfordshire

THE FOX AT WILLIAN

In a quiet village mentioned in the Domesday Book, this inviting pub by the parish church is a 'popular' gathering place for locals and townies on a getaway. On a sunny spring day this year, Guide inspectors found 'a very jolly Friday-afternoon atmosphere'. All-day refreshments, well-cooked pub classics and inspired-by-the-seasons dishes are served in the pared-back bar and dining room, or under heated parasols in the landscaped garden. Overnight guests sleep in one of the contemporary bedrooms, where rustic features mix with modern amenities (air conditioning, a rainfall shower). Dog-friendly garden rooms have a terrace, too. Part of Anglian Country Inns; see The White Horse, Brancaster Staithe (main entry).

MAP 2:C4
Willian SG6 2AE
T: 01462 480233
W: foxatwillian.co.uk

BEDROOMS: 8. 4, in garden annexe, on ground floor.
OPEN: all year, restaurant closed Sun eve (bar food available).
FACILITIES: bar (Sky TV), restaurant, conservatory, in-room TV (Freeview), 2 terraces, garden; restaurant, bar, garden bedrooms wheelchair accessible.
BACKGROUND MUSIC: in bar.
LOCATION: in village, 2 miles S of Letchworth Garden City.
CHILDREN: all ages welcomed.
DOGS: small dogs (and cats) allowed in garden bedrooms, bar.
CREDIT CARDS: Amex, MC, Visa.
PRICES: per room B&B single £110–£130, double £130–£165. À la carte £35.

WOLTERTON Norfolk

THE SARACEN'S HEAD

'The most welcoming staff make this a pleasant stop.' Tim and Janie Elwes's 'enjoyable' inn stands in 'a beautifully rural setting' not far from the north Norfolk coast. The ivy-covered 19th-century building was designed to mimic a Tuscan farmhouse; it has bright public spaces, cosy-making wood burners, and books and maps to browse. Simply and cheerily decorated, bedrooms have a well-supplied drinks tray, plus natural Norfolk toiletries; a family room comfortably accommodates four people. At mealtimes, plates of local produce – Brancaster-smoked salmon, Cromer crab, East Anglian cheeses – are 'very well served'. Beaches, stately homes, and day boats along the River Bure are all within reach.

MAP 2:A5
Wall Road
Wolterton NR11 7LZ
T: 01263 768909
W: saracenshead-norfolk.co.uk

BEDROOMS: 6.
OPEN: all year except 5 days over Christmas.
FACILITIES: lounge, bar, restaurant, in-room TV (Freeview), courtyard, 1-acre garden, restaurant and bar wheelchair accessible, no adapted toilet.
BACKGROUND MUSIC: in bar and dining rooms.
LOCATION: 5 miles N of Aylsham.
CHILDREN: all ages welcomed.
DOGS: allowed in bedrooms, back bar (booking required), not in restaurant.
CREDIT CARDS: MC, Visa.
PRICES: per room B&B single £80, double £120. À la carte £36.

WOODBRIDGE Suffolk
THE CROWN

Within easy reach of the Suffolk coast, this style-conscious 16th-century coaching inn in the centre of an animated riverside town has a coolly contemporary air. Decorated in a minimalist palette, bedrooms (some snug) have a 'well-stocked' hospitality tray; British-made toiletries are 'a definite plus'. (Some traffic noise may be audible.) Downstairs, the wooden sailing skiff in the glass-roofed bar is a nod to the area's nautical heritage. Eat in: pub classics and more modern dishes – perhaps crispy pork belly, squash purée, mushroom and truffle bubble 'n' squeak – are served in the split-level restaurant and on the wide terrace. Part of The Hotel Folk; see also The Swan Hotel & Spa, Lavenham (Shortlist entry).

MAP 2:C5
Thoroughfare
Woodbridge IP12 1AD
T: 01394 384242
W: thecrownatwoodbridge.co.uk

BEDROOMS: 10.
OPEN: all year, restaurant closed Sun eve.
FACILITIES: restaurant, bar, private dining room, in-room TV (Sky), terrace, parking, restaurant and bar wheelchair accessible.
BACKGROUND MUSIC: in public areas, plus regular live music.
LOCATION: in town centre.
CHILDREN: all ages welcomed.
DOGS: allowed in bar.
CREDIT CARDS: Amex, MC, Visa.
PRICES: per room B&B £110–£185. À la carte £34. 2-night min. stay at weekends.

WOODCHESTER Gloucestershire
WOODCHESTER VALLEY VINEYARD

Surrounded by the green fields of the Stroud valleys, Fiona Shiner's family-owned vineyard and winery shelter a modern B&B. Spacious duplex suites in a sympathetically restored barn each have a mini-kitchenette and a log burner-warmed sitting area; a trio of private terraces takes in far-reaching views across the valley and vine-covered hills. Set off on the walking or cycling routes that wind through this part of the south Cotswolds; return for a pre-booked vineyard tour and a tasting of the award-winning wines. Breakfast hampers (charged extra) include freshly baked bread, croissants, preserves, yogurt, fruit and juice. At the Cellar Door shop, stock up on bottles of wine before heading home.

MAP 3:E5
Convent Lane
Woodchester GL5 5HR
T: 07808 650883
W: woodchestervalleyvineyard.co.uk

BEDROOMS: 3. 1 suitable for disabled, plus 2-bed farmhouse available for self-catering.
OPEN: all year.
FACILITIES: tasting room, in-room TV (Sky), 40-acre vineyard, winery (tours, tutored tastings), electric car charging point.
BACKGROUND MUSIC: none.
LOCATION: 3 miles from Stroud.
CHILDREN: not under 12.
DOGS: allowed in farmhouse.
CREDIT CARDS: Amex, MC, Visa.
PRICES: per room £120–£180. Continental breakfast hamper £20. 2-night min. stay at weekends.

WOOLACOMBE Devon

WATERSMEET

Perched above Combesgate beach, this former Edwardian gentleman's retreat benefits from 'wonderful' clifftop views. Run with 'friendly, helpful staff', the 'comfortable, relaxed' hotel makes full use of its location. Its lounges, large, glass-fronted terrace and gardens have spectacular seascapes and glorious sunsets; all but three bedrooms look out to Lundy Island and Baggy Point. In the informal bistro and candlelit restaurant (every table with a view over the sea), local produce features on British menus – whole sole, brown shrimps, asparagus; duck breast, dauphinoise potato, duck roll. Breakfast is 'plentiful'. To stretch the legs, there are walks through National Trust land, or steps down to the sandy beach.

MAP 1:B4
Mortehoe
Woolacombe EX34 7EB
T: 01271 870333
W: watersmeethotel.co.uk

BEDROOMS: 27. 3 on ground floor, 1 suitable for disabled.
OPEN: all year.
FACILITIES: lift, lounge, snug, bar, restaurant, bistro, in-room TV (Freeview), civil wedding licence, function facilities, terrace, ½-acre garden, indoor and heated outdoor swimming pools, treatment room, restaurant wheelchair accessible.
BACKGROUND MUSIC: in public areas.
LOCATION: behind beach, slightly N of village centre.
CHILDREN: all ages welcomed.
DOGS: not allowed.
CREDIT CARDS: MC, Visa.
PRICES: per room B&B £160–£490. À la carte (bistro) £35, 2- and 3-course table d'hôte menus (restaurant) £42 and £50.

WORCESTER Worcestershire

THE MANOR COACH HOUSE

In a 'peaceful' rural hamlet, just right for 'a good night's sleep', Chrissie Mitchell's well-cared-for B&B is within easy reach of the town centre and Worcester cathedral. Returning guests know to expect a warm welcome, with tea and cake, from the enthusiastic, hands-on hostess. Set around a courtyard, 'immaculate' bedrooms in converted outbuildings each have their own entrance. 'The facilities are excellent': there's fresh milk for tea and coffee; bathrobes and toiletries are supplied. A duplex family suite (suitable for children over four because of the stairs) also has a kitchenette. Special diets can be catered for at breakfast; at dinner, pubs are within walking distance. Local information is readily provided.

MAP 3:C5
Hindlip Lane
Hindlip
Worcester WR3 8SJ
T: 01905 456457
W: manorcoachhouse.co.uk

BEDROOMS: 5. All in converted outbuildings, 3 on ground floor, plus 2 self-catering units.
OPEN: all year except Christmas.
FACILITIES: breakfast room, in-room TV (Freeview), 1-acre garden.
BACKGROUND MUSIC: none.
LOCATION: 2 miles from city centre.
CHILDREN: all ages welcomed.
DOGS: not allowed.
CREDIT CARDS: MC, Visa.
PRICES: per room B&B single from £74, double from £89.

YELVERTON Devon

CIDER HOUSE

In the sprawling grounds of the National Trust's
Buckland Abbey, this handsomely decorated
property is run with bonhomie by Bertie and
Bryony Hancock. Once the medieval abbey's brew
house – the granite supports for the old cider
press are still in place – the stone-built home is a
bright, birdsong-accompanied place to be. There
are flowers and deep sofas in the drawing room;
country-chic bedrooms have restorative views
through mullioned windows. Residents receive
passes for the abbey, and can explore its gardens
outside public visiting times. NOTE: As the
Guide went to press, the Hancocks announced
that the house will be run on a self-catering basis
for up to eight guests. Home-cooked meals on the
Aga may be provided on request.

MAP 1:D4
Buckland Abbey
Yelverton PL20 6EZ
T: 01822 259062
w: cider-house.co.uk

BEDROOMS: 4. Plus 2 adults-only self-
catering shepherd's huts.
OPEN: all year.
FACILITIES: drawing room, in-room
TV (Freeview), terrace, garden,
700-acre grounds, parking.
BACKGROUND MUSIC: none.
LOCATION: 1 mile from village, 4 miles
N of Plymouth.
CHILDREN: all ages welcomed.
DOGS: not allowed.
CREDIT CARDS: MC, Visa.
PRICES: from £1,468 for a long
weekend in low season.

YORK Yorkshire

BAR CONVENT

By the city's medieval walls, England's oldest
active convent houses a community of sisters,
who share their peaceful garden, domed chapel
and antique religious texts with B&B guests.
Immaculate, up-to-date bedrooms in the Grade
I listed building vary in size; two accommodate
a family of three. In a Victorian atrium, the café
serves hearty breakfasts, morning coffees, light
lunches and afternoon teas, plus a selection of
daily specials. On a warm day, the suntrap garden
is ideal for alfresco meals and snacks. There's
a communal kitchen for DIY dinners; York's
eateries are on the doorstep. Guests receive a
discount on entry to the on-site Living Heritage
Centre and the 17th-century convent.

MAP 4:D4
17 Blossom Street
York YO24 1AQ
T: 01904 643238
w: bar-convent.org.uk

BEDROOMS: 20. 4 with shared
bathrooms.
OPEN: all year except some days over
Christmas, café closed Sun except for
residents' breakfast.
FACILITIES: lift (to 1st and 2nd floors),
sitting room, kitchen, licensed
café, meeting rooms, in-room TV
(Freeview), ¼-acre garden, Victorian
atrium, 18th-century chapel, museum,
shop.
BACKGROUND MUSIC: none.
LOCATION: 5 mins' walk from the
railway station.
CHILDREN: all ages welcomed (guest
kitchen, with use of washing machine
for small additional charge).
DOGS: only assistance dogs allowed.
CREDIT CARDS: MC, Visa.
PRICES: per room B&B single £40–£86,
double £105–£150.

ABERDEEN
ATHOLL HOTEL

The spires of this Victorian Gothic Revival building make this traditional hotel an easy-to-spot beacon in a quiet location within reach of the city centre. It is popular with business travellers, though returning guests of all stripes praise the friendly welcome and fuss-free accommodation. Bedrooms range in size, from single rooms to family suites; in-room amenities include a tea and coffee tray, a hairdryer, an iron and ironing board. The restaurant, bar and lounge serve straightforward, generously portioned dishes such as roast rib of beef or a prawn and smoked salmon platter. At breakfast, try tattie scones or smoked Finnan haddie. Convenient for the airport; castles, distilleries and golf courses are close by.

MAP 5:C3
54 King's Gate
Aberdeen AB15 4YN
T: 01224 323505
W: atholl-aberdeen.co.uk

BEDROOMS: 34. 2 suitable for disabled.
OPEN: all year, restaurant closed 1 Jan.
FACILITIES: lift (to 1st floor), lounge, bar, restaurant, in-room TV (Sky Sports), wedding/function facilities, patio, parking.
BACKGROUND MUSIC: in restaurant.
LOCATION: 1½ miles W of city centre.
CHILDREN: all ages welcomed.
DOGS: only assistance dogs allowed.
CREDIT CARDS: Amex, MC, Visa.
PRICES: per room B&B single £80–£99, double £99–£109. À la carte £30.

ABERFELDY Perth and Kinross
FORTINGALL HOTEL

'Good food, spacious rooms, and friendly and efficient service continue to make this an excellent place,' say returnees this year of Mags and Robbie Cairns's unpretentious, 'enjoyable' country hotel. At the entrance to Glen Lyon, sheep-dotted fields stretching before it, the old coaching inn is in a 'beautiful, tranquil' part of Highland Perthshire. The convivial bar has pictures and photographs, pickled eggs and crisps, and live folk and blues music on Friday nights. Chef David Dunn's substantial dishes use local meat and game, plus lobster 'from a friend's boat on the Forth'. Bright bedrooms are supplied with coffee, shortbread and a decanter of whisky. Walking, cycling and fishing are on the doorstep.

MAP 5:D2
Old Street
Fortingall
Aberfeldy PH15 2NQ
T: 01887 830367
W: fortingall.com

BEDROOMS: 11.
OPEN: Wed–Sun all year.
FACILITIES: bar, lounge, library, dining room, function room, in-room TV, wedding facilities, garden, secure bicycle storage.
BACKGROUND MUSIC: in restaurant, live folk music in bar on Fri nights.
LOCATION: 8 miles W of Aberfeldy.
CHILDREN: all ages welcomed.
DOGS: allowed.
CREDIT CARDS: MC, Visa.
PRICES: per room B&B single £100, double £190–£230.

ALLANTON Scottish Borders
ALLANTON INN

In a sleepy village with a spirited history, Katrina and William Reynolds's 18th-century coaching inn is a 'good-value' base for walkers, cyclists, fisherfolk and visitors in search of a tranquil rural break. Family run for more than a decade, the relaxed restaurant-with-rooms has 'a happy blend of modern furnishings and artwork, and the feel of a traditional country pub'. At mealtimes, Borders produce is the taste of the day: expect home-baked breads and Scottish seafood platters among the 'generous portions of first-class food' served in the dining rooms and rear garden. Up-to-date bedrooms are supplied with Scottish biscuits, Highland toiletries and information on local walks; the helpful owners have tips to share.

MAP 5:E3
Main Street
Allanton TD11 3JZ
T: 01890 818260
W: allantoninn.co.uk

BEDROOMS: 6.
OPEN: all year except 25–26 Dec.
FACILITIES: bar, 2 restaurant areas, in-room TV (Freeview), wedding/function facilities, large garden, bicycle storage, drying room.
BACKGROUND MUSIC: in bar, restaurant.
LOCATION: in village centre.
CHILDREN: all ages welcomed.
DOGS: allowed in some areas, by prior arrangement.
CREDIT CARDS: Amex, MC, Visa.
PRICES: per room B&B £80–£105.

APPLECROSS Highland
APPLECROSS INN

Well worth taking, the scenic, single-track Bealach na Ba winds across the remote Applecross peninsula to reach Judith Fish's unpretentious hostelry, where low-key charm and cheer spill on to the shoreside terrace. Outside, the views stretch across the Inner Sound of Raasay; inside, malt whiskies, Scottish gins and Applecross ale are just right for sipping by the peat fire. In the small dining room or alfresco, ultra-fresh seafood, perhaps prawns and king scallops, come straight from the bay; in spring and summer, a food truck sells fish and chips, coffees and sweet treats. Freshly spruced bedrooms have no TV, but superlative water views (and perhaps some pub noise). Cyclists, walkers and kayakers welcomed.

MAP 5:C1
Shore Street
Applecross IV54 8LR
T: 01520 744262
W: applecrossinn.co.uk

BEDROOMS: 7. 1 on ground floor.
OPEN: all year, no accommodation for 2 weeks over Christmas, New Year, restaurant closed 25 Dec, 1–2 Jan.
FACILITIES: bar, dining room, beer garden, bicycle storage, bar, dining room wheelchair accessible, adapted toilet.
BACKGROUND MUSIC: 'easy listening' and traditional Scottish in bar.
LOCATION: 85 miles W of Inverness, opposite the Isle of Skye, approx. 2 hours' drive.
CHILDREN: all ages welcomed, not in bar after 9 pm.
DOGS: allowed in bedrooms (own bedding required), in bar/dining area.
CREDIT CARDS: Amex, MC, Visa.
PRICES: per room B&B single £90–£170, double £140–£170. À la carte £35.

BALLYGRANT Argyll and Bute
KILMENY COUNTRY HOUSE

'Fabulous hosts' Margaret and Blair Rozga are hailed for the warm hospitality, and home-baked treats, they extend to their guests at this 19th-century farmhouse on the southernmost of the Inner Hebrides islands. Surrounded by green acres of family farm, the Rozgas' home is handsomely furnished in country house style. The traditionally decorated bedrooms have antiques and 'spectacular views' across hills and glen. Some rooms are capacious (a suite with its own kitchen suits a family); others have access to a sheltered garden; all have tea, coffee, home-made biscuits, and fresh milk in the mini-fridge. Substantial breakfasts with home-made oatcakes and preserves are 'worth getting up for'.

MAP 5:D1
Ballygrant
Isle of Islay PA45 7QW
T: 01496 840668
W: kilmeny.co.uk

BEDROOMS: 5. 2 on ground floor.
OPEN: Mar–Oct.
FACILITIES: drawing room, dining room, sun lounge, in-room TV (Freeview), ½-acre garden.
BACKGROUND MUSIC: none.
LOCATION: ½ mile S of Ballygrant, 10 mins' drive to Port Askaig.
CHILDREN: not under 6.
DOGS: allowed in some bedrooms, not in public rooms.
CREDIT CARDS: none accepted.
PRICES: per room B&B £160–£190. 1-night bookings sometimes refused.

BARCALDINE Argyll and Bute
ARDTORNA

Light and bright inside, Karen and Sean O'Byrne's super-modern, eco-friendly house by Loch Creran has 'lovely views' over the water. B&B guests are welcomed with scones fresh from the oven; home-made whisky cream liqueur is further temptation. Spruced-up, loch-view bedrooms have a king-size bed and under-floor heating, plus chocolates and good toiletries. Fruit smoothies accompany the 'good' breakfast in the glass-fronted dining room. Choose among sweet and savoury pancakes, griddled waffles and a Scottish platter with Stornoway black pudding and tattie scones. The 'very helpful' hosts assist with planning day-trips to castles and islands, and can point out the best spots for a dram. 'Thoroughly recommended.'

MAP 5:D1
Mill Farm
Barcaldine PA37 1SE
T: 01631 720125
W: ardtorna.co.uk

BEDROOMS: 4. Plus self-catering accommodation in adjacent building.
OPEN: Apr–Nov.
FACILITIES: sitting room, dining room, in-room TV (Freeview), 1-acre farmland.
BACKGROUND MUSIC: traditional in dining room.
LOCATION: 12 miles N of Oban.
CHILDREN: not under 12.
DOGS: not allowed.
CREDIT CARDS: MC, Visa.
PRICES: per person B&B £80–£110.

BRIDGEND Argyll and Bute

BRIDGEND HOTEL

On the Inner Hebrides island of Islay, this stone-built hotel – a village landmark where two main roads meet – has welcomed visitors for more than 150 years. Recent refurbishments have given the public areas and bedrooms a facelift, while retaining some tweedy accents; the log burner crackles on. In the restaurant, local produce includes Loch Gruinart oysters and game from Islay estates; more casual dining, plus whiskies, gins and ales from the island, is in the public bar. Upstairs, simply, airily decorated bedrooms are supplied with local toiletries and Scottish tablet. After a breakfast kipper, set out to spot seal and sea eagle, visit distilleries, or follow any of the 'lovely' walking trails nearby.

MAP 5:D1
Bridgend
Isle of Islay PA44 7PB
T: 01496 810212
W: bridgend-hotel.com

BEDROOMS: 11. 1 family room with bunk bed.
OPEN: all year except 25 Dec and 1 Jan.
FACILITIES: lounge bar, public bar, restaurant, in-room TV (Freeview), wedding facilities, drying room, terrace, garden, ½-acre grounds, public areas wheelchair accessible, adapted toilet.
BACKGROUND MUSIC: a mix of traditional and modern Scottish music in public areas.
LOCATION: in village centre.
CHILDREN: all ages welcomed.
DOGS: well-behaved dogs allowed in bedrooms, bar.
CREDIT CARDS: Amex, MC, Visa.
PRICES: per room B&B £120–£205. À la carte £30.

BRUICHLADDICH Argyll and Bute

LOCH GORM HOUSE

On this southernmost island of the Inner Hebrides, Fiona Doyle runs her 'clean, comfortable' B&B in a stone-built house, steps from the shores of Loch Indaal. Cosily decorated and 'excellently appointed', the bedrooms have 'stunning views' over the bay or across the garden. 'Our room had fresh flowers, an amazing selection of teas and a good shower.' 'Delicious' scones are offered on arrival; breakfasts are praised, too. 'Friendly and helpful', the hostess has a wealth of local information to share, and can recommend restaurants and walking routes. Wellies, coats and beach towels may be borrowed for coastal wanderings. A bonus: 'The B&B's proximity to the wonderful Bruichladdich distillery makes a visit a necessity.'

MAP 5:D1
Bruichladdich
Isle of Islay PA49 7UN
T: 01496 850139
W: lochgormhouse.com

BEDROOMS: 3.
OPEN: all year.
FACILITIES: drawing room, dining room, in-room TV (Freeview), 1-acre garden, drying facilities.
BACKGROUND MUSIC: none.
LOCATION: on seafront, outside village.
CHILDREN: all ages welcomed.
DOGS: well-behaved dogs by special arrangement, not in bedrooms.
CREDIT CARDS: MC, Visa.
PRICES: per room B&B £145–£165.

COVE Argyll and Bute

KNOCKDERRY HOUSE HOTEL

By the shores of Loch Long, romantic turrets and towers add to the Scottish country house experience of Beth and Murdo Macleod's dog-friendly hotel. The listed baronial building stands in manicured lawns near the Arrochar Alps, surrounded by coastal walks and forest paths; within it are handsome rooms with original fireplaces, wood panelling, tartan carpets and notable stained glass. Several of the freshly redecorated bedrooms have views over the water towards the Argyllshire hills. Imaginative four-course dinners are served in the loch-facing restaurant; more informal meals may be taken in the lounge bar. There are novels and board games to entertain; in nearby Helensburgh, Charles Rennie Mackintosh's Hill House.

MAP 5:D1
Shore Road
Cove G84 0NX
T: 01436 842283
W: knockderryhouse.co.uk

BEDROOMS: 15.
OPEN: all year except Christmas.
FACILITIES: lounge bar, 2 dining rooms, library/billiard room, in-room TV, civil wedding licence, function facilities, terrace, ½-acre garden, dining areas wheelchair accessible, private moorings.
BACKGROUND MUSIC: 'soft classical' in restaurant.
LOCATION: on a peninsula in the Firth of Clyde, 17 miles from Helensburgh.
CHILDREN: all ages welcomed (no special facilities).
DOGS: in 5 bedrooms, public rooms, dog-friendly dining room.
CREDIT CARDS: Amex, MC, Visa.
PRICES: per room £95–£225.
À la carte £44.50. 1-night bookings refused over New Year.

NEW

DORNOCH Sutherland

LINKS HOUSE

At once grand and intimate, this sumptuously refurbished hotel overlooking the green at the Royal Dornoch Golf Club has a relaxed, country house feel. Bucolic landscapes and paintings of Highland cows decorate the Victorian manse; traditionally, but unstuffily, decorated bedrooms and suites are spread across the main house, the Georgian-styled Mews and the late Victorian-styled Glenshiel. At mealtimes, pick an ambience to suit: Mara restaurant has fine, modern menus; the bar/brasserie serves informal dishes. The sandy beach is within a five-minute stroll, and the diversions (fishing expeditions, whisky tours, etc) are many, but guests might choose to simply sink, in comfort and contentment, into a deep armchair by a peat fire.

MAP 5:B2
Golf Road
Dornoch IV25 3LW
T: 01862 810279
W: linkshousedornoch.com

BEDROOMS: 13. 5 in Glenshiel, 3 in Mews, 5 on ground floor, 1 suitable for disabled. Plus 2 apartments.
OPEN: all year except 2–3 months in winter.
FACILITIES: 2 drawing rooms (honesty bars), library, bar/brasserie, restaurant, in-room TV (Sky), wedding facilities, meeting/function facilities, terraces, lawns, putting green, sporting bothy, salmon fishing beat.
BACKGROUND MUSIC: in public areas, live music in bar/brasserie.
LOCATION: 10 mins' walk from town centre.
CHILDREN: all ages welcomed.
DOGS: only service dogs allowed.
CREDIT CARDS: Amex, MC, Visa.
PRICES: per room B&B from £225.
À la carte (brasserie) £30, (restaurant) £60, tasting menu £75.

MAP 5:C2
Lewiston
Drumnadrochit IV63 6UW
T: 01456 450991
W: staylochness.co.uk

BEDROOMS: 11. 4 in annexe, 1 on ground floor suitable for disabled, plus bunkhouse.
OPEN: all year except 25 Dec.
FACILITIES: bar, restaurant, in-room TV, wedding facilities, beer garden, 'courtesy bus' for local pick-ups and drop-offs.
BACKGROUND MUSIC: in bar, restaurant.
LOCATION: off the A82, in village 16 miles SW of Inverness.
CHILDREN: all ages welcomed.
DOGS: clean, well-behaved dogs allowed in 1 bedroom, bar.
CREDIT CARDS: Amex, MC, Visa.
PRICES: per room B&B £95–£200. À la carte £25.

DRUMNADROCHIT Highland
THE LOCH NESS INN

Hikers and cyclists stop for the simple comforts of this 'friendly' 160-year-old coaching inn, a 'busy and bustling' local gathering place in a village on the Great Glen Way. There are Scottish whiskies and gins, hand-pulled ciders and locally brewed real ales in the bar; in the slate-floored restaurant, ingredients for classic pub dishes are drawn from nearby waters, farms and estates. Throughout, nature paintings add interest. Accommodation is in fuss-free bedrooms made homely with wool throws and tweedy cushions, tea and coffee, Scottish toiletries; budget-friendly bunkhouse rooms overlooking the River Coiltie suit groups or a family. Hearty breakfast choices include porridge, smoked haddock and a 'full Highland'.

MAP 5:D2
Kirkstyle Square
Dunning PH2 0RR
T: 01764 684248
W: thekirkstyleinn.co.uk

BEDROOMS: 4. All in adjacent building.
OPEN: all year except 25–26 Dec, 1 Jan.
FACILITIES: bar, snug, lounges, dining room, Garden Larder café/farm shop, pizza bar, in-room smart TV (Freeview), wedding facilities, beer garden.
BACKGROUND MUSIC: in public areas, occasional live fiddle music.
LOCATION: in village, 10 miles SW of Perth.
CHILDREN: all ages welcomed.
DOGS: 'very welcome' in all areas, not on beds.
CREDIT CARDS: Amex, MC, Visa.
PRICES: per room B&B £105–£155. À la carte £40.

DUNNING Perth and Kinross
THE KIRKSTYLE INN & ROOMS

In a conservation village with history in its ancient stones, this well-liked, log fire-warmed village inn brims with genial hospitality and a traditional pub ethos. Well-worn leather armchairs and eclectic bits and pieces dot the stone-walled bar, where the wide range of drinks includes the pub's own Risky Kelt beer. Modern pub favourites feature on the weekly changing menu; a blackboard lists daily specials. Ten paces from the door, simply furnished bedrooms in a separate building have a large orthopaedic bed and, perhaps, a slipper bath in the modern bathroom. A continental breakfast (freshly baked croissants, muesli, yogurt, fruit) may be delivered to the room; the café/farm shop has sandwiches and sweet treats.

EDINBURGH
THE BALMORAL

An Edinburgh icon fronted by a kilted doorman, this Victorian railway stop-over is today a grand 21st-century hotel (Rocco Forte Hotels) with a Michelin-starred restaurant, a chic brasserie, an award-winning spa and a choice of inviting places to take tea. (Whisky, too, if that's your preference.) In bespoke Balmoral tartan, Hebridean blues and heather hues, many of the elegant bedrooms and suites look towards Edinburgh Castle and Arthur's Seat. Each room has an 'extremely comfortable' bed, a marble bathroom, robes and slippers. Lounge under the glass dome and Venetian chandelier of the Palm Court and savour the place: the hotel's landmark clock has been set three minutes fast since 1902, so no one misses their train.

MAP 5:D2
1 Princes Street
Edinburgh EH2 2EQ
T: 0131 556 2414
W: roccofortehotels.com/hotels-and-resorts/the-balmoral-hotel

BEDROOMS: 187. 3 suitable for disabled.
OPEN: all year.
FACILITIES: drawing room, tea lounge, 2 bars, restaurant, brasserie, in-room TV (Freeview), wedding facilities, conferences, 15-metre indoor swimming pool, spa, gym, valet parking.
BACKGROUND MUSIC: in public areas.
LOCATION: in city centre.
CHILDREN: all ages welcomed.
DOGS: allowed in bedrooms, public areas where food and drink are not served.
CREDIT CARDS: Amex, MC, Visa.
PRICES: per room B&B from £200. À la carte £80 (restaurant), £42.50 (brasserie).

NEW

EDINBURGH
BARONY HOUSE

The romantic ideals of the Arts and Crafts movement colour this restored Victorian terraced house, which is enthusiastically run as a B&B by Brisbane natives Susan and Paul Johnson. The hostess, an artist and a descendant of John Ruskin, has painted decorative friezes in the elegant, high-ceilinged bedrooms; William Morris fabrics adorn eye-catching oversized headboards. Down stone steps, a separate entrance leads to two rooms (one with a private garden) that share a lounge and a kitchen. Served on linen-dressed tables, breakfast includes home-baked bread and Aussie pikelets. The hosts have a wealth of local information; buses and taxis easily connect the conservation neighbourhood to the city centre.

MAP 5:D2
20 Mayfield Gardens
Edinburgh EH9 2BZ
T: 0131 662 9938
W: baronyhouse.co.uk

BEDROOMS: 7. 2 in 'Servants' Quarters' with shared lounge and kitchen.
OPEN: all year except 1 week over Christmas; open for Hogmanay.
FACILITIES: honesty bar, dining room, in-room TV (Freeview).
BACKGROUND MUSIC: classical in public rooms.
LOCATION: in Mayfield, 20 mins' walk from the centre; buses and taxis available.
CHILDREN: not under 10.
DOGS: not allowed.
CREDIT CARDS: MC, Visa.
PRICES: per room B&B £119–£200. 3-night stays preferred in summer.

EDINBURGH
THE DUNSTANE HOUSES

Two handsomely refurbished Victorian villas –
Dunstane House, and Hampton House, opposite
– make up one smart hotel, in a peaceful area just
beyond the city centre. From 'cosy wee singles
and doubles' to luxurious, high-ceilinged suites,
bedrooms (some dog friendly) are kitted out in
heather-toned heritage style and supplied with
pampering Scottish bath products and home-
made shortbread. In Ba' Bar, find monochrome
photographs and a wide selection of rare and
vintage craft spirits; in the clubby lounge, velvet
armchairs and sofas. A short menu of modern
Scottish dishes, including promising vegan and
vegetarian options, is available all day. Buses to
the centre and the airport stop right outside.

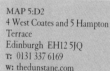

MAP 5:D2
4 West Coates and 5 Hampton
Terrace
Edinburgh EH12 5JQ
T: 0131 337 6169
W: thedunstane.com

BEDROOMS: 35. 18 in Hampton House,
opposite.
OPEN: all year.
FACILITIES: lounge/bar, conservatory,
residents' lounge and breakfast
room in Hampton House, in-room
smart TV, wedding facilities, garden,
parking.
BACKGROUND MUSIC: in bar, lounge.
LOCATION: in Murrayfield, just west of
city centre.
CHILDREN: all ages welcomed.
DOGS: allowed in some bedrooms (not
unattended), conservatory, garden.
CREDIT CARDS: Amex, MC, Visa.
PRICES: per room B&B single
£145–£295, double £175–£650.
Prix fixe menu £28 (3 courses), £34
(4 courses). 2-night min. stay preferred
Sat in peak season.

EDINBURGH
FINGAL

In shipshape and Bristol fashion, this plushly
revamped former Northern Lighthouse supply
ship is berthed in a working dock, moments
away from a lively district of waterfront cafés
and restaurants. Once serving Scottish islands,
the now-luxury liner today serves up cocktails
and refined dining before rocking guests to sleep
in decadent berths. All curving wood, thick
carpets and glossy brass, the Art Deco interiors
glamorously gleam. Porthole-lined cabins have
a huge bed draped in a custom-woven throw;
bathrobes, a rain shower, under-floor heating.
First-class cabins open on to the deck; those on the
starboard have the best views. At breakfast, haggis
and black pudding complete the full Scottish.

MAP 5:D2
Alexandra Dock
Leith
Edinburgh EH6 7DX
T: 0131 357 5000
W: fingal.co.uk

BEDROOMS: 23.
OPEN: all year except 25 Dec.
FACILITIES: bar, dining room, ballroom,
in-room TV, deck.
BACKGROUND MUSIC: none.
LOCATION: berthed at the port of Leith.
CHILDREN: all ages welcomed.
DOGS: not allowed.
CREDIT CARDS: Amex, MC, Visa.
PRICES: per room B&B £220–£1,200.
À la carte £25.

ELGOL Highland

CORUISK HOUSE

A welcome glass of sparkling wine awaits guests at Clare Winskill and Iain Roden's romantic restaurant-with-rooms, reached down a scenic, single-track road in a wild and remote part of the island. The original Skye 'black house' has quaintly low ceilings, a stone-walled snug and a conservatory dining room with views towards mountains and the islands of Rum and Eigg. Modern-rustic bedrooms and suites are upstairs and in the house next door. A four-course set menu of flavoursome, island ingredient-led cooking is served at 7 pm; dishes might include lobster bisque or venison fillet, pear and thyme crumble, sweet potato game chips. After a fortifying breakfast, set off on a scenic walk or take a dip in a loch or river nearby.

MAP 5:C1
Elgol
Isle of Skye IV49 9BL
T: 01471 866330
w: coruiskhouse.com

BEDROOMS: 5. 2 suites (one with 2 bedrooms) in The Steading, next door.
OPEN: Mar–end Oct/early Nov.
FACILITIES: sitting room/snug, 2 dining rooms (1 conservatory), in-room TV (Freeview) in 2 suites, humanist wedding facilities, front lawn, restaurant wheelchair accessible.
BACKGROUND MUSIC: none.
LOCATION: ½ mile NE of Elgol, 22 miles SW of Kyle of Lochalsh.
CHILDREN: not under 14.
DOGS: well-behaved dogs allowed in hall of 1 suite.
CREDIT CARDS: MC, Visa.
PRICES: per room B&B single £160–£275, double £160–£430. 4-course set menu £60.

NEW

FORRES Moray

CLUNY BANK AND FRANKLIN'S RESTAURANT

In a quiet residential area within a small, arty town, Julia and Lloyd Kenny run their affable restaurant-with-rooms with a personal touch. The refurbished Victorian building stands on a slope, with woodland walks from the door; inside are candlelit dinners, restful bedrooms and an impressive range of malt whiskies. Lloyd Kenny's award-winning classical cooking uses plenty of local produce – lamb and beef from the town butcher, lobster landed in nearby Lossiemouth, cheese from a family-owned farm in Ardersier. (Special diets are happily catered for, with advance notice.) Overnight guests stay in spacious bedrooms; in the morning, an extensive menu of hot dishes is cooked to order.

MAP 5:C2
69 St Leonard's Road
Forres IV36 2DW
T: 01309 674304
w: clunybankhotel.co.uk

BEDROOMS: 7. 1, on ground floor, with own entrance.
OPEN: all year.
FACILITIES: bar/lounge, restaurant, in-room TV, ½-acre garden, parking.
BACKGROUND MUSIC: 'low-key' contemporary jazz in public areas.
LOCATION: 10 mins' walk from High Street.
CHILDREN: all ages welcomed.
DOGS: not allowed.
CREDIT CARDS: MC, Visa.
PRICES: per room B&B single £85–£130, double £130–£175. À la carte £43.

GLASGOW
15GLASGOW

Opposite private gardens, Lorraine Gibson's 'guest-centred' B&B occupies an 'elegant' 19th-century terrace house close to Kelvingrove Park. Original fireplaces, sash windows and intricate cornicing in the former merchants' home are complemented by fresh, well-considered modern decor. Spacious, high-ceilinged bedrooms have a large bed, mood lighting and a Scottish cast; from two vast suites, huge windows overlook gardens front or rear. Ordered the night before, breakfast is eaten in the room, or communally in the lounge. Expect freshly squeezed orange juice, a fruit salad 'bursting with variety', a 'piping hot' full Scottish – 'all first class'. Museums are within walking distance; recommended eateries are close.

MAP 5:D2
15 Woodside Place
Glasgow G37 QL
T: 0141 332 1263
W: 15glasgow.com

BEDROOMS: 5.
OPEN: all year.
FACILITIES: lounge, in-room TV (Freeview), small garden, limited parking.
BACKGROUND MUSIC: none.
LOCATION: between town centre and West End.
CHILDREN: not under 6.
DOGS: allowed in bedrooms, not in public rooms.
CREDIT CARDS: MC, Visa.
PRICES: per room B&B £150–£180.

GLENEGEDALE Argyll and Bute
GLENEGEDALE HOUSE

Graeme and Emma Clark's much-praised guest house on the Isle of Islay basks in uninterrupted views over the Mull of Oa; guests often bask in the comfort – and home baking – the hosts provide. Handsome bedrooms with tweedy touches are stocked with spoiling extras (Scottish-blended teas; Highland chocolates); a residents' bar holds Islay malts and Scottish gins. Evenings, a platter of charcuterie, cheese or local seafood with home-baked bread and oatcakes is available for the asking. Breakfast, and its whisky-laced porridge, wins awards. The consummate hosts have local knowledge to share, perhaps over a dram by the peat fire. Close to the island's small airfield; ferry terminals are a short drive away.

MAP 5:D1
Glenegedale
Isle of Islay PA42 7AS
T: 01496 300400
W: glenegedalehouse.co.uk

BEDROOMS: 4. 1 on ground floor, plus 4-bed self-catering house.
OPEN: all year except Christmas and New Year.
FACILITIES: bar, morning room, drawing room, dining room, music room, in-room TV (Freeview), wedding facilities, garden, public rooms wheelchair accessible.
BACKGROUND MUSIC: classical, jazz and instrumental music, 'played very low', in dining room.
LOCATION: 4 miles from Port Ellen, 6 miles from Bowmore.
CHILDREN: not under 12.
DOGS: not allowed.
CREDIT CARDS: Amex, MC, Visa.
PRICES: per room B&B £115–£198. À la carte £45.

GLENFINNAN Highland
THE PRINCE'S HOUSE

Seventeenth-century travellers along the Road to the Isles once stopped in at this former coaching inn close to Loch Shiel. Today, it is a welcoming small hotel run by 'friendly, attentive' hosts Ina and Kieron Kelly. Traditionally decorated bedrooms are all on the first floor, under sloped ceilings. The best, with a Jacobean four-poster bed, is equipped with bathrobes, fresh flowers, a decanter of whisky mac. Book ahead to dine on Kieron's six-course tasting menu in the panelled restaurant: his well-regarded dishes highlight locally sourced ingredients such as fish and shellfish from the boats at Mallaig, and beef from Highland butchers. Simpler fare is found in the Stage House Bistro. The ferry to Skye is within easy reach.

MAP 5:C1
Glenfinnan PH37 4LT
T: 01397 722246
w: glenfinnan.co.uk

BEDROOMS: 9.
OPEN: mid-Mar–end Oct, restaurant open Easter–end Sept.
FACILITIES: restaurant, bistro/bar, in-room TV (Freeview), small front lawn.
BACKGROUND MUSIC: in public rooms.
LOCATION: 17 miles NW of Fort William, 330 yards from Glenfinnan station.
CHILDREN: all ages welcomed.
DOGS: not allowed.
CREDIT CARDS: Amex, MC, Visa.
PRICES: per room B&B single £95–£130, double £175–£275. 6-course set menu (restaurant) £65, à la carte (bistro) £35.

GRANDTULLY Perth and Kinross
THE GRANDTULLY HOTEL BY BALLINTAGGART

Artfully restored, this stone-built Victorian hotel is the sophisticated hub of a small Perthshire village surrounded by 'spectacular' scenery. It is run by chef/patron Chris Rowley, his wife, Rachel, and his brother, Andrew. Locals and visitors gather in the convivial bar and informal dining room for cocktails and inventive small and large plates that highlight locally sourced and home-grown ingredients – perhaps rib-eye, Balnaguard chanterelles, foraged salsa verde. In the modern bedrooms, adventurous colour schemes contrast with crisp white sheets on wide beds draped with locally woven tweeds; some rooms overlook the River Tay. Breakfast is best walked off in the surrounding glens.

MAP 5:D2
Grandtully PH9 0PL
T: 01887 447000
w: ballintaggart.com

BEDROOMS: 8. Some interconnecting, suitable for a family.
OPEN: all year except Christmas.
FACILITIES: bar, library, restaurant, private dining room, in-room TV (Freeview), civil wedding licence, terrace, garden, shop.
BACKGROUND MUSIC: in public areas.
LOCATION: in village.
CHILDREN: all ages welcomed.
DOGS: not allowed.
CREDIT CARDS: MC, Visa.
PRICES: per room B&B £155–£200. À la carte £37.

INNERLEITHEN Scottish Borders

CADDON VIEW

'An excellent base' for exploring the Tweed valley,
Lisa and Steve Davies's 'great-value' guest house
is in a small town surrounded by 'beautiful rolling
countryside'. Guests, including many returnees,
laud the friendly welcome and home-baked
treats on offer. 'Clean, pleasant and comfortable',
bedrooms have a simple country air, a modern
bathroom and all the amenities (tea- and coffee-
making facilities, fresh milk, a radio/alarm clock);
secondary glazing reduces traffic noise. There are
'lovely' walks to be had nearby; indoors, the hosts
provide books, board games, and a blazing fire in
the drawing room. Seasonal Scottish dishes are
served at dinner in the conservatory café several
nights a week; breakfast is 'beautiful'.

MAP 5:E2
14 Pirn Road
Innerleithen EH44 6HH
T: 01896 830208
w: caddonview.co.uk

BEDROOMS: 8.
OPEN: all year except Christmas, café
closed Mon, Tues, dinner available
Wed–Sat ('reservations strongly
advised').
FACILITIES: snug bar, drawing room,
breakfast room, café/bistro, in-room
TV (Freeview), ½-acre mature
garden, storage for bicycles and
fishing gear, parking.
BACKGROUND MUSIC: local radio in
café during the day, 'a CD at night if
people want it'.
LOCATION: 400 yards from town centre.
CHILDREN: well-behaved children of all
ages welcomed.
DOGS: allowed in 1 bedroom, drawing
room, café and bar, not in breakfast
room.
CREDIT CARDS: MC, Visa.
PRICES: per room B&B £60–£135. Set
menus £22–£28.

INVERNESS Highland

BUNCHREW HOUSE

On the tranquil shore of the Beauly Firth, this
'very pleasant' 17th-century mansion stands in
large grounds that lead into woodland laced with
walking paths. Within the hotel are traditionally
styled bedrooms and suites with period details,
each looking over garden or lake; one has its
own conservatory. There are two fireplaces in
the drawing room, and a fine collection of malt
whiskies in the clubby bar; in the wood-panelled
restaurant overlooking the water, Scottish dishes
at dinner might include salmon, wild mushrooms,
kale, samphire. At breakfast, fuel up on a
Highland Scottish grill or pancakes with maple-
glazed bacon, then set out to spot the brown hares
and roe deer who like to visit.

MAP 5:C2
Bunchrew
Inverness IV3 8TA
T: 01463 234917
w: bunchrewhousehotel.com

BEDROOMS: 16. 1 on ground floor.
OPEN: all year except 15–30 Jan.
FACILITIES: bar, drawing room,
restaurant, private dining room,
civil wedding licence, in-room
TV (Freeview), terrace, garden,
woodlands, electric car charging
points, public areas wheelchair
accessible.
BACKGROUND MUSIC: in public areas.
LOCATION: on the A862 Beauly/
Dingwall road, 3 miles from Inverness
city centre.
CHILDREN: all ages welcomed.
DOGS: allowed in bar, not in restaurant.
CREDIT CARDS: Amex, MC, Visa.
PRICES: per room B&B £95–£395. Prix
fixe dinner £45 (2 courses), £55 (3
courses), 7-course tasting menu £75.

KELSO Scottish Borders
THE OLD PRIORY BED AND BREAKFAST

In the heart of the cobbled market town, the genial Girdwood family run their B&B in this characterful Georgian house near the old parish church. Comfortable and spacious, the bedrooms are traditionally furnished with antiques and supplied with silk-filled duvets, large, fluffy towels and a hospitality tray. Most rooms overlook the pretty walled garden; a suite with a separate twin-bedded room is ideal for a family. In the morning, light fills the wood-floored breakfast room, where guests find a wide range of teas and plenty of cooked choices. The helpful hosts share local knowledge, and can advise on castles and cask ales, bookshops and sandy beaches. Kelso Abbey and many restaurants are a stroll away.

MAP 5:E3
33/35 Woodmarket
Kelso TD5 7AT
T: 01573 223030
w: theoldpriorykelso.com

BEDROOMS: 5. 2 on ground floor, suitable for disabled.
OPEN: Feb–Dec, New Year.
FACILITIES: dining room, conservatory/sitting room, in-room TV (Freeview), garden, parking.
BACKGROUND MUSIC: none.
LOCATION: in town centre.
CHILDREN: all ages welcomed (in family room).
DOGS: allowed in 1 bedroom (resident dogs).
CREDIT CARDS: not accepted.
PRICES: per room B&B single £80–£110, double £90–£120. 2-night min. stay.

KINLOCH RANNOCH Perth and Kinross
DUNALASTAIR HOTEL SUITES

The grandeur of the surrounding scenery – its hills, crags, forests and glens – sweeps in to this stone-built Victorian hotel, in a remote village on the edge of Loch Rannoch. From sleek lounge to modern eating areas, natural materials and tawny tones inform the contemporary, design-led interior. Each understated suite is equipped with tea, coffee, shortbread and fresh milk, plus robes, slippers and toiletries in a gleaming bathroom; some have a mini-kitchen with a microwave and a fridge. Many superior suites look toward Highland peaks. Back from a day's walking, cycling or general wilderness exploring, guests have a choice between two restaurants: relaxed but refined Monadh and the fine-dining Library.

MAP 5:C2
1 The Square
Kinloch Rannoch PH16 5PW
T: 01882 580444
w: dunalastairhotel.com

BEDROOMS: 32. 2 suitable for disabled.
OPEN: all year.
FACILITIES: lounge, 2 restaurants, in-room TV, room service, concierge service, wedding/function facilities, boot room, courtyard, parking, electric car charging point.
BACKGROUND MUSIC: in public rooms.
LOCATION: in village at eastern end of Loch Rannoch.
CHILDREN: all ages welcomed.
DOGS: not allowed.
CREDIT CARDS: Amex, MC, Visa.
PRICES: per room B&B (continental) £160–£800. Cooked breakfast £12. À la carte (Monadh) £55, 7-course tasting menu (Library) £69.95. 2-night min. stay at bank holiday weekends.

MEIKLEOUR Perth and Kinross

THE MEIKLEOUR ARMS

In a Victorian fishing lodge on the Meikleour estate, owned by the same Franco-Scottish family since 1362, this characterful country inn benefits from a verdant woodland setting and a double-bank salmon beat on the River Tay. The dog-friendly pub and oak-beamed restaurant have pleasingly rustic touches; a cheering wood-burner blazes between the two. At mealtimes, produce from the estate's fields, forest and kitchen garden is cooked with Gallic zest in dishes such as rillettes of loch trout; cheddar soufflé, leek fondue. Spacious bedrooms in the main building are charmingly decorated with a rural French ambience; more modern rooms, with a private garden, are in outlying cottages and the newly converted stables.

MAP 5:D2
Meikleour PH2 6EB
T: 01250 883206
W: meikleourarms.co.uk

BEDROOMS: 24. 7 in converted stables, 6 in cottages by walled garden of Meikleour House, a short distance away.
OPEN: all year.
FACILITIES: residents' lounge, pub, restaurant, private dining room, in-room TV, beer garden, large grounds and woodlands, 1.7-mile salmon fishing beat on river, restaurant wheelchair accessible.
BACKGROUND MUSIC: 'at a very low level' in pub.
LOCATION: 12 miles N of Perth.
CHILDREN: all ages welcomed.
DOGS: welcomed in ground-floor and cottage bedrooms, pub.
CREDIT CARDS: MC, Visa.
PRICES: per room B&B single £75–£140, double £85–£150. À la carte £29. 2-night min. stay in cottages.

MELROSE Scottish Borders

BURT'S

The Henderson family's well-established hotel stands on the main square of a pretty Borders town, a welcoming landmark for locals and visitors alike. Bedrooms in the listed 18th-century building are decorated in soothing shades and tweedy accents; each room has tea- and coffee-making facilities and Scottish toiletries. The restaurant and bistro bar are popular destinations for light lunchtime bites and hearty suppers – spiced pork belly, black pudding bonbon, creamed cabbage, perhaps. A sustaining breakfast supports the next day's activities: golfing, walking, fishing on the River Tweed, or wandering the lively town. The Hendersons also own The Townhouse, across the street.

MAP 5:E3
Market Square
Melrose TD6 9PN
T: 01896 822285
W: burtshotel.co.uk

BEDROOMS: 20.
OPEN: all year, no accommodation 24–26 Dec.
FACILITIES: lobby lounge, residents' lounge, bistro bar, restaurant, private dining room, in-room TV (Freeview), wedding facilities, function facilities, ½-acre garden, parking.
BACKGROUND MUSIC: in public areas.
LOCATION: in town centre.
CHILDREN: all ages welcomed, not under 8 in restaurant.
DOGS: allowed in some bedrooms, bistro bar, not in restaurant.
CREDIT CARDS: Amex, MC, Visa.
PRICES: per room B&B single from £79, double from £148. À la carte £42.

MOFFAT Dumfries and Galloway

HARTFELL HOUSE & THE LIMETREE RESTAURANT

Robert and Mhairi Ash offer 'good-value' accommodation in their 'lovely' 1850s Gothic Revival-style house, in a conservation town popular for outdoor activities. A highlight here is the Michelin-rated food in the Limetree restaurant (Tues–Sat, booking essential), where chef Matt Seddon cooks 'thoroughly enjoyable' modern Scottish dishes. Vegetarian and other diets are well catered for, with advance notice. Traditionally furnished bedrooms have tea- and coffee-making facilities and Scottish toiletries. Some rooms are snug; others accommodate a family. Breakfast is 'excellent'. Easy access to the M74; the Southern Upland Way passes nearby.

MAP 5:E2
Hartfell Crescent
Moffat DG10 9AL
T: 01683 220153
W: hartfellhouse.co.uk

BEDROOMS: 7. Plus self-catering cottage in the grounds.
OPEN: all year except Mon, Christmas, restaurant closed Sun, Mon.
FACILITIES: lounge, restaurant, in-room TV (Freeview), garden, cooking classes, bicycle storage, parking.
BACKGROUND MUSIC: in restaurant.
LOCATION: 5 mins' walk from town centre.
CHILDREN: all ages welcomed.
DOGS: not allowed.
CREDIT CARDS: MC, Visa.
PRICES: per room B&B single £55–£75, double £85–£95. Set menu £26 (2 courses), £33 (3 courses).

NAIRN Highland

SUNNY BRAE

John Bochel and Rachel Philipsen's 'good-value' B&B on the Moray coast stands before 'the panorama of the sea', within easy reach of dolphins, dunes and whisky distilleries. There's 'a domestic feel' at this house across the road from the beach: books are available for borrowing; the pretty suntrap gardens have plentiful seating. 'Airy, comfortable' bedrooms, some with views over the Moray Firth, are supplied with bathrobes and a hospitality tray. Local produce features in the 'very good' breakfast, with sausages from the town butcher and seasonal fruit from a farm shop nearby; vegetarian and vegan diets are happily catered for. 'Friendly and personable', the hosts have a wealth of local information to share.

MAP 5:C2
Marine Road
Nairn IV12 4EA
T: 01667 452309
W: sunnybraenairn.co.uk

BEDROOMS: 8. 1 suitable for disabled.
OPEN: Mar–end Oct.
FACILITIES: lounge, dining room, in-room TV (Freeview), terrace, front and rear gardens, parking.
BACKGROUND MUSIC: none.
LOCATION: 5 mins' walk from town centre, 2 mins from beach.
CHILDREN: all ages welcomed.
DOGS: only guide dogs allowed.
CREDIT CARDS: MC, Visa.
PRICES: per room B&B £85–£145. À la carte £35.

PEEBLES Scottish Borders
CRINGLETIE HOUSE

In springtime, daffodils blanket the lawns around this secluded baronial mansion; in all seasons, the extensive grounds – the historic walled garden, mile-long nature trail, sculptures and outdoor games – invite exploration. Inside, log fires, a frescoed ceiling, custom-created tartan and an old service bell in the public rooms add to the grand ambience, though 'friendly' staff encourage an easy, home-away-from-home feel. Individually decorated bedrooms and suites vary in size and style: some are snug, some more modern; all have views over the green grounds. At lunch and dinner, sit down to seasonal Borders produce in the Sutherland restaurant, whose vista stretches down the valley to Peebles.

MAP 5:E2
off Edinburgh Road
Peebles EH45 8PL
T: 01721 725750
W: cringletie.com

BEDROOMS: 13. 1 suitable for disabled, plus 2-bed cottage, with hot tub, in grounds.
OPEN: all year except 2–3 weeks Jan.
FACILITIES: lift, bar, lounge, conservatory, garden room, restaurant, in-room TV (Freeview), wedding facilities, 28-acre grounds (nature trail, walled garden, woodland), electric car charging points, hotel fully wheelchair accessible.
BACKGROUND MUSIC: in public areas.
LOCATION: 2 miles N of Peebles.
CHILDREN: all ages welcomed.
DOGS: allowed in most bedrooms, not in public rooms.
CREDIT CARDS: Amex, MC, Visa.
PRICES: per room B&B single from £197.50, double £230–£270. Prix fixe menu £55.

PEEBLES Scottish Borders
THE TONTINE

In the heart of a busy, arty town on the River Tweed, Kate and Gordon Innes's comfortable hotel is liked for its 'first-class atmosphere'. Locals and tourists pop in for afternoon teas and evening cocktails; at weekends, keen cyclists and golfers gather over real ales beside the open fire in the lounge. Informal bistro food might include a katsu curry (chicken, aubergine or monkfish) or pie of the moment. Seasonal menus are served in the high-ceilinged, chandelier-lit restaurant. Bedrooms are spread between the main 19th-century building and a more modern annexe (connected by a glass-sided corridor); dogs in annexe rooms have a blanket, a bowl and a treat. Maps point the way to country walks.

MAP 5:E2
High Street
Peebles EH45 8AJ
T: 01721 720892
W: tontinehotel.com

BEDROOMS: 36. 20 in Riverside Lodge annexe.
OPEN: all year.
FACILITIES: lift, bar, lounge, bistro, restaurant, private dining/meeting room, in-room TV (Freeview), wedding facilities, 2 garden areas, drying room, secure bicycle storage, parking, all public rooms wheelchair accessible.
BACKGROUND MUSIC: in public areas.
LOCATION: in town centre.
CHILDREN: all ages welcomed.
DOGS: allowed in 10 annexe bedrooms, bar, bistro, garden.
CREDIT CARDS: MC, Visa.
PRICES: per room B&B single £75–£135, double £125–£155. À la carte from £25.

PITLOCHRY Perth and Kinross

CRAIGATIN HOUSE AND COURTYARD

Keep an eye out for wandering pheasants: this Victorian house, once the home of a respected community doctor, stands amid a spread of gardens and woodland. Now owned and amiably run as a modern B&B by Lynne Fordyce and John Watters, it has been brought up to date with bright rooms and a lofty, glass-fronted extension facing the neat lawn. In the main house and converted stables, contemporary bedrooms are thoughtfully supplied with hot drinks, bottles of water and locally made biscuits. A log-burning stove warms the spacious lounge. Accompanied by home-made compotes and Perthshire honey, there's plenty of choice at breakfast: omelettes, apple pancakes, a traditional Scottish and more.

MAP 5:D2
165 Atholl Road
Pitlochry PH16 5QL
T: 01796 472478
W: craigatinhouse.co.uk

BEDROOMS: 14. 7 in courtyard, 2 on ground floor, 1 suitable for disabled.
OPEN: Feb–Oct, New Year.
FACILITIES: lounge, 2 breakfast rooms, in-room TV (Freeview), 2-acre garden, parking, lounge/breakfast room wheelchair accessible.
BACKGROUND MUSIC: in lounge, breakfast rooms.
LOCATION: 10 mins' walk to town centre.
CHILDREN: not under 14.
DOGS: not allowed.
CREDIT CARDS: Amex, MC, Visa.
PRICES: per room B&B single £105–£135, double £115–£145. 1-night bookings sometimes refused Sat.

PITLOCHRY Perth and Kinross

DALSHIAN HOUSE

In gardens and woodland on the outskirts of town, this 'blissfully remote', good-value B&B attracts wild birds, red squirrels and many regular guests, who appreciate its 'warm, friendly' atmosphere. From the comfy lounge, with a wood-burning stove and magazines, to the individually decorated bedrooms, Heather and Martin Walls, the owners, have given their white-painted Georgian house the feel of a private home. 'Outstanding' breakfasts feature home-baked breads, local honey and compotes; hot dishes, including veggie options, are cooked to order. After a bowl of whisky-laced Scottish porridge, set off to explore: the hosts helpfully advise on forest rambles and hilly hikes, and can pack a picnic lunch on request.

MAP 5:D2
Old Perth Road
Pitlochry PH16 5TD
T: 01796 472173
W: dalshian.co.uk

BEDROOMS: 7.
OPEN: all year except Christmas.
FACILITIES: lounge, dining room, in-room TV (Freeview), 1-acre garden.
BACKGROUND MUSIC: none.
LOCATION: 1 mile S of centre.
CHILDREN: not under 8.
DOGS: not allowed.
CREDIT CARDS: MC, Visa.
PRICES: per room B&B single £79, double £90–£99. 1-night bookings refused at New Year.

PITLOCHRY Perth and Kinross
PINE TREES HOTEL

There's old-world charm aplenty at this white-painted Victorian mansion, in 'a delightful setting' on the outskirts of town. Roe deer are regular visitors to the wooded grounds; inside the hotel, stately public spaces have oriental carpets, deep armchairs, single malt whiskies and a judicious use of tartan. An impressive wood-and-wrought iron staircase leads to individually decorated main-house bedrooms. Ground-floor rooms are in a converted coach house or annexe nearby, and have dedicated parking. In the garden-facing restaurant, hearty dishes use Scottish produce, perhaps Orkney herring or Isle of Mull cheeses. The town centre is a 10-minute walk away; fishing, golf and hill walking are within reach.

MAP 5:D2
Strathview Terrace
Pitlochry PH16 5QR
T: 01796 472121
W: pinetreeshotel.co.uk

BEDROOMS: 31. 3 in annexe, 6 in coach house, 7 on ground floor, plus 2-bed apartment.
OPEN: all year.
FACILITIES: bar, 3 lounges, restaurant, in-room TV (Freeview), 7-acre grounds.
BACKGROUND MUSIC: in bar, restaurant.
LOCATION: ¼ mile N of town centre.
CHILDREN: all ages welcomed.
DOGS: well-behaved dogs allowed in bedrooms, 1 lounge; only guide dogs allowed in restaurant, bar lounge.
CREDIT CARDS: Amex, MC, Visa.
PRICES: per room B&B £139–£269. Prix fixe menu £32.50 (2 courses), £39 (3 courses).

PITLOCHRY Perth and Kinross
SAORSA 1875

A thoughtful take on modern hospitality, the McLaren-Stewart family's vegan hotel and restaurant bring together a deeply considered environmental ethos with contemporary style. Everything in the Victorian gabled house has been sustainably sourced: the plump pillows, fine linens and Scottish toiletries in the zesty bedrooms; the vegan liqueurs and biodynamic wines at the bar; the eco-friendly cleaning products used behind the scenes. A supper-club atmosphere reigns each evening, as guests, including the 'plant-curious', mingle at a communal table for an inspired five-course menu. Characteristic dishes: sweet yellow pepper soup, crispy sage leaves; wild mushroom agnolotti pasta. Breakfast is a lavish cold spread.

MAP 5:D2
2 East Moulin Road
Pitlochry PH16 5DW
T: 01796 475217
W: saorsahotel.com

BEDROOMS: 11.
OPEN: all year.
FACILITIES: bar, snug, lounge, restaurant, 2-acre grounds.
BACKGROUND MUSIC: in public areas.
LOCATION: in town.
CHILDREN: all ages welcomed.
DOGS: allowed (resident dogs).
CREDIT CARDS: MC, Visa.
PRICES: per room B&B (continental) £150–£250. 5-course set dinner £50. 1-night bookings refused Christmas/New Year, Etape Caledonia weekend.

PORTREE Highland

MARMALADE HOTEL

A short walk from the bustle of the island's main harbour town, this refurbished Edwardian country house in landscaped gardens has a coolly contemporary interior and views that stretch to the bay. Bedrooms vary in size, with one room ideal for a family of three; all are equipped with welcome extras such as handmade Scottish soaps and a capsule coffee machine. Rooms in a modern extension have floor-to-ceiling windows to take in the best views. Choose Skye mussels or a Perthshire pork fillet at dinner in Chargrill restaurant; a full Scottish or porridge with a dash of whisky in the morning. In sunshine, the garden terrace, its vista reaching to the Cuillin hills, is the place to be. Part of the Perle Hotels group.

MAP 5:C1
Home Farm Road
Portree
Isle of Skye IV51 9LX
T: 01478 611711
W: marmaladehotel.co.uk

BEDROOMS: 34. 23 in extension, some on ground floor, 1 suitable for disabled.
OPEN: all year except 24–26 Dec.
FACILITIES: bar/restaurant, lounge, in-room TV (Freeview), wedding facilities, terrace, 2-acre grounds.
BACKGROUND MUSIC: in lounge, bar/restaurant.
LOCATION: in town centre.
CHILDREN: not under 12.
DOGS: not allowed.
CREDIT CARDS: Amex, MC, Visa.
PRICES: per room B&B £150–£370. À la carte £35.

RATHO Midlothian

THE BRIDGE INN AT RATHO

Guests receive a 'cheerful welcome' at this pub-with-rooms, which stands by a bridge over the Union Canal in a conservation village. Fires burn in a bar popular with locals; in the 'inviting' dining room, produce from local suppliers and the walled garden influences the menu of pub classics (pie of the day; Mull Cheddar macaroni) and more elaborate dishes (pheasant and Ayrshire smoked bacon terrine, pickled beets, apple gel). Upstairs, 'snug', pleasingly simple bedrooms have a canal view. Breakfast brings sausages from rare-breed pigs, and freshly laid chicken and duck eggs from Ratho Hall, just across the canal. Convenient for Edinburgh Airport. Sister hotel The Ship Inn is in Elie (see main entry).

MAP 5:D2
27 Baird Road
Ratho EH28 8RA
T: 0131 333 1320
W: bridgeinn.com

BEDROOMS: 4.
OPEN: all year except 25–26 Dec.
FACILITIES: 2 bars, restaurant, in-room TV (Freeview), wedding facilities, terrace (beer garden, boat shed), bar and restaurant wheelchair accessible, adapted toilet.
BACKGROUND MUSIC: 'relaxed' all day, monthly live music nights.
LOCATION: in village, 7 miles W of Edinburgh.
CHILDREN: all ages welcomed.
DOGS: allowed in main bar only.
CREDIT CARDS: MC, Visa.
PRICES: per room B&B £115–£220. À la carte £35.

ST ANDREWS Fife
RUFFLETS

Traditional standards are upheld at this turreted 1920s mansion, one of Scotland's first country house hotels, which has been owned by the same family for 70 years. 'It's not inexpensive, but the staff are welcoming and helpful, the food is good, the guest lounges, bar and dining areas are attractive and comfortable, and the grounds are delightful – what more can you ask of a hotel?' writes an admiring Guide reader this year after a return visit. Those who do ask for more find 'superb' dog- and family-friendly bedrooms packed with thoughtful touches; a popular afternoon tea; and modern Scottish lunches and dinners, served inside and out, featuring produce from the kitchen garden. Just beyond: the historic seaside town.

MAP 5:D3
Strathkinness Low Road
St Andrews KY16 9TX
T: 01334 472594
W: rufflets.co.uk

BEDROOMS: 23. Some in Gatehouse and Rufflets Lodge, 4 on ground floor, 1 suitable for disabled, plus 3 self-catering cottages in gardens.
OPEN: all year.
FACILITIES: bar, drawing room, library, restaurant, in-room TV (Freeview), wedding/function facilities, yoga studio, 10-acre grounds (formal gardens, kitchen garden and woodland), bicycle hire.
BACKGROUND MUSIC: in bar, restaurant.
LOCATION: 2 miles W of town.
CHILDREN: all ages welcomed.
DOGS: allowed in some bedrooms, bar.
CREDIT CARDS: Amex, MC, Visa.
PRICES: per room B&B £145–£375. À la carte £40.

ST FILLANS Perth and Kinross
ACHRAY HOUSE

Watch the osprey swoop over the water from this 'likeable' small hotel, which stands beside Loch Earn within Loch Lomond and the Trossachs national park – a 'beautiful part of Perthshire'. 'Quiet and peaceful', up-to-date bedrooms are supplied with teas, a coffee machine, biscuits and Scottish-made toiletries; most of the rooms have 'wonderful views' over the loch. Deep sofas in the lounge invite guests to settle in; in the 'lovely' restaurant, Scottish ingredients (Isle of Mull scallops, Loch Duart salmon, etc) dot the à la carte and tasting menus. 'The food at our dinner was delicious, well presented and unusual; the matched wines, interesting.' Next day, an 'enjoyable' breakfast is 'very good – all home-made or local'.

MAP 5:D2
On Loch Earn
St Fillans PH6 2NF
T: 01764 685320
W: achrayhouse.com

BEDROOMS: 9. Plus self-catering cottage.
OPEN: all year.
FACILITIES: lounge, bar, conservatory, restaurant, in-room TV (Sky), civil wedding licence, terrace, large foreshore, electric car charging point, bar and restaurant wheelchair accessible.
BACKGROUND MUSIC: in lobby, bar, restaurant.
LOCATION: at eastern end of Loch Earn, 6 miles W of Comrie.
CHILDREN: 'not ideal for small children, but call to discuss'.
DOGS: allowed in 5 bedrooms, conservatory, bar.
CREDIT CARDS: Amex, MC, Visa.
PRICES: per room B&B £79–£190. À la carte £35, tasting menu £49.

SCOURIE Highland
SCOURIE HOTEL

Genuine Scottish hospitality, and the chance to catch giant hill loch brown trout, lure visitors to the Campbell family's old coaching inn, in an area known for its spectacular mountain scenery, white sandy bays, and lochs and lochans teeming with wild trout and salmon. Bonhomie begins with tea and scones by roaring fires in lounges full of fishing memorabilia; tall tales are exchanged over drinks in the bar. At 7.30 pm, a gong summons diners to a set dinner focused on seafood and shellfish, Highland game and meat, home-grown vegetables. Drift off to peaceful sleep in a recently refurbished, TV-less bedroom. Large grounds encompass walled gardens and an orchard; a path leads down to the harbour.

MAP 5:B2
Scourie IV27 4SX
T: 01971 502396
W: scouriehotel.com

BEDROOMS: 21. 2 in garden annexe.
OPEN: mid-Apr–mid-Oct.
FACILITIES: 2 bars, 2 lounges, restaurant, 7-acre grounds (gardens, paddock, orchard), fishing beats (permits supplied, boats to hire, ghillies available).
BACKGROUND MUSIC: none.
LOCATION: in a village on the North Coast 500 route.
CHILDREN: all ages welcomed.
DOGS: allowed, not in dining area.
CREDIT CARDS: MC, Visa.
PRICES: per room B&B £120–£195. Set menu £37.

SOUTH GALSON Western Isles
GALSON FARM GUEST HOUSE

On the north-west coast of the Isle of Lewis, Elaine Fothergill and Richard Inger run their 'high-quality' guest house in a traditional Hebridean farmhouse, a short walk from the water's edge. The sky is vast here; the birds, wild. Recently refreshed bedrooms with views of rugged coast or moorland crofts have a modern rustic feel, with handcrafted ceramics and works by local artisans. Organic coffee and tea are supplied, along with fresh milk and cold drinks. Guests have use of a TV lounge (with a fire, in chilly weather) and a reading room overlooking the surging Atlantic. Served communally, a hearty, Aga-fresh dinner may be arranged in advance. 'Excellent' breakfasts fuel exploration of beaches, mountains and burns.

MAP 5:B1
South Galson
Isle of Lewis HS2 0SH
T: 01851 850492
W: galsonfarm.co.uk

BEDROOMS: 4. Plus 6-bunk hostel available for sole occupancy, self-catering.
OPEN: all year except Christmas, New Year.
FACILITIES: 2 lounges, dining room, ¼-acre garden, drying facilities, bicycle storage.
BACKGROUND MUSIC: in dining room, lounge.
LOCATION: on the coast, 7½ miles SW of the port of Ness, 20 miles from Stornoway.
CHILDREN: not under 16.
DOGS: only assistance dogs allowed (animals on site).
CREDIT CARDS: Amex, MC, Visa.
PRICES: per room B&B single £96–£98, double £96–£125. Dinner £25 (2 courses). 2-night min. stay in peak season.

STIRLING
VICTORIA SQUARE

Kari and Phillip Couser's serene Victorian guest
house overlooks a tree-lined square, a ten-minute
walk from the city centre. Individually decorated
bedrooms feature William Morris-designed
wallpapers and some period-style furnishings;
superior rooms might have bay-window seating
or a view towards Stirling Castle. Among the
modern comforts in each room: bottles of Scottish
mineral water in a silent mini-fridge; bathrobes
and upmarket toiletries in an underfloor-heated
bathroom. A two- or three-course dinner is
available Wednesdays to Saturdays; guests who
opt for a pyjama night in might ask for a 'room
picnic' of Scottish pastrami and Morangie brie,
with a bottle of wine or champagne.

MAP 5:D2
12 Victoria Square
Stirling FK8 2QZ
T: 01786 473920
W: victoriasquare.scot

BEDROOMS: 10. 1 on ground floor.
OPEN: all year except Christmas,
restaurant closed Sun, Mon.
FACILITIES: lounge, breakfast room,
orangery restaurant, in-room smart
TV (Freeview), limited parking.
BACKGROUND MUSIC: quiet, in
restaurant.
LOCATION: ½ mile from town centre.
CHILDREN: not under 12.
DOGS: not allowed.
CREDIT CARDS: MC, Visa.
PRICES: per room B&B £75–£190. Prix
fixe menu £29.95 (2 courses), £38.95
(3 courses).

THORNHILL Dumfries and Galloway
TRIGONY HOUSE

Relaxed and relaxing, Jan and Adam Moore's
dog-friendly country hotel is in 'a lovely setting
looking out over the hills – very green and
surrounded by trees'. Past fire-warmed sitting
areas, the 18th-century sporting lodge has
'perfectly pleasant and comfortable' bedrooms
supplied with home-made shortbread, fresh
coffee and organic toiletries; a garden suite has a
conservatory and private garden. Guests sensitive
to noise (an A road runs close by) should ring in
advance to discuss best options. Dinner has good
choice for vegetarians and vegans; breakfast is
'excellent'. Arm yourself with the hotel's richly
informative guide of walks before striding out, or
simply stay in: a Finnish sauna cabin and hot tub
are in the grounds.

MAP 5:E2
Closeburn
Thornhill DG3 5EZ
T: 01848 331211
W: trigonyhotel.co.uk

BEDROOMS: 9. 1 on ground floor.
OPEN: all year except 24–26, 31 Dec.
FACILITIES: bar, lounge, 2 dining
rooms, in-room TV (Freeview), spa
treatment room in private garden
(outdoor wood-fired hot tub, sauna
cabin), wedding facilities, 4-acre
grounds, electric car charging points.
BACKGROUND MUSIC: in bar in evening.
LOCATION: 1 mile S of Thornhill.
CHILDREN: all ages welcomed.
DOGS: well-behaved dogs 'not only
allowed but welcomed' in bedrooms,
bar, 1 dining room, grounds.
CREDIT CARDS: Amex, MC, Visa.
PRICES: per room B&B single
£105–£150, double £130–£175.
À la carte £35. 1-night bookings
sometimes refused Sat.

ABERYSTWYTH Ceredigion

NANTEOS MANSION

Standing in graceful seclusion in wooded grounds, this Grade I listed manor house is a tranquil country retreat from the vibrant university town on the coast. Sympathetically restored, the Georgian property retains vestiges of its past in its stained glass, carved fireplaces and grand staircase. Bedrooms and sumptuous suites are decorated in keeping with the period of the house, but hold thoughtful modern comforts, including activity packs for young guests. In the chandelier-lit dining room, the food is keenly contemporary: Welsh lamb rump, miso leeks, celeriac fondant, say. Afternoon tea and evening cocktails may be taken in the library bar. In the morning, breakfast includes grilled kippers and a full Welsh.

MAP 3:C3
Rhydyfelin
Aberystwyth SY23 4LU
T: 01970 600522
W: nanteos.com

BEDROOMS: 22. 3 on ground floor, 1 suitable for disabled. Plus 4-bed mews house.
OPEN: all year.
FACILITIES: lounge, bar, restaurant, private dining room, billiard room, in-room smart TV (Freeview), civil wedding licence, 30-acre grounds (gardens, woodland), electric car charging point.
BACKGROUND MUSIC: in reception, bar.
LOCATION: 4 miles SE of Aberystwyth.
CHILDREN: all ages welcomed.
DOGS: allowed in 4 bedrooms, not in restaurant.
CREDIT CARDS: Amex, MC, Visa.
PRICES: per room B&B single £99–£150, double £139–£300. À la carte £49.

AMROTH Pembrokeshire

MELLIEHA GUEST HOUSE

In a forested valley, with easy access to the Pembrokeshire Coast Path and the beach, Julia and Stuart Adams 'warmly welcome' B&B guests with tea and a home-baked treat. The house stands in large, well-cared-for grounds with a natural pond – a tranquil scene to take in from the sunny terrace. 'Comfortable' bedrooms have views over the garden and green valley, or towards Carmarthen Bay. They vary in size, but all of them are 'thoughtfully' supplied with fresh milk for morning coffee or tea. One room has a private terrace, another, its own balcony. Breakfast (perhaps of cockles and laverbread) is ordered the night before. The 'excellent, informative hosts' have circular walks to share.

MAP 3:D2
Amroth Hill
Amroth SA67 8NA
T: 01834 811581
W: mellieha.co.uk

BEDROOMS: 4.
OPEN: all year except over Christmas, New Year.
FACILITIES: lounge, breakfast room, in-room TV, no mobile signal, 1-acre garden, parking.
BACKGROUND MUSIC: none.
LOCATION: 150 yards from Amroth seafront, 2 miles E of Saundersfoot.
CHILDREN: not under 12.
DOGS: only assistance dogs allowed.
CREDIT CARDS: MC, Visa.
PRICES: per room B&B £100–£125. 2-night min. stay preferred at weekends May–Sept.

BALA Gwynedd
PALE HALL

Rich in antiques, wood panelling and fine original features, this historic Victorian country house on the edge of Snowdonia national park stands in a woodland garden that stretches to the River Dee. Sustainably run, the hotel is powered by one of the country's oldest-running hydro-electric plants, and bottles its own spring water. Seasonal produce from local suppliers inspires tasting menus in the Henry Robertson fine dining room and more informal meals in the Huntsman bistro. Gracefully decorated, bedrooms and newly converted suites (some dog friendly) have little luxuries, such as organic toiletries and complimentary Madeira. Outside, there are lawn games in the grounds, and a pond whose every fish is named Alan.

MAP 3:B3
Llandderfel
Bala LL23 7PS
T: 01678 530285
W: palehall.co.uk

BEDROOMS: 22. 4 in converted barn, coach house and cottage, 1 suitable for disabled.
OPEN: all year.
FACILITIES: Grand Hall, lounge, library, restaurant, bar/bistro, Venetian dining room, in-room TV (Freeview), function facilities, civil wedding licence, 50-acre grounds, electric car charging points.
BACKGROUND MUSIC: in Grand Hall, restaurants.
LOCATION: 2 miles from Bala.
CHILDREN: all ages welcomed.
DOGS: allowed in 7 bedrooms, Grand Hall, bistro, on lead in gardens and public areas.
CREDIT CARDS: Amex, MC, Visa.
PRICES: per room B&B single £260–£845, double £275–£1,000. Tasting menu £70 (5 courses), £90 (8 courses), à la carte £45–£50.

CARDIFF
NEW HOUSE COUNTRY HOTEL

In the gentle hills just north of the centre, this dog-friendly hotel takes in panoramic views over the city and the Severn estuary. A tiered fountain fronts the creeper-covered, Grade II listed manor house; stone steps lead to elegant rooms that look out on to lush greenery. Afternoon tea may be taken in the lounges; at mealtimes, modern Welsh dishes in the restaurant or under the new glass pergola might include Pant Ys Gawn goat's cheese, pickled baby beetroot, or braised feather blade of Welsh beef. Colourful and contemporary, bedrooms are supplied with ethically produced toiletries. Part of the Town & Country Collective; see also The Bear, Cowbridge, and The West House, Llantwit Major (Shortlist entries).

MAP 3:E4
Thornhill Road
Cardiff CF14 9UA
T: 02920 520280
W: townandcountrycollective.co.uk/newhouse

BEDROOMS: 37. 29 in annexe, connected via lounges.
OPEN: all year except 26 Dec, 1 Jan.
FACILITIES: 3 lounges, library, restaurant, in-room TV (Freeview), civil wedding licence, meeting/function facilities, gym, 9-acre grounds.
BACKGROUND MUSIC: in restaurant.
LOCATION: in Thornhill suburb, 7 miles from Cardiff city centre.
CHILDREN: all ages welcomed.
DOGS: allowed in 3 bedrooms, 2 lounges, parts of garden, not in restaurant.
CREDIT CARDS: Amex, MC, Visa.
PRICES: per room B&B £99–£165. À la carte £35.

COWBRIDGE Vale of Glamorgan

THE BEAR

For centuries, this centrally located former coaching inn has been the hub of the fashionable market town. The panelled lounge and grill bar (look out for the remains of a medieval fireplace) are a local gathering spot; when the sun's out, find a table in the courtyard. From light lunches to grill dinners, modern dishes in the bar and atmospheric Cellars restaurant feature Welsh produce. Up-to-date bedrooms have tea, coffee and Welsh toiletries; some can accommodate a dog or a family. Room service is available. Residents have gym access at a leisure centre nearby. Part of the Town & Country Collective; see also The West House, Llantwit Major, and New House Country Hotel, Cardiff (Shortlist entries).

MAP 3:E3
63 High Street
Cowbridge CF71 7AF
T: 01446 774814
W: townandcountrycollective.co.uk/thebear

BEDROOMS: 33. Some on ground floor, some in annexe, plus self-catering apartments.
OPEN: all year.
FACILITIES: lounge/bar, grill/bar, restaurant, in-room TV, civil wedding licence, conference facilities, courtyard, secure bicycle storage, parking.
BACKGROUND MUSIC: in restaurant.
LOCATION: in town centre.
CHILDREN: all ages welcomed.
DOGS: allowed in bedrooms, bar.
CREDIT CARDS: MC, Visa.
PRICES: per room B&B £90–£165. À la carte £35.

HARLECH Gwynedd

CASTLE COTTAGE INN

At the top of one of the world's steepest streets, this inn occupies two 16th-century buildings just above Edward I's formidable castle (faint hearts, take the High Street route). Darryl Jenkins is the new owner; former chef/patron Glyn Roberts still heads up the kitchen. Recent refurbishment has seen the creation of an aviation-themed bar serving snacks and small plates alongside local ales and spirits. New, too: a more casual approach to dining, with an à la carte menu of seasonal ingredient-led dishes – dressed local crab, say, or a wild mushroom risotto. In the bedrooms, contemporary decor and modern oak furniture contrast with original features; ask for a room with a view of sea, castle or Mount Snowdon.

MAP 3:B3
Y Llech
Harlech LL46 2YL
T: 01766 780479
W: castlecottageinnharlech.com

BEDROOMS: 7. 4 in annexe, 2 on ground floor.
OPEN: all year.
FACILITIES: bar/lounge, restaurant, in-room TV (Freeview), limited parking, public car park within 30 yards.
BACKGROUND MUSIC: in bar and restaurant at mealtimes.
LOCATION: in town centre.
CHILDREN: all ages welcomed.
DOGS: not allowed.
CREDIT CARDS: MC, Visa.
PRICES: per room B&B single £85–£125, double £130–£175. À la carte £27.

LAUGHARNE Carmarthenshire

BROWN'S HOTEL

Once a favourite watering hole of Dylan Thomas, this coolly refurbished 18th-century inn, in the centre of a lively coastal town, remains a characterful place. The timber-beamed pub is inviting with its wood stove, candle-topped tables, old photos and Thomas memorabilia; there are Welsh ales, Penderyn whisky, board games, books. Hearty steaks are served in Dexters, the handsome, wood-panelled restaurant. Dapper bedrooms decorated in deep shades are equipped with all the modern amenities (mini-fridge, coffee machine, eco-friendly toiletries, etc). Each different from the other, they have charm in their creaky wood floors, exposed stonework and beams. Down a green lane, Thomas's boathouse is a 10-minute stroll away.

MAP 3:D2
King Street
Laugharne SA33 4RY
T: 01994 427688
W: browns.wales

BEDROOMS: 14. 2 on ground floor.
OPEN: all year.
FACILITIES: bar, restaurant, in-room TV, function facilities, beer garden, electric car charging points, parking.
BACKGROUND MUSIC: occasional live music at weekends.
LOCATION: in town centre.
CHILDREN: all ages welcomed.
DOGS: allowed in most bedrooms, not in areas where food is served.
CREDIT CARDS: MC, Visa.
PRICES: per room B&B single from £75, double £130–£180. À la carte £35.

LLANBRYNMAIR Powys

THE ROYSTON

In acres of gardens and pasture, views of the green valley spreading in all directions, this Victorian gentleman's residence is today a smartly updated guest house and a fine base for Mid Wales exploration. Welcoming hosts Rob Perham and Clive Sweeting have filled their home with deep hues, contemporary artwork and vintage-inspired style. There's a wood-burning stove and an honesty bar in the lounge; bedrooms, moody-toned and well-equipped, are dotted with ornaments picked up during the owners' travels. There's no TV – instead, gaze through the windows at the Cambrian mountains or surrounding fields. From breakfast and dinner to packed lunches and picnics, much of the food is home made or home grown.

MAP 3:B3
Llwynaire
Llanbrynmair SY19 7DX
T: 01650 519228
W: theroystonwales.com

BEDROOMS: 7.
OPEN: all year except Christmas, New Year.
FACILITIES: lounge, dining room, 10-acre grounds.
BACKGROUND MUSIC: 'ambient chilled music' in lounge and dining room.
LOCATION: off a single-track road, in rural setting N of Llanbrynmair.
CHILDREN: not under 12.
DOGS: small to medium-size dogs allowed by prior arrangement in 2 bedrooms, not in lounge, on lead at all times.
CREDIT CARDS: MC, Visa.
PRICES: per room B&B £129–£159. À la carte £22 (2 courses), £25 (3 courses).

LLANDDEINIOLEN Gwynedd

TY'N RHOS

The Murphy family's 'friendly' hotel, a former farmstead turned country house, stands in the tranquil foothills of Snowdonia, overlooking the Isle of Anglesey. Sheep and cattle graze in fields beyond the gardens; binoculars are provided for watching the varied bird life. 'Comfortable, well-equipped' bedrooms are in the creeper-covered house or around the courtyard; some open on to the garden. Take pre-dinner drinks in the bar, lounge or conservatory, or on the terrace in fine weather, then sit down to a hearty meal, perhaps of Menai mussels or freshly caught lobster. At breakfast, the buffet has yogurts, pastries and home-made granola; cooked dishes include smoked haddock with Welsh rarebit.

MAP 3:A3
Seion
Llanddeiniolen LL55 3AE
T: 01248 670489
W: tynrhos.co.uk

BEDROOMS: 19. 7 in converted outbuilding, some on ground floor.
OPEN: all year except Sun, Mon, Christmas, New Year.
FACILITIES: lounge, bar, restaurant, conservatory, in-room TV, terrace, 1-acre garden.
BACKGROUND MUSIC: in public areas.
LOCATION: 12 mins' drive from the Llanberis train, 4 miles from Bangor and Caernarfon.
CHILDREN: all ages welcomed, no 'small children' in restaurant in evening.
DOGS: allowed in some bedrooms, garden.
CREDIT CARDS: MC, Visa.
PRICES: per room B&B single £85–£100, double £95–£205. 2-night min. stay.

LLANDUDNO Conwy

ESCAPE

Up the street from the Great Orme Tramway, Gaenor Loftus and Sam Nayar's design-conscious B&B occupies a white stucco Victorian villa filled with more than a touch of fun. Modern and vintage furnishings are set against a backdrop of period features such as stained-glass windows and oak panelling; bedrooms have plenty of personality. Choose a room decorated with beside-the-seaside flair or one in the loft with a cosy lounge area; two of the best rooms have seating in a wide bay window. In every room: high-end toiletries and high-spec technology. Breakfast, with veggie options alongside sausages from the local butcher, is served at the table. The beach and the pier are a short stroll away.

MAP 3:A3
48 Church Walks
Llandudno LL30 2HL
T: 01492 877776
W: escapebandb.co.uk

BEDROOMS: 9.
OPEN: all year except 18–26 Dec.
FACILITIES: lounge (honesty bar), breakfast room, in-room TV (Freeview), front garden, limited parking.
BACKGROUND MUSIC: at breakfast.
LOCATION: 1 mile from town and coast.
CHILDREN: not under 10.
DOGS: not allowed.
CREDIT CARDS: Amex, MC, Visa.
PRICES: per room B&B £105–£160. 2-night min. stay at weekends, 3 nights on bank holidays.

LLANDUDNO Conwy
OSBORNE HOUSE

Furnished with 'impressive grandeur', this small hotel on the promenade has 'splendid' public rooms decorated with oil paintings and gilded mirrors; on the upper floors, most of the 'characterful' suites take in the panorama of the sea. The hotel has been owned for more than 20 years by the Maddocks and Waddy families, Llandudno hoteliers who have been at the helm of neighbouring sister hotel The Empire since 1946. Each well-supplied suite has a sitting room, a marble bathroom, and a working gas fire in a marble fireplace; continental breakfasts are taken in the room. There's a brasserie-style menu in the 'ornate' Victorian dining room; guests may also eat, swim and step into the sauna at The Empire, 200 yards away.

MAP 3:A3
17 North Parade
Llandudno LL30 2LP
T: 01492 860330
W: osbornehouse.co.uk

BEDROOMS: 7 suites.
OPEN: all year except Sun, Mon, Christmas.
FACILITIES: lounge/bar, restaurant, in-room TV (Freeview), small patio, parking.
BACKGROUND MUSIC: in public rooms.
LOCATION: on the promenade.
CHILDREN: only allowed in rear family suite.
DOGS: not allowed.
CREDIT CARDS: Amex, MC, Visa.
PRICES: per room B&B £150–£225. À la carte £26.50. 2-night min. stay at weekends, 3-night min. stay over bank holidays.

LLANSTEFFAN Carmarthenshire
MANSION HOUSE LLANSTEFFAN

On a wooded headland overlooking the Tywi estuary, this contemporary restaurant-with-rooms is in a thoughtfully restored Georgian mansion as freshly inviting inside as out. It is owned and run by Carmarthenshire native Wendy Beaney and her husband, David. Stylish, uncluttered bedrooms with garden or river views are supplied with bathrobes and Welsh toiletries; one room opens on to a private garden terrace. From the period dining room, the 'excellent' view is fine accompaniment for Paul Owen's seasonal menus of locally farmed vegetables, Welsh meats and Carmarthen Bay seafood. Norman castles at Llansteffan and Laugharne are within reach; Dylan Thomas's contemplative boathouse is a half-hour's drive away.

MAP 3:D2
Pantyrathro
Llansteffan SA33 5AJ
T: 01267 241515
W: mansionhousellansteffan.co.uk

BEDROOMS: 9. 2 interconnecting rooms on ground floor, 1 suitable for disabled.
OPEN: all year, restaurant closed Sun eve except for residents, also Mon, Nov–mid-Feb.
FACILITIES: large open-plan bar/reception area, lounge, restaurant, in-room TV (Freeview), civil wedding licence, conference facilities, 5-acre grounds, electric car charging points, parking.
BACKGROUND MUSIC: in public areas.
LOCATION: 2 miles to Llansteffan village, beach and castle.
CHILDREN: all ages welcomed.
DOGS: not allowed.
CREDIT CARDS: Amex, MC, Visa.
PRICES: per room B&B £145–£220. À la carte £30. 1-night bookings refused at Christmas.

LLANTWIT MAJOR Vale of Glamorgan

THE WEST HOUSE

There's a relaxed atmosphere at this modern
hotel, in a quiet town within meandering reach,
down green lanes and pathways, of the dramatic
cliffs and secluded coves of the Glamorgan
Heritage Coast. Updated bedrooms vary in size
and decor; guests travelling with their dog may
request (at extra charge) one of the Fido-friendly
rooms – they're supplied with a dog bed, towel
and treats, and have access to the walled garden.
Sandwiches, light bites and straightforward
British classics are served in the restaurant, along
with interesting vegetarian options, perhaps a
falafel and spinach burger with hummus. Part
of the Town & Country Collective; see also New
House Country Hotel, Cardiff, and The Bear,
Cowbridge (Shortlist entries).

MAP 3:E3
West Street
Llantwit Major CF61 1SP
T: 01446 792406
W: townandcountrycollective.co.uk/
west-house

BEDROOMS: 17. 1 on ground floor.
OPEN: all year, restaurant closed Sun
eve.
FACILITIES: bar, restaurant, snug,
conservatory, in-room TV, civil
wedding licence, meeting/function
facilities, terrace, front and rear
gardens, parking.
BACKGROUND MUSIC: in public areas.
LOCATION: 10 mins' walk from town
centre.
CHILDREN: all ages welcomed.
DOGS: allowed in some bedrooms,
separate eating area.
CREDIT CARDS: MC, Visa.
PRICES: per room B&B £129–£149.
À la carte £25.

MOYLEGROVE Pembrokeshire

THE OLD VICARAGE B&B

Close to the craggy cliffs and pebbled coves of the
Pembrokeshire Coastal Path, Meg and Jaap van
Soest's modern B&B is in a hilltop Edwardian
vicarage that has peered down the valley for well
over a century. Restored and recently refreshed,
the house has an airy, uncluttered feel. There are
books, maps and guides in the spacious sitting
room, plus chess for a fireside game. Upstairs,
clean-cut bedrooms have Welsh woollen blankets
on a large bed, and a supply of fresh milk, coffee
and quality teas. Any evening, a Spanish tapas
hamper – with a bottle of wine, if you'd like – can
be arranged. At breakfast: home-baked breads;
local bacon and sausages; good veggie options; a
stretch of valley views.

MAP 3:D2
Moylegrove SA43 3BN
T: 01239 881711
W: oldvicaragemoylegrove.co.uk

BEDROOMS: 5. Plus birch huts in
grounds available for self-catering.
OPEN: all year.
FACILITIES: sitting room, dining room,
in-room TV (Freeview), 1-acre
garden.
BACKGROUND MUSIC: in dining room
in evening.
LOCATION: 500 yards from village,
13 miles N of Fishguard.
CHILDREN: all ages welcomed.
DOGS: allowed, not in dining room.
CREDIT CARDS: MC, Visa.
PRICES: per room B&B £100–£120.

NARBERTH Pembrokeshire
CANASTON OAKS

A short drive from the flourishing market town, this 'very good' B&B is liked for its spacious, modern bedrooms and award-winning breakfasts. It is run by friendly owners Eleanor and David Lewis, with their daughter, Emma Millership. Accommodation is in a lake-view lodge and converted barns set around a courtyard. Freshly redecorated, each thoughtfully supplied room (dressing gowns, candles, etc) is different: some have a conservatory seating area; a family suite opens on to a terrace with wide countryside views. Breakfast has thick Welsh yogurt, heather honey and poached fruit; hot dishes include porridge with Penderyn whisky, and smoked haddock fishcakes. Easy access to the A40.

MAP 3:D2
Canaston Bridge
Narberth SA67 8DE
T: 01437 541254
W: canastonoaks.co.uk

BEDROOMS: 10. 7 on ground floor around courtyard, 2 suitable for disabled, plus 1-bed self-catering apartment.
OPEN: all year except Christmas.
FACILITIES: lounge (honesty bar), dining room, in-room TV (Freeview), 1-acre grounds, parking.
BACKGROUND MUSIC: 'mainly easy listening or classical' in dining room.
LOCATION: 2 miles W of Narberth.
CHILDREN: all ages welcomed.
DOGS: well-behaved dogs allowed in 3 barn suites, not in dining area, on lead in all public areas.
CREDIT CARDS: MC, Visa.
PRICES: per room B&B £90–£175. Set menu £21 (2 courses), £26 (3 courses). 1-night bookings sometimes refused at peak times.

PORTMEIRION Gwynedd
HOTEL PORTMEIRION

Enveloping exotic woodland, sandy beaches and a riot of colour, Sir Bertram Clough Williams-Ellis's Italianate village on the edge of a tidal estuary is an architectural astonishment. Amid it all, this early Victorian villa with 'friendly' staff is a 'comfortably furnished' hotel whose traditional bedrooms have 'wonderful' views. (More contemporary accommodation is in Castell Deudraeth, overlooking a restored walled garden; other rooms, in cottages in the grounds, have a private patio or terrace.) Visitors have plenty of options at mealtimes, including the hotel's Art Deco dining room, where the modern menu has 'good choice'. Busy during the day, the village, come evening, is 'a delightful haven in which to wander in relative solitude'.

MAP 3:B3
Minffordd
Penrhyndeudraeth
Portmeirion LL48 6ER
T: 01766 770000
W: portmeirion.wales

BEDROOMS: 14. Plus 11 in Castell Deudraeth, 34 in village. Some on ground floor, 1 suitable for disabled.
OPEN: all year except 2 weeks Jan/Feb for annual maintenance.
FACILITIES: lift, 4 lounges, bar, restaurant, brasserie in Castell, in-room TV, civil wedding licence, terrace, 130-acre grounds, outdoor heated swimming pool (summer), electric car charging points, free shuttle service around village.
BACKGROUND MUSIC: in public areas, occasional live music in lounges.
LOCATION: 2 miles SE of Porthmadog.
CHILDREN: all ages welcomed.
DOGS: only assistance dogs allowed.
CREDIT CARDS: Amex, MC, Visa.
PRICES: per room B&B £124–£344. 2-night min. stay most weekends.

ROCH Pembrokeshire

ROCH CASTLE HOTEL

Rugged stone gives way to clean-cut, contemporary B&B accommodation at this 12th-century Norman castle. It stands on a rocky outcrop before a panorama that stretches from St Brides Bay around to the Preseli hills. Reached via a curving staircase, bedrooms are supplied with all the modern comforts; the best room has double-aspect windows to soak in the views. Still higher, the Sun Room, with glass walls and an open-air viewing platform, merits the climb. Throughout, modern artworks inspired by Welsh history and landscapes provide extra visual interest. At dinnertime, free transfers take residents to sister hotel Twr y Felin, St Davids (see main entry); in the morning, breakfast includes laverbread and local honey.

MAP 3:D1
Church Road
Roch SA62 6AQ
T: 01437 725566
W: rochcastle.com

BEDROOMS: 6.
OPEN: all year.
FACILITIES: lounge, study, breakfast room, Sun Room (honesty bar), in-room TV (Freeview), civil wedding licence, 19-acre grounds, electric car charging points.
BACKGROUND MUSIC: classical and 'easy listening' in lounges, breakfast room.
LOCATION: 7 miles NW of Haverfordwest.
CHILDREN: not under 12.
DOGS: not allowed.
CREDIT CARDS: Amex, MC, Visa.
PRICES: per room B&B £230–£280. 2- or 3-night min. stay at weekends and peak times; also available for exclusive use.

ST DAVIDS Pembrokeshire

CRUG-GLAS

In peaceful countryside within easy reach of the Pembrokeshire Coastal Path, the Evans family run their relaxed restaurant-with-rooms with 'warm concern for their guests'. 'They went out of their way to prepare a favourite dish for our birthday celebration,' a Guide reader reports this year. In this Georgian farmhouse on the family farm, photographs and inherited pieces lend character; a generations-old dresser houses the honesty bar. The bedrooms each have their own country style, though all share tranquil rural views. A short walk through the grounds, a spacious suite in a converted barn offers extra privacy. Seasonal dinner menus include beef from home-reared cows; breakfast has good choice.

MAP 3:D1
Abereiddy
St Davids SA62 6XX
T: 01348 831302
W: crug-glas.co.uk

BEDROOMS: 7. 1 in converted barn, 1 on ground floor.
OPEN: all year except 23–27 Dec.
FACILITIES: drawing room, dining room, in-room TV (Freeview), civil wedding licence, function facilities, hair salon, 1-acre garden on 600-acre farm.
BACKGROUND MUSIC: in public rooms.
LOCATION: 3½ miles NE of St Davids.
CHILDREN: babes-in-arms and over-11s welcomed.
DOGS: allowed in coach house suite.
CREDIT CARDS: MC, Visa.
PRICES: per room B&B £150–£190. À la carte £35.

ST DAVIDS Pembrokeshire

PENRHIW PRIORY

A tranquil retreat within easy walking distance of Britain's smallest city, this late Victorian vicarage stands in acres of landscaped gardens, enveloped by woodland paths, a river and a wildflower meadow. It is modern inside, with soberly decorated rooms and dramatic abstract artwork inspired by local landscapes. Bedrooms are supplied with cosseting extras (bathrobes and slippers, aromatherapy toiletries, quality bedding); a suite in the coach house has a private terrace and views of Carn Llidi. Drinks and snacks are available in the honesty bar. At dinnertime, complimentary transfers to and from the well-regarded Blas restaurant at sister hotel Twr y Felin (see main entry), on the other side of town, can be arranged.

MAP 3:D1
St Davids SA62 6PG
T: 01437 725588
W: penrhiwhotel.com

BEDROOMS: 8. 2 in coach house, 1 on ground floor.
OPEN: all year except Christmas, New Year.
FACILITIES: lounge, drawing room, breakfast room, study, in-room TV, treatment room, civil wedding licence, 12-acre grounds, electric car charging points.
BACKGROUND MUSIC: soft jazz/classical in breakfast room.
LOCATION: 10 mins' walk from St Davids cathedral and town centre.
CHILDREN: not under 12, except for exclusive-use bookings.
DOGS: not allowed.
CREDIT CARDS: Amex, MC, Visa.
PRICES: per room B&B £200–£280. À la carte £55. 2-night min. stay in summer months.

SAUNDERSFOOT Pembrokeshire

ST BRIDES SPA HOTEL

Seaside splendour comes to the fore at this modern hotel above Carmarthen Bay. Light floods in through floor-to-ceiling windows; ocean air, through glass doors. The seascapes of Saundersfoot harbour and the coastline are 'exceptional' – as restorative, perhaps, as the calm that washes over guests in the award-winning spa. 'Very pleasant' bedrooms are styled in breezy hues; some rooms have a balcony. A bonus: residents get a 90-minute session in the spa's thermal suite and hydrotherapy pool. In the restaurant and bar, or on the terrace, Pembrokeshire produce and locally landed fish feature on regularly changing menus. A downhill stroll away, a modern chippy and beach barbecue in the village are offshoots.

MAP 3:D2
St Brides Hill
Saundersfoot SA69 9NH
T: 01834 812304
W: stbridesspahotel.com

BEDROOMS: 34. 1 suitable for disabled. Plus six 2-bed apartments in grounds, 12 self-catering in village.
OPEN: all year.
FACILITIES: lift, lounge, bar, restaurant, Gallery dining area, meeting/function rooms, in-room TV, civil wedding licence, terraces, art gallery, spa (treatments, infinity hydropool), electric car charging point.
BACKGROUND MUSIC: all day in public areas.
LOCATION: 3 mins' walk to village.
CHILDREN: all ages welcomed.
DOGS: allowed in some ground-floor apartments.
CREDIT CARDS: Amex, MC, Visa.
PRICES: per room B&B single £145–£230, double £195–£360. À la carte £40.

ST ANNE Alderney

THE BLONDE HEDGEHOG

Down the cobbled street from the old clock tower at the Alderney Society Museum, this contemporary hotel is a chic base from which to experience island life. The popular restaurant, marble-topped bar and modish bedrooms span a Victorian pub, a Georgian town house and an 18th-century cottage; a modern rustic ambience connects them all. Driven by the seasons, unfussy dishes (perhaps local lobster and crab ravioli; pulled local ox cheek, potato mousse) are served in the stylish restaurant and terraced garden. Eat well, then retire to one of the well-equipped, handsome-hued bedrooms or suites. Island activities (bird-watching, island-hopping, sea kayaking, etc) can be arranged, with a picnic to take along.

MAP 1: inset D6
6 Le Huret
St Anne GY9 3TR
T: 01481 823230
W: blondehedgehog.com

BEDROOMS: 9. 5 in adjacent town house, 2 on ground floor, plus 3-bed cottage opposite.
OPEN: all year.
FACILITIES: bar, snug, restaurant, in-room TV, cinema/games room, terrace, ¼-acre garden, ground-floor public rooms wheelchair accessible.
BACKGROUND MUSIC: in bar, restaurant.
LOCATION: in town centre.
CHILDREN: all ages welcomed.
DOGS: allowed in bar, garden, cottage, assistance dogs allowed throughout.
CREDIT CARDS: Amex, MC, Visa.
PRICES: per room B&B from £230. À la carte £36. 1-night bookings refused during Alderney Week.

ST PETER PORT Guernsey

LA COLLINETTE HOTEL

There's a relaxed, family-friendly atmosphere at this unpretentious hotel, a short uphill stroll from the boats in the harbour. The 19th-century house has been owned and run by the Chambers family since 1960; walls of black-and-white photos in the newly refurbished Colly's bar capture island history. Up the stairs, bedrooms are brightly, if simply, decorated, and most have views of the sea. Uncomplicated dishes, perhaps with Guernsey lobsters and scallops, are served in the refreshed restaurant; in good weather, eat alfresco on the poolside terrace. Visit the German Naval Underground Museum, in former bunkers under today's self-catering accommodation, then head, with calling seagulls, to historic Candie Gardens.

MAP 1: inset E5
St Jacques
St Peter Port GY1 1SN
T: 01481 710331
W: lacollinette.com

BEDROOMS: 23. Plus 14 self-catering cottages and apartments.
OPEN: all year.
FACILITIES: lounge, bar, restaurant, in-room TV (Sky, Freeview), 2-acre garden, outdoor heated swimming pool, children's pool, play area, gym, sauna, spa treatments, restaurant and bar wheelchair accessible.
BACKGROUND MUSIC: in bar, restaurant.
LOCATION: less than 1 mile W of town centre.
CHILDREN: all ages welcomed.
DOGS: allowed only in self-catering accommodation, by arrangement.
CREDIT CARDS: MC, Visa.
PRICES: per person B&B £60–£160. Set dinner £20, à la carte £30.

BELFAST
THE OLD RECTORY

In a conservation area just south of the centre, Mary Callan's guest house is a welcoming home away from home. The late Victorian former rectory is set back from the road behind a row of mature trees; inside, the 'nicely furnished' drawing room has books, board games, and a hot whiskey for cool days. Bedrooms are supplied with tea, coffee, biscuits and magazines; there's fresh milk in a mini-fridge on each landing. A light supper (home-made soup, beef chilli, frittata, etc) may be requested in advance. In the morning, 'splendid' breakfasts by an open fire 'cater for vegetarians as generously as they do for meat-eaters'. The bus to the city stops right outside; the hostess has local knowledge to share.

MAP 6:B6
148 Malone Road
Belfast BT9 5LH
T: 028 9066 7882
w: anoldrectory.co.uk

BEDROOMS: 7. 1 on ground floor, suitable for disabled.
OPEN: all year except Christmas, New Year, 2 weeks mid-July.
FACILITIES: drawing room, dining room, in-room TV (Freeview), garden, parking.
BACKGROUND MUSIC: none.
LOCATION: 2 miles from city centre.
CHILDREN: all ages welcomed.
DOGS: not allowed.
CREDIT CARDS: MC, Visa.
PRICES: per room B&B single £58–£68, double £88–£98. 2-night min. stay May–Sept.

BELFAST
RAVENHILL HOUSE

Close to shops, restaurants and a leafy park, this handsomely restored red-brick B&B is just a short bus ride from the city centre. It is owned by Olive and Roger Nicholson, who welcome arriving guests with tea and oven-fresh treats. Individually decorated in keeping with the style of the Victorian house, bedrooms have good seating, home-baked shortbread, a vintage Hacker radio; all the modern facilities. A wide-ranging breakfast, including seasonal specials, is served in a book-lined room with a wood-burning stove. The Nicholsons mill their own flour from organic Irish wheat grain for the freshly baked sourdough bread; there are also home-made jams, spiced fruit compotes and good vegetarian options.

MAP 6:B6
690 Ravenhill Road
Belfast BT6 0BZ
T: 028 9028 2590
w: ravenhillhouse.com

BEDROOMS: 5.
OPEN: Feb–15 Dec.
FACILITIES: sitting room/breakfast room, in-room TV (Freeview), small garden, parking.
BACKGROUND MUSIC: classical music at breakfast.
LOCATION: 2 miles S of city centre.
CHILDREN: not under 10.
DOGS: not allowed.
CREDIT CARDS: Amex, MC, Visa.
PRICES: per room B&B £90–£145. 2-night min. stay preferred at busy weekends.

BUSHMILLS

BUSHMILLS INN

Travellers have been making their way to this
coaching inn along the Causeway Coastal Route
since the 17th century, drawn by its peat fires, cosy
nooks and convivial, wonky-timbered bar. Today,
the up-to-date bedrooms, each with a sitting area,
have all the modern amenities (tea and coffee,
bathrobes and slippers); many have a partial
view of the River Bush. 'Our room was excellent,
and very quiet.' In the public rooms, choose
an ambience to suit. Eat modern dishes in the
garden-facing restaurant or alfresco on the patio;
hunker down in the Gas bar, still lit by Victorian
gas light, for a Guinness-and-oyster pairing and
a Saturday-night live music session – 'a real plus'.
The world's oldest distillery is a short stroll away.

MAP 6:A6
9 Dunluce Road
Bushmills BT57 8QG
T: 028 2073 3000
W: bushmillsinn.com

BEDROOMS: 41. Some, on ground floor,
suitable for disabled.
OPEN: all year, no accommodation
24–25 Dec.
FACILITIES: lift, bar, lounge, restaurant,
loft, cinema, in-room TV (Freeview),
conference facilities, patio, 2-acre
garden, parking.
BACKGROUND MUSIC: in public areas,
live traditional Irish music sessions
every Sat in bar.
LOCATION: in village centre, 2 miles
from Giant's Causeway.
CHILDREN: all ages welcomed.
DOGS: allowed on patio.
CREDIT CARDS: Amex, MC, Visa.
PRICES: per room B&B £130–£460.
À la carte £60.

CARAGH LAKE Co. Kerry

ARD NA SIDHE
COUNTRY HOUSE HOTEL

The extensive gardens of this Irish sandstone-
built manor house on the wooded shores of
Lough Caragh are ripe for discovery: hidden
paths open on to the water, and the mountains
beyond. The serene hotel, once a grand private
home, has handsome bedrooms in the main
house and around a rustic courtyard. Each has
antique furnishings and a deep mattress; no TV,
but, perhaps, the sound of the water coming to
shore. Candlelit dinners are served in the elegant
restaurant; afternoon tea is taken in the fire-
warmed lounge, or on the terrace in fine weather.
Boating and fishing on the lake can be arranged,
along with a picnic hamper. Guests have access to
leisure facilities at a sister hotel.

MAP 6:D4
Caragh Lake
Killorglin V93 HV57
T: 00 353 66 976 9105
W: ardnasidhe.com

BEDROOMS: 18. 1 on ground floor,
suitable for disabled, 8 in Garden
House.
OPEN: Apr–Oct.
FACILITIES: lounge, library, restaurant,
terrace, 32-acre grounds.
BACKGROUND MUSIC: in lounge, library.
LOCATION: on Lough Caragh, 8 km
SW of Killorglin.
CHILDREN: all ages welcomed.
DOGS: not allowed.
CREDIT CARDS: Amex, MC, Visa.
PRICES: per room B&B double
€235–€360. À la carte €55.

CARLINGFORD Co. Louth
GHAN HOUSE

In shades of heather and bracken, Slieve Foy rises behind the Carroll family's listed Georgian house. Standing within walled gardens, a tree's length from the medieval town, the house is filled with family photographs and heirlooms, freshly cut flowers and squashy sofas. Traditionally decorated bedrooms, some with an antique bed, have home-made biscuits to go with garden or mountain views; most have a roll-top bath and a power shower in a modern bathroom. Enjoy walks on the slopes or along the seashore; in cool weather, return to the wood fire-warmed drawing room or 'elegant' dining room, where modern Irish menus are based on produce from lough and countryside. At breakfast: home-made jams and marmalades.

MAP 6:B6
Old Quay Lane
Carlingford A91 DXY5
T: 00 353 42 937 3682
W: ghanhouse.com

BEDROOMS: 12. 8 in garden annexe, 4 on ground floor.
OPEN: all year except 24–26, 31 Dec, 1–2 Jan; restaurant closed Mon, most Tues in autumn and winter ('best to book in advance').
FACILITIES: bar, lounge, restaurant, 3 private dining rooms, in-room smart TV (Freeview), wedding facilities, 3-acre garden, parking, electric car charging point.
BACKGROUND MUSIC: in bar, restaurant.
LOCATION: 'a tree length' from town.
CHILDREN: all ages welcomed.
DOGS: allowed in kennels in converted stables.
CREDIT CARDS: Amex, MC, Visa.
PRICES: per person B&B €90–€125. 6-course tasting menu from €45, 4-course menu from €57.50, 3-course early dinner €35.

CLIFDEN Co. Galway
BLUE QUAY ROOMS

Its facade an eye-catching blue, Paddy and Julia Foyle's jauntily refurbished B&B is above the harbour, a few minutes' walk from the centre of the small market town. Sister to The Quay House on the waterfront (see main entry), it is managed by the Foyles' son, Toby, and Pauline Petit. The 200-year-old building has been decorated with spirited flair (spot the gold lobster on the wood-burning stove); in the cosy sitting areas, board games, a TV and a DVD player are provided for guests' entertainment. All but one of the pretty, simply decorated bedrooms upstairs look towards the harbour. Over an imaginative breakfast, the engaging hosts have much local information to share. An ideal base for walkers and cyclists.

MAP 6:C4
Seaview
Clifden H71 WE02
T: 00 353 87 621 7616
W: bluequayrooms.com

BEDROOMS: 8. Plus 2-bed self-catering apartment.
OPEN: Apr–Oct.
FACILITIES: sitting area, breakfast room, garden.
BACKGROUND MUSIC: none.
LOCATION: close to town centre.
CHILDREN: not under 10.
DOGS: not allowed.
CREDIT CARDS: none accepted.
PRICES: per room B&B single €65–€75, double €70–€100.

COLLINSTOWN Co. Westmeath

LOUGH BAWN HOUSE

'Divine' views stretch down rolling meadows
to a spring-fed lough from this 'impressive'
Georgian house, which has been home to Verity
Butterfield's family for four generations. An
enthusiastic cook, the 'lovely hostess' lays out tea
and cake to welcome B&B guests. There's an open
fireplace in the 'cosy' drawing room packed with
family heirlooms, books and an abundance of
flowers; in the elegant dining room, home-cooked
dinners (by pre-arrangement) are 'a real treat'.
Pretty, country house-style bedrooms overlook the
garden or lake; two share a 'wonderful' bathroom
(wooden floors, a vast bathtub, a 'glorious' walk-
in shower). At breakfast, soda bread, granola and
marmalade are all home made. Walks abound.

MAP 6:C5
Lough Bane
Collinstown N91 EYX4
T: 00 353 44 966 6186
W: loughbawnhouse.com

BEDROOMS: 4. 2 share a bathroom.
OPEN: all year except Dec.
FACILITIES: 2 sitting rooms, dining
room, 50-acre parkland, wild
swimming lake.
BACKGROUND MUSIC: none.
LOCATION: by Lough Bawn, 3 miles
from village.
CHILDREN: all ages welcomed.
DOGS: allowed by prior arrangement
in 2 bedrooms, public rooms (resident
dogs).
CREDIT CARDS: MC, Visa.
PRICES: per room B&B single from
€100, double €140–€175. Dinner €50.
2-night min. stay at weekends in
May, June.

CORK

MONTENOTTE HOTEL

Above tiered gardens, this large, modern hotel
with an artistic bent takes in an impressive
panorama over the city and the harbour.
Colourful china dogs greet visitors; the plushly
furnished public spaces have a stylish sense of
fun. Diners gather in curving booths in the
bistro or on sofas on the spacious heated terrace
for creative cocktails, and dishes off the all-
day menu: salads, sharing platters and heartier
options with some international flavours. Brightly
decorated bedrooms, some suitable for a family,
are equipped with bathrobes and slippers, bottled
waters and hot drinks. There are nightly cinema
screenings, and treatments in the spa; the restored
Victorian sunken garden is worth a wander.

MAP 6:D5
Middle Glanmire Road
Cork T23 E9DX
T: 00 353 21 453 0050
W: themontenottehotel.com

BEDROOMS: 107. Some suitable
for disabled, plus 26 self-catering
apartments.
OPEN: all year except 24–27 Dec.
FACILITIES: lobby, bistro, in-room TV
(Sky), wedding facilities, room service,
gym, spa (20-metre heated indoor
swimming pool, sauna, steam room,
hot tub, treatments), cinema, terrace,
Victorian gardens, woodland.
BACKGROUND MUSIC: in lobby and
bistro.
LOCATION: St Luke's Cross district.
CHILDREN: all ages welcomed.
DOGS: only assistance dogs allowed.
CREDIT CARDS: Amex, MC, Visa.
PRICES: per room €160–€395. Breakfast
€15, à la carte €55.

DUBLIN
SCHOOLHOUSE HOTEL

Within walking distance of Dublin's many
attractions, this 19th-century schoolhouse by the
Grand Canal is today a hotel with a restaurant
and a 'very jolly' bar. The 'interesting' Victorian
building flaunts distinctive turrets and high
chimneys; an original wooden staircase, panelled
walls and a stone fireplace within. Period-style
bedrooms (some in the basement) are decorated
with William Morris patterns; the best rooms
have canal or garden views, or access to the lawn.
Pub classics and bistro dishes (seafood chowder;
sage and onion chicken en croûte) are served all
day under a vaulted ceiling in the restaurant and
lively bar, or alfresco on the terrace. The hotel
is in tree-lined Ballsbridge; Aviva Stadium is 15
minutes' walk away.

MAP 6:C6
2–8 Northumberland Road
Dublin 4
T: 00 353 1 667 5014
W: schoolhousehotel.com

BEDROOMS: 31. Some on ground floor.
OPEN: all year except 24–26 Dec.
FACILITIES: bar, restaurant, private
dining/meeting room, in-room TV,
wedding facilities, ½-acre garden,
limited parking.
BACKGROUND MUSIC: in bar, restaurant.
LOCATION: in Ballsbridge
neighbourhood, 15 mins' walk from
St Stephen's Green.
CHILDREN: all ages welcomed.
DOGS: only assistance dogs allowed.
CREDIT CARDS: Amex, MC, Visa.
PRICES: per person B&B €149–€239.
À la carte €42.

INIS MEAIN Co. Galway
INIS MEAIN RESTAURANT AND SUITES

Remote and remarkable, Ruairí and Marie-
Thérèse de Blacam's sustainably run restaurant-
with-suites blends in to the rugged landscape of
its Aran island setting. Wood, lime, stone and
wool define the large, architectural suites; each
has vast views from an outdoor seating area.
In the Michelin green star-winning restaurant,
succinct menus use prime produce from the
greenhouse, the island and the surrounding
waters. Characteristic dishes: lobster, golden beet;
scallop tartare, toasted hazelnut. Breakfast is
delivered to the door. The two- and four-night
booking packages include hotpot lunches and use
of an exploration kit with fishing rods, swimming
towels, binoculars, maps and nature guides.

MAP 6:C4
Inis Meáin
Aran Islands H91 NX86
T: 00 353 86 826 6026
W: inismeain.com

BEDROOMS: 5 suites.
OPEN: Wed–Sat, Apr–Aug; Mon–
Thurs, Mar, Sept–Nov.
FACILITIES: restaurant, 3-acre grounds.
BACKGROUND MUSIC: none.
LOCATION: centre of a small island,
15 miles off the Galway coast; 40-min.
ferry from Ros a' Mhíl; 7-min. flight
from Connemara airport.
CHILDREN: not under 12.
DOGS: not allowed.
CREDIT CARDS: MC, Visa.
PRICES: per suite B&B €300–€650,
includes daily hotpot lunch,
exploration kit (bicycles, fishing
rods, walking sticks, binoculars, etc),
collections to and from ferry port
or airport. Set 4-course dinner €75.
2-night or 4-night stays Apr–Aug,
4-night stay only Mar, Sept–Nov.

KINSALE Co. Cork

GILES NORMAN TOWNHOUSE

Soak up harbour scenes from this stylishly renovated Georgian town house in the centre of a historic town along the Wild Atlantic Way. It is owned by landscape photographer Giles Norman and his wife, Catherine, who have hung fine black-and-white photographic prints throughout the listed building. Above the gallery and shop on the ground floor, urbane, understated bedrooms are equipped with teas and a coffee machine, plus organic Irish toiletries; most look over the water. A spacious suite with handsome beams is under the eaves. No meals are served, but the cafés and notable restaurants of the foodie town are within a few minutes' walk. From the harbour front, hop on a cruise for panoramic views of the town.

MAP 6:D5
45 Main Street
Kinsale P17 K651
T: 00 353 21 477 4373
W: gilesnormantownhouse.com

BEDROOMS: 5.
OPEN: mid-Mar–mid-Dec.
FACILITIES: in-room TV.
BACKGROUND MUSIC: none.
LOCATION: in town centre.
CHILDREN: not allowed.
DOGS: not allowed.
CREDIT CARDS: MC, Visa.
PRICES: per room €150–€230. 1-night bookings refused at bank holiday weekends.

LISDOONVARNA Co. Clare

WILD HONEY INN

In a spa town on the edge of the Burren, a landscape of ash and hazel woodland, of grassland, cliffs and fen, this Michelin-starred pub-with-rooms attracts discerning diners with its refined bistro cooking and country-cosy accommodation. It is owned and run by chef/patron Aidan McGrath and his partner, Kate Sweeney. In the informal bar and dining room, frequently changing, fixed-price menus feature flavourful Irish produce – organic vegetables, freshly picked berries, seasonal game, wild fish straight off the day boat. Uncluttered bedrooms, some snug, have traditional charm and many fine touches: duck-down duvets, hand-woven throws, glossy magazines. Delicious breakfasts fuel nature walks along the Wild Atlantic Way.

MAP 6:C4
Kincora Road
Lisdoonvarna V95 P234
T: 00 353 65 707 4300
W: wildhoneyinn.com

BEDROOMS: 13. 3 on ground floor.
OPEN: Mar–Oct, closed Sun, Mon.
FACILITIES: bar, lounge, restaurant, in-room TV, courtyard garden.
BACKGROUND MUSIC: classical music in reception and at breakfast; 'an eclectic playlist' in bar.
LOCATION: on the edge of town.
CHILDREN: not allowed.
DOGS: not allowed.
CREDIT CARDS: MC, Visa.
PRICES: per room B&B €150–€220. Prix fixe menu €80.

RAMELTON Co. Donegal
FREWIN

Creeper-covered on the outside, and filled with
quiet, old-world charm on the inside, this B&B is
owned and run by Regina Gibson and Thomas
Coyle, who have restored the former rectory with
period flair. There are stained-glass windows,
interesting pictures and antiques, and shelves
of books to flip through; upstairs, spacious,
traditionally decorated bedrooms, each with a
compact bathroom, might have a four-poster
bed, a roll-top bath or a separate sitting area.
Communal breakfasts have a view on the mature
wooded grounds. The B&B is on the outskirts of
a Georgian port town on the Wild Atlantic Way;
the congenial hosts can help arrange golf, fishing
and guided hikes in the Bluestack mountains.

MAP 6:B5
Rectory Road
Ramelton F92 DW77
T: 00 353 74 915 1246
W: frewinhouse.com

BEDROOMS: 3. Plus cottage in grounds.
OPEN: Mar–end Oct, by special
arrangement for small groups in Feb
and Nov.
FACILITIES: sitting room, library, dining
room, 2-acre garden.
BACKGROUND MUSIC: none.
LOCATION: on the outskirts of town.
CHILDREN: not under 16.
DOGS: not allowed.
CREDIT CARDS: MC, Visa.
PRICES: per room B&B single
€120–€125, double €170–€180.

RATHNEW Co. Wicklow
HUNTER'S

'A special place.' Said to be Ireland's oldest
coaching inn, this rambling, 'extremely comfy'
hotel stands in 'lovely' grounds by the River
Vartry. Enveloped in olde-worlde charm, with
'staff who really make an effort', it has been
owned by the same family for almost 200 years.
'It's like walking back in time.' The current
stewards, the Gelletlie brothers, run it with
'acceptable eccentricity': antiques, old prints and
floral fabrics decorate the rooms; most of the
chintz-filled bedrooms overlook the 'inspiring'
garden. 'Delicious' classic cuisine is served on
crisp table linens in the dining room. 'Well worth
a stop-over from the Rosslare ferry.' Gardens and
golf courses are close.

MAP 6:C6
Newrath Bridge
Rathnew A67 TN30
T: 00 353 404 40106
W: hunters.ie

BEDROOMS: 16. 1 on ground floor.
OPEN: all year except 24–26 Dec.
FACILITIES: drawing room, lounge, bar,
dining room, private dining room, in-
room TV (Freeview), 5-acre grounds,
golf, tennis, fishing nearby.
BACKGROUND MUSIC: none.
LOCATION: 1 mile SE of Ashford.
CHILDREN: all ages welcomed.
DOGS: allowed in bedrooms only, by
arrangement.
CREDIT CARDS: MC, Visa.
PRICES: per person B&B from €85. Set
dinner from €35.

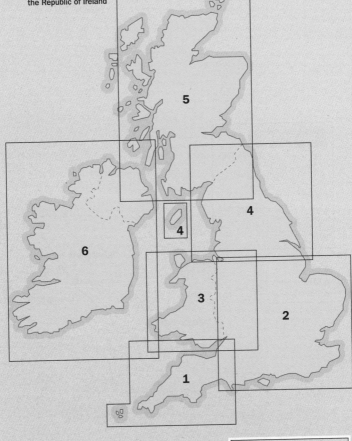

Map 1	South-West England
	including the Channel Islands
Map 2	Southern England
Map 3	Wales and the Cotswolds
Map 4	The North of England
	and the Lake District
	including the Isle of Man
Map 5	Scotland
Map 6	Northern Ireland and
	the Republic of Ireland

Channel Islands

1

Not to scale

MAP 1 · SOUTH-WEST ENGLAND

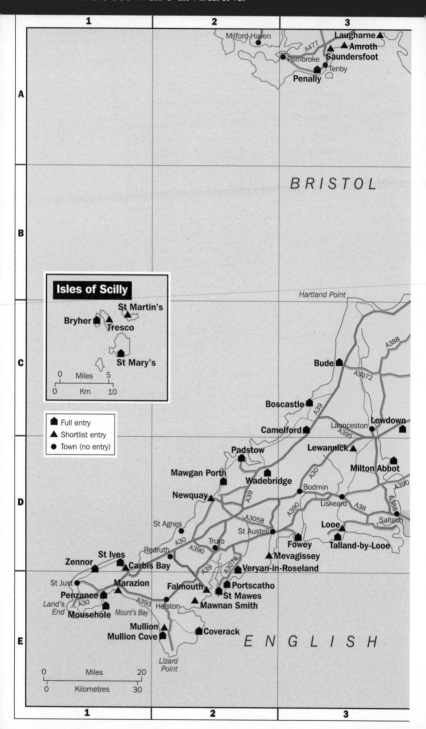

Milford Haven

A477

Laugharne ▲

Amroth ▲
Saundersfoot ▲
Pembroke ●
Tenby ●
Penally ■

A

BRISTOL

B

Isles of Scilly

St Martin's ▲
Bryher ■
Tresco ▲

St Mary's ■

0   Miles   5
0   Km   10

■ Full entry
▲ Shortlist entry
● Town (no entry)

Hartland Point

C

Bude ■

A3072

Boscastle ■

A39

Lewdown ■

Camelford ■

Launceston ●
A395

Lewannick ▲

Milton Abbot ■

Padstow ■

Mawgan Porth ▲

Wadebridge ■

A30

Bodmin ●

A390

Newquay ▲

A3058

Liskeard ●   A38

Saltash ●

A388

St Agnes ●

St Austell ●

A390

Looe ▲

D

St Ives ■
Zennor ■

Carbis Bay ▲

Redruth ●   A390   Truro ●

Fowey ■

Talland-by-Looe ■

Mevagissey ▲

A39   A3078

Veryan-in-Roseland ▲

St Just ●

Marazion ▲

Falmouth ■

Portscatho ■

St Mawes ■

Mawnan Smith ▲

Penzance ■

A30

A393   Helston ●

Land's
End

Mousehole ■   Mount's Bay

Mullion ▲
Mullion Cove ■

Coverack ■

E

Lizard
Point

ENGLISH

0   Miles   20
0   Kilometres   30

1   2   3

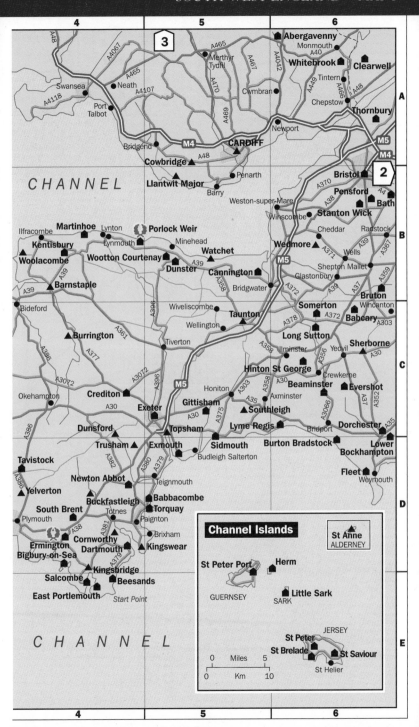

MAP 2 · SOUTHERN ENGLAND

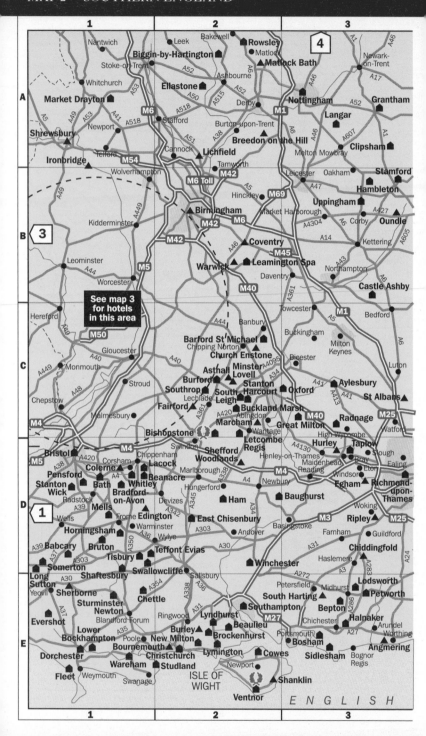

4

1   2   3

Nantwich
Leek
Bakewell
Rowsley
Biggin-by-Hartington
Matlock
Newark-on-Trent
Stoke-on-Trent
Matlock Bath
Whitchurch
Ashbourne
Ellastone
A52
Nottingham
Grantham
Market Drayton
Derby
Langar
A52
Clipsham
Shrewsbury
Newport
Stafford
Burton-upon-Trent
Melton Mowbray
Ironbridge
Telford
Cannock
Lichfield
Tamworth
Leicester
Oakham
Stamford
Wolverhampton
M6 Toll
M42
Hinckley
M69
Uppingham
Hambleton
Kidderminster
Birmingham
Market Harborough
Corby
Oundle
M42
M6
Coventry
M45
Leominster
M5
Warwick
Leamington Spa
Kettering
Northampton
Worcester
Daventry
Castle Ashby

See map 3
for hotels
in this area

Hereford
M50
Towcester
M1
Bedford
Gloucester
Banbury
Buckingham
Milton Keynes
Monmouth
Barford St Michael
Chipping Norton
Bicester
Luton
Chepstow
Stroud
Church Enstone
Minster Lovell
Asthall
A34
Aylesbury
Burford
Stanton Harcourt
Oxford
St Albans
Southrop
Lechlade
South Leigh
Malmesbury
Fairford
Buckland Marsh
M40
Radnage
Watford
Abingdon
Great Milton
High Wycombe
Bishopstone
Marcham
Wantage
Hurley
Taplow
Bristol
M4
Swindon
Shefford Woodlands
Letcombe Regis
Slough
M5
A420
Chippenham
Henley-on-Thames
Maidenhead
Ealing
Pensford
Corsham
Lacock
Marlborough
M4
Reading
Windsor
Richmond-upon-Thames
Colerne
Beanacre
Hungerford
Newbury
Egham
Stanton Wick
Bath
Whitley
Radstock
Bradford-on-Avon
Devizes
Ham
Baughurst
Woking
M25
Mells
Edington
Basingstoke
Ripley
Guildford
Horningsham
Frome
East Chisenbury
Andover
Farnham
M3
Wells
Warminster
Wylye
Babcary
Bruton
Teffont Evias
A30
Chiddingfold
Somerton
Tisbury
Winchester
Haslemere
Long Sutton
Shaftesbury
Swallowcliffe
Salisbury
Petersfield
Lodsworth
Yeovil
Sherborne
Chettle
Midhurst
Petworth
Sturminster Newton
South Harting
Bepton
Eversholt
Blandford Forum
Ringwood
Lyndhurst
Southampton
Chichester
Halnaker
Lower Bockhampton
Burley
Beaulieu
M27
Arundel
Worthing
Poole
New Milton
Brockenhurst
Portsmouth
Bosham
Angmering
Dorchester
Bournemouth
Christchurch
Lymington
Cowes
Sidlesham
Bognor Regis
Fleet
Wareham
Studland
Newport
Weymouth
Swanage
ISLE OF WIGHT
Shanklin
Ventnor
ENGLISH

1   2   3

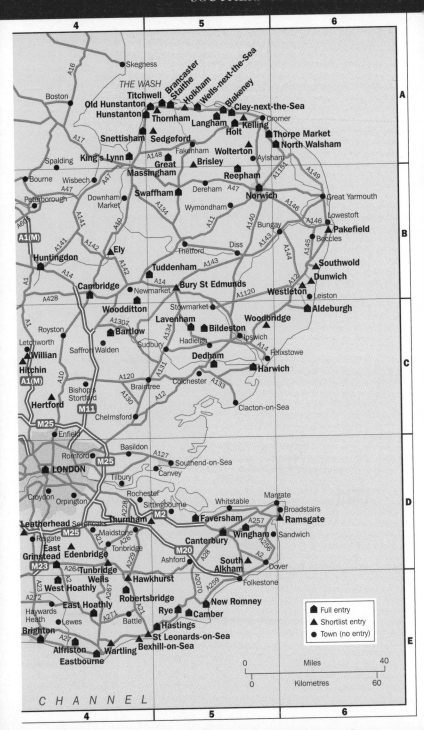

4 **5** **6**

Skegness

Boston

THE WASH

Old Hunstanton
Hunstanton
A17
Snettisham
King's Lynn
A148
Spalding

Bourne
Wisbech
Peterborough
A605

Downham Market
A141

Huntingdon
A14
A1
A1(M)

Royston
Letchworth
Willian
Hitchin
A1(M)
A10

Hertford
M25

Enfield
Romford
M25
LONDON

Croydon
Orpington

Leatherhead
Reigate
M25
East Grinstead
M23
A264

West Hoathly
A272
East Hoathly
Haywards Heath
Lewes
A271

Brighton
A27
Alfriston
Eastbourne
Wartling

Titchwell
Brancaster Staithe
Holkham
Wells-next-the-Sea
Blakeney
Cley-next-the-Sea
Thornham
Langham
Kelling
Cromer
Thorpe Market
Sedgeford
Holt
North Walsham
Fakenham
Wolterton
Aylsham
Great Massingham
Brisley
A149
Swaffham
Dereham
Reepham
A1131
Norwich
A149
Wymondham
A47
A140
A146
Great Yarmouth
A11
A140
Lowestoft
Bungay
A146
Pakefield
A143
Beccles
Ely
Thetford
Diss
A145
A12
A144
Southwold
Tuddenham
A143
Dunwich
Cambridge
Newmarket
Bury St Edmunds
A1120
Westleton
A428
A14
Leiston
Woodditton
Stowmarket
Aldeburgh
Bartlow
A1307
Lavenham
Woodbridge
Saffron Walden
A134
Bildeston
Ipswich
Hadleigh
A14
Felixstowe
A120
Sudbury
Dedham
Bishop's Stortford
Braintree
A131
Colchester
A133
Harwich
Chelmsford
A130
A12
Clacton-on-Sea

Basildon
A127
Southend-on-Sea
Canvey
Tilbury
Rochester
Margate
Sittingbourne
Whitstable
Broadstairs
M2
Faversham
Ramsgate
Thurnham
A257
Maidstone
Canterbury
Wingham
Sandwich
A26
Tonbridge
A229
Ashford
A256
Edenbridge
A2
A20
Dover
Tunbridge Wells
M20
South Alkham
A264
Hawkhurst
A267
A2070
A259
Folkestone
Robertsbridge
A21
New Romney
A23
Rye
Camber
Battle
Hastings
St Leonards-on-Sea
Bexhill-on-Sea

■ Full entry
▲ Shortlist entry
● Town (no entry)

0   Miles   40
0   Kilometres   60

C H A N N E L

4 **5** **6**

A   B   C   D   E

MAP 3 · WALES AND THE COTSWOLDS

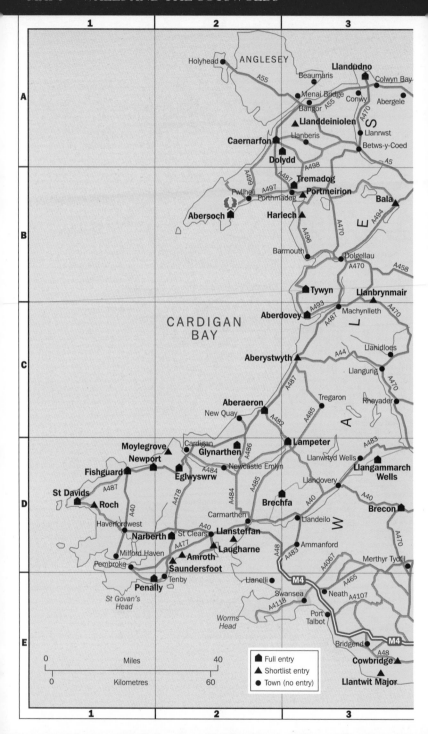

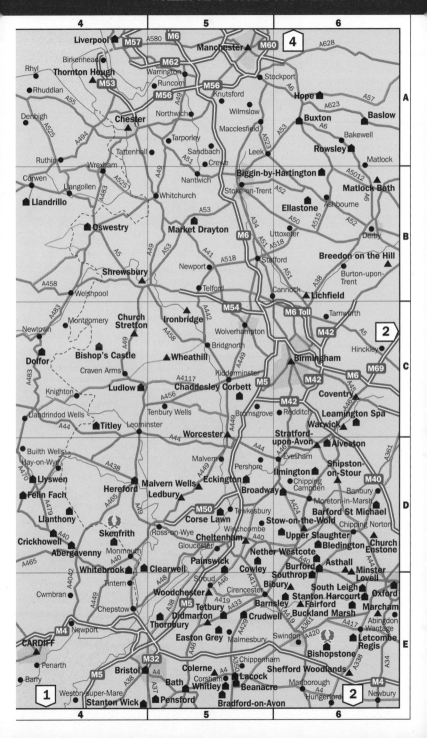

MAP 4 • THE NORTH OF ENGLAND AND THE LAKE DISTRICT

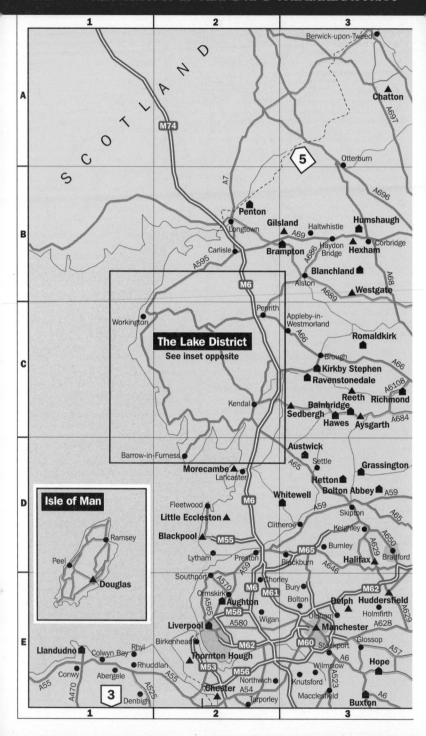

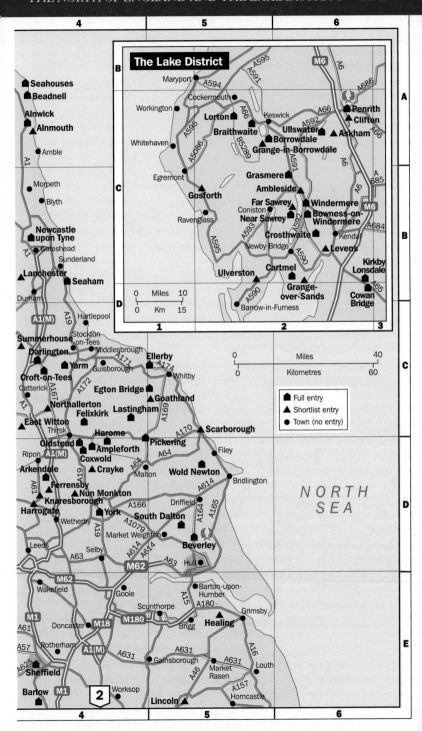

The Lake District

Maryport
Cockermouth
Workington
Keswick
Lorton
Braithwaite
Whitehaven
Borrowdale
Grange-in-Borrowdale
Egremont
Grasmere
Gosforth
Ambleside
Ravenglass
Far Sawrey
Windermere
Coniston
Bowness-on-Windermere
Near Sawrey
Crosthwaite
Newby Bridge
Kendal
Levens
Ulverston
Cartmel
Penrith
Clifton
Ullswater
Askham
Kirkby Lonsdale
Cowan Bridge
Grange-over-Sands
Barrow-in-Furness

0 Miles 10
0 Km 15

Seahouses
Beadnell
Alnwick
Alnmouth
Amble
Morpeth
Blyth
Newcastle upon Tyne
Gateshead
Sunderland
Lanchester
Seaham
Durham
Hartlepool
Summerhouse
Stockton-on-Tees
Darlington
Middlesbrough
Ellerby
Yarm
Guisborough
Whitby
Croft-on-Tees
Catterick
Egton Bridge
Northallerton
Goathland
Felixkirk
Lastingham
East Witton
Thirsk
Harome
Oldstead
Pickering
Scarborough
Ampleforth
Ripon
Filey
Coxwold
Arkendale
Crayke
Malton
Wold Newton
Ferrensby
Bridlington
Nun Monkton
Knaresborough
Driffield
Harrogate
York
Wetherby
South Dalton
Leeds
Market Weighton
Selby
Beverley
Hull

NORTH SEA

Full entry
Shortlist entry
Town (no entry)

0 Miles 40
0 Kilometres 60

Wakefield
Goole
Barton-upon-Humber
Scunthorpe
Grimsby
M1
Doncaster
Brigg
Healing
Rotherham
Gainsborough
Market Rasen
Louth
Sheffield
Barlow
Worksop
Lincoln
Horncastle

MAP 5 · SCOTLAND

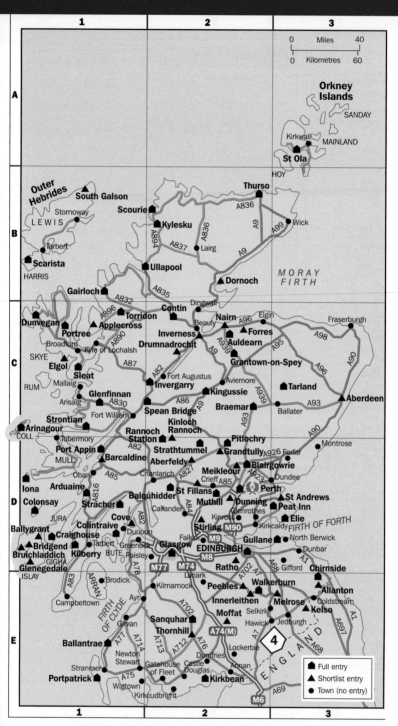

1   **2**   **3**

0   Miles   40
0   Kilometres   60

A

Orkney Islands
SANDAY
Kirkwall   MAINLAND
St Ola

HOY

Outer Hebrides   **Thurso**
South Galson   A836
Stornoway   **Scourie**   A836   A9   A99   **Wick**
L E W I S   **Kylesku**   A837   Lairg

B   Tarbert   A894   A9
Scarista   **Ullapool**   A9   *M O R A Y FIRTH*
HARRIS   Dornoch

Gairloch   A832   A835   Dingwall
Dunvegan   A896   **Contin**   **Nairn**   Elgin   Fraserburgh
Torridon   Beauly   A96   A98
Portree   **Applecross**   **Inverness**   **Forres**   A95
Broadford   A890   **Drumnadrochit**   **Auldearn**   A90
SKYE   Kyle of Lochalsh   A939
Elgol   A87   **Grantown-on-Spey**   A96

C   **Sleat**   A82   Fort Augustus   Aviemore
RUM   Mallaig   **Invergarry**   **Kingussie**   A939   **Tarland**
Glenfinnan   A86   **Braemar**   A93   **Aberdeen**
Arisaig   A830   Ballater
Fort William   **Spean Bridge**   A9
Strontian   **Kinloch Rannoch**   A93
Arinagour   **Rannoch Station**   **Pitlochry**   Montrose
COLL   Tobermory   A82   **Strathtummel**   Forfar
Port Appin   **Aberfeldy**   **Grandtully**   A926
MULL   **Barcaldine**   Crianlarich   **Meikleour**   **Blairgowrie**   A923
Oban   A85   A827   **Perth**   Dundee
Iona   **Arduaine**   **Balquhidder**   **St Fillans**   A85

D   **Colonsay**   **Strachur**   **Muthill**   **Dunning**   **Peat Inn**
Callander   A84   Kinross   **Elie**
JURA   **Cove**   A82   Glenrothes   FIRTH OF FORTH
Ballygrant   **Colintraive**   Dunoon   **Stirling**   M90   Kirkcaldy
Craighouse   Tarbert   Falkirk   M9   North Berwick
Bridgend   **Kilberry**   Greenock   **Glasgow**   **Gullane**   Dunbar
Bruichladdich   BUTE   Paisley   **EDINBURGH**   A1
GIGHA   M77   M8   A68
Glenegedale   **Ratho**   Gifford   **Chirnside**
ISLAY   ARRAN   Brodick   M74   A702   A7
Campbeltown   A83   Kilmarnock   Lanark   **Peebles**   **Walkerburn**   **Allanton**
A78   **Innerleithen**   **Melrose**   Coldstream
Ayr   A702   **Moffat**   Selkirk   **Kelso**
Ballantrae   **Sanquhar**   Hawick   Jedburgh   A697   A1
A77   A714   **Thornhill**   A74(M)   E N G L A N D

E   Newton Stewart   A713   A712   A76   4
Girvan   Lockerbie   A68
Portpatrick   Gatehouse of Fleet   Castle Douglas   Dumfries   Annan
Stranraer   A75   **Kirkbean**   A69
Wigtown   M6
Kirkcudbright

■ Full entry
▲ Shortlist entry
● Town (no entry)

1   **2**   **3**

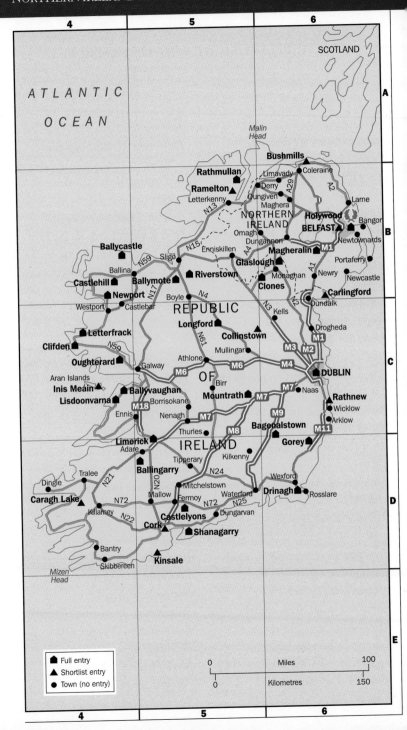

SCOTLAND

ATLANTIC

OCEAN

Malin
Head

Bushmills

Rathmullan
Limavady   Coleraine
Ramelton   Derry
Letterkenny Dungiven
N13   Maghera
            NORTHERN
            IRELAND   Larne
                             Holywood
Ballycastle Omagh   Dungannon   BELFAST   Bangor
N59   Enniskillen   Newtownards
Ballina Sligo N15   Magheralin   M1
Castlehill   Riverstown Glaslough   Portaferry
Newport Ballymote   Monaghan A1   Newcastle
Westport Castlebar Boyle N4 Clones   Newry
                                Carlingford
         REPUBLIC   Kells Dundalk
Letterfrack   Longford   N3   Drogheda
Clifden   N59   Collinstown   M1
Oughterard   Galway Mullingar   M3 M2
Aran Islands OF   Athlone M6   M4   DUBLIN
Inis Meáin   Birr   Naas
Ballyvaughan Borrisokane Mountrath M7   Rathnew
Lisdoonvarna M18   M7   Wicklow
Ennis Nenagh   M9   Arklow
IRELAND Thurles   M8 Bagenalstown   M11
Limerick   Gorey
Adare   Tipperary Kilkenny
Ballingarry   N24   Wexford
Tralee N21 Mallow Mitchelstown Waterford Drinagh
Dingle   N20 Fermoy   N72 N25   Rosslare
Caragh Lake N72 Killarney Dungarvan
N22   Castlelyons
       Cork Shanagarry
Bantry
Skibbereen Kinsale
Mizen
Head

Full entry
Shortlist entry
Town (no entry)

0   Miles   100
0   Kilometres   150

A

B

C

D

E

4   5   6

ALPHABETICAL LIST OF HOTELS
(S) indicates a Shortlist entry

INDEX OF HOTELS BY COUNTY
(S) indicates a Shortlist entry

FREQUENTLY ASKED QUESTIONS

HOW DO YOU CHOOSE A GOOD HOTEL?

The hotels we like are relaxed, unstuffy and personally run. We do not have a specific template: our choices vary greatly in style and size. Most of the hotels in the Guide are family owned and family run. These are places where the needs and comfort of the guest are put ahead of the convenience of the management.

YOU ARE A HOTEL GUIDE – WHY DO YOU INCLUDE SO MANY PUBS AND B&BS?

Attitudes and expectations have changed considerably since the Guide was founded in the 1970s. Today's guests expect more informality, less deference. There has been a noticeable rise in the standards of food and accommodation in pubs and restaurants. This is demonstrated by the number of such places suggested to us by our readers. While pubs may have a more relaxed attitude than some traditional hotels, we ensure that only those that maintain high standards of service are included in our selections. The best B&Bs have always combined a high standard of accommodation with excellent value for money. Expect the bedrooms in a pub or B&B listed in the Guide to be well equipped, with thoughtful extras. B&B owners invariably know how to serve a good breakfast.

WHAT ARE YOUR LIKES AND DISLIKES?

We like
* Flexible times for meals.
* Two decent armchairs in the bedroom.
* Good bedside lighting.
* Proper hangers in the wardrobe.
* Fresh milk with the tea tray in the room.

We dislike
* Intrusive background music.
* Stuffy dress codes.
* Bossy notices and house rules.
* Hidden service charges.
* Packaged fruit juices at breakfast.

WHY DO YOU DROP HOTELS FROM ONE YEAR TO THE NEXT?

Readers are quick to tell us if they think standards have slipped at a hotel. If the evidence is overwhelming, we drop the hotel from the Guide or perhaps downgrade it to the Shortlist. Sometimes we send inspectors just to be sure. When a hotel is sold, we look for reports since the new owners took over, otherwise we inspect or omit it.

WHY DO YOU ASK FOR 'MORE REPORTS, PLEASE'?

When we have not heard about a hotel for several years, we ask readers for more reports. Sometimes readers returning to a favourite hotel may not send a fresh report. Readers often respond to our request.

WHAT SHOULD I TELL YOU IN A REPORT?

How you enjoyed your stay. We welcome reports of any length. We want to know what you think about the welcome, the service, the building and the facilities. Even a short report can tell us a great deal about the owners, the staff and the atmosphere.

HOW SHOULD I SEND YOU A REPORT?

You can email us at editor@goodhotelguide.com. Or you can write to us at the address given on the report form at the end of the book, or send a report via the GHG's website: goodhotelguide.com.